Fodor's
BERKELEY
budget
guides

Critical accl   s

CW00835772

"[The Berkeley Guid   or
the low-budget trav....   ....   ly,
and often irreverent way."   —*The Philadelphia Inquirer*

"The [Berkeley Guides] are deservedly popular because of their extensive coverage, entertaining style of writing, and heavy emphasis on budget travel...If you are looking for tips on hostels, vegetarian food, and hitchhiking, there are no books finer."
—*San Diego Union-Tribune*

"Straight dirt on everything from hostels to look for and beaches to avoid to museums least likely to attract your parents... they're fresher than Harvard's Let's Go series."   —*Seventeen*

"The [Berkeley Guides] give a rare glimpse into the real cultures of Europe, Canada, Mexico, and the United States...with in-depth historical backgrounds on each place and a creative, often poetical style of prose."   —*Eugene Weekly*

"More comprehensive, informative and witty than Let's Go."
—*Glamour*

"The Berkeley Guides have more and better maps, and on average, the nuts and bolts descriptions of such things as hotels and restaurants tend to be more illuminating than the often terse and sometimes vague entries in the Let's Go guides."
—*San Jose Mercury News*

"These well-organized guides list can't-miss sights, offbeat attractions and cheap thrills, such as festivals and walks. And they're fun to read."   —*New York Newsday*

"Written for the young and young at heart...you'll find this thick, fact-filled guide makes entertaining reading."
—*St. Louis Dispatch*

"Bright articulate guidebooks. The irreverent yet straight-forward prose is easy to read and offers a sense of the adventures awaiting travelers off the beaten path."   —*Portland Oregonian*

On the Loose
On the Cheap
Off the Beaten P

New York City Area

New York City Area

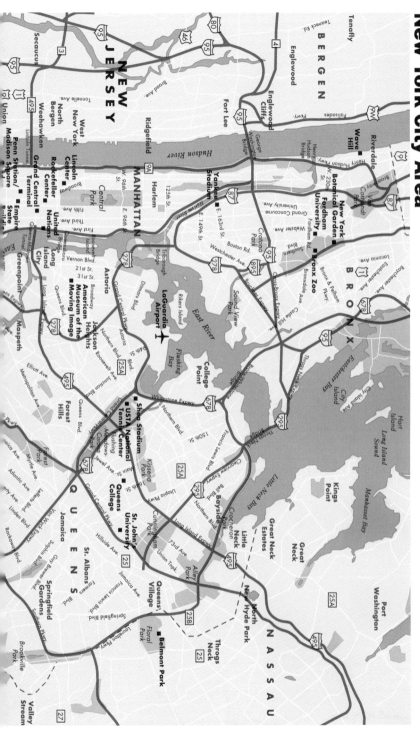

Downtown Manhattan

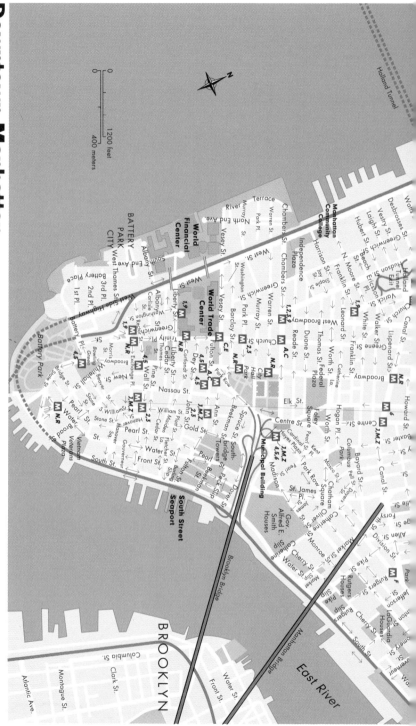

Downtown Manhattan

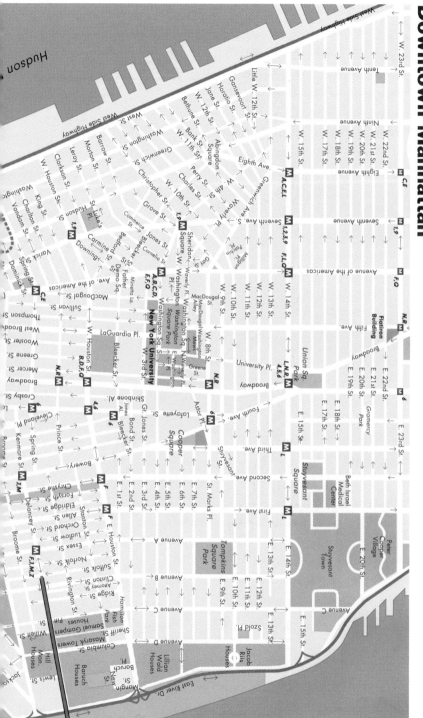

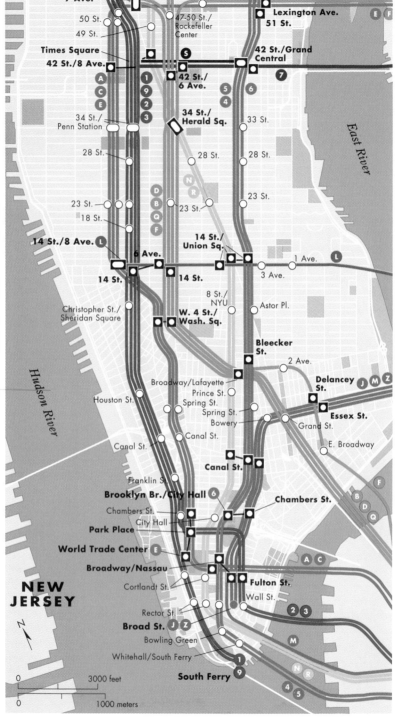

Manhattan Subways Below 42nd Street

7 Ave.
50 St.
49 St.
5 Ave.
47-50 St./
Rockefeller
Center
Lexington Ave.
51 St.
Times Square
42 St./8 Ave.
42 St./Grand
Central
S
A
C
E
1
9
2
3
42 St./
6 Ave.
7
5
6
4
34 St./
Penn Station
34 St./
Herald Sq.
33 St.
East River
28 St.
28 St.
28 St.
N
R
D
B
Q
F
23 St.
23 St.
23 St.
18 St.
14 St./8 Ave.
L
6 Ave.
14 St./
Union Sq.
1 Ave.
L
14 St.
14 St.
3 Ave.
8 St./
NYU
Astor Pl.
Christopher St./
Sheridan Square
W. 4 St./
Wash. Sq.
Bleecker
St.
2 Ave.
Broadway/Lafayette
Prince St.
Delancey
St.
J M Z
Houston St.
Spring St.
Spring St.
Bowery
Essex St.
Canal St.
Canal St.
Grand St.
E. Broadway
Canal St.
Franklin St.
Canal St.
F
B
D
Q
Brooklyn Br./City Hall
6
Chambers St.
Chambers St.
City Hall
Park Place
World Trade Center
E
A C
Broadway/Nassau
Fulton St.
NEW
JERSEY
Cortlandt St.
Wall St.
2 3
Rector St.
M
Broad St.
J Z
Bowling Green
Whitehall/South Ferry
1
South Ferry
9
N R
4 5

Hudson River

N

0   3000 feet
0   1000 meters

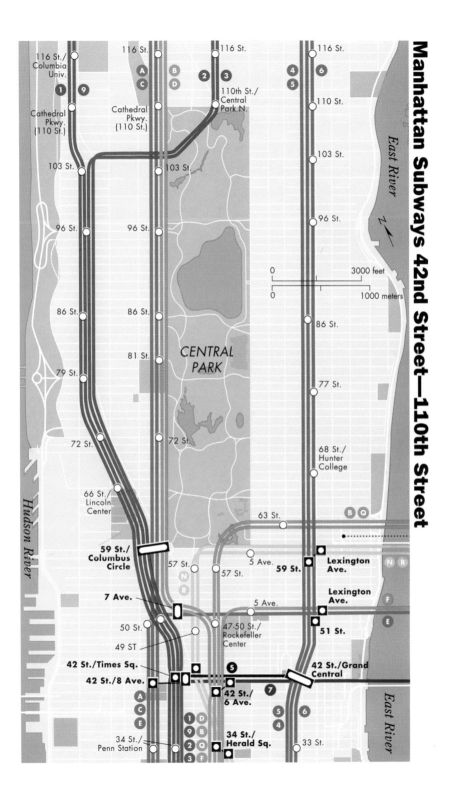

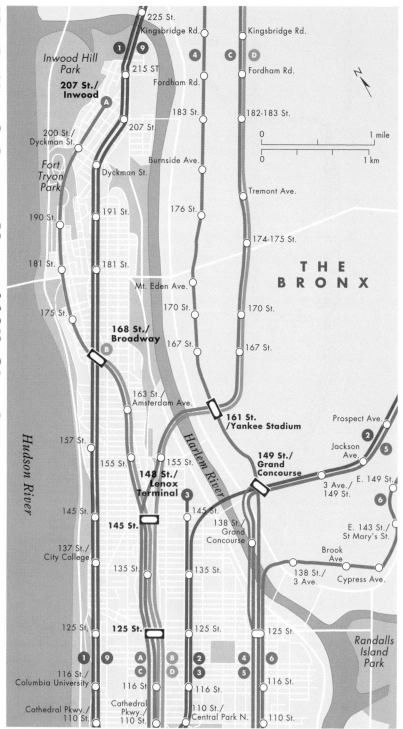

225 St.

Kingsbridge Rd. ❶ ❾ ④ ⒞ ⒟ Kingsbridge Rd.

Inwood Hill Park

215 ST Fordham Rd. Fordham Rd.

207 St./ Inwood

Ⓐ

200 St./ Dyckman St.

207 St. 183 St. 182-183 St.

Fort Tryon Park

Dyckman St. Burnside Ave.

191 St. Tremont Ave.

190 St.

176 St. 174-175 St.

181 St. 181 St.

THE BRONX

175 St. Mt. Eden Ave.

170 St. 170 St.

168 St./ Broadway 167 St. 167 St.

Ⓑ

163 St./ Amsterdam Ave.

Hudson River 161 St. /Yankee Stadium

157 St. Prospect Ave. ❷

Harlem River Jackson Ave. ❺

155 St. 155 St. 149 St./ Grand Concourse E. 149 St.

148 St./ Lenox Terminal ❸ 3 Ave./ 149 St. ❻

145 St. 145 St. 138 St./ Grand Concourse E. 143 St./ St Mary's St.

145 St. Brook Ave

137 St./ City College 135 St. 135 St. 138 St./ 3 Ave. Cypress Ave.

Randalls Island Park

125 St. 125 St. 125 St. 125 St.

❶ ❾ Ⓐ Ⓑ ❷ ④ ❻
Ⓒ Ⓓ ❸ ❺

116 St./ Columbia University 116 St 116 St. 116 St.

Cathedral Pkwy./ 110 St. Cathedral Pkwy./ 110 St. 110 St./ Central Park N. 110 St.

0 | 1 mile
0 | 1 km

Fodor's **BERKELEY** budget guides

new york city '97

On the Loose
On the Cheap
Off the Beaten Path

WRITTEN BY BERKELEY STUDENTS IN COOPERATION WITH
THE ASSOCIATED STUDENTS OF THE UNIVERSITY OF CALIFORNIA

ISBN 0–679–03135–9

THE BERKELEY GUIDE TO NEW YORK CITY

Editor: Jennifer Brewer
Managing Editors: Nicole Harb, Kristina Malsberger, Sharron Wood
Executive Editor: Scott McNeely
Map Editor: Robert Blake
Creative Director: Fabrizio La Rocca
Cartographers: David Lindroth Inc.; Eureka Cartography
Text Design: Tigist Getachew
Cover Design: Fabrizio La Rocca
Cover Art: Poul Lange (3-D art), The Automobile Association (photo in frame), Paul D'Innocenzo (still life)

SPECIAL SALES

The Berkeley Guides and all Fodor's Travel Publications are available at special discounts for bulk purchases for sales promotions or premiums. Special editions, including personalized covers, excerpts of existing guides, and corporate imprints, can be created in large quantities for special needs. For more information, contact your local bookseller or write to Special Markets, Fodor's Travel Publications, 201 East 50th Street, New York, NY 10022. Inquiries from Canada should be directed to your local Canadian bookseller or sent to Random House of Canada, Ltd., Marketing Department, 1265 Aerowood Drive, Mississauga, Ontario L4W 1B9. Inquiries from the United Kingdom should be sent to Fodor's Travel Publications, 20 Vauxhall Bridge Road, London SW1V 2SA, England.

PRINTED IN THE UNITED STATES OF AMERICA

10 9 8 7 6 5 4 3 2 1

Contents

Thanks to You

Putting together a spanking-new guidebook covering all of New York City is no easy task. From figuring out the Metropolitan Museum of Art to getting the lowdown on East Village dive bars, our six writers (and one beleaguered editor) relied on helpful souls along the way. We'd like to thank the following people—as well as the hundreds of others whom our writers met fleetingly on subway platforms, in cafés, or while dodging cabs on Sixth Avenue—for their advice and encouragement. You can help us in updating this book by giving us feedback; just drop us a line—a postcard, a scrawled note on some toilet paper, whatever. Our address is 515 Eshleman Hall, University of California, Berkeley, CA 94720.

Lauren Adams; Steven Amsterdam; Marianne Anderson; Chris Baty (Portland, OR); Bed-and-Breakfast on the Park; Marshall Berman; Karen Boyer; Gray Brechin (Berkeley, CA); Broadway–American Hotel; Angela Cairelli; Chelsea Center Hostel; Chelsea International Hostel; Greg Christensen; Mike D and the Boys; de Hirsch Residence; Sunny Delaney (Berkeley, CA); Shashi Dipanjan (San Francisco, CA); James Dresser (VT); Jeffrey Escoffier; Ray Franco; Beth Freeman; Lisa Freeman; Gershwin Hotel; Giselle at the Uptown Hostel; Paul Groth (Berkeley, CA); Nicole Harb (Los Angeles, CA); Brendan and Susie Healey; Sheila Healy-Jaimes; David Henschel (San Francisco, CA); Jodi Hernandez (Sacramento, CA); Hostelling International on 103rd Street; Hotel Milburn; Connie Hsia; Imaja and Karen (Albany, CA); Sara Jacobs; Jonathan; Michael Johns (Berkeley, CA); Katy at ICC (San Francisco, CA); Zita Kollar; Carole Levenson; Jonathan Lippincott; David Lowe; Sam Lu; Malibu Studios Hotel; Kim Marth; Mid-City Guesthouse; Andrea Milius; Fred Morris; Don Newton (Rockytown, CT); Fredrik Odegaard (Sweden); Russ Page and family (FL); John, Leslie, and Joseph Polizzi (NY and Los Angeles, CA); Larry Reilly; Jennifer Renk (San Francisco, CA); Pat Riedman; Andrew Riss; Byron Saunders; Anne Shelby (Ketchum, ID); Sugar Hill International House; David Szanto; Dolores Tarantino; B. Tyler; Caroline (Doll) Vollmer; Missy Wastila (Palo Alto, CA); Jennifer Wedel (Tucson, AZ); Westside YMCA; Jim Williams; Namshik Yoon; Shelley Zimmerman; and the people in seats 110 and 111 for the Metropolitan Opera's December 11, 1995, performance of *La Bohème*.

Back at the *Berkeley Guides*, Kathleen Dodge, Tara Duggan, Maureen Klier, Sora Song, and Suzanne Stein provided invaluable help in the final stages of the book. We'd also like to thank the Random House folks who helped us with cartography, page design, and production: Steven Amsterdam, Bob Blake, Denise DeGennaro, Janet Foley, Tigist Getachew, Fabrizio La Rocca, and Linda Schmidt.

And finally, a giant thank-you goes to Scott McNeely, former *Berkeley Guides* executive editor and onetime New Yorker, who never doubted this guidebook would be completed—and worked a great deal toward that end. Scott left his grieving coworkers in order to roam the far-flung corners of the earth, including Turkey, Romania, Jordan, Pakistan, India, and Nepal, and to eventually write a book.

Berkeley Bios

Behind every restaurant blurb and lodging review in this book lurks a student writer. You might recognize the type—perpetually short on time, money, and clean clothes. Our writers spent the spring and summer checking out the scene; every two weeks they sent their manuscript back to Berkeley, where it was whipped, squashed, and pummeled into shape by an occasionally dyspeptic editor.

The Writers

By the time that you read this, **Shon Bayer** may finally have given his last manuscript batch to his patient editor. Or maybe not. Growing up in Washington, D.C., Shon thought New York was a dirty, trashy metropolis. But, after contributing to sections on the East Village, Lower East Side, Chinatown, Little Italy, Lower Manhattan, and Brooklyn, he's changed his mind. Whether he returns to New York as an aspiring medical student or as a foul-tempered taxi driver after his final two semesters at Cal, he *will* return.

David Brown recently moved to New York after 20-odd years in California; he currently works as a freelance editor, writer, and researcher, and spends far too much money on things he doesn't need. David graduated from Berkeley with a B.A. in English, having read many books. He will probably never leave New York.

Matthew Jalbert, a tenderfoot raised in the wilds of Connecticut, was first set loose in New York City by an all-too-trusting teacher during a high school field trip to the United Nations. On his most recent voyage, he wrote about the Upper East Side, Chelsea, and that vast expanse of Manhattan known as Midtown. Now holding a brand-new B.A. in Geography, he's turned to a lucrative career in Internet development, but still dreams of writing about the vernacular landscape—or taking a second shot at rock-and-roll stardom. Above all, he hopes his summer in New York has taught him to be a modernist: To be, as it is said, at home in the maelstrom.

Until he wrote the chapter on Gay and Lesbian New York, **Matthew Lore**'s greatest travel achievement was falling asleep at the wheel of an overloaded Ryder truck going 70 miles an hour in the middle of Nebraska—and living to tell about it. He called the Bay Area home for six years, where he knew about Urban Ore before anyone else did. These days he'd like to say that he divides his time between Berkeley's Strawberry Canyon and Brooklyn's Prospect Park, but truthfully his time is divided between when he's riding the subway and when he's not. He hopes the book he's written, on lesbians and gay men and religion, will be published before he's gone completely gray.

Returning *Berkeley Guides* writer **Amy McConnell**, who edits Fodor's travel guides in Manhattan, will always remember the summer she spent uncovering the hidden charms of the Bronx, Queens, and Staten Island. After walking the length of the Bronx's Grand Concourse on scorching hot summer days, discovering ethnic cultures that she'd never even heard of in Queens, and discussing secessionist politics with folks in Staten Island, she's developed a protective fondness for New York City's forgotten boroughs. Now she just has to win over her Manhattan-centric friends.

Covering the West Village, SoHo, TriBeCa, the Upper West Side, Harlem, and the far north of Manhattan was native Californian **Mira Schwirtz**. She quickly learned to appreciate the pleasure of a cup of Cuban coffee in a Washington Heights greasy spoon, the go-go glitter of a TriBeCa dance club, the magnetic energy of a Harlem street, and the meditative beauty of Central Park—but without Angela Cairelli and Dolores Tarantino (the queens of Sullivan Street) and Jim Williams (certainly the best storyteller in Harlem), she would never have found New York's soul.

The Editor

After graduating from Berkeley, **Jennifer Brewer** sold her soul to Manhattan; she returned to California convinced a stint splashing her prose around the *Berkeley Guides* could be parlayed into a three-picture deal (with percent of the gross). Alas, Ovitz never called. So, choking back nostalgia for martinis, the Marathon, Don Mattingly, the Met, the Park, Page Six of the *Post*, readings at the 92nd Street Y, snow, the Strand, subways, and drunken sushi dinners at 3:30 AM, she labored like Sisyphus amped on ginseng drinks and clad in overalls to bring you, dear reader, this book. Now done, she hopes to visit Besham, Pakistan—a Muslim town where women are permitted to leave the house only on the event of their wedding, death, or hospitalization—during a year-plus odyssey through Europe, the Middle East, India, Nepal, and Tibet.

Introduction

By David Brown

In recent years, the city of New York has been hanging banners around town proclaiming that it's the Capital of the World. And despite the claims to fame of other cities—Tokyo has more banks, Seattle has more musicians, Vancouver is the new darling among moviemakers, and Kuala Lumpur, Malaysia, now has the world's tallest skyscraper—New York can still lay claim to the most grand-championship titles. It's home to the United Nations and is a longtime nucleus of such varied fields as advertising, art, publishing, classical music, fashion, cuisine, finance, law, and headline-grabbing corporate takeovers. Though naysayers the world over have been predicting New York's demise for decades, it still seems you can't turn on the TV or read a magazine without getting the impression that at least half of everything in the United States happens in New York. And if you were to ask someone in Bangkok or Berlin or Bujumbura to sketch an American city, it's at least even money that the Empire State Building or the Statue of Liberty would appear in the picture.

Which leads to another thing New York City is the capital of: attitude. True, Parisians are probably equally, um, brusque, but you'll find few other places on earth where people so clearly bear the imprint of their hometown. After a few days walking Manhattan streets you'll really know your New Yorkers. Be they foppish like Eustace Tilley, Rea Irvin's famed *New Yorker* cartoon cover model, or tough and street savvy as DeNiro in *Taxi Driver*, whether they're newly immigrated cabbies or megalomaniac financiers like Donald Trump, all seem to possess a real whoop-de-do enthusiasm (and wardrobe heavy on black clothes) for living here. Maybe it's survivor's mentality: The journalist Edward Hoagland once jokingly noted that annually the city's 7.3 million residents probably "see more death than most soldiers do."

Whatever the reason for the in-your-face attitude of New Yorkers, you'll have plenty of opportunities to mix and mingle with (or at least stand behind velvet ropes and stare at) this peculiar breed of urban dweller. For this is one of few American cities where people prefer to walk rather than drive (not surprising, given that traffic crossing Midtown averages 5.3 miles an hour), where face-to-face interaction has not been obliterated by cruise control and carpool lanes. New York sidewalks attract around 10,000 pedestrians per hour, making them some of the busiest on earth. By all means, take advantage of its 722 miles of convenient subway lines while you're visiting, but don't forget to get out and walk a few blocks; it's the best way to discover the city's 400 art galleries, 17,000 restaurants, 150 museums, and 200 skyscrapers—as long as you don't mind dodging the piles of doggie doo and, in the winter, crusty, black drifts of snow.

But long before these subways and skyscrapers were even a glimmer in New Yorkers' eyes, before the city became "the nation's thyroid gland," as Christopher Morley once described it, New York City was the tiny town of New Amsterdam, settled at the southern tip of Manhattan by the Dutch in 1624. In an astounding episode of flimflammery, the settlers had purchased Manhattan from the Indians for trinkets worth $24. This 22-square-mile island with the bargain-basement price exhibited an "anything goes" vibe from the get-go. When a missionary visited in 1643, he found an already cosmopolitan community of 500 settlers speaking 18 different languages. From its very inception, it was clear that New York would never become another lost-in-the-woods Roanoke.

Except for a decade or so break for the Revolutionary War (we won), the city, blessed with a commodious natural harbor, expanded into the corners of Manhattan Island and inched outward to swallow Brooklyn, the Bronx, Queens, and Staten Island. Canals and railroad built in the first half of the 19th century brought trade—and money—by the bushel, and the city soon became the largest and richest in the hemisphere, eclipsing its old rival, Philadelphia. But it wasn't until the second half of the 1800s that the city really started to percolate. With America as a whole, and New York in particular, shining as a beacon of prosperity for the rest of the world (Europe was suffering through a devastating famine), immigrants poured in, and then poured in some more. The melting pot that we alternately glorify and curse today took shape as some 16 million Italian, African, Irish, Jewish, and German immigrants arrived over the next six decades. All told, over 120 different nationalities now live here, including a new wave of immigrants from Central America and Southeast Asia, and each has left their mark on the city, whether it's a cool new cuisine or a special festival.

Ironically, as the teeming masses fled Europe for New York in the 19th century, the city's wealthiest residents were striving to re-create the splendor of a European capital right here at home. The upper crust made no secret of their envy of Paris when they lobbied city officials to create Central Park in the 1850s. Throughout the century, city planning and private philanthropy gave birth to powerhouse institutions like the Metropolitan Opera, the Metropolitan Museum of Art, the New York Public Library, and the American Museum of Natural History. This self-aggrandizing spirit continued through the next century, producing, among other things, the Museum of Modern Art, the Studio Museum in Harlem, and Lincoln Center for the Performing Arts. Of course, you can't have world-class cultural institutions without world-famous artists, writers, and performers. The city's literary giants have included Walt Whitman and Herman Melville in the 19th century; Marianne Moore, e.e. cummings, and Dorothy Parker in the 1920s; and Ralph Ellison, Carson McCullers, and Allen Ginsberg at mid-century. New York was the spot where "modern art" from Europe was introduced to an outraged public in 1913, and it's been synonymous with the avant-garde ever since—from abstract expressionists like Franz Kline to the pop art masters of the 1960s. Georgia O'Keeffe, Jackson Pollock, Mark Rothko, Agnes Martin, and Andy Warhol have all called the city home.

As much as New York can trumpet its economic, social, and cultural success, it also boasts an impressive array of things that suck: It's crowded, dirty, expensive as hell, and yes, occasionally dangerous. Newt Gingrich rightfully received flak for dissing New York as a "culture of waste" in 1995, but the fact is, organized crime, bloated bureaucracy, mounting debt, and crumbling infrastructure *are* ongoing problems here. Add to that the crash of the go-go '80s—which clipped the wings of many a high-rolling Wall Streeter—and the subsequent recession of the early '90s—which sent many big corporations scurrying for low-rent New Jersey—and you'll see why many people seem ready to kick New York in the kidneys and turn out the lights. But do you really think it would be that easy? As the millennium approaches, the city seems to be once again struggling back to life and cleaning up its act: FBI records show that violent crime rates in NYC fell by 6% from 1988 to 1993. Notoriously sleazy XXX-filled Times Square is being cleaned up and turned over to Disney; parks like Bryant Park and Tompkins Square have been reclaimed from drug peddlers; and farmers' markets and neighborhood cafés are flourishing. Better still, the city's transportation department swears it's got a handle on the 60,000 or so potholes that show up annually, and they've just finished adding air-conditioning to 99% of the city's subway cars. Whether or not you agree that New York deserves to be called Capital of the World, you can't dispute that it's one hell of a town.

BASICS 1

By Shon Bayer, Matthew Jalbert, and Mira Schwirtz

If you've ever traveled with anyone before, you know the two types of people in the world: the planners and the nonplanners. You also know that travel brings out the very worst in both groups: Left to their own devices, the planners will have you goose-stepping from attraction to attraction on a cultural blitzkrieg, while the nonplanners will invariably miss the flight, the bus, and the point. This Basics chapter offers you a middle ground, providing enough information to help plan your trip without saddling you with an itinerary or invasion plan. Keep in mind that companies go out of business, prices inevitably go up, and city buses rarely run on schedule. This is New York—if you want predictability, stay home and watch reruns of *The Brady Bunch*.

Planning Your Trip

USEFUL ORGANIZATIONS

If you call or write in advance, the **New York State Department of Tourism** will send you brochures on historical sites, recreational areas, and amusement parks around the state, as well as brochures on New York City. *1 Commerce Plaza, Albany, NY 12245, tel. 518/474–4116 or 800/225–5697.*

New York Convention and Visitors Bureau (NYCVB). The NYCVB's multilingual staff can set first-time visitors at ease with free subway and bus maps; discounts for museums, major attractions, hotels, restaurants, guided tours, Broadway shows, and many shops; plus the scoop on upcoming events. They occasionally offer free tickets to TV shows. Call, write, or drop by in person. *2 Columbus Circle, btw Broadway and Eighth Ave., Upper West Side, New York, NY 10019, tel. 212/397–8222 or 800/692–8474 for 24-hr interactive menu. Subway: A, B, C, D, 1, or 9 to W. 59th St. Open weekdays 9–6, weekends 10–3.*

WHEN TO GO

CLIMATE If you don't like the weather in New York, goes the old joke, wait a minute. Temperatures not only fluctuate dramatically from season to season, they often change from balmy to miserable and back again in a single afternoon. In winter, lows can hit 15°F (-9°C), with or without wicked winds and blizzards of snow. Summers bring hotter-than-hell temperatures coupled with 99.9% humidity. Because New York is so awfully hot in summer, many locals get the hell out June–August, when the streets are quieter, the bars are less crowded, and the ratio of tourists to locals jumps way up.

Without a doubt, fall and spring are the best times of year to visit New York, both in terms of the weather and the scenery. In fall the city's parks turn golden, and there's something about the smell of roasting chestnuts carried on a crisp autumn breeze that makes you feel at peace with the world. In spring, usually by early April, the snow melts for good, flowers start blooming, and the birds start singing—ah, sylvan Manhattan. The following chart shows the average highs and lows in Manhattan:

Jan.	41°F	5°C	May	70°F	21°C	Sept	76°F	24°C
	29	–2		54	12		61	16
Feb.	43°F	6°C	June	81°F	27°C	Oct.	67°F	19°C
	29	–2		63	17		52	11
Mar.	47°F	8°C	July	85°F	29°C	Nov.	56°F	13°C
	34	1		70	21		43	6
Apr.	61°F	16°C	Aug.	83°F	28°C	Dec.	43°F	6°C
	45	7		68	20		31	–1

PUBLIC HOLIDAYS Just about everything—including banks, museums, stores, and some restaurants—close on the following national holidays: **New Years Day** (Jan. 1), **Martin Luther King Jr.'s Birthday** (third Mon. of Jan.), **Presidents' Day** (third Mon. of Feb.), **Memorial Day** (last Mon. in May), **Independence Day** (July 4), **Labor Day** (first Mon. of Sept.), **Columbus Day** (second Mon. in Oct.), **Veteran's Day** (Nov. 11), **Thanksgiving** (fourth Thurs. in Nov.), and **Christmas** (Dec. 25). Buses and trains follow weekend schedules on holidays.

FESTIVALS Every month of the year finds some kind of celebration or happening, whether it's a daylong parade up Fifth Avenue or a summer-long series of performances. The huge diversity of people in New York adds plenty of spice to the mix—a wild proliferation of events celebrating different groups and all kinds of ethnic holidays, from the huge St. Patrick's Day parade to the Festival of San Gennaro in Little Italy. For more festival info ask at the NYCVB (*see* Useful Organizations, *above*) for a calendar of events or get a copy of the *Village Voice*, *Time Out*, *The New Yorker*, or the Friday edition of the *New York Times*. For info on free **summer concerts** and **music festivals**, *see* Summer Arts, in Chapter 7.

➤ **JANUARY** • For **New Year's Eve** you have two very different options: Hang out with drunken out-of-towners on Times Square and watch the famous ball drop at midnight, or catch a free midnight fireworks display in Central Park. On **New Year's Day** the Polar Bear Club takes its annual swim in the frigid Atlantic, at Coney Island.

The **Winter Antiques Show** (tel. 212/665–5250), held near the end of the month at the Seventh Regiment Armory (Park Ave., at E. 67th St.), is one of the nation's largest. It sounds dull, but it's actually pretty cool if you like antiques.

➤ **FEBRUARY** • **Chinese New Year.** In Chinatown the streets crackle with firecrackers, hailing the Chinese New Year, on the first full moon after January 21, with processions and a dragon parade. The main parade starts on Mott Street in Chinatown and continues down Canal Street and East Broadway. *Tel. 212/267–5780 or 212/744–8188.*

Westminster Kennel Club Dog Show. It's a dog-eat-dog world (not literally) at Madison Square Garden the second Monday and Tuesday of the month, as Schnauzers, Rottweilers, and Afghan hounds compete for the title of champion. Believe it or not, this is a big deal in New York.

➤ **MARCH** • The gargantuan **Art Expo** (tel. 212/216–2000 or 800/827–7170), at the Jacob K. Javits Convention Center, includes cultural performances from around the world. The Earth Society's **Earth Day** (tel. 212/730–4960) festival at the United Nations includes a ringing of the Peace Bell as the sun crosses the equator on the spring equinox. For blooms, check out the **New York Flower Show** (tel. 212/757–0915), at Piers 90 and 92 on the Hudson River, and in the Bronx at the New York Botanical Gardens' **Spring Flower Show** (tel. 718/817–8700). The **Sunday Easter Parade** (March 30 in 1997) is all about people in extravagantly odd hats sauntering along Fifth Avenue from 49th Street to 59th Street.

The **St. Patrick's Day Parade** is the city's biggest event, held every March 17 on Fifth Avenue between 44th and 86th streets. The four-hour parade features lots of beer, green hats, and woozy marchers. In the past few years it's also featured an unsanctioned band of Irish gays and lesbians protesting their exclusion from the official ceremonies. *Tel. 212/484–1200.*

➤ **APRIL** • For the entire month, an elaborate **chocolate Easter sculpture** is on display at the Waldorf-Astoria Hotel (301 Park Ave., at E. 50th St.); the hotel management will be very, very angry if you attempt to lick their work of art. The **Cherry Blossom Festival** (tel. 718/622–4433), held at the Brooklyn Botanic Garden, includes haiku readings, taiko drumming, the ancient tea ceremony, and exhibits of Japanese art.

➤ **MAY** • On the first Sunday after May 17, Brooklyn's thriving Scandinavian community parties down at the annual **Norwegian Constitution Day Parade** in Bay Ridge. The **Loisada Street Fair** takes place on the last weekend in May, celebrating those hip and funky inhabitants of the Loisada (Lower East Side).

Dance Africa. The Brooklyn Academy of Music (*see* Arts Centers, in Chapter 7) hosts the largest annual gathering of African dance companies in the States. Accompanying the performances are classes, discussions, and a bazaar with African-American crafts and foods.

Fleet Week. Navy ships from the United States and abroad are joined by Coast Guard ships for a parade up the Hudson River, then a docking in Manhattan during which ships are open to the public. It all happens at the *Intrepid* Air, Sea, and Space Museum (*see* Museums and Galleries, in Chapter 2) during the week before Memorial Day.

Ninth Avenue International Food Festival. Ninth Avenue, site of the most varied ethnic foods in the city, closes to traffic between West 34th and West 57th streets for an entire weekend so chefs can show off their stuff. *Tel. 212/581–7217 or 212/581–7029.*

Ukrainian Festival. New York's Ukrainian community whoops it up at this East Village festival, held on the weekend between Mother's Day and Memorial Day. *E. 7th St., btw Second and Third Aves., tel. 212/674–1615.*

Washington Square Art Show. Artists display their work around this Village park on Memorial Day weekend and the following weekend, and then again during the first two weekends of September. *Fifth Ave., at Washington Square North, West Village, tel. 212/982–6255.*

➤ **JUNE** • Harlem celebrates the 1865 signing of the Emancipation Proclamation with **Juneteenth** (tel. 212/368–8400), with music, food, and dance. East Broadway between Rutgers and Montgomery streets is the site of the **Lower East Side Jewish Spring Festival**, held on the second Sunday in June.

New York's **Gay Pride Parade**, held on the last Sunday in June, commemorates the 1969 Stonewall riots—considered by many the birth of the gay rights movement. (For other gay and lesbian festivities, *see* Chapter 8.) *Tel. 212/463–9030 or 212/807–7433.*

Mermaid Parade. This wild and wacky parade along the Coney Island boardwalk celebrates the summer solstice; marching bands and antique cars share the procession with people dressed like creatures of the sea. *Tel. 718/372–5159.*

During the annual **Museum Mile Festival**, Fifth Avenue from 82nd Street to 104th Street is closed to traffic 6 PM–9 PM. Admission to the Mile's museums is either free or greatly reduced. *Tel. 212/603–9868 or 212/397–8222.*

During the raucous **Puerto Rican Day Parade**, flag-waving Puerto Ricans jam the streets for an exuberant celebration of one of New York's biggest immigrant groups. Join the crowds on Fifth Avenue between 44th and 86th streets. *Tel. 212/484–1200.*

St. Anthony of Padua Feast. This two-week Italian festival is held on Sullivan Street from Spring to Houston streets in SoHo; carnival rides, street vendors, and general joviality climax in a grand pageant. *Tel. 212/777–2755.*

➤ **JULY** • On **American Independence Day** (July 4), the city explodes with illicit fireworks (the East Village sounds like a war zone), while the legit blasts are put on by Macy's: Its works are shot off from Battery Park and Midtown just after 9 PM. The best view may be from the

Promenade in Brooklyn (Subway: 2 or 3 to Clark St.). And keep an eye out for the **African Street Festival** in Brooklyn's Bedford-Stuyvesant neighborhood, a weeklong block party celebrating black culture.

➤ **AUGUST** • The Caribbean Cultural Center produces **Carnival** (tel. 212/307–7420), held the first weekend in August and celebrating people of the African diaspora. The last Sunday in August sees **Fiesta Folklorica**, a Latin American festival in Central Park. Harlem celebrates its heritage with **Harlem Week** (tel. 212/427–7200), a weeklong bash of cultural events.

➤ **SEPTEMBER** • The wild and wacky **Wigstock** transvestite festival—yes, the one canonized in that 1995 film documentary—happens the first weekend in September, in the West Village. New York's biggest German-American event is the **Steuben Day Parade** along Fifth Avenue from 61st to 86th streets on the third weekend in September (tel. 516/239–0741). Mulberry Street in Little Italy is the site of the hugely popular **Festival of San Gennaro** (tel. 212/226–9546), an Italian street carnival—the entire street is lined with arcade games, sellers of Italian kitsch, and stands selling greasy snacks or cotton candy.

The three-day **New York Is Book Country** fair, in mid-September, celebrates books of all kinds. On one afternoon, Fifth Avenue from 48th to 57th streets is closed and handed over to publishers, bookstores, and small presses displaying their wares. *Tel. 212/207–7242.*

Council Travel Offices in the United States

ARIZONA: Tempe (tel. 602/966–3544). CALIFORNIA: Berkeley (tel. 510/848–8604), Davis (tel. 916/752–2285), La Jolla (tel. 619/452–0630), Long Beach (tel. 310/598–3338), Los Angeles (tel. 310/208–3551), Palo Alto (tel. 415/325–3888), San Diego (tel. 619/270–6401), San Francisco (tel. 415/421–3473 or 415/566–6222), Santa Barbara (tel. 805/562–8080). COLORADO: Boulder (tel. 303/447–8101), Denver (tel. 303/571–0630). CONNECTICUT: New Haven (tel. 203/562–5335). FLORIDA: Miami (tel. 305/670–9261). GEORGIA: Atlanta (tel. 404/377–9997). ILLINOIS: Chicago (tel. 312/951–0585), Evanston (tel. 847/475–5070). INDIANA: Bloomington (tel. 812/330–1600). IOWA: Ames (tel. 515/296–2326). KANSAS: Lawrence (tel. 913/749–3900). LOUISIANA: New Orleans (tel. 504/866–1767). MARYLAND: College Park (tel. 301/779–1172). MASSACHUSETTS: Amherst (tel. 413/256–1261), Boston (tel. 617/266–1926), Cambridge (tel. 617/497–1497 or 617/225–2555). MICHIGAN: Ann Arbor (tel. 313/998–0200). MINNESOTA: Minneapolis (tel. 612/379–2323). NEW YORK: New York (tel. 212/822–2700, 212/666–4177, or 212/254–2525). NORTH CAROLINA: Chapel Hill (tel. 919/942–2334). OHIO: Columbus (tel. 614/294–8696). OREGON: Portland (tel. 503/228–1900). PENNSYLVANIA: Philadelphia (tel. 215/382–0343), Pittsburgh (tel. 412/683–1881). RHODE ISLAND: Providence (tel. 401/331–5810). TENNESSEE: Knoxville (tel. 423/523–9900). TEXAS: Austin (tel. 512/472–4931), Dallas (tel. 214/363–9941). UTAH: Salt Lake City (tel. 801/582–5840). WASHINGTON: Seattle (tel. 206/632–2448 or 206/329–4567). WASHINGTON, D.C. (tel. 202/337–6464). For U.S. cities not listed, call 800/2–COUNCIL.

The **New York Film Festival**, held late September–early October, is the premier showcase for dozens of films from around the world—and your best bet for seeing directors and actors at the opening of their films. The **New York Video Festival runs** concurrently. *140 W. 65th St., at Broadway, tel. 212/875–5050.*

➤ **OCTOBER** • The **Columbus Day Parade** (tel. 212/249–9923), the second-largest in New York after St. Paddy's Day, is held around October 12 on Fifth Avenue between 44th and 86th streets. The Cathedral of St. John the Divine (Amsterdam Ave., at W. 112th St., tel. 212/316–7540) is the site of the **Feast of St. Francis** on the first Sunday in October, featuring a Blessing of the Animals. The **International Expressions Festival** is a monthlong affair highlighting Caribbean- and African-diaspora cultures (tel. 212/307–7420).

➤ **NOVEMBER** • The **New York City Marathon**, in early November, is one of the world's most prestigious, featuring racers from around the world. Starting at the Verrazano-Narrows Bridge in Staten Island, the race proceeds through Brooklyn, Queens, and the South Bronx before finishing at Tavern on the Green in Central Park. *Tel. 212/860–4455.*

Macy's Thanksgiving Parade takes place on Thanksgiving Day, beginning at Central Park West and 77th Street, down to Columbus Circle, then down Broadway to 34th Street. The night before finds many New Yorkers watching the whole shindig being prepared—somebody's gotta blow those balloons up—on Central Park West from 77th to 88th streets. *Tel. 212/695–4400.*

➤ **DECEMBER** • On December 2 a Christmas tree is lit up at **Rockefeller Center** (Fifth Ave., at 50th St., tel. 212/698–8684). The scene is *very* New York. With the annual **Christmas Spectacular** (tel. 212/247–4777), Radio City Music Hall puts on its Christmas bash through January 8; expect rapping elves and lots of lasers. The hyper-consumptive **Fifth Avenue** is closed to traffic on the two Sundays before Christmas so people can go berserk with their credit cards. **Kwanzaa**, an African-American holiday, celebrates the "first fruits of the harvest" (as the name means in Swahili) and includes various cultural events and fairs at the Jacob K. Javits Convention Center.

BUDGET TRAVEL ORGANIZATIONS

Council on International Educational Exchange (CIEE) is a private, nonprofit organization administering work, volunteer, academic, and professional programs worldwide. Its travel divi-

STA Offices

• **UNITED STATES. CALIFORNIA:** Berkeley (tel. 510/642–3000), Los Angeles (tel. 213/934–8722), San Francisco (tel. 415/391–8407), Santa Monica (tel. 310/394–5126), Westwood (tel. 310/824–1574). **FLORIDA:** University of Florida (tel. 352/338–0068), Miami (tel. 305/461–3444). **MASSACHUSETTS:** Boston (tel. 617/266–6014), Cambridge (tel. 617/576–4623). **NEW YORK:** Columbia University (tel. 212/865–2700), West Village (tel. 212/627–3111). **PENNSYLVANIA:** Philadelphia (tel. 215/382–2928). **WASHINGTON:** Seattle (tel. 206/633–5000). **WASHINGTON, D.C.** (tel. 202/887–0912).

• **INTERNATIONAL. AUSTRALIA:** Adelaide (tel. 08/223–2426), Brisbane (tel. 07/221–9388), Cairns (tel. 070/314199), Darwin (tel. 089/412955), Melbourne (tel. 03/349–2411), Perth (tel. 09/227–7569), Sydney (tel. 02/212–1255). **NEW ZEALAND:** Auckland (tel. 09/309–9995), Christchurch (tel. 03/379–9098), Wellington (tel. 04/385–0561). **UNITED KINGDOM:** London (tel. 0171/937–9962).

sion, **Council Travel**, is a full-service travel agency specializing in student, youth, and budget travel. They offer discounted airfares, rail passes, accommodations, guidebooks, budget tours, and travel gear. They also issue the ISIC, GO25, and ITIC identity cards (*see* Student ID Cards, *below*), as well as Hostelling International (HI) cards. Forty-six Council Travel offices serve the budget traveler in the United States (*see box, above*), and there are about a dozen overseas (including ones in Britain, France, and Germany). Council also puts out a variety of publications, including the free *Student Travels* magazine, a gold mine of travel tips (including information on work-abroad, study-abroad, and international volunteer opportunities). *205 E. 42nd St., New York, NY 10017, tel. 888/COUNCIL, info@CIEE.org.*

Educational Travel Center (ETC) books low-cost flights to destinations within the continental United States and around the world. Their best deals are on flights leaving the Midwest, especially Chicago. ETC also issues Hostelling International cards. For more details request their free brochure, *Taking Off. 438 N. Frances St., Madison, WI 53703, tel. 608/256–5551.*

STA Travel, the world's largest travel organization catering to students and young people, has over 100 offices worldwide and offers low-price airfares to destinations around the globe, as well as rail passes, car rentals, tours, you name it. STA issues the ISIC and the GO25 youth cards (*see* Student ID Cards, *below*), both of which prove eligibility for student airfares and other travel discounts. Call 800/777–0112 or the nearest STA office (*see box, above*) for more info.

Student Flights, Inc. specializes in student and faculty airfares and sells rail passes and travel guidebooks. *5010 E. Shea Blvd., Suite A104, Scottsdale, AZ 85254, tel. 602/951–1177 or 800/255–8000.*

Travel CUTS is a full-service travel agency that sells discounted airline tickets to Canadian students and issues the ISIC, GO25, ITIC, and HI cards. Their 25 offices are on or near college campuses. Call weekdays 9–5 for information and reservations. *187 College St., Toronto, Ont. M5T 1P7, tel. 416/979–2406.*

HOSTELLING ORGANIZATIONS

HOSTELLING INTERNATIONAL **Hostelling International (HI)**, also known as the IYHF, is the umbrella group for a number of national youth hostel associations. HI offers single-sex dorm-style beds ("couples" rooms and family accommodations are available at many hostels) and self-service kitchen facilities at nearly 5,000 locations in more than 70 countries around the world. Membership in any HI national hostel association (*see below*), open to travelers of all ages, allows you to stay in HI-affiliated hostels at member rates (about $10–$25 a night). Members also have priority if the hostel is full and are eligible for discounts around the world, including rail and bus travel in some countries. A one-year membership is $25 for adults (renewal $20) and $10 for those under 18. *733 15th St. NW, Suite 840, Washington, D.C. 20005, tel. 202/783–6161.*

National branches of Hostelling International include **Hostelling International–American Youth Hostels (HI–AYH)** (733 15th St., Suite 840, Washington, D.C. 20005, tel. 202/783–6161); **Hostelling International–Canada (HI–C)** (400-205 Catherine St., Ottawa, Ont. K2P 1C3, tel. 613/237–7884 or 800/663–5777); **Youth Hostel Association of England and Wales (YHA)** (Trevelyan House, 8 St. Stephen's Hill, St. Albans, Herts. AL1 2DY, England, tel. 01727/855–215); **Australian Youth Hostels Association (YHA)** (Level 3, 10 Mallett St., Camperdown, New South Wales 2050, tel. 02/565–1699); and **Youth Hostels Association of New Zealand (YHA)** (Box 436, Christchurch 1, tel. 3/379–9970).

YMCA **Y's Way International.** This network of YMCA overnight centers offers low-cost accommodations (average overnight rate of $26) in New York City and around the United States to travelers of all ages. Their booklet, "The Y's Way," details locations, reservation policies, and package tours. *224 E. 47th St., New York, NY 10017, tel. 212/308–2899.*

STUDENT ID CARDS

Students traveling around the United States should not expect big discounts—except possibly on air travel, if tickets are purchased through special student-travel agencies such as Council

Travel or STA (*see* Budget Travel Organizations, *above*). Still, you'll want to bring your student ID card for those occasional discounts on bus travel, club cover charges, and admission to some museums and movie theaters.

The $19 **International Student Identity Card (ISIC)** entitles students to discount student air-fares, special fares on local transportation, and discounts at museums, theaters, sports events, and many other attractions. In the United States, apply to Council Travel or STA; in Canada, the ISIC is available for C$15 from Travel CUTS (*see* Budget Travel Organizations, *above*). In the United Kingdom, students can purchase the ISIC at any student union or student-travel company. Applicants must submit a photo as well as proof of current full-time student status, age, and nationality.

The **Go 25: International Youth Travel Card (GO25)** is issued to travelers (students and non-students) between the ages of 12 and 25 and provides services and benefits similar to those given by the ISIC card. The $19 card is available from the same organizations that sell the ISIC. When applying, bring a passport-size photo and your passport as proof of your age.

The $20 **International Teacher Identity Card (ITIC)**, sponsored by the International Student Travel Confederation, is available to teachers of all grade levels, from kindergarten to graduate school. The services and benefits you get when buying the card are similar to those for the ISIC. When you buy the card, ask for the *International Teacher Identity Card Handbook*, which has all the details.

MONEY

New York is, was, and will always be one of the most expensive cities in the United States. Stores and restaurants usually accept traveler's checks but prefer cash, and some turn up their noses at credit cards. At least there are plenty of banks.

HOW MUCH IT WILL COST In New York it's easy to get swept up in a debt-inducing cyclone of $50 dinners, $40 theater tickets, $25 club covers, $10 cab rides, and $100 hotel rooms. Don't do it. Stay in hostels, get around on the subway, check out Off-Broadway performances, and take advantage of lunch specials at restaurants and no-cover nights at clubs and bars. In this case, you'll have a fabulous time for about $50 per day.

Many New Yorkers advise that you keep at least $10 in cash handy as "mugging money"; this may be enough to send away an assailant without violence.

➤ **ACCOMMODATIONS** • Hostels are the best deal for solo travelers, with dorm beds for $12–$25. Singles and doubles cost $40–$90 at even the cheapest (and, predictably, skanki-est) hotels, though groups of three or more can find decent hotels offering triples, quads, and suites for a bargain $75–$100. If you're planning a longer visit, university housing can be yours for as little as $20 per night. Note: Temperatures really soar in New York during summer, so you might want to plunk down a few extra dollars to stay at a hotel or hostel that offers rooms with air-conditioning; many (but not all) do.

➤ **FOOD** • It's easy to gorge yourself at a cool restaurant in the East Village for under $10, but in other neighborhoods you'll probably spend twice that. That said, many restaurants cut prices drastically for their "lunch specials" (typically weekdays 11 AM–6 PM). Hot dogs, falafel sandwiches, tacos, pizza slices, and bagels are easy to find and all cost under $2. The city's many greenmarkets (*see* Chapter 4) also offer inexpensive, fresh produce.

➤ **ENTERTAINMENT AND NIGHTLIFE** • This is where you can go broke fast. Cover charges for nightclubs can hit $20 or more, not including drinks ($2–$5 each). Tickets to *Les Mis* or *Phantom* are $25–$100 a pop. A beer in a bar usually costs $2–$3.50, though some Manhattan bars serve $1 pints during weekday "happy hours." Movies are a ridiculous $8.50 most places. Crazy, huh? If you steer clear of the big names you can find live music and dance clubs with covers under $10, Off-Broadway shows with tickets for $5–$25, and, especially in summer, tons of concerts and performances for free.

➤ **TIPPING** • The customary tipping rate is 15% for taxi drivers and waiters. You can do the math quickly in restaurants by just doubling the tax noted on the check—it's 8¼% of your bill—and rounding up or down. Bartenders should get between 50¢ and $1 per drink, or more if you're sloshed. Hotel maids and porters should be tipped about $1. Tip $1 per coat checked.

TRAVELING WITH MONEY You can protect yourself by carrying cash in a money belt or necklace pouch; keeping accurate records of traveler's checks' serial numbers; and recording credit-card numbers and an emergency number for reporting the cards' loss or theft. You'll need at least some cash for cabs, buses, the subway, and some restaurants—but the bulk of your funds are most safely carried as traveler's checks.

TRAVELER'S CHECKS American Express card members can order traveler's checks by phone, free of charge (with a gold card) or for a 1% commission (with the basic green card). In three to five business days you'll receive your checks: Up to $1,000 can be ordered in a seven-day period. Checks can also be purchased through many banks, in which case both cardholders and non-cardholders can expect to pay 1%–4% in bank fees. AmEx also issues **Traveler's Cheques for Two**, checks that can be signed and used by either you or your traveling companion. If you lose

Rumor has it that even the city's drug dealers accept AmEx traveler's checks.

your checks or are ripped off, just like that guy on TV says, American Express has the resources to provide you with a speedy refund—often within 24 hours. For info on American Express offices in New York, *see* Staying in New York City, *below. Tel. 800/221–7282 in the U.S. and Canada.*

Citicorp traveler's checks are available from Citibank and other banks worldwide. For 45 days from date of check purchase, purchasers have access to the 24-hour International S.O.S. Assistance Hotline, which can provide English-speaking doctor, lawyer, and interpreter referrals; assistance with loss or theft of travel documents; traveler's check refund assistance; and an emergency message center. *Tel. 800/645–6556.*

MasterCard International traveler's checks are offered through banks, credit unions, and foreign-exchange booths. **Thomas Cook**, a brand of MasterCard, sells checks in all denominations; if purchased through one of the Thomas Cook Foreign Exchange offices in New York, there is no commission. *Tel. 800/223–7373.*

Visa traveler's checks are readily accepted in all New York banks. *Tel. 800/227–6811.*

CREDIT CARDS Whether you regard credit cards as tools of the bourgeois or the most convenient invention since zippered trousers, they're one way to survive a vacation in New York. Use them to rent a car, reserve a flight, or keep a roof over your head when your pockets are empty. Keep in mind that many of the city's restaurants refuse credit cards (or only take AmEx).

GETTING MONEY ON THE ROAD

Provided there is money at home to be had, there are at least five ingenious ways to get it:

- Have it sent through a large **commercial bank**. Unless you have an account with that large bank, though, you'll have to initiate the transfer at your own bank—which could prove slow and expensive.

- If you're an **American Express** cardholder, cash a personal check at an American Express office for up to $1,000 (usually given in traveler's checks rather than cash). **Express Cash** further allows AmEx cardholders to withdraw up to $1,000 every seven days from their personal checking accounts via ATMs (*see* Cash Machines, *below*).

- The *MoneyGram*^SM service can be a dream come true if you can convince someone back home to go to a MoneyGram^SM agent and fill out the necessary forms. Simply pay up to $1,000 with a credit card or cash (and anything over that in cash) and, as quick as 10 minutes later, it's ready to be picked up. Fees vary but average about 3%–10%. You have to show ID when picking up the money. For locations, call 800/926–9400.

- **MasterCard** and **Visa** cardholders can get cash advances (typically about $300 daily) from many banks and currency exchange offices. The commission for this handy-dandy service hovers around 7%, so contact your credit-card company before you leave for information. If you have a PIN number for your card, you might even be able to make the transaction with an ATM machine. For more info on this useful trick, *see* Cash Machines, *below.*

- Have funds sent through **Western Union** (tel. 800/325–6000), which has offices scattered around the city. These folks offer three ways to feed your hungry wallet, two of them requiring a friend with deep pockets on the other side of the wire. Said friend can transfer funds from a MasterCard, Visa, or Discover card (up to the card's limit, or $10,000) by calling from a home or business. Alternatively, your friend can trot some cash or a certified cashier's check over to the nearest office. Your third option is to bring your own plastic to certain Western Union locations for up to $500 in "FlashCash."

CASH MACHINES Virtually all U.S. banks belong to a network of **ATMs** (automated teller machines), which gobble up bank cards and spit out cash 24 hours a day. Most banks in New York accept cards affiliated with Star, Cirrus, Plus, and Nyce. To receive a card for an ATM system you must apply at a bank and select a PIN (personal identification number). There are ATMs on practically every corner of New York's shopping and commercial districts. For safety reasons, almost all are located inside a bank lobby or other locked enclosure that you can only open with an ATM card, and many are manned at night by a security guard. Hours are generally 6 AM–midnight, though some stay open 24 hours.

A **Visa** or **MasterCard** can also be used to access cash through certain ATMs (provided you have a PIN for it), but the fees for this service are usually higher than bank-card fees. Also, a daily interest charge usually begins to accrue immediately on these credit-card "loans," even if monthly bills are paid up.

In one current scam, a thief will create a distraction as you leave an ATM machine—by "accidentally" breaking an egg or popping a packet of ketchup in your face. Amidst confusion, apologies, and a hasty cleanup, your wallet will mysteriously disappear.

Express Cash allows AmEx cardholders to withdraw up to $1,000 in a seven-day period from their personal checking accounts via ATMs. Gold cardholders can receive up to $2,500 in a seven-day period. Each transaction carries a 2% fee, with a minimum charge of $2.50 and a maximum of $20. Set up the linking of your accounts at least two to three weeks before departure. Call 800/528–4800 for an application.

WHAT TO PACK

As little as possible. Besides the usual suspects—clothes, toiletries, camera, and a good book—you'll want to bring a day pack to stash essentials in while you're out exploring the city. If you're traveling in summer, buy a half-liter water bottle ($1.50) and refill it each day. You'll save big bucks, help heal the planet, and enjoy some of the finest tap water in the United States.

THE SLEEP SHEET:

Take a big sheet. Fold it down the middle the long way. Sew one short side and the long, open side. Turn inside out. Get inside. Sleep.

BEDDING Hostels require that you use a sleep sheet, and, though some rent them, some don't. If you have a backpack, consider a sleeping mat that can be rolled tightly and strapped onto the bottom of your pack, then unrolled and planted firmly under your ass. In New York, most hostels supply sheets, pillows, and blankets—but not towels.

CAMERAS AND FILM The higher the film speed, the more susceptible it is to damage by airport scanning machines. If you're a serious photographer, consider packing your unprocessed film in your carry-on luggage and ask security to inspect it by hand. (Keep your film in a plastic bag and you can just whip it out for quick inspection.) And if your camera is new (or new to you) shoot and develop a few rolls before leaving home to avoid spoiling travel footage with prominent thumb shots or miscalculated f-stops.

CLOTHING The first thing you may notice when you arrive in New York: Everyone here wears black, lots of black, year-round. This is considered chic. Whether you do the same is up to you, but you should keep in mind that New York is a fashionable city, and residents do not—as *Seinfeld* would have you believe—wear white Reeboks and windbreakers. Though it's important to pack pragmatically (bring comfortable, easy-to-clean clothes), you may feel awkward if you're always dressing down. It's better to have one decent shirt you can wear every other day than a whole slew of tacky T-shirts. Summers are gruesomely hot, so bring lightweight clothes, as well as something warm for overly air-conditioned subway cars and museums. In winter, you'll need a coat and shoes that can handle snow, sleet, and ice, plus a hat, gloves, and scarf to protect you from those -10° winds. And you should be prepared for rainfall any time of year.

MISCELLANEOUS Stuff you might not think to take but will be damn glad to have: (1) day pack; (2) flashlight; (3) Walkman; (4) pocket knife for as many purposes as there are doodads sticking out of it; (5) water bottle; (6) sunglasses; (7) towel; (8) several large zip-type plastic bags, useful for wet swimsuits, leaky bottles, and rancid socks; (9) travel alarm clock; (10) needle and small spool of thread; (11) umbrella; (12) an interesting book.

STAYING HEALTHY

HEALTH AND ACCIDENT INSURANCE Some general-health plans cover expenses incurred while traveling, so review your existing policy (or a parent's policy, if you're a dependent) before leaving home. Most university health insurance plans stop and start with the school year, so don't count on school spirit to pull you through. Canadian travelers, lucky to have a single-payer system with universal coverage, should check with their provincial ministry of health to see if their resident health insurance plan covers them in New York.

Carefree Travel Insurance is, in fact, pretty serious about providing coverage for emergency medical evacuation and accidental death or dismemberment. It also offers 24-hour medical phone advice. *100 Garden City Plaza, 5th Floor, Garden City, NY 11530, tel. 516/294–0220 or 800/323–3149.*

Globalcare Travel Insurance. Covers up to $20,000 for trip cancellation, delay, or interruption and up to $5,000 for individual medical treatment or hospitalization. Local legal and medical referrals are also given. *220 Broadway, Lynnfield, MA 01940, tel. 800/821–2488.*

Travel Guard offers an excellent variety of insurance plans, many of which are endorsed by the American Society of Travel Agents. Most policies include coverage for sickness, injury (or untimely death), lost baggage, and trip cancellation. *1145 Clark St., Stevens Point, WI 54481, tel. 800/826–1300 or 715/345–0505.*

CONTRACEPTIVES AND SAFE SEX Remember that you can contract AIDS and other STDs just as easily on vacation as you can at home. Just about every pharmacy and grocery store in New York sells condoms of every strength and texture. A pack of two costs about $2.50; a pack of 12 goes for around $8.

CRIME AND PUNISHMENT

Crime in New York has dropped like a rock in recent years: The New York crime rate of 1995 was ranked 22nd among major U.S. cities, down from 18th in 1993. And this has a lot to do with the increasing vigilance of New York's cleaned-up cop force. Petty offenses like public drinking or urination or petty drug-peddling won't get the nudge-and-a-wink treatment these days, and the biggies will land you in jail for sure. Many young New Yorkers are tolerant (even enthusiastic) about drug use: Heroin, LSD, amphetamines, cocaine, and marijuana are all bought and sold here (there are even free delivery services that'll bring a bag of pot right to your door). Drug possession and/or consumption, however, warrants arrest and fines. Crack is a major problem downtown, and you'll see plenty of people along Houston Street and First Avenue selling at all hours of the day. Stay on the right side of the law unless you want your vacation to include a stay on Riker's Island (you don't).

ALCOHOL The legal drinking age in New York state is 21. It's unevenly enforced, and corner stores ("bodegas" in New York lingo) are likely to sell beer to anyone who looks like they've graduated junior high. Most bars and clubs do not ask for ID, which translates into lots of college freshmen getting tanked in bars on the weekends. However, if you're underage and you're caught drinking, you may be fined and/or prosecuted. Likewise, despite the fact that people from Wall Streeters to derelicts can be seen drinking in public, the punishment—spending a few hours in a holding tank—might not be worth the thrill.

SMOKING The way most New Yorkers puff away, you'd think they were in Paris. Few bars, cafés, or clubs place any restrictions on smoking—in some, it may even seem like part of the dress code. Restaurants are another story: Recent laws have banned smoking in the larger ones (over 35 seats) except in separate, well-ventilated areas. Die-hard nicotine fiends tend to feign ignorance; don't be shy about standing up for your rights if you're a nonsmoker.

WOMEN TRAVELERS

Unfortunately, not everyone is as open-minded about women travelers as we know they should be—solo women travelers often have to put on a tough and surly facade to avoid unwelcome advances. You can take some comfort in knowing that some 1.1 million single women call New York home, but you'll still need to take some precautions, especially at night. Obviously, avoid situations where you're alone with a stranger—in a subway car, for example, or at an ATM machine. On city streets, walk briskly and with confidence, even if you're lost; you can duck into a café or subway station to discreetly check your map. Your best bet is to hook up with fellow travelers whom you feel you can trust, then enjoy exploring the city together.

PUBLICATIONS For a complete listing of women's periodicals, presses, and cafés, try the *Directory of Women's Media* ($30), published by the National Council for Research on Women. *530 Broadway, 10th Floor, New York, NY 10012, tel. 212/274–0730.*

Other than the lesbian-oriented *Women's Traveller* and *Are You Two...Together?,* major travel publications for women include *Women Travel: Adventures, Advice, and Experience* ($12.95), published by Prentice Hall and available at most bookstores. Over 70 countries receive some sort of coverage in the form of journal entries and short articles, though it offers few details on prices, phone numbers, and addresses. Thalia Zepatos's *A Journey of One's Own* ($13), available at most bookstores, is fun to read and a good resource for general travel info.

ORGANIZATIONS New York women have plenty of resources at their fingertips, including the **Women's Action Alliance** (370 Lexington Ave., tel. 212/532–8330); the **Young Women's Christian Association (YWCA)** (610 Lexington Ave., at E. 53rd St., Upper East Side, tel. 212/755–4500), which offers social-service programs and accommodation referrals for women; and the founding chapter of the **National Organization for Women (NOW)** (105 E. 22nd St., Suite 307, New York, NY 10010, tel. 212/260–4422), which offers regular meetings, support groups, lectures, and referrals. The **Guerrilla Girls** is a highly charged group of New York artists and art professionals dedicated to fighting discrimination—watch for their posters and happenings around town. They like to stay relatively anonymous, but you can reach them by e-mail at guerrillagirls@voyagerco.com.

TRAVELERS OF COLOR

A wealth of resources support, educate, celebrate, and bring together New York City's rich mix of ethnicities. In addition to community centers, look into student services and groups at the city's many universities.

AFRICAN-AMERICAN The **Schomburg Center for Research in Black Culture** (*see* Museums and Galleries, in Chapter 2) hosts forums, lectures, films, and exhibitions, and is the main resource library in the country for black culture. The **Afro Arts Cultural Center** (163 W. 125th St., Harlem, tel. 212/749–0827) is another leading center for African culture in New York, with exhibits, discussions, and a notice board listing community services. **Liberation Bookstore** (421 Malcolm X Blvd., at W. 131st St., Harlem, tel. 212/281–4615) and **Black Books Plus**

(702 Amsterdam Ave., at W. 94th St., Upper West Side, tel. 212/749–9632) are great places to get info on local happenings.

ASIAN-PACIFIC The **Asia Society** (725 Park Ave., at E. 70th St., Upper East Side, tel. 212/288–6400) holds cultural performances and shows works by Asian artists. The **China Institute** (125 E. 65th St., btw Park and Lexington Aves., Upper East Side, tel. 212/744–8181) mounts shows of Chinese art and culture. The **Japan Society** (333 E. 47th St., btw First and Second Aves., Midtown, tel. 212/832–1155) and the **Nippon Club** (145 W. 57th St., btw Sixth and Seventh Aves., Midtown, tel. 212/581–2223) present exhibitions and events highlighting Japanese culture. The **Asian American Arts Centre** (26 Bowery, btw Bayard and Doyers Sts., Chinatown, tel. 212/233–2154) stages performances and exhibitions of contemporary Asian-American art.

CHICANO-LATINO **El Museo del Barrio** (1230 Fifth Ave., at 104th St., East Harlem, tel. 212/831–7272) is the city's leading Puerto Rican and Latino cultural center. The **Association of Hispanic Arts** (173 E. 116th St., btw Lexington and Third Aves., East Harlem, tel. 212/860–5445) has a directory of Latino arts organizations and assists Latino artists with grants and shows. The **Caribbean Cultural Center** (408 W. 58th St., btw Ninth and Tenth Aves., Midtown, tel. 212/307–7420) produces lectures, performances, and other cultural events. They host an annual Carnival, held the first weekend in August, as well as the International Expressions Festival in October. **Intar** (420 W. 42nd St., btw Ninth and Tenth Aves., Midtown, tel. 212/695–6134) is an Off-Broadway theater specializing in Latin-American writers and translations of Latino writers. The **Americas Society** (680 Park Ave., tel. 212/249–8950) organizes educational programs about Western Hemisphere countries and shows artwork in their galleries. The new **Julia de Burgos Latino Cultural Center** is on Lexington Avenue, between 105th and 106th streets in East Harlem. It wasn't finished at press time; look in the phone book for the number.

NATIVE AMERICAN New York's American Indian community is served by the **American Indian Community House** (404 Lafayette St., 2nd Floor, at E. 4th St., East Village, tel. 212/598–0100), which offers programs in HIV/AIDS awareness/prevention, job placement, substance abuse, a Women's Wellness Circle, performing and visual arts, and tons of other services. The **National Museum of the American Indian** (*see* Museums and Galleries, in Chapter 2) also has a cultural resource center.

TRAVELERS WITH DISABILITIES

Although New York was largely built decades before the watershed Americans with Disabilities Act, most of the major sights, museums, and parks are accessible to those in wheelchairs. Hotels, hostels, restaurants, bars, and clubs are a different story: Generally, only the newest and most recently renovated are fully accessible. If you're in doubt about accessibility at a particular destination, your best bet is to call ahead. The **Mayor's Office for People with Disabilities** (52 Chambers St., Room 206, New York, NY 10007, tel. 212/788–2830) can also help with up-to-date info. The **Andrew Heiskell Library for the Blind and Physically Handicapped** (40 W. 20th St., btw Fifth and Sixth Aves., Midtown, tel. 212/206–5400 or TDD 212/206–5458) has a large collection of Braille, large-print, and recorded books.

COMING AND GOING The **American Public Transit Association** (tel. 202/898–4000) in Washington, D.C. has info on transportation options for travelers with disabilities. Most major airlines are happy to accommodate travelers with disabilities, provided they receive notification 48 hours in advance. Ask about possible discounts and check-in protocol when making reservations. *Access Travel: Airports*, a free publication describing facilities and services at more than 500 airports worldwide, is available by mail from the **Consumer Information Center** (Dept. 5804, Pueblo, CO 81009).

➤ **BY TRAIN AND BUS** • **Amtrak** (tel. 800/872–7245, TDD 800/523–6590) offers a 25% discount on one-way coach fares for travelers with disabilities. If notified when reservations are made, Amtrak will provide assistance for travelers at stations. **Greyhound-Trailways** (tel. 800/752–4841, TDD 800/345–3109) allows a traveler with a disability and a companion to ride for the price of a single fare. For both, you will need to show written proof of disability (such as a doctor's letter) to receive special fares.

> **BY CAR** • If you plan to rent a car, you'll find that some major car-rental companies are able to supply hand-controlled vehicles with a minimum of 24 hours' advance notice. Given a day's notice, **Avis** (tel. 800/331–1212) will install hand-controlled mechanisms at no extra charge. **Hertz** (tel. 800/654–3131, TDD 800/654–2280) asks for 48 hours advance notice and a $25 cash or credit-card deposit to do the same.

GETTING AROUND THE CITY Of the 469 subway stations in New York, a paltry 23 have elevators—and even those aren't very dependable. City buses are more convenient: All 3,700 buses kneel to the curb, 95% are equipped with wheelchair lifts, and drivers will announce stops for visually impaired riders. People with disabilities are eligible for reduced fares on public buses and subways with proper ID; call 212/878–7294 for info on obtaining a disability ID card. The Transit Authority's **Accessibility Hotline** (tel. 800/734–6772) has 24-hour recorded info regarding subway elevators and escalators, or you can speak directly to a Transit Authority representative about accessibility, daily 6 AM–9 PM, by calling 718/596–8585. Take note: Taxi drivers tend to avoid passengers who might cause them inconvenience or delay, while drivers for car services (which charge a per-trip flat rate) are more accommodating.

PUBLICATIONS The bible for New York visitors with disabilities is *Access for All* ($5), published by Hospital Audiences, Inc. (220 W. 42nd St., New York, NY 10036, tel. 212/575–7663, TDD 212/575–7673). It lists theaters, museums, and other cultural institutions that offer wheelchair access and services for the hearing or visually impaired. The free *I Love New York Travel and Adventure Guide,* describing access to the city's major sights, is available from the New York Division of Tourism (1 Commercial Plaza, Albany, NY 12245, tel. 518/474–4116 or 800/355-5697).

ORGANIZATIONS Several U.S. organizations provide travel info to people with disabilities, usually for a small annual membership fee. Among them are the **Information Center for Individuals with Disabilities** (Fort Point Pl., 27–43 Wormwood St., Boston, MA 02210, tel. 617/727–5540, TDD 617/345–9743); **Mobility International USA (MIUSA)** (Box 10767, Eugene, OR 97440, tel. and TDD 541/343–1284); and the **Society for the Advancement of Travel for the Handicapped (SATH)** (347 Fifth Ave., Suite 610, New York, NY 10016, tel. 212/447–7284).

Info for Foreign Visitors

Just as you'd expect from the city where the United Nations is permanently headquartered, New York hosts a consulate for just about every country on the map, except New Zealand (sorry, Kiwis): **Australia** (650 Fifth Ave., near 51st St., tel. 212/408–8400); **Canada** (125 Sixth Ave., btw 49th and 50th Sts., tel. 212/596–1600); **Ireland** (345 Park Ave., 17th Floor, at 51st St., tel. 212/319–2555); **United Kingdom** (845 Third Ave., near E. 51st St., tel. 212/745–0200). For other consulates, check the New York *Yellow Pages.*

CURRENCY EXCHANGE

The United States uses dollars ($) and cents (¢). Commonly used paper currency comes in denominations of $1, $5, $10, $20, $50, and $100; many places in the city will not accept bills greater than $20. Coins come in denominations of 1¢ (penny), 5¢ (nickel), 10¢ (dime), and 25¢ (quarter). Pennies are almost useless, but you should horde quarters for pay telephones, self-service laundromats, and bus fare. When you plan your budget, allow flexibility for fluctuating exchange rates; at press time, the exchange rates were:

Canada	Britain	Australia	New Zealand
C$1=69¢	£1=US$1.47	AUS$1=75¢	NZ$1=63¢
US$1=C$1.44	US$1=68p	US$1=AUS$1.33	US$1=NZ$1.58

You'll have no trouble finding currency exchange services in Manhattan—try touristy areas like the South Street Seaport, World Trade Center, Herald Square, Times Square, or Grand Central Terminal. All three airports also offer currency exchange (*see* Getting Around New York City, To and From the Airports, *below*). Currency-exchange offices are less common in the outer boroughs, so try a bank; they have good rates but short hours (they typically close by 3 PM on weekdays and shut entirely on weekends). In addition to the options listed below, exchange companies with late hours (relatively speaking) include **Freeport Currencies** (132 W. 45th St., tel. 212/223–1200; open weekdays 8:30–6, weekends 9:30–5); **Harold Reuter & Co.** (200 Park Ave., Room 332E, tel. 212/661–0826 or 800/258–0456; open weekdays 7–7, Sat. 8–3); or one of 22 citywide **AmEx** offices (*see* Staying in New York City, *below*).

Chemical Bank Foreign Currency Exchange has over a dozen offices throughout Manhattan, plus branches in Queens and the Bronx. Each offers a multilingual staff and wheelchair access. For locations, call 800/935–9935.

Chequepoint USA has three branches in Midtown. *Main Office: 22 Central Park S, at Fifth Ave., tel. 212/750–2400. Subway: N or R to Fifth Ave. Open weekdays 8–8, weekends 8–9.*

Thomas Cook Currency Services has seven offices throughout Manhattan, including one at Grand Central Station. *Main Office: 1590 Broadway, at W. 48th St., tel. 212/757–6915. Subway: 1 or 9 to W. 50th St. Open Mon.–Sat. 9–8, Sun. 9–5. Other locations: 317 Madison Ave., at E. 42nd St., Grand Central Station, tel. 212/883–0400; open Mon.–Sat. 9–5. 779 Broadway, btw E. 9th and 10th Sts., East Village, tel. 212/614–9690; open weekdays 9:30–5:30. 1271 Broadway, at W. 32nd St., Chelsea, tel. 212/679–4365; open Mon.–Sat. 10–6.*

PASSPORTS AND VISAS

If your passport is lost or stolen, you should immediately notify both the city police and your consulate. A consular officer should be able to wade through some red tape and issue you a new one, or at least get you back into your country of origin without one. The process will be slowed up considerably if you don't have other forms of identification on you, so you're well advised to carry other forms of ID—a driver's license, a copy of your birth certificate, a student ID—separate from your passport, and tuck a few photocopies of the front page of your passport in your luggage and your traveling companion's pockets. The **British consulate** (*see above*) requires a police report, any form of identification, and three passport-size photos. They will replace the passport in four working days. The **Australian consulate** (*see above*) requires three passport-size photos and can usually replace a passport in 24 hours. There is no consulate for New Zealand in the city, so Kiwis should contact their embassy in Washington, D.C.

CANADIAN CITIZENS Canadian citizens must show proof of citizenship and identity to enter the United States for up to 90 days (a passport, birth certificate with raised seal, or voter registration card are preferred). Passport applications, available at any post office or passport office, cost C$60 and take one to two weeks to process.

U.K. CITIZENS You need a valid 10-year, £18 passport to enter the United States. Application forms, which take about four weeks to process, are available from the **Passport Office** (Clive House, 70 Petty France, London SW1H 9BR, tel. 0171/279–4000 or 0990/210–410 for recorded info), or from most travel agents, main post offices, and regional passport offices. A British Visitor Passport is not acceptable.

Visas are required for visits of more than 90 days. Apply four weeks in advance to a travel agent or the **U.S. Embassy Visa and Immigration Department** (5 Upper Grosvenor St., London W1A 2JB) or, for residents of Northern Ireland, to the **U.S. Consulate General** (Queen's House, Queen St., Belfast BT1 6EO). Visas can be given only to holders of 10-year passports—although visas in expired passports remain valid. Submit a completed Nonimmigrant Visa Application (Form 156), a copy of your passport, a photograph, and evidence of your intended departure from the United States.

AUSTRALIAN CITIZENS Australian citizens need a valid passport and visa to enter the United States. Passports cost AUS$81 for adults. Children under 18 may purchase a five-year passport for AUS$41. Applications are available at any post office or passport office, or call toll-free in Australia 008/131–232 weekdays for additional info.

NEW ZEALAND CITIZENS New Zealand citizens need a valid passport to enter the United States. Ten-year passports, which cost NZ$80 and take about three weeks to process, are available from the **New Zealand Passport Office** (Documents of National Identity Division, Department of Internal Affairs, Box 10526, Wellington), as well as regional passport offices and post offices. To stay more than 90 days you'll also need a visa; contact the American Embassy or Consulate nearest you. In the United States, you can get more info from the **New Zealand Embassy** (36 Observatory Circle NW, Washington, D.C. 20008, tel. 202/328–4800).

CUSTOMS AND DUTIES

Visitors 21 and older can bring into the United States (1) 200 cigarettes or 100 non-Cuban cigars (sorry Fidel) or 2 kilograms of smoking tobacco, (2) 1 U.S. liter of alcohol, and (3) duty-free gifts to a value of $400 (this includes the value of your tobacco, cigars, and alcohol). Also, you may ship gifts valued up to $100 duty-free. Forbidden are meat and meat products, seeds, plants, and fruits. Avoid illegal drugs like the plague—if you get caught with them you can be banned from the United States for the rest of your life, no kidding. Make sure any legit bottles of pills are clearly labeled and that you have a copy of the written prescription handy.

CANADIAN CUSTOMS Exemptions for returning Canadians range from C$20 to C$500, depending on how long you've been out of the country: For two days out, you're allowed to return with C$200 worth of goods; for one week out, you're allowed C$500 worth. Above these limits, you'll be taxed about 15%. Duty-free limits are up to 50 cigars, 200 cigarettes, 400 grams of tobacco, and 1.14 liters of liquor. All must be declared in writing upon arrival at customs and must be with you or in your checked baggage. To mail back gifts, label the package: "Unsolicited Gift–Value under C$60." For more details, call the automated info line of the **Revenue Canada Customs, Excise and Taxation Department** (2265 St. Laurent Blvd. S, Ottawa, Ont., K1G 4K3, tel. 613/993–0534 or 613/991–3881), where you may request a copy of the Canadian Customs brochure "I Declare/Je Déclare."

U.K. CUSTOMS Travelers age 17 or over who return to the United Kingdom may bring back the following duty-free goods: 200 cigarettes or 100 cigarillos or 50 cigars or 250 grams of tobacco; 1 liter of alcohol over 22% volume or 2 liters of alcohol under 22% volume, plus 2 liters of still table wine; 60 ml of perfume and 250 ml of toilet water; and other goods worth up to £136. For further information or a copy of "A Guide for Travellers," which details standard customs procedures and other boring but important stuff, contact **HM Customs and Excise** (Dorset House, Stamford St., London SE1 9PY, tel. 0171/928–3344).

AUSTRALIAN CUSTOMS Australian travelers 18 and over may bring back, duty free: 1 liter of alcohol; 250 grams of tobacco products (equivalent to 250 cigarettes or cigars); and other articles worth up to AUS$400. If you're under 18, your duty-free allowance is AUS$200. To avoid paying duty on goods you mail back to Australia, mark the package: "Australian goods returned." For more rules and regulations, request the pamphlet "Customs Information for Travellers" from a local **Collector of Customs** (GPO Box 8, Sydney NSW 2001, tel. 02/226–5997).

NEW ZEALAND CUSTOMS Although you'll be greeted with the usual "*Haere Mai*" ("Welcome to New Zealand"), homeward-bound travelers face a number of restrictions. Travelers over age 17 are allowed, duty-free: 200 cigarettes or 250 grams of tobacco or 50 cigars or a combo of all three up to 250 grams; 4.5 liters of wine or beer and one 1,125-ml bottle of spirits; and goods with a combined value up to NZ$700. If you want more details, request the pamphlet "Customs Guide for Travellers" from a New Zealand consulate.

USEFUL ORGANIZATIONS

For "official" tourist information about the whole United States or its specific regions, check with the **U.S. Travel and Tourism Administration (USTTA)**. *Dept. of Commerce, 14th and Constitution Aves. NW, Washington, D.C. 20230, tel. 202/482–3811. AUSTRALIA: Level 59*

MLC Centre, King and Castlereagh Sts., Sydney, NSW 2001, tel. 02/233–4666. CANADA: Suite 602, 480 University Ave., Toronto, Ont. M5G 1V2, tel. 416/ 595–5082 or 1095 W. Pender St., 20th Floor, Vancouver, BC, tel. 604/685–1930. UNITED KINGDOM: American Embassy, 24 Grosvenor Sq., London WIA IAE, tel. 0171/495–4466.

HOMESTAY ASSOCIATIONS **World Learning**, part of the Experiment in International Living, arranges stays with American families for a week ($450) to a month ($600) for anyone—not just students—between the ages of 15 and 85. They also arrange intensive language programs and semester-long homestays for foreign high-school students. *41 Sutter St., Suite 518, San Francisco, CA 94104, tel. 800/858–0292 or 415/288–1380. Also: 419 Boylston St., 7th Floor, Boston, MA 02116, tel. 800/662–2967 or 617/247–0350. Also: British Experiment Association, W. Mavern Rd., Mavern, Worcest. WR14 4EN, England, tel. 01684/562–577, fax 01684/562–212.*

Institute of International Education (IIE) has a "Homestay Information Sheet" that lists homestay opportunities throughout the United States, including Manhattan and the boroughs. *809 United Nations Plaza, New York, NY 10017, tel. 212/883–8200.*

WORK PROGRAMS In order to work legally in the United States, you must have a social security number, which is the birthright of U.S. citizens. Obtaining a green card, which entitles foreigners to work and reside in the United States, is a long shot for most visitors.

A more promising option is to participate in an **Exchange Visitor Program (EVP).** These are authorized by the U.S. government to provide foreign students with legal jobs. Most jobs are not big moneymakers and come with restrictions, usually on the amount you can earn and the length of time you can stay. Council (*see* Budget Travel Organizations, in Planning Your Trip, *above*) publishes two excellent resource books with complete details on work/travel opportunities; Council's *Work, Study, Travel Abroad: The Whole World Handbook* ($13.95) gives the lowdown on scholarships, grants, fellowships, study-abroad programs, and work exchanges.

The U.K.-based **Vacation Work Press** publishes two other first-rate guides: *Directory of Overseas Summer Jobs* (£9) and Susan Griffith's *Work Your Way Around the World* (£12). The first lists over 45,000 jobs worldwide; the latter has fewer listings but makes a more interesting read. Look for them at bookstores or contact the publisher directly. *9 Park East End, Oxford OX1 1HJ, England, tel. 01865/241–978.*

The "Au-Pair in America" program offered by the **American Institute for Foreign Study (AIFS)** places foreign nannies in American households. *102 Greenwich Ave., Greenwich, CT 06830, tel. 203/869–6188 or 800/727–6188.*

Air Passes

If you want to cover a lot of ground in the United States, consider one of the two airfare deals offered exclusively to foreign visitors: The "Visit America Pass," offered by most major U.S. airlines, entitles the holder to three stops (traveling in one direction only) over a 60-day period for $200–$300; the catch is that you can only stop in cities served by the issuing airline. The "Discover America Pass," offered by Delta airlines (tel. 800/325–1447 in U.S.), consists of a coupon book good for flights over a 60-day period to U.S. cities served by Delta. You tear off a coupon for each flight, including any connecting flights. A book of three coupons costs $359; you pay $100 for each additional coupon. You must purchase either of these passes before arriving in the States; contact a budget travel agency in your home country before leaving.

For British travelers, **British Universities North America Club (BUNAC)** operates in conjunction with Council to provide temporary work permits to British citizens. *16 Bowling Green Ln., London EC1R OBD, England, tel. 0171/251–3472.*

Australians and New Zealanders should look into the **SWAP Program**, which arranges temporary work visas valid for up to six months in the United States. *Box 399, Carlton South, Melbourne, VIC 3053, Australia.*

Canadians should contact **Travel CUTS**, which offers a version of the CIEE program to Canadian students who want to work abroad for up to six months. *SWAP, 243 College St., 5th Floor, Toronto, Ont. M5T 2Y1, tel. 416/977–3703.*

VOLUNTEER PROGRAMS If you can afford to work for nothing, more power to you. And the first call you should make is to Council's **Voluntary Service Department**, which can get you a two- to four-week job as a teacher, house builder, archaeological dig helper, whatever, throughout the United States. Another excellent resource is Council's *Volunteer!* ($8.95), a comprehensive guide to volunteer opportunities worldwide. *205 E. 42nd St., New York, NY 10017, tel. 888/COUNCIL, http://www.ciee.org.*

STUDYING IN NEW YORK American universities welcome applications from foreign students, although you should contact the admissions office of your prospective school about specific requirements. If English is not your native language, you may be required to take the **Test of English as a Foreign Language** and **Test of Spoken English (TOEFL/TSE)**, which is administered at locations around the world several times a year. For more info, contact the **TOEFL/TSE Application Office** (Box 6155, Princeton, NJ 08541-6155, tel. 609/951–1100).

Coming and Going

FINDING THE CHEAPEST FLIGHT

While a last-minute, round-trip ticket to New York can cost $849 from San Francisco or Los Angeles, bargain-basement prices can go as low as $159. Flexibility is the key to getting a serious bargain on airfare. If you can play around with your departure date, destination, amount of luggage carried, and return date, you will probably save money. A useful resource is Michael McColl's *The Worldwide Guide to Cheap Airfares* (Insider Publications, 2124 Kittredge St., 3rd Floor, Berkeley, CA 94704, tel. 800/782–6657; $14.95), an in-depth account of how to find cheap tickets and generally beat the system. As a rule, the further in advance you buy the ticket, the less expensive it is.

If you're in New York and shopping for a ticket out, you'll find dozens of companies advertising unbelievably cheap flights in the *Village Voice* and in the Sunday travel section of the *New York Times*. Most are legit, but call around, and check with the Better Business Bureau (tel. 212/533–6200) before you purchase. A few to try: **Travel Abroad, Inc.** (47 W. 34th St., Suite 535, at Broadway, tel. 212/564–8989 or 800/700–TRVL), **ABS Travel Inc.** (347 Fifth Ave., btw 33rd and 34th Sts., tel. 212/447–1717), and **Air Travel, Inc.** (5 W. 36th St., Room 304, at Fifth Ave., tel. 800/938–4625).

APEX TICKETS If you're not a student nor the kind of person who enjoys scouring newspapers for the lowest fare, APEX (Advance Purchase Excursion) tickets bought directly from the airline or from your travel agent are the simplest way to go. Regular APEX fares normally apply to tickets bought at least 21 days in advance; you can get Super-APEX fares if you know your travel plans at least one month in advance. Here's the catch: If you cancel or change your plans, you'll pay a penalty, anywhere from $50 to $100.

STANDBY AND THREE-DAY-ADVANCE-PURCHASE FARES Flying standby—where you purchase an open ticket and wait for the next available seat on the next available flight—is almost a thing of the past. Most airlines have dumped standby policies in favor of three-day-advance-purchase youth fares, which are only open to people under 25 and (as the name states) can only be purchased within three days of departure. Return flights must also be booked no more than three days prior to departure. If you meet the above criteria, expect 10%–50% savings on published APEX fares. A number of brokers specializing in last-minute sales offer savings for unsold seats on commercial carriers and charter flights, as well as tour packages; try the **Last Minute Travel Club** (tel. 617/267–9800).

STUDENT DISCOUNTS Student discounts on airline tickets are offered through **Council**, the **Educational Travel Center**, **STA Travel**, and **Travel CUTS** (*see* Budget Travel Organizations, *above*). Keep in mind that you will often *not* receive frequent-flyer mileage for discounted tickets. For discount tickets based on your status as a student, youth, or teacher, you'll need to produce an International Student Identity Card (ISIC), Youth Identity Card, International Teacher Identity Card, or some other form of ID. **Campus Connection** (1100 E. Marlton Pike, Cherry Hill, NJ 08032, tel. 800/428–3235), exclusively for students under 25, searches airline computer networks for the cheapest student fares to worldwide destinations.

CONSOLIDATORS Consolidator companies, also known as bucket shops, buy blocks of tickets at wholesale prices from airlines trying to fill flights. Check out any consolidator's reputation with the Better Business Bureau before purchasing a ticket (most are perfectly reliable, but better safe than sorry). If everything works as planned, you'll save 10%–40% on the published APEX fare. And now the bad news: Consolidator tickets are often not refundable, and flights often feature indirect routes, long layovers in connecting cities, and undesirable seat assignments. If your flight is delayed or canceled, you'll also have a tough time switching airlines. As with APEX tickets, you risk a huge penalty if you change your travel plans. If possible, pay with a credit card, so that you don't have to pay if your ticket never arrives. Bucket shops generally advertise in newspapers—be sure to read the fine print and check restrictions, refund possibilities, and payment conditions. One last suggestion: Confirm your reservation with the airline both before and after you buy a consolidated ticket.

Both **Flytime Tours and Travel, Inc.** (45 W. 34th St., Suite 305, New York, NY 10001, tel. 212/760–3737, fax 212/594–1082) and **Michele Travel** (45 W. 34th St., Suite 206, New York, NY 10001, tel. 212/967–1149, fax 212/868–0299) specialize in flights between New York and other U.S. cities. Other consolidators to try include **Airfare Busters** (5100 Westheimer Ave., Suite 550, Houston, TX 77056, tel. 713/961–5109 or 800/232–8783, fax 713/961–3385); **Globe Travel** (507 5th Ave., Suite 606, New York, NY 10017, tel. 800/969–4562, fax 212/682–3722); and **Up & Away Travel** (347 Fifth Ave., Suite 202, New York, NY 10016, tel. 212/889–2345, fax 212/889–2350).

CHARTER FLIGHTS Depending on the company you're dealing with, a charter company either buys a block of tickets on a regularly scheduled commercial flight and sells them at a discount or leases the the whole plane and then offers relatively cheap fares to the public. Despite a few potential drawbacks—among them infrequent flights, restrictive return-date requirements, lickety-split payment demands, and frequent bankruptcies—charter companies often offer the cheapest tickets around, especially during high season when APEX fares are most expensive. Make sure to ask about the company's policy on refunds should a flight be canceled by either yourself or the airline. Summer charter flights fill up fast and should be booked a couple months in advance.

Tower Air consistently offers some of the lowest fares to New York from the West Coast—though the airline is notorious for overbooking. Still, a $200 round-trip ticket might be worth the risk. Call 800/34–TOWER for reservations.

If the company is offering tickets on a regular commercial flight, you generally deal with the airline directly after you've bought the ticket from the charter folks. Things get a little sketchier when a charter company has chartered the whole plane: Bankrupt operators, long delays at check-in, overcrowding, and flight cancellation are fairly common. You can minimize risks by checking the company's reputation with the Better Business Bureau and taking out enough trip-cancellation insurance to cover the operator's potential failure.

Charter companies to try include **Council Charter** (tel. 212/661–0311), **DER Tours** (tel. 800/782–2424), and **MartinAir** (tel. 800/627–8462). **Travel CUTS** (tel. 416/979–2406) is part of the CIEE umbrella, which means it's a reputable place for Canadians to book their charter. Check newspaper travel sections for more extensive listings.

COURIER FLIGHTS A few restrictions and inconveniences are the price you'll pay for the colossal savings on airfare offered to air couriers (travelers who accompany letters and packages between designated points). The way it works is simple. Courier companies list whatever flights are available for the next several months or so. After you book the flight, you sign a contract with the company to act as a courier (some places make you pay a deposit, to be refunded after the successful completion of your assignment). On the day of departure, you arrive at the airport a few hours early, meet someone who hands you a ticket and customs forms, and off you go. After you land, you simply clear customs with the courier luggage, and deliver it to a waiting agent. The main restrictions are (1) reservations are recommended (and sometimes required) two months in advance; (2) you are allowed carry-on luggage only, because the courier uses your checked-luggage allowance to transport the time-sensitive shipment; (3) returns are usually within one week to three months; and (4) most courier companies only issue tickets to travelers over the age of 18.

Check newspaper travel sections for courier companies, check in the yellow pages of your phone directory, or mail away for a telephone directory that lists companies by the cities to which they fly. One of the better publications is *Air Courier Bulletin* (IAATC, 8 South J St., Box 1349, Lake Worth, FL 33460, tel. 407/582–8320), sent to IAATC members every two months once you pay the $35 annual fee. Another good resource is the newsletter published by **Travel Unlimited** (Box 1058, Allston, MA 02134), which costs $25 for 12 issues. Publications you can find in the bookstores include *Air Courier Bargains* ($14.95), published by The Intrepid Traveler, and *The Courier Air Travel Handbook* ($9.95), published by Thunderbird Press. Courier companies frequently offering flights into (and out of) New York include: **Discount Travel International** (169 W. 81st St., New York, NY 10024, tel. 212/362–3636); **East-West Express** (tel. 718/656–6242); **Halbart Express** (tel. 718/656–8189); and **Now Voyager** (74 Varick St., Suite 307, New York, NY 10013, tel. 212/431–1616).

BY PLANE

Three major airports—**John F. Kennedy International**, **La Guardia**, and **Newark International**—serve New York City, though Newark is actually in the state of New Jersey. For a description of services at each, *see* Getting Around New York City, To and From the Airports, *below*. The Port Authority publishes the *Airport Flight Guide* (free), a comprehensive listing of airlines operating in the metropolitan area. Write to: Aviation Dept., The Port Authority of New York and New Jersey, One World Trade Center, 65N, New York, NY 10048. It's also available at the info desks in all terminals.

FROM THE OTHER 49 Just about every airline in the country schedules flights to and from New York. Try **American** (tel. 800/433–7300), **America West** (tel. 800/235–9292), **Continental** (tel. 800/525–0280), **Delta** (tel. 800/221–2500), **TWA** (tel. 800/221–2000), **United** (tel. 800/241–6522), **USAir** (tel. 800/428–4322), or the discount carrier **Tower Air** (tel. 800/221–2500). A number of domestic airlines also operate commuter-plane "shuttles" between New York and major East Coast cities of Boston, Philadelphia, and Washington, D.C.

FROM CANADA **Air Canada** (tel. 800/776–3000) flies into Newark from major Canadian airports. Additional service to Canada is provided by Delta and USAir (*see above*).

FROM EUROPE **Air France** (tel. 800/237–2747), **British Airways** (tel. 800/247–9297), and **Lufthansa** (tel. 800/645–3880) all have terminals at JFK and Newark. Many of the major American airlines—such as American, Continental, and Delta (*see above*)—also offer frequent flights from Europe to New York.

FROM DOWN UNDER **Qantas** (tel. 800/227–4500 in U.S., 02/9957–0111 in Australia) flies from all major Australian cities, plus some New Zealand cities, to JFK International (via Los Angeles or San Francisco). The U.S. carrier **United** (tel. 800/241–6522 in U.S.) has service from Australia and New Zealand to all three airports in the NYC area.

BY TRAIN

Unlike the rest of this car-obsessed country, people on the East Coast actually rely on trains to get from city to city or commute from home to work. Departures are frequent and fares are cheap. New York City has two major railroad stations: **Pennsylvania Station** (W. 31st–34th Sts., btw Seventh and Eighth Aves.; subway: A, C, E, 1, 2, 3, or 9 to W. 34th St.), and **Grand Central Terminal** (W. 42nd–45th Sts., at Park Ave.; subway: 4, 5, 6, or 7 to Grand Central). Trains bound for Grand Central also stop at the tiny **125th Street Station** (125th St. at Park Ave.; subway: 4, 5, or 6 to E. 125th St.).

AMTRAK   Amtrak is the only passenger rail service in the United States. It's also a damn fine way to travel; you get a dining car, a smoking lounge, and lots of pretty scenery. Trains arrive daily at Pennsylvania Station (*see above*) from Boston (3¾ hrs, $39 one-way); Philadelphia (1½ hrs, $30); Washington, D.C. (3¾ hrs, $51), Chicago (17 hrs, $134), Seattle (2¾ days, $259), Los Angeles (3 days, $259), and many other American cities. Fares fluctuate according to time of the year and other factors (they're generally higher on Fridays and holidays), so call ahead for the latest ticket info. *Tel. 212/582–6875 or 800/USA–RAIL.*

➢ **AMTRAK PASSES** • Amtrak's **All-Aboard America Fare**, actually a booklet of tickets, allows riders special rates for three stops made in 45 days of travel. Ticket agents need to know your dates of travel and intended destinations for ticketing. Cost is $198–$378, depending on season and number of regions traveled. Amtrak's **USARail Pass** is terrific for the foreign budget traveler (it's not available to U.S. or Canadian citizens) because it allows unlimited travel on any of Amtrak's U.S. routes, with no formal itinerary required. A 15-day pass costs $355 ($245 Sept.–May), a 30-day pass $440 ($350). You can buy one at a travel agency in your home country before you leave, or from an Amtrak office in the States. A passport is required for purchase, and reservations are recommended several months in advance.

REGIONAL TRAIN SERVICES   Whether you're a freshman at Yale or a visitor crashing at your aunt's house in Greenwich, CT, there's a train to take you into New York City. One-way fares from most destinations cost less that $12; purchase your ticket before you board to avoid a $1–$3 lazy person's surcharge. The **Metro-North Commuter Railroad** (tel. 212/532–4900) serves New York's northern suburbs and southern Connecticut, terminating in New Haven. The **Long Island Railroad (LIRR)** (tel. 718/217–LIRR) runs through Long Island, smarty. **New Jersey Transit** (tel. 201/762–5100) offers service from towns in northern and central New Jersey, including Princeton. In Manhattan, Metro-North trains stop at Grand Central Terminal and at 125th Street; the LIRR and New Jersey Transit lines terminate at Pennsylvania Station.

➢ **PATH** • The PATH trains run between New York City and terminals in New Jersey (including Hoboken, Jersey City, and Newark). In Manhattan, PATH stations are located at the World Trade Center; on Christopher Street (at Greenwich Street); and along Sixth Avenue at West 9th, 14th, 23rd, and 33rd streets. Trains run 24 hours and depart every 10–30 minutes. The fare is $1. *Tel. 800/234–PATH.*

BY BUS

All long-distance bus companies depart from the **Port Authority Bus Terminal**. This huge terminal, which services more than 35 bus companies and nearly 200,000 people a day, is situated in a somewhat squalid neighborhood. For **New York City buses** going uptown, board the M10 on the east side of Eighth Avenue; board the downtown M11 on Ninth Avenue across the street from the south wing entrance; board the cross-town M42 on 42nd Street at Eighth Avenue. You are expected to tip the terminal's Red Caps if they help you haul your 200-pound suitcase to a ticket window. *625 Eighth Ave., at W. 41st St., Midtown, tel. 212/564–8484. Subway: A, C, or E to W. 42nd St. Open 24 hrs.*

GREYHOUND   Bus service in North America can be grungy and depressing—but it *is* cheap. Greyhound-Trailways has routes throughout the United States, including service between New York and Boston (4½ hrs, $25), Philadelphia (2½ hrs, $13), Washington, D.C. (4½ hrs, $25), Chicago (18 hrs, $59), Atlanta (21 hrs, $89), San Francisco (2½ days, $109), and Los Angeles (3 days, $129). If you have a credit card, you can purchase tickets in advance over the tele-

Your vacation.

Your vacation after losing your hard-earned vacation money.

Lose your cash and it's lost forever. Lose American Express® Travelers Cheques and you can get them quickly replaced. They can mean the difference between the vacation of your dreams and your worst nightmare. And, they are accepted virtually anywhere in the world. Available at participating banks, credit unions, AAA offices and American Express Travel locations. *Don't take chances. Take American Express Travelers Cheques.*

do more

Travelers Cheques

All the best trips start with Fodor's.

EXPLORING GUIDES
Like the best of all possible travel magazines

"As stylish and attractive as any guide published." —*The New York Times*

"Worth reading before, during, and after a trip." —*The Philadelphia Inquirer*

More than 30 destinations available worldwide. $19.95 - $21.00 ($27.95 - 28.95 Canada)

BERKELEY GUIDES

The hippest, freshest and most exciting budget-minded travel books on the market.

"Berkeley's scribes put the funk back in travel."
—*Time*

"Fresh, funny, and funky as well as useful."
—*The Boston Globe*

"Well-organized, clear and very easy to read."
—*America Online*

14 destinations worldwide. Priced between $13.00 - $19.50. ($17.95 - $27.00 Canada)

AFFORDABLES

"All the maps and itinerary ideas of Fodor's established Gold Guides with a bonus—shortcuts to savings." —*USA Today*

"Travelers with champagne tastes and beer budgets will welcome this series from Fodor's." —*Hartford Courant*

"It's obvious these Fodor's folks have secrets we civilians don't." —*New York Daily News*

Also available: Florida, Europe, France, London, Paris. Priced between $11.00 - $18.00 ($14.50 - $24.00 Canada)

At bookstores, or call **1-800-533-6478**

The name that means smart travel.™

phone (though you can usually still score a seat if you wander into the terminal on the day of departure). Cheapest fares are offered during the low season (January–June). You're allowed two carry-on and two checked pieces of luggage. *Tel. 212/971–6300 or 800/231–2222.*

➢ **GREYHOUND PASSES** • Greyhound's **Ameripass**, valid on all U.S. routes, can be purchased in advance in cities throughout the States; spontaneous types can also buy it up to 45 minutes before the bus leaves the terminal. The pass allows purchasers unlimited travel within a limited time period: seven days ($179), 15 days ($289), 30 days ($399), or 60 days ($599). Foreign visitors get slightly lower rates.

GREEN TORTOISE Green Tortoise Adventure Travel is the Magic Bus alternative to humdrum public transportation. Buses are equipped with sleeping pads, kitchens, and stereos, and often stop for a gourmet cookout, hike, or swim. In summer, buses make 10-day cross-country trips between San Francisco and New York or Boston, passing through Chicago and such scenic wonders as Pyramid Lake, the Grand Tetons, and the Badlands. In spring and fall, the 14-day trip goes through the Southern California deserts, Texas, the South, and around the Appalachian Mountains. The cost is about $35 a day (meals included). Make reservations at least a week in advance. *Tel. 415/956–7500 or 800/TORTOISE, fax 415/956–4900.*

REGIONAL BUS SERVICES For bus travel into and around New Jersey, contact **New Jersey Transit** (tel. 201/762–5100 or 800/772–2222). **East Coast Explorer** (tel. 718/694–9667 or 800/610–2680) runs backroad trips to Boston ($29 one-way) and Washington, D.C. ($32), with stops at places of natural, historical, and cultural interest—like Newport, Rhode Island and the Pennsylvania Amish country. Buses depart New York for Boston on Monday and for Washington, D.C. on Thursday; returns are on the following day and travel a different route.

BY CAR

If you're planning to tool around the United States by car, the best investment you can make is to become a member of the **Automobile Association of America (AAA)** (1000 AAA Dr., Heathrow, FL 32746, tel. 800/222–4357) or one of its affiliates. Membership generally costs $58 for the first year and $41 annually thereafter, though rates vary from state to state. Members receive free maps, tour books, and personalized itinerary plans; free emergency road service; discounts at hotels, motels, and some restaurants; and no-fee purchase of traveler's checks. If you belong to any type of auto club abroad, AAA may honor your membership; otherwise, consider joining while you're here.

DRIVEAWAYS Not to be confused with drivebys, a driveaway is a car that you are responsible for delivering cross-country to its owner—a great way to get in and out of New York for relatively little cash. You'll have to deal with plenty of restrictions: The car's owner decides departure date, travel time, and final destination. You must be over 21, and you'll need three good references, several forms of ID, a clean driving record, and $200–$300 cash for the deposit (refundable on satisfactory return of the car). You should apply at least three weeks before you intend to travel. Try **A Economy Auto Transporters Inc.** (tel. 800/466–7775); the **Auto Driveaway Co.** (tel. 212/967–2344 or 800/487–2343), which charges a $10 non-refundable processing fee per application; or **A Anthony's Driveaway Truckaway Co. Inc.** (tel. 800/659–9903), which requires prospective drivers to fill out an application in person at their office in New Jersey.

RIDESHARES To take advantage of this deliciously cheap alternative, your skin must not crawl at the thought of sharing a vehicle for days or weeks with a complete stranger (and his or her equally strange taste in music). You'll be expected to contribute gas money and pay for your own expenses as a rider. The best places in New York to scout for rideshare opportunities are around colleges and universities. At **Columbia University** (tel. 212/854–1754) check Ferris Booth Hall. At the **Fashion Institute of Technology** (tel. 212/760–7710) look for the "personal bulletin boards" in Building B (first floor) and Building A (seventh floor). At **New York University** (tel. 212/998–4636) visit the lower level of Loeb Student Center, or hunt around dorm lobbies. Also check for ads in weeklies like the *Village Voice*. And like your mom warned you, be wary of nutcases.

INTERNATIONAL DRIVER'S PERMIT Foreign visitors itching to get behind the wheel of a fine American automobile may want to obtain an International Driver's Permit before arriving in the United States. It's not required by law, but it could save you some hassle if you're ever pulled over by the police. The automobile association in your home country will issue one for a small fee. The law *does* require that you carry automobile insurance—make sure that yours is valid in the United States.

Getting Around New York City

The **Metro Transit Authority (MTA)** publishes excellent fold-out maps that show all the subway and bus routes and stops; ask for one in any subway station. You might also want to request the MTA's booklet, "Token Trips: New York City Subway and Bus Travel Guide," which lists every conceivable attraction in the city with easy-to-follow travel directions. The tiny "Transit-wise NY Metropolitan Commuter Rail Map" ($4.95) is worth purchasing if you don't want to advertise your tourist status, because it shows all Manhattan subways and buses, but tri-folds to fit in a pocket. It's available at bookstores and newsstands. For general city bus and subway travel info, call the **MTA/New York City Transit hotline** (tel. 718/330–1234), staffed daily 6 AM–9 PM, or the **Multilingual Transit hotline** (tel. 718/330–4847), staffed daily 6 AM–9:30 PM. For info on **ferry service** to the Statue of Liberty, Ellis Island, and Staten Island, *see* Chapter 2.

TO AND FROM THE AIRPORTS

Call the Port Authority's **Air Ride hotline** (tel. 800/AIR–RIDE) for detailed, up-to-the-minute recorded info on how to reach your destination from New York's three major airports via car, private bus, shuttle service, or public transportation. The cheapest option is the public transit system, although what you save in dollars you'll pay for with time and effort, since routes can take an hour or more and may involve transferring between bus and subway. Private shuttle services travel between all three airports and many Manhattan hotels. Taxis and car services are the most expensive option, with fares running as high as $35 one-way, plus $3–$4 in bridge tolls. When all is said and done, you'll find that one of the easiest and most reasonable ways to get to the airport is with a bus service—either **NJ Transit** to Newark or **Carey Transportation** to La Guardia and JFK (*see* Shuttle Buses, *below*).

JFK INTERNATIONAL John F. Kennedy International (tel. 718/244–4444 or 800/247–7243 in NYC area) is the largest of New York's three airports, with five terminals located about 15 miles southeast of Manhattan, in Queens. There's a **currency exchange** booth on the second floor of the JFK International building and one in the Delta terminal. **Luggage storage** (tel. 718/656–8617) facilities are at three locations: By Gate 4 in the Delta terminal, and in the International building near Gates 10 and 32. Rates are $3.50–$5 per bag, per day. There are **information booths** in the east and west wings of the International building, on the first floor. Each terminal has its own **parking lot**. Six lots are for long-term parking with a 30-day maximum stay at a cost of $6 per day. Taxi or car service to JFK costs a flat $30 from Manhattan.

➤ **SHUTTLE BUSES** • The private bus line **Carey Airport Express** (tel. 718/632–0500 or 800/678–1569) picks up outside all JFK terminals every 30 minutes between 6 AM and midnight and stops in Manhattan at the Port Authority Bus Terminal (W. 42nd St., at Eighth Ave.), Grand Central Station (E. 42nd St., at Park Ave.), and a few major hotels. The ride costs $13 to or from JFK and takes anywhere from 30 minutes to an hour depending on traffic. Outbound Carey buses (from Manhattan to JFK) operate 24 hours a day, 365 days a year. **Gray Line Air Shuttle** (tel. 212/315–3006 or 800/451–0455) is slightly more expensive ($16 one-way from JFK) but is also slightly faster and stops at any major hotel between 23rd and 63rd streets. Make reservations at the airport's transportation center.

➤ **PUBLIC TRANSPORT** • Taking the subway to JFK is fairly simple and cheap ($1.50). Take the **A train** to the Howard Beach Station, from where you can catch a free shuttle run by the Port Authority. The shuttle makes the trip to JFK every 10 minutes and takes about 20 minutes to reach the terminals. All told, it's about a 70-minute trip from Midtown.

LA GUARDIA La Guardia Airport (tel. 718/533–3400) is the smallest New York airport, 8 miles northeast of Manhattan, in Flushing, Queens. There are **currency-exchange windows** on the upper level between the American and United terminals, and at the USAir Terminal. There are no luggage storage facilities. **Parking** costs $4 for the first four hours and $2 per hour after that, maxing out at $18 per day. There is no long-term parking at La Guardia. On average, taxi and car service to La Guardia costs about $20–$25 plus tax and tip.

➤ **SHUTTLE BUSES AND PUBLIC TRANSPORT** • The **Carey Airport Express** (tel. 718/632–0500 or 800/678–1569) picks up outside all La Guardia terminals every 30 minutes from 6 AM to midnight and stops at the Port Authority Bus Terminal (W. 42nd St., at Eighth Ave.), Grand Central Station (E. 42nd St., at Park Ave.), and many hotels downtown. The ride costs $10 to or from La Guardia and takes anywhere from 20 minutes to an hour depending on traffic. **Gray Line Air Shuttle** (tel. 212/315–3006 800/451–0455) costs $13 one-way from La Guardia but stops at any major hotel between 23rd and 63rd streets. Make reservations at the airport's ground transportation center or use the courtesy phone. The **Triboro Coach Corp.** (tel. 718/335–1000) runs its **Q-33** line from the airport to the Jackson Heights subway stop in Queens every 10 minutes during peak morning and evening hours. Their **Q-47** line services the Marine Air Terminal at La Guardia. The ride costs $1.50 and the buses run daily 4 AM–2 AM. The NYC Transit Service runs its **M60** line to La Guardia; catch it in Manhattan on 118th Street at Broadway. The route follows 125th Street across town and runs every half hour. The fare is $1.50.

NEWARK Newark International Airport (tel. 201/961–6000 or 800/247–7243 in New Jersey) is about 16 miles southwest of New York City, in New Jersey. Newark has four **currency-exchange windows**, and all but one are open daily 7 AM–8 PM. Terminal A offers a mobile currency exchange service (basically, a golf cart) for Japanese and German currency. Terminal B has a buy-back counter on the arrivals level between doors five and six (open daily 1–8) and a regular exchange counter on the concourse level. Terminal C also has its own exchange center on the concourse level next to the bank. **Luggage storage** (tel. 201/961–4720) at Newark is at Terminal B on the ground-floor level, open daily 7 AM–8 PM. Rates are $2.50–$5 per bag, per day. **Parking** is divided into hourly, daily, and long-term lots. Hourly parking is $4 for the first four hours and then $2 per hour after that. Daily parking costs $22 for 24 hours, with a maximum stay of three days. Long-term parking costs $7 per 24 hours. On average, car or taxi service to Newark is about $26 plus tax and tip.

➤ **SHUTTLE BUSES AND PUBLIC TRANSPORT** • The **NJ Transit Airport Express** (tel. 201/762–5100) departs every 15–20 minutes for the Port Authority Terminal in Manhattan (W. 42nd St., at Eighth Ave.). Buses run weekdays 6:15 AM–midnight, with reduced weekend service. The ride takes 30–45 minutes and costs $7 one-way. **Olympia Trails Airport Express** (tel. 212/964–6233, 718/622–7700, or 908/354–3330) picks up every 20 minutes outside all Newark terminals and stops at Grand Central Station, Penn Station, and the World Trade Center between 6:15 AM and midnight. The ride takes 30–45 minutes and costs $7. The **Gray Line Air Shuttle** (tel. 212/315–3006 or 800/451–0455) costs $18 one-way from Newark and stops at any major hotel between 23rd and 63rd streets. Make reservations at the airport's ground transportation center or use the courtesy phone. The cheapest option ($1) is a **PATH** train from Newark to various stops in Manhattan (for more info *see* Coming and Going, By Train, *above*).

BY SUBWAY

New York's subway system is amazing—it covers Manhattan and the outer boroughs thoroughly, it's quick and easy to use, it's air-conditioned, and it's one of the best places in the world to people-watch. Despite the horror stories you may have heard, the city's subways trains are used 24 hours a day, by over three million people daily. To enter the subway, simply drop a **token** ($1.50) into the turnstile; you can now ride anywhere you want and transfer as many times as you wish before exiting. Most of New York's 469 subway stations have 24-hour staffed booths where you can purchase single tokens and packs of 10—happily, these very same tokens are also valid on city buses. Some stations also have vending machines that take $5 bills. There are no discounts for quantity purchases.

A quick orientation for the first-time straphanger: **Express** trains only stop at major stations and transfer points, while **local** trains stop at every station. You can transfer to another subway line free of charge at many express stations—just follow the easy-to-read signs from platform to platform. Also, maps are posted at every subway station and inside every car. Subway station entrances are often specific to uptown or downtown trains; be sure you enter on the correct side. If there's a green globe light outside the station, that means the station is open and there's a transit clerk inside. A red globe means the station is closed (okay, some stations do close at night). All stations have off-hours waiting areas (usually near the staffed booth), designated by bright yellow signs. If you're at all concerned about your safety, wait in one of these areas rather than wandering off alone.

At press time, the MTA had recently announced its plan to allow free transfers between subways and buses and vice versa, starting July 1997. When (if?) this happens, the subway token and the cash fare will be a thing of the past, and the Metrocard will be the only way to pay your fare.

In 1994, the Transit Authority introduced the **MetroCard**, a plastic card with a magnetic stripe that lets you enter the subway at approximately 70 stations. The minimum card purchase is $5 and the maximum is $80. Sadly, there's no real advantage to using the card: If you lose it, you've lost all the credits you paid for, and it only works in some of the busiest stations. Also, using the MetroCard doesn't save you any money: Rides are still $1.50 each. For some reason the Transit Authority thinks these cards will catch on anyway. For info, call 212/638–7622; outside New York City call 800/METROCARD.

BY BUS

Though New York's subway system is amazingly comprehensive and quick, there are a few reasons to venture above ground and onto a city bus. For one thing, it's a good way to sightsee while you travel, and you'll probably feel a great deal more cheery if you're not spending all your time in a dark, dank, subterranean tunnel. Second, buses provide better door-to-door service if you just want to go a few blocks and can't find (or don't want to pay for) a cab. Say you want to skip from the Metropolitan Museum (Fifth Ave. at 82nd St.) to Sak's Fifth Avenue (Fifth Ave. at 50th St.) for some shopping; that's a 15-minute bus ride, but it'd be 40 minutes or more of walking and waiting and riding if you wanted to go by subway. You'll find that in some neighborhoods where subway lines are scarce—like the Upper East Side, Chelsea west of Eighth Avenue, and the East Village—you'll be practically forced to grab a bus to quickly move from point A to B. Ditto for crossing Central Park. A final reason, valid only in summer: All buses are air-conditioned (subway cars are air-conditioned, too, but subway platforms are typically sweltering hot). Keep in mind that during rush hours all the nice things we've told you about buses will still make for a pleasant trip—but not if you're in any kind of hurry. Manhattan's snarled traffic makes for slow going weekday mornings and evenings.

In Manhattan, buses run along virtually every **north–south avenue**, with several lines running up heavily used routes like Fifth Avenue, Madison Avenue, and Broadway. **Cross-town buses** run at least every 10 blocks, and across Central Park at 66th, 72nd, 79th, 86th, and 96th streets. Stops are every two or three blocks on north–south streets and every block on crosstown streets. Bus stops are indicated by a red, white, and blue sign on a pole, plus a yellow-painted curb. You'll also find a route schedule and map posted at each stop (you can pick up a map detailing *all* of the Manhattan bus routes at any subway station). Ideally, buses run every five minutes, but you can easily end up waiting 10–15 minutes or more, particularly in bad weather, during rush hours, and under Republican mayors. At night many bus routes run less frequently (or not at all); check the posted route schedule for info.

Bus fare is $1.50 per person, just like the subway, and buses accept subway tokens. You can also pay the fare with coins—but not pennies or dollar bills. But remember: Drivers will not make change, ever, even if you rend your clothing and weep loudly. You can use the **MetroCard** (*see* By Subway, *above*) on some routes. Don't forget to ask for your free **transfer ticket** after you've paid. It's good on one intersecting bus route (from a list on the back of the ticket) and must be used within the hour.

BY TAXI AND CAR SERVICE

The only real difference between taxis and car services is that a taxi is yellow, and a car-service sedan is not. Taxis run on a meter (charging by the amount of time a trip takes) while car services charge a flat fee based on distance, no matter how long the trip takes. Most of the time, the price ends up being about the same. The only times car services come in handy are if you're going crosstown (which tends to be slower going), if you're traveling during commute-hour traffic (especially to and from the airports), or if you're in the outer boroughs late at night and can't find a taxi.

There are 11,787 yellow cabs and 30,000 private cars (including limos) for hire in the city. The **New York City Taxi and Limousine Commission (TLC)** (tel. 212/840–4734 for lost property or 212/221–8294 for complaints) calculates that there are about 30,000 "gypsy" taxi drivers out there as well; these drivers are not licensed by the taxi commission and often do not even have a driver's license, much less insurance. Licensed private cars must display a black decal in the shape of a diamond on the right-hand side of their windshields—look for it. In 1996 the TLC set a flat $30 fee for travel between JFK and Manhattan for taxis and private car services.

TAXIS Taxis cost $1.50 for the first ⅕ mile, 25¢ for each ⅕ mile thereafter, 25¢ for each 75 seconds in standing traffic, plus a 50¢ surcharge Monday–Saturday 8 PM–6 AM and all day Sunday. There is no surcharge for additional people or luggage. Still, taxi fare adds up pretty quickly, so unless you're rich stick with public transportation—unless it's late night or you don't feel safe in a particular neighborhood. Because a taxi's meter calculates time as well as distance, the meter should click, adding another 25¢, about every four blocks while you're moving at a good clip. In slow traffic, the meter may click as often as every block. Sadly, drivers have been known to manipulate their meters in all kinds of crafty ways to speed them up and stick you with a higher fare—like the one chap who connected his meter to the radio, so that every time he turned up the volume, his meter increased the rate.

Be sure to ask for, and save, your receipt so if you have a complaint about a taxi, or wish to compliment the driver, or if you leave something in the car, the Taxi Commission can locate the car and driver easily. Some reputable taxi companies are: **Key Kab Service Inc.** (tel. 212/283–6000), **Love Taxi Inc.** (tel. 212/691–1234), and **Manhattan Checker** (tel. 800/236–6267).

CAR SERVICES Most companies have a flat-rate chart they consult for different distances and for different times of the day; call ahead to inquire if you're concerned about costs. The rate per mile is about $2. Some charge extra for large luggage and additional passengers. A few reliable services include **Highbridge Car Service** (tel. 212/927–4600), **Carmel** (tel. 212/666–6666), and **Tel-Aviv** (tel. 212/777–7777).

BY CAR

The biggest mistake you could make while living in or visiting New York is driving a car—New Yorkers typically only use cars to *leave* the city, not drive around in it. So consider this: If the city's Department of Transportation doesn't get you (with unfilled potholes and outdated signs), a carjacker just might. We don't want to scare you, but . . . the New York Police Department reported that in Manhattan there were 12,387 carjackings (meaning a vehicle taken by force) in 1994 alone. The most notorious carjacking of recent years was when rap and TV star Queen Latifah had her BMW stolen at gunpoint while driving in Harlem in the summer of 1995. Reports of grand larceny (or vehicles stolen when the driver was not around) totaled 12,978 in 1994 . Also keep in mind that traffic in New York is simply awful: On a good day, it can take

30 minutes to travel 30 blocks during the rush-hour commute. Though it is possible to see Manhattan by car, you should definitely get to know the city a little before committing to the four-wheel experience.

RENTING A CAR The minimum age for renting from a major company is usually 25, although some companies will rent to drivers as young as 21 as long as they pay an "age sur-charge" (which can be as much as $29.99 extra per day). Rates vary according to car model and pickup location. Rental companies located near JFK, for example, are about $6–$7 cheaper than companies in Manhattan. Either way, rates range from $41.95 to $53 per day, with weekend rates a little higher. Cars usually come with 100 or so free miles; additional miles are about 25¢ each. The moral: If you plan to drive long distances, make sure you ask for a car with unlimited free mileage. Most companies demand a driver's license and a credit card deposit before they'll rent to you. Reserving a car a few days in advance and renting it for a week or more may get you a better rate. Some companies charge nothing to return the car to another location, others charge $100–$150 extra. Optional insurance ($9–$12 a day) is a good idea. (Your credit card may provide automatic auto-insurance coverage if you charge your rental, but be sure to read the fine print.)

If you want to splurge, **Village Rent-A-Car** (19 E. 12th St., near Fifth Ave., tel. 212/633–1191) rents convertible BMWs ($109 per day) and Mustangs ($99 per day). More likely, you'll be renting from a national company like **Alamo** (tel. 800/327–9633), **Budget** (tel. 800/527–0700), or **Thrifty** (tel. 800/367–2277). **Rent-A-Wreck** (tel. 800/535–1391), specializing in cheaper, older, and uglier cars, sometimes undercuts the national companies on rates—but make sure the lower cost is not eclipsed by added mileage charges. Otherwise, try one of the following New York–based companies:

Allstar Rent A Car. You must be at least 22 to rent a car here, though unless you're 25 or older you'll pay a surcharge of $11 per day. The daily rate is $55 with 200 free miles, $269 per week with 1,000 free miles. After that, each extra mile costs 20¢. *325 W. 34th St., btw Eighth and Ninth Aves., Midtown, tel. 212/563–8282. Open weekdays 7:30 AM–6:30 PM.*

Amcar Discount Car Rentals. The minimum rental age is 23, with a daily surcharge of $10 for people under 25. The daily rate is $50 for a compact with 250 free miles. The weekly rate is $290 with 1,000 free miles. *315 W. 96th St., btw West End Ave. and Riverside Dr., Upper West Side, tel. 212/222–8500. Open weekdays 7:30–7:30, weekends 9–5.*

Elite Car Rental. This Brooklyn-based rental agency requires renters to be at least 23 with a valid license and credit card. The daily rate is $40 for a compact car with 100 free miles. The weekly rate is $210. *1041 Coney Island Ave., btw Foster and 18th Sts., Brooklyn, tel. 718/859–8111. Open Mon.–Thurs. 8–7, Fri. 8–5.*

BUYING A CAR If you must have a car in New York—or are planning to travel the country for a few months and hope to beat the cost of renting—first consider hassles and expenses like registration, insurance, and repairs. Registration means enduring long lines at the **Department of Motor Vehicles (DMV)** (155 Worth St., btw Center and Baxter Sts., Lower Manhattan, tel. 212/645–5550), where you must present the car title, bill of sale, proof of in-state insurance, and a state-required smog certificate, then fork over registration fees proportional to the weight of the car (just kidding). If you're looking at a car that needs repair work, ask yourself whether you want to pay mechanic labor fees of $50–$80 an hour.

Before you purchase, read up in *Consumer Reports* or check CompuServe and America Online for auto prices and info. You should also check auto magazines like the *Auto Trader*, available at most newsstands. Deals also lurk in the classified sections of the *New York Times* and the *Post.* If you don't want to buy directly from a person, most of the city's used-car lots are in the outer boroughs, on "automobile rows" like the Bronx's **Bruckner Boulevard** or **Northern Boulevard** in Queens.

PARKING Whether you opt for a garage or take your chances parking on the street, you'll have a few headaches to contend with. The first is price: Parking lot and garage rates vary from neighborhood to neighborhood, but you should expect to pay upwards of $6–$14 per hour or

$25–$31 per day. The highest rates are on the Upper East Side and in Midtown around Times Square. Long-term parking in a garage is almost equal to putting up another person, with average monthly costs ($250–$400) equal to half the rent on a studio apartment; the cheapest garages are on the Lower East Side. Or you can make the long trek north on the B or C train to **WD Lot** (304 W. 135th St., at Amsterdam Ave., Harlem), which offers rock-bottom prices: $3 an hour, $10 a night, or $100 a month.

If you want to conserve cash you can park on the streets for free. Most New York street-parkers tape hand-lettered signs inside their vehicles reading, NO RADIO, NOTHING OF VALUE INSIDE CAR to discourage thieves. It sometimes works. New Yorkers also contend with a mind-boggling number of posted parking restrictions, including the dreaded **alternate side of the street** system—which means moving your car across the street every morning at 6 AM to make way for street sweepers (wouldn't you rather have kids at this point?). The moral here is always read curbside signs, and if you're serious about parking on the street, send a SASE to the **New York City Department of Transportation** (Office of Public Affairs, 40 Worth St., Room 1009, New York, NY 10013, tel. 212/442–7033) for its free "SCR (Street Cleaning Rules) Suspension Calendar." This lists all the days when you can sleep in.

BRIDGE AND TUNNEL TOLLS New York City has dozens of bridges and tunnels. Manhattan is built on an island, remember? And while we're at it, so are Brooklyn and Queens. Tolls are levied one-way only, usually on traffic headed into Manhattan. **Bridges** leading into Manhattan and charging a toll are the George Washington Bridge ($4), which connects New York with New Jersey, and the Triboro Bridge ($3), which leads from the Bronx and Queens into Harlem. Around a dozen other bridges connect the outer boroughs and charge tolls ranging from $1.50 to $4. **Tunnels** leading into Manhattan include the Brooklyn Battery Tunnel ($3), Holland Tunnel ($4), Lincoln Tunnel ($4), and Queens Midtown Tunnel ($3). For more info, contact the Triborough Bridge and Tunnel Authority (tel. 212/360–3000) or the Port Authority of New York and New Jersey (tel. 212/435–7000).

Staying in New York City

AMERICAN EXPRESS AmEx has 22 offices throughout New York City, including branches at JFK Airport, Macy's Herald Square, Bloomingdale's, and the South Street Seaport. Even if you're not a cardholder, you can make travel arrangements, exchange foreign currencies, or purchase traveler's checks (available in six major currencies). Cardholders may receive mail free of charge (for everyone else it's $2 per piece) and can also cash personal checks. Mail is held only at the following AmEx office: *150 E. 42nd St., btw Lexington and Third Aves., NY 10017, tel. 212/640–5130, 800/937–2639, or 800/528–4800.*

EMERGENCIES Dial **911** for police, fire, and ambulance—as in any major American city, this may or may not result in a quick response. If you are the victim of an assault or rape, call the 24-hour **Sex Crimes Hotline** (tel. 212/267–7273) to report it and get help. The office is staffed by female investigators of the New York Police Department. The 24-hour **Crime Victims Hotline** (tel. 212/577–7777) provides over-the-telephone counseling and referrals. A few other numbers you'll hopefully never need: the **New York City Department of Health AIDS Hotline** (tel. 212/447–8200); **Poison Control Center** (tel. 212/764–7667 or 212/340–4494); **Drug Abuse Information Line** (tel. 800/522–5353); and the **Sexually Transmitted Disease Hotline** (tel. 212/788–4415).

The **Travelers' Aid Society** can help stranded travelers get home. Their office on the main floor of the International Arrivals Building at JFK Airport (tel. 718/656–4870) offers help making flight changes, communicating with relatives, and arranging local transportation. They will provide translators for most languages. It also gives out medical referrals. *1451 Broadway, 2nd Floor, btw 41st and 42nd Sts., tel. 212/944–0013. Open weekdays 9–7, Sat. 11–6, Sun. noon–6.*

MEDICAL AID

➤ **PHYSICIAN REFERRAL SERVICES** • Referral services can usually refer you to doctors offering sliding-scale fees, meaning that you are charged based on your ability to pay. To use a referral service is absolutely free, so try calling around to a few of the following hospital referral lines if you're worried about getting a giant doctor's bill: **Beth Israel** (tel. 800/420–4004); **Columbia-Presbyterian** (tel. 212/305–5156); **Cornell** (tel. 800/822–2694); **Lenox Hill** (tel. 212/434–2046); **Mount Sinai** (tel. 800/MD–SINAI); **New York Downtown** (tel. 800/822–6934); **New York University** (tel. 212/263–5000); or **St. Luke's–Roosevelt** (tel. 212/876–5432).

➢ **HOSPITALS AND CLINICS** • Heaven help you if you should get sick or injured in New York and not have insurance—low-cost care is really hard to come by. Fortunately, most hospitals take credit cards. If you need health care, call a referral service (*see above*) or try one of the following hospitals: **Bellevue** (First Ave., at E. 27th St., tel. 212/561–4141 or 212/561–4347 for emergency room); **Cabrini** (227 E. 19th St., btw Second and Third Aves., Gramercy, tel. 212/995–6000); or **St. Vincent's** (153 W. 11th St., at Seventh Ave., West Village, tel. 212/604–7000).

The **Margaret Sanger Planned Parenthood Clinic** is a great resource for women seeking individual counseling, birth control, gynecological exams, pregnancy testing, HIV testing, and abortion advice. Appointments are required; call weekdays 8:30–4:30. *380 Second Ave., btw E. 21st and 22nd Sts., Gramercy, tel. 212/677–6474. Subway: 6 to E. 23rd St. Open weekdays 8–5, Sat. 8–3.*

The **Women's Care Clinic** handles most gynecological and obstetrical health needs by appointment only, although they do handle some emergency situations. The clinic is cheaper than most, even when you factor in the $100 visit fee (cash and plastic accepted). *235 E. 67th St., Room 204, at Second Ave., Upper East Side, tel. 212/734–5700. Subway: 6 to E. 68th St. Open Mon. 2 PM–6:30 PM, Tues. 9 AM–1 PM, Thurs. 10–6:30.*

➢ **DENTISTS** • Two New York area medical schools have low-cost dental clinics where you can be the patient of a DDS student. **New York University** (421 First Ave., at E. 24th St., tel. 212/998–9800) charges about ⅓ of regular dentists' fees and is open Monday–Thursday 8–9, Friday 9–7:30. **Columbia Presbyterian Medical Center** (622 W. 168th St., btw Broadway and Ft. Washington, tel. 212/305–2648) has a dental clinic with fees 20%–50% lower than private practices. It's open weekdays 8:30–2. The **Dental Referral Service** (tel. 800/91–SMILE) doesn't include low-cost clinics, just standard-rate private practices. .

➢ **PHARMACIES** • Need drugs? We won't even touch the funny kind in this book, but for legitimate stuff try a **Duane Reade** discount drugstore. Of their 50 stores citywide, several are open 24 hours: 57th Street and Broadway (tel. 212/541–9708), 47th Street and Lexington Avenue (tel. 212/682–5338), 91st Street and Broadway (tel. 212/799–3172), and 74th Street and Third Avenue (tel. 212/744–2668). A few pharmacies even deliver; try 24-hour **Kaufman Pharmacy** (tel. 212/755–2266) or **McKay Drugs** (East Village, tel. 212/254–1454; West Village, tel. 212/255–5054; Upper East Side, tel. 212/794–7000).

LAUNDRY Finding a Laundromat is no problem in New York; they're on practically every block. Self-service machines typically cost $1.50 per wash and 75¢–$1.50 for 10 or 15 minutes of dryer time. Most machines only accept quarters. Drop-off service (where you leave your stinky stuff in the morning and pick it up clean and folded at the end of the day) costs 60¢–$1.50 per pound. Bleach and softener cost an additional 50¢ each. Dry cleaning will set you back $3–$6 per pair of pants, or $4 each for blouses and shirts. At **Ecowash** (72 W. 69th St., btw Columbus Ave. and Central Park W, Upper West Side, tel. 212/787–3890) you can clean your clothes without hurting the planet.

LUGGAGE STORAGE City officials removed all train, subway, and bus station luggage lockers after the 1993 World Trade Center bombing, and a few more recent bomb scares ensure that cheap and convenient luggage storage isn't returning anytime soon. However, most hotels will look after your luggage before check-in and after checkout for free, or stash it for a few days for a small fee. The **Portland Square Hotel** (132 W. 47th St., btw Sixth and Seventh Aves., Midtown, tel. 212/382–0600 or 800/388–8988) and **Herald Square Hotel** (19 W. 31st St., btw Fifth Ave. and Broadway, Midtown, tel. 212/279–4017) both have lockers ($1) in their lobbies that *theoretically* could be used by anybody. As a last resort, try a self-storage facility (check the New York *Yellow Pages* under "Storage"). They typically offer daily, weekly, and monthly rates on compartments of all sizes. Though it's expensive, at least your valuables won't wander off into the sunset. Luggage storage is also available at two airports, JFK and Newark; *see* Getting Around New York City, To and From the Airports, *above*.

MAIL The city's main post office is **J. A. Farley General Post Office** (Eighth Ave., btw W. 31st and 33rd Sts., Midtown, tel. 212/967–8585), open 24 hours. Other Manhattan post offices are generally open weekdays 10–5. For locations, look in the New York phone book's blue Government Pages under "United States Government Offices, Postal Service," or call the **Postal Information Line** (tel. 212/967–8585). You can also get info on zip codes and postal rates over the phone—saving you hours of standing in line.

➤ **SENDING MAIL** • Domestic first-class mail is 32¢ for up to one ounce, 23¢ for each additional ounce. Domestic postcards are 20¢. International rates begin at 60¢ for the first ½ ounce. Rates are slightly cheaper for mail to Canada. Ready-to-mail aerogrammes are 50¢. Postcards cost 40¢ to Canada and 50¢ to all other international destinations. Allow one to two weeks delivery time for international mail. For both domestic and international packages, the **United Parcel Service (UPS)** often proves to be cheaper than the post office; call 800/222–8333 for more info.

➤ **RECEIVING MAIL** • Yes, you can get that million-dollar royalty check while visiting New York, via the U.S. Postal Service's **General Delivery** (tel. 212/330–3099) department, at the back of the main post office (*see above*). Have mail addressed to: YOUR NAME, c/o General Delivery, 390 Ninth Ave., New York, NY 10001. Mail is held for 10 days only. Pickup hours are Monday–Saturday 10 AM–1 PM, and you must present a valid photo ID. **American Express** (*see above*) will hold mail (but not packages) for up to 30 days.

PHONES The area code for Manhattan is **212**. Any call from Manhattan to another area code must be dialed like so: 1 + (Area Code) + (seven-digit number). The Bronx, Brooklyn, Queens, and Staten Island are in area code **718**. Most cellular phones and pagers in New York City are in area code **917**. For local directory assistance, dial 411. For long-distance help, dial the area code plus 555–1212. If you don't know the area code or need help with a local call, dial 0 for the operator; for long-distance or international calls, dial 00. To find out if a particular business has an 800 number, call 800/555–1212.

There are more than 58,000 public telephones in New York, which translates to one on almost every street corner. Of those that work (probably around half), most allow you to place international calls and use a calling card. Pay phones cost 25¢ for the first three minutes of a local call (this includes calls between 212 and 718 area codes); an extra deposit is required for each additional minute. Local directory-assistance calls are free. At the **AT&T Public Calling Center**, on the Main Concourse level of Grand Central Terminal (E. 42nd St. and Park Ave., Midtown), you can make long-distance calls in relative quiet using a credit card or calling card. It's open weekdays 7 AM–9 PM.

Charges for collect calls are higher than for normal long-distance calls, so if you want to keep your friends, give them your number so they can call you back. (Not all pay phones accept incoming calls, so read the fine print on the phone before trying this.) Station-to-station is the standard collect call; anyone answering at the number you dial can accept the charges. Less common, and even more expensive, is a person-to-person call, which authorizes only the person whose name you give to the operator to accept the charges. On the upside, you won't be charged if the person you want to reach is out. Collect calls can be made by dialing 0 + (the number) or, more cheaply, by dialing 800/COLLECT.

➤ **CALLING CARDS** • Calling cards are issued by national long-distance companies to U.S. and Canadian citizens with current telephone service and allow you to make calls from any phone (and get billed at a later date). There's no fee to get a card, but each time you use it you pay for the call plus a service charge (40¢–80¢). For more info, contact long-distance carriers **AT&T** (tel. 800/CALL-ATT), **U.S. Sprint** (tel. 800/877–4646), or **MCI** (tel. 800/444–3333). Allow several weeks for them to process your new card.

➤ **INTERNATIONAL CALLS** • Calls to Canada can be dialed as regular long-distance calls. To reach any other country, dial 011, the country code, the city code (dropping the initial zero if there is one), then the actual number. The country code for **Great Britain** is 44, **Ireland** 353, **New Zealand** 64, and **Australia** 61. Rates vary widely depending on the hour of your call; ask a long-distance operator for exact rates.

PUBLIC REST ROOMS For travelers with tiny bladders, New York is a cold and stingy town. In Midtown, there are clean pleasant rest rooms at **Bryant Park** (W. 42nd St., btw Fifth and Sixth Aves.), decent ones in **Grand Central Terminal** (E. 42nd St. at Park Ave.), and grit-your-teeth options at the **Port Authority Bus Terminal** and **Penn Station**. Downtown near **City Hall** you'll find a single funky, coin-operated toilet kiosk modeled after those on the streets of Paris. There are no rest room facilities in subway stations, but you can boldly visit the bathrooms in diners, cafés, large hotels, public buildings, and department stores. The plush, unguarded rest rooms at **Bloomingdale's** (Third Ave., at E. 59th St.), for example, are no secret to shoppers. If you're looking for the ultimate bathroom read, check out *Where To Go: A Guide to Manhattan's Toilets*, by Vicki Rovere. It's available at most city bookstores.

Resident Resources

LIBRARIES

Budget cuts have weakened the city's public library system—but they haven't killed it off entirely. The **Mid-Manhattan Library** (455 Fifth Ave., at 40th St., Midtown, tel. 212/340–0833) is the best lending branch in the public system. They also have a decent reference room. The **New York Public Library for the Performing Arts** (40 Lincoln Center Plaza, at W. 65th St., Upper West Side, tel. 212/870–1630) is a research library specializing in dance, music, and theater.

Several museums offer excellent research (i.e., non-lending) libraries, including the Frick Collection; Goethe House, which collects material relating to Germans and German-Americans; and the Schomburg Center for Research in Black Culture. For more info, *see* Museums and Galleries, in Chapter 2.

Buttenwieser Library at the 92nd Street Y. The Y has a vast archive of recorded lectures and readings by decades of the biggest names in politics, literature, and the arts. *1395 Lexington Ave., btw E. 91st and 92nd Sts., Upper East Side, tel. 212/415–5544 for recordings archives or 212/415–5542 for main library. Admission free. Open by appointment only.*

New York Public Library–Central Research Library. The city's main library beautifully houses one of the largest collections in the world. Though you can't take any of the books home, you can take a free tour or pass a few hours in the spectacular reading room. *Fifth Ave. and 42nd St., tel. 212/930–0800. Open Tues.–Wed. 11–7:30, Thurs.–Sat. 10–6.*

Science, Industry and Business Library. The brand-spanking-new SIBL is a dazzling display of interactivity, featuring 250 computers for the patrons' use. Of course, you can still find some good, old-fashioned books here, both in their research facilities and sizable circulating collection. *188 Madison Ave., at 34th St, tel. 212/592–7001. Open Mon., Fri., and Sat. 10–6, Tues.–Thurs. 11–7.*

MEDIA

New York is a news- and gossip-intensive town—not surprising for this home of international movers and shakers. What other city in the country boasts four (count 'em quickly, before one goes bankrupt) daily papers? The city also has its own 24-hour TV news station, **New York One** (Channel 1), with local and international news announcements around the clock and daily recaps at 6:30, 9:30, 10, and 11 PM. City weather reports are broadcast "on the ones" (1:01, 1:11, 1:21, etc.). For gay and lesbian publications, *see* Chapter 8.

NEWSSTANDS The best newsstands for browsing include **Hotaling's** (142 W. 42nd St., near Sixth Ave., Midtown, tel. 212/840–1868), around since 1905 and great for foreign publications and obscure titles; **Nikos Magazine & Smoke Shop** (462 Sixth Ave., at W. 11th St., West Village, tel. 212/255–9175), which stocks some 2,500 titles, from scholarly stuff to 'zines like *Paranoia: The Conspiracy Reader*; and **Universal News Ltd.** (676 Lexington Ave., at E. 56th St., Midtown, tel. 212/750–1855), which boasts some 4,000 foreign and domestic rags. The citywide café/newsstand chain **News Bar** (*see* Cafés, in Chapter 4) is also great for a CNN fix or if you want to browse a rack of over 400 foreign and domestic publications.

NEWSPAPERS *New York Daily News.* This tabloid-style paper bills itself oxymoronically as "New York's Hometown Newspaper." Look for lots of slang and lurid headlines. *Cost: 60¢.*

New York Observer. The city's peach-colored weekly has some of the better in-depth reporting on New York arts, media, and political scenes, with an often tongue-in-cheek tone. Its "Eight-Day Week" is a quirky listing, equal parts uptown society and downtown hip. *Tel. 212/755–2400. Cost: $1. Published Wed.*

New York Post. World War III-size headlines bark out the "news" in Rupert Murdoch's cheap, gritty tabloid that's way more in line with most New Yorkers than the *Times*. It's got the quick and dirty on local murders and national scandals, plus "Page Six," the city's premier gossip column. *Tel. 800/552–POST. Cost: 50¢. Published Mon.–Sun.*

New York Press. This free weekly rag features some of the most acerbic writing in all of New York: Check out the front page's brilliant ditties on life in NYC and Perry McMahon's "Bigmouth." Plus comprehensive restaurant, film, art, theater, and music listings. *Tel. 212/941–1130. Published Wed.*

New York Times. The nation's newspaper of record is ultimately a tool of the establishment, and it shows in its high-falutin' business, arts, social, and fashion pages. Still, for quality writing and in-depth reporting you can't beat the Grey Lady. Special sections include Science (Tuesdays); Living (Wednesdays); Home (Thursdays); and Weekend (Fridays). The Sunday paper, bigger than a Britannica, is required reading for most New Yorkers. *Tel. 800/631–2500. Cost: Mon.–Sat. 60¢, Sun. $2.50.*

Village Voice. For political coverage that's strongly left of center, arts coverage that tends toward the avant-garde, and personals ads so hot they seem to smoke on the printed page, pick up the weekly bible for the downtown set. Must-reads include "Voice's Choices," for unbeatable cinema, music, and club listings, and gossip columnist Michael Musto's "La Dolce Musto." *Tel. 800/875–2997. Cost: Free ($1.25 outside Manhattan). Published Wed.*

Wall Street Journal. This business-only paper (it's published by Dow Jones & Company) won't familiarize you with New York beyond the world of Wall Street mergers and acquisitions. *Tel. 800/778–0840. Cost: 75¢. Published weekdays.*

MAGAZINES *Paper* ($3), a monthly, isn't specifically about New York, but it's a great resource for what's happening in the downtown art/music/club scene.

New York. This glossy magazine delivers weekly reports on city politics and endless looks at how the monied "other half" lives. Its "Cue" section is great for arts listings and reviews, its "Best Bets" and "Sales & Bargains" required reading for shopaholics. *Tel. 800/535–1168. Cost: $2.95.*

The New Yorker. The nation's revered literary weekly, founded in 1925, has shaken off its stodgy reputation and gotten a hell of a lot more modern under sassy Brit editor-in-chief Tina Brown, once of *Vanity Fair*. Which means a lot more coverage of Roseanne and photos by *Rolling Stone* star Annie Leibovitz, and fewer contributions by American humorists like Garrison Keillor and Ian Frazier. Its "Goings On About Town" is a critical listing of theater, gallery shows, readings, dance, film, and concerts. *Tel. 800/825–2510. Cost: $3.50.*

Time Out. A brand-new arrival in New York (other versions thrive in London and Amsterdam), the weekly *Time Out* offers the city's most comprehensive and easy-to-read listings and reviews for theater, music, film, readings, sports, art exhibitions, you name it. It's hip, but not intimi-dating. *Tel. 212/539–4444 or 800/457–4364. Cost: $1.95.*

RADIO STATIONS Here's a sampling of what's going out over the FM airwaves in New York City: **WNYU** (89.1) whatever's cool at New York University; **WXCR** (89.9) whatever's cool at Columbia University; **WNYC** (93.9) National Public Radio; **WQXR** (96.3) classical music; **WQHT** (97.1) the phattest hip-hop jams; **WRKS** (98.7) soul; **WBAI** (99.5) cutting-edge music of all sorts; **WHTZ** (100.3) alternative rock, but with annoying DJs and repetitive programming; **WCBS** (101.1) news; **WNEW** (102.7) alternative rock with some harder stuff; and **WAXQ** (104.3) lots of '80s rock. New York's infamous "shock jock" Howard Stern broadcasts live weekday mornings from **WXRK** (92.3).

CYBER NEW YORK

You can surf the Web for a few bucks an hour from @Cafe, Cyber Café, and Internet Café, all in the East Village; *see* Cafés in Chapter 4 for more info. A few cool New York–specific sites to browse include: **Museums New York** at http://www.museumsny.com/; the **New York Public Library** at http://www.nypl.org/; mega-New York dance club **Webster Hall** at http://cyberactive-1.com/webster-hall/; **Movielink 777–FILM Online** at http://www.777film.com/; and Columbia University's **Web Music Archive** at http://www.columbia.edu/hauben/music-index.html.

East Coast Hangout (ECHO). This hip New York BBS is popular for its lively chats with leading figures of the counterculture and arts communities; it also goes out of its way to provide space for women (who account for some 45% of its 3,500 users). Rates are $19.95 per month (stu-dents, $13.75) for local services, or $25 per month for Web access. *Tel. 212/292–0900 (voice) or 212/292–0910 (modem).*

Pipeline. If you've just learned how to turn on your computer and are all fired up to explore the Web, start here. They'll hook you up with incredibly easy-to-use software for Mac or Windows and tons of tips and advice. Unlimited Internet and e-mail access is $19.95 per month. *Tel. 212/267–3636 (voice).*

EXPLORING NEW YORK CITY

2

By Shon Bayer, Matthew Jalbert, Amy McConnell, and Mira Schwirtz

On returning from a visit, Charles Dickens once described New York City as "a vast amount of good and evil intermixed and jumbled up together." Though he pissed off a great number of his American readers, he made an excellent point. You'll need to endure a bit of evil, whether it's a rude taxi driver or a heavy-breathing guy standing next to you at an ATM, to discover the beauty of this city. Don't be scared by the throngs of tourists lined up to make the trip to the top of the World Trade Center or the Empire State Building—nowhere on earth can you get views so vertigo-inducing. Though your bladder may rupture before you find one of its hidden rest rooms, the Metropolitan Museum of Art has days worth of stunning art and artifacts to view, and a stroll over the Brooklyn Bridge at sunset has to be one of the best 1-mile walks anywhere.

Don't forget to stray off the beaten path: Hop on the subway to Fort Tryon Park, get up at 5 in the morning to see the fishmongers close shop at the Fulton Fish Market, or spend the afternoon in a Hell's Kitchen Irish pub drinking Guinness with regulars who probably have been glued to their bar stools for the past four decades. The outer boroughs have major attractions, too: The mammoth Brooklyn Museum, the world-famous Bronx Zoo, and the New York Botanical Gardens are just a few examples, and all are certainly worth day trips.

Wherever you go, you'll find New York's subway system extremely efficient, perfect for those of you engaged in the see-and-flee mode of sightseeing. That said, moving around Manhattan by bus or, better yet, on your own two feet is the ideal way to get a real feel for the city. New York's street life—its glamour, its frenetic pace, even its occasional hints of evil—is an important element of any visit.

There are two types of must-see attractions in New York: those that lifelong New Yorkers dismiss with "never been there," and the kind over which they gush, "you must go there first." Do them both.

GUIDED TOURS

If you were planning to skip this section because you bristle at the thought of being led around by the nose like a show pony, stop and reconsider. Not all guided tours will treat you like you're on a fourth-grade field trip. Indeed, if you're new to New York and unfamiliar with its offerings, doesn't it make sense to turn to an expert? Many of the museums, historical buildings, parks, and other attractions described in this chapter offer guided tours that will give you a rare, behind-the-scenes look at how they operate, or enchant you with historical tidbits and lore. Best of all, many of these tours are absolutely free once you've paid your admission (if any). Some of the most fascinating tours include those at

The Five Boroughs

STATEN ISLAND

Goethals Bridge

Newark International Airport

Bayonne Bridge

Newark Bay

Kill Van Kull

Snug Harbor Cultural Center

ST. GEORGE

Jaques Marchais Museum

Ferry Terminal

ROSEBANK

Alice Austen House

Verrazano Narrows Bridge

Liberty I.

Statue of Liberty

Ellis I.

Brooklyn-Battery Tunnel

Pulaski Skyway

Holland Tunnel

Lincoln Tunnel

M A

Brooklyn Bridge

Manhattan Bridge

Williamsburg Bridge

East River

GREENPOINT

WILLIAMSBURG

BROOKLYN HEIGHTS

FORT GREENE

COBBLE HILL

BROOKLYN HEIGHTS

Atlantic Ave.

BEDFORD-STUYVESANT

PARK SLOPE

Prospect Park

FLATBUSH

Brooklyn Museum and Botanic Gardens

Eastern Pkwy.

CROWN HEIGHTS

CANARSIE

QUEENS

BAY RIDGE

SUNSET PARK

Queens Expwy.

Belt Pkwy.

BENSONHURST

Ocean Pkwy.

B R O O K L Y N

Flatbush Ave.

Linden Blvd.

Inter Boro Pkwy.

Woodhaven Blvd.

Forest Park

CONEY ISLAND

NY Aquarium

BRIGHTON BEACH

MANHATTAN BEACH

SHEEPSHEAD BAY

Rockaway Inlet

Marine Park

Floyd Bennett Field

Jacob Riis Park

Gateway National Recreation Area

Jamaica Bay Wildlife Refuge

Cross Bay Blvd.

Van Wyck Expwy.

Southern Pkwy.

J.F.K. International Airport

Rockaway Beach

ATLANTIC OCEAN

17

280

95

78

9

1

495

The Five Boroughs

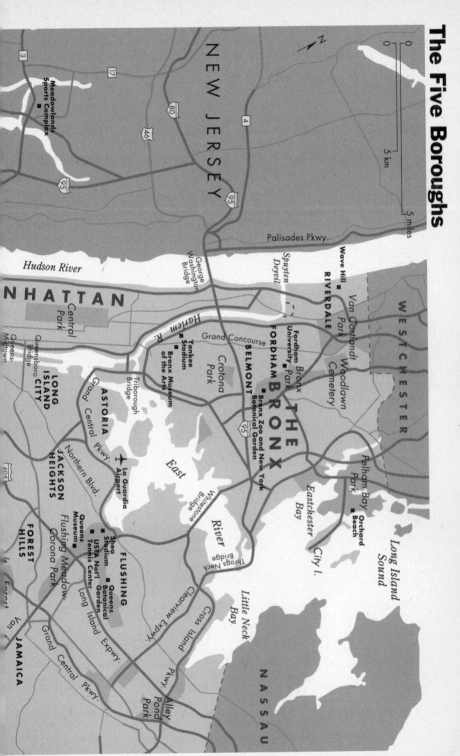

NEW JERSEY

Meadowlands
Sports Complex

3

17

80

46

4

95

95

Palisades Pkwy.

Hudson River

Spuyten
Duyvil

George
Washington
Bridge

Harlem R.

Wave Hill

RIVERDALE

Van Cortlandt
Park

Woodlawn
Cemetery

WESTCHESTER

NHATTAN

Central
Park

Queens-
Midtown

Queensboro
Bridge

LONG
ISLAND
CITY

ASTORIA

Grand Concourse

Fordham
University

Bronx

Yankee
Stadium

Bronx Museum
of the Arts

Crotona
Park

BELMONT

FORDHAM

THE BRONX

Bronx Zoo and New York
Botanical Garden

95

Pelham Bay
Park

Orchard
Beach

Long Island Sound

Triborough
Bridge

Grand Central Pkwy.

Northern Blvd.

JACKSON
HEIGHTS

La Guardia
Airport

Whitestone
Bridge

Eastchester
Bay

East

River

City I.

FOREST
HILLS

Flushing Meadow-
Corona Park

Queens
Museum

FLUSHING

Shea
Stadium

Queens
Botanical
Garden

USTA Nat'l
Tennis Center

Throgs Neck Bridge

Clearview Expwy.

Cross Island Pkwy.

Long Island Expwy.

Little
Neck
Bay

NASSAU

JAMAICA

Grand Central Pkwy.

Van

Alley Pond
Park

Forest

5 km

5 miles

35

Lincoln Center, the New York Stock Exchange, Carnegie Hall, Times Square, the American Museum of Natural History, the United Nations, the Fulton Fish Market, the Steinway & Sons Piano Factory, the Brooklyn Botanical Garden, the Federal Reserve Bank, and the Historic Orchard Street Bargain District, but of course there are dozens of others. For times and locations, see below.

NBC Studio Tour. What could be better for a TV junkie than a one-hour tour ($8.25) of the sets of NFL Live and Saturday Night Live? Plus, you'll peek at behind-the-scenes stuff like the producer's rooms and tons of technical gizmos, and look at all of NBC's broadcast milestones. Tours depart weekdays every 15 minutes between 9:30 and 4:30, but arrive early because tickets are usually sold out by noon. For info on free tickets to studio tapings, see box You, Too, Can Be a Member of a Live Studio Audience, below. 30 Rockefeller Plaza, at Fifth Ave., Midtown, tel. 212/664–7174. Subway: B, D, F, or Q to W. 47th–50th Sts./Rockefeller Center.

Police Department Headquarters Tour. The free 40-minute tour of police facilities includes a look at the firing range, central booking, and the 911 communications center. One Police Plaza, near Park Row, Lower Manhattan, tel. 212/374–3804. Subway: N or R to City Hall. Tours Oct.–May, weekdays 10:30–2:30.

WALKING TOURS Walking tours are one of the best ways to learn about New York and make new friends, all at the same time. And they're not just for tourists: Longtime New Yorkers rely on walking tours to get into some of New York's most inaccessible places, and into places they might not feel comfortable going to on their own. For a guide, you'll usually get some sort of expert, like a professor, graduate student, historian, or author. Most walking tours are held on weekends year-round and require reservations. Walking tours are listed in the "Above and Beyond" section of The New Yorker's "Goings On About Town" listings, the "Around Town" section of Time Out, and New York's "Cue" pages.

Several museums offer walking tours focusing on their particular neighborhood or area of expertise. For tours focusing on New York history, check out the Cooper-Hewitt Museum (tel. 212/860–6321) or the Museum of the City of New York (tel. 212/534–1672, ext. 206), which both charge around $15, or the New-York Historical Society (tel. 212/873–3400), which asks for a donation of $3 ($1 students). If you want out of Manhattan, try the Brooklyn Historical Society (tel. 718/624–0890). The tours offered by the Lower East Side Tenement Museum (tel. 212/431–0233) focus on the history and culture of Lower East Side immigrant groups—Chinese, Latino, Italian, Irish, German, or Jewish—and are sometimes led by costumed actors. The New York Transit Museum (tel. 718/243–3060) offers tours most Saturdays through spooky, abandoned Brooklyn subway tunnels. For more details on each museum, see Museums and Galleries, below.

92nd Street Y. The Y's excellent tours range from two hours to a full day, and can range from "Chinatown's Herb Markets" and "Hell's Kitchen: A Political History" to a look inside the Harvard Club or a walk through artists' studios. Tickets cost $15–$48, which includes brunch, train fare, and other related expenses. 1395 Lexington Ave., New York, NY 10128, tel. 212/996–1100. Tours given year-round; call for schedule. Reservations recommended.

Adventures on a Shoestring. For a bargain $5 you get a 1½-hour tour of the city's less touristed neighborhoods, like Hell's Kitchen; Jamaica, Queens; the German community of Yorkville; or Roosevelt Island. Tours usually end with lunch. 300 W. 53rd St., New York, NY 10019, tel. 212/265–2663. Tours given weekends.

Big Onion Walking Tours. Grad students pursuing degrees in American history are your enthusiastic guides to attractions such as the Brooklyn Bridge, Governor's Island, or New York's Revolutionary War sites. The 2½-hour tours are $9–$12 ($7–$10 students). Columbia University Station, Box 250201, New York, NY 10025-1533, tel. 212/439–1090. Tours given weekends at 1 PM.

Harlem Your Way! These 2½- to three-hour tours explore Harlem's historic districts and landmarks, like Sugar Hill, Hamilton Grange, and the Apollo Theater. On Sundays, the tour takes in a gospel church service. Cost is $25 ($23 students). 129 W. 130th St., near Adam Clayton

Powell Jr. Blvd., Harlem, tel. 212/690–1687 or 212/866–6997. Tours given Mon.–Sat. at 1:30 or 3 PM, Sun. at 10:30 AM. Reservations required.

Municipal Art Society. The Municipal Art Society's "Discover New York Tours" focus on architecture, history, and urban planning, with offerings like "57th Street: Culture and Kitsch" or "New York's Contemporary Architecture." Tours are 1½ hours and usually cost $10–$15 ($8 students). *Tel. 212/935–3960. Tours given Mon.–Sat. year-round. Reservations recommended for Sat. tours.*

Sidewalks of New York. These two-hour tours ($12) offer a mix of high camp and history: You may get a literary tour of the Village, the city's most famous murder sites, or a tribute to Jackie Onassis. *Box 1660, Cathedral Station, New York, NY 10025, tel. 212/662–5300 or 212/517–0201 for recorded schedule. Tours given year-round; call for schedule.*

Ever look at Sheep Meadow in Central Park and imagine all the edible stuff that must be growing there? So has "Wildman" Steve Brill, who was once arrested on charges of eating a dandelion.

Wildman Steve Brill. The Wildman leads four-hour tours of New York's parks, on which you'll learn how to identify, harvest, and prepare edible and medicinal plants, including berries, mushrooms, roots, herbs, seeds, and seaweed. Suggested donation is $10. *143–25 84th Dr., Suite 6C, Jamaica, NY 11435, tel. 718/291–6825. Tours given weekends Mar.–Nov.; send SASE for schedule. Reservations required.*

BY BUS Bite the bullet, because you're going to be branded a tacky, cheesy tourist the second you board a tour bus. That said, an air-conditioned bus ride is one of the better ways to explore the city during the summer heat (though keep in mind that many double-deck buses don't have air-conditioning). Tours generally zip around on one of 10–20 different routes, stopping for a quick look-see from ground level before hustling off to the next big attraction.

Sightseeing on the Cheap

If you want a motorized overview of Manhattan but don't want the perky commentary, save some cash by joining New York's cranky commuters on a standard city bus. You won't get the tape-recorded rundown on the sights, but you can use a single subway token ($1.50) for any of the following routes:

- **Bus M1:** Battery Park, the World Trade Center, Wall Street, SoHo, Union Square, the New York Public Library, Rockefeller Center, Central Park, the Metropolitan Museum of Art, Museum Mile.

- **Bus M4:** Empire State Building, Central Park, Columbia University, Harlem, the Cloisters Museum, and Fort Tryon Park.

- **Bus M10:** Central Park West, the American Museum of Natural History, Times Square, Chelsea, the West Village, and the World Trade Center.

- **Bus M11:** West Village, Chelsea, Hell's Kitchen, Lincoln Center, the Upper West Side, Columbia University, Riverbank State Park.

- **Bus M101:** City Hall, Chinatown, Little Italy, the East Village, Gramercy, Murray Hill, Grand Central Terminal, the Upper East Side, Martin Luther King Jr. Boulevard in Harlem, and Washington Heights.

Gray Line Tours. Gray Line aims to please: They offer 26 different routes, with stops at block-busters like the Metropolitan Museum, Central Park, the Empire State Building, the World Trade Center, and Chinatown. Reservations for the two- to nine-hour tours are unnecessary; just call for the day's schedule and show up at the Gray Line headquarters 30 minutes before departure. They'll also show you New York by helicopter ($75) and trolley car. *1740 Broadway, btw W. 55th and 56th Sts., Midtown, tel. 212/397–2620. Subway: N or R to W. 57th St. Tickets: $17.50–$50. Tours daily 8:30–6:30.*

Harlem Spirituals, Inc. These multilingual tours of Harlem and other uptown neighborhoods include stops at Hamilton Grange, the neighborhood of Sugar Hill, and a Baptist church service. The jazz tour ($69) includes dinner and club cover charge. *1697 Broadway, at 53rd St., Suite 205, Midtown, tel. 212/757–0425. Subway: B, D, or E to 7th Ave. Tickets: $32–$75.*

New York Apple Tours. Want to ride around New York in an authentic London double-decker? Here's your chance. These big, bright-red buses run daily 9–6 on three loops: uptown, down-town, and along the Hudson River. A two-day pass with unlimited stops is $25 for the uptown route, $16 for the downtown or river routes. They also offer nighttime "city lights" tours. **New York Doubledecker Tours** (Empire State Building, at 34th St. and Fifth Ave., tel. 212/967–6008) offers similar services. *Tel. 212/348–5300.*

Rock and Roll Tour of New York. The founder of this tour company has worked with the Doors, Cream, the Ramones, and Iggy Pop, so he knows what he's talking about. The 50 sites covered include famous clubs like Max's Kansas City, CBGB & OMFUG, and the China Club; the Dakota apartments, where John Lennon was shot; the Chelsea Hotel, where Sex Pistol Sid Vicious did himself in; and the secondhand clothing shop Screaming Mimi's, where many stars get their concert gear. *Tel. 212/807–7625. Tickets: $25. Reservations required.*

BY BOAT One of the best, and cheapest, ways to see New York by boat is aboard the **Staten Island Ferry** (*see* The Outer Boroughs, Staten Island, *below*); it costs just 50¢ round-trip. From Pier 16 at the South Street Seaport (*see* Manhattan Neighborhoods, Lower Manhattan, *below*) you can take two- or three-hour voyages ($16, $12 students) to New York's past aboard the 1885 iron cargo schooner *The Pioneer* (tel. 212/669–9400), or one-hour sightseeing tours ($12, $10 students) of New York Harbor and Lower Manhattan with **Seaport Liberty Cruises** (tel. 212/425–3737). For info on ferry service to the Statue of Liberty and Ellis Island, *see* Major Attractions, Statue of Liberty, *below*.

Circle Line. More than 40 million passengers have steamed around Manhattan on the eight 165-foot Circle Line yachts since the cruises were inaugurated in 1945. It's one of those true New York experiences—Conan O'Brien and crew even taped an episode of *Late Night* from the deck of a moving Circle Line ship in 1995. Once you've finished the three-hour, 35-mile cir-cumnavigation of Manhattan, you'll have a good idea of where things are and what you want to see next, and your hair will possess that sought-after windblown quality. *Pier 83, Twelfth Ave. at W. 42nd St., Midtown, tel. 212/563–3200. Subway: A, C, or E to W. 42nd St. (Port Author-ity). Fare: $18. Call for schedule.*

BY HORSE-DRAWN CARRIAGE Whether it's a frosty, crisp winter morning or a warm sum-mer night, one of the most romantic ways to see the city is by horse-drawn cab. Carriages occa-sionally go as far as Times Square, but a spin through the southern stretch of Central Park is perfect. Carriages line up on Grand Army Plaza (at the corner of Fifth Avenue and 59th Street), and along 59th Street between Fifth and Seventh Avenues. The cost is city-regulated at $34 for the first half hour, $10 for each quarter hour after that; the fare is calculated by time, not per passenger. In recent years, PETA (People for the Ethical Treatment of Animals) and other animal-rights groups have agitated for better working conditions for the city's carriage horses. Reforms mean the horses are treated better than they have been in the past, but the question of whether or not to ride is ultimately yours to answer.

Major Attractions

It takes months, or even years, to really get to know New York, but if you're only in town for a few days you'll want to check out the city's "bests"—its top museums, tallest skyscrapers, most stirring monuments, and best-loved park. Just don't try to do them all in one afternoon.

EMPIRE STATE BUILDING

The Empire State Building may no longer be the world's tallest building, or even the tallest building in New York, but it's certainly one of the world's best-loved skyscrapers. Some 2½ million visitors a year make the trip up to its observatory decks on the 86th and 102nd floors, where they gawk and snap photos and speculate about whether a penny dropped from this height would really bore a hole through the skull of someone on the sidewalk below. So, you ask, what's to love about a 1,250-foot-tall skyscraper? For one, the building's stats are pretty impressive: Approximately 20,000 people fill its offices (which includes the state's largest sperm bank), and its 73 elevators cruise 7 miles of shafts at speeds ranging from 600 to 1,200 feet per minute. In its framework you'll find 60,000 tons of steel, enough to lay tracks from New York City to Baltimore, and on its top you'll find the world's greatest TV tower, which reaches eight million television sets in four states. Then there are the windows, all 6,500 of them, which are continuously being hand-washed by people who we can only presume are unafraid of heights. Beyond size, the Empire State Building has beauty going for it: Zoning laws of the 1930s required that its design include numerous setbacks to allow sunlight to reach the street, and this step-like effect delights the eye. With its graceful Art Deco embellishments, it's 10 times more attractive than the boxy World Trade Center. No wonder the Empire State Building has appeared in over 90 movies during its lifetime, including 1933's unforgettable *King Kong*.

For the 1933 movie "King Kong," a scale model was used, but to celebrate the film's 60-year anniversary the real Empire State Building was decorated with an 84-foot-tall inflatable plastic gorilla.

Hard to imagine, isn't it, that the whole thing started with a pencil. Yes, the design of the most imitated building in the world was inspired by a large pencil one of the principal architects noticed sitting on his desk. Construction started weeks before the stock market crash of 1929 and was completed a record one year and 45 days later, at a cost of $41 million. The framework rose at a rate of 4½ stories per week, making the Empire State Building the fastest-rising major skyscraper ever built. Of course, the Great Depression put a damper on opening day ceremonies, and for the next few decades New Yorkers referred to it as the "Empty State Building." To further sour things, the original plan to make the building into a mammoth blimp launching pad was a total failure. Two blimps briefly made contact in 1931, but barely. Eventually, the 102nd floor (where the blimps were to moor) and the 86th floor (where the blimp ticket agencies and baggage rooms were to be situated) were turned into observation decks.

The blimp world's loss is a tourist's gain, because the views from the two observation decks are absolutely incredible. The better is on the 86th floor, with amazing *plein air* views of the city and far, far beyond. On a clear day you can see as far as 80 miles, meaning you've got stellar views of not just New York City, but also parts of New Jersey, Pennsylvania, Connecticut, and Massachusetts. Another thing to look for: In certain atmospheric conditions, the 86th floor's outdoor deck experiences enormous buildups of static electricity, and quite a few couples have experienced "shocking" kisses. Unless you're a fiend for high spots, don't bother with the extra wait at the elevators to go up 200 more feet to the cramped 102nd floor observatory; you really won't see much more, and you'll have to look out through badly vandalized windows at that. It's worth timing your visit to the Empire State Building for early or late in the day, when the sun is low on the horizon and the shadows are deep across the city. Morning is the least crowded time, while at nighttime the views of the city's lights are absolutely dazzling.

If you're lucky enough to visit the Empire State Building around a major holiday, you'll notice the top 30 floors are lit up at night with seasonal colors. What started in 1976 with red, white, and blue lights for the American bicentennial has grown to include: Christmas (red and green lights); Easter (white and yellow); Rosh Hashanah and Yom Kippur (blue and white); Thanksgiving (red and orange); Martin Luther King Jr. Day (red, black, and green); Valentine's Day (red and white); Pulaski Day (red and white); Columbus Day (red, white, and green, the colors of the Italian flag); baseball season (blue and white, the Yankees' colors); and of course, the Fourth of July (red, white, and blue). *350 Fifth Ave., at 34th St., Midtown, tel. 212/736–3100. Subway: 6 to E. 33rd St. Admission: $4. Open daily 9:30 AM–midnight.*

NEW YORK SKYRIDE The Empire State Building's brand-new motion simulation ride ain't cheap, but it's the hairiest eight minutes you'll have in New York outside a cab. After being subjected to a Comedy Central video laced with subliminal messages (e.g., "Buy your kid NY stuff") and a *Blade Runner*–like "pre-flight" briefing in English and Japanese, strap yourself into the cramped flight seats and look up at the two-story-tall movie screens for a bucking, rough ride through New York City. *Tel. 212/279–9777 or 212/564–2224. Admission: $8, $10 for Skyride and Observatory. Open daily 10–10.*

STATUE OF LIBERTY

The Statue of Liberty is one of America's most potent icons—the thing Batman rappelled off in *Batman Forever*, that Charlton Heston viewed with rising dread (well, the crown part, anyway) in *Planet of the Apes*, and that author David Foster Wallace fancied as a product spokesmodel (holding aloft Tuck's medicated pads and Whoppers instead of a torch) in his epic *Infinite Jest*. Of course, to New Yorkers, this great monument is practically a cliché—the thing that you visit when you're baby-sitting out-of-towners. But France's gift to America, officially entitled *Liberty Enlightening the World*, still impresses even the most jaded. The only way you could avoid a rush of patriotism as you chug through New York harbor toward this great green toga-covered lady is if you've gotten so seasick you're stuck in the ferry's loo.

Behind every 151-foot-tall, 225-ton woman, of course, stands a much smaller man. For Ms. Liberty that's Frédéric-Auguste Bartholdi, a renowned 19th-century French sculptor. An odd fellow ruled by strong passions (after a trip to the Sphinx and Great Pyramids he became infatuated with the idea of building a Suez Canal colossus, which Egypt's king squelched), Bartholdi executed the statue as a monument to French–American solidarity. During a trip to New York he chose tiny, uninhabited Bedloe Island, where "people get their first view of the New World," as the perfect spot to display his work. Bartholdi made a few sketches with his mother as model, and 15 years later, on October 28, 1886, the statue was unveiled to an adoring public. Of course, the man wasn't acting entirely alone. The framework inside the statue was designed by Alexandre-Gustave Eiffel, of Eiffel Tower fame. The 89-foot-tall pedestal on which the statue stands was completed thanks to the efforts of Joseph Pulitzer, publisher of the *New York World*. In a savvy marketing coup, Pulitzer promised the working poor of New York that he would publish in his paper the name of every contributor, no matter how small the donation. The money for the pedestal was raised and Pulitzer increased the *World*'s circulation by 50,000. Inscribed on a bronze plaque attached to the statue's base is the sonnet *The New Colossus* ("Give me your tired, your poor, your huddled masses . . . "), written by the radical socialist Emma Lazarus.

Once you've strolled around Liberty Island, you have two choices at the ground-floor entrance of the monument: You can take an elevator 10 stories to the top of the pedestal, or, if you've got the cardiovascular strength of a Himalayan sherpa, you can climb 354 steps to the crown (visitors are not allowed to climb into the torch). It usually takes two or three hours to walk up to the crown because of the long lines, and the trip is not recommended for claustrophobes. Exhibits on the ground floor illustrate the statue's history, including videos of the view from the crown for those too wimpy to make the ascent. There's also a model of the statue's face for the blind to feel. *Tel. 212/363–3200 or 212/363–8340. Admission free. Open daily 9–5.*

COMING AND GOING The ferry to the Statue of Liberty and Ellis Island (*see below*) departs from Castle Clinton in **Battery Park** (*see* Manhattan Neighborhoods, Lower Manhattan, *below*), at the southern tip of Manhattan. The ferry ride is one loop; you can get off at Liberty Island, visit the statue, then reboard any ferry and continue on to Ellis Island, boarding another boat once you are ready to return. Ferries depart every 45 minutes on weekdays and every 30 minutes on weekends 9:30–3:30, with more frequent departures and extended hours in summer. *Tel. 212/269–5755 for ferry info. Subway to Battery Park: 1 or 9 to South Ferry. Also 4 or 5 to Bowling Green. Round-trip fare to Statue of Liberty and/or Ellis Island: $7.*

ELLIS ISLAND

From 1892 to 1924 some 16 million immigrants—men, women, and children—took their first steps on U.S. soil at Ellis Island in New York harbor. In all, by the time the island's federal immigration facility closed for good in 1954, it had processed the ancestors of more than 40% of Americans living today. Now, after many years of restoration, this 27½-acre island has become a museum devoted to immigration. Even if your ancestors didn't arrive here, the visit leaves a powerful impression. At its heart is the **Registry Room**, where inspectors once attempted to screen out "undesirables," like polygamists, criminals, poor people, and people suffering from contagious diseases. The cavernous **Great Hall**, where immigrants were registered, has amazing tiled arches by Rafael Guastavino; white-tiled dormitory rooms overlook this grand space. The **Railroad Ticket Office** at the back of the main building houses exhibits on the "Peopling of America," recounting 400 years of immigration history, and "Forced Migration," focusing on the slave trade. The old kitchen and laundry building has been stabilized, rather than restored, so that you can see what the whole place looked like just a few years ago.

Immigrants who have passed through Ellis Island include: Charles Atlas, Irving Berlin, Frank Capra, Claudette Colbert, Father Edward Flannagan, Marcus Garvey, Samuel Goldwyn, Bob Hope, Al Jolson, Bela Lugosi, Hyman G. Rickover, Knute Rockne, Rudolph Valentino, and Maria von Trapp and her singing family.

The most moving exhibit is outdoors to the west of the Main Building: the **American Immigrant Wall of Honor**, a circular wall covered in stainless steel and engraved with the names of 420,000 immigrants of all stripes and colors. The names include Miles Standish, Priscilla Alden, George Washington's grandfather, and Irving Berlin; they include people who came to the South on slave ships, to San Francisco on Chinese junks, and to Plymouth, Massachusetts, on the *Mayflower*. A $100 fee was charged for each name on the wall, to pay for Ellis Island's restoration. Guided 30-minute tours of the island are given daily. For info on ferries to Ellis Island, *see* The Statue of Liberty, Coming and Going, *above*. *Tel. 212/363–3200 for recorded info. Admission free. Open winter, daily 9–5; summer, daily 9–6.*

WORLD TRADE CENTER

In a city where practically everything is described in superlatives like "biggest" and "most," the mammoth World Trade Center—which boasts the two tallest buildings in the city and the third-tallest in the entire world—is the *maxi-plus-ultra-*most. It's more like a miniature city than an office complex, really, with a daytime population of 130,000 (including 50,000 employees and 80,000 visitors); several train stations; dozens of restaurants; an 800-room hotel; and a huge performance space. Hey, it's even got its own blood bank and the world's largest air-conditioning system. Besides those famous 1,360-foot-high twin towers, it has five other buildings arranged around an enormous plaza, modeled after Venice's St. Mark's Square. Below that, you'll find a giant subterranean shopping mall. There's lots to explore, but what you're really here to do is ride one of the warp-speed elevators to the Observation Deck (*see below*) on the 107th floor of Tower Two.

The World Trade Center's "twin" towers are actually different heights. One World Trade Center is 1,368 feet tall, and Two World Trade Center is 1,362 feet tall.

Unlike some of the city's other skyscrapers—the Empire State Building, the Chrysler Building in Midtown, or the Flatiron Building in Gramercy—the Trade Center towers are more an engineering marvel than architectural masterpiece. Completed in 1976, they've since been criticized as being nothing more than boring glass-and-steel boxes. But something about their brutalist design and sheer magnitude gives them the beauty of modern sculpture, and at night, when they're lit from within, they dominate the Manhattan skyline. Where the towers differ most radically from other office buildings is hidden inside; they were engineered so that each of the nearly 1-acre floors is completely open, free of beams, pillars, and other visible means of support. Think about this for a minute and you might wonder how the whole thing keeps from collapsing like a house of cards. Don't worry. Structurally, the towers are capable of withstanding sustained winds of over 100 miles per hour. It probably would take a nuclear bomb to level them.

Of course, anyone who watches CNN knows that the World Trade Center is not invincible. On February 26, 1993, a Ryder van loaded with explosives detonated in one of the underground parking garages, killing six and injuring thousands. Today, the damage has been fixed and the main suspects are serving life sentences in prison. The only reminders are the metal detectors that all employees and visitors must now pass through before entering the center, and a small, granite **memorial** imbedded in the sidewalk of the outdoor plaza.

VISITOR INFO The New York Visitor Information Center, located on the mezzanine of Two World Trade Center, is an excellent place to begin your visit. Helpful if eccentric little old ladies will furnish you with an abundance of info on the Trade Center and other Big Apple sights. On the same level, you'll find the ticket booth for the Trade Tower's observation deck and the downtown branch of **TKTS** (see Chapter 7), your one-stop shop for cheap theater tickets. *Subway: C or E to World Trade Center. Also: 1 or 9 to Cortlandt St. Open weekdays 9–5; also Sat. 9–4:30 in summer. Wheelchair access.*

How big is the World Trade Center? Enough aluminum was slapped onto the exteriors of the twin towers to side 7,000 homes, and enough concrete was poured for the foundations to build a 5-foot-wide sidewalk from New York to Washington, D.C.

OBSERVATION DECK The best views in Manhattan are from the 107th-floor Observation Deck at Two World Trade Center. And if you look at the line of tourists waiting to buy tickets at the mezzanine-level office, you'll see that this is no big secret (the line is shortest weekday mornings and evenings). The elevator ride alone is worth the price of admission, as you hurtle a quarter-mile into the sky in only 58 seconds. Once you reach the top you can, if you dare, press your nose to the glass of the floor-to-ceiling windows and look out upon the entire island of Manhattan, or across the New York Bay to the Statue of Liberty and Ellis Island (the view potentially extends 55 miles, although signs at the ticket window disclose how far you can see that day). There's a café here, with prices elevated to correspond with the height: A can of Coke costs $2, sandwiches $7.50. On nice days you can ride up another few floors to the **Rooftop Observatory**, the world's highest outdoor observation platform. It's offset 25 feet from the edge of the building and surrounded with a barbed-wire electric fence, to thwart spontaneous hurlers of bowling balls. You'll notice that planes and helicopters are flying *below* you. *Tel. 212/323–2340. Admission: $8. Open June–Sept., daily 9:30 AM–11:30 PM; Oct.–May, daily 9:30 AM–9:30 PM. Wheelchair access.*

COMMODITIES EXCHANGE At Four World Trade Center, one of those other, shorter Trade Center buildings, you can spy on the capitalist equivalent of circus clowns: commodities traders, who roll up their sleeves and then sweat, shout, and shove their way through a day handling millions of dollars worth of petroleum, livestock, precious metals, and agricultural products (the exchange started in 1886 as the New York Butter and Cheese Exchange). Pick up a pass (free) from the security checkpoint at the southeast corner of the Trade Center's Mall. Warning: You'll be exposed to an endlessly repeating tape—espousing the glory of the free market—that only a Young Republican could love. *Open weekdays 10:30–3. Wheelchair access.*

CENTRAL PARK

Central Park is probably America's best-loved and best-known park, an 843-acre rectangle of green smack in the middle of Manhattan. You've probably spied it in Absolut Vodka ads, various episodes of *Seinfeld*, and countless movies old and new. If you care, it's the reason behind "Central Perk," the name of the café in *Friends*, and is the place where Robin Williams danced nude in *The Fisher King*. On the flip side, it's also made national headlines as the place where teenage gangs go "wilding," though these days the park is pretty safe—so long as you don't go wandering around its northern woods after dark.

Conceived in 1853, Central Park was America's first landscaped public park. Wealthy New Yorkers lobbied hard for its creation so that they'd have as pretty a place for carriage rides as their rivals in London and Paris, and also because they felt it would get the working classes out of the saloons. Besides, the stretch of land between 59th and 110th streets was at the time a swampy no-man's-land filled with squatters and roving packs of wild pigs and dogs. Leading the campaign was *New York Post* editor and part-time writer of nature poetry William Cullen Bryant, who later got a fine park named after himself in Midtown (*see* Parks and Gardens, *below*). Ultimately, master landscape architects Frederick Law Olmsted and Calvert Vaux (*see box* They Built This City, *below*) were teamed to draw up its design. The two met at night, walking over every acre of the land as they drew up plans to reconfigure it. What resulted, called the "Greenward Plan," cultivates the impression of rural English countryside, with wide sweeps of forest and lawn interspersed with beautiful cast-iron bridges and elaborate fountains. It took 15 years to mark out the park and another 40 for the trees to grow and fill in the outline. Over the decades the park has continued to grow, and it now includes 22 playgrounds, 26 ball fields, 30 tennis courts, and 58 miles of paved pedestrian paths.

You'll probably want to start your exploration at the south end of the park. Between Center and East Drives is the first of a few small bodies of water in the park, **The Pond** and **Hallett Nature Sanctuary**. The area between 59th and 65th streets is largely devoted to children: The **Conservatory Water** is a small pond usually cluttered with model boats and their child captains. Races and regattas are held here every weekend. On the west end of the basin is a statue of **Hans Christian Andersen** with his pet goose; on the north end, saddling a huge mushroom, sits **Alice in Wonderland** with a few of her eccentric friends. The park's **Children's Zoo** has been closed since 1992 and is due to reopen in the summer of 1997 with a design more friendly to its animal residents. At 79th Street, the landscape jogs upward to the top of **Vista Rock**, which forms the foundation for playful **Belvedere Castle** (*see below*). Just off to the left is the **Shakespeare Garden**, a beautiful plot crammed with flowering plants immortalized by the bard. East of the garden is the **Swedish Cottage**, where the **Marionette Theater** (tel. 212/988–9093) performs weekdays at 10:30 and noon. At the edge of the park at Fifth Avenue and 82nd Street is the grand **Metropolitan Museum of Art** (*see below*). Above 86th Street things start getting a little wilder, partly due to the original design, which called for footpaths through small rocky gorges and along creek beds, and partly due to lapsed supervision, although this area is undergoing a cleanup. While you're up here, look for the stone **Blockhouse**, the oldest building in the park. It dates from the War of 1812; you can still see gun ports in its decaying walls.

Public rest rooms are scattered throughout the park: at Bethesda Terrace, the Loeb Boathouse, the North Meadow Recreation Center, the Conservatory Garden, the Charles A. Dana Discovery Center, and north of the Reservoir near the tennis courts. For food, there's a restaurant/café at the Loeb Boathouse and the Ice Cream Café at the Conservatory Water. During summer, the park is home to numerous free arts performances, including the enormously popular **Summerstage** and **New York Shakespeare** festivals; for more info *see* Summer Arts, in Chapter 7. Year-round, the park draws all sorts of sporting enthusiasts for rock-climbing, tennis, horseback-riding, softball, you name it, including winter ice-skating on its famous **Wollman Rink**; for more info, *see* Ice Skating and Ice Hockey, in Chapter 9. *Tel. 212/360–3456 or 800/201–PARK for park events, 212/572–4820 for emergencies, or 800/281–5722 for TDD. Park open daily 30 min before sunrise–1 AM.*

THE DAIRY If you're planning to make a day of exploring Central Park, make this charming Victorian-style cottage your first stop. Back in the 19th century, when cows grazed on what's since become an ice-skating rink, the cottage was a dairy selling milk by the glass. It now houses the **Central Park Reception Center**, where you can pick up maps and info on park events, or check out exhibits on the park's history and wildlife. The striped-brick **Chess and Checkers House**, a short walk south of the Dairy, is perched atop a large rock named the *Kinderberg*, or "children's mountain." You'll find plenty of chess tables; with a $20 deposit, you can pick up pieces to play with at the Dairy. *Mid-park at 65th St., tel. 212/794–6564. Subway: N or R to Fifth Ave. Open Tues.–Sun. 11–5 (shorter hrs in winter).*

Jacqueline Kennedy Onassis
Reservoir

W. 88th St. / E. 88th St.
W. 87th St. / E. 87th St.
W. 86th St. / E. 86th St.
W. 85th St. / E. 85th St.
W. 84th St. / E. 84th St.
W. 83rd St. / E. 83rd St.
W. 82nd St. / E. 82nd St.
W. 81st St. / E. 81st St.

B,C **S**

Great Lawn

0 ———— 200 yards
0 ———— 200 meters

N

West Dr.

Turtle Pond

79th St. Transverse

E. 80th St.
W. 77th St. / E. 79th St.
W. 76th St. / E. 78th St.
W. 75th St. / E. 77th St.
W. 74th St. / E. 76th St.
W. 73rd St. / E. 75th St.

The Lake

Bow Bridge

East Dr.

Conservatory Water

E. 74th St.
E. 73rd St.
W. 72nd St. / E. 72nd St.

B,C **S**

E. 71st St.

Sheep Meadow

Central Park West

W. 70th St. / E. 70th St.
W. 69th St. / E. 69th St.
W. 68th St. / E. 68th St.
W. 67th St. / E. 67th St.
W. 66th St. / E. 66th St.
W. 65th St. / E. 65th St.

65th St. Transverse

Fifth Avenue

West Dr.

Center Dr.

Heckscher Playground

E. 64th St.
W. 64th St. / E. 63rd St.
W. 63rd St. / E. 62nd St.
W. 62nd St. / E. 61st St.
W. 61st St.

East Dr.

The Pond

W. 60th St. / E. 60th St.

Columbus Circle

S *A,B,C,D, 1,9*

Central Park South

Grand Army Plaza

S *N,R*

W. 58th St. / E. 58th St.
W. 57th St. / E. 57th St.

Broadway

Seventh Ave.

Sixth Ave.

KEY

i Tourist Information

American Museum of Natural History and Hayden Planetarium, **1**

Belvedere Castle (tourist info), **5**

Bethesda Fountain and Terrace, **11**

Chess and Checkers House, **17**

Children's Zoo, **22**

Cleopatra's Needle, **6**

Croquet Grounds and Lawn Bowling Greens, **12**

The Dairy (tourist info), **18**

Delacorte Theater, **4**

Friedsam Memorial Carousel, **15**

Hallett Nature Sanctuary, **20**

Literary Walk, **16**

Loeb Boathouse, **10**

The Mall, **14**

Metropolitan Museum of Art, **8**

The Ramble, **7**

Shakespeare Garden, **2**

Strawberry Fields, **9**

Swedish Cottage/ Marionette Theater, **3**

Tavern on the Green, **13**

Wildlife Conservation Center (Zoo), **21**

Wollman Rink, **19**

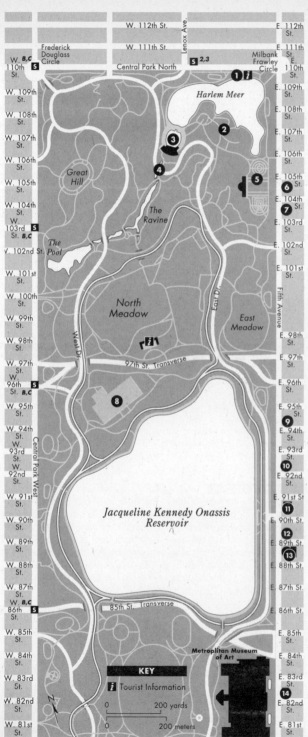

Conservatory
Garden, **5**

Huddlestone
Bridge, **4**

Charles A. Dana
Discovery Center, **1**

Lasker Rink
and Pool, **3**

McGowan's Pass, **2**

Tennis Courts, **8**

Museum Mile

Cooper-Hewitt
National Design
Museum, **11**

El Museo del
Barrio, **6**

Goethe House, **14**

Guggenheim
Museum, **13**

International Center
of Photography–
Uptown, **9**

The Jewish
Museum, **10**

Museum of the City
of New York, **7**

National Academy
of Design, **12**

45

FRIEDSAM MEMORIAL CAROUSEL This turn-of-the-century carousel was brought to the park from Coney Island (*see* The Outer Boroughs, Brooklyn, *below*) in 1951. Its 58 beautiful, hand-carved jumping steeds, three-quarters the size of real horses, go 'round to music by a wheezy but cheerful pipe organ. *Mid-park at 65th St., just west of Center Dr., tel. 212/879–0244. Admission: 90¢. Open weekdays 10:30–5, weekends 10:30–6.*

WILDLIFE CONSERVATION CENTER (ZOO) The Zoo has given itself a snappy new eco-friendly name and labored long and hard to give its small collection of furred and feathered residents more natural habitats, like in the **Tropic Zone**, where birds and reptiles cavort among jungle vines and palm fronds. There's also **Temperate Territory** for monkeys, and **Edge of the Ice Pack** for a flock of penguins. But there's been trouble in the **Polar Circle**, where Gus, the 700-pound polar bear, was recently diagnosed as suffering from depression; like every other New Yorker, he now has a therapist. Just outside the Zoo's gates look for the **Delacorte Musical Clock**. Every hour its six-animal band circles around and plays a tune while monkeys on the top hammer their bells. *E. 64th St., at Fifth Ave., tel. 212/861–6030. Subway: N or R to Fifth Ave. Admission: $2.50. Open Apr.–Oct., weekdays 10–5, weekends 10:30–5:30; Nov.–Mar., daily 10–4:30.*

SHEEP MEADOW Look around Sheep Meadow on a sunny summer Sunday and you'll see 15 acres full of sunbathers and Frisbee players. Stick around for an hour or two and you'll eventually meet the genius who walks around in a flapping red cape, selling cold cans of beer out of a paper bag. Unlike at the park's other grassy fields, team sports are prohibited here, so it's the perfect place to picnic or fly a kite. And, as you might have guessed from the name, the meadow was indeed once home-sweet-home to a woolly flock, evicted in 1934. Around that time the nearby sheepfold was turned into a glitzy restaurant, **Tavern on the Green** (Central Park W, at W. 67th St., tel. 212/873–3200), which is expensive but just the tiniest bit tacky, with lots of trees wrapped in twinkling lights and deer antlers on the walls. Just north of Sheep Meadow are the manicured **Croquet Grounds** and **Lawn Bowling Greens**. You must have a permit ($30) to play on them; call 212/360–8133 for info. *Mid-park btw 65th and 69th Sts.*

THE MALL Sorry, this isn't the kind of "mall" that has a Macy's and Mrs. Field's Cookies. It's a wide avenue shaded by tall elms and made for strolling; pretend you're in a painting by Seurat. At its southern end is the **Literary Walk**, so named because statues of dead white scribes like William Shakespeare, Robert Burns, and Sir Walter Scott line the path. One welcome addition was **The Indian Hunter**, sculpted in 1869 by John Quincy Adams Ward; this was the first piece of made-in-America sculpture to stand in the park. There must have been a very good reason for sticking it off to one side rather than placing it along the path with all the rest. *Mid-park btw 66th and 72nd Sts.*

BETHESDA FOUNTAIN AND TERRACE Not many New York views are more romantic than the one from the top of the magnificent stone staircase that leads down to Bethesda Fountain. And it makes an excellent place to meet when the weather's nice—you can either sit on the fountain's edge and let preteens soak you with their splashings, or choose one of the benches scattered around the elaborately patterned terrace. The fountain itself was created in 1873 and named for the biblical pool in Jerusalem that was supposedly given healing powers by an angel. The four figures around Bethesda Fountain's base symbolize Temperance, Purity, Health, and Peace. Beyond the terrace stretches the Lake (*see* Loeb Boathouse, *below*), filled with drifting swans and amateur rowboat captains. *Mid-park at 72nd St.*

LOEB BOATHOUSE At the Loeb Boathouse, on the eastern side of the park's 18-acre **Lake**, you can rent a dinghy (or the one authentic Venetian gondola) for $10 per hour (plus $20 deposit), or pedal off on a bicycle for $8 per hour. There's also an open-air café/bar that's packed with a crowd of tipsy professionals on summer evenings. *Mid-park at 74th St., near East Dr., tel. 212/517–2233 for boat rentals and café or 212/861–4137 for bike rental. Subway: 6 to E. 77th St. Rental shop open daily 11:30–6; café closed dinner fall–spring.*

STRAWBERRY FIELDS Also known as the International Garden of Peace, Strawberry Fields is a memorial to the late John Lennon, donated by his wife Yoko Ono. Every year on December 8, Beatles fans gather around the star-shaped, black-and-white tiled IMAGINE mosaic set into one of the sidewalks to mourn Lennon's 1980 murder, which took place across the street at the

Dakota apartments (*see box* Don't You Wish You Lived Here?, *below*), where he lived. The curving paths, well-tended shrubs, and orderly flower beds of this small garden are supposed to look a bit British. *W. 72nd St., near Central Park W.*

THE RAMBLE Yearning for romantic, Gothic wilderness? The Ramble comprises 37 acres of narrow footpaths that snake through thickets of trees, wind around a tiny stream, and even lead to a secret cave. It's one of the best parts of the park to wander (or ramble) because you're absolutely, positively guaranteed not to encounter any Rollerbladers. The Ramble is particularly popular with bird-watchers—and among some of the city's gay men, who come here to do something besides looking for titmice and warblers. The **Urban Park Rangers** lead bird-watching tours here; call 212/772–0210 for more info. *Mid-park btw 74th and 79th Sts.*

BELVEDERE CASTLE What park would be complete without a fanciful turreted castle? The Belvedere's a mishmash of styles—Norman, Gothic, Moorish—and deliberately built small so that when it was viewed from across the nearby lake, the lake would seem bigger. Now that the trees have grown you can't see the lake at all. Since 1919 the castle has housed a U.S. Weather Bureau station—look for twirling meteorological instruments on top of its tower. Inside is a **visitor information bureau** and some geology exhibits. *Mid-park at 79th St., tel. 212/772–0210. Subway: B or C to W. 81st St. Open Tues.–Sun. 11–5 (shorter hrs in winter).*

CLEOPATRA'S NEEDLE Over the centuries this sturdy relic has really racked up the mileage: It began life as a giant obelisk in Heliopolis, Egypt, around 1600 BC, was eventually carted off to Alexandria by the Romans in 12 BC, passed a little time hither and yon, and was ultimately presented to the city of New York by the khedive of Egypt on February 22, 1881. Ironically, a century in New York has done more to ravage the Needle than millennia of globe-trotting, and the hieroglyphics have sadly worn away to a *tabula rasa*. Thank Ra it wasn't the Rosetta Stone. *Mid-park at 81st St., behind the Metropolitan Museum of Art.*

JACQUELINE KENNEDY ONASSIS RESERVOIR This 106-acre reservoir (named for the former First Lady after her death in 1994) takes up most of the center of the park, from 86th to 97th streets. Around its perimeter is a 1.58-mile track popular with runners year-round. Even if you're not training for the New York Marathon, it's worth visiting for the stellar views of surrounding high-rises. *Mid-park btw 86th and 97th Sts.*

CONSERVATORY GARDEN The formal, symmetrical Conservatory Garden (laid out during the Depression as a WPA project) is a nice contrast to the rustic wilderness of the rest of Central Park. It's a favorite with couples and mournful poets. The **Central Garden** is bordered by flowering crab-apple trees (beautiful in spring), and has a reflecting pool and wisteria arbor. The **North Garden**, built around a pleasant fountain, explodes with some 20,000 tulip blossoms in spring and 5,000 chrysanthemums in fall. The **South Garden**, dedicated to *The Secret Garden* author Frances Hodgson Burnett, offers 175 kinds of perennials marshaled into proper British rows. Those impressive wrought-iron gates you passed through to enter the garden from Fifth Avenue once graced the mansion of Cornelius Vanderbilt II. *Fifth Ave., btw E. 103rd and 106th Sts. Subway: 6 to E. 103rd St. Open daily 8 AM–dusk.*

HUDDLESTONE BRIDGE If you're exploring the north end of the park, take a few minutes to look at Huddlestone Bridge, made from boulders weighing up to 100 tons. No mortar was used in its construction—instead, the sheer weight of the rocks "huddling together" keeps it from falling apart. Head southwest on one of the footpaths and you'll pass several small waterfalls before arriving at the **Pool**, a romantic spot surrounded by weeping willows and clusters of tall reeds. *Mid-park at 105th St., just south of Lasker Rink and Pool.*

HARLEM MEER AND THE CHARLES A. DANA DISCOVERY CENTER First, before you ask: *Meer* is the Dutch word for lake. This particular meer has been recently spruced up and stocked with 50,000 bluegills, largemouth bass, and catfish, which you're allowed to catch and release (what would you do with a dead fish at your hostel anyway?). Pick up fishing poles (free) at the **Charles A. Dana Discovery Center** (tel. 212/860–1370), disguised as a petite Swiss chalet; the center is closed Mondays. Just south of the meer is **McGowan's Pass**, through which American troops fled from the British on September 15, 1776, and returned victoriously at the end of

They Built This City

- *Olmsted and Vaux. Frederick Law Olmsted (1822–1903), a farmer from Staten Island, and Calvert Vaux (1824–1895), a talented young architect from England, first teamed up in 1853 to design Central Park. Together the dynamic landscape architects went on to create Morningside Park, Prospect Park, Fort Greene Park, the Eastern Parkway, and many others. Their designs tended to be naturalistic rather than formal, recreating the look of the English countryside, for example, with rustic stone walls, wide lakes, and scattered groves of trees. Eventually, the partnership dissolved in 1872 as Olmsted became increasingly antagonistic toward city politicians he felt were cramping his style; he bitterly opposed city-mandated additions to his parks by McKim, Mead & White (see below). Insanity forced his retirement in 1895. Vaux formed his own practice after the breakup, and worked on the Metropolitan Museum of Art and American Museum of Natural History, with architect Jacob Wrey Mould. As the years passed he became increasingly bitter over the lack of recognition for what he considered his greatest works—Central Park and Prospect Park—and drowned under mysterious circumstances in Gravesend Bay.*

- *McKim, Mead & White. Just about every landmark Beaux Arts and neo-Renaissance building in town dating between 1880 and 1915 was designed by the architecture firm of McKim, Mead & White. Most notably: the Tiffany's showroom, the Plaza Hotel, the Harvard Club, the mammoth Brooklyn Museum, J. P. Morgan's private library (which later became the Pierpont Morgan Library), City's Hall's Municipal Building, Judson Memorial Church, portions of the grand Metropolitan Museum of Art, and the entire campus of Columbia University. At its busiest, the firm employed almost a hundred, even though a penchant for alabaster marble rather than cheap brownstone made their buildings fairly expensive.*

William Rutherford Mead (1846–1928) had a fairly low profile, but Stanford White (1853–1906) and Charles McKim (1847–1909) lead busy lives outside the firm. White, lover of Italian Renaissance design and the firm's acknowledged "master of effects," was solo designer for the triumphal Washington Square arch, Striver's Row houses in Harlem, and the original Madison Square Garden. A lusty man who collected antiquities and women, he met an ironic end at a party on the roof of the Garden when he was shot point-blank by one Harry K. Shaw. White had been having an affair with Thaw's showgirl wife since she was 16; "Vanity Fair" magazine marked his passing with an article titled, "Stanford White, Voluptuary and Pervert, Dies the Death of a Dog." Meanwhile, White's partner, Charles McKim, was regarded as the most talented and influential architect of his day; he designed many beautiful New York mansions but lived alone in a modest rented flat. He suffered a nervous breakdown when White was shot and died soon after at the home of White's widow.

the Revolutionary War led by General Henry Knox. *Near Fifth Ave., btw E. 106th and 110th Sts. Subway: 6 to E. 110th St.*

BROOKLYN BRIDGE

"The complete work, when constructed in accordance with my designs, will not only be the greatest bridge in existence, but it will be the greatest engineering work on this continent, and of the age." So wrote John Augustus Roebling, the visionary architect, legendary engineer, metaphysical philosopher, fervid abolitionist, and unabashed egotist who practically willed the Brooklyn Bridge into existence in the mid-1800s. At a length of 6,016 feet, it was four times longer than the longest suspension bridge of its day. Its twin Gothic-arched towers rise 268 feet from the river below, while the roadway is supported by a web of human-sized steel cables, hung from the towers and attached to block-long anchorages on either shore. From roadway to water is about 133 feet, high enough to allow the tallest ships to pass. Though it is hardly the longest suspension bridge in the world anymore, the Brooklyn Bridge is still a beautiful sight and one of New York's most emblematic structures.

Roebling first conceived of the bridge on an icy winter's day in 1852, angry because he couldn't get to Brooklyn—the East River had frozen solid, and the ferry had as much chance of crossing it as the proverbial snowball in hell. Roebling spent the next 30 years designing, raising money for, and building the bridge. But tragically, two years into construction, a falling timber crushed his foot, and the stubborn visionary died of gangrene a week later. Roebling's son Washington rose valiantly to the task, only to suffer extensive nerve damage during the underwater phase of construction and end up in a wheelchair. Ultimately, the job of foreman fell to another Roebling, Washington's wife. In 1883, under her supervision, the bridge was finally completed. The public was so captivated by the long struggle to build this mighty bridge that it was quickly crowned the "Eighth Wonder of the World."

A walk across the **Great Bridge promenade**, a pedestrian walkway and bike path elevated slightly above the roadway, is a New York experience on par with the Statue of Liberty trip or the Empire State Building ascent. It's a 40-minute walk from Manhattan's civic center to the heart of charming Brooklyn Heights (*see* The Outer Boroughs, *below*). Most days the promenade is quite busy, with camera-toting tourists and a variety of New Yorkers speeding by on foot, bike, or 'blades. At dusk the views of Manhattan's twinkling skyline will make you yelp with delight. And, for a real treat, walk out on the bridge before sunrise, when Lower Manhattan glows golden in the early light. As always, though, keep your wits (and preferably a friend or two) about you. *Subway: 4, 5, or 6 to Brooklyn Bridge/City Hall (Manhattan). Also: A or C to High St./Brooklyn Bridge (Brooklyn).*

METROPOLITAN MUSEUM OF ART

The Met, as it's known to New Yorkers, is a gargantuan treasure trove of art from around the world. This sucker is *big*—a collection to end all collections. In fact, it's not really a single museum at all, but instead a vast network of many museums all under one roof. In its permanent collections are nearly three million works of art, from reconstructed Egyptian temples to delicate Han dynasty dishes, spanning time from the good old Paleolithic days right up to the present. At any given time, only a quarter of the Met's permanent collection is on display. This is hardly surprising, considering holdings include 2,000 European paintings, 3,000 European drawings, an equal number of American paintings and statues, 4,000 medieval objects, a comparable group of musical instruments, and a million prints. Add to that more than 30 special exhibitions each year and you'll see why even longtime city residents answer evasively when asked if they've seen everything in this 1½-million-square-foot megamuseum.

Despite the size and breadth of its collection, the Met does have its detractors. Its reputation as a bastion of Eurocentric art was only slightly improved back in 1969, when oil magnate Nelson Rockefeller donated significant cash to improving the collections of art from Africa, Oceania, and the Americas. More recently, after viewing a 1995 exhibition of the Met's newest acquisitions, a reviewer for the *New York Times* carped that the museum seems to be "studiously avoiding the hip, the trendy, the conceptual, the political, and the installational," which is basically artspeak for saying that its curators are pretty out of it.

It's hard to believe that the whole thing began in 1870 at a building south of its present location with a modest 174 works of art, and an assumption by New York's power brokers than the metropolis would be all the more metropolitan if it had, rather than decent living conditions for its poorest citizens, a really cool art museum. The Met moved to its current home along posh Fifth Avenue, in Central Park, a decade later, and there it began to grow. The first permanent building was designed by architects Calvert Vaux and Jacob Wrey Mould; most of this has since been swallowed up by additions (if you look just inside the Robert Wood Johnson, Jr. Gallery you can see one of the original pointed Gothic archways). Some of New York's most noted architects have had a hand in the Met's expansion, including R. M. and R. H. Hunt, and McKim, Mead & White. Beginning in the '70s, the museum's separate buildings were unified by bridging the spaces between them with huge glass-and-grid walls and roofs. Unlike most things from that style-challenged decade, this has resulted in some of the museum's most exuberant spaces. Finally, the huge stone steps out front, which had for decades terrorized those wanting in youthful energy (and to some embodied the museum's attitude toward its public), were redesigned to include landings where climbers could stop for rest. These days you'll find the steps crowded with citizens from all over the world, resting their weary feet and watching cabs jockey on Fifth Avenue.

The biggest mistake you can make at the Met is to try to see everything (or even most things) in one visit. Unless you're on Rollerblades, you should really focus on two to four sections rather than attempting the whole shebang. Because of reduced funding and ongoing renovations, some galleries are closed on a rotating schedule; inquire at the Information Desk (*see below*) when you pick up your trusty museum map. *1000 Fifth Ave., at 82nd St., Upper East Side, tel. 212/879–5500. Subway: 4, 5, or 6 to E. 86th St. Open Sun., Tues.–Thurs. 9:30–5:15, Fri.–Sat. 9:30–8:45. Wheelchair access.*

PRACTICALITIES The $7 ($3.50 students) admission is only a suggested amount, so if you're really broke, you can pay less—do as your conscience tells you. Your admission here also entitles you to a free same-day visit to the Cloisters (*see* Museums and Galleries, *below*), the Met's annex for medieval art. But that's a hell of a lot of art to absorb in one day.

The museum's **Information Desk** is in the center of the Great Hall—you can't miss it. You'll want to pick up a Floor Plan (without this you'll never make it out alive) and the calendar of special programs. The **International Visitors Desk** (tel. 212/650–2987), also in the Great Hall, assists those speaking Chinese, French, German, Italian, Japanese, or Spanish. For info on **services for visitors with disabilities**, call 212/535–7710 or TDD 212/879–0421.

Check with the Information Desk (*see above*) for the day's schedule of walking tours, which are usually free with your museum admission. Self-guided **audio tours** (tel. 212/570–3821) focus on the highlights of a particular wing or gallery, including European paintings, ancient Egypt, Greek and Roman art, and musical instruments, as well as major special exhibitions. The 45-minute tapes rent for $4 from the Audio Tour Desk in the Main Hall.

Special exhibits scheduled for 1997 are too numerous to list, but among the most important are works by 18th-century Venetian painters Giambattista and Domenico Tiepolo from January 23 to April 27; "Masterpieces from a European Foundation," including renowned impressionist and postimpressionist works, from January 30 to May 4; and "The Glory of Byzantium," from March 18 through July 6. Lectures, films, and panel discussions take place almost hourly in the **Grace Rainey Rogers** and **Uris Center** auditoriums on topics as diverse as the collections. Classical music concerts are also regularly scheduled at the Met; *see* Music, in Chapter 7.

COLLECTION HIGHLIGHTS The **20th-Century Art** galleries (first and second floors) span everything from Grant Wood's *The Ride of Paul Revere* to totally abstract stuff like gigantic Clyfford Still canvases of black and red, and Ellsworth Kelly's *Curve XXXII*, a gigantic slab of Corten steel. In the **Islamic Art** galleries (second floor) you'll find a reconstructed room from an Ottoman Empire upper-class home. Nearby are the **Ancient Near Eastern Art** galleries, where you'll see portions of the Persepolis monument and the famous Assyrian reliefs from the palace of Ashurnasirpal II. A narrow hallway is all that is devoted to **Drawings, Prints, and Photographs**; if you're interested in photography, you're better off heading to the Museum of Modern Art (*see below*).

➤ **AMERICAN WING** • The American Wing offers room after reconstructed room of early American interiors and some of the museum's best-known paintings. In **Gallery 223** you'll view Emanuel Leutze's famous *Washington Crosses the Delaware*, and undoubtedly walk away happily sated with your dose of early-Republic hypernationalism. Two whole rooms are

Don't miss the Met's collection of vintage baseball cards, on display in the American Wing. They date from the late 1800s to the 1950s.

devoted to the artists of the Hudson River School; in Frederic Edwin Church's 1859 masterwork *The Heart of the Andes*, look for Church's signature "carved" into a tree. You'll also find a room from one of Frank Lloyd Wright's Prairie-style homes. *First, second, and third floors.*

➤ **EUROPEAN SCULPTURE AND DECORATIVE ARTS** • The Met's collection of European sculpture and decorative arts includes sculpture, glass, ceramics, textiles, and jewelry that date from the 16th to 20th centuries. It's housed in a new five-story south wing.

➤ **COSTUME INSTITUTE** • One floor below the Great Hall, you'll find the Costume Institute, a relatively small suite of rooms that exhibits a rotating array of items from the Met's huge collection of fashions—everything from 19th-century royal wedding gowns to see-through plastic dresses. *Ground floor.*

➤ **LEHMAN PAVILION** • The 1,000-piece **Robert Lehman Collection** of 18th-century French furniture and Flemish, Italian, and French paintings, drawings, and tapestries is arranged around a skylit courtyard. At the center of the courtyard is a 15th-century Florentine fountain with an unhappy provenance: It was commissioned by a merchant who lost his life trying to snuff out a rival family, and his unhappy heirs ended up hawking it to pay the bills. *Ground floor.*

➤ **THE EGYPTIAN WING** • The Met owns one of the most comprehensive collections of Egyptian Art outside Cairo, with objects from every facet and era of Egyptian life: crumbly yellow household linens, stone tools dating back some 6,000 years, and even a mummified gazelle that was once the pet of a royal court singer. Adjacent to the Egyptian Collection is the magnificent **Temple of Dendur**, an ancient temple donated by the Egyptian government. The whole shebang was transported here block by giant block. *First floor.*

➤ **PRIMITIVE ART** • In the Michael C. Rockefeller Wing you'll find the somewhat sparse galleries devoted to the **Arts of Africa, Oceania, and the Americas**. The 7,000 sculptures, ritual objects, and everyday artifacts span 3,000 years. *First floor.*

➤ **ARMS AND ARMOR** • The Arms and Armor galleries hold some impressive European armor—for both men and their horses. There's also a wild collection of Japanese arms and armor, plus a model trebuchet, used for flinging diseased carcasses over castle walls (mankind's first attempts at chemical warfare). *First floor.*

➤ **MEDIEVAL ART** • The galleries housing art from the Dark Ages are dimly lit, appropriately enough, and home to a wicked-looking choir screen from Spain's Cathedral of Valladolid—the ultimate home-security fence. Especially noteworthy is the cavernous sculpture hall, built to resemble a church. *First floor.*

➤ **GREEK AND ROMAN ART** • If they're not shut down for major renovations, check out the Greek and Roman Art galleries' dazzling displays of gold and silver tableware, ceremonial vessels, and Grecian urns. *First and second floors.*

➤ **ASIAN ART GALLERIES** • The entrance to the Asian Art galleries is dominated by a huge Buddhist wall painting of the *Paradise of Bhaisajyaguru*. The **Chinese Art** galleries were being renovated at press time, but the elegant Astor Court, based on the 16th-century Garden of the Master of the Fishing Nets in Suzhou, was due to open soon. Galleries containing Chinese

Ask a museum guard to direct you to the Met's Astor Court, a peaceful courtyard constructed by Chinese craftsman in the style of a Ming-dynasty scholar's retreat.

paintings, jades, textiles, and metalwork are scheduled to open in fall 1997. In the **South and Southeast Asian Art** galleries, pick up a brochure on "Recognizing the Gods" to read while you stroll past bronze statues of Hindu gods like the elephant-headed *Ganesh*. Some of the quietest galleries in the Met are the rooms holding art of Nepal and Tibet. *Second floor.*

➤ **DUTCH PAINTERS** • In **Galleries 11–15** hang the Dutch painters (or at least their paintings), including creations by Jan Vermeer, Frans Hals, and Gerard Ter Borch. There are 19—count 'em, 19—Rembrandts. *Second floor.*

➤ **MUSICAL INSTRUMENTS** • The Musical Instruments collection, featuring an extraordinary array of world instruments, is a must-see for music lovers. Rent an "Acoustiguide" cassette tape ($4) on your way into the museum, and you can hear how exquisite craftsmanship translates into sound. *Second floor.*

➤ **19TH-CENTURY PAINTINGS AND SCULPTURE** • The newly renovated Beaux Arts galleries displaying 19th-century European paintings and sculpture are one of the glories of New York. They also draw the biggest crowds. This is where you'll find painting after world-famous painting by Corot, Millet, Turner, Rodin, Renoir, Pissaro, Van Gogh, Cézanne, and many others. During the latter half of every year these galleries showcase *TV Guide*–magnate Walter Annenberg's collection of impressionist and postimpressionist masterpieces; upon Annenberg's death the installation becomes permanent. *Second floor.*

➤ **SCULPTURE GARDEN** • If you've made it this far, then you owe it to yourself to visit the **Iris and B. Gerald Cantor Roof Garden**, generally open May through October. From atop the museum, you'll have a millionaire's view of Central Park.

MUSEUM OF MODERN ART (MOMA)

The Museum of Modern Art, or MoMA, has long been the world's premier showcase for modern art. Opening on the heels of the 1929 stock-market crash, the museum's first exhibition, *Cézanne, Gauguin, Seurat, van Gogh*, was revolutionary—those now-famous artists were, at the time, unknowns in the United States, and their postimpressionist style had few admirers. Fortunately, scholar and founding director Alfred H. Barr, Jr.'s aesthetic agenda found an enthusiastic audience in New York City, and as the collections grew the museum expanded several times. It moved to its current location in 1939, and its gallery space was doubled in 1984. Then, in early 1996, after years of fractious negotiations, the museum closed a $50-million deal to purchase three adjoining buildings, which will double its present-day gallery space in the next decade. Still, the museum is currently able to show only 10% of its vast collection at any given time. Among its treasures are many famous paintings of the modern era,

The MoMA continues to grapple with questions of relevancy and the true meaning of "modern art" as many of its original pieces turn 100 years old.

including a good collection of surrealist works, several huge canvases of Monet's *Waterlilies*, and van Gogh's *Starry Night*. Drawings, prints, books, film, video, and design are also well represented. And you'll find a few surprises, like a helicopter, lamps, and models of landmarks in modern architecture such as Frank Lloyd Wright's "Falling Water." Photography, too, has long been richly acknowledged by the MoMA, well before it acquired fine-art status, and its collection is one of the best around. *11 W. 53rd St., near Fifth Ave., Midtown, tel. 212/708–9480. Subway: E or F to Fifth Ave. Admission: $8, $5 students (pay what you wish Thurs. and Fri. 5:30–8:30). Open Sat.–Tues. 11–6, Thurs. and Fri. noon–8:30. Wheelchair access.*

PRACTICALITIES Brown bag lunch lectures (tel. 212/708–9795 or 212/333–1117) happen Tuesdays and Thursdays from 12:30 to 1:15; pay the $5 and learn while you eat. **Gallery talks** are conducted daily and are free with admission. Other programs include **Conversations with Contemporary Artists** and **Special Exhibition Programs**; for more information call

212/708–9795 or 212/708–9798. Any galleries may be temporarily closed while new or changing exhibitions are installed.

COLLECTION HIGHLIGHTS The **René d'Harnoncourt Galleries** and the **Theater Gallery** house temporary exhibitions. Films and videos (often related to what's hanging on the museum's walls) are presented in the **Roy and Niuta Titus Theater 1** and **2**. Tickets (free) are distributed in the main lobby; for more info, *see* Movie Houses, in Chapter 6.

➤ **GROUND FLOOR** • Besides the information desk, checkroom, and bookstore, you'll find two galleries showing temporary exhibitions on the ground floor: the **International Council Galleries** and the small **Projects Gallery**. The **Garden Café** serves up decent cafeteria food ($3.50–$9.50) in a pleasant setting, while the **Sette MoMA** (tel. 212/708–9710) serves up really pricey stuff and usually requires reservations. Outside is the serene **Abby Aldrich Rockefeller Sculpture Garden**, a wonderful courtyard with trees, fountains, pools, and (of course) sculpture. Julliard Music School students perform free concerts in the garden during summer; for more info *see* Music, in Chapter 7.

➤ **SECOND FLOOR** • The **photography** galleries hold a rotating display of the museum's renowned collection. The main collection of **painting and sculpture** is exhibited in galleries 1–22, and begins with postimpressionism, romps through Dada, and continues on to Mexican art of the 1930s. Included are gems like Rousseau's *The Sleeping Gypsy* and Picasso's famous *Les Demoiselles d'Avignon*, which renders three female nudes by mixing cubist forms with primitivism. You may also see Marcel Duchamp's *Bicycle Wheel*, and will probably wonder if such a work is mocking or serious. Also on this floor is Monet's *Waterlilies* series, housed in one of the museum's most peaceful interior spaces.

➤ **THIRD FLOOR** • The **painting and sculpture** collection continues on the third floor in galleries 23–31. The art picks up in 1940s Europe, continues through abstract expressionism, and finally ends with a rotating selection of contemporary art. The third floor also carries rotating exhibits from the museum's collections of **drawings**, **prints**, and **illustrated books**.

➤ **FOURTH FLOOR** • This floor holds the **architecture and design** collection—that is, all the 3-D stuff that doesn't sit flat against the wall. Included is an elegant Tizio lamp, a Formula One race car, and a Bell-47 helicopter suspended over the escalators.

Manhattan Neighborhoods

Regardless of who you are or what you're after, New York City has a neighborhood to fulfill your every whim. Virtually all of the major "touristy" sights are in **Midtown**, including the Theater District, Rockefeller Center, and Times Square. If museums are what you want, the **Upper East Side**'s Museum Mile has more than enough for even the most energetic art lover, while the **Upper West Side**, home to Lincoln Center, holds all the cards when it comes to the performing arts. If you're looking for a little boho culture, you might want to spend your time in the bar- and café-crowded **East Village** or **Chelsea**. There's great people-watching in the **West Village**, home to New York University students, the city's gay community, and a bunch of aging Beat poets. **SoHo** and **TriBeCa** have long been the haunts of artists and the people who profit from them, and both are packed with art galleries. For a vicarious taste of the good (or at least expensive) life, head to the ritzy blocks of **Gramercy** and **Union Square**. The **Lower East Side**, **Harlem**, **Little Italy**, and **Chinatown** are miniature cities in their own right, having been settled by Jewish, African, Italian, and Asian immigrants respectively. If you're interested in New York's legal and financial institutions, make your way to **Lower Manhattan**.

UPPER WEST SIDE

If you can believe it, the Upper West Side was actually a bunch of small villages until the late 1860s, an area the Dutch referred to as Bloemendael (Vale of Flowers). In those days wealthy

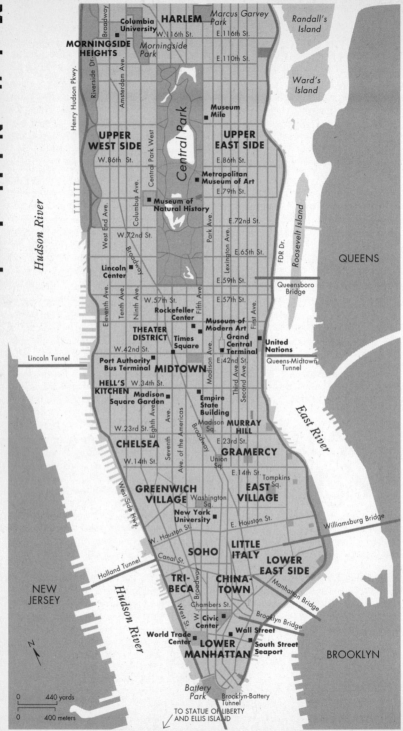

Manhattan Neighborhoods

HARLEM

Marcus Garvey Park

Randall's Island

Columbia University

W.116th St.   E.116th St.

MORNINGSIDE HEIGHTS

Morningside Park

Ward's Island

E.110th St.

Museum Mile

UPPER WEST SIDE

Central Park

UPPER EAST SIDE

W.86th St.

E.86th St.

Metropolitan Museum of Art

E.79th St.

Museum of Natural History

Park Ave.

E.72nd St.

W.72nd St.

Lexington Ave.

E.65th St.

Roosevelt Island

QUEENS

Lincoln Center

E.59th St.

Queensboro Bridge

W.57th St.

E.57th St.

Rockefeller Center

THEATER DISTRICT

Museum of Modern Art

Times Square

Grand Central Terminal

United Nations

W.42nd St.

E.42nd St.

Queens-Midtown Tunnel

Lincoln Tunnel

Port Authority Bus Terminal

MIDTOWN

HELL'S KITCHEN

W.34th St.

Madison Square Garden

Empire State Building

W.23rd St.

Madison Sq.

MURRAY HILL

CHELSEA

E.23rd St.

GRAMERCY

W.14th St.

Union Sq.

E.14th St.

Tompkins Sq.

GREENWICH VILLAGE

Washington Sq.

EAST VILLAGE

New York University

E. Houston St.

Williamsburg Bridge

W. Houston St.

SOHO

LITTLE ITALY

LOWER EAST SIDE

Canal St.

Holland Tunnel

TRI-BECA

CHINA-TOWN

Manhattan Bridge

NEW JERSEY

Chambers St.

Brooklyn Bridge

Civic Center

Wall Street

World Trade Center

South Street Seaport

LOWER MANHATTAN

BROOKLYN

Battery Park

Brooklyn-Battery Tunnel

Hudson River

East River

Henry Hudson Pkwy.

Riverside Dr.

Broadway

Amsterdam Ave.

Central Park West

Columbus Ave.

West End Ave.

Eleventh Ave.

Tenth Ave.

Ninth Ave.

Eighth Ave.

Seventh Ave.

Ave. of the Americas

Fifth Ave.

Madison Ave.

Broadway

Third Ave.

Second Ave.

First Ave.

FDR Dr.

West Side Hwy.

W. Broadway

West St.

0   440 yards

0   400 meters

TO STATUE OF LIBERTY AND ELLIS ISLAND

54

islanders would take sleigh and carriage trips to Bloemendael and crash for the night in mansions converted into guest inns. The main thoroughfare was tree-lined Bloomingdale Road, which connected "urban" Manhattan (that is, everything below 23rd Street) to Bloomingdale Village (around 114th Street). As Central Park West quickly developed into a fashionable address, many of the area's pig farms and slaughterhouses were converted into low-income apartments. And by the end of World War II, the area west of Broadway was a slum ridden with drugs and prostitution. The government poured tons of money into building large plots of low-rent housing during the 1950s and '60s, but it wasn't until the building of Lincoln Center (*see below*) and the Fordham University campus that the area cleaned up its act. Today, famous folk like Ethan Hawke, Madonna, John MacEnroe, and Liam Neeson live in the Upper West's giant luxury apartment buildings. Less hyped are the methadone clinics and soup kitchens between 90th and 110th streets.

In an attempt to confuse you, some streets change their name at 59th Street, the southern boundary of the neighborhood: Eighth Avenue becomes **Central Park West**, Ninth Avenue becomes **Amsterdam Avenue**, Tenth Avenue becomes **Columbus Avenue**, and Eleventh Avenue becomes **West End Avenue**. The main drag on the Upper West Side is **Broadway**, and the main cross streets are 72nd, 79th, 86th, and 96th streets. Yet the real action happens on Amsterdam Avenue, which is crammed with funky bars, restaurants, and boutiques. Beyond **Riverside Park** (*see* Parks and Gardens, *below*), there's little action or excitement on the primarily residential streets of West End Avenue and Riverside Drive. For info on the neighborhood's **Nicholas Roerich Museum**, *see* Museums and Galleries, *below*.

COLUMBUS CIRCLE At all hours of the day and night, traffic zooms around Columbus Circle, which is where West 59th Street, Broadway, Central Park West, and Eighth Avenue intersect. Besides acting as a sort of gateway from Midtown to the Upper West Side, it's home to that miraculous dispenser of bus maps and free TV tickets, the **New York Convention and Visitors Bureau** (*see* Useful Organizations, in Chapter 1). At the center of the circle (atop a marble pillar, gift of the city's Italian Americans) stands an 1894 sculpture of Mr. Round Earth himself, Christopher Columbus. *Subway: A, B, C, D, 1, or 9 to W. 59th St./Columbus Circle.*

BROADWAY Broadway is home to one of the city's greatest food shrines—namely **Zabar's** (*see* Markets and Specialty Shops, in Chapter 4), which stocks everything from reasonably priced deli items to expensive Belgian chocolates. It's always packed with New Yorkers who shop like they're stocking up for Armageddon. The massive **Sony IMAX Theater** (1998 Broadway, btw W. 67th and 68th Sts., tel. 212/336–5000) is a ten-plex movie theater and "urban entertainment center" where you can see 3-D movies on eight-story-high screens (with the aid of heavy plastic viewing helmets), or movies of the usual 2-D variety.

A few "parks" along Broadway offer benches where you can munch sandwiches and rubberneck at careening taxis: Across from Lincoln Center, **Dante Park** is a tiny triangle named for the Italian poet; **Sherman Square** (south of the W. 72nd St. subway station) is a tiny triangle named for the Civil War general; **Verdi Square** (north of the W. 72nd St. subway station) is a tiny triangle named for the Italian opera composer—but was better known as "Needle Park" during the height of its popularity with drug dealers in the '70s. Really, you're better off heading a few blocks east to Central Park or a few blocks west to Riverside Park.

COLUMBUS AVENUE Columbus Avenue, once just a street where residents of Central Park West stopped to pick up a few pints of Häagen-Dǎzs, has blossomed in the last decade as a tony stretch of cafés, boutiques, and restaurants. Watch for your favorite soap star or news anchor from the sidewalk facing the headquarters of the **American Broadcasting Company (ABC)** (56 W. 66th St., btw Columbus Ave. and Central Park W); for info on getting tickets to tapings of some of its TV shows, *see box* You, Too, Can Be a Member of a Live Studio Audience, *below*. Nearby are two museums: the **Museum of American Folk Art** and the mammoth **American Museum of Natural History** (for both, *see* Museums and Galleries, *below*), which has over 36 million artifacts, including a newly renovated dinosaur exhibit on the cutting edge of exhibition design. If you're around on a Sunday, check out the flea market/greenmarket on the corner of West 77th Street and Columbus Avenue.

Upper West Side

0   880 yards
0   800 meters

KEY

i Tourist Information

American Broadcasting Company (ABC), **13**
American Museum of Natural History/ Hayden Planetarium, **6**
The Ansonia, **8**
Apthorp Apartments, **5**
Boat Basin, **3**
The Dakota, **10**
Dante Park, **16**
Julliard School of Music, **14**
Lincoln Center, **17**
Lotus Gardens, **2**
Museum of American Folk Art, **15**
New-York Historical Society, **7**
Nicholas Roerich Museum, **1**
Sherman Square, **11**
Sony IMAX Theater, **12**
Verdi Square, **9**
Zabar's, **4**

Henry Hudson Parkway

RIVERSIDE

PARK

Riverside Dr.

Hudson River

West End Ave.

Amsterdam Ave.

Broadway

Columbus Ave.

Central Park W.

CENTRAL PARK

West End Ave.

Cathedral Pkwy.
W. 109th St.
W. 108th St.
W. 107th St.
W. 106th St.
W. 105th St.
W. 104th St.
W. 103rd St.
W. 103rd St.
W. 102nd St.
W. 101st St.
W. 100th St.
W. 99th St.
W. 98th St.
W. 97th St.
W. 96th St.
W. 94th St.
W. 93rd St.
W. 92nd St.
W. 91st St.
W. 90th St.
W. 89th St.
W. 88th St.
W. 87th St.
W. 86th St.
W. 86th St.
W. 85th St.
W. 84th St.
W. 83rd St.
W. 82nd St.
W. 81st St.
W. 80th St.
W. 79th St.
W. 78th St.
W. 77th St.
W. 76th St.
W. 75th St.
W. 74th St.
W. 73rd St.
W. 72nd St.
W. 71st St.
W. 70th St.
W. 69th St.
W. 68th St.
W. 67th St.
W. 66th St.
W. 65th St.
W. 64th St.
W. 63rd St.
Damrosch Park
W. 62nd St.
W. 61st St.
W. 60th St.
Columbus Circle
W. 59th St.

Manhattan Ave.

1,9
1,9
1,2,3,9
1,9
1,9
1,2,3,9
1,9
A,B,C,D,
1,9

B,C
B,C
B,C
B,C
B,C
B,C
B,C

CENTRAL PARK WEST The *real* Central Park West has very little to do with that soapy, sleazy TV series *CPW*. It's basically just a quiet residential street bordering Central Park, where multimillionaires raise their families in peace and quiet. Besides the famous **Dakota** (*see box* Don't You Wished You Lived Here?, *below*), there are plenty of stately apartment buildings dating back to the late 19th century. Also here is the **New-York Historical Society** (*see* Museums and Galleries, *below*).

LINCOLN CENTER FOR THE PERFORMING ARTS Lincoln Center, the largest performing arts center in the United States, is the year-round home for ballet, opera, musical, and drama performances of all kinds—some are even free. When it was conceived of in the late 1950s to meet "some of the needs of an anxious age," the idea of a single city center for the arts was considered pretty radical; neighbors protested the construction of the $165 million

On Thanksgiving eve, thousands of New Yorkers crowd the blocks around the American Museum of Natural History to watch giant balloons like Bart Simpson and the Cat in the Hat being inflated for the annual Macy's Thanksgiving Day parade.

Don't You Wish You Lived Here?

For the last century or so, the Upper West Side has competed with the Upper East Side for that rather limited pool of New Yorkers able to afford apartments equipped with live-in maids' quarters, grand ballrooms, and wall-to-wall priceless antiques. A few of the West's best:

- *The Ansonia. This Beaux Arts beauty, built in 1904, has turrets, ornamented balconies, and rooftop gargoyles; live seals once played in the entrance hall's enormous fountain. Soundproof walls have made it especially attractive to musicians, like Enrico Caruso, Igor Stravinsky, and Arturo Toscanini, as well as theater producer Florenz Ziegfeld and writer Theodore Dreiser. More recently it served as the setting for the movie "Single White Female." 2108 Broadway, btw W. 73rd and 74th Sts.*

- *The Apthorp Apartments. Designed to look like a pumped-up Italian Renaissance palazzo, this giant complex has shown up in a half-dozen films, including "The Cotton Club" and "The Money Pit." It was built in 1908 by major New York landowner William Waldorf Astor (think Astor Place and Waldorf Astoria Hotel). 2101–2119 Broadway, btw W. 78th and 79th Sts.*

- *The Dakota. Most famous of all the apartment buildings along Central Park West is the Dakota. Squint at it and it looks like a dark, spooky castle. The design is by Henry Hardenbergh, who later did the famous Plaza Hotel; Singer sewing-machine heir Edward S. Clark ponied up the cash. When it was finished in 1884 it was so far uptown that it was jokingly described as being "out in the Dakotas." Ha, ha, ha—it rented anyway. A 10-room apartment originally cost $250 per month, which included service by the building's 150-person staff. In December 1980 resident John Lennon was fatally shot by a deranged fan on the sidewalk outside. Yoko Ono still keeps an apartment here, and Lennon is memorialized across the street in Central Park's Strawberry Fields. 1 W. 72nd St., at Central Park W.*

complex as disruptive, while the literati pronounced its design boring and limited. At its completion in the mid-'60s, a critic for the *New York Times* sniffed that the halls "are lushly decorated, conservative structures that the public finds pleasing and most professionals consider a failure of nerve, imagination, and talent." Nonetheless, it's responsible for transforming the Upper West Side from urban ghetto to gourmet ghetto. For the complete scoop, consider one of the daily hour-long guided tours ($7.75, $6.75 students) led by excitable Carol Channing look-alikes. For more info on various Lincoln Center activities, *see* Movie Houses, Walter Reade Theater, in Chapter 6, and just about everything in Chapter 7. *W. 62nd to 66th Sts., btw Columbus and Amsterdam Aves. Subway: 1 or 9 to W. 66th St./Lincoln Center.*

Stand on Columbus Avenue, facing the central court with its huge fountain (where, incidentally, Cher and Nicholas Cage cavorted in *Moonstruck*). The three concert halls on this plaza are all made of pale travertine marble. To your left is the **New York State Theater** (tel. 212/870–5570), home to the New York City Ballet and the New York City Opera. The interior, designed to look like a jewel box, is covered in red plush with diamondlike light fixtures. In the lobby is a $20-million Jasper Johns creation, *Numbers*. Straight ahead, at the rear of the plaza, is the grand **Metropolitan Opera House** (tel. 212/362–6000), where the Metropolitan Opera and American Ballet Theatre perform. Its crystal chandeliers were a gift of the Austrian government; the brilliantly colored tapestries are by Marc Chagall. To your right, abstract bronze sculptures distinguish **Avery Fisher Hall** (tel. 212/875–5030), host to the New York Philharmonic Orchestra. The hall was originally plagued with sound problems; technicians struggled with bizarre makeshift solutions like hanging giant sheets of metal around the stage. In 1976, a rich guy named Avery Fisher donated a big sum of cash and the problem was fixed for good.

Wander through the plaza, then head left past the Opera House into **Damrosch Park**, where summer open-air festivals like "Mostly Mozart" are often accompanied by free concerts at the Guggenheim Bandshell. Walk right from the plaza, between the Opera House and Avery Fisher, and you'll come to the North Plaza and a reflecting pool with a massive reclining sculpture by Henry Moore. To the rear is the **Library and Museum of the Performing Arts**. Visitors can listen to any of their 50,000 records and tapes, or check out its four galleries. Next to the library is the **Vivian Beaumont Theater**, officially considered a Broadway house. Below it is the smaller **Mitzi E. Newhouse Theater**, where many award-winning plays have originated.

An overpass leads from the North Plaza across 65th Street to the world-renowned music and theater school, **The Julliard School** (tel. 212/769–7406), alma mater of Robin Williams, Christopher Reeves, Itzhak Perlman, and other famous folk far too numerous to mention. There's usually something going on at its theater and recital hall. To the left is Lincoln Center's newest venue, the **Walter Reade Theater** (tel. 212/875–5600), screening avant-garde films. Take the elevator down to street level to find **Alice Tully Hall** (tel. 212/875–5050 or 212/875–5788), home to the Chamber Music Society and the New York Film Festival.

COLUMBIA UNIVERSITY AND MORNINGSIDE HEIGHTS

The neighborhood of **Morningside Heights** covers the highest hill in Manhattan. To the east, Harlem sprawls below you; to the west is **Riverside Park** (*see* Parks and Gardens, *below*) and the mighty Hudson River. These days, the neighborhood is 99% geared toward serving the students of Columbia University. The area's main thoroughfares—Broadway and Amsterdam Avenue—are more a conglomeration of résumé services, textbook exchanges, and all-night diners than any kind of community. But before it became a college town, Morningside Heights was the sight of a pivotal victory (1776) for General Washington's forces during the American Revolution, in a buckwheat field since replaced by the all-women Barnard College (*see* Columbia University, *below*).

Besides Columbia University, several theological institutions are based here, as well as the respected **Manhattan School of Music** (*see* Music, in Chapter 7). Cut into the steep gorge beneath the Morningside cliffs is **Morningside Park** (Morningside Dr., btw W. 110th and 123rd

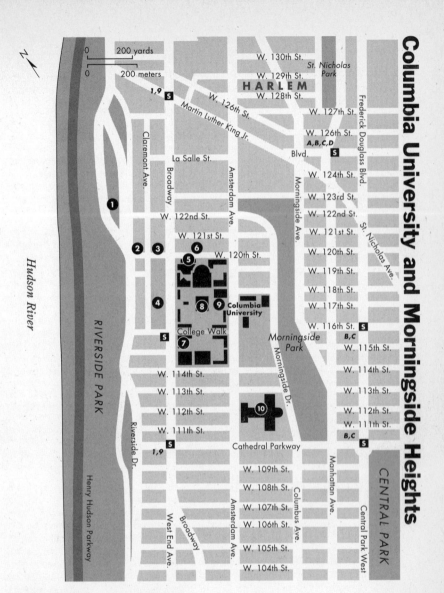

W. 130th St.

W. 129th St.

HARLEM

W. 128th St.

St. Nicholas Park

W. 127th St.

Martin Luther King Jr.

W. 126th St.

1,9 S

W. 126th St.

A,B,C,D

La Salle St.

Blvd. S

W. 124th St.

Claremont Ave.

W. 123rd St.

Broadway

W. 122nd St.

W. 122nd St.

Amsterdam Ave.

W. 121st St.

W. 121st St.

6

W. 120th St.

W. 120th St.

5

W. 119th St.

Morningside Ave.

W. 118th St.

2 **3**

4

W. 117th St.

8 **9**

Columbia University

W. 116th St. S

B,C

S

College Walk

7

Morningside Park

W. 115th St.

St. Nicholas Ave.

W. 114th St.

W. 114th St.

RIVERSIDE PARK

W. 113th St.

W. 113th St.

W. 112th St.

10

W. 112th St.

Morningside Dr.

W. 111th St.

W. 111th St.

B,C

S

1,9 S

Cathedral Parkway

Riverside Dr.

W. 109th St.

W. 108th St.

Henry Hudson Parkway

W. 107th St.

Manhattan Ave.

Amsterdam Ave.

Columbus Ave.

W. 106th St.

CENTRAL PARK

West End Ave.

W. 105th St.

Central Park West

Broadway

W. 104th St.

Hudson River

0   200 yards
0   200 meters

Morningside Heights

Cathedral of St. John the Divine, **10**
Grant's Tomb, **1**
Manhattan School of Music, **3**
Riverside Church, **2**

Columbia University

Barnard College, **4**
Low Memorial Library, **8**
Pupin Hall, **5**
St. Paul's Chapel, **9**
School of Journalism, **7**
Teachers College, **6**

Sts.), an overgrown and littered lot that was once a prime piece of greenery designed by Central Park's Frederick Law Olmsted and Calvert Vaux.

COLUMBIA UNIVERSITY Founded by British royal charter in 1754 as King's College (the name changed after the Revolutionary War), Columbia University is the fifth-oldest institution of higher learning in the United States and the oldest in New York state. It's also wealthy, private, and a member of the Ivy League. At least their football team sucks. Original alumni include John Jay, the first Chief Justice of the Supreme Court, and Alexander Hamilton, the first Secretary of the Treasury. The university's current campus was designed by McKim, Mead & White (*see box* They Built This City, *above*) and completed in 1897. Yes, its neoclassical and Renaissance-style buildings are covered with ivy, as you'd expect; they've also got copper roofs, used specifically because they'd turn green with oxidation over the years and create the illusion of lush vegetation (grass being fairly sparse at the time). The university's underground tunnel system—third largest in the world, after the Kremlin and the Massachusetts Institute of Technology—was recently closed indefinitely, due to "mischievous goings-on."

Start your exploration of Columbia in the central quad at the **Low Memorial Library**. Outside, it's styled to look like the Greek Parthenon; inside is the spectacularly domed, templelike Reading Room. At the visitors center (Room 213, tel. 212/854–4900) you can pick up maps, or hook up with one of the free, student-led campus tours, given at 11 AM and 2 PM daily. Low's steps, presided over by the statue *Alma Mater* (designed by Daniel Chester French, who also did the statue of Abraham Lincoln in Washington, D.C.'s Lincoln Memorial), were a rallying point for students during the riots of '68. East of the library is the exquisite Byzantine-style **St. Paul's Chapel**, with a student-run art gallery (tel. 212/854–1953) on the ground level. Saturday nights the gallery hosts poetry readings. At the north edge of campus is **Pupin Hall**, where the world's first successful splitting of an uranium atom took place on January 22, 1939—launching the Manhattan Project and ultimately leading to the development of the atom bomb. The university's renowned **School of Journalism**, founded by Joseph Pulitzer, holds classes in the building just south of the campus's west gates.

Across Broadway from Columbia is its sister institution, **Barnard College**, established in 1889. One of the former Seven Sisters of women's colleges, Barnard has steadfastly remained a single-sex institution and maintained its independence from Columbia, although its students can take classes there. Follow Broadway north to 120th Street, where you'll see the redbrick Victorian building of Columbia's **Teachers College**, founded in 1887 and today still the world's largest graduate school in the field of education.

CATHEDRAL OF ST. JOHN THE DIVINE Someday, the Cathedral of St. John the Divine will be the largest cathedral in the world. But first they have to finish it: Construction has been off and on since 1892. Still unbuilt are three towers, the transept, and a "bioshelter," a plant-filled skylight that will create the effect of stained glass. What is done is the mammoth, soaring nave, the length of two football fields and with enough space for 5,000 worshippers. It's bigger than the nave in St. Peter's in Rome. Way bigger. Lining either side of the nave are small chapels dedicated to American history, the arts, people with AIDS, even lawyers. In some of the

The ornate stone carvings on the facade of St. John the Divine feature the usual saints and biblical scenes, plus a few modern details—like a tiny Manhattan skyline.

niches you'll find very unchurchly things like a 2,000-pound quartz crystal, a menorah, and a 100-million-year-old fossilized sea creature. The great front doors, called the Portal of Paradise, are opened only twice a year: once at Easter, and once so that elephants and chihuahuas can walk the main aisle for the Blessing of the Animals. Other festivities include Halloween (with silent horror flicks and ghouls rappelling from the ceiling) and summer solstice (with ringing of a giant bronze gong). Tours ($3) of the cathedral are offered daily, and, on the first and third Saturday of each month, the cathedral offers super-cool vertical tours ($10), which allow you to climb around its towers and other tall parts. Next door, the **Children's Sculpture Garden** features a giant statue of a gruesome-looking angel triumphing over the devil, with surrounding inscriptions by Georgia O'Keeffe, John Lennon, Ray Charles, and Gandhi. *Amsterdam Ave. and W. 112th St., tel. 212/316–*

7540 or 212/932–7347 for tour reservations. Subway: 1 or 9 to W. 110th St. Suggested donation: $2. Open Mon.–Sat. 7–5, Sun. 8–5. Wheelchair access.

RIVERSIDE CHURCH Riverside Church has a groovy neo-Gothic exterior modeled after the cathedral in Chartres, France, plus vaulted ceilings and archways so pretty they'll make you weep. Its congregation is nondenominational, interracial, extremely political, and socially conscious; live music and theatrical productions are a big thing here year-round (see Music, in Chapter 7). If you're here on Sunday, take the elevator ($1) to the top of the 356-foot tower, which is topped with a 74-bell carillon—the largest in the world. *Riverside Dr. and W. 120th St., tel. 212/222–5900. Subway: 1 or 9 to W. 116th St. Open Mon.–Sat. 9–5, Sun. noon–4.*

GRANT'S TOMB The final resting place of Ulysses S. Grant, Civil War general and 18th U.S. president, and Julia Dent Grant, his wife, is a white-marble rotunda influenced by the tomb of King Mausolus at Halicarnassus, the tomb of Roman Emperor Hadrian, and Napoleon's tomb in the Hôtel des Invalides. It's the second-largest mausoleum in the western hemisphere (try to imagine what this place would look like if he'd been elected to a second term). Inside are various Civil War artifacts and, of course, his-and-hers black marble sarcophagi. Tours are given on request, and on the weekends the staff here wear Civil War costumes. Recently cleaned and restored, the monument will celebrate its centennial on April 27, 1997. *100 W. 122nd St., at Riverside Park, tel. 212/666–1640. Subway: 1 or 9 to W. 116th St. Open daily 9–5.*

HARLEM

Harlem is the birthplace of what was once a purely American art form—jazz. It's also awash with crack and blighted housing projects. The difficulty is in separating the misconceptions from the reality. Many areas in Harlem, from the main commercial spine of Martin Luther King Jr. Boulevard to the residential enclaves along St. Nicholas Avenue, are experiencing a commercial and civic renaissance. Rastafarian and Senegalese restaurants overflowing with customers, Dominican families listening to *musica* on their front stoops—these are some of the sights of Harlem today. Note that the city's numbered north–south avenues acquire different names up here, commemorating heroes of black history: Sixth Avenue becomes **Malcolm X Boulevard** (formerly Lenox Avenue); Seventh Avenue is **Adam Clayton Powell Jr. Boulevard**; and Eight Avenue is **Frederick Douglass Boulevard**. One of the major east–west streets, 125th Street, is now **Martin Luther King Jr. Boulevard**. Many people still use the streets' former names, but street signs (and this book) use only the new names.

Harlem's sights are clustered together, making exploring easy: The majority are along Martin Luther King Jr. Boulevard. Farther north are the historic and affluent neighborhoods of **Sugar Hill** (Edgecomb Ave., btw W. 145th and 155th Sts.; Subway: A, B, C, or D to W. 145th St.) and **Striver's Row** (see below), and, at **155th Street**, a cluster of museums and a spacious riverside park. East of Park Avenue is the predominantly Puerto Rican neighborhood of **East Harlem** (a.k.a. el barrio).

MARTIN LUTHER KING JR. BOULEVARD Once a vacant strip, Martin Luther King Jr. Boulevard is fast becoming a lively, engaging street. At its intersection with Malcolm X Boulevard you'll find two worthwhile museums: The **Studio Museum in Harlem** (see Museums and Galleries, *below*) features exhibitions on African, Caribbean, and African-American art, while one block to the north, the **Black Fashion Museum** (see Museums and Galleries, *below*) has over 3,000 pieces in its collection—including all the costumes from *The Wiz*.

Across Malcolm X Boulevard from the Fashion Museum is the famed **Sylvia's Restaurant** (see Chapter 4), a 20-year-old institution run by the self-proclaimed "Queen of Soul Food." Incidentally, the intersection of Malcolm X Boulevard with Martin Luther King Jr. Boulevard is also called **Africa Square**. A block away is the **National Black Theater** (see Theater, in Chapter 7), which produces new works by contemporary African-American writers.

APOLLO THEATER When it opened in 1913 this was a burlesque hall for white audiences only, but after 1934 music greats such as Billie Holiday, Ella Fitzgerald, Duke Ellington, Count Basie, James Brown, and Aretha Franklin performed (or even got their first break) here. After

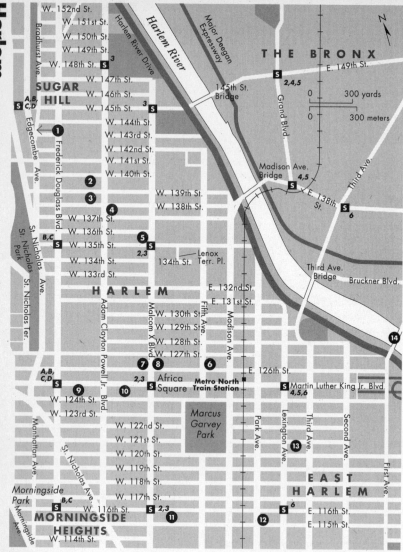

Harlem

W. 152nd St.
W. 151st St.
W. 150th St.
W. 149th St.
W. 148th St.
W. 147th St.
W. 146th St.
W. 145th St.
W. 144th St.
W. 143rd St.
W. 142nd St.
W. 141st St.
W. 140th St.
W. 139th St.
W. 138th St.
W. 137th St.
W. 136th St.
W. 135th St.
W. 134th St.
W. 133rd St.
W. 130th St.
W. 129th St.
W. 128th St.
W. 127th St.
W. 124th St.
W. 123rd St.
W. 122nd St.
W. 121st St.
W. 120th St.
W. 119th St.
W. 118th St.
W. 117th St.
W. 116th St.
W. 114th St.

E. 149th St.
E. 138th St.
E. 132nd St.
E. 131st St.
E. 126th St.
E. 116th St.
E. 115th St.

SUGAR HILL
THE BRONX
HARLEM
EAST HARLEM
MORNINGSIDE HEIGHTS

Harlem River
Harlem River Drive
Major Deegan Expressway
145th St. Bridge
Madison Ave. Bridge
Third Ave. Bridge
Willis Avenue Bridge

Bradhurst Ave.
Edgecombe Ave.
Frederick Douglass Blvd.
St. Nicholas Ave.
St. Nicholas Ter.
St. Nicholas Park
Adam Clayton Powell Jr. Blvd.
Malcom X Blvd.
Fifth Ave.
Madison Ave.
Manhattan Ave.
St. Nicholas Ave.
Morningside Ave.
Morningside Park
Grand Blvd.
Third Ave.
Park Ave.
Lexington Ave.
Second Ave.
First Ave.
Bruckner Blvd.

Lenox Terr. Pl.
134th St.
Africa Square
Metro North Train Station
Marcus Garvey Park
Martin Luther King Jr. Blvd.
La Marqueta

300 yards
300 meters

A,B C,D
B,C
A,B C,D
B,C
2,4,5
4,5
6
2,3
2,3
4,5,6
6
2,3
3
3

Abyssinian Baptist Church, 4
Apollo Theater, 9
Black Fashion Museum, 7
Harlem Court House, 13
La Marqueta, 12
Malcom Shabazz Mosque, 11
National Black Theater, 6
Riverbank State Park, 1

St. Nicholas Historic District, 2
Schomburg Center for Research in Black Culture/ American Negro Theatre, 5
Striver's Row, 3
Studio Museum in Harlem, 10
Sylvia's Restaurant, 8
Willis Avenue Bridge, 14

falling on hard times in the '70s it roared back to life in 1986 and is now a TV studio. The regular Wednesday "amateur night" (7:30 PM) is as wild and raucous as it was in the theater's heyday. *253 MLK Jr. Blvd., btw Adam Clayton Powell Jr. and Frederick Douglass Blvds., tel. 212/749-5838. Subway: A, B, C, or D to MLK Jr. Blvd. (W. 125th St.).*

MARCUS GARVEY PARK Though this rocky, terraced park has fallen into disrepair, it offers spectacular views of the surrounding old Victorian homes and neoclassical churches, part of a designated historical district. Look for the park (renamed in 1973 for the Jamaica-born black nationalist leader of the 1920s) just south of Martin Luther King Jr. Boulevard. Farther south is the onion-domed **Malcolm Shabazz Mosque** (102 W. 116th St., near Malcolm X Blvd.), a former casino turned Black Muslim temple; in the '60s it rang with the preachings of Malcolm X. Several stores operated by Muslims are located nearby.

STRIVER'S ROW The handsome set of town houses known as Striver's Row was designed by powerhouse turn-of-the-century architects like Stanford White, who did the north side of West 139th Street. Since 1919, they've been the homes of African-American professionals and entertainers, including musicians W. C. Handy ("The St. Louis Blues") and Eubie Blake ("I'm Just Wild About Harry"). And that's how they got their name: Less affluent Harlemites felt its residents were "striving" to become well-to-do. The surrounding quiet, tree-lined streets of the **St. Nicholas Historic District** are a remarkable reminder of the Harlem that used to be. *W. 138th and W. 139th Sts., btw Adam Clayton Powell Jr. and Frederick Douglass Blvds. Subway: B or C to W. 135th St.*

ABYSSINIAN BAPTIST CHURCH One block east of Striver's Row is the Gothic-style Abyssinian Baptist Church. Founded in 1808, it's New York's oldest black church. Adam Clayton Powell, Jr., the first black U.S. congressman, once preached here; you'll find a tribute to him (including photos of him with Dwight D. Eisenhower, John F. Kennedy, and Lyndon B. Johnson) on the second floor. Stop in on Sunday at 9 or 11 AM to hear the gospel choir and a fiery sermon. A few blocks farther south is the **Schomburg Center for Research in Black Culture** (*see* Museums and Galleries, *below*). *132 W. 138th St., at Adam Clayton Powell Jr. Blvd., tel. 212/862-7474.*

EAST HARLEM East of Park Avenue and north of 96th Street, all the way to the East River, is **el barrio**, a district with a radically different past from that of central Harlem. Historically home to some of New York's poorest, East Harlem has never known stately brownstone mansions or drawn wealthy inhabitants. In the 1880s, East Harlem's population was two-fifths foreign born: Working-class Germans, Jews, Irish, and enough Italians to earn it the nickname "Italian Harlem" lived in shoddy tenements in the shadow of the elevated railroads (the "El"). Immigration patterns shifted after World War II; by 1990 half of East Harlem's residents were Latin American, and the neighborhood became known as "Spanish Harlem." Housing projects, empty lots (some converted to carefully tended community gardens), burned-out buildings, and graffiti murals eulogizing victims of crack or gang violence all bear testimony to the neighborhood's struggles with chronic unemployment and capital flight. Even locals claim that many of the corner bodegas survive by peddling drugs. It's not the safest neighborhood in the city, but if you show respect to the residents you'll likely be treated with the same.

Harlem Renaissance author Langston Hughes lived at 20 E. 127th Street for the last two decades of his life.

Most of el barrio's action is along **East 116th Street**, where tiny Puerto Rican cafés with blaring salsa music do quick business in deep-fried *orejas* (pigs ears), and delicious *jugas tropicales* like *horchata* (a sweet rice drink). Botánicas sell herbs and stuff for religious ceremonies. The intersection of East 116th Street with Lexington Avenue was Fiorello La Guardia's "lucky corner," where the beloved progressive mayor (and the first ever Italian-American elected to Congress, in 1923), always held his election-eve rallies. *Subway: 6 to E. 116th St.*

A few blocks south under the elevated railroad tracks is **La Marqueta** (Park Ave., btw E. 111th-115th Sts.; closed Sun.), a once-thriving indoor market where vendors have been selling clothing and Latin American foods since 1936. These days, sadly, there's little business.

You'll also find two northern outposts of the Museum Mile here: **El Museo del Barrio** and the **Museum of the City of New York**. For more on both, see Upper East Side, Museum Mile, *below*.

North of 116th Street, the sturdy **Harlem Court House** (170 E. 121st St., btw Lexington and Third Aves.), built in 1891, is the area's most handsome structure and its only designated landmark. For views of East Harlem and the Bronx, cruise up the pedestrian lane of the **Willis Avenue Bridge** (E. 125th St., at First Ave.), spanning the Harlem River.

WASHINGTON HEIGHTS

Washington Heights, a.k.a. "Little Santo Domingo," is a mostly Latino neighborhood at the northern tip of Manhattan; its boundary with Harlem is West 155th Street. While wealthy New Yorkers built fanciful country estates here in the 19th century, in the 20th the area has been plagued with urban woes like poverty and drugs: In 1992, several days of rioting followed the shooting of a drug dealer by the police. In the past century, immigrant Greeks, Irish, Jews, Africans, Puerto Ricans, and Cubans have called the Heights their first American home.

In Washington Heights, passersby will casually answer a ringing pay phone and then search out the callee. Take this as a sign of a close-knit community—or a thriving drug trade.

Presently, the largest Dominican population in the United States—plus a growing number of Salvadoreans—live here. Though it won't win a prize as the nicest neighborhood in Manhattan, it's safe to visit Washington Heights during the day. Wander up **Broadway** and you'll find Spanish music blaring, discount merchandisers hawking cut-rate belts, shoes, or electronics, and random pay phones ringing off the hook.

The main attraction here is **The Cloisters** (see Museums and Galleries, *below*), the Metropolitan Museum's amazing collecting of medieval European art and artifacts. It's housed in an imposing, atmospheric "castle" at the center of **Fort Tryon Park**, which offers inspiring views of the Hudson River. **Fort Washington Park**, near the George Washington Bridge, and **Inwood Hill Park**, much farther north, also offer open space and greenery rare in the rest of Manhattan. For more on all three parks, see Parks and Gardens, *below*.

The **Audubon Ballroom** (W. 165th St. and Broadway) is where Malcolm X was assassinated February 21, 1965, during a rally of his Organization of Afro-American Unity. It's recently been swallowed up by a Columbia University biotechnology research facility, and only portions of the original facade and ballroom remain. Nearby is the oldest standing house in Manhattan, the **Morris-Jumel Mansion** (see Museums and Galleries, *below*). On Broadway at West 178th Street is the 14-lane **George Washington Bridge**, which links Manhattan with New Jersey. When it opened in 1931 it was the longest suspension bridge in the world. *Subway: A to W. 175th St.*

AUDUBON TERRACE At Harlem's northern boundary stands Audubon Terrace, which houses the underappreciated museums of the **Hispanic Society of America** and the **American Numismatic Society** (for both, see Museums and Galleries, *below*). The **American Academy of Arts and Letters** (tel. 212/368–5900), also here, opens its doors to the public three times annually to exhibit sculpture, painting, and prints by promising young American artists; call for dates. The whole Beaux Arts compound was built on the former game preserve of artist/naturalist John James Audubon by a turn-of-the-century railroad magnate turned student of Hispanic culture. In the courtyard are a bas relief of Don Quixote on his emaciated horse and a monumental sculpture of El Cid on his more muscular steed; both are works of the founder's wife. *W. 155th St. and Broadway. Subway: 1 to W. 157th St.*

TRINITY CEMETERY Across the street from Audubon Terrace, Trinity Cemetery was established in the 19th century by Wall Street's venerable Trinity Church. Famous long-term residents include fowl-lover John James Audubon; rapacious real-estate magnate John Jacob Astor; and Alfred Dickens, son of the late, great British author. Pick up a free map of famous burial sites at the cemetery office (W. 153rd St. and Broadway; open daily 8 AM–dusk). A bit father west along the Hudson River, **Riverbank State Park** (see Parks and Gardens, *below*) has plenty to offer sports fanatics and view seekers. Who would guess such a gorgeous park and

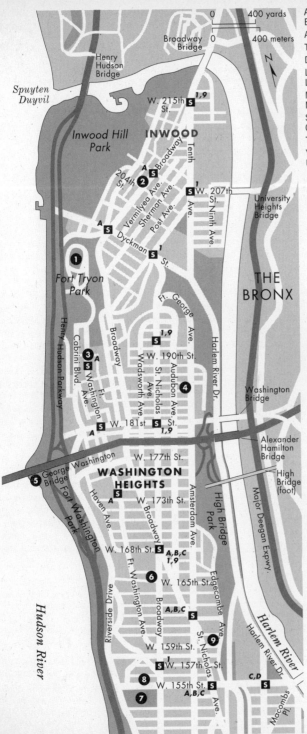

Washington Heights

Audubon
Ballroom, **6**
Audubon Terrace, **8**
The Cloisters, **1**
Dyckman House, **2**
Little Red
Lighthouse, **5**
Morris-Jumel
Mansion, **9**
St. Francis Xavier
Cabrini Chapel, **3**
Trinity Cemetery, **7**
Yeshiva
University, **4**

Broadway
Bridge

Henry
Hudson
Bridge

Spuyten
Duyvil

Inwood Hill
Park

W. 215th St.

INWOOD

Tenth

Broadway

204th St.

Vermilyea Ave.
Sherman Ave.
Post Ave.

W. 207th St.

University
Heights
Bridge

Dyckman St.

Ninth Ave.

St.

THE
BRONX

Fort Tryon
Park

Ft. George Ave.

W. 190th St.

Broadway

Wadsworth Ave.
St. Nicholas Ave.
Audubon Ave.

Harlem River Dr.

Washington
Bridge

Cabrini Blvd.

Ft. Washington Ave.

W. 181st St.

Alexander
Hamilton
Bridge

W. 177th St.

WASHINGTON
HEIGHTS

George Washington
Bridge

Fort Washington Park

Henry Hudson Parkway

W. 173rd St.

Haven Ave.

Broadway

Amsterdam Ave.

High Bridge Park

High
Bridge
(foot)

Major Deegan Expwy.

W. 168th St.

A,B,C
1,9

Ft. Washington Ave.

W. 165th St.

Edgecombe Ave.

Broadway

A,B,C

W. 159th St.

St. Nicholas Ave.

Harlem River

Harlem River Dr.

Hudson River

Riverside Drive

W. 157th St.

W. 155th St.
A,B,C

C,D

Macombs Pl.

65

recreation complex was situated above a sewage treatment plant? *W. 153rd–155th Sts., btw Amsterdam Ave. and Riverside Dr., tel. 212/368–1600.*

ST. FRANCIS XAVIER CABRINI CHAPEL This is the final resting place of Mother Cabrini, clothed in her habit and lying in a crystal casket. Her smiling face is a wax replica; her real head is locked away somewhere in Rome. According to legend, a lock of the saint's hair supposedly cured a blind infant who grew up to be a priest in Texas. *Ft. Washington Ave. and W. 190th St. Subway: A to W. 190th St.*

YESHIVA UNIVERSITY Founded in 1886, Yeshiva University is the oldest and largest Jewish studies center in the country. On campus you'll find a small **museum** displaying Hebrew treasures from around the world. The main building, Tannebaum Hall, has a fun-to-look-at facade combining modernist touches with Middle Eastern fancies like turrets, minarets, and pointy arches. *2520 Amsterdam Ave., at W. 185th St., tel. 212/960–5390. Subway: 1 or 9 to W. 181st St. Museum admission: $3. Open Tues.–Thurs. 10:30–5, Sun. noon–6. Closed Aug.*

UPPER EAST SIDE

For most of its recent history the Upper East Side has been the domain of the super-rich, from old-money types, like the Rockefellers, whose names pop up on buildings all over town, to *nouveau riche* types like the Trumps and Hollywood celebrities. Luxury co-ops and condominiums, immaculate *fin de siècle* mansions and town houses, private schools, posh galleries, world-class museums, five-star restaurants, and international shops fill its blocks. You may find the people who live and work in this neighborhood a bit snobbish compared with other New Yorkers, but take it in stride—they treat everybody that way. On **Fifth Avenue** (which borders Central Park) and **Park Avenue** are the homes of the wealthy: **998 Fifth Avenue**, at East 81st Street, was the city's first giant luxury apartment building, built in 1910. Prior to that, rich folk scraped by in giant mansions like the one that now houses the **Polo/Ralph Lauren** (*see* New Clothes, in Chapter 5) store. Quite a few of the grandiose apartment buildings you'll see were designed in the 1920s and '30s by Rosario Candela, a Sicilian-born son of a plasterer. If you dig that kind of thing, check out the most fantastic ones at 720, 740, 770, and 778 Park Avenue, and 834 and 960 Fifth Avenue. And if you're around in spring, stop to smell the tulips planted along the median of Park Avenue—the Metro North Railroad's tracks run underneath it after they dip underground at 96th Street. Sandwiched between Park and Fifth avenues is **Madison Avenue**, which is the main commercial strip and slathered with ostentatious displays. Here you'll see boutique after over-priced boutique and, behind the second-floor windows, the theater of hairdressing performed before your eyes. For the best of the lot, *see box* Window-Shopping With The Rich and Famous, in Chapter 5. Note that Fifth Avenue in the Upper East Side is also known as **Museum Mile** (*see below*) for its astounding concentration of, well, museums.

The Upper East Side is an alternative universe where you might spot a starving-artist type walking 15 or more pedigreed pooches (this person is a professional dog-walker), and sidewalks where the snow never piles up, even in a blizzard. Expensive residences like 9 East 71st Street boast special heated sidewalks.

While the blue bloods and their debutante children dominate the blocks immediately adjoining Central Park, walk east all the way to the river and you'll find squat brownstones, cheap diners, and lots of just-out-of-the-fraternity types a bit puzzled why their tiny apartments don't look like the huge ones on *Friends*. **Lexington Avenue** tends to show a little grit, while Third, Second, and First Avenues are lined with moderately upscale restaurants and bars frequented by yuppies living in homogenous apartment buildings.

86TH STREET A major crosstown artery, 86th Street used to be the center of the neighborhood's German and Austrian immigrant populations. One of the few holdouts in this area, called Yorkville, is **Kleine Konditorei** (234 E. 86th St., btw Second and Third Aves., tel. 212/737–7130), a classic German restaurant virtually unchanged since the '50s. At the east end of 86th Street is **Carl Schurz Park** and the mayor's home, **Gracie Mansion** (for more on both, *see* Parks and Gardens, *below*), where the sounds of birds replace the roar of traffic. It's

Upper East Side and Museum Mile

998 Fifth
Avenue, **14**
Abigail Adams
Smith Museum, **25**
Asia Society, **21**
China House
Gallery, **22**
Cooper–Hewitt
Museum, **6**
El Museo del
Barrio, **1**
Frick Collection, **19**
Goethe House, **13**
Gracie Mansion, **10**
Henderson Place
Historic District, **11**
International Center
of Photography
(ICP), **4**
Islamic Cultural
Center, **3**
Jewish Museum, **5**
Metropolitan
Museum of Art, **12**
Museum of
American
Illustration, **23**
Museum of the City
of New York, **2**
National Academy
of Design, **8**
Polo/Ralph
Lauren, **18**
Roosevelt Island, **26**
Solomon R.
Guggenheim
Museum, **9**
Whitney Museum of
American Art, **17**

Galleries
Bonni Benrubi, **16**
M. Knoedler, **20**
Robert Mann, **15**
Stone, **7**
Throckmorton, **24**

E. 106th St.
E. 104th St.
E. 102nd St.
E. 101st St.
E. 100th St.
E. 99th St.
E. 98th St.
E. 97th St.
E. 96th St.
E. 95th St.
E. 94th St.
E. 93rd St.
E. 92nd St.
E. 91st St.
E. 90th St.
E. 89th St.
E. 88th St.
E. 87th St.
YORKVILLE
E. 86th St.
E. 85th St.
E. 84th St.
E. 83rd St.
E. 82nd St.
E. 81st St.
E. 80th St.
E. 79th St.
E. 78th St.
E. 77th St.
E. 76th St.
E. 75th St.
E. 74th St.
E. 73rd St.
E. 72nd St.
E. 71st St.
E. 70th St.
E. 69th St.
E. 68th St.
E. 67th St.
E. 66th St.
E. 65th St.
E. 64th St.
E. 63rd St.
E. 62nd St.
E. 61st St.
E. 60th St.
E. 59th St.
E. 58th St.
E. 57th St.

FDR Dr.
Carl
Schurz
Park
East End Ave.
East River
FDR Dr.
First Ave.
Second Ave.
York Ave.
Third Ave.
Lexington Ave.
Park Ave.
Madison Ave.
Fifth Ave.
CENTRAL PARK
Queensboro
Bridge
Roosevelt
Island
Tramway

N,R
4,5,6
B,Q
N,R
4,5,6
6
6

0   440 yards
0   400 meters

67

a sweet place to be, even if the view across the river is of industrial zones. At East End Avenue and 86th Street is **Henderson Place Historic District**, a delightful (but partially amputated) enclave of 1880s brick Queen Anne houses.

ISLAMIC CULTURAL CENTER Dig on this postmodern mosque, built in 1991 on Manhattan's best-kept lawn. If you conform to Islamic dress standards (long pants and shirt for men, neck to ankle *and* hair coverage for women), you can take a short tour of the mosque; call 212/722–5234. Walking south on Third Avenue from here you'll find a slew of restaurants (some of them actually cheap) and bars. *E. 96th St., at Third Ave. Subway: 6 to E. 96th St.*

MUSEUM MILE So studded with museums is Fifth Avenue as it runs along Central Park, that this stretch between 59th and 110th streets has been quasi-officially dubbed Museum Mile. In addition to the museums listed below, this area includes the unparalleled **Metropolitan Museum of Art** (*see* Major Attractions, *above*). The **Whitney Museum of American Art** (*see* Museums and Galleries, *below*) is one block east on Madison Avenue, which means it isn't technically part of Museum Mile, but it's easy to include in your afternoon museum orgy. If you're in town in June, check the local listings for the **Museum Mile festival**, when, for three brief hours one weekday evening, the museums along Fifth Avenue throw open their doors, and the strip between 82nd and 104th streets becomes a festival for highbrow types.

➢ **COOPER–HEWITT NATIONAL DESIGN MUSEUM** • The former mansion of steel magnate Andrew Carnegie provides the setting for the Cooper–Hewitt, one of few museums in the country dedicated solely to design. Constructed in 1902 when this stretch of Fifth Avenue was still all squats and tenements, the mansion—all 64 rooms of it—was built according to Carnegie's simple directive: To have "the most modest, plainest, and most roomy house in New York." OK, so his idea of "modest" is a bit different than yours—get over it. In this ornate space (which just underwent major renovations in 1995–96), Smithsonian curators have assembled brilliant exhibitions covering all aspects of design: graphic, industrial, architecture, urban, decorative, etc. Also not to be missed are the gardens, found by walking straight through the main hall from the entrance. The Cooper–Hewitt also sponsors a number of educational programs, including tours, lectures, seminars, and workshops; for information call the Education Department at 212/860–6321. *2 E. 91st St., at Fifth Ave., tel. 212/860–6868. Subway: 4, 5, or 6 to E. 86th St. Admission: $3, $1.50 students (free Tues. 5–9). Open Tues. 10–9, Wed.–Sat. 10–5, Sun. noon–5.*

➢ **EL MUSEO DEL BARRIO** • The northern outpost of Fifth Avenue's Museum Mile is this museum dedicated to the art of Latin America. Located in a portion of the Heckscher Building (1921), El Museo really *is* in el barrio (*see* Harlem, *above*), which begins at about 96th Street—though el barrio is less evident along Fifth Avenue than just a block east. The exhibition space was handsomely renovated in 1994, and now provides over 8,250 square feet of simple white-walled galleries, several illuminated by natural light.

When El Museo was founded in 1969, it comprised only a single classroom in East Harlem. Since then, it has shifted locations several times as it assembled a permanent collection that today includes nearly 8,000 pieces of art, from pre-Columbian objects to contemporary videotapes. The museum also produces numerous temporary exhibitions, drawing from its permanent collection as well as borrowed works; several shows are staged each year. Hour-long **gallery tours** are given Wednesdays at 12:30 and Thursdays–Sundays at 1. *1230 Fifth Ave., at 104th St., tel. 212/831–7272. Subway: 6 to E. 103rd St. Suggested donation: $4, $2 students. Open Oct.–Mar., Wed.–Sun. 11–5; May–Sept., Thurs. noon–7. Wheelchair access.*

Millionaire industrialist Henry Clay Frick sought aesthetic and spiritual harmony in his collection, and apparently he found it—the Frick museum is often cited as one of the most peaceful spaces in New York City.

➢ **THE FRICK COLLECTION** • How did an uneducated American industrialist who made a million bucks in coke (the kind used for steel manufacturing, not sniffing) by his 30th birthday attain the cultural sophistication of a European aristocrat? He bought it, of course. Henry Clay Frick (1849–1919) began amassing his fabulous personal collection of paintings, sculptures, and decorative arts after his first trip to Europe in the 1890s, and continued up until his death. The elegant

Fifth Avenue mansion (built in 1914) where he lived was converted to a museum in 1935—yet it still looks like a rich person's house. Rather than echoing halls with sterile display cabinets, you get rooms decorated with 18th-century European furnishings, velvet- and wood-paneled walls, and art hung exactly as the industrialist hung it, brazenly mixing styles and schools and times, so that an ancient Chinese vase rests on a 19th-century French cabinet.

The collection itself (one-third of which was added by trustees after Frick's death) is a remarkable if Eurocentric sampling from the early Renaissance through the late 19th century: masterworks by Bellini, Constable, Gainsborough, Goya, Holbein, Rembrandt, Renoir, Titian, Turner, Van Dyck, Velázquez, and Whistler, surrounded by exquisite candlesticks, tables, vases, and bronze and marble sculpture. In particular, look for the Vermeers and Fragonards, Hans Holbein the Younger's *Sir Thomas More*, a work of intoxicating luminosity; Rembrandt's *Self-Portrait*, which reveals the artist beaten by age; and the furious *Samson and Two Philistines*, a 16th-century bronze study by Michelangelo Buonarroti. In keeping with the home-rather-than-museum effect, none of the art carries detailed labels, so pick up the *Guide to Works of Art on Exhibition* ($1) before you start exploring; an introductory video shows in the Music Room at half-past the hour from 10:30 to 4:30 Tuesday–Saturday and 1:30 to 4:30 on Sunday. The museum's downstairs galleries house temporary exhibitions. The Frick's also famous for hosting concerts in its Music Room and Garden Court; for more info, *see* Music, in Chapter 7.

If you're in need of a serious research library, you came to the right place: The **Frick Art Reference Library** (10 E. 71st St., tel. 212/288–8700) is right behind the museum. Open to scholars and art professionals, the Frick library contains an archive of over 800,000 photographs of works of art; 186,000 books, exhibition catalogs, and pamphlets; and 67,000 art-auction sale catalogs. *1 E. 70th St., at Fifth Ave., tel. 212/288–0700. Subway: 6 to E. 68th St. Admission: $5, $3 students. Open Tues.–Sat. 10–6, Sun. 1–6. Wheelchair access.*

➤ **GOETHE HOUSE** • As the home of the German Cultural Center, the Goethe House exhibits art relating to the German experience in its two small galleries. There's also a library open to the public, as well as language, lecture, and film programs. *1014 Fifth Ave., btw 82nd and 83rd Sts., tel. 212/439–8700, http://cultural.tolerance.org/GH/GHNY. Subway: 4, 5, or 6 to E. 86th St. Admission free. Open Mon.–Thurs. 9–5, Fri. 9–4.*

➤ **INTERNATIONAL CENTER OF PHOTOGRAPHY (ICP)–UPTOWN** • Housed in a 1915 neo-Georgian mansion that was once home-sweet-home to the founder of the *New Republic*, the ICP features photographic installations culled from its collection of 45,000 works, as well as special exhibitions that change on a regular basis. You'll easily work your way through the modest paneled galleries in a few hours. For information about the ICP's photography education programs, call 212/860–1776, ext. 156. *1130 Fifth Ave., at 94th St., tel. 212/860–1777. Subway: 4, 5, or 6 to E. 86th St. Admission: $4, $2.50 students (pay what you wish Tues. 6–8). Open Tues. 11–8, Wed.–Sun. 11–6.*

➤ **THE JEWISH MUSEUM** • Found in a French Gothic Fifth Avenue mansion built in 1908, this museum assembles Jewish art and artifacts in a beautifully designed (and recently renovated) interior. The exquisite permanent exhibition, "Culture and Continuity," tracing the 4,000-year history of Judaism, begins on the fourth floor and continues on the third. Also not to be missed is the "audio café," where you can listen to reenacted conversations of Jews confronting modernity in cities such as New York, Fez, and Tel Aviv. The first two floors carry changing exhibitions, displayed amidst the setting of the original mansion's interior. A small café is on the bottom floor. *1109 Fifth Ave., at 92nd St., tel. 212/423–3230. Subway: 4, 5, or 6 to 86th St. Admission: $7, $5 students (free Tues. 5–8). Open Sun.–Thurs. 11–5:45 (Tues. until 8).*

➤ **MUSEUM OF THE CITY OF NEW YORK** • One of the best ways to start any visit to this daunting metropolis is with a visit to the Museum of the City of New York. Set in a Colonial Georgian mansion built in 1930, the museum provides a venue in which the rich history and contemporary events of New York can be viewed and interpreted. The museum—the first in America dedicated to a city's history—was founded in 1923 and was then housed in Gracie Mansion (now the mayor's residence, found in Carl Schurz Park).

Depending on the installation, the galleries occupy four to five spacious floors. The permanent exhibitions include several reconstructed New York residential interiors (sadly, no working-class homes are shown), toys, decorative arts, a survey of Broadway productions, and the **Marine Gallery**, which features models, dioramas, and paintings of early New York port life. There's also the **Fire Gallery**, which has one of New York's first water pipes—made from a hollowed-out pine log. In addition, the museum produces nearly a dozen excellent temporary exhibitions every year, which tend to be more intriguing than the permanent installations. The museum has an extensive **program schedule**, including various tours of New York, performances, film screenings, continuing education opportunities, and symposia. *1220 Fifth Ave., at 103rd St., tel. 212/534–1672. Subway: 6 to 103rd St. Suggested admission: $5, $3 students. Open Wed.–Sat. 10–5, Sun. 1–5. Wheelchair access.*

➤ **NATIONAL ACADEMY OF DESIGN** • The Academy has a tradition of art exhibition and instruction that goes back over 170 years. At its location in a 1914 mansion (which in this case makes the layout confusing and sometimes claustrophobic), the Academy shows off its permanent collection of 19th- and 20th-century American art and architecture, including works by Richard Diebenkorn, Mary Cassatt, I. M. Pei, and John Singer Sargent. In addition to changing installations highlighting its permanent collection, the museum also presents loan exhibitions of all sorts, from Old Masters to contemporary artists. The Academy also produces a small number of lectures, tours, and performances; call for information. *1083 Fifth Ave., at 89th St., tel. 212/369–4880. Subway: 4, 5, or 6 to 86th St. Admission: $3.50, $2 students (free Fri. 5–8). Open Wed.–Sun. noon–5 (Fri. until 8).*

➤ **SOLOMON R. GUGGENHEIM MUSEUM** • The Frank Lloyd Wright building housing the Guggenheim (opened in 1959) is a controversial work of architecture—even many who love its assertive six-story spiral rotunda will admit that it does not result in the best space in which to view art. Inside, under a 92-foot-high glass dome, a quarter-mile-long ramp spirals down past changing exhibitions of modern art. The Wright way to see the Guggenheim (if you'll pardon the pun) is to take the elevator to the top floor and walk *down* the spiral. Otherwise, it's quite a hike. The museum, originally conceived as the Museum of Non-Objective Painting, has especially strong holdings in Wassily Kandinsky, Paul Klee, and Pablo Picasso; the oldest pieces are by the French impressionists. A new (non-round) annex called the Tower Galleries opened in June 1992, creating an additional 20,000 square feet of gallery space to display the recently acquired Panza di Buomo collection of minimalist art, and touching off frenzied yapping among art-world critics. In its defense, the boring 10-story annex was based on Wright's original designs, and accommodates the extraordinarily large art pieces that the Guggenheim owns but previously had no room to display.

Several **gallery talks and tours** are offered on exhibitions and the building itself. Inquire at the information desk or call 212/423–3600. Recorded **audio tours** are available for most major exhibitions. A **reading room** on Ramp 2 in the main rotunda is a good place to sit back and relax while perusing museum publications. The small **museum café** has some pretty ritzy food

The Museum That Frank Built

As much a piece of modern art itself as the works it was designed to house, Frank Lloyd Wright's Guggenheim Museum can be a startling sight to unwary tourists strolling up Fifth Avenue towards 88th Street—it's like a huge, bright-white child's spiral top planted between traditional brown, rectangular apartment houses. Wright's design for the museum was over 15 years in the planning and wasn't fully completed until a few years after the architect's death in 1959. An earlier version of the trademark spiral was tested out in San Francisco, where Wright built the Circle Gallery, just off Union Square. Much later the Guggenheim became the obvious inspiration for the Pavilion of Japanese Art, designed by Bruce Goff, at the Los Angeles County Museum of Art.

for not too much money (sandwiches run $4–$6). Stop by if only to view the hung photos of the museum under construction. *1071 Fifth Ave., at 88th St., tel. 212/423–3500. Subway: 4, 5, or 6 to E. 86th St. Admission: $7, $4 students (pay what you wish Fri. 6–8). Open Sun.–Wed. 10–6, Fri. and Sat. 10–8. Wheelchair access.*

ROOSEVELT ISLAND In the middle of the East River, straddled by the Queensborough Bridge, looms Roosevelt Island. For many years it was called Blackwell Island, after the English farmer who bought the property in the 18th century (and whose 1796 home still stands here). It was renamed Welfare Island in 1921, and finally Roosevelt Island in 1973. For much of its history, the island has been a repository for lunatics, criminals, smallpox victims, the elderly, and studying nurses; among the briefly incarcerated notables (no, the nurses weren't incarcerated) were Mae West and Tammany Hall honcho Boss Tweed. It was quite a swinging place in the early decades of this century: Prisoners pretty much ran their own coops and narcotics trafficking was rampant, until a penal crackdown sent the troublemakers off to Riker's Island. For a few decades the island's buildings lay empty; not until the 1970s did savvy developers move in to create one of the most successful high-density areas in the city, one that consciously mixes persons of all incomes in a postmodern idyll. The composition designed by Philip Johnson and John Burgee is strikingly pleasant: The winding, brick-paved **Main Street**, despite being flanked by some rather huge apartments, feels perfectly welcoming. And cars are mercifully kept all in one place, in an attractive parking structure (forgive the oxymoron) near the bridge that connects the island to Queens.

A walk north from the tram stop will lead you through the island's main residential area, past an 1889 Victorian Gothic chapel, and to the island's lighthouse, designed by James Renwick, the architect who designed St. Patrick's Cathedral. There's also a small, serene park at the north end. To visit Roosevelt Island, take the B or Q subway to Roosevelt Island. Or better yet, pay $1.40 and take the **Roosevelt Island Tram** (tel. 212/832–4543), which runs parallel to the Queensborough Bridge. Board the tram at Second Avenue and East 60th Street. A brochure describing the island and its history is available for 25¢ at the Manhattan tram station, or on the island at 591 Main Street.

MIDTOWN

If Manhattan has a heart, it is in Midtown, where nearly everything you think of as New York is found: the Empire State Building, Times Square, Rockefeller Plaza, the glitzy stretch of Fifth Avenue and schmaltzy length of Broadway, the United Nations, and skyscrapers, by God, like you've never seen before. Fifth Avenue in the 50s looks like one obscenely posh mall, where tourists with fat wallets spend up a storm. Sixth Avenue is America's corporate heartland, a menacing tunnel of skyscrapers. Seventh and Eighth avenues in the 50s—and Broadway, which cuts the block between them—is tourist hell, where souvenir shops mix with expensive restaurants where certain visitors are titillated by the possibility of a star sighting.

The west side of Midtown, on the other hand, has long had a dicey reputation. In the 30s and 40s, **Hell's Kitchen** is an area with little to attract tourists—unless they're in search of an hour's furtive interlude. Here, the history of ethnic poverty and barroom slashings near the docks shows through the current gloss of gentrification. Ninth Avenue, populated by a comfortable mélange of ethnic eateries, shops, and small apartments, is the heart of Hell's Kitchen. For info on the veritable buffet of cheap ethnic restaurants in this area, *see* Midtown West of Fifth Avenue, in Chapter 4.

One last note: Even though they're all in Midtown, we've covered the **Empire State Building** and the **Museum of Modern Art (MoMA)** *above*, in Major Attractions. You'll find reviews of Midtown's myriad museums in Museums and Galleries, *below*: the **American Craft Museum**, **International Center of Photography–Midtown**, *Intrepid* **Air, Sea, and Space Museum**, **Japan Society, Museum of Television and Radio, Pierpont Morgan Library**, and **Sony Wonder Technology Lab**. Midtown's only good-sized park, **Bryant Park**, is in Parks and Gardens, *below*.

GRAND ARMY PLAZA What was once a splendid public plaza, Grand Army Plaza is now the scene of intolerable traffic and tourist trappings—note the drivers of horse-drawn cabs (*see*

Guided Tours, *above*) jockeying for potential fares. On the north half of the plaza is a massive gilded statue of Civil War general William Tecumseh Sherman and an unnamed, lithe Nubian; the southern half is dominated by the Pulitzer Memorial Fountain, now in a state of disrepair. Appropriately enough for this ritzy area, the lady on top is *Pomona*, the goddess of abundance. The palatial **Plaza Hotel** (768 Fifth Ave., at 59th St., tel. 212/759–3000), at the western edge of the plaza, is New York's finest hotel building, home to Frank Lloyd Wright when he was in town building the Guggenheim Museum. It's difficult to believe that the architect who dreamt up the sinister-looking Dakota apartments (*see box* Don't You Wish You Lived Here?, *above*), Henry Hardenbergh, could have concocted this confection with white-glazed brick and copper-and-slate roof. The hotel has been featured in notable films like *Plaza Suite* and *North by Northwest*, as well as less notable ones like *Crocodile Dundee* and *Home Alone 2*.

Next to the plaza, the **General Motors Building** (767 Fifth Ave., btw 58th and 59th Sts.) is a much-maligned, 50-story tower of white Georgia marble and glass. Spoil your inner child by going into the building's mammoth **F.A.O. Schwarz** (*see* Specialty Stores, in Chapter 5) for an $8,000 teddy bear or similarly extravagant toy. Beware overly enthusiastic employees who feel the need to make you "play," tossing balloons or balls in your direction as you descend the stairs. If your inner grown-up is screaming for attention, don't forget about nearby **Bergdorf Goodman** (754 Fifth Ave., at 58th St., tel. 212/753–7300), where outrageously expensive clothing and housewares are sold by employees with an attitude. For more info on the shrines to consumerism that start here and stretch to the north, *see* Chapter 5.

CARNEGIE HALL New York's premier concert hall, Carnegie Hall, has been hosting musical headliners since 1891, when its first concert was conducted by no less than Tchaikovsky. Audiophiles the world over have a lot to say about the hall's acoustics—though no two seem to be saying the same thing: Some have always said that it's a rare example of an acoustically perfect space. Others say that this has been true only since the 1995 discovery and removal of several tons of cement below the stage. Still others say the removal damaged the acoustics. And don't get them started on the effects of the 1990–1991 centennial renovations. Don't ask us. For info on performances and tickets, *see* Music, in Chapter 7, or consider taking a one-hour tour ($6, $5 students) of the building. Tours are given mid-September through mid-June on Mondays, Tuesdays, Thursdays, and Fridays. *881 Seventh Ave., at W. 57th St., tel. 212/903–9790 for tours. Subway: N or R to W. 57th St.*

A block north and worth a look is the **Alwyn Court Apartments** (180 W. 58th St., at Seventh Ave.), an example of what happens when architects get a hold of some terra-cotta and cheap labor. Built in 1909, this was the ultimate luxury apartment house of the time, with up to 34 rooms per apartment. Abandoned by the 1930s, it was renovated in 1985 as three- to five-room apartment units.

ROCKEFELLER CENTER When movies and TV shows are set in Manhattan, they often start with a shot of Rockefeller Center. To many, this glitzy, 19-building complex *is* New York City. Begun during the Great Depression by John D. Rockefeller (who made his fortune in oil by age 26), Rockefeller Center occupies nearly 22 acres of prime real estate between Fifth and Seventh avenues and 47th and 52nd streets. At the time, it was the largest urban design project ever undertaken in the city. At its center is the 850-foot tall RCA Building—now the **GE Building**, and also called "The Slab"—which borrowed from Le Corbusier's "tower in the park" concept. But the real genius of its design was its intelligent use of public space: plazas, concourses, and street-level shops that create a sense of community for the nearly 250,000 human beings who use it daily. Headquartered here are such giants as NBC, Time-Warner, RCA, Paramount Publishing/Simon & Schuster, General Electric, and the Associated Press (for more info on NBC, *see* Guided Tours, *above*, and *box* You, Too, Can Be A Member of A Live Studio Audience, *below*). Ironically, despite the appearance of so much wealth, one of the center's latest owners, Mitsubishi Estate Company, was forced to file bankruptcy in 1995.

Diego Rivera's original murals in Rockefeller Center's RCA building were removed because of his sympathetic depiction of socialism.

You can skip all the fancy, expensive shops here—they're filled with luxury tchotchkes you wouldn't want and can't afford. But take a stroll through the **Channel Gardens** (Fifth Ave., btw

49th and 50th Sts.), so named because they separate the British building to the north from the French building to the south. Artists, floral designers, and sculptors give the flower beds a fab new look monthly. At the foot of the gardens is the center's most famous sight, the gold-leaf statue of **Prometheus** (more familiarly known as "Leaping Louie"), surrounded by 50 jets of water and flags from the United Nations and United States. He's sprawled above a sunken plaza that holds an open-air café in summer and a romantic ice-skating rink (*see* Ice Skating and Ice Hockey, in Chapter 9) in winter. Around Christmas, this is where they set up the enormous Christmas tree; the tree-lighting ceremony (tel. 212/632–3975) during the first week of December draws huge crowds. Inside and around all the center's buildings are innumerable Art Deco flourishes and artwork: The buff bronze *Atlas* stands guard outside the International Building (Fifth Ave., btw 50th and 51st Sts.). Walking tour brochures and maps for Rockefeller Center are available in the lobby of the GE building (30 Rockefeller Plaza). *Subway: B, D, F, or Q to W. 47th–50th Sts.*

> **THE RAINBOW ROOM** • On the 65th floor of the GE Building is the über-expensive, super-capitalistic restaurant the Rainbow Room, which routinely gets described as the "Ultimate New York Experience." If you can afford it, congratulations—the views are fantastic. Of course, gents need to wear coat and tie. *30 Rockefeller Plaza, tel. 212/632–5100.*

> **RADIO CITY MUSIC HALL** • This 6,000-seat auditorium was the largest in the world when it was built and is considered one of the Art Deco jewels of New York City. It's also got singing elves at Christmastime. What more could you want? Behind-the-scenes tours, offered daily, are $12. *1260 Sixth Ave., btw W. 50th and 51st Sts., tel. 212/247–7777 for events or 212/632–4041 for tours.*

ST. PATRICK'S CATHEDRAL Across from Rockefeller Center, St. Patrick's Cathedral is an anatomically incorrect Gothic cathedral; it's got the ornate white spires, but totally lacks flying buttresses. Even so, as the Roman Catholic Cathedral of New York, it is the site of countless society weddings. If you can get past the limos and Armani-clad throngs, take a spin around the interior. Among the statues in the alcoves around the nave is a striking modern interpretation of the first American-born saint, Mother Elizabeth Seton. The cornerstone was laid in 1858, but the cathedral didn't achieve its present form until 1906, when the Lady Chapel (behind the altar) was built. *Fifth Ave., btw 50th and 51st Sts., tel. 212/753–2261. Subway: B, D, F, or Q to W. 47th–50th Sts.*

SEAGRAM BUILDING Built in 1958 by Bauhaus founder Mies van der Rohe, the **Seagram Building** is the high point of high modernism. Its austerity set the tone for dozens of skyscrapers that followed in New York and other cities, though few have come close to the perfection of details in the Seagram. High priest of modern architecture Philip Johnson eats lunch daily at the Four Seasons restaurant (*see box* Serious Splurges, in Chapter 4) off the main lobby, which he designed. The stark plaza out front—which works around New York's setback zoning laws—became an oft-copied model for high-rise buildings. By setting the base of their building back from the street, architects were free to construct a uniform glass box with sheer, unbroken sides. Free tours of the Seagram Building are given every Tuesday at 3 PM; meet in the lobby. *375 Park Ave., btw 52nd and 53rd Sts. Subway: 6 to E. 51st St.*

URBAN CENTER Housed inside a wing of the Villard Houses, an 1884 complex of some of New York's ritziest brownstones, the Urban Center acts as the locus of the urban design arts. New York's premier architectural preservation and education organization, the **Municipal Art Society** (*see* Walking Tours, *above*) has its headquarters here; so too the **Architectural League** (tel. 212/753–1722) and the **Parks Council** (tel. 212/838–9410). The Center has three **galleries** that feature exhibitions focusing on contemporary planning, design, and preservation issues. Panel discussions and lectures are scheduled throughout the year, and a library of clippings, leaflets, and books on New York City is open to the public weekdays 10–1. *457 Madison Ave., btw 50th and 51st Sts., tel. 212/935–3960. Subway: E or F to W. 53rd St.*

UNITED NATIONS The United Nation's site on the East River was an industrial slum district until oil magnate John D. Rockefeller gave $8.5 million to help build the high-modernist complex we know, fronted by the flags of all the member nations, neatly lined up, from Afghanistan to Zimbabwe. The buildings of this "workshop for peace" were finished in 1962,

73

Alwyn Court
Apartments, **1**

American Craft
Museum, **4**

Carnegie Hall, **2**

Chrysler
Building, **17**

Empire State
Building, **21**

Grand Army Plaza, **3**

Grand Central
Terminal, **16**

International Center
of Photography–
Midtown, **22**

Intrepid Air, Sea,
and Space
Museum, **25**

Japan Society, **14**

Museum of
Modern Art, **5**

Museum of
Television and
Radio, **8**

New York Public
Library, **19**

Pace Wildenstein, **6**

Pershing Square
Park, **18**

Pierpont Morgan
Library, **20**

Radio City
Music Hall, **10**

Restaurant Row, **26**

Rockefeller
Center, **11**

St. Patrick's
Cathedral, **12**

Seagram Building, **9**

Sony Wonder
Technology Lab, **7**

Theater Row, **23**

Times Square, **24**

United Nations, **15**

Urban Center, **13**

The Pond

Grand Army Plaza

S N,R

3 **S**

B,Q

E. 62nd St.
E. 61st St.
E. 60th St.

E. 59th St.

4,5,6,
S N,R

E. 58th St.

E. 57th St.

6

E. 56th St.

7

E. 55th St.

5 E,F

E. 54th St.

S

4 **8**

E,F

9 **S**

E. 53rd St.

E. 52nd St.

E. 51st St.

10

Rockefeller Center

S

6 **S**

E. 50th St.

11

E. 49th St.

12 **13**

E. 48th St.

W. 48th St.

E. 47th St.

W. 47th St.

W. 46th St.

E. 46th St.

14

W. 45th St.

E. 45th St.

15

W. 44th St.

E. 44th St.

W. 43rd St.

Grand Central Terminal

E. 43rd St.

16

7

E. 42nd St.

S

S

17

E. 41st St.

18 4,5,6,7,S

Bryant Park

19

E. 40th St.

E. 39th St.

MURRAY HILL

E. 38th St.

E. 37th St.

E. 36th St.

20

old are

E. 35th St.

E. 34th St.

21

E. 33rd St.

S **6**

E. 32nd St.

E. 31st St.

Kipps Bay Plaza

E. 30th St.

E. 29th St.

NYU Medical Center

N,R

S

E. 28th St.

S **6**

Bellevue Hospital

E. 27th St.

Fifth Avenue
Madison Ave.
Vanderbilt Ave.
Park Ave.
Park Avenue
Lexington Ave.
Third Ave.
Second Ave.
First Ave.
Sutton Place
Beekman Pl.
United Nations Plaza
FDR Drive
Broadway
Park Ave. S.

Queensboro Br.

Roosevelt Island

Queens-Midtown Tunnel

East River

Founded in 1945, the U.N. occupies land that is the domain of no nation—when you're there, you aren't really here in New York. Rather, you'll be on land that belongs to the U.N.'s 185 member states and has its own police force and fire department.

the collaborative product of 11 international architects led by Wallace Harrison. By running FDR Drive underneath the grounds, the architects created one of the most peaceful riverfront portions of Manhattan, including a large grassy expanse from which sunbathers and picnickers are banned (bummer).

Though it seems every tourist makes a trip to the U.N., a visit can be disappointing. The main visitor attraction is the hour-long guided tour. On an ideal day, you'll get to see the General Assembly Hall, the Security Council Chamber, the Trustee Council Chamber, and the Economic and Social Council Chamber, though some rooms may be closed on any given day. Still, a visit to one room is like a visit to any of them: They all look more or less like a big auditorium. The **tour**, offered in 20 languages, takes you through several fascinating installations that, unfortunately, are not accessible to those not on a tour. You'll see some terrifying artifacts of the atomic bombing of Hiroshima and Nagasaki, and displays on war, nuclear energy, and refugees, but you'll have little time to absorb it all. The tour guides give you their spiel, hurry you along, and dutifully deposit you in the lower-level gift-shop area. Besides the usual bric-a-brac with the U.N. logo on it, there's the **U.N. Postal Administration** (stamps and postcards bought here *must* be mailed from this post office), a coffee shop, and a bookstore that sells travel books and some of the U.N.'s technical publications.

Even if you decide not to take the tour, you can still visit the shops and the main General Assembly lobby. Its luminous north wall and long curving balconies make it one of New York's great modernist interiors. In the plaza outside, check out Carl Fredrik Reutersward's twisted gun sculpture, perhaps the best antiwar statement of them all. And if the weather's nice, stroll over to the river for a look at Queens and Roosevelt Island. *United Nations, First Ave. and E. 46th St., tel. 212/963–7713, http://www.undp.org. Subway: 4, 5, 6, or 7 to Grand Central. Admission free. Tours: $6.50, $4.50 students. Open weekdays 9–5, weekends and holidays 9:15–5.*

CHRYSLER BUILDING Although the Chrysler Corporation itself moved out a long time ago, the Art Deco Chrysler Building is a New York icon. The stainless-steel frills, a decorative band emblazoned with cars, and a lobby practically paved in African marble are just a few highlights of William Van Alen's 1930 tour de force. The 480 fluorescent tubes on the spire were added only recently; apparently, technology of the '30s wasn't up to Van Alen's designs for the illumination back then. *405 Lexington Ave., at 42nd St. Subway: 4, 5, 6, or 7 to Grand Central.*

GRAND CENTRAL TERMINAL More than just a train station, Grand Central Terminal is an architectural jewel, one of the world's greatest public spaces. The disdain with which Isabella Rosellini uttered this name in *Blue Velvet* is undeserved, for it stands as a masterpiece of urban design, a 1913 Beaux Arts shrine to space and transportation. Its main concourse is a billowing, reverberating hall where the sound of street musicians mixes smoothly with the bustle of commuters taking the Metro-North to Westchester County.

Currently Grand Central is undergoing a four-year, $175-million restoration, scheduled to be completed in 1998. A major cleaning, on par with that given to the Sistine Chapel, will restore the brilliance of the celestial map on the 120-foot ceiling, while part of the lower level will be converted to a food market. The building will also get outfitted with air-conditioning and complete wheelchair access (currently almost nonexistent). Free **tours** (donation requested) of the terminal are given Wednesdays at 12:30 by the Municipal Art Society (*see* Walking Tours, *above*); meet at the Chemical Bank Commuter Express on the main concourse. *E. 42nd St., at Park Ave., tel. 212/439–1049. Subway: 4, 5, 6, or 7 to Grand Central.*

One of the niftier additions to the terminal's Main Concourse is the **New York Transit Museum Gift Shop** (next to the Track 30 entrance, tel. 212/682–7608). If you love the subways but can't make it to the New York Transit Museum in Brooklyn (*see* Museums and Galleries, *below*), at least come here to check out the books, T-shirts, and ephemera relating to the magnificent subway system. On the terminal's lower level is the famous, ancient **Oyster Bar and Restaurant** (tel. 212/490–6650; open weekdays 11:30–9:30), an eatery that seems far too tony to be located in a train station. The scallops will set you back a cool $25, the bouillabaisse $26. The interior is cavernous and really cool, except for some nasty 1970s renovations. The take-out counter, found up the ramp from the main entrance, has sandwiches for about $7.

Just south of Grand Central Terminal is the perfect alfresco dining area, **Pershing Square Park**. Just show up on the south side of Park Avenue (btw E. 41st and 42nd Sts.) on summer weekdays from 11 to 3; the city provides the tables, chairs, umbrellas, and live music, and all you need to bring is the food. As you dine among the suits, get a load of the Park Avenue viaducts routing auto traffic above you—how oddly pleasing.

NEW YORK PUBLIC LIBRARY A research and exhibition facility rather than a lending library, the **New York Public Library**, built in 1911, is rarely matched in Beaux Arts splendor anywhere in the city. Surely you've seen those two crouching marble lions—dubbed "Patience" and "Fortitude" by Mayor Fiorella La Guardia—on TV before? Tours of the building, beautifully restored in the 1980s, are given for free Monday through Saturday at 11 AM and 2 PM; sign up in advance at the Information Desk. If you're going it on your own, be sure to peek into the Periodicals Room, decorated with trompe l'oeil paintings by Richard Haas commemorating New York's importance as a publishing center. For information on current exhibits being shown in the library, call 212/869–8089. If it's a nice day, though, you'd probably just enjoy sitting on the library's steps, an even livelier stage than the Metropolitan Museum of Art 40 blocks to the north. For the real scene, though, go behind the library to **Bryant Park** (*see* Parks and Gardens, *below*). *Fifth Ave., btw 40th and 42nd Sts., tel. 212/930–0800. Subway: B, D, F, or Q to W. 42nd St. Open Tues.–Wed. 11–7:30, Thurs.–Sat. 10–6.*

TIMES SQUARE While it may not exactly be the Crossroads of the World, as it is often called, Times Square is one of New York's white-hot energy centers. Hordes of people, mostly tourists and the pickpockets who prey on them, crowd it day and night to gawk and walk. Though it's called a "square," it's actually a triangle, formed by the angle of Broadway slashing across Seventh Avenue at 42nd Street—and the roadways are so wide here that it can be hard to tell where that darned "square" really is. However, the former Times Tower, now clad in white marble and called **One Times Square Plaza**, should be immediately obvious—you may've seen it on TV. When the *New York Times* moved into this, its new headquarters, on December 31, 1904, it publicized the event with a fireworks show at midnight. Fireworks of a different sort have since taken place every New Year's Eve at Times Square. Drunk and rowdy revelers mob the intersection below, and when the 200-pound ball being lowered down the flagpole hits bottom on the stroke of midnight, pandemonium ensues (savvy New Yorkers stay far away). Recently, Times Square promoters have been soliciting ideas for the Year 2000 bash, and a few suggestions include lowering a diapered David Letterman with the ball, painting the ball like an olive and lowering it into a giant martini glass, and inviting the Pope.

Times Square is hardly more sedate on the other 364 nights of the year, mesmerizing visitors with its zillion kilowatts of flashing neon, a mammoth digital display offering world news and stock quotes, a 42-foot-tall bottle of Coke, and the occasional way, way larger-than-life Calvin Klein billboard of a 16-story-tall waif in nothing but panties. Could it get any glitzier? Possibly. The city has made quite an effort in recent years to eradicate Times Square's sex shops, porn palaces, and other elements of XXX sleaze to make the area more palatable to tourists (and maybe even New Yorkers). New stores are opening up almost every month, replete with blazing neon signs, required by the city for all new businesses here. The biggest hype surrounded the April 1996 opening of the Virgin Megastore Times Square (*see* Records, Tapes, and CDs, in Chapter 5), a 75,000-square-foot shrine to pop culture consumerism. A Disney Store is expected to open at the southwest corner of 42nd Street and Seventh Avenue in spring 1997. Free walking tours of Times Square are given Fridays at noon; meet at the Times Square Visitors Center (Seventh Ave. and W. 42nd St.). *Subway: N, R, 1, 2, 3, 7, or 9 to Times Sq.*

THEATER DISTRICT Near Times Square, about 30 major Broadway theaters are clustered in an area bounded roughly by Sixth and Ninth avenues and 41st and 53rd streets. There aren't too many reasons to spend time here, unless you're on your way to a show or looking to buy an inflatable sheep: 42nd Street, especially between Seventh and Eighth avenues, is still chock-full of porn shops, peep shows, and prostitutes, despite the city's recent renovation efforts. Try to imagine it as a scene out of the movie *Taxi Driver*, lyrical in its squalor.

The bulk of live theater of 42nd Street is provided by a group of thriving Off-Broadway playhouses, called **Theater Row**, between Ninth and Tenth avenues. Peek into No. 330, between Eighth and Ninth avenues, behind the Port Authority Bus Terminal. Originally the McGraw-Hill building, it was designed in 1931 by Raymond Hood, who later worked on Rockefeller Center. The lobby is an Art Deco wonder of opaque glass and stainless steel. Over 20 restaurants crowd block-long **Restaurant Row** (*see* Midtown West of Fifth Avenue, in Chapter 4) on 46th Street between Eighth and Ninth avenues, but most are pricey and cater to an upscale theater-going crowd.

CHELSEA

The increasingly hip neighborhood of Chelsea (bounded by 14th Street to the south, 30th Street to the north, Fifth Avenue to the east, and the Hudson River to the west) was not named after its equally hip counterpart in London—though both were frequented by the thoroughly soused Sid "Sex Pistols" Vicious before, well, you know. According to lore, it was actually named after the Chelsea Royal Hospital, an old soldiers' home *in* London. Go figure. The whole damn thing was at one time the country estate of one very lucky Clement Clarke Moore, a clergyman and classics professor better known for writing *'Twas the Night Before Christmas* in 1822. Moore saw the city moving north and, intuitive urban planner that he was, decided to divide his land into sub-lots in the 1830s. He dictated a pattern of development that ensured street after street of graceful row houses. Manhattan's first elevated railroad was built on Ninth Avenue in 1871—look for its remains around Tenth Avenue at West 17th Street. The motion picture industry flourished briefly in Chelsea before heading west to Hollywood around World War I. And during the Depression, drama of a different sort flourished on the Chelsea waterfront: Longshoremen and ship owners went head-to-head in some vicious conflicts.

With the 1990s came gentrification: **Eighth Avenue** between West 14th and 23rd streets now rivals Christopher Street in the Village as the city's main gay street, with a slew of groovy restaurants, bars, cafés, gyms, and shops. The action continues on many side streets, particularly **West 18th Street**. Wander east on 18th Street to the block between Fifth and Sixth avenues to find a number of new bookstores (*see* Chapter 5). The stretch of **22nd Street** between Tenth and Eleventh avenues is a good bet for finding galleries displaying art so new the paint is still wet. If you're traveling with gold credit cards you can stop by **Barneys New York** (106 Seventh Ave., at W. 17th. St., tel. 212/929–9000), a hyperexpensive department store that to some New Yorkers is reason enough to live in the city. At least look at the window displays—always outrageous, quirky, and well accessorized. Tenth through Twelfth avenues is the land of warehouses, with a sprinkling of dance clubs; use caution when exploring around here at night. If you're here on a weekend, check out the **Annex Antiques Fair and Flea Market** (*see* Flea Markets in Chapter 5), the city's longest-running outdoor market with over 300 vendors of treasure.

Ladies' Mile

Sixth Avenue, once known as Ladies' Mile, has nothing on the Champs-Elysées now. But during its heyday in the gaslight era it was lined with palatial department stores offering dazzling window displays to rival the best in London and Paris. Most relocated to Fifth Avenue when their wealthy customers moved uptown, and the grand old buildings stood empty until sharp-eyed developers rediscovered them just a few years ago. The fixed-up ones are worth a look: The 1895 Seigel-Cooper Dry Goods Store (Sixth Ave., at W. 18th St.) is elaborately embellished with Corinthian and Doric pilasters, Romanesque arches, lion heads, et cetera. When it opened it had a giant fountain, dental parlor, and art gallery (in addition to those ho-hum "dry goods") on 18 acres of floor space.

Chelsea

Annex Antiques Fair
and Flea Market, **8**
Barneys
New York, **9**
Chelsea Hotel, **7**
Cushman Row, **5**
London Terrace, **4**

St. Peter's
Episcopal Church, **6**
Seigel-Cooper Dry
Goods Store, **10**

Art Galleries
Annina Nosie, **1**
Geenenaftali, **3**
Matthew Marks, **2**

Hudson River

West Side Highway

Eleventh Ave.

Twelfth Ave.

Eleventh Ave.

Tenth Ave.

Ninth Ave.

Eighth Ave.

Seventh Ave.

Sixth Ave.
(Ave. of the Americas)

Fifth Ave.

Broadway

Madison
Square
Park

CHELSEA
HISTORIC
DISTRICT

Clement Clarke
Moore Park

W. 15th St.
W. 16th St.
W. 17th St.
W. 18th St.
W. 19th St.
W. 20th St.
W. 21st St.
W. 22nd St.
W. 23rd St.
W. 24th St.
W. 25th St.
W. 26th St.
W. 14th St.

A.C.,
E,L
1,2,
3,9
C,E
1,9
1,9
F,L
F
N,R

0   400 yards
0   400 meters

CHELSEA HISTORIC DISTRICT In Chelsea's historic district—West 20th to 23rd streets between Eighth and Tenth avenues—you'll find examples of all of Chelsea's architectural periods, dating back to the days of Clement Clarke Moore. Just think of how excited your loved ones will be when you've learned to distinguish Gothic Revival from Italianate. Too boring? Check out **467 West 21st Street**, at Tenth Avenue; its live-in landlord was the late Anthony Perkins, of *Psycho* fame. And now, here we go: The houses of **Cushman Row** (406–418 W. 20th St., at Ninth Ave.) are some of the country's most perfect examples of Greek Revival town houses. Look for tiny pineapple decorations on Nos. 416 and 418. **St. Peter's Episcopal Church** (344 W. 20th St., btw Ninth and Tenth Aves.) "welcomes all faiths and uncertain faiths." Its fieldstone building is one of New York's earliest examples of Gothic Revival architecture. Built in the 1930s, **London Terrace** (W. 23–24th Sts., btw Ninth and Tenth Aves.) is a 1,670-unit apartment complex that isn't Revival-anything. It's just big—really, really big. The theme-crazed management used to dress up the doormen as London bobbies.

CHELSEA HOTEL Chelsea's most famous landmark is the Chelsea Hotel, a slightly seedy redbrick building with lacy wrought-iron balconies. Though the street it stands on is now run down, when the Chelsea opened in 1884 this was the center of New York's theater industry. It has traditionally catered to long-term (and often eccentric) tenants, including Mark Twain, Eugene O'Neill, O. Henry, Thomas Wolfe, Tennessee Williams, Vladimir Nabokov, Mary McCarthy, Arthur Miller, Dylan Thomas, William S. Burroughs, and Arthur C. Clarke (who wrote the script for *2001: A Space Odyssey* while living here). Andy Warhol filmed *The Chelsea Girls* here in 1966; in the '80s, the film *Sid and Nancy* (1986) revisited Sid's old haunts. *222 W. 23rd St., btw Seventh and Eighth Aves., tel. 212/243–3700. Subway: 1 or 9 to W. 23rd St.*

GRAMERCY AND UNION SQUARE

Unless you'd like to sit on a curb and stare longingly at rich people walking their miniature poodles, there's little reason to visit the wealthy residential neighborhood of Gramercy (roughly defined as everything east of Fifth Avenue between 14th and 30th streets). The blocks along **Broadway**, particularly where it meets bustling Union Square, are home to some of New York's most exclusive bars, shops, and restaurants.

Originally, 17th-century Dutch settlers called this part of Manhattan island *Krom Moerasje* (little crooked swamp), and much of the area remained marshy swampland until developer Samuel Ruggles got his hands on it. Ruggles drained the swamp, replaced it with 66 beautiful town houses, and lured the rich with the promise of a private garden, **Gramercy Park** (E. 20th to 21st Sts., at Lexington Ave.), accessible only with a golden key. Over 150 years later it's still one of the most exclusive addresses in New York. And though the keys are no longer golden, the private park is still off-limits and residents fiercely guard this privilege (ironically, the park is almost always empty). And here's another thing you're excluded from: The **Players Club** (16 Gramercy Park S), an actor's club with notable alumni, including Mark Twain, Lionel Barrymore, Irving Berlin, Winston Churchill, Sir Laurence Olivier, Frank Sinatra, Walter Cronkite, and—the David among these Goliaths—Richard Gere.

The Union Square Greenmarket (see Chapter 4) is the place where New York's finest chefs come to purchase farm-fresh produce, bread, cheese, and fruit.

UNION SQUARE During the Civil War, Union troops paraded around, were reviewed in, and embarked from Union Square. History buffs will also recall that Union Square was the home of America's labor, socialist, and anarchist movements. In fact, a list of Union Square's former tenants reads like a who's who of America's radical left; the newspaper *Socialist Call*, the *Daily Worker*, the ACLU, the International Ladies Garment Workers' Union, and the League for Peace and Democracy all had their headquarters here. If that fails to interest you, at least come to Union Square to pay homage to an event that paved the way for a three-day weekend: On September 21, 1882, the Knights of Labor, a union that even during the 19th century included women and minorities, held a rally here. This rally was later commemorated as Labor Day.

During the early 20th century, demonstrations became increasingly large, and often violent, as city officials started calling in the heavy-handed NYPD to bash heads. At a vigil on the night

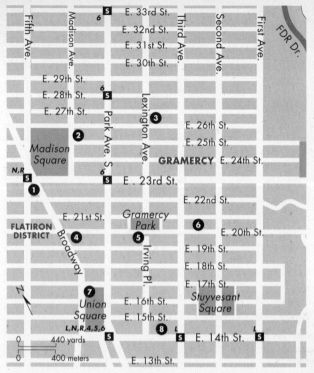

69th Regiment Armory, 3
Con Edison Energy Museum, 8
Flatiron Building, 1
New York City Police Museum, 6
New York State Supreme Court, 2
Players Club, 5
Theodore Roosevelt Birthplace, 4
Union Square Greenmarket, 7

that scapegoat anarchists Sacco and Venzetti were to be executed, National Guardsmen manned machine guns from the roofs of surrounding buildings. Drop by the square in the 1940s and you'd find big banners draped across the Communist party headquarters, urging DEMONSTRATE AGAINST IMPERIALIST WAR! FOR DEFENSE OF THE SOVIET UNION!

By mid-century, the left left and Union Square became an entertainment center, full of bars and movie houses—a working-class Times Square (back before it became a den of sleaze). During the '60's, Andy Warhol had his famous Factory off Union Square, and Marcel Duchamp, expatriate French dadaist, lived a block off it. Today it's home to some of the city's finest (read: most expensive) restaurants, including **Union Square Cafe** (*see box* Serious Splurges, in Chapter 4). Just north of here is a mini-neighborhood, the **Persian Rug District**, where many shops hang richly patterned rugs in their windows. Check out every New Yorker's favorite store, **ABC Carpet and Home** (*see* Chapter 5), which arranges its expensive goodies in big jumbles like in grandma's attic. *Subway: N, R, 4, 5, or 6 to Union Sq.*

FLATIRON BUILDING .Christened the Fuller Building, this dramatic neo-Renaissance building was popularly called the Flatiron Building because of its resemblance to the clothes-pressing device popular at the time. Built on a triangular wedge of land in 1902, it rose 286 feet (20 stories), a height unprecedented at the time; it is often considered the world's first skyscraper. Its internal steel frame structure was revolutionary, allowing for taller and taller buildings (Otis's elevator also helped). Its unusual shape also had the effect of creating unusually strong winds at its tip at 23rd Street. Dirty old men (and young ones, too) would gather to watch the wind raise the ankle-length skirts of passing women. To these men policemen gave the warning "23-skidoo." *175 Fifth Ave., btw 23rd and 24th Sts. Subway: N or R to E. 23rd St.*

South of the Flatiron Building, between Fifth Avenue and Park Avenue South, lies the **Flatiron District**, where some of the trendiest—and most expensive–restaurants and boutiques in New York have recently been popping up. It's definitely one of the nicest areas to do some window shopping and gawk at the rich enjoying small, beautifully arranged portions of overpriced food. See how uncomfortable you can make them by drooling a little.

MADISON SQUARE Most days this 7-acre park is full of activity: children playing, bums snoozing, and Fox TV execs rushing to lunch (the Fox offices are on the park's northwest corner). Statues in the park include Admiral David G. Farragut, Civil War hero, and one of those patently forgettable presidents, Chester A. Arthur. More important is the park's history: On this spot in 1842, a group of men calling themselves the Knickerbockers started playing a game known as New York ball—which was later to be known as baseball.

Right off the park, between East 26th and 27th streets—where the New York Life Building now stands—was where the original incarnation of **Madison Square Garden** stood (it's since moved a few blocks farther west). Designed by Stanford White, an illustrious architect who helped design much of Columbia University, the Garden was the place where New York society gathered for hedonistic post-theater revelries. During a boisterous party at the Garden, White was shot through the head by Harry Thaw, a partner in White's firm. For the sordid details of White's, um, affairs, *see box* They Built This City, *above. E. 23rd to 26th Sts., btw Fifth and Madison Aves. Subway: N or R to W. 23rd St.*

Right across the street from Madison Square Park is the Appellate Division of the **New York State Supreme Court** (35 E. 25th St., at Madison Ave.), a gem of a courthouse, built on the heels of the City Beautiful movement in 1900. Flanking the portal are figures representing "Wisdom" and "Force"; among the other figures on the building are "Peace" and "Justice." Go inside to see the exhibitions of New York historical ephemera (including a share in the stock of the City Lunatic Asylum) and the gorgeous murals. If it seems like there's a statue missing from the balustrade, there is: In the 1950s, the statue of Mohammed was removed at the request of local Islamic groups, as Islamic law forbids the representation of humans in sculpture or painting. *35 E. 25th St., at Madison Ave.*

69TH REGIMENT ARMORY Today, the only crowds moving in and out of the ugly, warehouselike 69th Regiment Armory are uniformed National Guardsmen. But over 85,000 New Yorkers caught the controversial 1913 Armory Show, which brought modern art by Picasso, Duchamp, and other artists to the American public for the first time. The stuffy American press roundly criticized the show: The European art was labeled subversive, and the American art too derivative of the European art. *E. 26th St., at Lexington Ave. Subway: 6 to E. 23rd St.*

WEST VILLAGE

The West Village is also known as **Greenwich Village**, or sometimes just **The Village**. Greenwich Village used to encompass everything between 14th Street and Houston Street, from the Hudson to the East River. Nowadays, east of Broadway is considered the East Village, and everything west is the West Village. The Village really did begin life as its own little village, named Grin'wich, in the early 1700s. The people of New York City (who then lived much farther south, at the tip of Manhattan) regarded this as a resort town. When a series of nasty smallpox and yellow fever epidemics struck the city from 1799 to 1822, residents fled north to Grin'wich. Eventually, the area became a neighborhood of blue bloods who built lofty Greek Revival and Italianate style homes (some of which still survive) before continuing their migration north.

By the start of the 20th century, the Village had earned a pretty dicey reputation. The area around **Washington Square** (*see below*) became known as "Frenchtown" and was site of the city's highest concentration of brothels and rough bars. Writers and artists moved into its ornate brownstones anyway, because rent was cheap. A few you may have heard about: in the 19th century, Henry James, Edgar Allen Poe, Mark Twain, Walt Whitman, and Stephen Crane; at the turn of the century, O. Henry, Edith Wharton, Theodore Dreiser, and Hart Crane; and during the 1920s and '30s, John Dos Passos, Norman Rockwell, Sinclair Lewis, Eugene O'Neill, Edward Hopper, Margaret Sanger, and Edna St. Vincent Millay. In the late 1940s and early '50s, the abstract expressionist painters Franz Kline, Jackson Pollock, Mark Rothko, and Willem de Kooning congregated here, as did the Beat writers Jack Kerouac, Allen Ginsberg, and Lawrence Ferlinghetti. The 1960s brought folk musicians and poets, notably Bob "Posi-

West Village

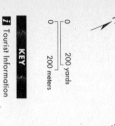

KEY

i Tourist Information

0 ____ 200 yards
0 ____ 200 meters

N

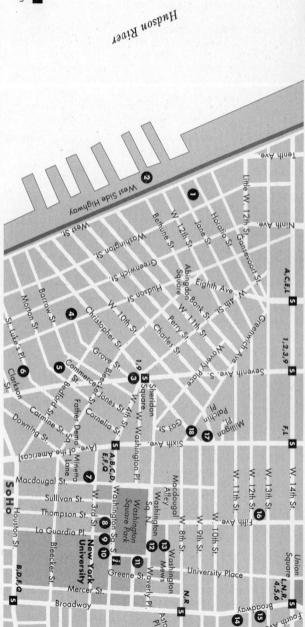

83

tively 4th Street" Dylan and Peter, Paul and Mary. In the 1970s a burgeoning gay community helped make this the crucible for a national gay-rights movement. Today it's still a center for radical politics and tolerant attitudes, a home to AIDS activists and video artists, a place where the elderly First Bohemians mingle in cafés with those newly minted at **New York University** (*see below*).

Bleecker Street is one of the Village's main drags. Where it intersects with **MacDougal Street** (*see below*) it's jammed with cafés, jazz clubs, and bars. Between Seventh Avenue and Abingdon Square you'll find a more mellow Bleecker Street, with cozy little restaurants and purveyors of everything from Japanese furniture to African art. Consider making a detour off Bleecker Street to visit **18 West 11th Street**; the radical group The Weathermen had their bomb-making factory here until they accidentally blew it up in 1970. (At the time, Dustin Hoffman lived next door—he was seen on TV news coverage frantically trying to rescue his possessions.) Or follow Bleecker Street east of Seventh Avenue, to **Leroy Street**, to find an old Italian neighborhood that's a hell of a lot livelier than Little Italy these days: Italian butchers, bakers, and pizza-pie makers abound. To the west, Bleecker Street ends at **Hudson Street**, which has a lot of small, slick restaurants and a handful of lesbian bars and clubs. Beyond that, way over on **West Street**, you'll find druggies and prostitutes hangin' by the piers.

In addition to the must-sees listed below, be sure to check out the **Forbes Magazine Galleries** (*see* Museums and Galleries, *below*) and brand-new **Hudson River Park** (*see* Parks and Gardens, *below*). The Village is also home to the monthlong **Gay Pride** festivities, and the ultra-fabulous **Wigstock Festival**; for more on these, *see* Festivals, in Chapter 1.

WASHINGTON SQUARE At the heart of the Village is Washington Square. Before it became a public park in 1827, this was a cemetery for victims of yellow fever (an estimated 10,000–22,000 were buried below), then a military parade ground (bad idea—the heavy artillery kept collapsing into old graves), and finally a site of public executions during the late 18th and early 19th centuries. Quite a few citified desperadoes met their maker at the **Hanging Elm**, which stands at the park's northwest corner. These days, the square is a maelstrom of playful activity, shared by a truly bizarre mix of people: earnest-looking NYU students, ruthless chess players, businesslike drug dealers, homeless hippie folk singers, bongo-drum players, joggers, skateboarders, vociferous protesters—and people like you, sitting on benches, witnessing the grand opera of it all. At the center of the square is a perpetually broken and waterless **fountain**: It's the New York City equivalent of Speaker's Corner in London, a theater in the round for musicians, magicians, and ranting amateur politicians. Dominating the square's northern end is the triumphal **Washington Arch**, beyond which lies the start of glorious Fifth Avenue. Originally, a wood-and-plaster arch was erected in 1889 to celebrate the 100th anniversary of George Washington's presidential inauguration; it proved so popular that a Tuckahoe marble version (designed by the irrepressible Stanford White) was thrown up in 1895. Below it you'll find two pollution-corroded statues of the President who hated to pose for portraits and such because it meant wearing those dreadful wooden teeth: "Washington at Peace," sculpted by Alexander Stirling Calder, and the Ying to Calder's Yang, "Washington at War," by Hermon Mac-Neil. Bodybuilding legend Charles Atlas was the model for "Peace." *Btw Waverly Pl. and W. 4th St., at Fifth Ave. Subway: A, B, C, D, E, F, or Q to W. 4th St. (Washington Sq.).*

Most of the beautiful old buildings bordering Washington Square belong to **New York University** (*see below*). The **Row**, a line of well-preserved, Federal-style town houses lining the north side of the square between Fifth Avenue and University Place, now serves as offices and housing for lucky NYU faculty. Ditto for **Washington Mews** (half a block north), a cobblestone private street lined on one side with the former stables of the houses on the Row. Because Washington Square has long been considered tony real estate, it's had its share of famous residents: Author Willa Cather once lived at 60 Washington Square South, and Henry James's grandmother made her home at 18 Washington Square North (now demolished); James used it as the setting for his creatively titled, bodice-ripping novel *Washington Square*. Eugene O'Neill wrote *The Iceman Cometh* between trips to the pub from his home at 38 Washington Square South.

The **Judson Memorial Church**, a Romanesque Revival masterwork built in 1892 by McKim, Mead & White, is known as much for the social activism of its congregation as its impressive stained glass and marble reliefs: The Baptist church has supported AIDS research and abortion rights. Its tower is now an NYU dormitory. *55 Washington Square S, at Thompson St.*

MACDOUGAL STREET Pick up MacDougal Street on the west side of Washington Square to watch Village people do their thing. South of the Square, between West 3rd and Bleecker streets, you'll find a row of ancient cafés that all claim to have been the Beats' "favorite" hangout (*see* Cafés, in Chapter 4). The intersection with Bleecker Street is a major bar scene—well, for the bridge-and-tunnel crowd, anyway. North of Washington Square you'll find the **Provincetown Playhouse** (133 MacDougal St., tel. 212/477–5048), which helped to start the career of the great playwright Eugene O'Neill; the gracious Federal homes at **127-131 MacDougal Street** were once owned by former Vice President and unfortunately accurate marksman Aaron Burr. Fiorello La Guardia, the enormously popular mayor of the 1930s and '40s who passed major social reforms (and also read "Dick Tracy" comic strips over the radio) was born at **177 Sullivan Street**, a block east of MacDougal Street. MacDougal Street ends to the north at **West 8th Street**, a.k.a. "The Shoe Street." It's filled with cheapie footwear boutiques and a sprinkling of head shops.

NEW YORK UNIVERSITY New York University was founded 1831 by a group of prominent citizens fed up with what they saw as a ridiculous infatuation with Greek and Latin among the colleges of their day. NYU, they proclaimed, would cater to the common person. Today, it's the largest private university in the United States, offering over 2,500 courses (including Greek and Latin) and 25 degrees to both graduate and undergraduate students. Almost all of the programs at NYU are top in the nation, but its film school—which has graduated the likes of Spike Lee and Martin Scorcese—is the sexy one. Most of the buildings you'll see around Washington Square belong to the school—just look for the purple flags.

Your first task is to look at the **Elmer Holmes Bobst Library** (70 Washington Sq. S, at La Guardia Pl.), repository of some 2.5 million books. In the 1960s, well-intentioned but aesthetically impaired university officials planned (with aid of architects Philip Johnson and Richard Foster) to reface *all* its Washington Square buildings in ugly red sandstone, just like this one. Thankfully, cost proved prohibitive and they soon abandoned the plan. Next door, the **Loeb Student Center** (566 La Guardia Pl., at Washington Sq. S, tel. 212/998–4900) stands on the site of a famous boardinghouse, nicknamed the House of Genius for the talented writers who lived there over the years—Stephen Crane, O. Henry, and Theodore Dreiser, to name a few. Check its North Lobby for flyers about cool happenings around NYU. Pop by the university's Main Building (entrances at 100 Washington Sq. E and 33 Washington Pl.) to check out the exhibits, usually of contemporary art, at **Grey Art Gallery** (*see* Museums and Galleries, *below*). For maps and such, stop by **NYU information**, on the first floor of Shimkin Hall (50 W. 4th St., at Washington Sq. E, tel. 212/998–4636). It's open weekdays 8:30–8, weekends 10–4. On weekdays during the school year, **free tours** of the university are given several times daily. Tours depart from the Office of Undergraduate Admissions (22 Washington Sq. N, tel. 212/998–4524). Reservations are not necessary. *Subway: N or R to E. 8th St.*

BROADWAY The Great White Way turns incredibly unglamorous around NYU. It's lined by ugly modern university high-rises, fast-food joints, and mallish clothing stores. Two shops are worth checking out: The **Strand** (*see* Used and Rare Books, in Chapter 5) offers over 8 miles of books. Across the street, **Forbidden Planet** (*see* Specialty Bookstores, in Chapter 5) claims the title of world's largest comic book and sci-fi store. And **Tower Records** (*see* Records, Tapes, and CDs, in Chapter 5) is just really damn big.

➤ **GRACE CHURCH** • Seeing this ornate Gothic church on a schlocky block of Broadway is a bit like spying a wedding dress in a rack of poly-blend T-shirts. James Renwick, Jr., a parishioner with a very odd hobby (some people collect model trains, he drew cathedrals) designed it for free; when it opened for business 1846, it was the first Gothic-style church in the United States. During the 19th century its flock was so rich "they literally shat money," according to one tour guide. Step inside and admire the glorious English stained-glass windows that bathe the interior in an otherworldly glow. Free

Much to the chagrin of its stuffy parishioners, the February 10, 1863, marriage of "General" Tom Thumb to Lavinia Warren, orchestrated by P. T. Barnum, temporarily turned Grace Church into a circus—literally.

brochures at the back of the church point out some of the church's architectural highlights. At press time, free tours of the church had been suspended indefinitely; call ahead to see if they have resumed. *802 Broadway, btw 10th and 11th Sts., tel. 212/254–2000. Admission free. Open weekdays 10–5:30, Sat. noon–4.*

WEST OF SIXTH AVENUE If you've been navigating Manhattan's efficient, numbered grid and just crossed over Sixth Avenue into the heart of the Village, you're in for a shock: Its tree-lined streets are short and narrow, oddly named, and cross each other at unfathomable angles. But don't let this vex you. It's one of the most beautiful neighborhoods in the city, with rows of ivy-covered brick town houses and nary a skyscraper in sight. Spend the afternoon wandering, then park yourself in one of its woodsy taverns (many former speakeasies) for a drink.

➤ **JEFFERSON MARKET LIBRARY** • The triangle formed by West 10th Street, Sixth Avenue, and Greenwich Avenue originally held a meat market, an all-women jail, and the magnificent 1877 courthouse that is now the Jefferson Market Library (a branch of the New York Public Library system). It's another fine design by the ubiquitous Calvert Vaux and Frederick Clarke Withers. A group of architects voted it one of the "ten most beautiful buildings in America" in 1885, but critics often have a hard time describing it. Some say it's "Venetian," others call it "High Victorian Gothic." Villagers, noting the alternating wide bands of red brick and narrow strips of white granite, dubbed it the "Lean Bacon Style." *425 Sixth Ave., at W. 10th St., tel. 212/243–4334. Subway: 1 or 9 to Christopher St. (Sheridan Sq.). Open Mon. and Thurs. 10–6, Tues. and Fri. noon–6, Wed. noon–8, Sat. 10–5.*

Around the corner you'll find two tiny, charming courtyards, **Patchin Place** (off W. 10th St., btw Greenwich Ave. and Sixth Ave.) and **Milligan Place** (off Sixth Ave., just north of W. 10th St.). Both were built in the 1850s for the waiters (mostly Basques) who worked at a posh Fifth Avenue hotel. **No. 4 Patchin Place** was the onetime home of e. e. cummings. Also worth a quick look is the gourmet wonderland **Balducci's** (424 6th Ave., btw 9th and 10th Sts., tel. 212/673–2600), which began decades ago with the lowly vegetable cart of the late Louis Balducci, and **Bigelow's Pharmacy** (414 Sixth Ave., btw W. 8th and 9th Sts., tel. 212/533–2700), which looks the same as the day it opened in 1838, right down to the wooden display cases.

➤ **GAY STREET** • This short, crooked lane is lined with small row houses circa 1810. It was originally a black neighborhood and later a strip of speakeasies. Ruth McKenney wrote *My Sister Eileen* (based on her sister and her brother-in-law, Nathaniel West) in the basement of **No. 14 Gay Street**. Howdy Doody was designed in the basement of **No. 12 Gay Street**. *Btw Christopher St. and Waverly Pl., just west of Sixth Ave.*

➤ **SHERIDAN SQUARE** • In 1863, this was the site of one of the nastiest riots in American history; a mob outraged with the Civil War draft turned against the city's freed slaves and some 125 people were killed. You'll find a statue of the mighty and heavily mustached military man for whom the square is named, Civil War general Philip "Little Phil" Sheridan, near the north end. *Seventh Ave. S, at the intersection of Christopher, W. 4th, and Grove Sts. Subway: 1 or 9 to Christopher St. (Sheridan Sq.).*

Southwest of Sheridan Square is **Christopher Street**, chock-full of gay bars and shops and strolling gay couples. Whatever your sexual orientation, you should stop by the **Li-Lac Chocolate Shop** (120 Christopher St., tel. 212/242–7374) for homemade chocolate and buttercrunch. The national gay-rights movement was born not far from Sheridan Square in 1969, when riots broke out over a police raid of the now-defunct gay club, **Stonewall Inn** (53 Christopher St.). The Inn is long gone, but a plaque marks the site. In tiny **Christopher Park** (Christopher St., north of Sheridan Sq.) you'll find a statue by sculptor George Segal of a lesbian couple sitting on a bench and gay male partners standing nearby.

➤ **BEDFORD STREET** • The narrowest house in the Village is at **75½ Bedford Street**, a scant 9½ feet wide. It led a fine life as an alley until soaring real-estate prices inspired someone to put it to good use in 1873. Pulitzer-winning poet Edna St. Vincent Millay and actor Cary Grant have both called it home (at different times, natch). Next door, **77 Bedford Street** is the oldest house in the Village (1799), while **86 Bedford Street** was the site of a Prohibition-era speakeasy that served the likes of Thornton Wilder and Ernest Hemingway. The bar that stands here now, **Chumleys** (*see* Chapter 6) keeps the tradition by leaving its entrance unmarked. At the intersection with Grove Street, look for the funny-looking 1835 house that Villagers call **Twin Peaks** (102 Bedford St.).

➤ **COMMERCE STREET** • Walk two blocks south of Grove Street on Bedford Street to find the homes of more famous dead folk: Aaron Burr at **17 Commerce Street**, Washington Irving at **11 Commerce Street**. The two identical brick houses separated by a garden are popularly known as the **Twin Sisters** (39–41 Commerce St.). Local legend has it that they were built by an indulgent sea captain for his two spoiled daughters, who loathed each other. The **Cherry Lane Theater** (38 Commerce St., tel. 212/989–2020) is one of the city's very first Off-Broadway houses and site of American premieres of works by O'Neill, Beckett, Ionesco, and Albee.

➤ **ST. LUKE'S PLACE** • St. Luke's Place (the proper name for Leroy Street between Hudson Street and Seventh Avenue South) is *the* place to go to check out classy 1860s town houses with famous pasts: Poet Marianne Moore lived at **No. 14**; Jimmy Walker, mayor of New York during the '20s and one of its most colorful political figures, lived at **No. 6** (the lampposts out front are special "mayor's lamps"); **No. 12** was shown as the Huxtables' home on *The Cosby Show* (although the family ostensibly lived in Brooklyn); and **No. 4** was the setting of the Audrey Hepburn movie *Wait Until Dark*. Before 1890 the playground on the south side of the street was a graveyard where, according to legend, the dauphin of France—the lost son of Louis XVI and Marie Antoinette—is buried. *Subway: 1 or 9 to Houston St.*

The Church of St. Luke-in-the-Fields (487 Hudson St., btw Christopher and Barrow Sts.), a simple chapel built in 1821, has a small garden area that is open to the public during the day. It's a pleasant spot for a picnic lunch.

MEAT-PACKING DISTRICT Believe it or not, New York City was the largest center of beef production in America during the mid-1800s. But with the advent of refrigeration, most meat packers quit trying to wrangle whole dead heifers into Manhattan and instead moved out West where the cows were. Still, more than a few have stuck around to serve the city's large Jewish community, since kosher meat can be kept only three days after butchering. Wholesale meat markets—fragrant enough to make your nose quiver even if you've never read anything by Upton Sinclair—can still be found sandwiched along the cobblestone streets west of Washington Street and south of 12th Street. (The men you see lingering at corners here work a different kind of meat market.) Photographers love the grit and rawness (no pun intended) of the meat-packing district, and if you stroll around you're bound to see a few fashion shoots in progress. Quite a few late-night restaurants and clubs have sprung up here in recent years. *Subway: A, C, E, or L to W. 14th St.*

EAST VILLAGE AND ALPHABET CITY

The East Village, originally considered part of the Lower East Side, was colonized by the young artists and intellectuals of the 1950s and '60s who'd abandoned Greenwich Village because it was too damn expensive. Beats like Jack Kerouac, Allen Ginsberg, and William S. Burroughs, jazz greats Charlie Parker and Charles Mingus, and artists like Willem de Kooning and Mark Rothko cruised these streets for inspiration or, sometimes, a little smack. Which is not to say the East Village didn't exist before the cool cats got here: In 1925 George Gershwin penned "I'm Something on Avenue A," and prior to the Civil War rich folks like the Vanderbilts made **Astor Place** (*see below*) one of the city's most exclusive addresses.

While neighborhoods like the West Village, SoHo, and TriBeCa have recently morphed into overpriced yuppielands, the East Village—bounded to the west by Fourth Avenue and Lafayette Street, to the north by 14th Street, to the south by Houston Street, and to the east by the East River—has miraculously remained the domain of nihilists, starving artists, and people with lots of dyed hair, pierced body parts, and tattoos. Main drags in the East Village are **St. Marks Place** and **Avenue A**, littered with bars, clubs, cafés, avant-garde galleries, hole-in-the-wall theaters, and purveyors of secondhand kitsch. Along the East River is the blissfully

East Village and Alphabet City

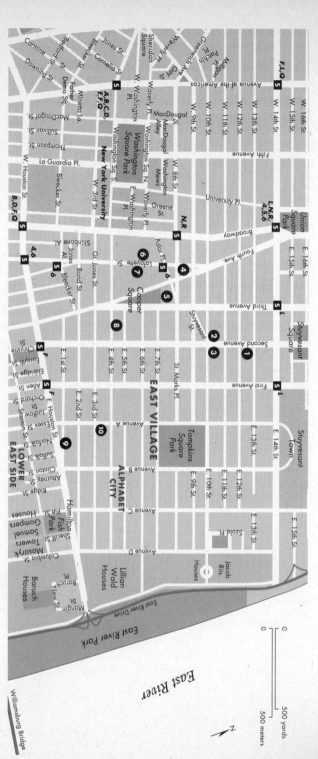

uncrowded **East River Park** (*see* Parks and Gardens, *below*), where the views of the Brooklyn Bridge can't be beat.

Add to the mix a few thriving ethnic enclaves: **Little Ukraine** (First and Second Aves., near E. 7th St.) features a handful of amazing Ukrainian diners, a few Eastern Orthodox cathedrals, the **Ukrainian Museum** (*see* Museums and Galleries, *below*), and a bunch of dives where elderly Ukrainian women tend bar. **Little India** (6th St., btw First and Second Aves.) is jam-packed with restaurants vying to serve you the cheapest tandoori in the most garish surroundings. For more on neighborhood restaurants, *see* Chapter 4.

ASTOR PLACE At the intersection of Fourth Avenue and Lafayette Street, Astor Place is the gateway to the East Village: Teen skaters hang out, self-consciously checking their pagers; and the occasional band sets up to grind out a few Eagles covers. The subway entrance here is a cast-iron replica of the Beaux Arts original. Next to it is *Alamo*, a huge black steel cube sculpted in 1967 by Bernard Rosenthal. It balances on one corner and was designed to pivot, but, alas, pivots no more. The **Mosaic Trail** of decorated lampposts on Astor Place (and continuing east along St. Marks Place) is the creation of an anonymous local artist. *Subway: 6 to Astor Pl.*

The street's namesake, John Jacob Astor, made his first millions by trading furs in the Pacific Northwest (bas-relief beavers on the tiles at the Astor Place subway station are fuzzy little reminders). Once settled in New York City he degenerated into a human Jabba the Hut, amassing enough land and wealth to be considered the richest man in America by 1840—all with a girth too great to get out of bed and on a steady diet of human milk. On his deathbed he expressed the desire to buy every foot of land in Manhattan.

One of the bloodiest riots in New York history occurred on Astor Place in 1849, over a disparaging remark made by Charles Macready, an English tragedian (popular with the city's Anglophilic elite), about the abilities of Edwin Forrest, an American actor worshipped by the working classes. Hundreds of protesters armed with rotten eggs, fruit, and rocks interrupted Macready's performance of *MacBeth* at the Astor Place Opera House. The ensuing riot left 31 dead, over 150 injured, and painfully underscored the chasm between New York's classes.

COLONNADE ROW These days, Colonnade Row's four remaining town houses resemble Greek ruins more than Greek Revival masterpieces. The original 1833 development of nine homes—named "La Grange Terrace" after the country estate of the Marquis de Lafayette—was derided as tacky by New York elites until bigshots like John Jacob Astor, Cornelius Vanderbilt, and Charles Dickens moved in. Current tenants are much less impressive. *428–434 Lafayette St., btw Astor Pl. and E. 4th St. Subway: 6 to Astor Pl.*

The Corinthian columns fronting the town houses at Colonnade Row were built by the talented inmates of Sing Sing Penitentiary.

➤ **JOSEPH PAPP PUBLIC THEATER** • The imposing Italian Renaissance–style building across the street began life as the city's first free library (a gift from the usually miserly John Jacob Astor in 1854), then became offices for the Hebrew Immigrant Aid Society (HIAS) before being renovated in the '60s to serve as the New York Shakespeare Festival's Joseph Papp Public Theater. Under the leadership of the late Joseph Papp, the Public's five playhouses and one cinema built a reputation for innovative performances: The Aquarian hippie-fest *Hair* started here, as well as *A Chorus Line*, and it helped launch the careers of Meryl Streep, Raul Julia, Kevin Kline, James Earl Jones, and David Mamet. For more info, *see* Arts Centers, in Chapter 7. *425 Lafayette St., at Astor Pl., tel. 212/598–7150. Subway: 6 to Astor Pl.*

COOPER UNION AND COOPER SQUARE If self-made millionaire, railroad industrialist, and inventor Peter Cooper were still alive (he isn't), every year he'd get 1,000 big, wet, sloppy kisses from the engineers, artists, and architects in training at the Cooper Union, a totally *tuition-free* college. Cooper himself came from a poor family and learned to read late in life, so he plowed his big bucks back into an institute of higher learning for working folks, opened in 1859. Lectures in its **Foundation Building** (the city's first internal steel-frame building, which was Cooper's own invention) helped launch the NAACP and catapulted Abraham Lincoln to the presidency—Abe gave his famous "Might Makes Right" speech here in 1860. Call or check the paper for the current lecture and concert schedule. *41 Cooper Sq., btw Third and Fourth Aves., tel. 212/254–6374. Subway: 6 to Astor Pl.*

Cooper Union stands, logically, on **Cooper Square** (bordered by St. Marks Place, Third and Fourth Aves., and the Bowery), an immaculate—and locked—park with a regal-looking statue of Peter Cooper at its center. To the west stands **Carl Fisher Music Publishers** (42–62 Cooper Sq., tel. 212/677–0821), which sells sheet music and, more importantly, keeps a large monthly calendar with the birthdates of every major and minor musician on the planet (Boy George and Burl Ives share a special day, if nothing else).

ST. MARKS PLACE St. Marks Place, as 8th Street is called between Third Avenue and Avenue A, is the most *happenin'* street in the East Village. Hippies and acid heads tripped here in the '60s, and disco fever found its first NYC outlet here in the '70s at a club called Get Down. Green-haired neo-punks blasting the Boredoms are now makin' the scene. You can buy just about anything in the string of cluttered shops or at the de facto flea market that appears daily along the sidewalk, from dope to vintage clothes to a new guitar. What a pisser: There's even a Gap. *Subway: 6 to Astor Pl.*

ST. MARK'S-IN-THE-BOWERY CHURCH This 1799 fieldstone country church was built over the family chapel of Peter Stuyvesant (who is buried here), and is the city's oldest continually used church. Its liberal clergy has sponsored voter-registration drives, preached for civil rights, and opened the nation's first lesbian health-care clinic. In the '20s, one pastor livened up the boring Episcopalian ceremonies with American Indian chants, Greek folk dancing, and recitation of Eastern mantras. It currently hosts dance, poetry, and musical performances; call for a schedule. *Second Ave., at E. 10th St., tel. 212/674–8194. Subway: L to Third Ave.*

The stretch of Second Avenue next to St. Mark's Church was known as the "Jewish Rialto" at the turn of the century, because its eight Yiddish theaters presented the best in comedy, melodrama, and musicals from the Old World. On the sidewalk in front of the **Second Avenue Deli** (*see* East Village and Alphabet City, in Chapter 4) are Hollywood-style squares commemorating luminaries of the Yiddish stage.

TOMPKINS SQUARE PARK Recently restored Tompkins Square Park is the physical, spiritual, and political heart of the radical East Village. It's a good-size park, and you can always find a drum circle or game of Rollerblade basketball or whatever. Look for two monuments: **Temperance Fountain**, oddly out of place given the number of people drinking beers out of brown bags, and the **General Slocum Memorial**, which commemorates 1,021 German immigrants from the East Village who perished on the way to a church picnic when their ship caught fire and sank.

The square takes its name from four-times governor Daniel Tompkins (Pataki, don't get any ideas), an avid abolitionist and vice president under James Monroe who once owned this land from Second Avenue to the East River. Its history is long and violent: The 1874 Tompkins Square Riot involved some 7,000 unhappy laborers and 1,600 police. The police gained control by beating bystanders and demonstrators indiscriminately. The 1988 Tompkins Square Riot involved police on horseback charging homeless-rights and anti-gentrification protesters armed with sticks and bottles—Mayor David Dinkens had ordered the square cleared of proliferating refrigerator-box castles and tent mansions. The park did not reopen until 1992, midnight curfew in place. In between, activist Abbie Hoffman and his New Left Yippies held a few rallies at the square in the '60s. *E. 7th–10th Sts., btw Aves. A and B. Subway: 6 to Astor Pl.*

ALPHABET CITY As you head toward the East River to the blocks along Avenues A, B, C, and D you enter Alphabet City. It's predominantly a Puerto Rican community, once known as the heroin capital of New York. Gentrification and a police crackdowns on drugs have made it a somewhat safer place—**Avenue A** has been recently annexed by East Village hipsters and is crowded with bars, cafés, and cheap nosh spots. But Avenues C and D are still places to use caution (or avoid) after dark. On abandoned buildings throughout the neighborhood look for graffiti murals, beautiful and poignant. Many eulogize members of the community who have fallen to gang violence. A towering sculpture built from old motorcycles, hubcaps, 55-gallon drums, half a rowboat, and wound with iridescent pink ribbon stands on Avenue B at E. 2nd Street. A 30-foot-tall sister sculpture, of welded-together children's toys, stands on Avenue C between E. 5th and 6th streets.

Other landmarks to look for: **Red Square** (Houston St., btw Aves. A and B) is a redbrick high-rise with a gloriously beaming statue of Vladimir Lenin (plundered from Russia after the fall of Communism) on its roof. The bland, blocklike **First Houses** (E. 3rd St., at Ave. A), built in 1935, have the dubious distinction of being the first public-housing projects in the entire country.

LOWER EAST SIDE

In the century before the Beats carved out their own special little neighborhood, the East Village, for radical' politics and experimental art, everything east of Broadway and from 14th Street south to Canal Street was considered the "Lower East Side." Today it's roughly confined by Houston Street to the north, the Bowery to the west, and Canal Street to the south. Almost every ethnic group to arrive in America has spent some time here: Italians, Eastern-European Jews, Russians, Ukrainians, Germans, Greeks, and Poles in the 1880s, and more recently Africans, Puerto Ricans, Chinese, Dominicans, Filipinos, Indians, and Koreans. Wander its streets and you can find octogenarian Senegalese playing dominoes, overhear a heated argument about the meaning of this or that verse in the Talmud, or purchase Spanish-language comics at a corner newsstand.

Despite Alphabet City's economic troubles, there's a sense of community here that many other neighborhoods in the city totally lack. On street corners, elderly Puerto Rican men play dominoes, children chase each other on beat-up banana bikes, and homeless young punks gather together to panhandle for the price of a forty.

Although waves of immigrants fresh from Ellis Island made this the most crowded neighborhood in the world around 1915, lately it's become nearly deserted. Impoverished artists and funksters have started drifting south from the East Village in search of cheaper rents and greater pathos; they're responsible for the downmarket hip bars and cafés that have recently sprung up along **Ludlow Street** and **East Houston Street**. *Subway: F to Second Ave.*

ESSEX STREET AND THE JEWISH COMMUNITY In the '20s a half million Jews comprised one of the largest ethnic enclaves on the Lower East Side. Many Jewish shops, delis, and temples still line Essex Street, particularly its intersection with **Hester Street**. An unparalleled junk shop, **Israel Wholesale** (21 Essex St., at Hester St., tel. 212/477–2310) supplies the diaspora with menorahs 'n' more. Buy your yarmulkes at **H&M Skullcap Company** (46 Hes-

Tenement Buildings

Tenements, cheap to build and easy to maintain (or neglect), were considered the perfect solution to the city's 19th-century immigration boom. Early tenements were typically six-story buildings with four tiny, windowless apartments per floor, and no indoor plumbing, heating, gas, or electricity. To afford rent, as many as 20 people would cram into each apartment—crowded, dangerous, and depressing as hell. Muckraking journalists like Jacob Riis and Stephen Crane helped expose the desperate conditions of tenement dwellers, leading to reforms in the 1870s and 1900s that mandated basics like ventilation, plumbing, and electricity. You can still see tenement buildings all over the Lower East Side; notice that the style of the time dictated that even low-cost housing come with ornate Italianate facades.

The fascinating Lower East Side Tenement Museum (see Museums and Galleries, below) has two carefully re-created tenement buildings with displays on the actual families that once lived here. The museum also offers weekly neighborhood walking tours for $10–$15, a must if you're into the history of the Lower East Side.

The Lower East Side, Little Italy, and Chinatown

Bleecker St.
E. 1st St.
Houston St.
Orchard St.
Ludlow St.
Essex St.
Norfolk St.
Suffolk St.
Stanton St.
Forsyth St.
Eldridge St.
Allen St.
Rivington St.
Broadway
Lafayette St.
Prince St.
Cleveland Pl.
Mulberry St.
Mott St.
Elizabeth St.
The Bowery
Chrystie St.
Sara D. Roosevelt Park

LOWER EAST SIDE

Delancey St.
Broome St.
Spring St.
Crosby St.
Kenmare St.
Broome St.
Grand St.

LITTLE ITALY

Grand St.
Howard St.
Lafayette St.
Hester St.
Canal St.
Sew
Pa
Walker St.
Centre St.
Baxter St.
Mulberry St.
Canal St.
Forsyth St.
Division St.
Pike St.

CHINATOWN

White St.
Bayard St.
Pell St.
Doyers St.
Division St.
East Broadway
Henry St.
Madison St.
Market St.
Franklin St.
Columbus Park
Mott St.
Mosco St.
Chatham Square
Oliver St.
Catherine St.
Monroe St.
Cherry St.
Water St.
Leonard St.
Catherine La.
Hogan Pl.
Worth St.
Foley Square
Pearl St.
Kent Pl.
Park Row
St. James Pl.
James St.
Federal Plaza
Duane St.
Elk St.

CIVIC CENTER
Reade St.
Cardinal Hayes Plaza
Pearl St.

B, D, F, Q
N, R
N, R
J, M
J, M, Z
J, M, Z
B, D, Q
F
F

Lower East Side
CBGB & OMFUG, 1
Eldridge Street
Synagogue, 12
Essex Pickles, 14
Gertel's Bakery, 13
Lower East Side
Tenement
Museum, 15
Orchard Street
Bargain District, 17
Schapiro's
Winery, 16

Little Italy
Ferrara, 3
D&G Bakery, 2
San Gennaro
Church, 6
Umberto's Clam
House, 4

Chinatown
Buddhist
Temple, 10
Chinatown Fair, 8
Confucius Plaza, 11
First Shearlith Israel
graveyard, 7
Pearl River
Department Store, 5
Quong Yuen Shing
& Co., 9

92

The Lower East Side, Little Italy, and Chinatown

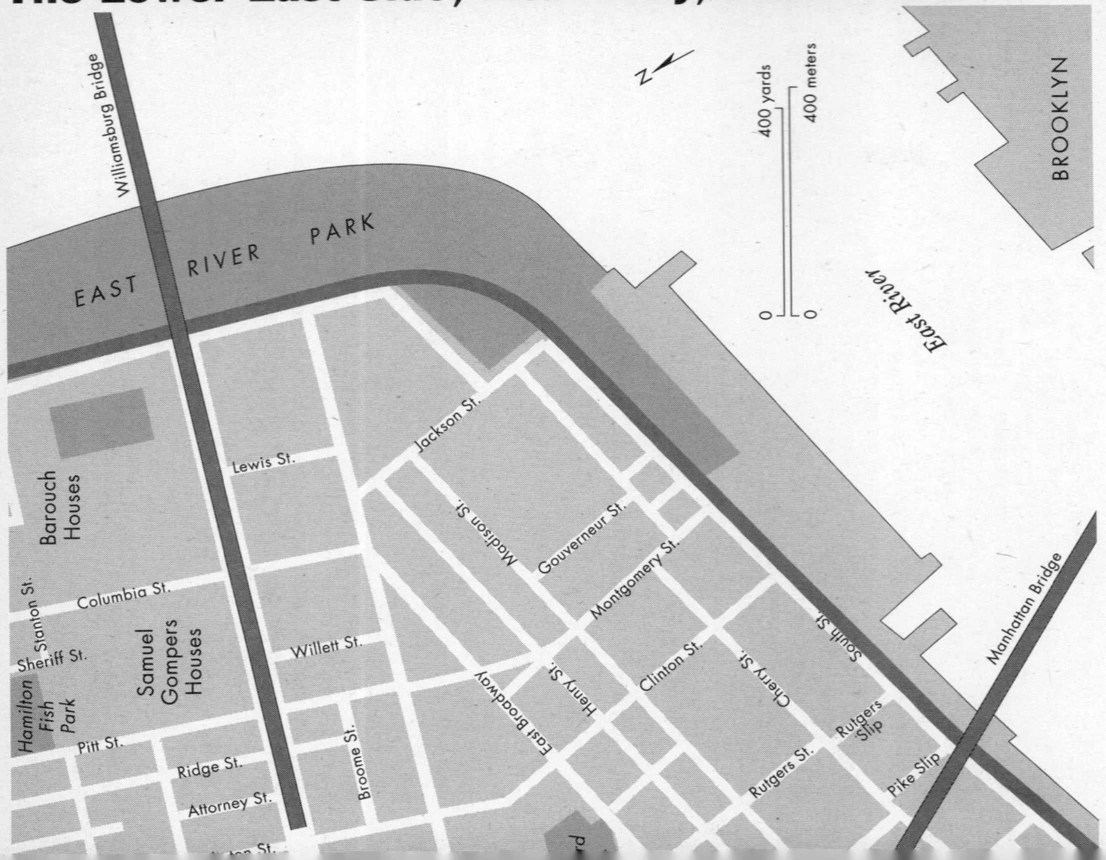

Williamsburg Bridge
EAST RIVER PARK
BROOKLYN
400 yards
400 meters
0
0
East River
Barouch Houses
Lewis St.
Jackson St.
Madison St.
Gouverneur St.
Montgomery St.
Columbia St.
Stanton St.
Sheriff St.
Samuel Gompers Houses
Willett St.
Hamilton Fish Park
Pitt St.
Ridge St.
Attorney St.
Broome St.
East Broadway
Henry St.
Clinton St.
Cherry St.
South St.
Rutgers Slip
Rutgers St.
Pike Slip
Manhattan Bridge

ter St., near Essex St.), or some rich kosher confections at **Gertel's Bakery** (53 Hester St., at Essex St., tel. 212/982–3250). **Essex Pickles** (35 Essex St., btw Grand and Hester Sts., tel. 212/254–4477) sells 'em straight from the barrel and is an essential New York experience.

➤ **SCHAPIRO'S WINERY** • Also worth a visit is America's first kosher winery. Though it's been around since 1899, Schapiro's will never steal the thunder from France's Châteauneuf-du-Pape; the original Schapiro's slogan was SO THICK YOU CAN ALMOST CUT IT WITH A KNIFE. The old-time store doles out free samples (Sundays 11–5) and offers free half-hour tours of its cellars from September to Passover on Sundays; call for exact times. *126 Rivington St., btw Essex and Norfolk Sts., tel. 212/674–4404. Subway: J, M, or Z to Essex St.*

➤ **ELDRIDGE STREET SYNAGOGUE** • Four blocks west of Essex Street is one of the Lower East Side's largest and grandest remaining Jewish temples. The Eldridge Street Synagogue, which is currently being restored as a cultural heritage center, remains open for interesting guided tours, given every Sunday on the hour noon to 4, and by appointment Tuesdays–Thursdays. Tours cost $4, $2.50 for students. *12–16 Eldridge St., at Canal St., tel. 212/219–0888. Subway: J, M, or Z to Essex St.*

ORCHARD STREET BARGAIN DISTRICT Orchard Street is lined with old-time mom-and-pop stores selling ersatz leather goods, linens, bootleg tapes, fabrics, "designer" watches, clothing, housewares, and just plain junk. Originally, immigrants came here to hawk buttons or heirloom diamonds or whatever else they owned. Scores of New Yorkers still come for cut-rate prices, or at least to wander: Where else can you hear bargaining in every tongue from Polish to Farsi to Hindi? Most shops are closed on Saturday—but that's okay. The big deal is Sunday, when Orchard Street is closed to traffic between Houston and Hester streets and the whole area takes on the air of an exotic bazaar. Between April and December, free **walking and shopping tours** (tel. 212/995–VALU) of the district are given on Sundays at 11 AM; meet at Katz's Delicatessen (Ludlow and Houston Sts.). *Subway: F to Second Ave.; walk 4 blocks east.*

LITTLE ITALY

Welcome to Little Italy. Did you expect to find Mafiosi chasing down narrow streets, like in Scorcese's *Mean Streets*? Or stoops filled with wizened old women in black, passing the days with talk of the Old Country? Maybe you expected to catch Italian-American actors like Tony Danza, Danny Aiello, and Robert DeNiro slurping down cannolli and espresso at a café? Sorry. All of that went *arrivederci* a long time ago, *bambino*. At the turn of the century, Piedmontese, Neapolitan, Genoan, Sicilian, Tuscan, and Calabrian settlements filled the blocks south of Houston Street; in 1932, an estimated 98% of the area's inhabitants were of Italian heritage. Though technically the neighborhood still occupies a corridor between Lafayette Street and the Bowery, from Houston Street south to Canal Street, in reality, Chinatown's continuing expansion has swallowed most of traditional Little Italy. What's left is confined to the blocks along **Mulberry Street**.

If you want to see a thriving Italian-American community populated by Italian Americans, not tourists, hop a subway to Carroll Gardens in Brooklyn or Arthur Avenue in the Bronx.

The best time to visit is during the 10-day **Feast of San Gennaro** (tel. 212/226–9546), a rollicking party held every mid-September to honor the patron saint of Naples. Streets are closed to traffic, decorated with tinsel, then packed with game booths and vendors of Italo-snacks. It's officially sponsored by the **San Gennaro Church** (113 Baxter St., near Canal St.), though just last year a few embarrassing Mob connections were discovered, causing a major scandal. In June is the smaller **Feast of St. Anthony of Padua**. For more on both, *see* Festivals, in Chapter 1.

What you get on Little Italy's main drag is a lot of souvenir shops sandwiched between tourist-filled trattorias and sidewalk cafés; looming above are the tenement buildings into which immigrant families once crowded. It's a street for strolling, gawking, and inhaling the aroma of garlic and olive oil, but you'll need an appetite to explore. The neighborhood's most famous landmark is **Umberto's Clam House** (*see* Little Italy, in Chapter 4), a restaurant that looks authentically

Italian—and was in fact where Mafia don Joey Gallo was fatally surprised by hit men in 1973, during a birthday dinner with family. He had the scungili. **Ferrara** (*see* Cafés and Coffee Bars, in Chapter 4) is a 100-year-old pastry shop. It's a truly wonderful place to eat tiramisù and sip cappuccino, even if you're sitting next to some bloke who thinks the Grand Canal is a sewage treatment plant in the Bronx. Also on Grand Street, the **Alleva Dairy** (188 Grand St., at Mulberry St., tel. 212/226–7990) has been selling its homemade mozzarella for over a century. Finally, **D&G Bakery** (45 Spring St., near Mulberry St., tel. 212/225–6688) is one of the last coal-oven bakeries in the United States. Everyone agrees that their bread is some of the best in the city, and they start selling it daily at 8 AM. *Subway: 6 to Spring St.*

CHINATOWN

When you walk into Chinatown, you'll know it: It's like magically being transported from Manhattan to Shanghai. Everywhere its streets are crowded, bustling, and vibrant; shopkeepers' signs and billboards are all written in Chinese characters, and sidewalk markets offer buckets of live fish, stacks of alien-looking vegetables, and bundles of refrigerated chicken feet. Even the smells are different, courtesy of street vendors serving up steaming chow mein and conch dumplings. Around half of the city's population of 300,000 Chinese live here; some 55% of its residents speak little or no English. In recent years, a flood of immigrants from Thailand, Korea, Vietnam, Taiwan, and especially Hong Kong have settled beyond the traditional boundaries of Chinatown and swallowed parts of Little Italy and the Lower East Side. **Canal Street** (which was once really a canal), formerly Chinatown's northern barrier, is now one of the busiest streets in the neighborhood and lined with interesting shops; check out the **Pearl River Department Store** (277 Canal St., at Broadway, tel. 212/431–4770) for kimonos and Maoist postage stamps. *Subway: J, M, N, R, Z, or 6 to Canal St.*

Other streets great for wandering include **Mott Street**, **Pell Street**, and **Bayard Street**; the intersection of Mott and Pell streets is the heart of Chinatown. On Mott Street you'll find the sleazy arcade **Chinatown Fair** (*see* Cheap Thrills, *below*); the super-cool curio shop **Quong Yuen Shing & Co.** (32 Mott St., at Mosco St., tel. 212/962–6280); and, across the street, the **Church of the Transfiguration**, a Georgian structure with Gothic windows and a Chinese Catholic congregation. Mass is said in Cantonese, Mandarin, and English. If Christianity's not your thing, you can always cruise the gift shop at the nearby **Buddhist Temple** (Pell St., at Mott St.). If you're looking for a place to chill, check out **Columbus Park** (Bayard St., btw Baxter and Mulberry Sts.). Where this tiny, paved park stands was once a tough, 19th-century slum of Irish and German immigrants.

CHATHAM SQUARE Eight different roads converge at Chatham Square, causing vehicular and pedestrian nightmares aplenty. On the center island is the **Kim Lau Arch**, a memorial to the Chinese Americans who died defending the United States in foreign wars (good luck getting across the street to take a closer look). North of the square, where Bowery and Canal Street come together, is called **Confucius Plaza**, possibly because a spectacular statue of Confucius stands guard. At the statue's base you'll find a long, thought-provoking quote from the 2,000-year-old wise man's treatise, *The Chapter of the Great Harmony (Ta Tung)*. Just south of Chatham Square on St. James Place you'll find the **First Shearlith Israel graveyard**, which was the first Jewish cemetery (1656) in the United States.

SOHO

Several of SoHo's streets have been spiffed up with quaint Belgian cobblestones, just like Europe. Or Disneyland.

SoHo (so-named because it's the area SOuth of HOuston Street), formerly industrial and now high-wattage hip, shed its working-class roots not so long ago. In the mid-19th century this was a light-industry district, with makers and sellers of goods like china, furs, textiles, glass, and lace; shops and factories and even sweatshops were housed in grand **cast-iron buildings** (*see box, below*). Unfortunately, the overcrowded area caught fire so frequently it was dubbed "Hell's Hundred Acres"; as late as 1962 a City Club of New York study called it "commercial slum number one." In the '70s, the city's restless population of artists—always looking for large, cheap, well-lit spaces—defied zoning laws to move into SoHo's run-down and

WEST VILLAGE

Leroy St.

Clarkson St.

W. Houston St.

King St.

Charlton St.

Vandam St.

Spring St.

Dominick St.

Broome St.

Canal St.

Watts St.

Desbrosses St.

Vestry St.

Laight St.

Hubert St.

Moore St.

Franklin St.

TRIBECA

Harrison St.

Jay St.

Staple St.

Independence Plaza

Washington Market Park

Chambers St.

Warren St.

Murray St.

Hudson River Park

West Side Hwy./West St.

Greenwich St.

Washington St.

Hudson St.

Varick St.

Downing St.

Ave. of the Americas (Sixth Ave.)

MacDougal St.

Sullivan St.

Thompson St.

West Broadway

Wooster St.

Greene St.

Mercer St.

Broadway

Crosby St.

Lafayette St.

Baxter St.

W. Houston St.

Prince St.

Spring St.

Broome St.

Grand St.

Howard St.

Canal St.

Lispenard St.

Walker St.

White St.

Franklin St.

Leonard St.

Worth St.

Thomas St.

Duane St.

Reade St.

Duane Park

Federal Plaza

City Hall Park

Church St.

West Broadway

Ericsson Pl.

Holland Tunnel Entrance

Holland Tunnel Exit

SOHO

B,D,F,Q

N,R

C,E

A,C,E

N,R

1,9

1,9

1,2,3,9

A,C

N,R

440 yards
400 meters

N

Alternative Museum, **7**

Ghostbusters' headquarters, **14**

Guggenheim Museum SoHo, **4**

Haughwout Building, **10**

Institute for Contemporary Art/Clocktower Gallery, **17**

King of Greene Street, **9**

Museum for African Art, **6**

New Museum of Contemporary Art, **5**

New York City Fire Museum, **18**

Queen of Greene Street, **11**

TriBeCa Film Center, **13**

Art Galleries

Art in General, **15**

The Drawing Center, **8**

Franklin Furnace 112, **16**

Holly Solomon, **2**

Leo Castelli, **3**

Paula Cooper, **1**

Thread Waxing Space, **12**

abandoned warehouses. By the '80s it was all over: Zoning laws changed, art-collecting debu-
tantes moved in, loft prices soared into the millions. Today the smallish, walkable neighborhood (which encompasses only 40 blocks from Houston Street south to Canal Street and from
Lafayette Street west to Sixth Avenue) is the epitome of postmodern chic. An amalgam of
black-clad art dealers, models, artists, celebrities, and other Beautiful People rush in and out
of galleries, bistros, and boutiques all day long. Some New Yorkers have lately taken to refer-
ring to the area as "like a shopping mall." This is not a compliment.

Naturally, SoHo is packed with zillions of galleries (*see* Museums and Galleries, *below*), which
look intimidating and in fact sell paintings you will never, ever be able to afford. Relax. No
one's going to object to your looking, and many complement whatever's currently hanging at
the Guggenheim, MoMA, or Met. Besides, they're free. Not surprisingly, artsy SoHo also brims
with artsy museums: The **New Museum of Contemporary Art**; the **Guggenheim Museum SoHo**;
the **Alternative Museum**; and the **Museum for African Art**. For more info on each, *see* Museums
and Galleries, *below*.

SoHo's shops offer clothing and furnishings and even toothbrushes so beautiful they could qualify as objets d'art, too. Of course they're priced accordingly. Great for wandering and window-
shopping are the blocks along **Prince Street**, **Spring Street**, and **West Broadway**, where you'll
find hip Euro-style boutiques like **Agnès B.** (116 Prince St., tel. 212/925–4649). But don't
max out your credit cards just yet: There are a few affordable things to buy in SoHo, provided
you find the right corner. On **Broadway** south of Spring Street you'll find vintage- and second-
hand-clothing stores, while vendors at the small vacant lot on the corner of Wooster and Spring
streets sell cheapie clothes and trinkets. For more info, *see* Chapter 5.

TRIBECA

Despite what you may have inferred from a certain much-hyped-but-short-lived TV drama of the
distant past, TriBeCa (a name savvy real-estate developers dreamed up for the TRIangle BElow
CAnal Street) does not crackle with illicit sex and spectacular crimes. Actually, as Manhattan
neighborhoods go, it's fairly sleepy. Like SoHo, this was historically a commercial neighborhood, once filled with fish-packing plants and chemical manufacturers. Like SoHo, its ware-

Cast-Iron Buildings

You know how used-car lots put out lots of flags and balloons to attract customers?
Well, the shop and factory owners of the 19th century wanted big, showy buildings with
large windows for that exact same reason. Between 1860 and 1890 most of these four-
to six-story buildings were made of cast iron, which was cheaper, stronger, and easier
to work with than brick. Cast iron could be molded to mimic any style—Italianate, Victorian Gothic, neo-Grecian, Second Empire, Star Wars, whatever. Even buildings that
housed sweatshops had beautiful façades with fantastic embellishments. Kind of a
depressing thought, isn't it?

Some of the finest remaining cast-iron buildings in the world are on Greene Street
between Canal and Grand streets: The "Queen of Greene Street" (28–30 Greene St.) is
only surpassed by its colossal neighbor the "King of Greene Street" (72–76 Greene St.).
The "Parthenon of Cast Iron," the Haughwout Building (488 Broadway), was originally a
china and glassware business with an exterior inspired by a Venetian palazzo. Inside, it
contained the world's first commercial passenger elevator, a steam-powered device
invented by Elisha Graves Otis.

houses and factories were all but abandoned in the 1960s. Like SoHo, they were recolonized as residential lofts by artists in the '70s, grew trendy in the '80s, and are now affordable only to investment bankers. Like SoHo, it still has its share of cool art galleries (see Museums and Galleries, below) and artsy shops, even if many of the artists have moved elsewhere. **The Institute for Contemporary Art/Clocktower Gallery** (see Museums and Galleries, below) houses a few lucky artists and their works. Unlike SoHo, TriBeCa (bounded to the north by Canal Street, to the east by Broadway, to the south by Chambers Street, and to the west by the Hudson River) has a tendency to shut down entirely on weekends. But you can still have some fun.

You can cover TriBeCa's attractions in an afternoon, really: Along Broadway, White Street, and Thomas Street are cafés, restaurants, and some shops, many housed in charmingly detailed cast-iron buildings from the late 1800s. Follow White Street across West Broadway to Moore Street; the firehouse (114 Moore St.) you'll see was **Ghostbusters' headquarters** in the two movies of the same name. Do not disturb the firemen. A bit farther west is Robert DeNiro's **TriBeCa Film Center** (375 Greenwich St., at N. Moore St.), a movie-production complex housed in an old coffee-and-tea warehouse. You might even see the Big Guy himself dining at his restaurant downstairs, **TriBeCa Grill** (see Chapter 4). Farther south, interesting residential areas to explore include **Staple Street** (barely an alley) and **Jay Street**. Nearby **Duane Park** (Duane St., btw Staple and Hudson Sts.) has been preserved since 1800 as a calm, shady triangle; it is still surrounded by cheese, butter, and egg warehouses. In contrast, **Independence Plaza** (Greenwich St., near Harrison St.) is a bunch of ugly '70s high-rises. If it weren't for a bunch of building-hugging preservationists, the entire neighborhood would now look like that. At the southern edge of TriBeCa is **Washington Market Park** (see Parks and Gardens, below). On Saturdays a dozen or so vendors gather to sell fresh flowers, vegetables, fish, and baked goods (see Greenmarkets, in Chapter 4). Of course, it's not as cool as Bear Market, which flourished around these parts in the early 19th century. Then, you could buy wild game and caviar.

LOWER MANHATTAN

In Lower Manhattan, behemoth glass-and-steel skyscrapers lie mere blocks from ancient churches and cobblestone alleys. Walk a few blocks and it will seem like every building has a plaque recalling some event from the past quarter of a millennium. It was here, after all, that the Nieuw Amsterdam colony was established by the Dutch in 1625; the city did not really expand much above Canal Street until the middle of the 19th century. Today, this tiny section of Manhattan is a global financial center, and swarms of businesspeople clutching cellular phones crowd its sidewalks on weekdays. You can practically hear the wheels of commerce grinding, and the spirit of the place is pretty infectious—you might get struck with the urge to put on a power tie and renounce socialism if you stay too long. On evenings and weekends, however, the streets are eerily empty of everyone except tourists (and the handful of crazy New Yorkers who come down to Rollerblade the empty streets). Don't expect to find open restaurants, bars, bodegas, or even hot dog vendors after 5 PM or on weekends.

New York City's lights are beautiful at night, aren't they? Imagine how it must have looked when the world's first electrical generating station lit up Manhattan like a birthday cake on September 4, 1882. A plaque marks the spot of the former station at 40 Fulton Street.

Streets in Lower Manhattan were laid out back when heavy traffic was defined as a dozen yoked oxen pulling wagons. So, besides **Broadway**, which ends its 17-mile run down the length of Manhattan at **Bowling Green** (see Parks and Gardens, below), there really isn't a main drag. The most famous of lower Manhattan's labyrinthine streets is Wall Street (see box, Wonder Wall, below). **Pearl Street** was actually a shoreline drive before more land was reclaimed from the harbor. **Fulton Street** is named for Robert Fulton, whose steam ferry (the first in the world) carried passengers and cargo between Manhattan and Brooklyn.

At the very tip of Lower Manhattan is **Battery Park** (see Parks and Gardens, below), named for the battery of cannons that was originally placed along the shore to scare off those nasty Brits. It offers awe-inspiring views of the harbor. Stop by the visitors center at **Castle Clinton National Monument** to look at historical exhibits or pick up ferry tickets to Ellis Island and the Statue of

Liberty (*see* Major Attractions, *above*). Castle Clinton has also held jobs as an island fort (land-fill has now made it part of Manhattan) and an immigration depot (nearly eight million immigrants passed through here).

The best way to see Lower Manhattan's sights is to follow the Heritage Trail. This self-guided tour winds through the streets of Lower Manhattan, passing important stuff like the New York Stock Exchange, Tweed Courthouse, and Castle Clinton. You can pick up the maps and brochures you'll need to start your tour at City Hall, the South Street Seaport, or Castle Clinton in Battery Park; just look for Heritage Trail kiosks. City Hall also offers free interactive video machines that dispense info on Lower Manhattan sights, City Hall history, and mass transit options. For more info on the Heritage Trail, call 212/767–0637.

Besides being the place where Michael Milken types sell their soul to the devil for pocket change and golden parachutes, Lower Manhattan is home to some fascinating museums: the **National Museum of the American Indian**, **New York Unearthed**, **Fraunces Tavern**, the **South Street Seaport Museum**, and the **Museum of American Financial History**. For more info, *see* Museums and Galleries, *below*. And don't forget to check out that massive magnet to terrorists and tourists alike, the World Trade Center (*see* Major Attractions, *above*).

NEW YORK STOCK EXCHANGE (NYSE) This hoary hall of high finance, the largest securities exchange in the world, had humble beginnings: Originally Wall Street traders were not tasseled-loafer types, but local merchants who gathered to buy and sell stocks under the shade of a nearby buttonwood tree (which has long since become firewood). In its earliest incarnation, stocks were called out and bid on one at a time. These days, the "Big Board" is capable of handling up to one trillion shares of stock per day, and when the NYSE sneezes, prime ministers in far-off countries murmur nervous "bless you"s. The NYSE's current home is a grand 1903 building with an august Corinthian entrance—a fitting temple to the almighty

Wonder Wall

Back in the 1650s, when hostile Indian territory started around 40th Street, Dutch settlers built a protective wooden stockade around the northern outskirts of their settlement. The colony grew so quickly they bagged the wall in 1699, but the name stuck to the street that followed. Today, Wall Street is both an actual street and a shorthand name for the vast, powerful financial community that clusters around the New York and American stock exchanges. While captains of industry, robber barons, and social Darwinists have long revered this street, radicals have cursed it as the heart of capitalist wrongdoing. Not surprisingly, when a horse-drawn wagon loaded with explosives detonated on September 16, 1920, in front of what is now Federal Hall, it was quickly blamed on anarchists bent on disrupting world financial markets. The noontime blast killed 30 and wounded 100, making it the deadliest American bombing of the century—until Oklahoma City in 1995. However, several bystanders (perhaps with cooler heads) testified that the wagon belonged to an explosives company who carelessly abandoned it. No culprits were found, and the explosion remains a mystery to this day.

The real Wall Street, you might be surprised to know, is only ⅓ of a mile long and not much wider than an alley. On all sides it's surrounded by unbelievably tall buildings. To best experience this trippy Grand Canyon effect, stand at the corner of Wall Street and William Street. Then look up. Subway: 4 or 5 to Wall St. (at Broadway). Also: 2 or 3 to Wall St. (at William St.).

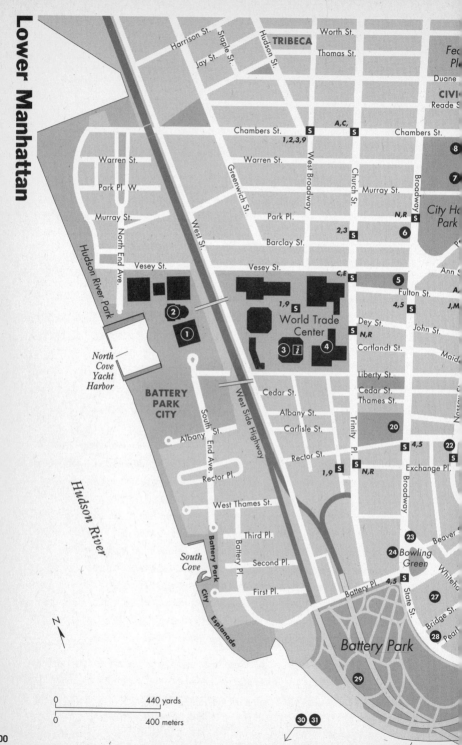

Lower Manhattan

TRIBECA

Harrison St.
Jay St.
Staple St.
Hudson St.
Worth St.
Thomas St.

Fed
Ple

Duane

CIVI
Reade S

Chambers St.   **S** 1,2,3,9   A,C,   **S**   Chambers St.

Warren St.
Warren St.

Park Pl. W.

Murray St.
Murray St.

Park Pl.   2,3 **S**   **6**

Barclay St.

Vesey St.   Vesey St.   C,E **S**

North End Ave.
Greenwich St.
West Broadway
Church St.
Broadway

City H
Park

8

7

N,R **S**

5
Fulton St.   A,
4,5 **S**   J,M
Ann S

West St.

Hudson River Park

North Cove Yacht Harbor

2
1

BATTERY PARK CITY

South St.
North End Ave.

Albany

Rector Pl.

West Side Highway

Cedar St.
Albany St.
Carlisle St.

Rector St.

West Thames St.

Third Pl.

Second Pl.

First Pl.

Battery Park City

South Cove

1,9 **S**   World Trade Center

3 **i**   **4**

Dey St.   **S** N,R
Cortlandt St.

Liberty St.
Cedar St.
Thames St.

Trinity Pl.

20

John St.

Maid

Nassau

S 4,5
22
S

Exchange Pl.

1,9 **S**   **S** N,R   Broadway

23

24 Bowling Green

Whiteha

27

Battery Pl.   4,5 **S**   State St.

Bridge

28 Pearl

Esplanade

Battery Park

29

Hudson River

N

0   440 yards
0   400 meters

30 **31**

Brooklyn Bridge, **14**

Castle Clinton National Monument, **29**

Charging Bull Statue, **23**

City Hall, **7**

Commodities Exchange, **4**

Criminal Courts Building, **13**

Ellis Island, **31**

Federal Hall National Memorial, **21**

Federal Reserve Bank, **19**

Fraunces Tavern, **25**

Fulton Fish Market, **15**

National Museum of the American Indian, **27**

Municipal Building, **10**

Museum of American Financial History, **24**

New York County Courthouse, **12**

New York Stock Exchange (NYSE), **22**

New York Unearthed, **28**

Pier 16, **17**

Pier 17, **16**

St. Paul's Chapel, **5**

Statue of Liberty, **30**

South Street Seaport Museum, **18**

Surrogate's Court, **9**

Trinity Church, **20**

Tweed Courthouse, **8**

U.S. Courthouse, **11**

Vietnam Veterans Memorial, **26**

Winter Garden Atrium, **2**

Woolworth Building, **6**

World Financial Center, **1**

World Trade Center Observation Deck, **3**

KEY

i Tourist Information

dollar. Don't miss a trip to the glass-enclosed **visitors' gallery** overlooking the immense trading hall, from which you can peer down at the chaos of video monitors and 1,500 madly gesticulating brokers some 50 feet below. (A free multilingual tape explains all the action.) The glass was installed in 1967 after members of Students for a Democratic Society staged a protest here, throwing $1 bills onto the trading floor. Same-day visitors tickets are issued from 9 AM on a first-come, first-served basis; to get one, arrive before 1 PM. *20 Broad St., at Wall St., tel. 212/656–5168. Subway: 4 or 5 to Wall St. Also: J, M, or Z to Broad St. Admission free. Open weekdays 9:15–3:15.*

TRINITY CHURCH The Trinity Church you're looking at now was built in 1846 on the site of the 1697 original. For 50-odd years it was the tallest building in the city, but today it's like a dollhouse in the shadow of the World Trade Center's towers. Trinity's medieval-looking sanctuary doesn't hold a candle to the dark Gothic ambience of Grace Church (*see* West Village, *above*) or the colossal grandeur of St. Pat's (*see* Midtown, *above*), but the 2-acre graveyard's a fascinating jumble of crumbling headstones. At rest here are notable dead folk like Alexander Hamilton (thanks to Aaron Burr) and Robert Fulton. A free 45-minute tour of the church is given daily at 2 PM. *74 Trinity Pl., at cnr of Broadway and Wall St., tel. 212/602–0800. Subway: 4 or 5 to Wall St. Open weekdays 9–11:45 and 1–3:45, Sat. 10–3:45, Sun. 1–3:45.*

ST. PAUL'S CHAPEL Six blocks north of Trinity Church on Broadway, St. Paul's Chapel is the oldest (1766) surviving church in Manhattan; it was modeled after London's St. Martin-in-the-Fields. George Washington said his prayers here immediately after being sworn in as America's first president (look for his pew in the north aisle). Both Trinity and St. Paul's offer live music at lunch time (*see* Music, in Chapter 7). *Broadway, at Fulton St., tel. 212/602–0874.*

VIETNAM VETERANS MEMORIAL On a large brick plaza near the eastern end of Battery Park, you'll find a 70-foot-long, 16-foot-high wall of greenish glass. It's etched with letters, diaries, and poems written by servicemen and servicewomen during the Vietnam War, as well as excerpts from news dispatches and public documents. *Next to 55 Water St., just north of Broad St. Subway: N or R to Whitehall St. (South Ferry).*

FEDERAL HALL NATIONAL MEMORIAL Federal Hall, built as a Customs House in 1842, is a mishmash of Europe's greatest hits: Its Doric-columned entrance is modeled after the Acropolis in Athens, and its rotunda is modeled after the Pantheon in Rome. Add to that a statue of George Washington (who was sworn in as president on this spot in 1789) that would look more at home in Washington, D.C. Inside, you'll find a few exhibits on New York and Wall Street. The original building served as our nation's great capitol building until the whole bureaucracy packed off to Philadelphia in 1790. Free concerts are given on Federal Hall's steps Wednesdays at 12:30. *26 Wall St., at Nassau St., tel. 212/264–8711. Subway: 2 or 3 to Wall St. Also: J, M, or Z to Broad St. Admission free. Open weekdays 9–5.*

FEDERAL RESERVE BANK Shakespeare may have said "all that glitters is not gold," but when you're in a room with enough gold to buy most medium-sized nations, you may beg to differ. The Federal Reserve Bank's got over 10,325 tons of the stuff (equal to one-seventh of the gold ever mined) in a vault carved from solid bedrock 80 feet below street level. Most of it belongs to foreign nations, but the United States lets them store it here for free. Yes, this is the bank that Jeremy Irons's character robbed with such ease in *Die Hard With a Vengeance*. No, such a thing would not be possible in real life. You can take the fascinating, free, one-hour tour, however, if you call for a reservation at least one day in advance. Tours are given weekdays four times daily. *33 Liberty St., btw Nassau and William Sts., tel. 212/720–6130. Subway: 2 or 3 to Wall St. Admission free. Reservations required.*

THE CHARGING BULL STATUE Soon after the stock-market crash of 1987, playful Italian artist Arturo DiModica dumped a 3½-ton bronze statue of a charging bull in front of the New York Stock Exchange under cover of night. It dismayed stock brokers (who didn't need reminding that the bull market of the '80s was over), but it irked city officials even more. So the statue was "temporarily" parked just north of **Bowling Green** (*see* Parks and Gardens, *below*) until a buyer could be found. And there it stands. Facing north, up Broadway, the Bull menacingly crouches, nostrils flared, large enough to gore a city bus. Some feel the city's cool reception to this fine piece of public art has to do with the bull's gargantuan genitals—tourists seem to take more pictures of the rear of the bull than the front. *Broadway, near Beaver St. Subway: 4 or 5 to Bowling Green.*

SOUTH STREET SEAPORT The closest thing Manhattan has to Disneyland is the 11-block South Street Seaport Historic District, with its snapping, brightly colored flags, smartly painted colonial-style buildings, and tethered flock of tall ships festooned with twinkling lights. If you think it looks a bit like Boston's Quincy Market, you're right; the same corporation "restored" them both. Over 12 million tourists from all over the world come to the Seaport annually to find they've been snookered into shopping at mall standbys like the Gap, Sharper Image, and J. Crew. That said, there are a few reasons to spend an hour or two here: The **South Street Seaport Museum** (*see* Museums and Galleries, *below*) and the **Fulton Fish Market** (*see below*) both give fascinating glimpses into the area's glorious past. This was, after all, a throbbing zone of brothels, boarding houses, gambling parlors, and saloons during the era of the clipper ship, and its cobblestone streets were once filled with randy sailors. Now, of course, it's the haunt of pimpled teens looking for the virtual-reality game center (hint: It's at Pier 17). As you walk along Fulton Street—which is closed to cars east of Water Street—look out for the historic 19th-century buildings of **Cannon's Walk Block** and **Schermerhorn Row**. The tiny white lighthouse you'll notice is the **Titanic Memorial** (Fulton and Water Sts.), commemorating the 1912 sinking of the "unsinkable" ocean liner. Check out **Pier 17** if you have a hankering for souvenir T-shirts and cheese fries, or **Pier 16** to see the tall ships, including the *Peking*, the second-largest sailing ship in existence. For info on boat tours that depart from Pier 16, *see* Guided Tours, *above. Tel. 212/SEA–PORT. Subway: J, M, Z, 2, 3, 4, or 5 to Fulton St. Also: A or C to Broadway–Nassau St.*

Herman Melville was born at 6 Pearl Street and worked as a customs officer on the Gansevoort Street pier while writing "Moby Dick."

➤ **FULTON FISH MARKET** • Strolling by, you might think that this is the smelliest place on earth. And you'd almost be right. Opened in 1831, Fulton is the oldest and largest fish market in the United States—but somewhere out there (we won't tell you where) there's a fish market that's *bigger* and *smellier*. Fishmongers at Fulton deal in a pungent 600 species of fish and shellfish, annually hauling in over eight million pounds. You'll need to arrive before 9 AM to catch the action; after that, the whole place shuts down. Behave nicely (i.e., don't gawk or ask fishmongers to take a picture of you with their fish) and you can sometimes score the catch of the day at wholesale prices. During summer, you can also hook up with a fascinating tour ($10). Tour guides will not answer questions about the fish market's alleged ties to the mob, and they suggest you don't wander around alone here before dawn. *South St., btw Fulton St. and Peck Slip, tel. 212/748–8590. Subway: J, M, Z, 2, 3, 4, or 5 to Fulton St. Also: A or C to Broadway–Nassau St. Market open daily midnight–9 AM. Tours given Apr.–Oct. on first and third Thurs. at 6 AM; reservations required.*

CIVIC CENTER New York City's civic center, just north of the financial district, is so filled with grand buildings it puts most of the nations' *state* capitals to shame, including the one in Albany, New York. But considering most New Yorkers' unshaken belief that their city is vastly superior to all others, does this really surprise you? You can spend a few hours wandering around the stately government and justice buildings, most of which have appeared in movies or TV. Besides those mentioned below, worth a quick look-see are the **New York County Courthouse** (40 Centre St.), backdrop for Henry Fonda's tirades in *12 Angry Men*; the spectacular Beaux Arts **Surrogate's Court** (31 Chambers St.); and the towering **U.S. Courthouse** (Foley Sq.). Though these buildings are all crowded together, it's easy to identify each: The U.S. Courthouse has imposing marble steps and a golden pyramid on top. The New York County Courthouse has imposing marble steps and a hexagonal shape (its pediment reads "The true administration of justice is the firmest pillar of good government"). Meanwhile, the grim-looking Art Deco **Criminal Courts Building** (100 Centre St.) got a bit part in Tom Wolfe's *Bonfire of the Vanities*. This is also where you'll find the entrance to the **Brooklyn Bridge** (*see* Major Attractions, *above*). *Subway: N or R to City Hall. Also: 4, 5, or 6 to Brooklyn Bridge–City Hall.*

➤ **CITY HALL** • Refreshingly, New York's City Hall looks more like a pastoral New England courthouse than a Politboro. Its exterior columns reflect the classical influence of Greece and

New York's most important federal court, housed in the U.S. Courthouse, is where Julius and Ethel Rosenberg were tried for espionage; where the owners of the "Titanic" were sued for gross negligence; where D. H. Lawrence's "Lady Chatterley's Lover" was declared obscene (and James Joyce's "Ulysses" was not); and where hotel queen Leona Helmsley was tried for tax evasion.

Rome, while its crowning statue of Lady Justice seems a nod to positive thinking. The whole thing was built in 1802 and touched up a bit in 1858, after fireworks launched from its roof set the top half aflame. At some point the back side was finished off with nice white limestone—city fathers originally assumed New York would never grow north of Fulton Street and had skimped on the part that wouldn't "show." Inside are the city council chambers and the offices of the mayor. Some rooms, including the Governor's Room, brimming with official tchotchkes, are open to the public. *Broadway, at Park Row. Subway: N or R to City Hall. Admission free. Open weekdays 10–4:30.*

➤ **CITY HALL PARK** • The triangular park surrounding City Hall started life as the town common and has seen its share of hangings, riots, and demonstrations. Look for the statue of Nathan Hale (hanged as a spy by the visiting Brits) on the Broadway side. **Park Row**, the street bordering the hypotenuse side of the triangle, is itself pretty historic. From the mid-19th to early 20th century it was dubbed "Newspaper Row" because most of the city's 20 or so daily papers had their offices here. A statue of Benjamin Franklin (who was, after all, a printer) stands in tribute across the street from the park near Pace Plaza.

➤ **TWEED COURTHOUSE** • The Tweed Courthouse, named after legendary "Boss" William Magear Tweed, stands north of City Hall in City Hall Park (*see above*). The swaggering, 300-pound Tweed, who wore an enormous diamond in his shirtfront, was adored by the poor as a do-no-wrong Robin Hood. This while he was apparently embezzling some $10 million of the $14 million budgeted to build the courthouse. The truth eventually caught up with Tweed and he died, ironically, in a jail that had earlier been a pet construction project. Peek inside the courthouse (which now houses municipal offices) to see its magnificent seven-story rotunda. *52 Chambers St., btw Broadway and Centre St. Subway: N or R to City Hall. Admission free. Open weekdays 9–4:30.*

➤ **WOOLWORTH BUILDING** • Rising 792 feet above the street like a Gothic church on steroids, the so-called Cathedral of Commerce was the world's tallest building when it opened in 1913. The finest in Gothic design is what Frank W. Woolworth wanted and got when he ponied up $13.5 million in cash to have architect Cass Gilbert build a suitable headquarters for his Woolworth Company (which is still the sole tenant). It's got gargoyles. It's got flying buttresses. It's also got one of the most ornate entryways ever constructed by a perfectly sober man. As you enter, notice on your left the two sculptures set into arches in the ceiling: One is of elderly F. W. Woolworth pinching his pennies, and the other is of Cass Gilbert holding a model of the building you are standing in. *233 Broadway, at Park Pl. Subway: N or R to City Hall.*

➤ **MUNICIPAL BUILDING** • This was the city government's first skyscraper, and if you've been paying any attention at all to this book, you know something of such monumental importance could only be entrusted to the architectural firm of McKim, Mead & White. And so, in 1914, it was. In the world of *Batman* the Municipal Building was stunt double for "Gotham City Police Headquarters." In the real world, it's where New Yorkers go to pay parking fines, obtain marriage licenses, and get hitched in civil ceremonies. You can make a quick buck if you hang around on weekdays with a Polaroid camera and offer to capture the moment for ill-prepared newlyweds. *1 Centre St., near entrance to Brooklyn Bridge. Subway: 4, 5, or 6 to Brooklyn Bridge–City Hall.*

BATTERY PARK CITY Battery Park City is connected to the World Trade Center (*see* Major Attractions, *above*) by a pair of pedestrian walkways spanning West Street. There's another, deeper connection, too: Developers needed someplace to stick all the extra dirt (about 1 million cubic yards of it) they had lying around after they dug the foundation for the World Trade Center's whopping twin towers. Rather than filling a barge and floating it to Jersey, they added landfill to lower Manhattan, and, voilà, Battery Park City was born. Battery Park City *is* like a separate city, sort of, with over 5,000 residents and 20,000 workers. It's just not a very exciting one to visit. The best thing about it is the 1.2-mile **Battery Park City Esplanade**, which runs along the Hudson River. It offers those rarest of rare things in lower Manhattan, trees and open space, plus stellar views of the Statue of Liberty and New Jersey's "Gold Coast." The **World Financial Center** (West St., btw Vesey and Liberty Sts., tel. 212/945–0505) dominates the rest of the landscape with its four geometric-capped towers, each 33 to 51 stories high. They're some of the least offensive modern architecture in the city and serve as world headquarters for companies such as American Express and Merrill Lynch. On the concourse level you'll find shops and restaurants, plus the gorgeous, glass-walled **Winter Garden Atrium** (open daily 7 AM–1 AM). The 120-foot-tall vaulted atrium hosts free concerts, dance recitals, and art exhibits. *Subway: 1 or 9 to Cortlandt St. Also: C or E to World Trade Center.*

The Outer Boroughs

When most people think of New York, they think of Manhattan as "The City," and Brooklyn, Queens, the Bronx, and Staten Island as one big peripheral blob—the sticky, brown caramel surrounding the real Big Apple. While Manhattan Island admittedly contains most of the sights that the city is known for, it's only one of the five boroughs (counties) that comprise New York City. Almost 80% of New York City's population *doesn't* live in Manhattan, and many will assure you that a trip to New York really isn't complete without a trip to the outer boroughs. After all, what could be more indicative of the city's diversity than a morning spent at the high-tech New York Stock Exchange, and an afternoon out in a sleepy Bronx fishing village, where shop owners leave signs saying GONE TO THE BEACH in their windows?

Even if your visit to New York is only a short one, there is no excuse for spending all your time on Manhattan Island: Most sights in Brooklyn, Queens, and the Bronx are less than 40 minutes away by subway, and the 20-minute, 50¢ ferry ride to Staten Island is a treat in itself. Even the most distant destinations, like City Island in the Bronx (an hour away), are definitely worth the schlep for those interested in expanding their horizons beyond the asphalt grid.

Many museums, parks, and historical sights in the outer boroughs warrant a special trip: the **Bronx Zoo**, **Coney Island**, **Prospect Park**, the **Brooklyn Museum**, **Yankee Stadium**, and the **American Museum of the Moving Image**, to name a few. Lesser-known gems include **Wave Hill** estate (where Franklin Roosevelt, Mark Twain, and Toscanini each lived); the **Steinway & Sons Piano Factory** (where you can watch a single piece of wood being shaped into a grand piano); the **Jacques Marchais Museum** (home to the largest private collection of Tibetan art outside Tibet, personally blessed by the Dalai Lama); and the Russian neighborhood of **Brighton Beach**. Additionally, the outer boroughs are where you'll find New York City's only **beaches**; for more info, *see box* New York City, Land of Skyscrapers and Sunny Beaches?!, *below.*

BROOKLYN

Hardly Manhattan's wimpy sidekick, Brooklyn is a metropolis in its own right, full of world-class museums, spacious parks, landmark buildings, five-star restaurants, and lively ethnic neighborhoods. In fact, it's the most populous of all the boroughs, with 2.3 million residents; even if it were sheared from the rest of New York, it would still be among the 20 largest cities in the United States. It's no wonder that an intense and long-standing rivalry exists between Brooklyn and Manhattan, a rivalry that recently led Brooklyn-born newspaperman Pete Hamill to refer to the 1898 unification of Brooklyn with the rest of the city as "the Great Mistake."

Not only does Brooklyn boast more residents, but more people visit it than any of the other outer boroughs, particularly the charming 19th-century neighborhoods of Brooklyn Heights, Cobble Hill, and Carroll Gardens. Manhattan residents frequently make the trip to visit Park Slope for the outstanding Brooklyn Museum, Botanic Gardens, and sprawling Prospect Park; others continue south to Coney Island for its beach boardwalk and Cyclone roller coaster. Even after hitting the biggie sights though, you've still got a hell of a lot of interesting territory to cover. For up-to-date listings of Brooklyn's cultural events, museum and gallery exhibits, street fairs and festivals, and walking and bike tours, the quarterly *Meet Me in Brooklyn* (30 Flatbush Ave., Suite 427, New York, NY 11217, tel. 718/855–7882, ext. 4, fax 718/802–9095) can't be beat. Write for a copy, or pick one up at the New York Convention and Visitors Bureau (*see* Useful Organizations, in Chapter 1). The best place to start a tour of Brooklyn is at the **Brooklyn Historical Society** (*see* Museums and Galleries, *below*) in Brooklyn Heights, which has been collecting weird and wonderful facts about the borough and its citizens since 1863.

BROOKLYN HEIGHTS "All the advantages of the country, with most of the conveniences of the city." So ran the ads for a real-estate development that sprang up in the 1820s just across the East River from downtown Manhattan. Brooklyn Heights (named for its enviable hilltop position) was New York's first suburb, linked to the city first by ferry and later by the mighty Brooklyn Bridge. In the 1940s and 1950s, the neighborhood was said to be home to the city's largest number of writers outside the Village, among them Carson McCullers, W. H. Auden, Arthur Miller, and Truman Capote. Today, Brooklyn Heights still has its share of famous scribes (keep an eye out for Norman Mailer), but the main reason to come here is to walk timeless streets lined with immaculate buildings, many dating back to the 1800s.

The main thoroughfare in Brooklyn Heights is **Montague Street**, which offers cafés, pubs, and plenty of prosperous-looking real-estate offices. Here you'll find the **Church of St. Ann and the Holy Trinity** (157 Montague St., at Clinton St., tel. 718/875–6960), which boasts the first stained-glass windows made in America (older windows were imported from Europe or were cheap substitutes made by painting over panes of plain glass). *Subway: 2 or 3 to Clark St. Also: M, N, or R to Court St.; or 2, 3, 4, or 5 to Borough Hall.*

Wander a few blocks north of Montague Street and you'll encounter unusual street names like Cranberry, Pineapple, and Orange. The names were bestowed by a Miss Sarah Middagh, who despised the practice of naming streets for the town fathers.

Just north of Brooklyn Heights proper is the up-and-coming Fulton Ferry landing area, where Robert Fulton's steam ferry once arrived carrying passengers from Manhattan. Though the ferry is gone, **Old Fulton Street** is getting cooler by the day as new restaurants, cafés, and bars spring up. The area is also dotted with old warehouses and Federal-style row houses, all watched over by the towering Brooklyn Bridge. In the vaults under the bridge look for the **Brooklyn Anchorage** (Hicks and Old Fulton Sts., tel. 718/802–1215), a funky art gallery/performance space with a stellar medicinal herb garden out front. If you're looking for a place to chill, cruise north to the **Empire Fulton Ferry State Park** (*see* Parks and Gardens, *below*). *Subway: A or C to High St./Brooklyn Bridge.*

➤ **BROOKLYN HEIGHTS PROMENADE** • From any one of the antique benches along this ⅓-mile, cobbled waterfront promenade, you can enjoy stunning views of the Lower Manhattan skyline, the South Street Seaport, and the majestic Brooklyn Bridge. If you're the kind of person who hates lovey-dovey, lip-locked couples, stay far away on moonlit summer nights. On the 4th of July, join the crowds here for the best views of the fireworks. *Subway: M, N, or R to Court St.; walk 1 block south to Remsen St., then west to the waterfront.*

COBBLE HILL AND CARROLL GARDENS A few blocks south of Brooklyn Heights, Cobble Hill is a slightly less manicured version of its northern neighbor, with equally charming old town houses. Most days you'll see an assortment of people on the residential streets, pushing strollers, walking dogs, or returning home laden with groceries. **Atlantic Avenue** (which separates Cobble Hill from the Heights) offers excellent window-shopping: It's lined with Middle Eastern spice shops and stores selling dirt-cheap antiques. If you've got a spare hour, you can hunt for **40 Verandah Place**, former home of novelist Thomas Wolfe, and **197 Amity Street**, where Jennie Jerome (Winston Churchill's mother) was born. *Subway: F or G to Bergen St.*

Still farther south, below Degraw Street, is the deeply Italian neighborhood of **Carroll Gardens**. Here you'll find octogenarians playing boccie in the parks or smoking and chatting on their stoops. On streets like **First Place**, **Carroll Street**, and **President Street**, the houses have tiny front yards, best seen around Christmas, when everyone puts out glow-in-the-dark nativity scenes and giant, plastic Virgin Marys. Your final stop should be the **Cammereri Brothers Bak-**

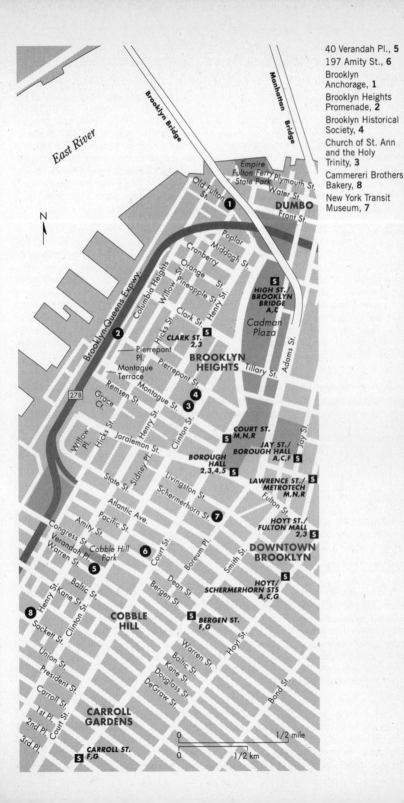

Brooklyn Heights, Cobble Hill, and Carroll Gardens

40 Verandah Pl., **5**
197 Amity St., **6**
Brooklyn Anchorage, **1**
Brooklyn Heights Promenade, **2**
Brooklyn Historical Society, **4**
Church of St. Ann and the Holy Trinity, **3**
Cammereri Brothers Bakery, **8**
New York Transit Museum, **7**

ery (502 Henry St., at Sackett St., tel. 718/852–3606), where Nicholas Cage slaved over a hot oven in *Moonstruck*. *Subway: F or G to Carroll St.*

DUMBO DUMBO—not Disney's flying pachyderm, but Down Under the Manhattan Bridge Overpass—is the place to go if SoHo's sterile, mall-like atmosphere has left you cold. Since the mid-1980s this has been a true struggling-artists' community, with turn-of-the-century brick industrial buildings, cobblestone streets crisscrossed with old railroad tracks, and the ever-present rumble of subway cars rattling across the Manhattan Bridge above. Needless to say, TV and film crews come here when they want "atmosphere." The best blocks to explore are north of **Front Street**, between Main Street and Hudson Avenue. Though you won't find any art galleries, there are several groovy art supply stores; check out **Chamber's Paper Fibers** (139 Plymouth St., btw Pearl St. and Anchorage Pl., tel. 718/624–8181) and **Pilot Pilot** (47 Pearl St., btw Plymouth and Water Sts.). DUMBO is also the international headquarters for the Jehovah's Witnesses—strange bedfellows for bohemian artists. *Subway: F to York St.*

FORT GREENE Bounded to the north by the East River, to the east by Vanderbilt Avenue, to the south by Atlantic Avenue, and to the west by Flatbush Avenue, Fort Greene is a neighborhood of brownstones and row houses, home to many of the city's African-American professionals, musicians, and artists. Among Fort Greene's residents is director Spike Lee; his store, **Spike's Joint** (1 S. Elliot Pl., at DeKalb Ave., tel. 718/802–1000), is full of clothing and movie memorabilia. In a nearby renovated firehouse you'll find Lee's production company, **40 Acres and a Mule** (256 DeKalb Ave.). To get a firsthand look at Fort Greene's artistic bent, check out the **Spiral Art Gallery** (637 Vanderbilt Ave., btw Prospect and St. Marks Pl., tel. 718/783–2891), which exhibits works by local African-American artists. Also worth your while is the **New York Experimental Glass Workshop** (647 Fulton St., near Flatbush Ave., tel. 718/625–3685), the only studio/gallery in New York devoted to glassblowing.

Beyond tiny, eclectic galleries, Fort Greene is home to a world-class avant-garde art space, the **Brooklyn Academy of Music (BAM)** (*see* Arts Centers, in Chapter 7). Adjoining BAM, the **Williamsburgh Savings Bank Tower** (1 Hanson Pl., btw Atlantic and Flatbush Aves.) is Brooklyn's tallest building at 512 feet. Completed in 1929, the tower was meant to signal Brooklyn's emergence as a commercial superpower. Of course these plans went down the toilet a few months later with the Black Tuesday stock market crash, leaving most floors standing empty for decades. Today the building's spectacular mosaic-tiled lobby is a fine place to use an ATM. *Subway: D, Q, 2, 3, 4, or 5 to Atlantic Ave.*

➤ **PRISON SHIP MARTYR'S MONUMENT** • A macabre chapter in Fort Greene's history is forever remembered at this 148-foot-tall monument, the world's tallest freestanding Doric column, which stands in shady **Fort Greene Park** (*see* Parks and Gardens, *below*). During the American Revolution, the Brits crowded their colonial prisoners into cattle ships moored in the bay just north of here; some 11,500 died. The corpses were dumped in trenches and continued, horribly, to wash ashore until 1792. *Subway: D, M, N, Q, or R to DeKalb Ave.*

WILLIAMSBURG Alternately an Orthodox Jewish neighborhood, a Latino community, and the home of hip young artists, the northern neighborhood of Williamsburg is suffering a delightful identity crisis that makes it one of New York's most interesting places to visit. To explore this mishmash, start at the **Bedford Avenue** subway station: The neighborhood around this part of Bedford Avenue feels positively small town, with an eclectic mix of organic-food stores, thrift shops, Polish butcher shops, and a few neighborhood bars. One of the more popular watering holes is **Mug's Ale House** (125 Bedford Ave., at N. 10th St.). Just north of Broadway is a cluster of Latino bodegas and cheap Puerto Rican and Mexican restaurants and coffee shops. Take note: Broadway runs underneath the elevated subway line and isn't a very pleasant place at night. *Subway: L to Bedford Ave.*

If you follow Broadway west to the water you'll find signs announcing LOFT FOR RENT, a good indication that you're entering Williamsburg's artist quarter—often called the "**Right Bank**." Artists and writers who've fled pretentious SoHo have been colonizing the industrial buildings near the water and under the ugly gray Williamsburg Bridge for the last 20-odd years. If you double back to Bedford Avenue and follow it south, you'll come to the heart of the second-largest Orthodox Jewish community in Brooklyn (the largest is farther east, in Crown Heights).

Lee Avenue, which runs parallel to Bedford Avenue, is Jewish Williamsburg's main street. Here you'll see men wearing identical black suits, prayer shawls, long beards, and black hats, alongside women with colorful but conservative dresses. Stop by the **Southside Kosher Bakery** (454 Bedford Ave., btw S. 9th and S. 10th Sts., tel. 718/218–8512) for a tasty kosher snack.

GREENPOINT The Polish community of Greenpoint (north of Williamsburg and just a stone's throw south of Queens) is one of the most thriving ethnic enclaves in the city. The main drag, **Manhattan Avenue**, is lined with Polish bakeries, Polish coffee shops serving up kielbasa and stuffed cabbage, and even a few Polish curio shops and clothing stores. Drop by **Zakopone** (714 Manhattan Ave., btw Nassau and Meserole Sts.) for weird souvenirs and framed photos of the Pope. **Stodycze Wedel** (722 Manhattan Ave., at Meserole St., tel. 718/349–3933) has sparkling clean shelves full of imported Polish candies, crackers, and other gourmet items.

There are lots of beautiful old churches in and around Greenpoint, but the 1916 **Cathedral of the Transfiguration of Our Lord** (N. 12th St. and Driggs Ave.), a Russian Orthodox church with five huge copper-clad onion domes, takes the cake. Although Greenpoint's ethnic flavor is its main draw, the neighborhood's many parks and tree-lined residential streets have earned it the nickname, "The Garden Spot of the Universe." Ironically, most of the greenery was paid for by Greenpoint's metal industry: In Greenpoint's shipyards, the Union's *Monitor* was given its iron sidings, and the 100-ton *Iwo Jima* memorial (now just outside Washington, D.C.) was cast at the **Bedi-Rassy Foundry** (227 India St.). *Subway: G to Greenpoint Ave.*

BEDFORD-STUYVESANT Bed-Stuy, as it's commonly known, is an inland neighborhood lying south of Williamsburg and just east of Fort Greene. Spike Lee fans will recognize it as the place where the shit went down in *Do the Right Thing*, and it's true that drugs and crime have plagued the area since the 1960s. These days, however, a community revival's afoot, and more and more African-American professionals are gentrifying the area. It's worth an afternoon visit to see some of the finest Victorian brownstones in the city, most of which line Chauncey, Dacatuer, MacDonough, and Hancock streets. Other notable sights include the **Billie Holiday Theater** (1368 Fulton St., at New York Ave., tel. 718/636–0918), a showcase for African-American playwrights and actors; and the **Simmons African Arts Museum** (1063 Fulton St., btw Classon and Grand Aves., tel. 718/230–0933), with a small collection of contemporary African artwork. If your empty belly takes precedence over cultural endeavors, try the **North Carolina Country Kitchen** (1991 Atlantic Ave., at Saratoga Ave., tel. 718/498–8033) for authentic southern cooking. In July, keep an eye out for the **African Street Festival**, a weeklong block party celebrating black culture. *Subway: A or C to Nostrand Ave.*

PARK SLOPE With row after row of gorgeous, meticulously maintained brownstones, Park Slope will either charm you into thinking you've entered a 19th-century village, or annoy the hell out of you with its ostentatious display of wealth. Indeed, this is one of Brooklyn's most sought-after addresses. Aside from the handsome architecture, the main draw here is **Prospect Park** (*see* Parks and Gardens, *below*), a 526-acre urban playground with a zoo, concert grounds, a boathouse, and more.

Park Slope is a center for the city's lesbian community, earning it the nickname "Dyke Slope."

But there's more to Park Slope than Prospect Park. You'll find pockets of hipness along **Seventh Avenue**, which is lined with cool restaurants and eclectic shops selling everything from rare Pez dispensers to pulp fiction paperbacks to Thai ceremonial masks. Record buffs might want to check out **Holy Cow** (442 9th St., at Seventh Ave., tel. 718/788–3631) for its selection of old vinyl. If you're an art fan, pay a visit to the **Brownstone Gallery** (76 Seventh Ave., at Berkeley Pl., tel. 718/636–8736), which generally displays the best of Brooklyn artwork. Also consider making a trip into the nearby neighborhood of Crown Heights to visit the fascinating **Chassidic Art Institute** (375 Kingston Ave., btw Carroll and Crown Sts., tel. 718/774–9149), which specializes in the folk art of Hasidic Jews. *Subway: D or Q to Seventh Ave.*

While you're in Park Slope you'll also want to check out **Grand Army Plaza** (Flatbush Ave., at Eastern Pkwy.) for its fantastic 80-foot-tall **Soldiers' and Sailors' Memorial Arch**—Brooklyn's answer to the Arc de Triomphe. On Saturdays a sprawling farmers' market sets up at its base. Also on the plaza are the stately **Brooklyn Museum** (*see* Museums and Galleries, *below*), the

PARK SLOPE

GRAND ARMY PLAZA 2,3

Grand Army Plaza

EASTERN PARKWAY 2,3

St. Johns Pl.

FRANKLIN AVE. 2,3,4,5

Brooklyn Botanic Garden

7TH AVE./ PARK SLOPE F

Prospect Park West

Flatbush Ave.

Washington Ave.

Franklin Ave.

Bedford Ave.

15TH ST./ PROSPECT PARK F

Prospect Park

PROSPECT PARK D,Q,S

Empire Blvd.

Prospect Lake

Ocean Ave.

Flatbush Ave.

Bedford Ave.

Rogers Ave.

PARKSIDE AVE. D

Parkside Ave.

Parade Grounds

Prospect Expwy.

11th Ave.

Park Southwest

Carroll St.

President St.

1st St.

6th Ave.

7th Ave.

8th Ave.

9th St.

9th St. Bandshell, **4**
Boathouse, **11**
Brooklyn Museum, **7**
Brooklyn Public Library, **6**
Brownstone Gallery, **2**
Chassidic Art Institute, **9**
Holy Cow, **1**
Kate Wollman Rink, **10**
Long Meadow, **5**
Soldiers' and Sailors' Memorial Arch, **3**
Wildlife Conservation Center, **8**

Brooklyn Public Library (tel. 718/780–7700), and the entrance to the lovely **Brooklyn Botanic Garden** (see Parks and Gardens, below), a favorite springtime destination. On weekends from noon to 5 PM, you can ride for free on the old-fashioned trolley (tel. 718/965–8967) that runs between the Public Library, the Brooklyn Museum, the Botanic Garden, and several points in Prospect Park. Subway: 2 or 3 to Grand Army Plaza.

BAY RIDGE Bay Ridge, just south of Sunset Park, is characterized by posh circa-1915 homes and a large Scandinavian population. Before the subway ruined the neighborhood's exclusivity, Brooklyn's wealthiest lived in Bay Ridge, and a few of their spectacular waterfront mansions remain: the **Gingerbread House** (82nd St., near Narrows Ave.), in the style of a thatch-roofed English cottage, and the **Fontbonne Hall Academy** (9901 Shore Rd., near 99th St.), a huge mansion turned private girls' school. Your best bets for shopping and eating in Bay Ridge are along **Third Avenue** and **Fifth Avenue**, between 70th and 90th streets. Try **Nordic Delicacies** (6909 Third Ave., at 69th St., tel. 718/748–1874) for authentic Scandinavian deli food. On the first Sunday after May 17, the whole 'hood parties down at the annual **Norwegian Constitution Day Parade**, which runs along Fifth Avenue between 67th and 90th streets. Subway: R to 77th St.

CONEY ISLAND During the late 1800s the sandy beach of Coney Island (actually not a separate island) was New York City's golden riviera, and the resort hotels lining its 2-mile-long boardwalk were patronized by presidents and captains of industry. With the introduction of the 5¢ elevated line in the early 20th century, fancy hotels were replaced by penny arcades, roller coasters, and oddities like a hotel built in the shape of an elephant. During this period as many as one million people (nearly 20% of New York's population at the time) would flock to Coney Island on hot summer Sundays. After World War II, as more people were able to afford cars and head elsewhere, Coney Island began its decline. In what is now a no-man's-land west of the boardwalk you can catch a glimpse of the park's forgotten past: Look for the looming, vine-covered remains of the Thunderbolt roller coaster and the abandoned Parachute Jump (which once lured patriotic post-war riders with the claim that it was used to train GIs).

Despite its decline, there is still a lot of charm in Coney Island, though it's of the seamy carnival-show variety. Video arcades, go-carts, merry-go-rounds, and kiddie rides dominate the Midway, at the heart of which towers the 70-year-old **Cyclone** (Surf Ave., at W. 10th St., tel. 718/266–3434), a legendary roller coaster ($4) still considered one of the world's scariest. Of course, you could attribute a portion of the fright factor to the fact that the coaster's rickety old wooden tracks seem ready to fall apart with every carload of screaming teenagers. Near the Cyclone, the **Astrotower** ($2) is a Seattle Space Needle wanna-be, providing panoramic views of Coney Island and Brighton Beach. The circa-1920s **Wonder Wheel** is more akin to a very angry Ferris wheel—instead of gently circling you around, it hurls you back and forth, giving you the delicious feeling that you are about to fall to a certain death. For a demolition-derby disco experience, complete with flashing lights and pumping house music, head to the **Eldorado Auto Skeeter** (Surf Ave., btw W. 12th and Hendrickson Sts.).

Freak shows are another big attraction along the Midway, and yes, they've all got a "two-headed" baby and the "world's largest" rat. If you're gonna give in to curiosity, the **Coney Island Circus Sideshow** (on the boardwalk, at W. 12th St., tel. 718/372–5159) gives you the best value for your $3, with acts like the human blockhead and the sword-swallowing bearded lady. Note that due to NEA budget cuts, owner Dick D. Zugin (a Yale graduate) may soon have to close up shop. Next door, the **Coney Island Museum** (99¢) has a funky hall of mirrors and a small café. North and west of the boardwalk is quite dodgy after dark, so stick to the well-lit Midway. *Subway: B, D, or F to Coney Island.*

➤ **NEW YORK AQUARIUM FOR WILDLIFE CONSERVATION** • This recently renovated aquarium (with a spiffy new politically correct name) may not be world-class, but don't tell that to the hordes of parents who tote their offspring here year-round. Activities include getting up close and personal with sharks and stingrays in their 90,000-gallon habitat; exploring **Sea Cliffs**, a coastal California habitat with playful sea otters; touching your slimy and spiky friends from the sea at **Discovery Cove**; or, at the **Beluga Whales** exhibit, pondering whether these intelligent marine mammals might be a tad pissed off that their entire world is limited to a 400,000-gallon tank. (Probably not, since recently two of the whales got pretty friendly and produced the first Beluga whale born in captivity). *Surf Ave. and W. 8th St., tel. 718/265–FISH. Subway: D or F to W. 8th St. Admission: $6.75. Open daily 10–5 (Memorial Day–Labor Day, weekends until 7). Wheelchair access.*

BRIGHTON BEACH Long before Brighton Beach was immortalized in the Neil Simon play-turned-movie, *Brighton Beach Memoirs*, it was just an old-fashioned Jewish community east of Coney Island, with lots of high-rise retirement towers lining the shore. These days, a flood of Russian, Ukrainian, and Georgian émigrés have earned it the nickname "Little Odessa." Along **Brighton Beach Avenue** (which runs under the rattling, rusting, elevated 'D' subway line) you'll find Russian merchants hawking fruit, bargain-priced caviar, lingerie, and Russian-language video tapes—it's an amazing scene. Stick around for nightfall, when many of the Russian restaurants (*see* Outer Borough Restaurants, in Chapter 4) along the avenue and on the boardwalk push their tables to the wall for a frenzied night of dancing and vodka drinking. *Subway: D or Q to Brighton Beach.*

SHEEPSHEAD BAY While Brighton Beach is Russian, neighboring Sheepshead Bay is an authentic Italian fishing community with a small-town, 1940s flavor. To get a real feel for the place, walk down **Emmons Avenue** (which runs parallel to the bay) and over the Ocean Avenue footbridge. Here you'll find old salts hunched over the sea wall, diligently fishing up tonight's dinner. Head to the north end of the pier to discover dozens of deep-sea fishing boats ready and willing to take you out for the day (if you can rally by around 7 AM) for the absurdly low price of $25, equipment and advice included; try the **Sea Queen** (tel. 718/646–6224). If you've literally missed the boat, you can sometimes purchase fish at the end of the day (lucky fishermen sell their catch from their boats). *Subway: D or Q to Sheepshead Bay.*

QUEENS

Most Manhattan residents only set foot in Queens en route to La Guardia or J.F.K. airport, but those who manage to get past the area's dull appearance will discover a few surprises. According to estimates, some 120 nationalities coexist in Queens (including people from Afghanistan, China, Colombia, the Dominican Republic, the Philippines, India, Pakistan, Bangladesh, Korea, Mexico, Uruguay, Argentina, Peru, Romania, Thailand, and Ireland), and the area's strong ethnic flavor is one of its main draws. A former British outpost, Queens was named for Queen Catherine of Braganza, wife of Charles II, the guy in charge when this area was plucked like a prized goose by eager British settlers (never mind that several American Indian tribes had lived here for centuries). Queens did its thing as an independent county until 1898, when it joined up with New York City. In its present-day incarnation, it's the largest of the city's five boroughs, accounting for a full third of the city's entire area. It's also the second most populous, surpassed only by Brooklyn.

Almost all of the sights in Queens are accessible by subway. Train rides take between 15 and 45 minutes from midtown Manhattan; the ride to the Rockaways takes more than an hour. The Greek community of Astoria lies over the Triborough Bridge from Manhattan, at the northwestern tip of Queens. Just south of here is the industrial center of Long Island City, which is emerging as a vital artists' community. To the east is the giant Flushing Meadows–Corona Park, bordered by Latino communities. Flushing, in the northeastern corner of Queens, is predominantly Asian. Near the center of the borough you'll find ritzy residential neighborhoods filled with Tudor-style houses and tree-lined streets, as well as stunning **Forest Park** (*see* Parks and Gardens, *below*). East of the park is the primarily African-American neighborhood of Jamaica, and beyond that is **Alley Pond Park** (*see* Parks and Gardens, *below*). To the south lies the uninhabited Jamaica Bay Islands, site of the 9,155-acre **Jamaica Bay Wildlife Refuge** (*see* Parks and Gardens, *below*), and the narrow, beach-lined Rockaway Peninsula.

ASTORIA Astoria, containing one of the largest Greek communities this side of the Adriatic, is packed with sidewalk cafés, family-run stores, and Greek tavernas offering live music and dancing. More recently, Colombian, Middle Eastern, and Thai immigrants have moved in and set up shop, but the Greek community still thrives along the old-fashioned blocks between **Broadway** and **Ditmars Boulevard**, from 21st Street to Steinway Street. *Subway: N to Broadway.*

If you're looking for a real behind-the-scenes experience, head for **Steinway & Sons Piano Factory**. On the free, two-hour tour you'll get to watch six hulking men make a $50,000 concert grand piano the old-fashioned (and scary) way, by bending and pressing 22-foot-long, ⅜-inch-

Brooklyn . . . Land of the Free and the Famous

Fact: One in seven famous Americans is from Brooklyn. If you're not convinced, consider this (very incomplete) list of famous Brooklynites, past and present:

Mickey Rooney, Jackie Gleason, George Gershwin, Lena Horne, Barbara Stanwyck, Spike Lee, Danny Kaye, Shelly Winters, Barbra Streisand, Neil Diamond, Buddy Hackett, Mary Tyler Moore, Woody Allen, Richard Dreyfuss, Neil Simon, Max Roach, Joan Rivers, Elliot Gould, Joseph Heller, Truman Capote, Maurice Sendak, Mike Tyson, John Steinbeck, Lenny Bruce, Harvey Fierstein, Eddie Murphy, Dom DeLuise, Thomas Wolfe, Bud Abbot, Philip Glass, Harry Houdini, Woody Guthrie, Barry Manilow, Alan Arkin, Henry Miller, Arthur Miller, Al Capone, Sandy Koufax, Isaac Asimov, Bobby Fisher, F. W. Woolworth, and W. E. B. DuBois.

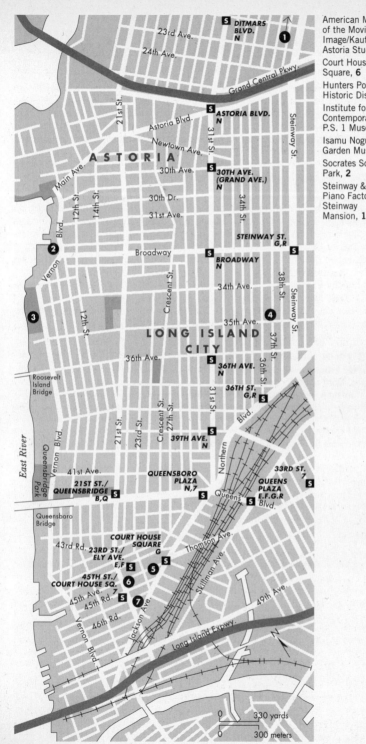

American Museum
of the Moving
Image/Kaufman–
Astoria Studios, **4**
Court House
Square, **6**
Hunters Point
Historic District, **5**
Institute for
Contemporary Art/
P.S. 1 Museum, **7**
Isamu Noguchi
Garden Museum, **3**
Socrates Sculpture
Park, **2**
Steinway & Sons
Piano Factory/
Steinway
Mansion, **1**

thick strips of maple into a curvy frame. Afterwards, visit the remains of the 400-acre company town that the original piano man William Steinway built for his workers in the 1870s; a row of workers' houses stands along 41st Street between 20th Road and 20th Avenue, not far from the imposing granite **Steinway Mansion** (18–33 41st St., btw Berrian Blvd. and 19th St.). *38th St. and 19th Ave., tel. 718/721–2600. Subway: N to Ditmars Blvd.*

But the really big deal in Astoria is movies: This was the center of the American motion-picture industry in the 1920s and '30s, until Hollywood took over. Gloria Swanson, W. C. Fields, and Claudette Colbert all got their starts at the **Kaufman-Astoria Studios** (36–11 35 Ave., at 36th St.), which is still used for major films like *The Age of Innocence*, *Scent of a Woman*, and the 1995 version of *Sabrina*, as well as for TV shows like *Sesame Street*. Peek through the windows (the actual studios are closed to the public) to see on-the-set stills of Rudolph Valentino, the Marx Brothers, and Maurice Chevalier, then head next door to the excellent **American Museum of the Moving Image** (*see* Museums and Galleries, *below*). *Subway: N to 36th Ave.*

LONG ISLAND CITY Until recently, the neighborhood just across the 59th Street (Queensborough) Bridge from Manhattan was known solely as a drab industrial wasteland of train yards, warehouses, and belching factories. Though its appearance is still pretty bleak, the area is home to a growing community of young artists who have fled SoHo and its outrageous rents. To get a feel for the Long Island City arts scene (plus great views of Manhattan), check out the **Socrates Sculpture Park** (*see* Parks and Gardens, *below*) and the **Isamu Noguchi Garden Museum** (*see* Museums and Galleries, *below*), both of which lie along the waterfront. Or cruise to **The Institute for Contemporary Art/P.S. 1 Museum** (*see* Museums and Galleries, *below*), a converted public school that houses a warren of galleries, studios, and performance spaces; it's closed for renovation, but will reopen in spring 1997. If you want to do a little gallery hopping, head to the intersection of **Vernon Boulevard** and **Jackson Avenue**.

Long Island City's business and historical districts also offer a few sights of interest. The **Hunters Point Historic District** (45th Rd., btw 21st and 23rd Sts.) consists of two uniform rows of houses from the 1880s; their solid Westchester stone facades, iron railings, and fancy cornices conjure up the Victorian era. At nearby 21st Street is a small park with a giant metal sculpture titled "Bigger Bird"—possibly a nod to the fact that the PBS children's program *Sesame Street* has been taped in the nearby neighborhood of Astoria for decades. From here, head down 21st Street to **Court House Square** (21st St., at 45th Ave.) and I. M. Pei's towering **Citicorp Building**. With 48 stories (663 feet) of green-tinted glass, it's the tallest structure in all of Queens, Brooklyn, and Long Island (of course, it'd literally be looked down upon in Manhattan). Across the street is the **New York State Supreme Court** (25–20 Courthouse Sq.), where murderer Ruth Snyder made history in 1928 as one of the first women to be executed in the United States. Together with her lover (a traveling corset salesman), she succeeded in murdering her husband, after seven bungled attempts, in order to collect a $95,000 insurance policy; for more details, rent Billy Wilder's *Double Indemnity*. *Subway: 7 to 45th Rd./Courthouse Sq. Also: 7 to Vernon Blvd./Jackson Ave.*

FLUSHING Settled by the Dutch in 1645 under the name of *Vlissingen*, Flushing today is home to sizable Korean, Chinese, Japanese, Indian, and Eastern European communities. The blocks around **Roosevelt Avenue** and the **Main Street** subway station are packed with wall-to-wall Asian shops and restaurants, including Hunan, Szechuan, Cantonese, Japanese, Korean, Taiwanese, Vietnamese, and Malaysian eateries; farther south on Main Street, the Indian community takes over. But there's more to Flushing than ethnic diversity: It's also one of New York City's most historically significant areas. Way, way back, before America was even a gleam in Washington's eye, this little village was a hotbed of religious debate. Quaker settlers, having been forbidden to worship in public, found a loophole in the governing patent that granted all villagers liberty of conscience. This finding was the basis for the religious freedom that is granted in the U.S. Constitution.

➤ **THE FLUSHING FREEDOM MILE** • All the important historical stuff in Flushing, including the surprisingly interesting **Bowne House** (*see* Museums and Galleries, *below*), is a short walk north of the subway station, in an area bounded by Parsons and Northern boulevards, Roosevelt Avenue, and Main Street. You can pick up maps and a self-guided tour brochure at the 1785 **Kingsland Homestead** (143–35 37th Ave., west of Parsons Blvd., tel.

718/939–0647), headquarters of the Queens Historical Society. While you're here, check out the **Weeping Beech Tree** in the garden out back; with a 14-foot trunk and an 85-foot branch spread, this hulking green giant looks virile enough to be the granddaddy of all American beech trees, which in fact it is. Planted in 1847 by an immigrant from Belgium, the tree is one of the two living landmarks in New York. (The other is not Ed Koch, but a magnolia tree in Brooklyn.) The nation's first nursery stood on this site, and today you'll still find rare trees throughout Flushing—golden larch, cedar of Lebanon, sassafras, mulberry, boxwood bush, and more. Three blocks away on Northern Boulevard, the shingled **Friends' Meeting House** (137–16 Northern Blvd.), in service since 1719, is the oldest house of worship in New York City. Turn up around 11 AM on a Sunday morn if you want to take part in a Quaker meeting. Across the street, the **Flushing Town Hall** (137–35 Northern Blvd., tel. 718/463–7700) houses a small art gallery/café, with live jazz ($10) on Thursday nights. *Subway: 7 to Main St.*

FLUSHING MEADOWS–CORONA PARK Once a city dump so desolate that F. Scott Fitzgerald referred to it as "a valley of ashes" in *The Great Gatsby*, Flushing Meadows–Corona Park is now a 1,255-acre park in northeastern Queens. As the 380-ton **Unisphere** (the largest known model of our beloved planet) in the center of the park attests, this was the site of two World's Fairs, in 1939 and 1964. Today there are a few good reasons to visit the site: For one, you can laugh at its sad, *Jetsons*-era attempts at space-age coolness. Skip the **New York Hall of Science** (47–01 111th St., at 46th Ave., tel. 718/699–0055), which also seems stuck in the days before the lunar landing, but consider a spin on the antique carousel ($1), said to be the fastest in the Northeast. Or check out the 9,335-square-foot model of New York City in the **Queens Museum of Art** (*see* Museums and Galleries, *below*), where you can also pick up maps and info on the rest of the park's attractions.

On a sunny day, the park offers plenty of outdoor diversions, including the tiny, 8-acre **Queens Wildlife Center** (tel. 718/271–1500), home to a bald eagle and other North American critters. For sports fans, there's Shea Stadium (home to the Mets) and the U.S.T.A. National Tennis Center, where the U.S. Open takes place every year (for more on both, *see* Chapter 9). For flower-lovers, there's the **Queens Botanical Garden** (*see* Parks and Gardens, *below*), which boasts the largest collection of roses in New York. At the southeastern end of the park you'll find the large, man-made **Meadow Lake** and the smaller **Willow Lake**. You can rent boats ($10 per hour) and bicycles ($6 per hour) from the boathouse (tel. 718/699–9596) at Meadow Lake. *Tel. 718/592–0711. Subway: 7 to Willets Point/Shea Stadium. Also: 7 to 111th St.*

JAMAICA The once-wealthy neighborhood of Jamaica slid into a funk around the turn of the century; **Jamaica Avenue**, which was once lined with country estates and gentleman's farms, became slowly overrun with fast-food restaurants, discount stores, and, in 1930, the world's first modern supermarket. Today, the largest African-American community in Queens (also home to many immigrants from South America and Asia) is experiencing something of a revival. The **Jamaica Arts Center** (161–04 Jamaica Ave., tel. 718/658–7400; closed July), housed in a landmark Renaissance Revival building, is worth checking out for its exhibits by artists of color, women artists, and artists outside the mainstream. Also worth a look is the fantastically gilded lobby of the **Tabernacle of Prayer** (Jamaica Ave., at 165th St.), a 1929 Art Deco movie palace turned fundamentalist church. Walk along the busiest section of Jamaica Avenue and you'll encounter the weirdly out-of-place **King Manor** (*see* Museums and Galleries, *below*), a Dutch-style farmhouse dating from the mid-1700s. If you're in Jamaica at lunchtime, the **165th Street Pedestrian Mall** is fantastic for strolling and snacking on beef patties ($1), a favorite West Indian treat.

THE BRONX

Burned-out tenement buildings, drug crimes, and general urban decay are what most people associate with the Bronx. While these images are true to some extent, New York City's northernmost borough is also home to some of the grandest mansions and greenest parks around, not to mention the much-loved **Yankee Stadium** (*see* Chapter 9), the famous Bronx Zoo, and the stunning **New York Botanical Garden** (*see* Parks and Gardens, *below*). The city's only mainland borough (the others are all on islands), the Bronx was first settled by Jonas Bronck, a Dane, in the 17th century. Legend has it that the Bronx got its name because other settlers

North Bronx

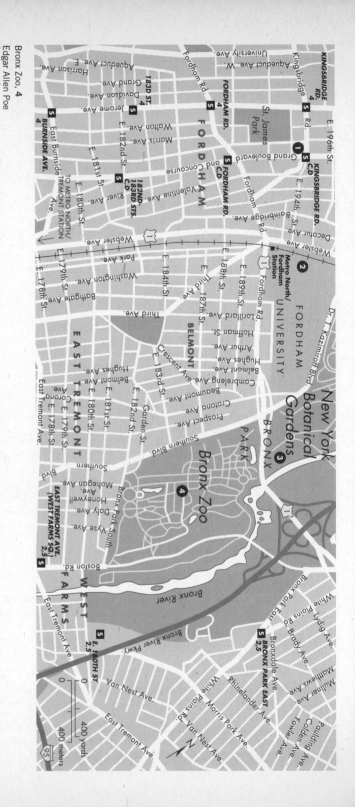

would say, "Let's go see the Broncks." (In fact, the Bronx River had its name long before the Bronck family came along.) Wealthy New Yorkers maintained rural retreats in the Bronx in the 19th century, when the area consisted of a picturesque patchwork of farms, market villages, and country estates. In the 1920s, the Bronx experienced a short-lived golden age: The new elevated subway line attracted an upwardly mobile population, and the **Grand Concourse** was fashioned as New York City's Champs-Elysées. But the Bronx declined as quickly as it had boomed; today, vestiges of its glory days are few and far between.

Aside from the Grand Concourse and the **Bronx Museum of the Arts** (*see* Museums and Galleries, *below*), the southwestern part of the Bronx is not the best place to be . . . unless, of course, you're a Yankee fan. Major attractions—the zoo, the botanical gardens, and the Italian community of Belmont—are clustered in Central Bronx. Riverdale, in the hilly, northwest corner of Bronx, is a wealthy community of estates, including Wave Hill (*see* Museums and Galleries, *below*). To the east, City Island is a quaint, slightly bohemian fishing community packed with boat repair shops and fish restaurants. The northern half of the Bronx is dominated by the vast **Van Cortlandt** and **Pelham Bay** parks (for both, *see* Parks and Gardens, *below*). And, if you're a big fan of the man who penned "The Raven," take a peek at the **Edgar Allen Poe Cottage** (*see* Museums and Galleries, *below*). Most Bronx sights are no more than 45 minutes from midtown Manhattan; Yankee Stadium is just a 15-minute ride. Within the Bronx, stick to subways and buses; this is not a place where you'd want to get lost on foot.

BRONX ZOO With 265 acres and more than 4,000 animals, this is the largest and most interesting of New York City's self-described "wildlife conservation centers." Most of the exhibits rely on moats rather than cages to keep animals (and humans) in their proper places, and are landscaped like natural habitats. A few exhibits you won't want to miss include **Wild Asia**, populated by Siberian tigers, elephants, rhinos, and sika deer (a species that was mistakenly declared extinct in 1977); **World of Birds**, where you can walk among your winged friends; and **World of Darkness**, a windowless building that reverses day and night so that you can see bats, leopard cats, and other nocturnal creatures in action. The zoo is also home to a troupe of around 16 gorillas, each with a unique personality. Free walking tours of the zoo are offered on weekends; call 718/220–5141 for reservations. *Bronx River Pkwy., at Fordham Rd., tel. 718/367–1010. Subway: 2 to Pelham Pkwy.; walk 3 blocks west. Also: Liberty Lines BXM11 Express Bus from midtown Manhattan; call 718/652–8400 for schedule and fares. Admission: $6.75, $3 children; free on Wed. Open weekdays 10–5, weekends 10–5:30.*

The Bronx Zoo strives to house animals in their natural habitats: Polar bears splash in Arctic pools, gibbons swing through the trees of a lush indoor rain forest, and lions lounge on their own personal Serengeti Plain.

A Trip to the South Bronx

The south Bronx, once a well-to-do neighborhood, has a sad history. After World War II industries began drifting out of New York City, forcing the many Bronx residents who depended on high-wage jobs in Manhattan to pick up and haul their possessions elsewhere. By the 1970s, some landlords took to torching their empty, run-down apartment buildings to collect the insurance money. Buildings rotted, crime flourished. Only recently have grassroots programs started to pull the south Bronx out of its long depression, and the Grand Concourse (its main drag) has once more flourished as a lively social strip. At one end of a four-block span (161 to 165 Sts.) you'll find the great "House that Babe Ruth Built," better known as Yankee Stadium; at the other is the Bronx Museum of the Arts. On Sunday afternoons, Joyce Kilmer Park (at 162nd St.) fills with salsa dancers and sellers of crafts for the Bronx Sunday Market.

BELMONT Though today's Belmont is populated mostly by African Americans and Hispanics, the short stretch of **Arthur Avenue** between 187th Street and Crescent Avenue remains the heart of an old Italian neighborhood, once home to more than 25,000 Italian Americans. The best time to visit is on a Saturday afternoon (the whole place shuts down on Sundays). Arrive hungry, since numerous bakeries, trattorias, and cafés (see Outer Borough Restaurants, in Chapter 4) line the streets, and tiny markets sell cured olives and giant slabs of salami. You can atone for your gluttony at the **Church of Our Lady of Mount Carmel** (627 E. 187th St., btw Hughes and Belmont Aves.) or drop by the **Catholic Goods Center** (630 E. 187 St., tel. 718/ 733–0250) for religious statuettes and Bibles in every tongue—Nigerian, Serbian, Albanian, and Creole, to name a few. Subway: D to Fordham Rd. (20 min); walk 1 mi east on E. Fordham Rd. to Arthur Ave., turn right and walk 3 blocks to E. 187th St. Also: Metro North to Fordham Rd. (10 min).

FORDHAM UNIVERSITY The 85-acre Fordham University campus is worth a look if you're visiting the botanical gardens (that is, if you can persuade the university's persnickety security guards to let you in). With its eerie Gothic-looking, ivy-covered buildings, the campus looks as if it should be populated only by cowled, medieval monks The university church, whose bells are said to have inspired for Bronx resident Edgar Allen Poe's poem, "The Bells," recall Fordham's origins as a Jesuit institution in the 1840s. Free one-hour campus tours are offered weekdays at noon and 2 PM. 441 E. Fordham Rd., at Webster Ave., tel. 718/817–4000. Subway: D to Fordham Rd. (20 min). Also: Metro North to Fordham Rd. (10 min).

CITY ISLAND City Island is probably the only place in New York where shop owners hang signs reading GONE TO THE BEACH. This mile-and-a-half long, half-mile-wide spit of land (connected by bridge to the rest of the Bronx) feels like a cross between ye olde New England fishing village and a California hippie commune from the '60s. First settled in the 1760s, the whole place might have dried up and blown away if it weren't for its highly profitable yacht-building industry (the Astors and Vanderbilts have shopped here) and dozens of boat-repair businesses. Today there's not much else going on here, which is precisely City Island's charm. Spend the day strolling along the marina, poking around the funky, ramshackle little shops, or scarfing fried seafood at seagull-infested picnic tables. Afterward, take a peek inside the **North Wind Undersea Institute** (610 City Island Ave., tel. 718/885–0701; open weekdays 10–5), whose ragtag collection includes whaling artifacts, scrimshaw art, and deep-sea diving gear (ask to see the video of Physty, the rescued sperm whale). At **Mooncurser Antiques** (229 City Island Ave., tel. 718/885–0302), you'll find a collection of 50,000 used LPs presided over by a bearded old eccentric. At the **Boat Livery** (663 City Island Ave., tel. 718/885–1843) you can grab a beer ($1) or bait and tackle (they're sold over the same counter), or rent a four-person dinghy ($20 per day) and row out into Pelham Bay. Subway: 6 to Pelham Bay Park (45 min). Also: Bus BX29 to City Island Ave. (20 min).

STATEN ISLAND

Ask New Yorkers what's fun to do in the Big Apple for 50¢ or less, and they'll either shake their heads and tell you to stop dreaming, or they'll brightly mention the ferry ride to Staten Island. Ask them what's on Staten Island and they'll stare blankly and shove off. This ignorance is infectious: Every day, hordes of tourists join commuters on the Staten Island Ferry (see below) for panoramic views of the Statue of Liberty, Ellis Island, and Lower Manhattan. Once there, most get right back on the next boat to Manhattan.

Staten Island is truly the forgotten borough. Though it's twice the size of Manhattan Island, its claims to fame (if it has any) are as the city's official garbage dump, and as the borough that is perpetually agitating to secede from New York City. The two are not unrelated: Islanders resent being dumped on (literally) and fear the environmental ramifications of having the world's largest landfill in their backyard. In addition, they resent paying New York City taxes, which they feel benefit Manhattan and the other boroughs far more than themselves.

Garbage dumps notwithstanding, Staten Island can be a lovely place to visit. It has more natural, unpaved areas than any of the other boroughs, including coastline beaches and the hiker's paradise, **High Rock Park** (see Parks and Gardens, below). It's also got a whole lot less

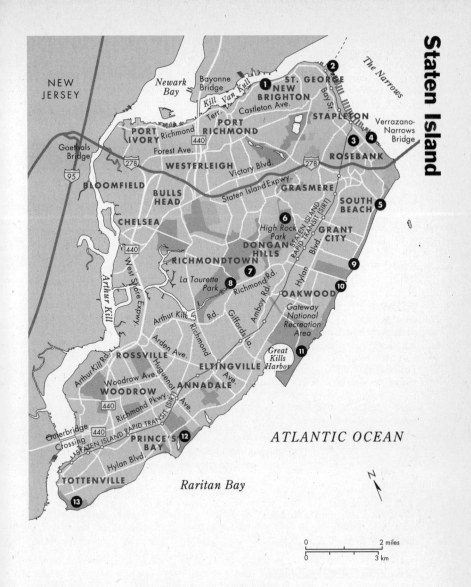

Staten Island

NEW JERSEY

Newark Bay

Bayonne Bridge

Kill Van Kull

Terr. Richmond

PORT RICHMOND

ST. GEORGE 1 **NEW BRIGHTON**

2

The Narrows

Bay St.

STAPLETON

Castleton Ave.

PORT IVORY

PORT RICHMOND 440

Forest Ave.

Goethals Bridge

95

278

WESTERLEIGH

Victory Blvd.

Staten Island Expwy.

278

ROSEBANK

3

4 Verrazano-Narrows Bridge

BLOOMFIELD

BULLS HEAD

CHELSEA

GRASMERE

SOUTH BEACH 5

High Rock Park

6

DONGAN HILLS

GRANT CITY

440

RICHMONDTOWN

7

La Tourette Park

8

Richmond Rd.

9

10

OAKWOOD

Hylan Blvd.

Arthur Kill

West Shore Expwy.

Arthur Kill Rd.

Richmond

Amboy Rd.

Giffords La.

Gateway National Recreation Area

ROSSVILLE

Arden Ave.

Huguenot Ave.

ELTINGVILLE

Great Kills Harbor

11

Woodrow Ave.

ANNADALE

Ave.

WOODROW

440

Richmond Pkwy.

STATEN ISLAND RAPID TRANSIT (SRT)

Outerbridge Crossing

440

STATEN ISLAND RAPID TRANSIT (SRT)

PRINCE'S BAY

12

Hylan Blvd.

TOTTENVILLE

13

ATLANTIC OCEAN

Raritan Bay

N

0   2 miles
0   3 km

Ferry Terminal, **2**

Alice Austen House, **4**

Conference House, **13**

Garabaldi–Meucci Museum, **3**

High Rock Park/ Todt Hill, **6**

Jacques Marchais Museum of Tibetan Art, **7**

Richmondtown Restoration/Staten Island Historical Society Museum, **8**

Snug Harbor Cultural Center, **1**

Beaches

Great Kills Park **11**

Midland Beach, **9**

New Dorp Beach, **10**

South Beach Park, **5**

Wolfe's Pond Park, **12**

people: The island's population in the late 1980s was comparable to Manhattan's in 1845. You'll find it's still got an old-time, rural feel, especially in the re-created 18th-century village of Richmondtown and in the 19th-century sailors' haunt of Snug Harbor. Oddly enough, Staten Island is also home to an excellent museum of Tibetan art, the **Jacques Marchais Museum of Tibetan Art**, as well as the **Conference House**, onetime meeting place of Benjamin Franklin and his revolutionary crew (for both, *see* Museums and Galleries, *below*).

If you do disembark the ferry on Staten Island, plan on spending at least half a day there, since the island is vast and the sights spread apart. From the **Ferry Terminal** (*see below*) you can catch a bus directly to Snug Harbor (20 min), Richmondtown (40 min), and most other sights. At the Ferry Terminal you can also pick up the Staten Island Railway (SIRT), which makes limited stops on its way to Totenville, at the south end of the island. Pick up bus maps and train schedules inside the terminal.

➢ **COMING AND GOING BY FERRY** • The Staten Island Ferry costs a bargain 50¢ round-trip, which you pay when you arrive in Staten Island. Ferries run 24 hours, departing every 15 minutes during morning and evening rush hours, hourly after 11 PM and on weekend mornings, and every 30 minutes most other times; call for current schedules. In Manhattan the ferry departs from the **Staten Island Ferry Terminal** in Battery Park (South St., near State St., Lower Manhattan; Subway 1 or 9 to South Ferry). Passengers disembark in Staten Island at the Ferry Terminal in St. George, on the northeastern tip of the island (from there it's easy to catch a bus or train to all of the island's attractions). The trip is 20–30 minutes one-way, but you'll be so busy gasping at the incredible views of the Manhattan skyline and the Statue of Liberty that you'll swear it's less than five minutes long. A tip: The newer boats are super-fast, but try to get a ride on one of the older ones, which have big open-air decks that are great for snapping photos. *Tel. 718/727–2508 or 718/390–5253.*

At the Ferry Terminal in Staten Island, you'll find a small museum of ferry paraphernalia, including antique ships' wheels and scale models of ferries. Check it out if you have a few minutes to kill.

SNUG HARBOR CULTURAL CENTER Once home to a colony of "aged, decrepit and worn-out sailors," Snug Harbor is now an 83-acre cultural center full of landmark Greek Revival and Victorian buildings, artists' workshops and studios, a pleasant **Botanical Garden** (tel. 718/273–8200), a **Children's Museum** (tel. 718/273–2060), and the **Newhouse Center for Contemporary Arts** (tel. 718/448–2500). Wealthy shipowner Robert Richard Randall founded the colony in 1831, and for the next 140 years it served as the nation's first maritime hospital and home for retired seamen. Free weekend tours (departing from the visitor center daily at 2 PM) will fill you in on the history of the colony. For snacks, head to **Melville's Cafe**, named in honor of Herman Melville's brother, who was once Snug Harbor's governor. *1000 Richmond Terr., tel. 718/448–2500. From Ferry Terminal, take Bus S40 (10–15 min). Museums open Wed.–Sun. noon–5; grounds open daily dawn–dusk.*

RICHMONDTOWN RESTORATION Sure, it sounds hokey: A living history museum with a bunch of people dressed in silly costumes and lots of 18th-century buildings. But the Richmondtown Restoration is so well done it's cool. Many of the buildings in this 100-acre village are over 200 years old; one you won't want to miss is the **Guyon-Lake Tysen House**, one of the best surviving examples of Dutch Colonial architecture anywhere in the country (stick around to see the authentic-looking scullery maids whip up snacks in a beehive oven). The **Voorlezer's House**, built in 1695, is thought to be the oldest elementary school in the country. Here the *voorlezer*, or lay minister, conducted church services and taught children how to read the Bible. You can also watch people weave baskets at the **Basketmaker's House**, or drop by an old print shop and a restored general store. Also in Richmondtown, the **Staten Island Historical Society Museum** (*see* Museums and Galleries, *below*) has a slew of surprisingly interesting historical stuff. Free tours of the village depart from the visitors center on the hour. *441 Clarke Ave., tel. 718/351–1611. From Ferry Terminal, take Bus S74 (45 min). Admission: $4, $2.50 students. Open Wed.–Fri. 1–5 (July and Aug., Wed.–Fri. 10–5, weekends 1–5).*

ROSEBANK The Italian community of Rosebank, centered around Tompkins and Bay streets near the Verrazano Bridge, has been around since the late 1800s. Besides trattorias, markets, and trim Catholic churches, it's got three really cool sights: The **Garibaldi–Meucci Museum** (*see* Museums and Galleries, *below*), which commemorates Rosebank's most famous residents; Alice Austen House (*see* Museums and Galleries, *below*), full of works by this photographer of the early 20th century; and the wonderful shrine to **Our Lady of Mount Carmel** (Amity St., at White Plains Ave.). The shrine is a fabulously gaudy thing, studded with garishly painted plaster statuettes of various saints, strings of light bulbs, and eternally burning candles. Reach it from Tompkins Avenue by following St. Mary's Street to White Plains Avenue and then turning right onto Amity Street. *From Ferry Terminal, take Bus S78 Tompkins Ave. (15 min).*

Museums and Galleries

Despite the recent rise of high-art quotients in metropolises like Los Angeles and Chicago, New York City is still the museum capital of the United States. And, New York being New York, overkill is key. Most cities would be ecstatic just to host the likes of the Metropolitan Museum of Art or the MoMA (*see* Major Attractions, *above*), but that's not nearly enough for New Yorkers. From the unabashedly Eurocentric Pierpont Morgan Library to the downright esoteric Jacques Marchais Museum of Tibetan Art, New York's museums and galleries successfully enshrine every imaginable object of human and nonhuman contrivance. Throw in an aircraft carrier, a preserved early-19th-century tenement, a giant collection of Fabergé eggs, and dozens of other collections large and small, and you'll begin to see why New York can rightly be considered the United State's museum capital. By some estimates, there are more than 150 museums in the city of New York. This chapter covers the best 73 of 'em.

Many of the city's blockbuster museums are conveniently clustered on Fifth Avenue between 82nd and 104th streets, also known as **Museum Mile** (*see* Manhattan Neighborhoods, Upper East Side, *above*). These include the **Solomon R. Guggenheim Museum**, **Frick Collection**, **National Academy of Design**, **Cooper-Hewitt National Design Museum**, **El Museo del Barrio**, **Goethe House**, **International Center of Photography (ICP)–Uptown**, **The Jewish Museum**, and the **Museum of the City of New York**. The behemoth **Metropolitan Museum of Art** (*see* Major Attractions, *above*) is also on Museum Mile, while the **Museum of Modern Art (MoMA)** (*see* Major Attractions, *above*) is in Midtown.

In addition to pretty pictures and fascinating artifacts, you'll find that museums offer guided tours, lectures, films (*see* Movie Houses, in Chapter 6), concerts (*see* Music, in Chapter 7), dance performances, and more. Often, these activities are free with museum admission, a deal that can turn even the most dedicated museum-hater into a true devotee. For info on current shows and events, check listings in one of the city's weeklies, like *The New Yorker* or *Time Out*, or the "Weekend" section of the Friday *New York Times*. In case your cultural pursuits span lunch hour, most major museums boast attractive cafeterias and/or cafés, where you may or may not get a decent value for your dollar—the one at the American Museum of Natural History is called the Diner Saurus. If you keep your admission ticket (or button), however, you can always pop outside for a cheap slice of pizza and reenter the museum. Some museums, like the Met, the MoMA, the Frick, and the Cloisters, offer stunning courtyards and gardens for your perusal. And, of course, all museums have gift shops.

Almost all of the city's museums are closed on Mondays. Otherwise, museum hours vary greatly; many major ones offer extended hours on Tuesday or Thursday, and further tempt weekday visitors by making admission free after 6 PM on those

If you're in town in June, check the local listings for the Museum Mile festival, when, for three brief hours one weekday evening, all the museums on Fifth Avenue throw open their doors, and the strip becomes a free block party for highbrow types.

In summer 1997, look for a new Museum of the Skyscraper to open somewhere downtown. Presumably, they'll display models instead of the real thing.

evenings. As you would expect, museums are closed on New Year's Day, Independence Day, Thanksgiving, and Christmas. If you want to visit a museum on other holidays, you should call ahead and confirm hours.

AMERICAN MUSEUM OF NATURAL HISTORY

The American Museum of Natural History, established by scientist Albert Bickmore in 1868, is one of the largest and most important museums of its kind. All of the "-ologies" are represented here—zoology, anthropology, vertebrate paleontology, ornithology, and evolutionary biology, to name a few—in a collection of more than 36 million artifacts and specimens enclosed in 40 halls and galleries. If you're expecting just a bunch of dead, stuffed elk displayed in stale, airless rooms, you're in for a big surprise. There's something here for everyone, from the world's largest collection of insects (17 million and counting) to the world's biggest sapphire (563 carats). Of course, there are also plenty of dead, stuffed elk. But the museum has long been on the cutting edge of research in its fields, and is constantly changing its exhibits to jive with the times: During the first decades of the 20th century, the museum president arranged exhibits in the Hall of the Age of Man to reflect his racist belief in the supremacy of northern Europeans, but curators in the 1960s completely revamped the displays and renamed them the Hall of the Biology of Man. More recently, the museum completed a much-needed $34-million overhaul of its world-famous **dinosaur halls** (*see below*).

The museum and the attached Hayden Planetarium (*see below*) dominate a four-block tract on the Upper West Side. Originally, architects Calvert Vaux and Jacob Wrey Mould (who both also designed the Metropolitan Museum of Art) were determined to make this the largest building in the United States. They finished one wing and, from 1892 to 1936, other architects finished the rest. The last and most grandiose section, the work of John Russell Pope, is the neoclassical facade that borders Central Park West. It's quite a striking backdrop for the giant statue of Teddy Roosevelt. *Central Park W, at W. 79th St., Upper West Side, tel. 212/769–5100. Subway: 1 or 9 to W. 79th St. Suggested donation: $7, $5 students. IMAX or Planetarium tickets, including museum admission: $7–$9. Open daily 10–5:45 (Fri. and Sat. until 8:45). Wheelchair access.*

PRACTICALITIES Free tours of the museum's highlights are given daily at 10:15, 11:15, 1:15, 2:15, and 3:15, beginning at the African Mammals Hall on the second floor. They provide an excellent overview if you've never been here before, or if you've only got one afternoon to explore. Year-round, the museum offers a number of special performances, films, and lectures; call for the schedule.

COLLECTION HIGHLIGHTS If you're pressed for time, skip everything else and head directly to the museum's famed **dinosaur halls** (*see below*). Otherwise, most of the good stuff is on the first floor, including the 94-foot-long (that's actual whale size) fiberglass model of a blue whale, which is suspended from the ceiling of the **Ocean Life Room**. In the **Hall of Minerals and Gems** you'll find the famous 563-carat Star of India sapphire, the largest in the world, while the adjoining **Hall of Meteorites** contains the Cape York Meteorite, which is smaller than a Volkswagen but so heavy that its supporting pillars go through the museum's floor and straight down into the bedrock below the building. The **Hall of Human Biology and Evolution** is all about man's favorite subject, namely, him- or herself; don't miss the "Visible Woman" hologram, a spooky life-size display that flashes from skeleton to internal organs to veins, arteries, and nerves to flesh-and-blood person, depending on the angle you look at her from. To see what a slice of a 1,300-year-old giant sequoia tree looks like, check out the **Hall of North American Forests**.

On the second and third floors, you'll find rooms devoted to the peoples of the world. Look for the **Chinese Wedding Chair** (Hall of Asian Peoples); the 3,000-year-old giant jade **Kunz Axe** and the silver-and-gold **Royal Llama of the Inka** (Hall of Mexico and Central America); and the amazing model of an **African Spirit Dancer** wearing a costume made of real snail shells (Hall of African Peoples). Sharing these floors are dioramas of animals in their natural habitats, many bagged by wealthy American taxidermist Carl Akeley in the 1920s—it's hard to think of

Akeley as a hero while you're staring at a whole herd of stuffed African elephants in the **Akeley Hall of African Mammals**. You'll have to admit, however, that the Hall of Reptiles and Amphibian's display of three **Komodo dragons** eating a large wild boar is kind of cool.

➤ **THE DINOSAUR HALLS** • In 1995, after four years and $34 million worth of work, the museum opened two spectacular new dinosaur halls: the **Hall of Suarischian Dinosaurs** and the **Hall of Ornithischian Dinosaurs**, both on the fourth floor. Then, in 1996, they opened the **Hall of Vertebrate Origins**, with displays of primitive fishes and pterodactyls. In these halls, interactive computer displays feature animated footage of how these monstrous beasts got around. More to the point, you'll find the single largest collection of real dinosaur fossils in the world: approximately 100 skeletons, 85% of which are real fossils (not that you would ever notice the difference). During the renovation process some of the skeletons were taken apart and rebuilt according to scientists' improved understanding of how the animals moved; for example, the **Apatosaurus**, previously known as Brontosaurus, got a new skull, additional neck bones, and a tail that has been lengthened by 20 feet. Other highlights include the **Warren Mastodon**, which was discovered in a bog less that 100 miles from New York City, and is one of the most complete skeletons of the hairy prehistoric

The American Museum of Natural History's fossilized dinosaur embryo on display is thought to be 70 to 80 million years old. Jurassic Park, anyone?

elephant ever found; a **Dinosaur Mummy**, important because it shows the skin and other soft tissues of a duck-billed dinosaur; the **Glenn Rose Trackway**, a series of 107-million-year old fossilized dinosaur footprints; and last but certainly not least, the mighty, meat-eating **Tyrannosaurus Rex**, which was reset in a stalking (as opposed to a standing) posture. The rest of the museum's dinosaur collection is on the second floor, and has also been recently restored.

➤ **HAYDEN PLANETARIUM** • The planetarium, adjacent to the museum, has two stories of outer space–related exhibits plus several different Sky Shows daily, projected on 22 wraparound screens. Show up for the laser-light shows on Friday or Saturday nights and drown in loud rock with an audience of red-eyed teenage fans. *Entrance at W. 81st St., btw Columbus and Central Park W, tel. 212/769–5920 for show times. Admission: $7, $5 students.*

➤ **IMAX THEATER** • Films on the IMAX Theater's 40-foot-high, 66-foot-wide screen are usually about nature, whether it's a jaunt through the Grand Canyon, a safari in the Serengeti, or a journey to the bottom of the sea to the wreck of the *Titanic*. If you've never watched a flick on a giant IMAX screen before, you're in for an awe-inspiring experience. *Tel. 212/769–5650 for show times. Admission: $10, $7 students. Purchase tickets at the IMAX ticket counter in the museum's W. 77th St. lobby.*

BROOKLYN MUSEUM

This institution would be a museum-lover's first stop in any other city; with Manhattan's myriad museums, however, it's easy to overlook the fact that the borough of Brooklyn boasts the seventh-largest museum in the United States. Now housed in a turn-of-the-century Beaux Arts monument by McKim, Mead & White, the Brooklyn Museum was founded in 1823 as the Brooklyn Apprentices' Library Association (Walt Whitman was one of its first directors). It has since grown to include 1.5 million items running the gamut from plastic-and-metal Elsa Shiaparelli jewelry to Brooklyn Dodgers uniforms to Winslow Homer watercolors. Initial plans made this the largest art museum in the world—larger even than the Louvre in Paris—and although it was never fully completed, a recent renovation and expansion project has added a new auditorium and nearly doubled its original 45,000 square feet. And many Manhattanites make a special trip here for its blockbuster exhibitions; special exhibits scheduled for 1997 include "Mistress of House, Mistress of Heaven: Women in Egypt" (February); "The Furniture of George Hunzinger" (March); "Working in Brooklyn" (fall); and "Kajar: 200 Years of Paintings from Royal Persian Courts" (fall). *200 Eastern Pkwy., Park Slope, Brooklyn, tel. 718/638–5000. Subway: 2 or 3 to Eastern Pkwy./Brooklyn Museum. Admission: $4, $2 students. Open Wed.–Sun. 10–5. Wheelchair access.*

COLLECTION HIGHLIGHTS The Brooklyn Museum pioneered the collection and study of non-Western art, and its **African and Pre-Columbian Art** galleries are outstanding. Make sure you view the 2,000-year-old *Paracas Textile*, which is considered by many to be the most important ancient Andean textile in the world. The museum's collection of **Asian Art** (second floor) includes pieces from Afghanistan, China,, India, the Islamic world, and much more. You'll also find an impressive number of European and American paintings and sculpture here: The galleries of **Old Masters and French impressionists** (fifth floor) show works by Hals, Monet, Degas, Pissarro, Cassatt, Toulouse-Lautrec, and others. On the first floor, the **Grand Lobby installations** feature work created by contemporary artists specifically for this grandiose space.

➤ **AMERICAN COLLECTION** • This collection, which rivals that of the Met, chronicles American art from its origins to the present with paintings by Copley, Sargent, Lafarge, Sloan, and Eakins. Don't miss *Brooklyn Bridge* by Georgia O'Keeffe. *Fifth floor.*

➤ **THE EGYPTIAN GALLERIES** • The newly renovated **Schapiro Wing** houses the museum's Egyptian art, considered the finest collection outside London and Cairo. The galleries, watched over by massive Assyrian wall sculptures, contain incredible treasures from ancient Egyptian tombs and royal cities dating from the Predynastic period (4,000–3,000 BC) to the Muslim conquest (7th century AD). Besides mummies in glorious sarcophagi, you'll see jewelry; pots; tools; solemn statues of queens, kings, cats, and dogs; and lots of small precious objects made from alabaster or ivory. *Third floor.*

➤ **FRIEDA SCHIFF WARBURG MEMORIAL SCULPTURE GARDEN** • This zany outdoor garden features relics from the "lost New York," such as a lion's head from Coney Island's old Steeplechase Park and the white goddess that once cradled the Penn Station clock. You'll find lots more cherubs, lions, scrolls, capitals, Medusas, and Greek-looking columns rescued from 19th-century buildings before they were torn down. During August, this is also a cool place to catch Sunday jazz concerts (3 PM).

➤ **IRIS AND GERALD CANTOR GALLERY** • This attractive gallery showcases 58 sculptures by Auguste Rodin, including works related to *The Gates of Hell*, *The Burghers of Calais*, and *Balzac. Fifth floor.*

➤ **PERIOD ROOMS** • Impressive are the 28 period rooms—parlors, sitting rooms, and dining rooms, from plantation mansions and New England cottages—that show how New Yorkers lived from 1675 to 1830. Viewing the Jan Martense Schenck House, the oldest, is like stepping into a painting by a Dutch master, and the somber, exotic Moorish Room from John D. Rockefeller's town house is a tycoon's Alhambra. Costume galleries and decorative arts displays complement the period rooms. *Fourth floor.*

THE CLOISTERS

Perched atop a wooded hill near Manhattan's northernmost tip, the Cloisters houses the medieval collection of the Metropolitan Museum of Art (*see* Major Attractions, *above*) in an appropriately medieval monastery-like setting. Colonnaded walks connect authentic French and Spanish monastic cloisters, a French Romanesque chapel, a 12th-century chapter house, and a Romanesque apse. The whole complex is spectacularly situated overlooking the Hudson River,

If you want to make a day out of your visit to the Cloisters Museum, catch Bus M4 "Cloister–Fort Tryon Park" along Madison Avenue below 110th Street. It's a lengthy but scenic ride.

at the high point of Fort Tryon Park; for more on Fort Tryon Park itself, *see* Parks and Gardens, *below.* The galleries that display the collection are organized chronologically, starting with pieces from AD 1000 to AD 1150, continuing through the Gothic period, and ending around 1520. Featured are chalices, altarpieces, sculptures, precious illuminated manuscripts, and works in stained glass, metal, enamel, and ivory. An entire room is devoted to the richly woven and extraordinarily detailed 15th- and 16th-century Unicorn Tapestries—a must-see. Just as noteworthy as the art on the walls are the museum's three **formal gardens:** The central courtyard offers a splashing fountain, flowering plants, and some piped-in choir music; the herb garden is full of strangely named greens once employed in medieval cures; and the Unicorn garden blooms with flowers and plants depicted in the famous Unicorn Tapestries. The Cloisters also frequently hosts special concerts of medieval and Renaissance music; for more info, *see* Music, in Chapter 7. *Fort Tryon Park, Broadway and W. 190th St., Washington Heights, tel. 212/923–3700. Subway: A to W. 190th St. Also: Bus M4 to last stop. Suggested donation: $7, $3.50 students (includes same-day admission to Metropolitan Museum of Art). Open Mar.–Oct., Tues.–Sun. 9:30–5:15; Nov.–Feb., Tues.–Sun. 9:30–4:45.*

PIERPONT MORGAN LIBRARY

This small, patrician museum is built around famous tycoon J. P. Morgan's own study and library, completed in 1906 by McKim, Mead & White—if you walk east past the neoclassical facade on 36th Street, you can see what is believed to be McKim's face on the sphinx in the righthand sculptured panel. The modern galleries at the museum's entrance contain temporary exhibits (often complementing shows at other New York museums), and beyond these, you'll encounter the opulent period rooms of Morgan's original library. These rooms house the permanent collection: Morgan's rare books, manuscripts, drawings, and other artifacts of Western civilization, dating from the Middle Ages to the 20th century, including letters penned by Thomas Jefferson and John Keats; handwritten music by Beethoven; a summary of the theory of relativity in Einstein's own elegant handwriting; a Gutenberg Bible; and Charlotte Brontë's leather gloves. To reach the upper levels of the three tiers of rare books that encircle the **East Room** (the main library), go through the hidden doors near the entrance. The **West Room**, Morgan's personal study, is so dark and sullen with red damask walls, heavy furniture, and medieval paintings that you wonder if he ever actually *read* here. And the **Rotunda**, with its psychedelic marble columns and Raphael-esque ceiling mosaics, is one of the most grandiose small spaces in New York. When you get hungry or tired, linger awhile at the museum's delightful new glass-roofed garden court, which offers salads and sandwiches ($8–$9). Free guided tours of the museum happen weekdays at 2:30. Around the corner, at 37th Street and Madison Avenue, is the latest addition to the library, an 1852 Italianate brownstone that was once the home of Morgan's son, J. P. Morgan, Jr. *29 E. 36th St., at Madison Ave., Murray Hill, tel. 212/685–0008. Subway: 6 to E. 33rd St. Suggested donation: $5, $3 students. Open Tues.–Fri. 10:30–5, Sat. 10:30–6, Sun. noon–6.*

WHITNEY MUSEUM OF AMERICAN ART

Gertrude Vanderbilt Whitney founded the Whitney Museum in 1930 with the noble notion of celebrating artists while they were still alive; the result is one of Manhattan's most dynamic institutions. Mrs. Whitney's own collection is the nucleus of the permanent collection of some 10,000 20th-century paintings, sculpture, and works on paper by more than 1,500 artists, including George Bellows, Stuart David, Edward Hopper, Jasper Johns, Willem de Kooning, Alex Katz, Ellsworth Kelly, Roy Lichtenstein, Georgia O'Keeffe, Maurice B. Prendergast, Jackson Pollock, Mark Rothko, John Sloan, Frank Stella, and Andy Warhol. And, though only a small percentage of the museum's permanent collection can be shown at any one time, the museum is preparing to undergo a $14-million expansion that will increase its gallery space by 33% and allow it to display many of its works for the first time in its 30-year history.

In addition, there are always lively special exhibits, which, in recent years, have included Jean-Michel Basquiat's paintings, Richard Avedon's photographs, and in-depth examinations of the Fluxus artists of the 1960s–1970s and the Beats of the 1950s–1960s. Pause for a moment before entering the museum, because this granite-clad building (1966), designed by the great Bauhaus/modernist architect Marcel Breuer, is a work of art in its own right. One of the biggest regular events at the Whitney is the **Biennial Exhibition**, which is held in the spring of every odd-numbered year (including 1997) and highlights what the museum considers the greatest creations by American artists during the previous two years. Biennial shows are a blast; they're always wildly controversial and usually generate some wicked banter within the art community. The Whitney

At the Whitney Museum, look for artist Charles Simonds's tiny, overlooked model based on an Indian pueblo, tucked into a corner of the stairwell.

also offers a film and video series; dial 212/570–3676 for more info, or check out the museum's web site at http://www.echonyc.com/~whitney/WMAA/INT4.html. If you still haven't had your fill, visit the Whitney's small Midtown outpost, the **Whitney Museum of American Art at Philip Morris** (120 Park Ave., at E. 42nd St., tel. 212/878–2550), which has galleries and a sculpture court. *945 Madison Ave., at E. 75th St., Upper East Side, tel. 212/570–3676. Subway: 6 to E. 77th St. Admission: $8, $6 students; free Thurs. 6–8. Open Wed. and Fri.–Sun. 11–6, Thurs. 1–8. Wheelchair access.*

MORE ART MUSEUMS

Alternative Museum. As the sign outside says, this two-room gallery SEEKS TO EXHIBIT THE WORK OF THOSE ARTISTS WHO HAVE BEEN DISENFRANCHISED BECAUSE OF IDEOLOGY, RACE, GENDER, OR ECONOMIC INEQUALITY. It boasts some of the most interesting and engaging (and occasionally gross or confrontational) art in SoHo. *594 Broadway, btw Houston and Prince Sts., SoHo, tel. 212/966– 4444. Subway: N or R to Prince St. Suggested donation: $3. Open Tues.–Sat. 11–6.*

American Craft Museum. Across the street from the famous Museum of Modern Art (MoMA), this small museum showcases contemporary American crafts in clay, fabric, glass, metal, wood, and even chocolate. Stop worrying about the distinction between "crafts" and "high art" while you're here—most of this stuff is just fun to look at. *40 W. 53rd St., btw Fifth and Sixth Aves., Midtown, tel. 212/956–3535. Subway: E or F to Fifth Ave. Admission: $5, $2.50 students. Open Tues. 10–8, Wed.–Sun. 10–5. Wheelchair access.*

Bronx Museum of the Arts. Don't expect pretty paintings in this progressive museum. The exhibits, by artists of African, Asian, and Latin American descent, range from "The Body in Contemporary Photography" (in which striking black-and-white photos depict cultural and religious practices associated with the body) to the architecture of the Bronx and the history of its residents. The museum is in a former synagogue, and the three-story, glass-enclosed atrium gives it an airy, unstuffy feel. *1040 Grand Concourse, at 165th St., Bronx, tel. 718/681– 6000. Subway: C, D, or 4 to 161st St./Yankee Stadium. Admission: $3, $2 students. Open Wed. 3–9, Thurs.–Fri. 10–5, weekends 1–6.*

Grey Art Gallery. New York University's museum has recently undergone major renovations; at press time it was scheduled to reopen in September 1996. It houses two major art collections: the NYU art collection, which includes a few works by Picasso, Miró, and Matisse; and the Abbey Weed Grey Collection, which showcases contemporary Asian and Middle Eastern art. *33 Washington Pl., at Washington Sq. E, West Village, tel. 212/998–6780. Subway: N or R to E. 8th St./NYU. Admission free. Open Tues.–Fri. 11–6:30 (Wed. until 8:30), Sat. 11–5.*

Guggenheim Museum SoHo. The SoHo outpost of the world-renowned Solomon R. Guggenheim Museum (*see* Manhattan Neighborhoods Upper East Side, *above*) has struggled to define itself since its 1992 opening in a landmark redbrick warehouse on one of the city's most chic blocks. It displays contemporary art and works from the permanent collection and, increasingly, cutting-edge multimedia and electronic exhibits. *575 Broadway, at Prince St., SoHo, tel. 212/423–3500. Subway: 6 to Spring St. Admission: $5, $3 students. Open Wed.–Sun. 11– 6 (Sat. until 8).*

The Institute for Contemporary Art/Clocktower Gallery. Ride up to the 13th floor to visit this gallery of avant-garde art and sculpture by resident artists (whose studios are closed to the public). For unique views of Manhattan, you can climb even farther up a twisting metal stairway and take a peek through the clock's massive cogs and gears. The building, which once housed the New York Life Insurance Company, is a 1895 design by McKim, Mead & White. *346 Broadway, at Leonard St., TriBeCa, tel. 212/233–1096. Subway: A or C to Chambers St. Suggested donation: $2. Open Wed.–Sun. 1–7.*

The Institute for Contemporary Art/P.S. 1 Museum. When this Queens public-school-turned-art-forum finally reopens in spring 1997, count on it for provocative paintings, performances, installations, and film and video screenings by an international cadre of "the world's hottest emerging visual artists" (as one enthusiastic brochure gushes). *46–01 21st St., btw 46th Rd.*

and 46th Ave., Long Island City, Queens, tel. 718/784–2084. Subway: 7 to 45th Rd./Court House Sq. Suggested donation: $2.

International Center of Photography (ICP)–Midtown. The ICP–Midtown presents several photography shows a year, as well as film and video screenings, in an ultracontemporary, multilevel space. Photography diehards will also want to visit the museum's larger uptown sibling (*see* Manhattan Neighborhoods, Upper East Side, *above*). *1133 Sixth Ave., at W. 43rd St., Midtown, tel. 212/768–4680. Subway: B, D, F, or Q to W. 42nd St. Admission: $4, $2.50 students. Open Tues. 11–8, Wed.–Sun. 11–6.*

Isamu Noguchi Garden Museum. More than 300 works by the famous late Japanese-American sculptor Isamu Noguchi are on display here, from abstract bronzes inspired by Brancusi (a mentor to Noguchi during the '20s) to traditional Japanese ceramic and cast-iron sculpture to surrealist-inspired works in marble, slate, and wood. The peaceful outdoor garden is graced by a traditional *tsukubai* (fountain). *32–37 Vernon Blvd., btw Broadway and 35th Ave., Long Island City, Queens, tel. 718/721–1932. Subway: N to Broadway. Admission: $4, $2 students. Open Apr.–Nov., Wed. and weekends 11–6.*

Museum for African Art. This is one of only two museums in the United States devoted exclusively to the arts of Africa, and its collection is incredible. The displayed wooden sculptures, masks and headdresses, jewelry, and religious relics are usually accompanied by printed narratives and photographs showing how the artifact was actually used. A small theater shows documentaries on tribal dances and customs. Exhibits change every five to seven months. *593 Broadway, btw Houston and Prince Sts., SoHo, tel. 212/966–1313. Subway: N or R to Prince St. Admission: $4, $2 students. Open Tues.–Fri. 10:30–5:30, weekends noon–6.*

Museum of American Folk Art. A trip to this museum would be a lot like a foray into your grandmother's attic, assuming she hoarded paintings, quilts, carvings, dolls, wooden decoys, furniture, silver pieces, altars, copper weather vanes, and a beautiful collection of carousel horses. You can read all about how these pieces were made, and which immigrant groups brought them here. *2 Lincoln Sq., on Columbus Ave., btw W. 65th and 66th Sts., Upper West Side, tel. 212/595–9533. Subway: 1 or 9 to W. 66th St. Admission free. Open Tues.–Sun. 11:30–7:30.*

Museum of American Illustration. The Society of Illustrators, founded in 1901, mounts exhibits of the commercial arts, such as children's book illustrations, book and magazine covers, postal stamps, and print advertisements. The museum's two small galleries are located in an 1875 carriage house. *128 E. 63rd St., btw Park and Lexington Aves., Upper East Side, tel. 212/838–2560. Subway: B or Q to Lexington Ave. Admission free. Open Tues. 10–8, Wed.–Fri. 10–5, Sat. noon–4. Closed Aug.*

New Museum of Contemporary Art. What you'll see here is experimental, often radically innovative work by unrecognized artists—and none of it is more than 10 years old. *583 Broadway, btw Houston and Prince Sts., SoHo, tel. 212/219–1222. Subway: B, D, F, or Q to Broadway–Lafayette St. Admission: $3.50, $2.50 students and artists; free Sat. Open Wed.–Sun. noon–6 (Sat. until 8).*

Curators at the New Museum of Contemporary Art feel that art, like fish and house guests, starts to smell if it hangs around too long.

Nicholas Roerich Museum. Housed in a beautiful Upper West Side town house (built in 1898), this small, eccentric museum displays the work of the prolific Russian artist who was also author, philosopher, explorer, archaeologist, and set designer (he designed sets for Diaghilev ballets). His vast paintings of the Himalayas are suffused with such a trippy mysticism that they give the whole place a cultish appeal. Also displayed are Roerich's books and travel treasures. Drop by on a winter weekend for poetry readings and chamber-music performances. *319 W. 107th St., btw Broadway and Riverside Dr., Upper West Side, tel. 212/864–7752. Subway: 1 or 9 to W. 110th St. Donations appreciated. Open Tues.–Sun. 2–5.*

Queens Museum of Art. If there's one reason to make the trek to Flushing Meadows–Corona Park, it's to see the knock-your-socks-off **New York City panorama** in the Queens Museum of Art. The 9,335-square-foot model, constructed for the 1964 World's Fair, faithfully replicates all five boroughs of the city, building by building, on a scale of 1 inch per 100 feet. The model's tiny brownstones and skyscrapers are updated periodically to look exactly like the real things. The museum's other exhibits examine the history of the World's Fair, and its biannual art exhibitions reflect the cultural diversity of Queens. The park's New York City Building, which houses the museum, was also the site of several United Nations meetings between 1939 and 1964. *Flushing Meadows–Corona Park, tel. 718/592–5555 or 718/592–9700. Subway: 7 to Willets Point/Shea Stadium. Admission: $3, $1.50 students. Open Wed.–Fri. 10–5, weekends noon–5.*

Studio Museum in Harlem. The museum's extensive collection of artifacts and art from the African diaspora includes sculptures, masks, headdresses, delicately beaded clothing, and religious tokens from Guinea, Tanzania, the Ivory Coast, Nigeria, Zaire, Ghana, Cameroon, Angola, and the Zulu people of South Africa. Also look for works by the Studio Museum's artists-in-residence, who come from all over the world. *144 W. 125th St., btw Adam Clayton Powell Jr. and Malcolm X Blvds., Harlem, tel. 212/864–4500. Subway: 2 or 3 to W. 125th St. Admission: $5, $3 students. Open Wed.–Fri. 10–5, weekends 1–6.*

MUSEUMS ABOUT NEW YORK

Brooklyn Historical Society. The Historical Society has been collecting weird and wonderful facts about the borough and its citizenry since 1863. Its Shellens Gallery of Brooklyn History boasts permanent exhibits (none of which are boring) on the Brooklyn Bridge, the Brooklyn Navy Yard, Brooklynites, Coney Island, and the Brooklyn Dodgers, plus special exhibits like "Volunteer Firefighting in 19th-Century Brooklyn" (which tells how volunteer fire departments were once so competitive that they brawled over the right to extinguish a fire). Its Donald F. and Mildred Topp Othmer Library houses some 110,000 books and 12,000 articles on Brooklyn in its Victorian splendor. The society also sponsors walking tours ($10) of various neighborhoods; reservations are recommended. *128 Pierrepont St., at Clinton St., Brooklyn Heights, tel. 718/624–0890. Subway: 2 or 3 to Clark St. Admission: $2.50; free Wed. Open Tues.–Sun. noon–5. Library closed Sun.*

Lower East Side Tenement Museum. This is the only museum in the country devoted to re-creating and remembering the urban squalor of the tenements (no-frills apartment buildings that opportunistic landlords constructed on the Lower East Side during the mid-1800's immigration boom). At the museum, you'll see photo exhibits and take a fascinating 45-minute tour of two restored 19th-century tenement apartments. For more information on the tenement buildings, *see box above. 90 Orchard St., btw Delancey and Broome Sts., Lower East Side, tel. 212/430–0233. Subway: F to Delancey St. Admission: $7, $6 students; free Tues. Open Tues.–Sun. 11–5.*

New York City Fire Museum. It may not be as exciting as a three-alarm blaze, but this museum's impressive collection of ornate old fire carriages and engines is a kick to look at—so are its photos of the horse-drawn fire wagons that once raced around New York, dousing flames and saving babies. There are exhibits devoted to all kinds of lore, including why firehouses have always favored black-and-white-spotted Dalmatians rather than, say, toy poodles. The museum itself is housed in a quaint old fire station that was active from 1904 to 1959. *278 Spring St., btw Varick and Hudson Sts., SoHo, tel. 212/691–1303. Subway: C or E to Spring St. Suggested donation: $4, $2 students. Open Tues.–Sun. 10–4 (Thurs. until 9).*

New York City Police Museum. *NYPD Blue* this isn't. The city's police museum doesn't celebrate lurid crimes (and there's nary a mention of a notorious Washington, D.C. convention during which New York's finest slid bare-assed and drunk down hotel banisters), but instead exhibits historical stuff like antique firearms, badges, and uniforms. There are cool collections of old mug shots—including ones of Al Capone—and drugs and funny money found on New York's mean streets. You'll need to show your photo ID to visit. *235 E. 20th St., btw Second and Third Aves., Gramercy, tel. 212/477–9753. Subway: 6 to E. 23rd St. Admission free. Open weekdays 9–2, by appointment only. Wheelchair access.*

New-York Historical Society. Since its founding in 1804, the Historical Society has collected over one million artifacts of the city's past, including Ben Franklin's glasses; the Louisiana Purchase contract, complete with Napoleon's signature; the first English Bible published in America; hundreds of busts and statues; 250 Tiffany lamps (the largest such collection in the world); and the remains of a leaden King George statue that had been melted down for bullets during the Revolutionary War. Concerts and walking tours are also part of the Society's program. *2 W. 77th St., at Central Park W, Upper West Side, tel. 212/873–3400. Subway: 1 or 9 to W. 79th St. Suggested donation: $3. Open Wed. noon–8, Thurs.–Sun. noon–5.*

New York Transit Museum. You don't have to be enraptured by public transportation to find this museum fascinating. Housed in a restored 1930's subway station, it shows off 20 retired subway cars (some with ceiling fans and fancy seats), a couple of funky elderly city buses, and exhibits on how the subway tunnels were built, or sometimes dynamited. Most Saturdays at 11 AM you can also catch a walking tour of abandoned Brooklyn subway tunnels. *Boerum Pl., at Schermerhorn St., Brooklyn Heights, tel. 718/243–3060. Subway: A, C, or F to Jay St./Borough Hall. Admission: $3. Open Tues.–Fri. 10–4 (Wed. until 6), weekends noon–5.*

New York Unearthed. Whenever they start raising a new glass-and-steel monstrosity in Manhattan, New York Unearthed's crack team of urban archaeologists rushes in to sift through the dirt. At this museum/laboratory, you'll see artifacts from the prehistoric days right up through the 1950s (interestingly, tobacco pipes seem to be the one artifact common to all eras)—and learn what lies where under New York's pavement. There's some pretty astounding stuff, including foot-long oyster shells from the Colonial era. *17 State St., btw Bridge and Pearl Sts., Lower Manhattan, tel. 212/748–8628. Subway: 4 or 5 to Bowling Green. Admission free. Open Mon.–Sat. noon–6 (Jan.–Mar., weekdays only).*

South Street Seaport Museum. In the middle of yuppified South Street Seaport stands this great museum, dedicated to New York's early history as an international port. You'll find a working 19th-century printing press, scrimshaw art, model ships, and temporary exhibits on lively topics such as 19th-century sailors' tattoos. Your ticket also lets you board six historic ships, including the *Peking*, a four-masted barque from 1911; the *Wanetree*, an 1885 three-masted tall ship; and the *Ambrose*, a 1908 lightship once used to guide other ships into port. *12–14 Fulton St., btw Front and South Sts., Lower Manhattan, tel. 212/748–8600. Subway: J, M, Z, 2, 3, 4, or 5 to Fulton St. Admission: $6, $4 students. Open daily 10–5.*

Staten Island Historical Society Museum. Bet you never knew that Crisco, Ivory soap, and dental drills were all made on Staten Island in the 19th century, or that Staten Island was the principal source of New York City's beer in the 1850s. This excellent little museum, in Staten Island's Richmondtown Restoration, displays all kinds of tools, furniture, toys, photos, and drawings that shed light on New York's forgotten borough. Its upper level is devoted to an exhibit on the Fresh Kills dump, which is one of only two man-made objects visible from outer space. FYI, the other is the Great Wall of China. *Tel. 718/351–1611. For directions and admission, see Outer Boroughs, Staten Island, above. Open Wed.–Sun. 1–5.*

ETHNIC AND CULTURAL MUSEUMS

The Asia Society. John D. Rockefeller III, great-grandson of the original gajillionaire Rockefeller, founded the Asia Society in 1956 to further the understanding of Asia in America. The Society's modest galleries display art from all reaches of Asia, as well as New Zealand, Australia, and the Pacific Islands. Free gallery talks are given Tuesday–Saturday at 12:30 (also at 6:30 on Thursday) and Sunday at 2:30. Shows change several times a year. *725 Park Ave., at E. 70th St., Upper East Side, tel. 212/288–6400 or 212/517–NEWS. Subway: 6 to E. 68th St. Admission: $3, $1 students; free Thurs. 6–8. Open Tues.–Sat. 11–6 (Thurs. until 8), Sun. noon–5. Wheelchair access.*

Black Fashion Museum. The recently renovated Black Fashion Museum has more than 3,000 pieces in its collection, including all the costumes from *The Wiz*, a few Michael Jackson outfits, a slave girl's original gingham dress, and a copy of Mary Todd Lincoln's second inaugural gown. A few of the designers featured include Lenny Varnadoe (creator of a number of Bobby Brown's getups), Anne Lowe (whose credits include Jacqueline Kennedy's wedding dress), and Willi Smith (the creative force behind WilliWear). *157 W. 126th St., btw Adam Clayton Powell Jr. (Seventh Ave.) and Malcolm X (Lenox Ave.) Blvds.,*

Spike Lee used some of the Black Fashion Museum's zoot suits in his film "Malcolm X."

Harlem, tel. 212/666–1320 or 212/666–4019. Subway: 2 or 3 to W. 125th St. Admission: $3. Open by appointment only.

China House Gallery. A pair of fierce, fat stone lions guard the doorway to the China Institute. Inside, you'll find the galleries where three or four museum-quality shows are mounted yearly, generally on historical topics. The Institute also offers film programs, lectures, and classes in language, calligraphy, cooking, and painting. *125 E. 65th St., btw Park and Lexington Aves., Upper East Side, tel. 212/744–8181. Subway: B or Q to Lexington Ave. Suggested donation: $5, $3 students. Open Mon.–Sat. 10–5 (Tues. until 8), Sun. 1–5.*

Hispanic Society of America. Relics and paintings from the 10th through the 15th centuries are displayed at this 90-year-old museum, housed in a Spanish Renaissance–style building. Don't miss the giant wall paintings by Joaquin Sorolla y Bastida, which colorfully depict the Spain of the 1860s–1920s. You'll also find two oil paintings by Spanish masters Goya and El Greco, and a bunch of altars and nifty marble sarcophagi. The library houses more than 200,000 books about (surprise, surprise) Spain and Portugal. *Audubon Terr., Broadway at W. 155th St., Washington Heights, tel. 212/926–2234. Subway: 1 to W. 157th St. Admission free. Open Tues.–Sat. 10–4:30, Sun. 1–4.*

In 1991 the Dalai Lama blessed the Jacques Marchais Museum, and since then, Buddhists have journeyed from around the world to worship here.

Jacques Marchais Museum of Tibetan Art. Find nirvana among the *bodhisattvas* (religious deities), *tankas* (ritual paintings used to aid meditation), *mani* stones (slates inscribed with Tibetan prayers), and other Tibetan artifacts at this hilltop temple museum, seeming totally out of place in Staten Island. It's the brainchild of Edna Coblentz (a.k.a. Jacques Marchais), an Asian art dealer from the Midwest, who indulged her passion for a country she never visited by building this Tibetan center next door to her home. Outside, you'll find a serene garden filled with ponds, statues, and strings of prayer flags. *338 Lighthouse Ave., Staten Island, tel. 718/987–3478. From Ferry Terminal, take Bus S74 to Lighthouse Ave. Admission: $3. Open Wed.–Sun. 1–5 (Dec.–Mar., by appointment only).*

Japan Society. Not far from the United Nations is the headquarters of the Japan Society, which produces a range of cultural events, including occasional gallery exhibits, film series, and lectures. In its lobby you'll find a touch of Kyoto: a pond, bamboo trees, and shoji screens. The gallery is scheduled to be closed through the end of September 1997; call ahead. *333 E. 47th St., btw Second and First Aves., Midtown, tel. 212/832–1155. Subway: 4, 5, 6, or 7 to Grand Central. Admission free. Lobby open weekdays 9–7:30; gallery open Tues.–Sun. 11–5.*

National Museum of the American Indian. This incredible museum, a branch of the Washington, D.C.–based Smithsonian Institute, houses George Gustav Heye's collection of more than one million American Indian artifacts. Wealthy and passionate collector Heye spent the first half of the 20th century traveling the world, gathering jade ornaments from the ancient Mayans, stone carvings from the peoples of the Pacific Northwest, and even a shrunken head or two. Whether you consider his activities grossly exploitative, you'll find the artifacts—games, clothing, religious items—displayed intelligently, each accompanied by an explanation written by a member of the tribe or group of its origin. The museum is located in the former **Alexander Hamilton U.S. Custom House**, one of the most spectacular examples of Beaux Arts architecture in New York: The first row of statues atop the pediment represents the various continents, while the second row symbolizes the major trading cities of the world. *1 Bowling Green, btw State and Whitehall Sts., Lower Manhattan, tel. 212/668–NMAI. Subway: 4 or 5 to Bowling Green. Admission free. Open daily 10–5. Wheelchair access.*

Schomburg Center for Research in Black Culture. Arturo Alfonso Schomburg, black scholar and bibliophile, dedicated his life to collecting evidence of and denouncing white prejudice. At his death in 1938 he had amassed some 100,000 items, including books, photographs, political cartoons, paintings, oral histories, and even the white robe and hood of a KKK member—it's an amazingly powerful collection. In addition to gallery space, the center (part of the New York Public Library system) holds a research library and the recently renovated **American Negro Theatre**, where Sidney Poitier, Ruby Dee, and Harry Belafonte have performed. *515 Malcolm X Blvd.*

(Lenox Ave.), at W. 136th St., Harlem, tel. 212/491–2265. Subway: 2 or 3 to W. 135th St. Admission free. Open Mon.–Wed. noon–8, Thurs.–Sat. 10–6, Sun. 1–5.

Ukrainian Museum. This museum's two tiny rooms were put together by Ukrainian Americans, obviously with much pride in their rich cultural heritage. On permanent display are Ukrainian ceremonial costumes, jewelry, and footwear. Seasonal exhibits include Christmas decorations and fabulously ornate Easter eggs (the latter are worth a special trip). *203 Second Ave., btw E. 12th and 13th Sts., East Village, tel. 212/228–0110. Subway: L to Third Ave. Admission: $1, 50¢ students. Open Wed.–Sun. 1–5.*

HISTORICAL HOUSES

Abigail Adams Smith Museum. Back when the Upper East Side was nothing but farmland, Abigail Adams Smith, daughter of President John Adams, set up a nifty 23-acre estate on the East River. Today, her 1799 house is hemmed in by massive brick buildings. Tours show off the *in situ* collection of Federalist furniture, art, and household implements, plus several rooms that are being restored to their original appearance when the house was the Mount Vernon Hotel, a ritzy resort for downtowners. *421 E. 61st St., btw. First and York Aves., Upper East Side, tel. 212/838–6878. Subway: N, R, 4, 5, or 6 to E. 59th St./Lexington Ave. Admission: $3, $2 students. Open weekdays noon–4, Sun. 1–5. Closed Aug.*

Alice Austen House. Whoever said that the Victorians were a repressed lot was not accounting for Alice Austen, a woman who was out photographing city life during an age when most sat around doing needlepoint. Here at "Clear Comfort," the harborfront cottage where Austen lived luxuriously (until she lost her fortune in the 1929 stock market crash), you'll see her striking and vivid photos. Compare those of tennis matches and other scenes of the "larky life" with those of the immigrant street sweepers, ash collectors, Irish policemen, and the many other laborers who flooded turn-of-the-century New York. *2 Hylan Blvd., at Bay St., Rosebank, Staten Island, tel. 718/816–4506. From Ferry Terminal, take Bus S51 to Hylan Blvd. (15 min). Admission: $2. Open Thurs.–Sun. noon–5; grounds open daily until dusk.*

Bowne House. U.S. citizens, thank Mr. John Bowne, the original owner of this 1661 house, for your freedom of religion. The defiant Bowne held Quaker meetings here despite the Dutch governor's ban on the sect, and was eventually thrown in jail. At his trial, Bowne successfully argued that the colony's patent granted its new citizens the right "to have and enjoy liberty of conscience," and the Quakers lived happily ever after—the freedoms they championed were later consecrated by the Bill of Rights. This house, with its slanting floors and low ceilings, is considered one of the finest examples of Dutch English architecture in the United States. *37–01 Bowne St., Flushing, Queens, tel. 718/359–0528. Subway: 7 to Main St. Admission: $3. Open Tues. and weekends 2:30–4:30.*

The bayberry candles you see in Bowne House were sort of like colonial chastity insurance. According to lore, when a bayberry candle burned out, all visiting males were supposed to pick up immediately and leave.

Conference House. One fateful day in 1776, Benjamin Franklin, John Adams, and Edward Rutledge met at this Staten Island house with British Admiral Lord Howe. The rabble-rousing revolutionaries pooh-poohed the Lord's offer of "clemency and full pardon to all repentant rebels," and the rest, as they say, is history. The Conference House's rooms have been fixed up to look the same as they did when American insurgents used them to talk war over "good claret, good bread, cold ham, tongues, and mutton." Outside, in Conference Park, is a small beach where Franklin allegedly took his post-lunch naps. *7455 Hylan Blvd., Tottenville, Staten Island, tel. 718/984–2086. From Ferry Terminal, take SIRT to Tottenville (40 min). Admission: $2, $1 students. Open Wed.–Sun. 1–4. Closed Jan.–Feb.*

Dyckman House. This 1784 Dutch farmhouse-turned-museum is the only attraction in Inwood, the teeny neighborhood north of Washington Heights. Not surprisingly, Dyckman House is the last farmhouse remaining in Manhattan. Surprisingly, there's more to see here than a few rusty hoes: The Relic Room features a Revolutionary War uniform and musketry. In the garden is a replica of a Revolutionary War military hut. *4881 Broadway, at W. 204th St., Inwood, tel. 212/304–9422. Subway: A to W. 200th St. Admission free. Open Tues.–Sun. 11–4.*

Edgar Allen Poe Cottage. In the hope that the fresh, clean country air of Fordham Village might improve the health of Virginia, his tuberculosis-stricken wife, the 37-year-old Poe moved to this cottage in 1846. Alas, Virginia soon passed away, leaving Poe alone with his mum-in-law until 1849, when he, too, succumbed. Not exactly a happy history, but at least fans of Poe's "Annabel Lee," "Ulalume," and "The Bells" can admire the room in which they were written. There's a small collection of manuscripts, a seedy surrounding park, and no rest rooms. *Grand Concourse and Kingsbridge Rd., Fordham, Bronx, tel. 718/881–8900. Subway: D to Kingsbridge Rd. Admission: $2. Open Sat. 10–4, Sun. 1–5.*

Fraunces Tavern. So central was Fraunces Tavern to the American Revolution, you'd think the entire insurrection was plotted here over a few pints and tavernkeep Samuel Fraunces's fancy desserts. During the war, the Sons of Liberty met at the tavern, and George Washington bid his officers farewell here in 1783. Later, it housed the fledgling U.S. government's departments of the Treasury, Foreign Affairs, and War. The whole thing was restored in 1904, patched up a bit in 1975 (when it was bombed by a Puerto Rican nationalist organization), and today contains a collection of 18th- and 19th-century paintings, decorative arts, prints, and documents. Downstairs is a re-creation of the original tavern, where you can eat an overpriced meal or down a pint yourself. *54 Pearl St., at Broad St., Lower Manhattan, tel. 212/425–1778. Subway: J, M, or Z to Broad St. Admission: $2.50, $1 students. Open weekdays 10–4:45, Sat. noon–4.*

Garibaldi–Meucci Museum. General Giuseppe Garibaldi, the man who established Italy as a nation, took refuge here in 1850 as the guest of Antonio Meucci, argued to be the true inventor of the telephone. This museum is full of informative exhibits about both men—you'll get to see a chair that clever Meucci carved out of tree branches, and the shirt and dagger that Garibaldi used in battle. A guided tour and video tell the sad tale of Meucci's invention of electromagnetism (he died before he was able to renew the costly patent, and Alexander Graham Bell sucked up all the glory). *420 Tompkins Ave., btw Vanderbilt and Hylan Aves., Staten Island, tel. 718/442–1608. From Ferry Terminal, take Bus S78 (15 min) to Tompkins Ave. Admission: $3. Open Tues.–Sun. 1–5.*

King Manor Museum. Yes, this white colonial house and the surrounding manicured lawns at the center of the tiny Rufus King Park look weird and kind of lonely on the main commercial drag in Jamaica, Queens. It's dedicated to reminding you of the great works of Rufus King, a founding father and statesman best known for successfully hedging the Louisiana Territory from slavery. This house was King's working country estate in the early 1800s—it's a pretty nice spread. Visit the newly revamped downstairs rooms for a look at what life was like back in the old days. *King Park, Jamaica Ave. at 153rd St., Jamaica, Queens, tel. 718/206–0547. Subway: E to Jamaica Center. Admission: $2. Open weekends noon–4, second and last Tues. of month 12:15–2.*

Morris-Jumel Mansion. This Palladian-style mansion, built in 1765, is the oldest standing house in Manhattan, and a lot has happened here in the last 200 years. During the Revolutionary War, it was used by the Brits, the Hessians, and George Washington and troops (not all at once, of course). Eliza Bowen Jumel—a former prostitute who in 1832 became the wealthy widow of French wine merchant Stephen Jumel—lived here during her short (1834–1836), unhappy marriage to former Vice President Aaron Burr. Since 1906, the mansion has been a museum of exquisitely refurbished rooms, some of Burr's desks, and a chaise rumored to have once belonged to Napoleon. The gorgeous rose garden offers spectacular views of the Harlem River, and the surrounding **Jumel Terrace Historic District** (W. 160th–162nd Sts., btw St. Nicholas and Edgecombe Aves.) encompasses blocks of beautiful 19th-century brownstones. *65 Jumel Terr., btw W. 160th and 162nd Sts., Washington Heights, tel. 212/923–8008. Subway: A, B, or C to W. 163rd St./Amsterdam Ave. Admission: $3, $2 students. Open Wed.–Sun. 10–4.*

Old Merchant's House. If you love looking at old houses, the Merchant's House is for you. It's a fully restored 1830 Federal-style town house, built with red bricks and marble trim. Seabury Treadwell and his descendants lived here from 1835 right up until it became a museum in 1933. All of the family's furniture remains, along with personal items such as clothing, needlepoint, and photographs. Concerts, lectures, readings, and cooking demonstrations are held throughout the year. *29 E. 4th St., btw Bowery and Second Ave., East Village, tel. 212/777–1089. Subway: 6 to Astor Pl. Admission: $3. Open Sun.–Thurs. 1–4.*

Theodore Roosevelt Birthplace. The building now standing isn't the actual house where the Bull Moose was born, but instead a brick-by-brick re-creation. The original brownstone was purchased for Teddy's father by Cornelius Roosevelt, who at the time was the fourth-richest man in New York. House tours, which are spiced up with anecdotes about Teddy's childhood in New York, look at five rooms filled with authentic furniture. There's also a small museum of Teddy's personal effects (the "big stick" is nowhere to be found). From Labor Day to Memorial Day, you can catch concerts (tel. 212/866–2086) Saturday at 2 PM. *28 E. 20th St., btw Broadway and Park Ave. S, Gramercy, tel. 212/260–1616. Subway: N or R to W. 23rd St. Admission: $2. Open Wed.–Sun. 9–5; tours given on the hour until 4.*

Wave Hill. This lavish estate, in the exclusive Bronx neighborhood of Riverdale, was home at various times to Teddy Roosevelt, Mark Twain, and Arturo Toscanini. It consists of two houses—the 1843 gray-stone Wave Hill House (where you'll find an open-air café) and the newer, neo-Georgian Glyndor House (which has an art gallery)—and 28 acres of beautifully landscaped gardens. The Pergola Overlook, a gazebo with a river view, is the ultimate spot for romance seekers. Garden tours (free) convene Sunday at 2:15 PM. *675 W. 252nd St., at Independence Ave., Bronx, tel. 718/549–3200. Subway: 1 or 9 to W. 231 St. (30 min); follow signs to Wave Hill (15 min). Also: Bus BX 7, 10, or 24 to 246 St. (30 min), or Metro North to Riverdale Station (30 min). Admission: $4, $2 students; free Tues. and before noon Sat. Grounds open Tues.–Sun. 9–5:30 (Fri. until dusk); shorter hrs in winter.*

MUSEUMS OF MOVIES AND TELEVISION

American Museum of the Moving Image. Housed in the historic Kaufman-Astoria studios, this museum of movies is absolutely worth the trip to Astoria, Queens. You can play with all kinds of high-tech gizmos to create your own special effects; dub your voice over Clint "go ahead, make my day" Eastwood's; or pose while a camera makes a video flip-book (the same kind that's used in cartoon animation) of you. Also check out "Behind the Screen," a cool exhibit in which actors and directors explain their secret tricks, and *Precious Images*, an Academy Award–winning short made from snippets of American film classics. The museum's **Riklis Theater** shows new and old films, with famous actors and directors as guest speakers. Most films are free with museum admission. *36–11 35th Ave., at 36th St., Astoria, Queens, tel. 718/784–0077. Subway: N to 36th Ave. Admission: $5, $2.50 students. Open Tues.–Fri. noon–4, weekends noon–6.*

Museum of Television and Radio. In this museum it's okay to lounge in cushy chairs watching old episodes of the *Brady Bunch* instead of traipsing past peeling paintings of Christs-on-the-cross and haloed Madonnas-with-Child. In fact, this museum has *60,000* of the best and most significant television and radio programs—from *Howdy Doody* to CNN broadcasts of Princess Di's wedding. And you're free to fast-forward, pause, rewind, whatever. All you have to do is stroll in, select up to four programs at a time from a computer index, then settle down at one of the unbelievably comfortable state-of-the-art viewing consoles (is this the greatest museum you've ever been to, or what?). The museum, which opened in 1991, also offers gallery exhibitions, lectures, and group screenings. *25 W. 52nd St., btw Fifth and Sixth Aves., Midtown, tel. 212/621–6600 or 212/621–6800. Subway: E or F to Fifth Ave. Admission: $6, $4 students. Open Tues.–Sun. noon–6 (Thurs. until 8). Wheelchair access.*

MUSEUMS OF THE SCIENCES

American Numismatic Society. The study of money is what goes on at this 130-year-old organization. Even if you don't have *mucho dinero* yourself, it's a pretty interesting place. They've got more than one million pieces of currency representing every period of history, from ancient Egypt to the Elizabethan age right up through the present. *Audubon Terr., Broadway at W. 155th St., Washington Heights, tel. 212/234–3130. Subway: 1 to W. 157th St. Admission free. Open Tues.–Sat. 9–4:30, Sun. 1–4.*

If you're hanging around Union Square and have a spare half hour, try to stop in at Con Ed's museum—they need your business.

Con Edison Energy Museum. This museum's emphasis is on Thomas Edison and early electrical power generation in New York City, and all the displays look like they were put together in 1978. Still, they're in great shape—presumably because of light traffic. Don't skip the "Underneath New York" exhibit, a kitschy pleasure with faux stone walls and funky psychedelic lights that make you feel like you're in line for a bad ride at a theme park. The five-minute presentation (multimedia in the '70s sense of the word) is okay, but it would be more fun to get naked and frolic under the colorful lights. It's doubtful that anyone would notice. *145 E. 14th St., btw Third and Lexington Aves., Gramercy, tel. 212/460-6244. Subway: L, N, R, 4, 5, or 6 to Union Sq. Admission free. Open Tues.–Sat. 9–5.*

New York Hall of Science. If you're into blowing giant bubbles and understanding the physics of sound, this museum is directly up your alley—but don't expect any cutting-edge technological wonders here. Educational hands-on exhibits (some computerized) demonstrate everything from the size of a microbe to how H.I.V. advances, but many exhibits may remind you of a sixth-grade science class—and not in a good way. *47–01 111th St., at 46th Ave., Flushing Meadows–Corona Park, Queens, tel. 718/699–0675. Subway: 7 to Willets Point/Shea Stadium. Admission: $4.50; free Wed.–Thurs. 2–5. Open Wed.–Sun. 10–5.*

Sony Wonder Technology Lab. This Sony product–filled place will really wow you, especially if you're one of those who can't program a VCR or considers the microwave oven cutting-edge technology. All the exhibits are interactive and hands on: Start in the lobby by recording your name, image, and voice on a plastic chip, which acts as your "key" to other exhibits too weird and astounding to describe here. One of the best is the High Definition Theater, where you and other audience members orchestrate a video adventure from your seats—you actually get to determine the outcome of the movie by voting with a futuristic joystick attached to the arm of your chair. *550 Madison Ave., btw E. 55th and 56th Sts., Midtown, tel. 212/833–8100. Subway: 4, 5, or 6 to E. 59th St. Admission free. Open Tues.–Sat. 10–6, Sun. noon–6.*

NONE-OF-THE-ABOVE MUSEUMS

Forbes Magazine Galleries. While millionaires Gertrude Vanderbilt Whitney and Henry Clay Frick collected oil paintings, sculpture, and drawings, magazine magnate Malcolm Forbes collected items that excited his boyhood fancy. On the ground floor of the Forbes Magazine headquarters you'll find Malcolm's collections displayed; they include: "Ships Ahoy," a flotilla of over 500 toy boats; "On Parade," an army of more than 12,000 toy soldiers arranged in battle; "Monopoly," with many versions of Forbes's favorite board game; "Presidential Papers," an impressive assembly of presidential correspondence; "Fabergé," the world's second-largest private collection of the famous jeweled Russian eggs; and, almost as an afterthought, "Pictures," a collection of paintings, photographs, and drawings. *62 Fifth Ave., btw 12th and 13th Sts., West Village, tel. 212/206–5548. Subway: L, N, R, 4, 5, or 6 to Union Sq. Admission free. Open Tues.–Wed. and Fri.–Sun. 10–4.*

Wealthy, flamboyant, and sexually ambiguous Malcolm Forbes amassed the world's second-largest private collection of Fabergé eggs (the largest belongs to Queen Elizabeth) during his lifetime; ergo Maureen Dowd of the "New York Times" dubbed his dorky son, Steve "Flat Tax" Forbes, "the Fabergé Egghead" during the 1996 presidential campaign.

Intrepid Air, Sea, and Space Museum. Maximum war glorification is yours for the asking at this World War II aircraft carrier–cum–floating museum. More than two dozen warplanes and helicopters are parked on the deck and inside, including a Grumman Avenger painted for World War II pilot George Bush (look for "Barbara" calligraphed near the cockpit window). Other exhibits cover this century's plentiful wars, outer-space exploration, and aircraft and nautical history. The 10- to 40-minute tours explore the *Intrepid*, plus a few other ships and a submarine docked nearby. *Twelfth Ave. and W. 46th St., at the Hudson River, Midtown, tel. 212/245–0072. Subway: A, C, or E to W. 42nd St. Admission: $10, $7.50 students age 12–17. Open summer, daily 10–5 (Sun. until 6); winter, Wed.–Sun. 10–5.*

Museum of American Financial History. Taking up the foyer of the former Standard Oil Building, the tiny Museum of American Financial History displays odd Wall Street–related memorabilia such as a bond certificate owned by George Washington; "Wall Street" brand cigars from the 19th century; and copies of the *Bawl Street Journal*, a satirical newspaper published by the Bond Club of New York. The paper's weather reports, which read "SECtional Showers" or "Wet, Followed by Hangover," prove once and for all that some people should keep their day jobs. *26 Broadway, at Bowling Green, Lower Manhattan, tel. 212/908–4110. Subway: 4 or 5 to Bowling Green. Admission free. Open weekdays 11:30–2:30.*

ART GALLERIES

Is New York the capital of the art world? Draw your own conclusions. It's been home to some of the 20th century's most famous and acclaimed artists and photographers, like Andy Warhol, Jackson Pollack, Keith Haring, Jasper Johns, Willem de Kooning, Mark Rothko, Roy Lichtenstein, Cindy Sherman, Alfred Stieglitz, and Diane Arbus to name a few. And it's probably got more art galleries than any other city in America: Approximately 500 fill Manhattan, mainly in SoHo and on 57th Street, but also in the neighborhoods of TriBeCa, the Upper East Side, and increasingly, Chelsea. Uptown galleries tend to be a bit more snobbish, especially to people who aren't looking to buy, while downtown galleries tend to be more laid-back affairs showing experimental art or just stuff that is way out of the mainstream and is happy to be there. That said, keep in mind that many artists and gallery owners have fled SoHo in recent years, claiming it's morphed into one big bland yuppie fantasyland. If you're after art with *real* edge, head to grittier neighborhoods like west Chelsea, or even Long Island City, Queens (*see* The Outer Boroughs, *above*).

Despite the high pretensions of many galleries, they're a great way to see art. First of all, they're free. And many coordinate their shows to complement special exhibitions at the big museums like the Met, MoMA, or the Guggenheim. For work that isn't normally accessible to the public, whether it's masterworks that are in private hands or work by contemporary artists who haven't made it into the museums yet, art galleries are your ticket. Most galleries open between 10 and 11 AM and close by 5 or 6 PM, Tuesday through Saturday. July through early September (the months when their customers leave New York for their summer châteaus), they're typically open by appointment only. On average, shows change every six to eight weeks, often less frequently during summer. For info on current shows, check *Time Out, New York*, or *The New Yorker*; they list many, but hardly all, galleries and their current exhibitions. The *Village Voice* and *New York Press* also list galleries, with an emphasis on downtown and experimental stuff. At galleries and major museums, you can pick up a copy of **Art Now Gallery Guide** (free), the most complete reference to the art scene you'll find. It lists addresses, phone numbers, and open hours of practically all the city's galleries and provides handy maps for gallery-hoppers.

SOHO AND TRIBECA SoHo possess the lion's share of the city's art galleries. Quite a few are clustered along Broadway between Houston and Spring Street, but you can wander almost anywhere and find dozens lining its blocks. TriBeCa, just south of Houston, has fewer galleries, but they're less commercial.

Art in General. This gallery, founded by a group of artists, shows experimental work with a heavy political message. It's got six floors of space and sometimes installs works in the elevator and windows, too. *79 Walker St., btw Broadway and Lafayette Sts., TriBeCa, tel. 212/219–0473. Subway: 6 to Canal St.*

The Drawing Center. The Drawing Center, as you may've guessed from the name, shows exclusively drawings—an art form long neglected by the rest of the world. Recent (and fascinating) shows have included tattoos, cartoons, and even drawings by sidewalk artists. *35 Wooster St., btw Broome and Grand Sts., tel. 212/219–2166. Subway: 1 or 9 to Canal St.*

Franklin Furnace 112. The in-your-face attitude here can be refreshing after a tour of the vacuum-packed art of SoHo galleries. *112 Franklin St., btw West Broadway and Church St., TriBeCa, tel. 212/925–4671. Subway: 1 or 9 to Franklin St.*

Holly Solomon. Solomon has been an art-world heavyweight since the '70s, though the gallery moved downtown only recently. Among the artists whose careers got a boost here are Robert Mapplethorpe (this was the first gallery to show his photos) and William Wegman. *172 Mercer St., at Houston St., tel. 212/941–5777. Subway: B, D, F, or Q to Broadway–Lafayette St.*

Leo Castelli. One of the most famous of all New York galleries, Castelli was where many pop art and abstract expressionist artists got their start. Jasper Johns's one-man show in 1958 is recognized by many as the birth of pop art and minimalism. *578 Broadway, at Prince St., 3rd Floor, tel. 212/431–6279. Subway: N or R to Prince St.*

Paula Cooper. You don't get much more exclusive than this, a gallery revered even by other snobby gallery owners. The shows here, of contemporary artists, are consistently outstanding. *155 Wooster St., btw Houston and Prince Sts., tel. 212/674–0766. Subway: B, D, F, or Q to Broadway–Lafayette St.*

Thread Waxing Space. Video installations and occasionally performance art take place at this esteemed nonprofit gallery. Past artists include Nam June Paik, Hiroshi Teshigahara, and Robert Rauschenberg. *476 Broadway, btw Grand and Broome Sts., tel. 212/966–9520. Subway: A, C, or E to Canal St.*

57TH STREET Midtown's 57th Street, between Sixth and Park avenues, is chock-a-block with galleries trying to retain a ritzy image while standing next to mall staples like the Warner Brothers Studio Store. A few buildings are devoted entirely to art galleries: **41 East**, **20 West**, **24 West**, and **50 West 57th Street**.

Of the approximately 500 galleries in New York, half are in SoHo, and one quarter are along 57th Street.

Pace Wildenstein. One of the city's top galleries, Pace is the place where you'll find all those million-dollar Dubuffets, as well as solo shows by the hottest contemporary artists. Separate fiefdoms under the same roof include **Pace Editions** for prints, **Pace Primitive** for "primitive" art, and **Pace/MacGill** for photography. *32 E. 57th St., at Madison Ave., tel. 212/759–7999. Subway: N or R to W. 57th St.*

UPPER EAST SIDE With few exceptions, the Upper East Side's galleries are clustered along Madison Avenue between 65th and 86th streets—which makes for convenient gallery-hopping if you're exploring the Museum Mile (*see* Manhattan Neighborhoods, Upper East Side, *above*). One of the most venerable galleries in the neighborhood is **M. Knoedler** (19 E. 70th St., btw Fifth and Madison Aves., tel. 212/794–0550), which you can count on for famous contemporary artists from Europe and America. If you're looking for art by someone other than the usual cast of Dead (and Living) White Males, head to **Stone** (113 E. 90th St., btw Park and Lexington Aves., tel. 212/988–6870), which offers shows of contemporary African painting and sculpture, or **Throckmorton** (153 E. 61st St., btw Lexington and Third Aves., tel. 212/223–1059), which specializes in Latin American art and photography. For contemporary photography, try **Bonni Benrubi** (52 E. 76th St., btw Madison and Park Aves., tel. 212/517–3766) or **Robert Mann** (42 E. 76th St., btw Madison and Park Aves., tel. 212/570–1223), which frequently shows works from Europe and Japan.

CHELSEA Most of the galleries in Chelsea are on 22nd Street, between Tenth and Eleventh avenues. The area's only become newly hip for galleries, so don't be afraid to wander around and drop in on whatever looks cool; chances are it may've just opened last week. Galleries here almost uniformly show emerging and on-the-edge art, photography, sculpture, and multimedia work, which makes it one of the best places in the city to get in touch with the current vibe. A few places to get you started: **Annina Nosie** (530 W. 22nd St., btw Tenth and Eleventh Aves., second floor, tel. 212/741–8695); **Matthew Marks** (522 W. 22nd St., tel. 212/861–9455); **Greenenaftali** (526 W. 26th St., tel. 212/463–7770).

Parks and Gardens

While there's no ignoring New York's soaring skyscrapers, concrete canyons, and yellow-cab pileups, you'll find that the city offers much more than an urban jungle. It's got some 29,000 acres of park land, playgrounds, gardens, forests, nature reserves, and even beaches—in fact, New York boasts the largest urban forest in the nation—no doubt you've already noticed **Central Park** (see Major Attractions, *above*), the 843-acre wonderland that occupies a large chunk of upper Manhattan. But you probably haven't yet discovered the enormous, pristine parks of Brooklyn, Queens, the Bronx, and Staten Island, where you can hike for miles without seeing another human being. You can get info on all the city's parks by calling the **City Parks Department hotline** (tel. 800/834–3832). Additionally, the city's **Urban Park Rangers** (tel. 212/772–0210 in Manhattan, 718/287–3400 in Brooklyn, 718/548–7070 in the Bronx, 718/699–4204 in Queens, and 718/667–6042 in Staten Island) have a wealth of info on the parks in their home boroughs. They also offer free guided park tours and nature walks.

The **Gateway National Recreation Area** and the **Staten Island Greenbelt** offer some of the best destinations in the city for would-be tree huggers and bird-watchers. Gateway encompasses 26,000 acres of beach, marsh, and woodlands in New Jersey and the New York boroughs of Staten Island and Queens; the most accessible portions are Jacob Riis Park (see box, New York City, Land of Skyscrapers and Sunny Beaches?!, *below*) and the Jamaica Bay Wildlife Refuge (see below). For info on other parts contact the National Park Service, Fort Tilden, New York, NY 11695, tel. 718/318–4300. The Staten Island Greenbelt is a 2,500-acre expanse of undeveloped land, including High Rock Park (see below). It was conceived by Central Park's designer Frederick Law Olmsted, who once owned a farm here, and currently has about 28 miles of trails through woods, meadows, wetlands, and beachfront. For particulars, contact the main Greenbelt office (200 Nevada Ave., Staten Island, tel. 718/667–2165).

If you're pining for just a few trees and a breath of fresh air, Manhattan has some unusual alternatives. Besides the decent-sized parks listed below, don't overlook the dozens of **"vest-pocket" parks**, less than a city block in size, that pepper its neighborhoods. In Midtown, you'll find these little parks at West 46th Street (btw Sixth and Seventh Aves.), East 53rd Street (btw Fifth and Madison Aves.), and East 51st Street (btw Second and Third Aves.). Other great places to kick back with a book and a brown-bag lunch are office building **atriums**, products of the 1980s building boom (you see, something good did come out of the Decade of Greed). In exchange for "giving" the public some open space at ground level, developers got to build even taller skyscrapers, from which they could garner more rent. Waterfalls, foliage, abundant benches, and a small café often complement the scene, and keep in mind that these indoor atriums are invariably air-conditioned. Most are open daily 8 AM–6 PM. Some of the most spectacular include the **Harkness Atrium** (Broadway, btw W. 62nd and 63rd Sts., Upper West Side), **IBM Garden Plaza** (E. 56th St., at Madison Ave., Midtown), and **Olympic Tower** (51st St., at Fifth Ave., Midtown). In a class by itself is the 120-foot-tall, glass-walled Winter Garden Atrium at the **World Financial Center** (see Manhattan Neighborhoods, Lower Manhattan, *above*), which also hosts art exhibits and live music.

MANHATTAN

In addition to the parks listed below, don't forget **Union Square** and **Madison Square** (for both, see Manhattan Neighborhoods, Gramercy and Union Square, *above*), **Washington Square** (see Manhattan Neighborhoods, West Village, *above*), **City Hall Park** (see Manhattan Neighborhoods, Lower Manhattan, *above*), and **Tompkins Square** (see Manhattan Neighborhoods, East Village and Alphabet City, *above*)—the latter two are arguably the liveliest parks in the city. If you're sick to death of competing for a patch of green with yuppies in Central Park, their newborns strapped on in some expensive papoose, buy a bumper of Bud, lean up against a tree, and watch the zany characters parade by in one of Manhattan's smaller parks. For flower gardens, don't overlook the formal beds at **The Cloisters** (see Museums and Galleries, *above*).

Battery Park. At the southernmost tip of Manhattan, skyscrapers and taxi-filled streets give way to green fields, trees, and footpaths filled with camera-toting tourists. Battery Park (so named because a battery of 28 cannons was placed along its shore in colonial days to fend off the British) is built on landfill and has gradually grown over the centuries. In fact, its main structure, **Castle Clinton National Monument**, originally stood on an island some 200 feet from shore—like the mountain coming to Mohammed, the island of Manhattan has gradually snuck up and encompassed it. Since its construction around 1810, Castle Clinton has been a defensive fort, entertainment hall (where P. T. Barnum presented the "Swedish Nightingale" Jenny Lind to an enchanted New York audience), immigration depot, and aquarium. It now holds a **visitor center** and the ticket booth for ferries to the Statue of Liberty and Ellis Island (for info on ferry service and tickets, *see* Major Attractions, *above*). The park is loaded with various other statues and monuments, some impressive, some downright obscure. The **East Coast Memorial**, a granite structure topped by a fierce-looking eagle, was dedicated by President Kennedy in 1963 to the American servicemen who died in the Atlantic during World War II. The **Netherlands Memorial Flagpole**, near Castle Clinton, bears a plaque that describes (in English and Dutch) a bead exchange that procured from American Indians the land used to establish Fort Amsterdam in 1626. Also look for a romantic statue of Giovanni da Verrazano, the Florentine merchant who piloted the ship that first sighted New York and its harbor in 1524, and the extraordinary **Hope Garden**, whose 100,000 rosebushes were planted in 1992 as a living memorial to people with AIDS. After wandering past these monuments, head for the waterfront to get unparalleled views of the New York harbor, including Lady Liberty and the onion-domed brick buildings of Ellis Island. *Broadway at Battery Pl., Lower Manhattan. Subway: 4 or 5 to Bowling Green. Also: 1 or 9 to South Ferry.*

Bowling Green. The benches at this tiny park, just north of Battery Park (*see above*), fill with brown-bagging business types on sunny weekday afternoons. Colonial lawn-bowling enthusiasts once leased this oval of green from the governor for the annual fee of one peppercorn; it became New York's first public park in 1733. Look closely at the iron fence around parts of the Green and you'll notice the height is uneven. That's because rioters stormed the place on July 9, 1776, after learning about the signing of the Declaration of Independence; they toppled a statue of King George III that had occupied the spot for 11 years and then melted most of its lead into bullets. *Lower Manhattan. Subway: 4 or 5 to Bowling Green.*

Bryant Park. For 20 years Bryant Park, Midtown's only major green space, was abandoned to crack addicts and muggers. An incredible $9-million renovation, however, has transformed it into one of the best-loved and most beautiful parks in all the city. (It also boasts New York's cleanest public bathrooms.) Century-old shade trees and formal flower beds line the perimeter of its grassy central square, which is scattered with hundreds of smart green folding chairs. The chairs aren't bolted down, and no one steals them; like we said, it's a pretty miraculous place. During summer, it draws thousands of lunching office workers; hosts live jazz and comedy concerts; and presents a free, summer-long, outdoor film festival (*see* Movie Houses, in Chapter 6) every Monday at dusk. Several times each year giant tents spring up when New York designers hold their fashion shows here (forget trying to sneak in, but you can look for supermodels hailing cabs on Sixth Avenue). Year-round it's home to a discount theater tickets booth, TKTS (*see* Chapter 7); a chic, expensive restaurant, the **Bryant Park Grill** (tel. 212/840–6500); and a semi-affordable restaurant, the **Bryant Park Café**. When money is tight, go west to the Sixth Avenue edge of the park, where kiosks sell sandwiches and salads for $4–$5. *From W. 40th to 42nd Sts., btw Fifth and Sixth Aves., Midtown. Subway: B, D, F, or Q to W. 42nd St.*

Carl Schurz Park. When Upper East Siders want fresh air and river views, they head for Carl Schurz Park. Once known as East End Park, it was renamed in honor of a German revolutionary and founder of the Republican party, who served as a U.S. senator, cabinet secretary, and editor of *Harper's Weekly* in the late 1800s. Joggers and dog walkers pace along the pleasant **John Finley Walk** (named for an editor of the *New York Times* who was also an avid stroller), while traffic rumbles just below on FDR Drive. The large, fenced-off home near 88th Street is **Gracie Mansion**, the mayor's residence. Built for Scottish merchant Archibald Gracie, the mansion housed the Museum of the City of New York until the early 1940s, when Parks Commissioner Robert Moses commandeered the mansion for political buddy (and mayor) Fiorello La Guardia. Tours ($3) are offered Wednesdays at 10, 11, 1, and 2. Call 212/570–4751 for reservations, which are required. *East River Dr., btw E. 82nd and 90th Sts., Upper East Side. Subway: 4, 5, or 6 to E. 86th St.*

Columbus Park. This Chinatown park isn't the nicest in Manhattan, but if you can deal with the glassy-eyed Village junkies sprawled on its benches, it's one of the best places in the city to people-watch. Mornings bring groups of elderly Chinese practicing the graceful movements of tai chi. During afternoons, the park's tables fill for heated games of mah-jongg; games are so intense that despite crowds, the only sounds you can hear are the clicking of the mah-jongg tiles. *On Bayard St., btw Baxter and Mulberry Sts. Subway: J, M, N, R, Z, or 6 to Canal St.*

East River Park. This 1½-mile stretch of green is perfect for running, biking, or just watching the garbage scows toil slowly up the East River. For some reason (maybe because you have to walk through a dicey section of the East Village to get here) the park's fields, baseball diamonds, and tennis courts are completely underutilized. What a shame—the views of Brooklyn Heights, Williamsburg, and the Brooklyn Bridge are unparalleled. *East River Dr., btw E. 14th St. and Delancey St. Subway: F to Second Ave.*

Fort Tryon Park. This phenomenal 62-acre spread of terraced walks and riotous gardens was another of Olmsted's landscape creations (*see box* They Built This City, *above*). Though it's a long haul north on the subway, it's definitely worth the trip. On a hill at the northern end of the park is **The Cloisters** (*see* Museums and Galleries, *above*), which houses the Metropolitan Museum of Art's collection of medieval art. The central plaza honors Revolutionary War heroine Margaret Corbin. Nearby are the remains of Fort Tryon, used during the Revolutionary War. Walk west along its meandering pathways for spectacular views of the Hudson River. *Entrance on Fort Washington Ave., at W. 190th St., Washington Heights. Subway: A to W. 190th St. Also: Bus M4 to last stop.*

Fort Washington Park. This northern Manhattan park is difficult to reach, but worth the trouble: From the foot of Washington Bridge (179th St. and Fort Washington Ave.), walk north to 181st Street, then west across a pedestrian overpass. Once across, follow the path through a tunnel and over some railroad tracks to eventually reach a shady, pleasant rest area. Here you'll find the **Little Red Lighthouse** (of storybook fame), which once guided ships away from this rocky outcrop, plus a few desolate remains of the old Fort Washington. You can also stare up into the steel framework of the mighty Washington Bridge. *Riverside Dr., btw 170th and 181st Sts., Washington Heights. Subway: A to W. 181st St.*

Hudson River Park. If you can ignore the blitzkrieg on 'blades and bikes coming at you from all directions, this newly opened park is just right for a stroll along the water. Or grab one of the dozens of benches and enjoy the spectacle of Lycra-clad weekend warriors huffing and puffing up and down the park's 1½-mile length. The park connects with the 1.2-mile-long Battery Park City Esplanade (*see* Manhattan Neighborhoods, Lower Manhattan, *above*) to the south. *On the Hudson River, from Gansevoort St. to Battery Park City, West Village/SoHo, tel. 212/353–0366. Subway: A, C, E, or L to W. 14th St.*

Inwood Hill Park. The 196-acre Inwood Hill Park covers the northern tip of Manhattan, an area once inexplicably dubbed *Spuyten Duyvil* ("Spitting Devil") by Dutch colonists. The whole place actually looks much as it did centuries ago, its thick forest a tangle of overgrown brambles. The handful of hilly trails provide an afternoon's escape from car horns and exhaust fumes. *Entrance at Dyckman St. and Seaman Ave., Inwood. Subway: A to Dyckman St. (200th St.).*

Lotus Garden. This small garden on the rooftop of an Upper West Side apartment complex has been kept up for over 20 years by a group of dedicated volunteers. It's a flower- and tree-filled oasis in the sky where you can enjoy a few moments of quiet. Look for the iron entrance gate marked LOTUS GARDENS on West 97th Street at Broadway, next to The Wiz music store. *W. 97th St. and Broadway, tel. 212/580–4897. Subway: 1, 2, 3, or 9 to W. 96th St. Open Sun. 1–4 and by appointment.*

Riverbank State Park. Riverbank is a park with a dark past. In the early 1990s city officials announced plans to build an enormous sewage plant along the Hudson River in Harlem, then flinched in surprise when Harlem residents protested. Then-governor Mario Cuomo brokered a truce by ordering that a park be built atop the sewage plant, and 28-acre Riverbank State Park opened for business in 1993. Amazingly, it's a lovely and stench-free stretch of grass and trees, with striking views of the Hudson River and athletic facilities, including a hockey rink, Olympic-sized pool, basketball courts, and track. The park's brand-new **carousel** is alone worth the trip. It has a zany menagerie of 32 brightly colored critters—a giraffe, flamingo, kangaroo, zebra, snail, bat, lizard, lobster, octopus, and swordfish—instead of the usual prancing horses. The animals were carved by an artist in Queens who used children's drawings as his patterns. The kids whose drawings he used get a lifetime of free rides. *Riverside Dr., btw W. 137th and 145th Sts, Harlem, tel. 212/694–3600. Subway: 1 or 9 to W. 145th St.*

Riverside Park. Stretching along the Hudson River from the heart of the Upper West Side north into Harlem, this narrow cliff-top park is a favorite of runners, dog-walkers, bicyclists, and Rollerbladers. Its picturesque terraces, rustic stone walls, and rambling paths were designed at the turn of the century by Frederick Law Olmsted and Calvert Vaux to look like a snippet of English countryside. The park's **Promenade** begins at 72nd Street and continues north for more than a mile, past formal gardens, statues, and a few lofty monuments. At 83rd Street, look for **Mt. Tom**, a boulder Edgar Allen Poe often climbed to ponder the passing river scene. You'll also find a memorial to firemen at 100th Street and a **Joan of Arc Statue** at 93rd Street, which was the first monument in New York dedicated to a woman when it was put up in 1915. At 121st Street is **Grant's Tomb** (if you want to find out who's buried in Grant's Tomb, *see* Manhattan Neighborhoods, Columbia University and Morningside Heights, *above*). Just beyond that at 123rd Street is the **Grave of an Amiable Child**, marking the spot where a five-year-old girl fell to her death in 1797. Though the Henry Hudson Parkway runs alongside most of the park, a pedestrian underpass at 79th Street will take you to the **Boat Basin**, where you can walk right along the river's edge. North of 100th Street the park gets a bit wild and woolly (as you might guess from the number of crack vials scattered under park benches), and isn't the best place to linger alone or at dusk. *Riverside Dr., btw W. 72nd and 135th Sts. Subway: 1, 2, 3, or 9 to W. 72nd St. Also: 1, 2, 3, or 9 to W. 96th St.*

Washington Market Park. TriBeCa's only park is a 1½-acre former vacant lot turned attractive public square, with a luxurious lawn, children's playground, and Victorian gazebo. It's a great place to stop for a picnic lunch, especially if you time your visit to coincide with the farmer's market (*see* Greenmarkets, in Chapter 4) held here every Saturday. *Greenwich St., btw Chambers and Duane Sts., TriBeCa. Subway: 1, 2, 3, or 9 to Chambers St.*

THE OUTER BOROUGHS

One of the most romantic gardens in the city can be found in the Bronx at **Wave Hill** (*see* Museums and Galleries, *above*), while awesome views of Manhattan can be had from the **Brooklyn Heights Promenade** (*see* The Outer Boroughs, Brooklyn Heights, *above*). For info on **Flushing Meadows–Corona Park**, home to two world's fairs, *see* The Outer Boroughs, Queens, *above*.

Alley Pond Park. In northeast Queens you'll find 635 acres of woodlands, meadows, fresh- and salt-water marshes, and kettle ponds (a type of lake created 21,000 years ago by melting glaciers). Though the park is crisscrossed by several busy expressways, you'll still find quiet,

Murder in Riverside Park

While it's true that just about every park in New York City has been the scene of a lurid crime at one time or another, the 1944 murder of David Kammerer by Lucien Carr in Riverside Park must be one of the most bizarre. Carr, an original Beat generation member famous for introducing Jack Kerouac and Allen Ginsberg to William Burroughs, murdered his former Boy Scout master after the lovesick older man followed him from Missouri to New York City—Kammerer had gone as far as to take a job as a school janitor when Carr enrolled at Columbia University. The crime made headlines for weeks; at his trial, Carr was found guilty of manslaughter. He served two years of his sentence before receiving a pardon from the governor.

tree-shaded hiking trails that stretch for miles. Pick up free trail maps at the Alley Pond **Environmental Center** (228–06 Northern Blvd., Douglaston, tel. 718/229–4000), at the north end of the park near Little Neck Bay. *Douglaston, Queens. Subway: 7 to Main St. (Flushing), then Bus Q12 to Northern Blvd. (25 min).*

Brooklyn Botanical Garden. At 52 acres, the Brooklyn Botanical Garden is only a fifth the size of the stunning New York Botanical Garden in the Bronx. Still, its collection of over 12,000 different plants is nothing to sneeze at (unless, of course, it's pollen season), and you can spend hours wandering its grounds. A few highlights include the **Shakespeare Garden**, which contains 80 plants immortalized by the bard; the **Japanese Garden** (50¢ on weekends) takes you out of Brooklyn and into Kyoto with winding paths around a lake shaped in the Japanese character for "heart"; the **Cranford Rose Garden** has over 1,000 varieties of the thorny things and has got to be *In spring, the Brooklyn Botanical Garden's Daffodil Hill and Cherry Esplanade are each so colorful you'll swear you're on hallucinogens.* one of the most romantic picnic spots in the city; and the **Fragrance Garden**, with placards written in English and Braille, is designed especially for the blind. Don't skip a peek into the $25-million **Steinhardt Conservatory**, a greenhouse encompassing 24,000 square feet. Its Trail of Evolution shows how plant life developed from the mosses of billions of years ago to the plants of present-day deserts, temperate lands, and tropics. In winter the steamy Tropical Pavilion is almost as good as a trip to Hawaii. Excellent free tours of the gardens depart weekends at 1 PM from the lily pools in front of the conservatory. *1000 Washington Ave., at Carroll St., Park Slope, Brooklyn, tel. 718/622–4433. Subway: 2 or 3 to Eastern Pkwy./Brooklyn Museum. Admission to gardens: $3, $1.50 students (free Tues.). Admission to Conservatory: $2, $1 students. Open Apr.–Sept., Tues.–Fri. 8–6, weekends 10–6; Oct.–Mar., Tues.–Fri. 8–4:30, weekends 10–4:30.*

Empire Fulton Ferry State Park. New York's ultimate waterfront park is located between the Brooklyn and Manhattan bridges on the East River. The views of Manhattan are spectacular and the park itself immaculate. Few people venture here besides sculptors from nearby warehouse studios, who bring their works out onto the grass on sunny days. *On Water St., west of Washington St., Brooklyn Heights, Brooklyn. Subway: A or C to High St./Brooklyn Bridge.*

Forest Park. The high hills of this 538-acre park in central Queens offer great views of Long Island Sound and the Atlantic Ocean. Its southwestern half has athletic fields, an antique carousel ($1), a golf course (tel. 718/296–7679), and a band shell that hosts Sunday concerts June through September. The northeastern half of the park has nature trails winding through stands of 150-year-old oaks. You can rent horses ($20 per hour) to explore the park at nearby **Dixie Drew Riding Academy** (70th Rd. and Sybilla St., tel. 718/263–3500). *Forest Hills/Kew Gardens, Queens, tel. 718/699–4204 for rangers' offices or 718/520–5911 for summer concert info. Subway: J to 85th St./Forest Pkwy. Also: E or F to Union Turnpike/Kew Gardens; take Bus Q37 to Union Turnpike and Park Ln. (1 hr).*

Fort Greene Park. This large, underutilized park—another fine product of Olmsted and Vaux—is just waiting for your lazy picnics and ultimate Frisbee games. Its towering hill has great views of both Manhattan and Brooklyn and a long, smooth slope, if you want to make use of your trash-can lid after a good snowfall. The two monuments you'll see are the Prison Ship Martyrs Monument (*see* The Outer Boroughs, Brooklyn, *above*) and a memorial to the 126 Spanish soldiers who died during the American Revolution and were buried in Brooklyn. *DeKalb Ave., just east of Flatbush Ave., Fort Greene, Brooklyn. Subway: D, M, N, Q, or R to DeKalb Ave.*

High Rock Park. At only 100 acres, High Rock is one of the smallest but prettiest parts of Staten Island's Greenbelt (*see* The Outer Boroughs, Staten Island, *above*). Trails meander through hardwood forest and lush wetlands dotted with glacial ponds; check out the ¼-mile loop around Marsh Pond for spring wildflowers, or take the arduous trek up **Todt Hill** for an eagle-eye view of the whole island. At the visitor center (open weekdays 9–5, weekends 10–4) you can pick up a trail map or join a ranger-led ecology walk weekends at 2 PM. *200 Nevada Ave., Staten Island, tel. 718/667–6042. From Ferry Terminal, take SIRT to New Dorp. Also: Bus S74 to Rockland Ave.*

Jamaica Bay Wildlife Refuge. You might spot any one of 325 bird species, plus butterflies, box turtles, and small mammals like muskrats and raccoons among the salt marshes, fields, woods, and mudflats of this 9,155-acre wildlife preserve just south of JFK International Airport.

There's something magical about standing in a marsh watching snowy egrets at the Jamaica Bay Wildlife Refuge, the World Trade Center visible in the distance through sepia-hued smog.

Spring and fall are the best times to catch migrating birds, and the wildflowers are tremendous in spring. In summer you'll need insect repellent or a giant fly swatter. Pick up a map and mandatory free permit at the **visitor center** (open daily 8:30–5) before hitting the trail. *Queens, tel. 718/318–4340. Subway: A (make sure it's marked "Rockaways" and not "Lefferts Blvd.") to Broad Channel; walk west to Cross Bay Blvd., turn right and walk ¾ mi north.*

New York Botanical Garden (NYBG). Of the city's many botanical gardens, this is the most stunning. Its 250 beautifully landscaped acres opened in 1891, patterned after Britain's Royal Botanical Gardens. Highlights include the formal rose garden, with 230 varieties; the rock garden ($1), with a man-made waterfall and alpine meadow; and the native plant garden, featuring flowers and shrubs of the eastern United States. You can also visit the Alfred E. Haupt Conservatory, built in 1902 and modeled after London's Crystal Palace, and a historic snuff mill that dates from the 1840s and now houses a café. Free guided walking tours depart weekends at 1, 1:30, 3, and 3:30. When you tire of strolling the gardens, you can hike a nearby 40-acre tract of virgin hemlock forest paralleling the Bronx River Gorge. *200th St. and Southern Blvd., Bronx, tel. 718/817–8500. Subway: C or D to Bedford Park Blvd. Also: Metro North to Botanical Gardens. Admission: $3; free Sat. 10–noon. Open Tues.–Sun. 10–6 (shorter hrs in winter).*

Pelham Bay Park. The highlight of New York City's largest park is **Orchard Beach**, created in 1936 when Parks Commissioner Robert Moses turned $8 million and 1,200,000 cubic yards of fine, white imported sand into the beach you see today. The crowds here are mostly Latin; if you don't like salsa music, stay away. But this 2,764-acre wooded sprawl has a handful of other attractions, including the **Bartow-Pell Mansion** (895 Shore Rd., tel. 718/885–1461; admission $2.50, $1.25 students), an elegant 1840s country estate built by a Thomas "Lord of Pelham" Pell; two golf courses; miles of hiking trails; and the **Thomas Pell Wildlife Refuge and Sanctuary**, whose wetlands attract thousands of birds in spring and fall. To see the entire park, follow the 6-mile Siwanoy Trail starting on Shore Road at the north side of Pelham Bridge. Or you can rent horses at **Pelham Bit** (tel. 718/885–0551) for $20 per hour. *Bronx, tel. 718/885–3466 or 718/430–1890. Subway: 6 to Pelham Bay Park.*

Prospect Park. Prospect Park is to Brooklyn what Central Park is to Manhattan: a vast, 526-acre green space where people gather to picnic, play ball, or just go for a stroll. Indeed, Olmsted and Vaux (who collaborated on the design of both) preferred Prospect Park to their Manhattan creation. As in Central Park, its roads are closed to motor traffic on weekends. One of the best places to chill is on **Long Meadow**, near the northern entrance to the park. If you can believe it, this is the largest open space in an urban park in the entire United States. Near the south end of the park, you'll find the 60-acre Prospect Lake, where you can tool around in pedal boats for $10 per hour during summer from **Pelican Boat Rentals** (tel. 718/282–7789) in the park's **Boathouse**. In winter, swirl around **Kate Wollman Rink** (tel. 718/287–6431) on a pair of ice skates ($3). There's a small zoo, the **Prospect Park Wildlife Conservation Center** (450 Flatbush Ave., tel. 718/399–7339), completely redesigned in 1993, with a tiny collection of sea lions, baboons, prairie dogs, wallabies, and red pandas; admission is $2.50. The park's antique **carousel**, near the zoo, was created by a Russian immigrant, and offers 56 horses, chariots, lions, and giraffes for your riding pleasure. During summer, Prospect Park's 9th Street Bandshell is home to the **Celebrate Brooklyn** festival; for more info, *see* Summer Arts, in Chapter 7. *West of Flatbush Ave. and south of Grand Army Plaza, Park Slope, Brooklyn, tel. 718/956–8999. Subway: D or Q to Prospect Park. Also: F to 15th St./Prospect Park, and 2 or 3 to Grand Army Plaza.*

Queens Botanical Garden. The 39-acre pride of Flushing, Queens has the largest collection of roses in all of New York. Its theme gardens—Herb, Bird, Bee, Woodland, Backyard, All-America, and Victorian Wedding—are super cheesy, and wedding parties just love 'em. *43–50 Main St., near Roosevelt Ave., Flushing, Queens, tel. 718/886–3800. Subway: 7 to Main St.*

New York City, Land of Skyscrapers and Sunny Beaches?!

Beaches in New York? It's not as strange as you'd think. Though you'd need to venture out to Long Island to find really great beaches (and if you're looking for a surfable swell, try the Left Coast), there are some decent stretches of sand in Brooklyn, the Bronx, Queens, and Staten Island. Just prepare yourself for 48° water, even in June, and lots of crowds.

- Brighton Beach. At Brighton Beach, a.k.a. "Odessa by the Sea," boardwalk stands hawk Russian snacks like pierogies alongside popsicles and hot dogs. Waves are small enough to let grandma get in the water. Brooklyn. Subway: D or Q to Brighton Beach; walk 2 blocks south.

- Coney Island Beach and Boardwalk. There's nothing quite like Coney Island in summer, with its Cyclone roller coaster, carnival side shows, annual Mermaid Parade, and savvy entrepreneurs covertly peddling cans of ice-cold beer. Brooklyn. Subway: B, D, or F to Coney Island (Stillwell Ave.); walk 2 blocks south.

- Jacob Riis Park. Besides a full mile of beachfront, Jacob Riis Park offers softball fields, paddleball courts, and a pitch-and-putt golf course, all free. At the eastern end of the park lies a gay (and until recently, nude) beach. Gateway National Recreation Area, Queens, tel. 718/318–4300. Subway: 2 or 5 to Flatbush Ave./Brooklyn College, then Bus Q35 (1 hr).

- Manhattan Beach. Though less than half a mile long, this is one of the city's nicest beaches for sunning and swimming. It's just east of Brighton Beach, off Oriental Boulevard, Brooklyn. Subway: D or Q to Brighton Beach.

- Rockaway Beach and Boardwalk. New York City's longest beach faces the Atlantic Ocean. That means decent-size waves and a minimum of pollution. Of course, these facts aren't secret, and during summer it can be difficult to find a spot to spread your towel. Follow the boardwalk past the last subway stop (116th Street) to the area where wealthy residents have tacked up NO PARKING signs in the hopes of scaring people away. This spot is actually public and much less crowded than the rest of the strand. Queens, tel. 718/318–4000. Subway: A (make sure it's labeled "Rockaway Park") to Beach 105th St./Seaside. Also: A to 116th St./Rockaway Park.

- Staten Island beaches. The entire southeast shore of Staten Island is Atlantic Ocean beach, much of it belonging to the Gateway National Recreation Area (tel. 718/351–6970). Surfable spots include Wolf's Pond Park and Beach (tel. 718/984–8266) and Great Kills Park. If you just want sun and sand, head to Oakwood Beach, New Dorp Beach, Midland Beach, or South Beach Park. For info on transport, see The Outer Boroughs, Staten Island, above.

Socrates Sculpture Park. Venture past rows of abandoned factories, and you'll come to this strange but peaceful 4-acre park on the East River. Formerly an illegal dump site, it's now filled with mammoth abstract sculptures made from scrap metal, broken pipes, and used tires—the perfect spot to contemplate weighty themes like Man vs. Nature, Man vs. Machine, and, of course, Art. The views of Manhattan are superb. *32–00 Vernon Blvd., at Broadway, Long Island City, Queens, tel. 718/956–1819. Subway: N to Broadway. Open daily 10 AM–sunset.*

Van Cortlandt Park. With 1,146 acres of forest and wetlands, this park offers much more than lots of green space and hiking trails. On the park's Parade Grounds stands the oldest building in the Bronx (1748), the chock-full-of-antiques **Van Cortlandt Mansion** (tel. 718/543–3344). It was twice used by George Washington as headquarters during the Revolutionary War. You can sometimes catch Anglophiles playing cricket on the Parade Grounds. Also here is the country's oldest municipal golf course—people have been putting around these greens since 1885. If you like to hike, follow the forest-lined **Old Croton Aqueduct trail**, the **Cass Gallagher Nature Trail**, or the tracks of the **Old Putnam Railroad line**, which once linked New York and Boston. The **John Kieran Nature Trail** circles Van Cortlandt Lake—New York City's largest—and offers great bird-watching. *Bronx, tel. 718/430–1890. Subway: 1 or 9 to 242 St./Van Cortlandt Park.*

Cheap Thrills

In summer, it's impossible not to stumble across some sort of free concert, play, or dance performance in the course of a day's exploration; check one of the city weeklies like the *New York Press* or *Time Out* to see what's going down, where. For more info, *see* Summer Arts, in Chapter 7. If you plan to be in New York for a while, you might want to invest in a yearly subscription to *Free Time* (20 Waterside Plaza, Suite 6F, New York, NY 10010; $13.50), a monthly guide that lists about 450 free concerts, lectures, dance recitals, and plays per issue. You can buy (nope, it's not free) a single copy at most newsstands and some bookstores for $1.

COOL VIEWS Once you've seen all the obvious cool views—from the **Empire State Building**, the **World Trade Center**, and inside the head of the **Statue of Liberty** (for all, *see* Major Attractions, *above*)—you're ready for the advanced stuff. If you want to work for it, consider the 14-floor climb up the building housing the **Clocktower Gallery** (*see* Museums and Galleries, *above*) in TriBeCa; in Brooklyn, you can climb up the inside of the 80-foot-tall **Soldiers' and Sailors' Memorial Arch** (*see* The Outer Boroughs, *above*); it's open to climbers weekends in warm weather. If you're feeling lazy, take the elevator ($1) to the top of the 22-story, 356-foot tower of **Riverside Church** (*see* Manhattan Neighborhoods, Columbia University and Morningside Heights, *above*) to spy on the Hudson River below. If you're just looking to stroll along, sopping up all the New York atmosphere, try one of these less-obvious spots: The 1.2-mile **Battery Park City Esplanade** (*see* Lower Manhattan, *above*) offers stellar views of the Statue of Liberty and New Jersey's "Gold Coast"; the ⅓-mile **Brooklyn Heights Promenade** (*see* The Outer Boroughs, *above*) is packed on summer evenings with New Yorkers whose gaping mouths and reverent stares at the skyline contradict their world-weary cynicism (perhaps they're marveling at just *how* phallic the Empire State Building is). In the very un-touristy neighborhood of Long Island City, Queens, you'll find breathtaking waterfront views of the Manhattan skyline at the quirky **Socrates Sculpture Park** (*see* Parks and Gardens, The Outer Boroughs, *above*).

HIGH CULTURE: THE FINE ARTS Unless you're planning to buy that Joan Miró instead of just admiring it, visiting **art galleries** is always free (*see* Museums and Galleries, *above*). For a taste of shopping, museum-going, people-watching, and high drama all rolled into one, New York's famous auction houses **Sotheby's** (1334 York Ave., at 72nd St., Upper East Side, tel. 212/606–7000) and **Christie's** (502 Park Ave., at 59th St., tel. 212/546–1000) are just the ticket. You can attend both the previews (where they display all the stuff about to be sold) and the auctions themselves for free; call for details. The most famous auctions (not counting the Jackie O frenzy in 1996) are those for paintings, which happen in November and May.

Many of the city's churches and museums bring string quartets and such into their courtyards and gardens for free performances. One of the best freebies is at the **Metropolitan Museum of Art**, which holds concerts Friday and Saturday evenings on its Great Hall balcony. For info on all your options, *see* Music, Other Spaces, in Chapter 7. And what could be more civilized than free Shakespeare in Central Park? *See* Summer Arts, in Chapter 7, for details on finagling free tickets to the yearly **New York Shakespeare Festival.**

LOW CULTURE: MOVIES AND TV You've a bunch of ways to get your daily fix of Low Culture for little or no cash. During summer, classic flicks are shown at dusk on a giant outdoor screen in **Bryant Park** (*see* Movie Houses, in Chapter 6), so pack the picnic basket. The **Museum of Television and Radio** (*see* Museums and Galleries, *above*) offers *60,000* episodes of radio- and TV-land for your viewing pleasure; admission is $6, $4 students. To satisfy your TV itch with a twist, turn off the tube and go join the studio audience (*see box, below*) for one of the many shows taped in the city.

JOY RIDES One of the best ways to see the Lower Manhattan skyline and New York Harbor is from the deck of the **Staten Island Ferry** (*see* The Outer Boroughs, *above*), which is only 50¢ round-trip. If you're looking for altitude, climb aboard the **Roosevelt Island Tram** (*see* Manhat-

---

You, Too, Can Be a Member of a Live Studio Audience

In New York you can not only watch TV, you can be on it. Numerous shows tape in New York, and they all need studio audiences to laugh, applaud, and answer embarrassing questions. To score a free ticket or two you'll need to plan ahead: Most shows require that you send a postcard (with number of tickets requested) weeks or months in advance. If you missed the boat, you can still score standby tickets if you're willing to spend a morning standing in line.

- *Fox TV. Fox always has a handful of shows open to studio audiences; call for the latest. Tel. 212/452–3600.*

- *Late Night With Conan O'Brien. Same-day standby tickets are available at the NBC Page Desk in the lobby of 30 Rockefeller Center. NBC Tickets, "Late Night With Conan O'Brien," 30 Rockefeller Plaza, New York, NY 10112, tel. 212/664–3055.*

- *The Late Show With David Letterman. Standby tickets are available weekdays at noon in front of the Ed Sullivan Theater. Arrive early. Ed Sullivan Theater, 1697 Broadway, New York, NY 10019, tel. 212/975–1003.*

- *Live With Regis and Kathy Lee. Standby tickets are available at 8 AM weekdays from the ABC headquarters; line up at the corner of 67th Street and Columbus Avenue. Live Tickets, Asonia Station, Box 777, New York, NY 10023, tel. 212/456–3537.*

- *Politically Incorrect with Bill Maher. Tapings of this funky and irreverent show are Tuesdays and Thursdays year-round. Tel. 212/512–8959.*

- *Saturday Night Live. Tickets for performances and dress rehearsals are available by lottery, and postcards are accepted only during the month of August. Standby tickets are available at 8 AM on the day of show on the mezzanine of Rockefeller Center (50th Street side). NBC Tickets, "Saturday Night Live," 30 Rockefeller Plaza, New York, NY 10112, tel. 212/664–3055.*

tan Neighborhoods, Upper East Side, *above*), which runs high in the air over the East River, parallel to the Queensborough Bridge. The trip is $1.40. The subway ride to **Rockaway Beach** (*see box, above*) is about an hour from mid-Manhattan, and for $1.50 pretty spectacular—the train emerges from below ground to run on elevated tracks through the borough of Queens and finally over the sandy marshes of the Rockaways.

TOTAL KITSCH-O-RAMA Freak shows are a big thing at the **Coney Island Beach and Boardwalk** (*see* The Outer Boroughs, Brooklyn, *above*) and they've all got a "two-headed" baby and the "world's largest" rat. Don't miss the **Coney Island Circus Sideshow**'s ($3) acts like the human blockhead and the sword-swallowing bearded lady.

Chinatown Fair. This sleazy arcade has all your favorite old video games, like PacMan, Galaxian, Frogger, and Space Invaders, plus a smattering of modern ones. Depending on your feelings about animal rights, you can also "play" tic-tac-toe (50¢ per game) against a pathetic-looking chicken. This genius fowl was once featured on *That's Incredible. 8 Mott St., near Mosco St., Chinatown. Subway: J, M, N, R, Z, or 6 to Canal St.*

THE SPORTING LIFE Believe it or not, Central Park boasts a lovely public **croquet grounds** (*see* Major Attractions, *above*) where you and your friends can gather together to act out your own version of *Heathers.* You must have a permit ($30) to play, which is good for an entire year; call 212/360–8133 for more info. If your sport of choice is **disco roller skating**, go to the **Roxy** (*see* Dance Clubs, in Chapter 6) on Tuesdays (gay) or Wednesdays (mixed).

Fishing in Central Park. Central Park's Harlem Meer has recently been spruced up and stocked with 50,000 bluegills, largemouth bass, and catfish. You can rent poles for free from the adjacent Charles A. Dana Discovery Center, then catch-and-release to your hearts' content. *Near Fifth Ave., btw E. 106th and 110th Sts., Central Park, tel. 212/860–1370. Subway: 6 to E. 110th St. Open Tues.–Sun. 11–5; shorter hrs in winter.*

Hashing. The New York Hash House Harriers is the club for self-described "drinkers with a running problem." Basically, it's a jolly group of folks who meet weekly to run around the city playing an alcohol-intensive version of the British children's game Hounds and Hares. Check out their World Wide Web site at http://mu.met.psu.edu. *Tel. 212/HASH–NYC for recorded info.*

Moonlight Bike Rides. On the last Friday of each month, **Time's Up** (tel. 212/802–8222) offers moonlight group rides through Central Park; for the October ride everyone's encouraged to come in Halloween costume.

TRIPPING THE LIGHT FANTASTIC If you've ever had a hankering to swing, waltz, foxtrot, salsa, two-step, lindy, or rumba under the stars, here's your chance. Show up at Lincoln Center's central plaza July 10–August 10 at 6:30 on Wednesdays through Fridays for a free hour of instruction; afterwards, you'll have several hours to whirl around practicing your new moves during the **Midsummer Night Swing Dance Extravaganza.** Saturdays the dancing starts at 8:15 (with no prior lesson). Admission is $8. Look for a printed schedule in the Center's concert halls, or call 212/875–5102 for a schedule update. *Lincoln Center, W. 66th St. btw Columbus and Amsterdam Aves., tel. 212/875–5400. Subway: 1 or 9 to W. 66th St.*

WHERE TO SLEEP   3

By Shon Bayer, Matthew Jalbert, Amy McConnell, and Mira Schwirtz

There's no way around the fact that lodging in New York City is pricier than a Pentagon hammer. In 1996, the *average* daily hotel room rate was $158, and the ritziest places cost hundreds more. If you can afford spending $100 a night, you won't have a problem finding a place to sleep; but if you define "splurge" as $50 a night, you'll have to look a bit harder. In fact, if it weren't for hostels (*see* Hostels, *below*) the lodging situation might force you to skip New York City entirely. Hostels are a big success here and are actually growing in number—and beds in hostels usually cost less than $20 a night. Also be sure to visit the New York Convention and Visitors Bureau (*see* Useful Organizations, in Chapter 1), since hotels and hostels often offer hefty savings coupons in the NYCVB "Big Apple Visitors Guide." Price categories listed in this book refer to the price of the hotels' least expensive double rooms.

If you're staying in New York for a week or more during summer, one of the best bets is to crash in a university dormitory (*see* Student Housing, *below*). Most of the dorms at **New York University (NYU)** are dirt cheap and located in the East and West Village, a very cool place to stay. **Columbia University** and the **Fashion Institute of Technology** are other student-housing options—apply for spaces here by May 1.

With so many New Yorkers getting the hell out of the city in summer, sublets in private apartments and short-term apartment shares are also feasible options (*see* Longer Stays, *below*). You may have to do some pretrip research, but won't you be glad to have your very own apartment for a month or two? For listings check the back of the weekly *Village Voice,* an invaluable resource for apartment hunting; if you live in a college town or major city, chances are you can purchase a copy at your local bookstore or newsstand before you leave home. Other long-term lodging options are the city's low-end hotels listed in this chapter: Hotels that target budget travelers are often eager to rent rooms by the week at cheap rates. Ask a manager for a discount contract of some kind.

When it comes to hotels, wouldn't you know that the coolest parts of Manhattan—the East and West Village, SoHo, TriBeCa—are devoid of them. In fact, the majority of New York's hotels are in Midtown, which means that you're going to get very familiar with the subways. Many parts of Midtown are fairly desolate after dark (especially east of Fifth Avenue), so exercise caution when stumbling home from that club or bar late at night. Wherever you stay, reservations are a good idea in summer, around Christmas, and during any of the city's major festivals (*see* Festivals, in Chapter 1).

Hotels

It's not much of an exaggeration to say that New York's hotel industry is little more than a scam operation: Air conditioners warm rooms rather than cool them, floors feel like they're going to give way any minute, and shared bathrooms are inevitably filthy by 10 AM. On the other hand, many of New York's hotels underwent major renovations following the economic recession in the early 1990s, and virtually every place we looked at had been recently remodeled. Yet the city also *lost* numerous hotel rooms, with the net effect of overall higher prices. Countering this was a lowering of the hotel tax, to 13½% plus a $2 occupancy tax. The bottom line? Hotel rooms are cleaner, newer, slightly less plentiful, and slightly more expensive than they were just a few years ago.

Over the years, New York's budget hotels have evolved into a strange breed—some of them do double duty as residential *and* tourist hotels. Much more of a problem is the prostitute activity in and around lower-end hotels, particularly near Eighth Avenue and Lexington Avenue. This is a cold reality of the city, and you'd better get used to it. More than a few budget hotels have a besieged look, with reception desks encased in bulletproof glass, security cameras scanning lobbies, and posted signs warning NO GUESTS. If security is a major concern, ask if the hotel has a security guard. If you're traveling with valuables (never a great idea), ask the reception desk if there's a safe-deposit box—several of the hotels listed below have them.

Groups of three or four people score big time in New York's hotels—triples and quads are always the cheapest options. And even if we don't list triples, quads, or studios below, always ask if a hotel has these larger (and often cheaper) rooms, because they often *do*—they just don't like to publicize them (especially to nosy travel writers). The next cheapest way to travel is in twos, splitting the double rate. If you're traveling alone and want to stay in hotels, prepare to pay top dollar.

More budget tips: Rooms without private baths often have at least a sink, so ask yourself if you really need your very own private toilet and shower. When checking in or making reservations, always ask for a cheaper room than what you were offered; hotels often have some unlisted rooms below the published rates, and you may get one if you pry a bit. And remember that many budget hotels offer major discounts for weeklong stays; just talk to the management.

UPTOWN

Forget about finding a bed on the **Upper East Side**: It ain't gonna happen unless your surname is engraved on a wing in the Met. Choices on the **Upper West Side** are few and fairly pricey, but if you can score a room here you'll be able to frolic in Central Park or hop a crosstown bus to the museums on Fifth Avenue. The Upper West Side also offers some good cheap bars and restaurants.

➤ **UNDER $75** • **Broadway American Hotel.** The best thing about the aging Broadway American is its location, smack in the middle of the Upper West Side. The handsome gray-

Why Pay Full Price?

New York City's hotels just got a wee bit cheaper, thanks to a program started in January, 1996 called AFTER 6. Here's the deal: When one of three dozen citywide hotels—from budget digs to fancy affairs like the Tudor, Ameritania, and Lexington—know they've got some empty rooms, they discount them up to 50% and turn them over to the folks at AFTER 6. Rates go as low as $50 per night (unlimited number of people). All you have to do is call the AFTER 6 hotline (tel. 800/515-2248) no earlier than 6 PM the day before you need a room. You'll need to specify price range and neighborhood, and they'll connect you with an appropriate hotel.

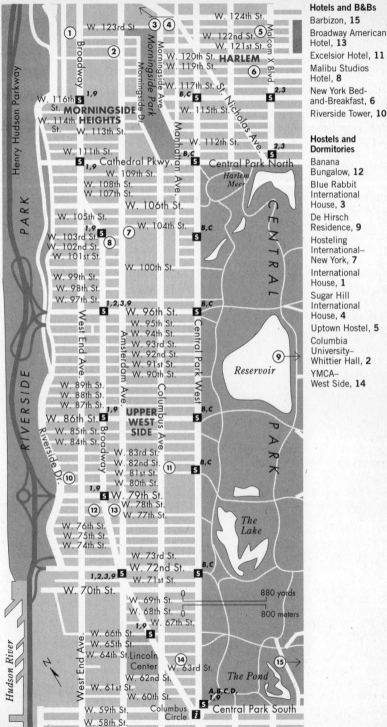

Hotels and B&Bs

Barbizon, **15**

Broadway American Hotel, **13**

Excelsior Hotel, **11**

Malibu Studios Hotel, **8**

New York Bed-and-Breakfast, **6**

Riverside Tower, **10**

Hostels and Dormitories

Banana Bungalow, **12**

Blue Rabbit International House, **3**

De Hirsch Residence, **9**

Hosteling International–New York, **7**

International House, **1**

Sugar Hill International House, **4**

Uptown Hostel, **5**

Columbia University–Whittier Hall, **2**

YMCA–West Side, **14**

149

toned rooms aren't too shabby, either. If none of the zillion or so cool restaurants in the neighborhood whets your appetite, the hotel has a kitchen for guest use. Singles start at $45 ($79 with private bath), doubles $65 ($89 with bath), triples $75 ($99 with bath). *2178 Broadway, at W. 77th St., Upper West Side, tel. 212/362–1100, fax 212/787–9521. Subway: 1 or 9 to W. 79th St.; walk 2 blocks south on Broadway. 350 rooms, some with bath. Kitchen, laundry, luggage storage. Wheelchair access.*

Malibu Studios Hotel. This tacky West Coast wanna-be could never be mistaken for Melrose Place, but the young and loud crowd of student interns who summer here would like to think so. Clean, shared-bath singles are $35, doubles $50, triples $60, and quads $80. Rooms with private bath average $20 more. For longer stays you can usually work a deal. Either way, you get all the comforts of home, including a minifridge and hot plate. Reservations require a $50 cash deposit. *2688 Broadway, at W. 102nd St., Upper West Side, tel. 212/222–2954 or 800/647–2227, fax 212/678–6842. Subway: 1 or 9 to W. 103rd St.; walk 1 block south on Broadway. 150 rooms, some with bath. Kitchenettes, luggage storage.*

Riverside Tower. If your room's above the sixth floor, you'll enjoy sweeping views of Riverside Park, the mighty Hudson River, and—don't get too excited—the New Jersey skyline. A liberal policy toward smoking (heartily embraced by the European backpackers who flock here) means that singles ($53), doubles ($65), and suites ($75–$100) are not only small and dark, they're also occasionally smoke-singed. The staff is young and easy to like, even if they do store luggage in a big, open sitting room where anyone could waltz off with it. *80 Riverside Dr., at W. 80th St., Upper West Side, tel. 212/877–5200 or 800/724–3136, fax 212/873–1400. Subway: 1 or 9 to W. 79th St.; walk 2 blocks west to Riverside Dr. then 1 block north. 120 rooms, some with bath. Air-conditioning, luggage storage, minifridges. Wheelchair access.*

➢ **UNDER $100** • **Excelsior Hotel.** The Excelsior is next to Central Park and the Museum of Natural History, and earnest paleontologists who've come to New York to scrutinize dinosaur clavicles love this place for its faded grandeur and tony address. Despite a lobby full of gold scrollwork and gilt-edged mirrors, singles ($65), doubles ($75), and four-person suites ($99) are disappointingly sterile; get one at the front of the hotel and you'll at least be rewarded with a stupendous view. Make reservations about a month in advance. You must possess a credit card to check in. *45 W. 81st St., btw Columbus Ave. and Central Park W, Upper West Side, tel. 212/362–9200 or 800/368–4575, fax 212/721–2994. Subway: B or C to W. 81st St.; walk ½ block west. 169 rooms, some with bath. Air-conditioning, kitchenettes, luggage storage.*

The owner of the Excelsior Hotel lets actors from theater companies (at least the ones he's invested in) stay here during their stints on Broadway, which explains all those guests who speak in rhymed couplets.

➢ **UNDER $150** • **Barbizon.** Here's your typically plush Upper East Side hotel, a former women's boarding house of the type that an Edith Wharton character might have chosen. Rooms are clean, though rather small. Singles run $105–$170, doubles $105–$190. You won't be wanting a suite ($295–$650). *140 E. 63rd St., at Lexington Ave., Upper East Side, tel. 212/838–5700 or 800/223–1020, fax 212/223–3287. Subway: N, R, 4, 5, or 6 to E. 59th St.; walk 4 blocks north. Also: B or Q to Lexington Ave. 345 rooms. Air-conditioning, cable TV, luggage storage, safe-deposit boxes. Wheelchair access.*

MIDTOWN

Midtown has the largest selection of hotels, and your choices range from grossly opulent to flea-infested, smelly joints where the bed linen is crunchy and yellow. Hotels around **Times Square** and in the **Theater District** will put you in prime tourist territory—meaning lots of ugly souvenir T-shirts and bad, expensive food. You'll also be bombarded with sleaze, sleaze, sleaze, thanks to the XXX storefronts and prostitutes wandering the streets. It goes without saying that these areas have New York's cheapest hotels. On the flip side, **Chelsea** is a hip and happening neighborhood with a few good hotels; try the **Chelsea Inn** (46 W. 17th St., btw Fifth and Sixth Aves., tel. 212/645–8989), a quaint old brownstone where rooms range from $79 (shared bath) to $150 (two-room suite). In the primarily residential Midtown neighborhood of **Murray**

Hill and the no-man's-land around the Empire State Building you'll find another cluster of budget hotels, though you'll want to catch a subway or cab to somewhere more interesting at night. When all else fails, consider **Hotel Carter** (250 W. 43rd St., btw Seventh and Eighth Aves., Theater District, tel. 212/944–6000). This grungy Times Square behemoth (would you believe 700 rooms?) charges only $46 a night.

➢ **UNDER $75** • **Allerton House.** This women-only hotel is an excellent deal. It's extremely secure and clean; it's near Midtown's museums, art galleries, and ritzy boutiques; and it even has the Grace Kelly stamp of approval (rumor has it that she stayed here before packing off to Monaco). Good-sized rooms with shared baths are $35–$50, and spacious top-floor doubles with private baths are $65. There's also a roof deck with views into the heart of Gotham. *130 E. 57th St., btw Lexington and Park Aves., Midtown East, tel. 212/753–8841. Subway: N, R, 4, 5, or 6 to E. 59th St.; walk 2 blocks south on Lexington Ave. then ½ block west. 407 rooms, some with bath. Laundry, luggage storage. No credit cards.*

> *According to a sign at the Allerton House's registration desk, men found above the third floor are promptly arrested.*

Carlton Arms. What do you get when you cross a pack of artists with a down-and-out hotel? You get the decades-old Carlton "It Ain't No Holiday Inn" Arms, where each room is done up with a way funky motif, from Astroturf to tropical to hip-hop to faux Grecian. Shared-bath singles run $44, doubles $57, triples $68. Rooms with bathtubs are $53 (singles), $65 (doubles), and $78 (triples). Students, foreigners, and those who stay for a week or more get a 5%–10% discount. It's got an international cult following, so reserve far in advance. *160 E. 25th St., near Third Ave., Gramercy, tel. 212/679–0680. Subway: 6 to E. 23rd St.; walk 2 blocks north on Park Ave. S then 2 blocks east. 54 rooms, some with bath. Luggage storage.*

Gershwin Hotel. This place caters to a younger and more cosmopolitan clientele than most budget places, offering impromptu barbecues and occasional live music. You can schmooze with fellow Gen Xers at the rooftop wine and beer bar, or over lattes in the hip little café. A bed in one of the sparkling four- to eight-person dorms costs $20. Doubles are $65, triples $82. A handful of designer rooms (with pop art on the walls and weirdly groovy furniture) are $82 (double) or

> *The Gershwin Hotel keeps a Campbell's Soup can in the lobby, but it's not for emergency snacking—this one is signed by Andy Warhol.*

$99 (triple). *7 E. 27th St., btw Madison and Fifth Aves., Midtown East, tel. 212/545–8000, fax 212/684–5546. Subway: 6 to E. 28th St.; walk 1 block south on Park Ave. S then 1½ blocks west. Also: N or R to W. 28th St.; walk 1 block south on Broadway then 1½ blocks east. 350 beds, some with bath. Linens, luggage storage ($1), 24-hr room service.*

Hotel Rutledge. Judge this place by its exterior alone and you'd go running. Fortunately, recent renovations have left the rooms—shared by a mix of tourists and long-term residents—some of the nicest around. Shared-bath singles are $40, doubles $50; rooms with private bath are an additional $10. *161 Lexington Ave., at E. 30th St., Murray Hill, tel. 212/532–2255, fax 212/481–7270. Subway: 6 to E. 33rd St.; walk 1 block east then 3 blocks south on Lexington Ave. 176 rooms, some with bath. Luggage storage. No credit cards.*

Hotel Wolcott. This place has a gilded lobby to rival Versaille's Hall of Mirrors, though the medium-sized rooms are as sterile as a city hospital. Downstairs is the Five Spot jazz club (*see* Live Music, in Chapter 6), the most exciting thing within a stone's throw of the Empire State Building. Singles cost $40 ($70 with bath), doubles $50 ($75 with bath). *4 W. 31st St., btw Fifth Ave. and Broadway, Midtown West, tel. 212/268–2900, fax 212/563–0096. Subway: B, D, F, N, Q, or R to W. 34th St. (Herald Sq.); walk 3 blocks south on Sixth Ave. then 1½ blocks east. Also: 6 to E. 33rd St.; walk 2 blocks south on Park Ave. S then 2½ blocks west. 300 rooms, most with bath. Air-conditioning, cable TV, laundry. Wheelchair access.*

Madison Hotel. The Madison distinguishes itself from other no-frills hotels by hanging an unexpected reproduction of Jasper Johns's *Three Flags* behind its bulletproof reception counter. Rooms are dingy but big, and all have private baths. Singles run $60, doubles $70, triples and quads $90. Telephones are available with a deposit ($40). *27 E. 27th St., at Madison Ave.,*

Midtown and Downtown Lodging

Hotels and B&Bs
Allerton House, **2**
Arlington Hotel, **18**
Broadway Bed-and-Breakfast Inn, **38**
Carlton Arms, **17**
Chelsea Hotel, **29**
Chelsea Inn, **24**
Chelsea Pines Inn, **26**
Edison Hotel, **41**
Gershwin Hotel, **15**
Gramercy Park Hotel, **19**
Herald Square Hotel, **6**
Holiday Inn Downtown, **22**
Hotel 17, **20**
Hotel Carter, **37**
Hotel Grand Union, **10**
Hotel Iroquois, **45**
Hotel Riverview, **27**
Hotel Rutledge, **12**
Hotel Stanford, **5**
Hotel Wolcott, **8**
Howard Johnson on 34th Street, **34**
Madison Hotel, **16**
The Manhattan, **7**
Martha Washington, **13**
New York Inn, **39**
Off SoHo Suites, **21**
Paramount Hotel, **40**
Park Savoy, **1**
Pickwick Arms Hotel, **3**
Portland Square Hotel, **42**
Roger Williams Hotel, **11**
Rosoff's Hotel, **44**
Senton Hotel, **14**
Washington Square Hotel, **25**
Webster Apartments, **35**

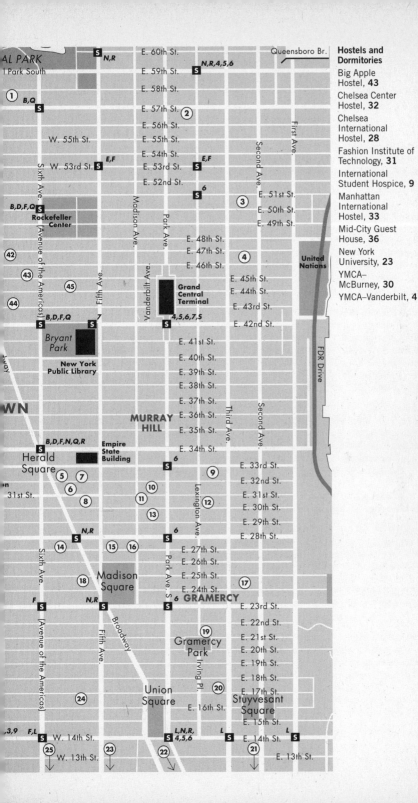

Hostels and Dormitories

Big Apple Hostel, **43**

Chelsea Center Hostel, **32**

Chelsea International Hostel, **28**

Fashion Institute of Technology, **31**

International Student Hospice, **9**

Manhattan International Hostel, **33**

Mid-City Guest House, **36**

New York University, **23**

YMCA–McBurney, **30**

YMCA–Vanderbilt, **4**

Gramercy, tel. 212/532–7373 or 212/595–9100, fax 212/799–5179. Subway: 6 to E. 28th St.; walk 1 block south on Park Ave. S then 1 block west. 75 rooms, all with bath. Air-conditioning.

Martha Washington. Renovations have brought flowery wallpaper and dainty furniture to this ancient, women-only hotel. Many of the guests are long-term residents in their 50s and 60s who appreciate the extra security and low rates. Singles are $40–$54 (weekly $160–$202), doubles $60–$80 (weekly $250–$290). The cheapest rooms share a bath. *30 E. 30th St., btw Park Ave. S and Madison Ave., Murray Hill, tel. 212/689–1900, fax 212/689–0023. Subway: 6 to E. 28th St.; walk 2 blocks north on Park Ave. S then ½ block west. 451 rooms, some with bath. Air-conditioning, kitchenettes, laundry.*

Park Savoy. This inexpensive hotel is just a block south of Central Park and only a few blocks from the Museum of Modern Art—and if you think that's no big deal, try strolling into the glittering lobby of the Plaza Hotel and asking for something "budget." Needless to say, the Park Savoy is a good find, even if the clean rooms are miniscule and devoid of air-conditioning or TVs. Shared-bath singles run $35, private singles $55, doubles $55–$75, quads $85. *158 W. 58th St., btw Sixth and Seventh Aves., Midtown West, tel. 212/245–5755, fax 212/765–0668. Subway: N or R to W. 57th St.; walk 1 block north on Seventh Ave. then ½ block east. Also: B or Q to W. 57th St.; walk 1 block north on Sixth Ave. then ½ block west. 110 rooms, some with bath. Kitchenettes, luggage storage.*

Roger Williams Hotel. If you're into traveling with cookware (aren't we all?), take advantage of the minikitchen located in your room's closet. The big, slightly musty rooms all have private baths, and the location is convenient to Midtown's sights and subways. Singles run $55–$65, doubles $60–$70, triples and quads $74–$90. Students get a 15% discount late December–March. *28 E. 31st St., at Madison Ave., Murray Hill, tel. 212/684–7500 or 800/637–9773, fax 212/576–4343. Subway: 6 to E. 33rd St.; walk 2 blocks south on Park Ave. S then 1 block west. 211 rooms. Wheelchair access.*

Senton Hotel. This aging hotel sits on a side street that bustles with commercial activity by day. But at night the street is creepy and desolate. The unaccommodating staff has adopted a few safety precautions like locking up late at night and banning unregistered guests. They've also painted the entire ground floor in-your-face, just-try-to-be-grumpy sky blue. Singles are $47–$53 (the cheapest ones share a bath), doubles $57–$70, suites $85 and up. *39–41 W. 27th St., btw Broadway and Sixth Ave., Midtown West, tel. 212/684–5800, fax 212/545–1690. Subway: N or R to W. 28th St.; walk 1 block south on Broadway then ½ block west. Also: 1 or 9 to W. 28th St.; walk 1 block south on Seventh Ave. then 1½ blocks east. 80 rooms, most with bath. Air-conditioning, cable TV. No credit cards.*

➤ **UNDER $100** • **Arlington Hotel.** The Arlington has signs in both English and Chinese, plus mediocre Asian art on the walls—a bow to the Chinese businesspeople who frequent the place on trips to Chelsea's warehouses. The rooms themselves are large but unspectacular; singles are $68, doubles $80, triples $86, suites $93. International students get a 10% discount. *18–20 W. 25th St., btw Broadway and Sixth Ave., Chelsea, tel. 212/645–3990, fax 212/633–8952. Subway: N or R to W. 23rd St.; walk 2 blocks north on Broadway then ½ block west. Also: F to W. 23rd St.; walk 2 blocks north on Sixth Ave. then ½ block east. 140 rooms. Air-conditioning, luggage storage.*

Herald Square Hotel. This hotel, located in the former *Life* magazine building, pays homage to the pre-MTV era with lots of framed *Life* covers. Rooms are bright, clean, and even equipped with telephone voicemail. Singles are $55, doubles $60–$95, triples and quads $100–$105. Singles with shared bath are $45. *19 W. 31st St., btw Fifth Ave. and Broadway, Midtown West, tel. 212/279–4017 or 800/727–1888, fax 212/643–9208. Subway: B, D, F, N, Q, or R to W. 34th St. (Herald Sq.); walk 3 blocks SE on Broadway then ½ block east. 130 rooms, most with bath. Air-conditioning, lockers ($1).*

Hotel 17. This trendy Euro-style hotel—with its colorful mélange of slackers, club kids, and European funksters—is reason enough to visit New York. Most rooms are small and share a bath, but there's plenty of space to ogle fashion victims or the parade of fabulous guests (among them, Madonna and David Bowie). Be prepared to look pouty and glamorous, and be sure to reserve far in advance. Doubles cost $75 (shared bath) or $90 (private bath). *225 E. 17th St., near Third Ave., Gramercy, tel. 212/475–2845, fax 212/677–8178. Subway: L, N, R, 4, 5, or 6 to E. 14th St. (Union Sq.). 140 rooms, some with bath. No credit cards.*

Hotel Grand Union. Though little distinguishes this hotel from others in Murray Hill, at least the newly renovated rooms are clean and spacious. Singles run $60–$70, doubles $74–$90, quads $105. Students with an ISIC card get a 10% discount. Pay for six days in advance and the seventh is free. *34 E. 32nd St., btw Park Ave. S and Madison Ave., Murray Hill, tel. 212/683–5890, fax 212/689–7397. Subway: 6 to E. 33rd St.; walk 1 block south on Park Ave. S then ½ block west. 95 rooms, some with bath. Air-conditioning, refrigerators.*

Hotel Iroquois. Stay here and spiffy singles cost $75, doubles $85, first-rate doubles with kitchenettes $99. They give a 10% discount to AAA members. You're right next to the historic **Algonquin Hotel** (59 W. 44th St., tel. 212/840–6800), where Dorothy Parker and her Round Table held forth in its Rose Room during the 1920s—and where double rooms currently run $240 per night. *49 W. 44th St., btw Fifth and Sixth Aves., Midtown West, tel 212/840–3080, fax 212/398–1754. Subway: 4, 5, 6, or 7 to E. 42nd St. (Grand Central); walk 2 blocks north on Madison Ave. then 1½ blocks west. Also: B, D, F, or Q to W. 42nd St.; walk 2 blocks north on Sixth Ave. then ½ block east. 100 rooms. Air-conditioning, kitchenettes, luggage storage.*

The Manhattan. Rooms here are decorated in one of three themes: Fifth Avenue (ritzy), Central Park (lots of florals), or SoHo (dramatic colors). Whether you find this corny or cool, they're brand new and equipped with coffeemakers. And you're just south of the Empire State Building in a bustling Korean neighborhood, near lots of shops and restaurants. Singles are $85, doubles $95, triples $100, quads $110. *17 W. 32nd St., btw Fifth Ave. and Broadway, Midtown West, tel. 212/736–1600 or 800/567–7720, fax 212/695–1813. Subway: B, D, F, N, Q, or R to W. 34th St. (Herald Sq.); walk 2 blocks SE on Broadway then ½ block east. 150 rooms. Air-conditioning, 24-hr room service.*

New York Inn. This small, shabby hotel straddles an uncomfortable corner—where the ersatz glamour of Restaurant Row meets sleazy, porn-spangled Eighth Avenue. Rooms are decent but nothing more, and to reach them you need to deal with creaky, narrow stairs (there's no elevator). Singles cost $65, doubles $75. *765 Eighth Ave., btw W. 46th and 47th Sts., Theater District, tel. 212/247–5400 or 800/777–6933, fax 212/586–6201. Subway: A, C, or E to W. 42nd St.; walk 4½ blocks north on Eighth Ave. 40 rooms. Air-conditioning, continental breakfast (free).*

Pickwick Arms Hotel. The Pickwick's recently homogenized rooms are clean and reasonably spacious, and when you tire of watching *Mork and Mindy* reruns on TV you can chill on the rooftop patio. Shared-bath singles start at $45, private singles $75, doubles $95, studios (with double beds and sofas) $110. Each additional person pays $12. *230 E. 51st St., btw Second and Third Aves., Midtown East, tel. 212/355–0300 or 800/PICKWIK, fax 212/755–5029. Subway: 6 to E. 51st St.; walk 1½ blocks east. 400 rooms, most with bath. Air-conditioning, luggage storage.*

Portland Square Hotel. The lobby of this renovated 1904 hotel has the besieged feel of a Tel Aviv airport: Signs everywhere warn against leaving baggage unattended (in this case, because Times Square thieves will grab it the moment you turn your head). Still, if you're tired of traveling, the Portland's small, antiseptic rooms are a welcome sight. You're also not too far from the Theater District's bars and restaurants. Shared-bath singles run $45, private singles $65, doubles $79–$89, triples $94, quads $99. *132 W. 47th St., btw Sixth and Seventh Aves., Theater District, tel. 212/382–0600 or 800/388–8988, fax 212/382–0684. Subway: N or R to W. 49th St.; walk 2 blocks south on Seventh Ave. then ½ block east. 130 rooms, most with bath. Air-conditioning, lockers ($1).*

Rosoff's Hotel. This small Times Square hotel is one of very few in New York City that didn't have its charm painted away or wallpapered over during renovations. The lobby and second-floor lounge are still circa 1908 (as are many of the permanent residents), the staff is genuinely friendly, and the rooms are spacious and clean. Singles cost $79, doubles $89, two-room triples $99. *147 W. 43rd St., btw Sixth Ave. and Broadway, Midtown West, tel. 212/869–1212, fax 212/944–6223. Subway: N, R, 1, 2, 3, 7, or 9 to W. 42nd St. (Times Sq.); walk 1 block north on Broadway then ½ block east. 32 rooms. Air-conditioning, luggage storage.*

➤ **UNDER $150** • **Chelsea Hotel.** The Victorian-era Chelsea is one of the city's most famous residential hotels, home to innumerable artists and other creative folk over the last century: Thomas Wolfe, Arthur Miller, Sarah Bernhardt, Robert Mapplethorpe, Christo, Bob Dylan, Dylan Thomas, Leonard Cohen, Sid Vicious, Eugene O'Neill, and maybe you. Some of the artists who called the Chelsea Hotel home left paintings and sculpture in lieu of paying their bill; there's a gallery of their work in the lobby. Its giant rooms vary widely in personality; some are regal and others are time capsules from the shag-carpet '70s. Per night, singles cost $85–$175, doubles $99–$175, suites $250. Naturally, the people who've lived here for decades pay a lot less. *222 W. 23rd St., btw Seventh and Eighth Aves., Chelsea, tel. and fax 212/243–3700. Subway: 1 or 9 to W. 23rd St. (Seventh Ave.). Also: C or E to W. 23rd St. (Eighth Ave.). 75 rooms.*

Edison Hotel. This mondo Art Deco hotel gets major business from big (and big-haired) tour groups. A relict from the Roaring '20s, it's got some over-the-top extras like a cool hotel bar, a magnificent mural-filled lobby, and a coffee shop inside a rococo ballroom. Rooms aren't cheap, but they are plush. Singles are $92, doubles $102, triples $112–$122, suites $115–$145. *228 W. 47th St., btw Broadway and Eighth Ave., Theater District, tel. 212/840–5000 or 800/637–7070, fax 212/596–6850. Subway: 1 or 9 to W. 50th St.; walk 3 blocks south on Broadway then ½ block west. Also: C or E to W. 50th St.; walk 3 blocks south on Eighth Ave. then ½ block east. 1,000 rooms. Air-conditioning, cable TV, luggage storage, safe-deposit boxes. Wheelchair access.*

Gramercy Park Hotel. The grand old Gramercy may be showing its age (e.g., worn carpets, peeling walls, and bathrooms clamoring for Tilex), but it's still an elite address. More to the point, it also has keys to the city's only private, locked park; grab a key, head across the street, and spend a day lounging in one of Manhattan's finest sylvan sanctuaries. Another plus: The suites ($135) are big enough to fit you, your backpack, your friends, and, say, the entire Italian men's soccer team. Singles cost $115, doubles $125. Additional guests pay $10 each. Budget alert: Rooms are $30 less on weekends January–May and July–September. *2 Lexington Ave., at E. 21st St., Gramercy, tel. 212/475–4320 or 800/221–4083, fax 212/505–0535. Subway: 6 to E. 23rd St.; walk 1 block west to Lexington Ave. then 2 blocks south. 500 rooms. Air-conditioning, luggage storage, refrigerators, safe-deposit boxes. Wheelchair access.*

Hotel Stanford. The impeccably renovated Stanford is in the center of Midtown's dynamic Korean enclave, its three lobby clocks set for London, New York, and Seoul/Tokyo time. The tidy rooms range from mini to monstrous: Singles are $80, doubles $90–$130, suites $180–$200. And your craving for a little karaoke can be satisfied, thanks to the hotel cocktail bar. *43 W. 32nd St., btw Fifth Ave. and Broadway, Midtown West, tel. 212/563–1500, fax 212/629–0043. Subway: B, D, F, N, Q, or R to W. 34th St. (Herald Sq.); walk 2 blocks SE on Broadway then ½ block east. 120 rooms. Air-conditioning, luggage storage, refrigerators.*

The manager at the Howard Johnson says his hotel is "environmentally friendly" because "we use shades of green in all the rooms: green carpet, green bedspreads, and green drapes." Way to go, eco-warrior.

Howard Johnson on 34th St. A major rehab by HoJo hoteliers turned the dumpy Penn Plaza Hotel into a businessman's wet dream, complete with modem hookups on all telephones. Singles run $85–$95, doubles $100–$110, plus $15 for each additional person. Students get a 10% discount. *215 W. 34th St., btw Seventh and Eighth Aves., Midtown West, tel. 212/947–5050 or 800/446–4656, fax 212/268–4829. Subway: A, C, E, 1, 2, 3, or 9 to W. 34th St. (Penn Station). 145 rooms. Wheelchair access.*

➤ **SPLURGE** • **Paramount Hotel.** When hip bicoastal types come to town (including quite a few celebrities), they often shack up at the Paramount. It's got funky furniture by ultra-cool French designer Philippe Starck, a children's rec room by the designer of Pee Wee's *Playhouse*, and the achingly cool Whiskey Bar (*see Bars, in Chapter 6*). Most impressively, the hotel trusts guests with VCRs and blindingly white bedspreads. Singles run $99–$165, doubles $135–$215. Special weekend rates are $120–$170. *235 W. 46th St., btw Broadway and Eighth Ave., Theater District, tel. 212/764–5500 or 800/225–7474, fax 212/354–5237. Subway: N, R, 1, 2, 3, 7, or 9 to W. 42nd St. (Times Sq.); walk 4 blocks NW on Broadway. Also: A, C, or E to W. 42nd St. (Port Authority); walk 4 blocks north on Eighth Ave. 610 rooms, some with bath. Air-conditioning, cable TV, gym. Wheelchair access.*

DOWNTOWN

Be they super-cheap or super-glitzy, hotels of any sort are hard to find below 14th Street. Don't believe us? Well, know that when the World Trade Center opened a hotel in 1982, it was Lower Manhattan's first new lodging in over a century. Village-bound hipsters are better off finding a bed in one of the dozens of cheap hotels filling Midtown. In a pinch, the **Holiday Inn Downtown** (138 Lafayette St., near Canal St., tel. 212/966–8898 or 800/HOLIDAY), in the never-never land between Chinatown and TriBeCa, can set you up with a wheelchair-accessible double for $155 ($144 for AAA members). The **Best Western Seaport Inn** (33 Peck Slip, at South St. Seaport, tel. 212/766–6600 or 800/HOTEL–NY) has wheelchair-accessible rooms with VCRs and saucy nautical decor priced $135–$155 ($99–$109 on weekends). For something with a bit more character or a lower price tag, you've got very few choices.

➤ **UNDER $50** • **Hotel Riverview.** Not only is this place cheap, it's also in the heart of the West Village. Too bad it looks like it hasn't been mopped since 1912, the year it put up American survivors from the wrecked *Titanic*. Some of the decrepit, musty, graffiti-scrawled rooms are temporary housing for welfare recipients, while others are under renovation. Every floor has a coed bathroom. Singles run $27–$29, doubles $42–$47, and weekly rates are even lower. *113 Jane St., at West St., West Village, tel. 212/929–0060, fax 212/675–8581. Subway: A, C, E, or L to W. 14th St.; walk 3 blocks south on Eighth Ave. then 4 blocks west on Jane St. 250 rooms, none with bath. Key deposit ($5), luggage storage.*

➤ **UNDER $100** • **Off SoHo Suites.** Amidst the urban decay of the Bowery, this self-described "European" hotel couldn't stand out more if it had been wrapped by Christo. The two-person suites ($79) share a kitchen and bath, while the four-person suites ($129) are completely private. All are extremely clean, if totally generic. Because of its small size you should reserve well in advance. *11 Rivington St., btw Chrystie St. and Bowery, Lower East Side, tel. 212/979–9808 or 800/OFF–SOHO, fax 212/979–9801. Subway: J or M to Bowery; walk 1 block north then ½ block east on Rivington. 37 rooms. Air-conditioning, kitchenettes, luggage storage, safe-deposit boxes. Wheelchair access.*

Washington Square Hotel. This turn-of-the-century hotel went modern a decade ago, and the result is rooms that are small and bland but quite clean. Every floor has a shower that is shared among single rooms ($70); doubles ($99) all have private baths. Extras include free breakfast at the hotel's full-service restaurant and access to a small gym. And it boasts a prime West Village location. *103 Waverly Pl., at MacDougal St., West Village, tel. 212/777–9515 or 800/222–0418, fax 212/979–8373. Subway: A, B, C, D, E, F, or Q to W. 4th St. (Washington Sq.); walk 2 blocks north on Sixth Ave. then 1 block east. 160 rooms, most with bath. Continental breakfast (free), gym, lockers ($1 per day).*

Bed-and-Breakfasts

Most of the bed-and-breakfast establishments in New York City are just regular apartments with clever owners—people who are paying their astronomically high rents with a little help from strangers like you. These B&Bs are booked through several reservation services, which act

If your idea of a B&B is a quaint Victorian with antiques and a great view of cows chewing their cud, you should be vacationing in New Hampshire, not New York.

as the liaison between travelers and residents who have rooms (or entire apartments) available. There are also a handful of traditional, independently owned B&Bs, for which you'll be competing with New York locals (city dwellers just *adore* the idea of a weekend "escape" where they can still get hot bagels and the *New York Times*). Wherever you stay, rates average $60–$100 a night. But be warned: Not all places serve breakfast, and many do not accept credit cards.

B&B RESERVATION SERVICES

You have two options when you use a B&B reservation service: a hosted or an unhosted apartment. A **hosted apartment** is simply an extra room or two in someone's apartment. Your host or hostess will probably feed you a continental breakfast, let you come and go as you please, and give you access to amenities such as a TV, phone, and private bath. Best of all, hosts are happy to offer the lowdown on where to dine, shop, or drink, and what to see. The more expensive **unhosted apartment** is unoccupied (but furnished), often with an owner out of town on business. Here you'll have the run of the place, including full kitchen privileges (remember to behave nicely). Apartments range in size from tiny walk-up studios to expensive penthouses with full-time doormen.

Reservation services list hundreds of apartments, so they can set you up in almost any Manhattan neighborhood (or, if you so desire, the outer boroughs). The earlier you make a reservation, the better your chance of scoring a pad in your favorite 'hood. To reserve, you usually need to send in a deposit equal to 25% of the total cost; ask about lower weekly and monthly rates, because they're often available. Refunds (minus a $25 service charge) are given up to 10 days before arrival. Each reservation service has several apartments outfitted for travelers in wheelchairs.

Abode Bed-and-Breakfast. Lists more than 150 locations throughout Manhattan. Hosted singles and doubles cost $70–$95. Unhosted apartments start at $99. Minimum stay is two nights. *Box 20022, New York, NY 10021, tel. 212/472-2000.*

Bed-and-Breakfast in Manhattan. The woman who runs this place couldn't be nicer—she goes out of her way to figure out what's best for her customers, be they virgin visitors to New York, travelers in wheelchairs, or gay/lesbian. Hosted singles and doubles cost $75–$90, unhosted studios and two-bedroom apartments $110–$200. *Box 533, New York, NY 10150, tel. 212/472-2528, fax 212/988-9818.*

Bed-and-Breakfast Network of New York. This service lists more than 300 apartments throughout Manhattan and Brooklyn. Hosted singles run $50–$70, doubles $80–$90. Unhosted apartments start at $80. *134 W. 32nd St., Suite 602, New York, NY 10001, tel. 212/645-8134 or 800/900-8134.*

City Lights Bed-and-Breakfast. Many of this service's hosts are gay friendly. Hosted doubles are $70–$85 ($95 with private bath). Unhosted studios and two-bedrooms are $95–$160. *Box 20355, Cherokee Station, New York, NY 10021, tel. 212/737-7049, fax 212/535-2755.*

New World Bed-and-Breakfast. This is the most budget-oriented reservation service of the bunch: Singles run $50–$75, doubles $60–$90. Unhosted apartments start at $70. They list 150 locations, all in Manhattan. *150 Fifth Ave., Suite 711, New York, NY 10011, tel. 212/675-5600, fax 212/675-6366.*

Urban Ventures. The oldest of the reservation services, Urban Ventures lists around 800 locations throughout Manhattan and the outer boroughs. Hosted doubles cost $70–$125. Unhosted apartments start at $75. *38 W. 32nd, Suite 1412, New York, NY 10001, tel. 212/594–5650, fax 212/947–9320.*

INDEPENDENT B&BS

MANHATTAN **Broadway Bed-and-Breakfast Inn.** This cozy inn, opened in 1995, musters country charm in the middle of Manhattan's Theater District. Rooms are small but immaculate, and those on the top floor have Jacuzzis and skylights. Your continental breakfast is served in the comfy lobby by a staff too friendly and helpful to be native New Yorkers. The ground-floor restaurant gives Broadway guests a 20% discount. Singles run $75–$85, doubles $85–$95. *264 W. 46th St., btw Broadway and Eighth Ave., Theater District, tel. 212/997–9200 or 800/826–6300, fax 212/768–2807. Subway: N, R, 1, 2, 3, 7, or 9 to W. 42nd St. (Times Sq.); walk 4 blocks north on Broadway then ½ block west. Also: A, C, or E to W. 42nd St. (Port Authority); walk 4 blocks west on Eighth Ave. then ½ block east. 45 rooms, some with bath. Air-conditioning.*

Chelsea Pines Inn. It may not be Aspen or even Fire Island, but for many gay and lesbian couples the Chelsea Pines ranks among the best B&Bs anywhere (straights are welcome, too). The tidy rooms are filled with kitsch items and vintage movie posters. The delicious breakfasts include fresh fruit and homemade bread. Doubles range from $55 (shared bath) to $85 (private bath). Each extra person pays $20. In summer and fall you should reserve a month in advance, especially for the less expensive rooms. *317 W. 14th St., btw Eighth and Ninth Aves., Chelsea, tel. 212/929–1023, fax 212/645–9497. Subway: A, C, E, or L to W. 14th St.; walk ½ block west. 22 rooms, some with bath. Air-conditioning, luggage storage, refrigerators.*

New York Bed-and-Breakfast. This beautiful old Harlem brownstone is owned by Gisele, a friendly Canadian who also runs the Uptown Hostel (*see* Hostels, *below*). It's got an ardent fan club of French tourists who return annually to enjoy its six rooms with shared bath. Singles cost $30, doubles $40. All that and a continental breakfast, to boot. *134 W. 119th St., btw Malcolm X and Adam Clayton Powell Jr. Blvds., Harlem, tel. 212/666–0559. Subway: 2 or 3 to W. 116th St.; walk 3 blocks north on Malcolm X Blvd. then ½ block west. 6 rooms, none with bath. No credit cards.*

BROOKLYN **Bed-and-Breakfast on the Park.** This spectacular brownstone is a great reason to leave Manhattan. Every detail is exquisite, from the rooms appointed with 19th-century antiques and oil paintings to the gourmet, four-course breakfasts. And if you ever manage to leave your bedroom, there's a full kitchen open to guests. Doubles with shared bath cost $75; private rooms start at $125. *113 Prospect Park W, btw 7th and 8th Sts., Park Slope, tel. 718/499–6115, fax 718/499–1385. Subway: F to Seventh Ave. (Park Slope); walk 2 blocks east on 9th St. then ½ block north on Prospect Park W. 7 rooms, most with bath. No credit cards.*

Hostels

On the whole, hostels are most popular with students and foreign backpackers and are great for hooking up with other travelers. But you'll need to be able to tolerate lots of noise. Both independent hostels and those affiliated with **Hostelling International (HI)** (*see* Hostelling Organizations, in Chapter 1) don't differ much in price or style, and almost all hostels offer private rooms as well as dorms that sleep four to 16 people. The three private hostels in Harlem charge $12–$14 per dorm bed, while Midtown joints cost $18 or more. From this, clever readers may draw the conclusion that the farther uptown a hostel is, the cheaper the rates. There are no hostels south of 14th Street.

Clubs and bars alike advertise happy hours and theme parties at hostels, so always check around the lobby and front desk for flyers.

Most people think that **YMCA**s (it stands for Young Men's Christian Association, though these places are not religious) are cheap alternatives to hotels. They're not—most are expensive and have only singles and doubles instead of dorms. And the atmosphere at most is fairly subdued, thanks to the preponderance of families, older single travelers, and long-term elderly residents. Their one big bonus is free use of their gym facilities with a night's stay.

The general rule about reservations is to make them at least two weeks in advance (more around Christmas and in late summer). Otherwise, you'll be in for a long, painful search for cheap accommodations. One final note for Americans only: Many private hostels (like Banana Bungalow) have an unadvertised policy of refusing Americans. Why? Well, it seems that Americans have an ugly reputation for being demanding and for destroying hostel property. If you can politely convince a private hostel that you're an exception, they may let you in.

UPTOWN

The hostels in **Harlem** are usually the least crowded, and the cheapest, of any type of lodging in New York City. While you may have some concerns about safety, know that neighborhood restaurants are cheap, and coming and going late at night is okay if you do so in a group. Hostels on the **Upper West Side** are more expensive but are within walking distance of more snazzy restaurants, lots of bars, Central Park, the Museum of Natural History, Lincoln Center—you get the picture. Hostels throughout upper Manhattan are usually only a block or two from a subway station; from Harlem it's a 20- to 30-minute subway ride (or a $10–$20 taxi ride) to downtown.

Banana Bungalow. If you're American and can convince the guy at the bamboo front desk that you're not an arsonist or psychopath, you may be allowed inside the magic Banana kingdom.

On Friday nights, you can drink all the beer you like—for free—on the rooftop garden at Banana Bungalow.

Otherwise, a foreign passport is your E-ticket for this ride. Semiprivate rooms (sorry, no bungalows) are $15 per person; a bed in one of the six-person coed dorms is $12. You have easy access to Upper West Side sights, plus all the beer you can drink at the hostel's free, Friday-night parties held on its fabulous rooftop garden. *250 W. 77th St., btw Broadway and West End Ave., Upper West Side, tel. 800/6–HOSTEL, fax 212/877–5733, bbhostel@bananabungalow.com. Subway: 1 or 9 to W. 79th St.; walk 1 block west. 100 beds. Reception open 24 hrs, check-in 11 AM, checkout noon. Key deposit ($5), kitchen, linens ($5), lockers (bring lock), TV lounge. Wheelchair access.*

Blue Rabbit International House. Ride the A-train to its end in the well-to-do Sugar Hill section of Harlem for this clean, comfortable, recently refurbished hostel, under the same management as the adjacent Sugar Hill International House (*see below*). Coed dorms (sleeping four to eight) are $12–$14 per night. Doubles are $14–$16 per person. There's a communal kitchen, friendly pet cats, and lots of European tourists. Reservations are essential in summer and fall. Send them an e-mail (InfoHostel@aol.com) for more info. *730 St. Nicholas Ave., btw W. 145th and 146th Sts., Harlem, tel. 212/491–3892 or 800/610–2030, fax 212/283–0108. Subway: A, B, C, or D to W. 145th St.; walk ½ block north on St. Nicholas Ave. 25 beds. Reception open 9 AM–10 PM, check-in 9 AM–11 AM and 7 PM–10 PM, checkout 9–11 AM. Kitchen, linens, luggage storage, safe-deposit boxes, TV lounge.*

De Hirsch Residence at the 92nd Street YMHA. Stay in the Upper East Side's only affordable lodging and you'll be able to see every Degas, Arbus, and Giacometti on Museum Mile, no prob. Despite the name (Young Men's Hebrew Association), this is a non-sectarian hostel with immaculate dorms and a kitchen, laundry, and shared bath on every floor. You'll also have access to the superb fitness facilities, library, community room, and all sorts of cultural and social events. Here's the catch: You must fill out an application at least three weeks in advance, and you must stay a minimum of three nights. Singles cost $45, doubles $66. Weekly and monthly rates are cheaper. *1395 Lexington Ave., btw E. 91st and 92nd Sts., Upper East Side, tel. 212/415–5650 or 800/858–4692, fax 212/415–5578. Subway: 4, 5, or 6 to E. 86th St.; walk 5½ blocks north on Lexington Ave. 300 beds. Reception open 9 AM–7 PM, check-in noon, checkout noon. Air-conditioning ($3 per night), laundry, linens, luggage storage. Wheelchair access.*

Hosteling International–New York. Despite the barbed wire, this monstrous landmark building (designed by big-deal 19th-century architect Richard Morris Hunt) manages to get beyond the "vacation in Baghdad" feel. The neighborhood is safe and filled with great bars, and the Big House itself boasts an entire city block's worth of clean, airy rooms, lawns and gardens, and an upper-level outdoor terrace. Four- to 12-person dorms run $20–$23 ($22–$25 in summer), while a handful of private singles with bath cost $75. Flash an HI card for a $3 discount. If you plan on coming in summer, reserve far, far, far in advance. *891 Amsterdam Ave., at W. 103rd St., Upper West Side, tel. 212/932–2300, fax 212/932–2574. Subway: 1 or 9 to W. 103rd St.; walk 1 block east. 540 beds. Reception open 24 hrs, check-in anytime, checkout 11 AM. Air-conditioning, kitchen, laundry, linens ($3), lockers, luggage storage ($1.50 per day), TV lounge. Wheelchair access.*

Sugar Hill International House. This hostel, brought to you by the same cheery folks as the Blue Rabbit International House (*see above*), is clean, comfortable, and friendly, with easy subway access and a sunny communal kitchen. Coed and women-only dorms (four to eight beds each) are $12–$14. Or try to score the Sugar Hill's lone private double ($16 per person). *722 St. Nicholas Ave., at W. 145th St., Harlem, tel. 212/926–7030, fax 212/283–0108, InfoHostel@aol.com. Subway: A, B, C, or D to W. 145th St. 20 beds. Reception and check-in 9 AM–10 PM, checkout 9–11 AM. Kitchen, linens, luggage storage, safe, TV room.*

Uptown Hostel. Sure, you're a traveler and you're tired, but think of poor Gisele: The hard-working owner of this beautiful brownstone has labored for months to refurbish it, so don't go messing it up with your smelly ol' socks and sad lack of personal hygiene. Predominantly single-sex dorms (four to six beds) are $12 per night. A private double is $15 per person. Gisele also operates the slightly more expensive New York Bed-and-Breakfast (*see above*), about three blocks away. *239 Malcolm X Blvd., at W. 122nd St., Harlem, tel. 212/666–0559. Subway: 2 or 3 to W. 125th St.; walk 3 blocks south on Malcolm X Blvd. 30 beds, some with bath. Reception open 9–9, check-in 10–9, checkout noon. Kitchen, luggage storage. No credit cards.*

YMCA–West Side. Live like a sultan in this attractive, vaguely Middle-Eastern style building mere blocks from Lincoln Center. Clean, comfortable doubles are $80 with bath or $55 without—and this princely sum entitles you to the Y's gym, sauna, pool, indoor track, and squash courts (you packed your racquet, right?). Or loaf around one of two outdoor terraces and have your silly *Cats* and *Les Misèrables* questions answered by the knowledgeable multilingual staff. Now the bad stuff: You must be at least 18 years old and can stay no longer than 25 days. Reservations (deposit required) are best made a month in advance. *5 W. 63rd St., btw Central Park W and Broadway, Upper West Side, tel. 212/787–4400, fax 212/875–1334. Subway: A, B, C, D, 1, or 9 to W. 59th St. (Columbus Circle); walk 4 blocks north on Broadway then ½ block east. 550 rooms, some with bath. Reception open 24 hrs, check-in 1 PM, checkout noon. Air-conditioning, airport shuttle to La Guardia ($11) and JFK ($14), cafeteria, gym, laundry, luggage storage ($1 per bag), pool.*

MIDTOWN

Conveniently, several hostels are in the heart (or at least on the fringe) of the myriad Midtown tourist attractions. Of them, the **Chelsea International Hostel** (*see below*) is the most "downtown"—in other words, it's the closest to good bars and restaurants and is only a short walk to the West Village. Another good option is the $20 dorms at the hip **Gershwin Hotel** (*see Hotels, Midtown, above*).

Big Apple Hostel. The Big Apple takes up seven floors of an old hotel with not a single air conditioner in sight—but who cares when you've got all of Times Square lying at your feet like a lathered, drooling beast? You'll also get brisk service, bathrooms that sparkle, and a big outdoor patio where you can sip free coffee with lots of overstimulated Europeans. Four-person dorms are $17, private doubles $45. You must show an out-of-state driver's license or foreign passport to stay here. *119 W. 45th St., btw Sixth and Seventh Aves., Theater District, tel. 212/302–2603, fax 212/302–2605. Subway: N, R, 1, 2, 3, 7, or 9 to W. 42nd St. (Times Sq.); walk 3 blocks north on Seventh Ave. then ½ block east. 104 beds. Reception open 24 hrs, check-in anytime, checkout 11 AM. Kitchen, laundry, linens, lockers (bring lock), TV lounge.*

Chelsea Center Hostel. You can take your shower in the bathroom or you can take your shower in the kitchen at this compact, homey hostel on the northern edge of Chelsea. They've also got two coed dorms and a lush back patio to enjoy. The owner (who is fluent in German, French, and English) prefers foreigners but will accept Americans during the off-season. Beds are $18 ($20 in summer). Arrive late in the day and you'll be shipped 10 blocks south to the hostel's annex. *313 W. 29th St., btw Eighth and Ninth Aves., Chelsea, tel. 212/643–0214, fax 212/473–3945. Subway: 1 or 9 to W. 28th St.; 36 beds. Lock out 11 AM–5 PM. Reception and check-in 8:30 AM–11 PM, checkout 11 AM. Continental breakfast (free), kitchen, luggage storage, linens. No credit cards.*

Chelsea International Hostel. This hostel compensates for cramped rooms with a decent Midtown location, comfortable bedding, and free pizza 'n' beer parties on Wednesday and Sunday nights (plus they finished some major renovations and repainting in 1996). It's a favorite with boisterous young Europeans. Space in a four-person dorm costs $18, doubles are $40. Flash your HI or ISIC card for a $1 per day discount. Under the same ownership, the brand-new **Manhattan International Hostel** (341 W. 30th St., btw Eighth and Ninth Aves., tel. 212/929–8248) offers beds at the same price, and a big backyard. *251 W. 20th St., btw Seventh and Eighth Aves., Chelsea, tel. 212/647–0010, fax 212/727–7289. Subway: C or E to W. 23rd St.; walk 3 blocks south on Eighth Ave. then ½ block east. Also: 1 or 9 to W. 23rd St.; walk 3 blocks south on Seventh Ave. then ½ blocks west. 200 beds, none with bath. Reception open 8 AM–9 PM, check-in anytime, checkout 1 PM. Common room, kitchen, linens.*

International Student Hospice (ISH). This Murray Hill hostel usually accepts only foreigners and always requires that you produce a current student ID. Every room is crammed full of beds, bunks, musty antique furniture, and haphazard piles of old books. It's pricey for a hostel that looks like it's falling apart ($25 per person), and indeed some parts are—watch your step on the stairs. *154 E. 33rd St., btw Third and Lexington Aves., Murray Hill, tel. 212/228–7470, fax 212/228–4689. Subway: 6 to E. 33rd St.; walk 1½ blocks east. 20 beds. Reception open 24 hrs. Linens, luggage storage. No credit cards.*

Mid-City Guest House. Despite its sleazy XXX locale a half block from the Port Authority, this hostel has a super-friendly staff and a few nice touches, like fireplaces and brick walls. The coed dorms have wimpy foam mattresses and an original soundtrack performed by the traffic on Eighth Avenue. There's no sign, so find the address and then go up two flights of stairs. Beds are $15 ($18 in summer) with a seven day maximum. You must brandish a passport and/or a backpack to stay. *608 Eighth Ave., btw W. 39th and 40th Sts., Midtown West, tel. 212/704–0562. Subway: A, C, or E to W. 42nd St.; walk 2½ blocks south on Eighth Ave. 24 beds. Midnight curfew (Fri. and Sat. at 1 AM), lockout noon–6 PM. Reception open daily 8 AM–midnight, check-in anytime, checkout noon. Continental breakfast (free), kitchen, linens, luggage storage. No credit cards.*

YMCA–McBurney. Many of McBurney's residents are long-term and mildly scuzzy. And, depending on your point of view, the security guard and glassed-in reception are either reassuring or depressing as hell. Still, you get free use of the Y's gym, a small but decent bedroom, and a bathroom down the hall. Two coed floors have been recently renovated; the others house men only. Singles cost $36 ($43 with TV), doubles $52, triples $66, quads $84. For reservations they require a $36 deposit. *206 W. 24th St. btw Seventh and Eighth Aves., Chelsea, tel. 212/741–9226, fax 212/741–0012. Subway: C or E to W. 23rd St.; walk 1 block north on Eighth Ave. then ½ block east. Also: 1 or 9 to W. 23rd St.; walk 1 block north on Seventh Ave., then ½ block west. 277 rooms, none with bath. Reception open weekdays 7 AM–11 PM (weekends from 8 AM), check-in anytime, checkout noon. Gym. Wheelchair access.*

YMCA–Vanderbilt. This popular Y packs in backpackers like the 42nd Street Shuttle at rush hour. The tiny, linoleum-floored rooms share bathrooms; the immaculate building itself is mere blocks from Grand Central Station. Best of all, a stay here entitles you to free use of the vast health facilities (pools, cardiovascular equipment, Nautilus machines, even a roving trainer) and shuttle service ($14) to the airports. Singles cost $45, bunk-style doubles $55, doubles and quads $73. *224 E. 47th St., btw Second and Third Aves., Midtown East, tel. 212/756–9600, fax 212/752–0210. Subway: 6 to E. 51st St.; walk 4 blocks south on Lexington Ave.*

then 1½ blocks east. Also: E or F to Lexington/Third Aves.; walk 4 blocks south on Third Ave. then ½ block east. 377 rooms, none with bath. Reception open 24 hrs, check-in 1 PM, check-out noon. Air-conditioning, key deposit ($10), luggage storage ($1 per bag), TV. Wheelchair access.

Student Housing

If you're planning a stay of a few weeks to a few months—and you aren't too fussy about sharing a bathroom with strangers—then you'll find one of the best deals in town is student housing. The colleges and universities that open their dormitories to the great unwashed typically do so while school is not in session (i.e., summer). You'll pay less than you would for a hotel room, and you won't have to deal with the noise and crowds that often come with staying in a hostel. In the case of **New York University** (*see below*), you also get a killer location in the East or West Village, smack in the middle of all the city's coolest clubs, bars, cheap restaurants, and cafés. The only catch is that you'll need to fill out an application far in advance (usually during spring) and then wait patiently a week or two for an answer.

Columbia University. From mid-May through mid-August, Columbia University offers small, clean single rooms at one of two Upper West Side/Morningside Heights dormitories for $24–$35, depending on length of stay (the lowest rates go to those spending 30 days or more). Nicer rooms with kitchen and bath are $25–$55. For $5 per day more they'll throw in air-conditioning. Applications are available at the end of February. Year-round, the university also offers a small number of shared-bath rooms at a nightly rate of $35 (single) or $45 (double), and private-bath rooms with kitchens at $55; maximum stay for these is six nights, and reservations are recommended a month in advance. *Whittier Hall, 1230 Amsterdam Ave., at W. 120th St., Morningside Heights, tel. 212/678–3235, fax 212/678–3222. Subway: 1 or 9 to W. 116th St. Mailing address: Residential Life Office, 525 W. 120th St., Box 312, NY 10027.*

Fashion Institute of Technology (FIT). FIT makes rooms available to travelers from mid-May through the end of July at its dormitory on the northern end of Chelsea—pretty close to the sleaze of Penn Station, but still okay. It's a great opportunity to meet and mingle with the next generation of Isaac Mizrahis and Anna Suis. Singles ($35) and doubles ($20 per person) are coed, share baths, and require a one-week minimum stay. Suites (which have kitchen and bath) are $25–$45, 30-day minimum stay required. Dorms have air-conditioning and laundry. Call in advance to request an application. *210 W. 27th St., btw Seventh and Eighth Aves., Chelsea, tel. 212/760–7885. Subway: 1 or 9 to W. 28th St. Mailing address: Residential Life Office, 210 W. 27th St., NY 10001.*

International House. Foreign grad students ages 21 and over who are attending nearby Columbia University get priority here, but during the summer this stately residence always has a few rooms ($20–$30 per night) available to Americans. Your clean and luxurious surroundings include a fitness center, billiard and TV rooms, a pub, and a cafeteria. Additionally, the I-House sponsors frequent fun weekend excursions and guest lecturers. Call in advance for an application. *500 Riverside Dr., at W. 122nd St., Morningside Heights, tel. 212/316–8436, fax 212/316–1827. Subway: 1 or 9 to W. 125th St. Laundry.*

New York University (NYU). NYU has a slew of dormitories in and around the East and West Village, making it the best choice for long-term stays. From mid-May through mid-August, the weekly rates are $70–$175, depending on whether you opt for so-called frills like air-conditioning, private bath, and kitchen, and depending on what type of room it is: single, double, triple, or suite. For this low rate you also get a mailbox, fitness facilities, laundry rooms, and the option to buy meals in the cafeteria. To be sure of getting a spot, apply by May 1 (late applications are considered through July 23). Anyone is eligible and the *minimum* stay is three weeks. *Mailing address: New York University Summer Housing Office, 14A Washington Pl., NY 10003, tel. 212/998–4621.*

Webster Apartments. This old but impeccably maintained apartment building offers small, clean shared-bath singles ($130–$178 per week, 2 meals per day included) for women only. Guests must fill out an application and show proof of internship or student status. The building has dining rooms, TV and rec rooms, a library, back garden, and roof deck. *419 W. 34th St., btw Ninth and Tenth Aves., Midtown West, tel. 212/967–9000, fax 212/268–8569. Subway: A, C, or E to W. 34th St. 383 rooms, none with bath. Laundry.*

Longer Stays

Finding convenient, affordable, and safe housing for an extended stay in New York City can seem like a Sisyphean task. For one, rents are astronomical: Peruse the rental listings in the *New York Times* classified pages and you may conclude that the only way to live cheaply here is on a bench in Central Park. Expect to pay a minimum of $500–$600 per month for a share or $700 for a studio, more for really desirable neighborhoods like the Upper West Side or the West Village. Furthermore, the cheap places go fast—really fast. It's not uncommon for an apartment to get rented the day it is advertised. Which leads to one pressing question: Is it even remotely possibly to find a cheap apartment? Yes and no. If you have a bit of time and money, you will inevitably find something suitable. Give yourself at least two weeks.

On Tuesdays around 6 PM, savvy apartment-seekers begin lining up at the Cooper Square newsstand in the East Village; it's always the first one in the city to receive the latest "Village Voice."

If you're willing to consider commuting from a neighborhood in Brooklyn—like Brooklyn Heights, Cobble Hill, or Williamsburg—or if you don't mind living in the somewhat sketchy territory east of Avenue B in the East Village/Alphabet City, you'll find places that are a tad cheaper. The weekly *Village Voice* has the most and lowest-priced listings. It pops off the presses at 7:30 PM on Tuesdays; wear running shoes and bring plenty of quarters for phone calls when you go to pick up your copy. If you have Web access, you can read the new edition about six hours earlier at http://www.villagevoice.com/. More limited but also geared toward starving artist types are the listings in the *New York Free Press*. And don't forget to check bulletin boards at Manhattan's two big colleges, Columbia University and New York University. Then, once you've won an appointment to see an apartment, make sure you're outfitted with referrals, proof of income, and bank account information.

If you're pressed for time and decide to use outside help, expect to pay through the nose. Real-estate companies charge anywhere from one to two months' rent. Roommate search services are a bit cheaper. The oldest of these is **Roommate Finders** (250 W. 57th St., near Broadway, tel. 212/489–6918). For a $200 fee, you have access to their listings for a full year (if you're not happy after a month of looking they'll refund you $100). Still feeling panicky? You can find more helpful hints in Karen Spinner's *How to Find an Apartment in New York City* (City Books, 1995; $12.95), available in most New York bookstores.

FOOD

4

By Shon Bayer, Matthew Jalbert, Amy McConnell,
and Mira Schwirtz, with Ada Vassilovski

Dining out is a big deal in New York. If you need proof, consider this: Ruth Reichl, the restaurant critic for the *New York Times*, spends around $350,000 a year reviewing restaurants. True, that's a lot more money than most normal people would spend on chow in an entire lifetime, but then again, there are more good restaurants here than in any other city in the world. Besides the high-end joints like Four Seasons and Union Square Cafe, with five-star chefs and waiters so obsequious they'd probably take a bullet for you, there are tons of humbler restaurants serving New York staples like pizza-by-the-slice and bagels—old-world creations perfected over the centuries in America's numero uno melting pot. It's impossible not to be impressed by the city's countless immigrant groups—Irish, Latin American, Eastern European, Italian, Asian, and more—who've introduced their respective culinary secrets to New York: pub grub, burritos, pierogie, dim sum, pad thai, tandoori chicken, and killer cannoli. Live a little while you're here; if you don't know what *feijoada* is, or have never tasted Burmese cuisine before, this is the place to give it a try.

The recession of the early 1990s caused restaurant owners to lower prices and improve the quality of their food in order to win back jaded diners. Happily, you'll find that this trend has continued unabated—as long as you know where to look. In New York you can easily spend $100 for mediocre food in a trendy restaurant; you could also spend $15 on the best meal of your life in some family-run joint that nobody's ever heard of. And another thing: You should sample some of New York's finer restaurants during the week, when most offer reduced-price lunch specials. This is especially true in Midtown, where a $15 lunch entrée could easily fetch $50 at dinner.

New Yorkers have a staggering 16,000 restaurants to choose from. Do three a day and you'd finish in around 14 years.

Throughout New York, it's hard to define places strictly as a bar, café, or restaurant—many spots tend to serve as all three. Cafés often pour beer and mix cocktails, while plenty of restaurants have bars frequented by resident barflies. Likewise, lots of bars have active kitchens. One rule that does apply across the board, however, is: The cheaper the establishment, the longer the hours. In fact, most places that charge less than $10 for a filling feast stay open until the wee hours—good news for bar crawlers who need a fix after the bars close at 4 AM.

After you've exhausted the reviews in this book, you're still left with about 16,000 restaurants to explore—and 8,000 of those are in Manhattan alone. Zealous New Yorkers on the prowl for a place to eat refer to **The Zagat Survey** ($11.95), an annual guide to some 1,800 restaurants in all price ranges; look for it at bookstores and some newsstands. In contrast are the often snooty and frequently controversial restaurant reviews in **The New York Times**. Every Friday, however, the *Times* stoops to reviewing budget restaurants in the "Under $25" column of its "The Living Arts" section. The **Village Voice** and the **New York Press** tend to review and list restaurants that are affordable, and even include stuff in the outer boroughs. Strict vegetarians visiting New York might want to invest in **The Vegan Guide to New York City**, available for $4.75 from Rynn Berry (159 Eastern Parkway, Apt. 2H, Brooklyn, NY 11238). If you're still not sure where to eat, your best bet is to cruise the streets of the East or West Village, the Upper West Side, or one of the city's many ethnic enclaves, and seek out a place overflowing with locals. Some final notes: The price categories in this chapter refer to the cost of a main course, including a non-alcoholic drink. If you insist on drinking lots of wine or finishing your meal with a flaming bananas Foster, all bets are off. Also, in our reviews we won't mention a restaurant's credit-card acceptance policy unless it takes either select credit cards (e.g., *AE only*) or none at all (i.e., *No credit cards*); otherwise, you can assume that the establishment takes all major cards.

Manhattan Restaurants

UPPER WEST SIDE

Restaurants are plentiful along the Upper West Side's three main north–south avenues: **Columbus Avenue**, **Amsterdam Avenue**, and **Broadway**. All three (and their surrounding side streets) offer just about anything your stomach might desire. Columbus Avenue has the most swank, expensive options, while Amsterdam Avenue draws a crowd that's semi-hip. On Broadway you'll discover an awful lot of nondescript diners offering cheapie Greek gyros and Italian hero sandwiches. If you're looking to dine before catching a performance at **Lincoln Center** (*see* Chapter 7), be warned: The restaurants in this area are pricey. After all, they're catering to people who think nothing of paying $115 for a single opera ticket.

UNDER $5 **Bagels on Amsterdam.** Top your circular sandwich with a stunning variety of shmears (75¢–$2.75), including chocolate chip, raisin-carrot, and three flavors of tofu cream cheese. For lunch, try a bagel with tuna salad ($3.75) or salami ($4.25). *164 Amsterdam Ave., at W. 67th St., tel. 212/799–0700. Subway: 1 or 9 to W. 66th St. Open daily 6:30 AM–8 PM (Sun. until 6 PM). No credit cards.*

Gray's Papaya. In this enlightened city the natural accompaniment to a couple of dogs is a big frothy cup of papaya juice. Total cost for two hot dogs and a drink: $1.95. *2090 Broadway, at W. 72nd St., tel. 212/799–0243. Subway: 1, 2, 3, or 9 to W. 72nd St. Open 24 hrs. Other location: 402 Sixth Ave., at W. 8th St., West Village, tel. 212/260–3532. No credit cards.*

Restaurants by Neighborhood

Zabar's. The Zabar's cafeteria, part of the city's famous gourmet food emporium (*see* Markets and Specialty Shops, *below*), dispenses quality eats at everyman prices: Bagels with lox, salmon chowder, and sandwiches are all about $4. Counter service is quick, though you'll suffer a long line of cranky New Yorkers. *2245 Broadway, at W. 80th St., tel. 212/787–2004. Subway: 1 or 9 to W. 79th St. Open weekdays 7:30–7:30, Sat. 7:30–8, Sun. 7:30–6.*

UNDER $10 **Big Nick's Burger/Pizza Joint.** Customers are urged to "confide their ultimate pizza fantasy," and the menu features hard-to-swallow combinations like Gyromania (gyro strips, onions, tomatoes, and cheese), Farmer's Pizza (fresh tomatoes and hard-boiled eggs), and Reuben, Reuben (pastrami, sauerkraut, cheese, and tomato sauce). Individual pizzas are $4.50, burgers $3–$5. *2175 Broadway, at W. 77th St., tel. 212/362–9238 or 212/724–2010. Subway: 1 or 9 to W. 79th St. Open 24 hrs. Other location: 70 W. 71st St., at Columbus Ave., tel. 212/799–4444; open daily 10 AM–5 AM. No credit cards.*

Big Nick's has been the self-proclaimed savior of "compulsive noshers and groovy happyfolk" since 1962.

Café con Leche. This cheery restaurant blends Dominican, Cuban, and Spanish cuisines to produce wildly popular dishes like *arroz con pollo y chorizo* (rice, chicken, and Spanish sausage; $9), *camarones en salsa de coco* (shrimp in coconut sauce; $9.25), and *filete de pollo al ron* (sautéed chicken in rum sauce; $8). Their Paella Festival (Mon. and Tues. 4 PM–midnight) features the special Spanish stew of rice, chicken, sausage, and seafood for $9.95 (regularly $13). *424 Amsterdam Ave., btw W. 80th and 81st Sts., tel. 212/595–7000. Subway: 1 or 9 to W. 79th St. Open daily 8 AM–midnight. Lunch special ($6) daily 11 AM–4 PM.*

The Cottage. This ancient, dark-paneled Chinese restaurant has a loyal following among young Upper West Siders, mainly because of its reasonably priced chef's specialties ($7–$9) and the "all the wine you can drink—free" policy at dinner. *360 Amsterdam Ave., at W. 77th St., tel. 212/595–7450. Subway: 1 or 9 to W. 79th St. Open daily 11:30–11 (Fri. and Sat. until midnight). Lunch special ($4.25–$5) weekdays 11–3. Wheelchair access.*

Eclair Bakery Cafe. An odd mix of elderly German immigrants and Hollywood celebs (Michael J. Fox, Sigourney Weaver, you get the idea) people Eclair's fraying, pink-upholstered booths, presumably for the cheap breakfast plates ($3.25), sandwiches ($4–$6), pastas ($6–$8), and hearty German dishes. And they do sell eclairs ($3), chocolate or mocha. *141 W. 72nd St., btw Broadway and Columbus Ave., tel. 212/873–7700. Subway: 1, 2, 3, or 9 to W. 72nd St. Open weekdays 7:30 AM–9 PM, weekends 7:30 AM–10 PM.*

La Caridad. The crowds keep coming back to this Creole/Chinese eatery—despite the high grease factor—because portions are huge and prices cheap. A small roasted chicken or side of beef with a mountain of fried rice is $5–$7; seafood dishes are $5 and up. Expect to wait hours for a table (or show some initiative and snag a counter seat). *2199 Broadway, at W. 78th St., tel. 212/874–2780. Subway: 1 or 9 to W. 79th St. Open daily 11:30 AM–1 AM (Sun. until 10:30 PM). No credit cards.*

Monsoon. Join Upper West Siders dining on skillfully prepared Vietnamese delicacies like *bun xao* (stir-fried noodles with shrimp, egg, and chopped peanuts; $7), spicy curries ($8–$11), and vegetarian dishes ($6–$8). Though large portions make an appetizer unnecessary, the *cha gio chay* (spring rolls; $4) are first-class. *435 Amsterdam Ave., at W. 81st St., tel. 212/580–8686. Subway: 1 or 9 to W. 79th St. Open Mon.–Thurs. 11:30–11:30, Fri. and Sat. 11–midnight, Sun. 11–11:30.*

UNDER $15 **Josie's.** This hip, earth-friendly restaurant does diner food the organic way. We really like the garlic-basil linguini with gulf shrimp ($12.75), the grilled-chicken salad with miso-tofu vinaigrette ($9.75), and the free-range hamburger on focaccia bread ($7). *300 Amsterdam Ave., at W. 74th St., tel. 212/769–1212. Subway: 1, 2, 3, or 9 to W. 72nd St. Open daily 5:30 PM–midnight (Sun. and Mon. until 11 PM). Wheelchair access.*

Luzia's. Your gregarious hosts Luzia and Murray serve up hearty Portuguese-influenced fare like white-bean salad ($4), baked ham with pineapple glaze ($11), and salmon poached in champagne ($13), all accompanied by (heavenly) fresh Portuguese bread. The brunch menu includes omelets ($7.50) and Portuguese sausage ($3). *429 Amsterdam Ave., btw W. 80th and 81st Sts., tel. 212/595–2000. Subway: 1 or 9 to W. 79th St. Open Tues.–Fri. 10–10, weekends 9:30 AM–10 PM.*

`UNDER $20` **Fujiyama Mama's.** This slick, loud sushi hot spot rocks nightly with young professionals doing the groove-and-food thing while a DJ spins tunes. Sushi à la carte averages $4.25; a variety of entrées are $16–$22. *467 Columbus Ave., btw W. 82nd and 83rd Sts., tel. 212/769–1144. Subway: 1 or 9 to W. 79th St. Open Mon.–Thurs. 6 PM–midnight, Fri. and Sat. 6 PM–1 AM, Sun. 5 PM–11 PM. AE only.*

Good Enough to Eat. On weekends, Volvo-deprived West Side couples pack this Manhattan substitute for a rustic Vermont farmhouse to feast on delicious blueberry pancakes ($7.75), Mexican scrambled eggs with tortillas ($6), or the formidable Lumber Jack special (two eggs, two strips of bacon, and two giant pancakes; $7.75). Hearty dinners like roast chicken, meat loaf, or stuffed brook trout cost $12–$17. Just up the street, **Popover Cafe** (551 Amsterdam Ave., at W. 87th St., tel. 212/595–8555) also does a mouthwatering country brunch. *483 Amsterdam Ave., btw W. 83rd and 84th Sts., tel. 212/496–0215. Subway: 1 or 9 to W. 86th St. Open daily 8–4 and 6–10:30 (weekends from 9 AM).*

COLUMBIA UNIVERSITY AND MORNINGSIDE HEIGHTS

Morningside Heights, the neighborhood surrounding **Columbia University** and **Barnard College**, caters to students who love to eat but hate spending all their hard-earned loan money on food. You'll find dozens of cheap snack shops and 24-hour diners on **Broadway** and **Amsterdam Avenue**, between West 110th and 116th streets. When that gets boring, head north along Broadway to the blocks around 125th Street (a.k.a. Martin Luther King Jr. Boulevard) to find some terrific West African eateries (*see Harlem, below*).

`UNDER $5` **Amir's Falafel.** Everything at this relaxed student hangout is pretty darn cheap. For less than $4 you can eat your fill of falafel, stuffed grape leaves, and baba ghanoush. Sandwiches, loaded with tahini and marinated chicken or beef, are also a steal at $4. *2911-A Broadway, btw W. 113th and 114th Sts., tel. 212/749–7500. Subway: 1 or 9 to W. 116th St. Open daily 11–11. No credit cards.*

The Bread Shop. Come to this hole-in-the-wall pizza shop/bakery to scarf down heavenly hot 'n' greasy slices ($1.30–$3) or any one of the dozens of pies and custard-filled delicacies. *3139*

Dinner, Family Style

The family-style Italian restaurant is a special New York institution—it provides the perfect setting for celebrating a birthday, graduation, suspended sentence, whatever. If you've got a big, hungry group of people who want lots of vino and garlicky food in a festive atmosphere, reserve a table at one of the following: CARMINE'S (2450 Broadway, btw W. 90th and 91st Sts., tel. 212/362–2200; 200 W. 44th St., btw Broadway and Eighth Ave., tel. 212/221–3800), SAMBUCA (20 W. 72nd St., btw Columbus Ave. and Central Park W, tel. 212/787–5656), or OSSO BUCO (88 University Pl., btw E. 11th and 12th Sts., tel. 212/645–4525).

Broadway, at La Salle St., tel. 212/666–4343. Subway: 1 or 9 to W. 125th St. Open daily 8 AM–9 PM. No credit cards.

Tamarind Seed Health Food Store. If you don't mind being surrounded by vitamin bottles and cans of soy milk, you'll learn to love this health-food store/deli. Sandwiches are $3.50, and everything at the bountiful salad bar (chow mein, tofu, pasta, plenty of raw vegetables) is $3.25 per lb. *2935 Broadway, btw W. 114th and 115th Sts., tel. 212/864–3360. Subway: 1 or 9 to W. 116th St. Open Mon.–Sat. 8 AM–10 PM, Sun. 10 AM–9 PM.*

`UNDER $10` **Bengal Cafe.** Count on this classy, little restaurant for delicious Indian dishes like shrimp curry ($7.50), chicken tandoori masala ($8.25), beef vindaloo ($6), and *aloo gobi motar* (sautéed cauliflower with tomatoes and onion; $5.75), accompanied by big helpings of basmati rice, cabbage, and a half dozen other relishes. *1028 Amsterdam Ave., btw W. 110th and 111th Sts., tel. 212/662–7191. Subway: 1 or 9 to Cathedral Pkwy. (W. 110th St.). Open daily 11:30–3 and 4–11. Lunch special ($5–$7) weekdays 11:30–3.*

Grandma's Kitchen. This diner feeds the penniless waifs of Columbia with an ungrandmotherly repertoire that includes pita sandwiches and burgers ($4.25–$6.75), pastas ($5.50–$9), and Greek and Mexican entrées ($4–$8). At breakfast there are omelets ($4.50–$7), waffles, bagels, cereal, and a big glass of good-for-you prune juice ($1.75). *2937 Broadway, at W. 115th St., tel. 212/662–5410. Subway: 1 or 9 to W. 116th St. Open 24 hrs. No credit cards.*

La Rosita. This Cuban joint's breakfast specials (rice, beans, eggs, juice, and toast) are served around-the-clock, along with *chuletas* (pork chops) and Cuban sandwiches. The crowd is all cab drivers and Columbia students. *2809 Broadway, at W. 108th St., tel. 212/663–7804. Subway: 1 or 9 to Cathedral Pkwy. (W. 110th St.). Open daily 9 AM–10 PMish. No credit cards.*

Obaa Koryoe. Tease your senses with African techno music and West African cuisine. The traditional chicken, tripe, fish, cowfoot, oxtail, and lamb dishes ($8.75–$10) come with *wachey* (rice and black eyed peas) or *jolloff* (rice with tomato sauce); both are delicious. Vegetarian meals are $7–$9. *3143 Broadway, at 125th St., tel. 212/316–2950. Subway: 1 or 9 to W. 125th St. Open daily 11 AM–midnight (Fri. and Sat. until 2 AM). No credit cards.*

Riverside Church Cafeteria. Students from the Manhattan School of Music, Columbia University, and Riverside Church's own theological school flock here for the $5.50 lunch platter (chicken, meat loaf, or fish, with greens and bread or potatoes). Breakfast costs even less. *490 Riverside Dr., at W. 120th St., tel. 212/222–5900. Subway: 1 or 9 to W. 125th St. Open weekdays 8 AM–3:30 PM. No credit cards.*

Tom's Restaurant. A mixed crowd of old-timers and Columbia students come here to chow on cheeseburgers ($2.75), salads ($5), southern-fried chicken ($5), and thick brain-freezing milk shakes. Curious *Seinfeld* fans just come in to gawk at the blown-up photo of the gang, complete with their signatures. *2880 Broadway, at W. 112th St., tel. 212/864–6137. Subway: 1 or 9 to Cathedral Pkwy. (W. 110th St.). Open Sun.–Wed. 6 AM–11:30 PM, Thurs.–Sat. 24 hrs. No credit cards.*

For those who worship at the house of Jerry (Seinfeld, not Garcia), Tom's Restaurant is a sacred place; its neon sign is featured at the beginning of every show.

`UNDER $15` **The Mill.** It's the side of *kimchee* (spicy pickled cabbage and onion) that makes Korean dishes like *dak bokum* (stir-fried chicken; $8), *haemul dolsott bibimbob* (seafood and rice in a hot earthen bowl; $10), and *bul goki* (barbecued beef; $10) so fiery hot. The decor is upscale and understated; you're more likely to see a Ph.D. holder here than a starving student. *2895 Broadway, btw W. 112th and 113th Sts., tel. 212/666–7653. Subway: 1 or 9 to Cathedral Pkwy. (W. 110th St.). Open daily 11 AM–10 PM. Lunch special ($5–$7) weekdays 11–3. Wheelchair access.*

HARLEM

You'll find East African, West African, Creole, Caribbean, and Southern restaurants aplenty along Harlem's main commercial arteries: **Malcolm X Boulevard** (Lenox Avenue), **Adam Clayton Powell Jr. Boulevard** (Seventh Avenue), **Martin Luther King Jr. Boulevard** (125th Street), and

138th Street. Many of the West African restaurants double as community centers for African immigrants—you can enjoy a really good meal while soaking up a little foreign culture. In **East Harlem** there are dozens of Latino restaurants on Lexington Avenue between East 116th and 125th streets that serve pupusas and tacos for a few bucks apiece. As a tourist, you'll have no problem visiting Harlem or East Harlem during the day. On the other hand, use caution at night and stay on main thoroughfares or take a cab.

UNDER $5 **Joseph's Food Basket.** Everything here is free of additives, preservatives, and chemicals (and sometimes free of dairy, wheat, and cholesterol). Breakfast is an unbelievable $2.50, while lasagna, stir-fried vegetables, macaroni pie, and savory stews are all $1.50–$3. There's also a wide selection of gourmet coffees and fresh organic juices ($1.25–$4). *471 Malcolm X Blvd., btw W. 133rd and 134th Sts., tel. 212/368–7663. Subway: 2 or 3 to W. 135th St. Open Mon.–Sat. 8–8. Lunch special ($5) weekdays 11–3. No credit cards.*

UNDER $10 **Darou Minan.** The only conversation you'll hear in English at this friendly Senegalese restaurant will probably be your own. For $5–$6 fill up on spicy entrées like *yassa ganaar* (lemon chicken with rice), vegetarian *mafe* (vegetables in peanut sauce), or *thiebou dieun* (stewed fish with rice and vegetables in tomato sauce). For dessert, go with the *tiacri* (sour cream, couscous, and milk; $2.50). *1943 Adam Clayton Powell Jr. Blvd., btw W. 117th and 118th Sts., tel. 212/665–4711. Subway: 2 or 3 to W. 116th St. Open 24 hrs. No credit cards.*

Ethel's Southern Quarters (ESQ). Hospitable Ethel and her daughters really know how to whip up superb home-cooked catfish and shrimp ($7.50), fried chicken ($6), and buffalo wings and ribs ($8). For breakfast try a gut-buster of bacon, eggs, grits, and home fries for only $3. *747 St. Nicholas Ave., btw W. 147th and 148th Sts., tel. 212/694–1686. Subway: A, B, C, or D to W. 145th St. Open Tues.–Sat. 6 AM–10 PM, Sun. 6 AM–7 PM. No credit cards.*

The Reliable. This ramshackle Sugar Hill favorite serves some fine, authentic Southern food: smothered chicken, barbecued ribs, sweet curried chicken, and salmon cakes, all priced at $5–$6.50 and served with tasty cooked greens and corn bread. Next door and under the same ownership, **Copeland's** (547 W. 145th St., tel. 212/234–2356) is a bit more upscale, with great Southern breakfasts and brunch. *549 W. 145th St., btw Broadway and Amsterdam Ave., tel. 212/234–2357. Subway: 1 or 9 to W. 145th St. Open daily 8 AM–11 PM (Fri. and Sat. until midnight). No credit cards.*

Singleton's Bar-B-Que. Singleton's claims to have the only brick-oven barbecue in the entire city, and the product is outstanding soul food. Try the hickory-smoked chicken ($6.25) slathered with barbecue sauce and paired with collard greens or yams. The $5 breakfast includes omelets, pancakes, and plenty of meat. *525 Malcom X Blvd., btw W. 136 and 137th Sts., tel. 212/694–9442. Subway: 2 or 3 to W. 135th St. Open daily 8 AM–4 AM. No credit cards.*

UNDER $15 **Sylvia's.** The most famous soul-food restaurant in New York remains popular with locals, despite having fed celebs like Dan "potatoe" Quayle. Dinner favorites, like deep-fried fish, smothered steak, and barbecued ribs, are $7–$12. Breakfast costs $2–$6, and on Sundays there's a gospel brunch ($13) with live music. Look for matronly Sylvia presiding over the two large dining rooms and outdoor seating area. *328 Malcom X Blvd., at W. 126th St., tel. 212/996–0660. Subway: 2 or 3 to W. 125th St. Open Mon.–Sat. 7:30 AM–10:30 PM, Sun. 1 PM–7 PM. AE only.*

WASHINGTON HEIGHTS

Washington Heights, at the very northern tip of Manhattan, is so far from most tourist attractions that you wouldn't want to make the trip just to get something to eat. But if you're in the neighborhood you can enjoy kosher bagels and lox, Salvadoran fried plantains, or a cup of syrupy Cuban coffee—at prices far lower than in the rest of Manhattan. The main thoroughfares—**St. Nicholas Avenue** and **Broadway**—are chockablock full of street carts and cheap, divey eateries offering Dominican, Salvadoran, Cuban, and other Latin fare. (It helps if you speak Spanish, though you'll find most places serve familiar stuff like tostadas and burritos. And you can always point.) The blocks around **Yeshiva University** (Audubon Ave., near 186th St.) cater to the Jewish student population with dozens of kosher restaurants. Another cluster of diners and bodegas lies a few blocks from **Fort Tryon Park**, around 204th Street. Remember, this isn't the most heavily touristed of neighborhoods, so use your street smarts and don't wander the streets alone after dark.

If you don't want to be branded a tourist in Washington Heights, eat your Salvadoran "pupusas" (fried, filled tortillas) with your hands.

UNDER $10 **La Cabaña Salvadoreña.** At $2 apiece, it's easy to fill up on à la carte Salvadoran snacks like *pupusas con queso* (fried tortillas, folded and filled with cheese), enchiladas, and tacos. Or get a combination plate ($6–$8) of *carne asada* (grilled steak) or *chuletas de cerdo* (pork chops); both come with fries, mashed potatoes, or rice and beans. *4384 Broadway, at W. 187th St., tel. 212/928–7872. Subway: A to W. 181st St. Open daily 7 AM–1 AM. No credit cards.*

Mambi #1. If you're a monolingual American, this place can be bewilderingly foreign; the wait-staff speaks *solamente español*. It's worth bridging the language barrier, though, because the food is excellent, especially the paella with squid ($9), *pescado frito* (fried fish; $8), and omelets ($3). The coffee, brewed Latin American–style, is strong enough to melt your spoon. *558 W. 181st St., btw St. Nicholas and Audubon Aves., tel. 212/923–9035. Subway: 1 or 9 to W. 181st St. Open 24 hrs. No credit cards.*

Wilson's Bakery and Restaurant. Wilson's Bakery began serving soul and diner food ($5–$9) when *Howdy Doody* was a cool new TV show. Nearly 40 years later, breakfast ($2–$6) still means eggs any style plus your choice of ham, bacon, sausage, smothered pork chops, beef bologna, grits, pancakes, and french toast. Weekend brunch is popular with neighborhood churchgoers, and seats get scarce after 11 AM. *1980 Amsterdam Ave., at W. 158th St., tel. 212/923–9821. Subway: A, B, or C to W. 155th St. Open daily 6 AM–9 PM. Wheelchair access. No credit cards.*

UPPER EAST SIDE

Upper East Siders have a lot of money to blow on grub, and it shows. For what you'd pay to eat in one of the schmancy restaurants lining Fifth and Madison avenues (where, naturally, all of the cool museums are), you could probably buy one of the smaller OPEC countries. That said, there are plenty of affordable options east of Lexington Avenue, along **Third Avenue** and **Second Avenue**. Here's a good rule of thumb: The farther east you walk from the subway line (which runs along Lexington Avenue), the cheaper the food gets. On York Avenue, way out by the East River, they practically give it away.

UNDER $5 **Soup Burg.** A few mirror tricks and a long counter constitute this tiny coffee shop, the quintessential greasy spoon. Breakfast costs about $4, soups are $1.50, and a fat chunk of cow meat with fries (the beef burger deluxe) is $4.25. Old-fashioned milk shakes are $2. *1150 Lexington Ave., btw E. 79th and 80th Sts., tel. 212/737–0095. Subway: 6 to E. 77th St. Open weekdays 4 AM–9 PM, Sat. 4 AM–8:30 PM, Sun. 4 AM–8 PM. No credit cards.*

Teriyaki Boy. The Japanese food here—like seaweed udon ($4.50) or the "chicken egg bowl" ($4)—tastes good mainly because it's cheap. On the other hand, the sushi selection is first-rate ($1–$2 à la carte). *1640 Third Ave., btw E. 91st and 92nd Sts., tel. 212/987–7150. Subway: 4, 5, or 6 to E. 86th St. Open weekdays 11–11, weekends 11–10. Other location: 885 Ninth Ave., btw W. 57th and 58th Sts., Midtown, tel. 212/307–7202. No credit cards.*

UNDER $10 **Candle Cafe.** Earth-friendly dining (at least an upscale version) means low-on-the-food-chain vegetarian and macrobiotic dishes. If you need a roughage boost, the Harvest Salad (romaine lettuce, vegetables, sprouts, and sesame seeds) comes in small ($4.25) or large ($7.25). To drink, try a glass of wheat grass ($1.75) or some organic coffee ($1.25). *1307 Third Ave., btw E. 74th and 75th Sts., tel. 212/472–0970. Subway: 6 to E. 77th St. Open Mon.–Sat. 7:30 AM–10:30 PM, Sun. 11:30 AM–9:30 PM. Wheelchair access.*

EJ's Luncheonette. At this amped-up '90s diner, you'll wait in long lines to chow stuff like the sautéed mushroom burger ($6.25), veggie club sandwich ($6.50), and milk shakes mixed with fruit or peanut butter ($3.50). For breakfast try flapjacks and waffles done 14 ways ($5–$7).

1271 Third Ave., at E. 73rd St., tel. 212/472–0600. Subway: 6 to E. 77th St. Open Mon.–Thurs. 8 AM–11 PM, Fri. and Sat. 8 AM–midnight, Sun. 8 AM–10:30 PM. Other location: 447 Amsterdam Ave., btw W. 81st and 82nd Sts., Upper West Side, tel. 212/873–3444; open Mon.–Thurs. 9 AM–11 PM, Fri. 9 AM–midnight, Sat. 8 AM–midnight, Sun. 8 AM–10:30. No credit cards.

El Pollo. Head here for killer Peruvian-style chicken, both grilled and marinated; you can eat your fill for less than $7. El Pollo doesn't look like much, but the food merits a visit. *1746 First Ave., btw E. 90th and 91st Sts., tel. 212/996–7810. Subway: 4, 5, or 6 to E. 86th St. BYOB. Open weekdays 11:30–11, weekends 12:30–11.*

Garlic Bob's. Everything at this "pizza bar" (translation: pizza joint with nine microbrews instead of Bud) comes with an optional blast of roasted garlic. Slices are $1.75, focaccia sandwiches $5.75, and vegetarian lasagna $7. The half-dozen specialty pizzas—try the Tuscan Vegetable with eggplant, zucchini, red peppers, sun-dried tomatoes, yellow squash, and red onions—cost $9–$14. *1325 Third Ave., btw E. 75th and 76th Sts., tel. 212/772–BOBS. Subway: 6 to E. 77th St. Open daily noon–10 PM. Other location: 508 Columbus Ave., btw W. 84th and 85th Sts., Upper West Side, tel. 212/769–2627. AE only.*

Samalita's Tortilla Factory. There's nothing factorylike about this lovable Cal-Mex restaurant squeezed between the Upper East Side's chichi restaurant drudgery. The soft tacos ($2.75) and burritos ($5.50–$7) are subtley spiced, and so is the decor. *1429 Third Ave., btw E. 80th and 81st Sts., tel. 212/737–5070. Subway: 6 to E. 77th St. Open daily noon–11 PM. Wheelchair access. No credit cards.*

UNDER $15 **Barking Dog Luncheonette.** Bring your favorite canine to the Barking Dog Luncheonette and park him or her at the "dog bar" (a trough of fresh water) outside. No kidding. Thanks to NYC health codes, only humans can order the hefty and inventive salads ($4.50–$9), burgers ($6–$8), and other carnivore specials ($10–$16). *1678 Third Ave., at E. 94th St., tel. 212/831–1800. Subway: 6 to E. 96th St. Open daily 8 AM–11 PM. Wheelchair and dog access. No credit cards.*

Bella Donna. This bustling, cramped pasta shop is not unlike a Tuscan country home inhabited by some nice Swiss folks. Incredibly tasty pizzas ($8–$9) and pastas ($7–$10) are served with fresh hot bread; salads and antipasti are $4–$5.50. Just down the street, **Caffé Buon Gusto** (236 E. 77th St., btw Second and Third Aves., tel. 212/535–6884) has equally scrumptious and cheap pastas. *307 E. 77th St., btw First and Second Aves., tel. 212/535–2866. Subway: 6 to 77th St. BYOB. Open daily 11 AM–midnight. Wheelchair access. No credit cards.*

Good Health Cafe. Like a United Nations of good cooking, this restaurant/health-food store dishes up a multitude of hearty entrées ($8.50–$10) ranging from Japanese soba noodles to artichoke spaghetti with Italian "wheatballs." Weekend brunch (11–4) is $4.75–$6 and includes wild-rice pancakes, blue-corn waffles, and spinach-and-mushroom omelets. *324 E. 86th St., btw First and Second Aves., tel. 212/439–9680. Subway: 4, 5, or 6 to E. 86th St. Open daily 11 AM–10 PM (Fri. and Sat. until 11).*

Mocca Hungarian. Chicken paprika ($10), veal goulash ($10), and cherry soup (summer only; $2.75) are among the savory items served up here daily. As if that weren't tempting enough, from 11:30 to 4 they also dish out the city's best $6 lunch special. *1588 Second Ave., btw E. 82nd and 83rd Sts., tel. 212/734–6470. Subway: 4, 5, or 6 to E. 86th St. Open daily 11:30–11.*

Viand. You must be the world's pickiest eater if you can't find something you like on Viand's menu. It lists more than 300 breakfast, lunch, and dinner items, including 70 Italian dishes ($4–$15), dozens of Greek specialties, and a ton of sandwiches, omelets, and salads for less than $10. *300 E. 86th St., at Second Ave., tel. 212/879–9425. Subway: 4, 5, or 6 to E. 86th St. Open 24 hrs. Other locations: 1011 Madison Ave., btw E. 78th and 79th Sts., tel. 212/249–8250; open daily 6 AM–10 PM. 673 Madison Ave., at E. 61st St., tel. 212/751–6622; open Mon.–Sat. 6 AM–10 PM, Sun. 7 AM–9 PM. No credit cards.*

UNDER $20 **The Velvet Room.** Purple-and-red lamps, chandeliers, velvet-draped walls, antique furniture, and the almost total absence of light create the Upper East Side's weirdest setting for sipping wine ($5 and up per glass). The menu includes luxe dishes ($14–$23) like baked chicken breast in a dry sherry sauce with apple, walnut, and honey compote. *209 E. 76th St., btw First and Second Aves., tel. 212/628–6633. Subway: 6 to E. 77th St. Open Sun. and Mon. 6 PM–1 AM, Tues. and Wed. 6 PM–2 AM, Thurs.–Sat. 6 PM–3 AM. Wheelchair access. AE only.*

Want a taste of the high-rolling, post-Perestroika lifestyle of a Moscow Mafia don—without the messy visa requirements? Order the house combo at the Velvet Room: For $90 you get three types of caviar with four glasses of chilled Russian vodka.

MIDTOWN WEST OF FIFTH AVENUE

West of Fifth Avenue, Midtown sometimes seems as charmless as an armpit. This is where cabs pile up, where skyscrapers tower, and where hundreds of hole-in-the-wall diners and delis feed working stiffs as cheaply and unoriginally as possible. Though it's a bit gritty, the neighborhood of **Hell's Kitchen** is where you should go to seek relief: Ninth Avenue in the 40s and 50s is loaded with ethnic restaurants offering some of the cheapest meals in Manhattan. One weekend every May, Hell's Kitchen is also home to an **International Food Festival** (*see* Festivals and Annual Events, in Chapter 1). **West 32nd Street** between Fifth Avenue and Broadway is sometimes referred to as "Korean Restaurant Row," thanks to its cheap Korean and Japanese diners. Two recommendations: **Won Jo** (23 W. 32nd St., btw Broadway and Sixth Ave., tel. 212/695–5815) and **Camelia** (17 W. 32nd St., tel. 212/290–2525), which offers an anytime, all-you-can-eat barbecue buffet ($13.95). Both are open 24 hours. **West 46th Street** around Broadway boasts a cluster of Brazilian restaurants, cafés, and markets.

Sadly, the **Theater District** is heavy on tourist traps boasting overpriced and often mediocre food. Consider this: Do you really want to blow $20 or more on a substandard pre-theater dinner, especially if you've already paid $35 for restricted-view seats? If so, check out **Virgil's Real BBQ** (152 W. 44th St., btw Broadway and Sixth Ave., tel. 212/921–9494) or the Midtown branch of **Carmine's** (*see box* Dinner, Family Style, *above*). They aren't particularly cheap, but the food at both is good and the size of the entrées obscene. The district's ritzy **Restaurant Row**—West 46th Street between Eighth and Ninth avenues—gets a lot of hoopla, and you can eat here without breaking the bank, particularly at a place like tiny **Hourglass Tavern** (373 W. 46th St., tel. 212/265–2060). All plates here are less than $10 and, after your table's 59-minute hourglass has run out, you are asked to move on.

Finally, there's **West 57th Street** between Fifth and Eighth avenues. Over the last few years it's undergone a Kafkaesque transmogrification—from plain ol' thoroughfare to one embraced by Disney and bland theme restaurants. As a tourist you may feel obliged to check it out, although real New Yorkers prefer to ignore **Planet Hollywood** (140 W. 57th St., tel. 212/333–7827), **Hard Rock Cafe** (221 W. 57th St., tel. 212/459–9320), **Jekyll and Hyde Club** (1409 Sixth Ave., at W. 57th St., tel. 212/541–9505), **Motown Cafe** (104 W. 57th St., tel. 212/581–8030), **Brooklyn Diner U.S.A.** (212 W. 57th St., tel. 212/581–8900), and **Harley-Davidson Cafe** (1370 Sixth Ave., at W. 56th St., tel. 212/245–6000). The point to all these places is never the food (typically $7–$20), but rather the stuff on the walls. Jekyll and Hyde has an electronically animated Great Sphinx and flapping gargoyles, Motown Cafe has its Motown Moments quartet singing Four Tops and Temptations songs, while Harley-Davidson has a revvable motorcycle upon which you can get your picture taken ($7). The **Russian Tea Room** (150 W. 57th St., tel. 212/265–0947), once the kind of place where Woody Allen had his own table, is due to reopen in 1997 with a redesign that will probably make it as cheesy as all the rest. And though it's not exactly on 57th Street, it's hard to ignore the **Fashion Cafe** (51 Rockefeller Center, W. 51st St., btw Fifth and Sixth Aves., tel. 212/765–3131), owned in part by supermodels Naomi Campbell, Claudia Schiffer, and Elle Macpherson.

UNDER $5 **Manganaro's Hero-Boy.** Come for fast-food Italian dishes, most notably the biggest and best sub sandwiches in the entire city. *492 Ninth Ave., btw W. 37th and 38th Sts., tel. 212/947–7325. Subway: A, C, or E to W. 34th St. (Penn Station). Open daily 9–7:30.*

Tachigui-Soba. A large Japanese lantern hangs in front of this Times Square nosh spot, the only indication of the cheap cafeteria-style food that lies within (there's no sign in English). Chicken tempura is $3, chicken teriyaki $4, and *udon* and *soba* soups $3–$5.50. Seating is upstairs in a zero-decor room. *732 Seventh Ave., btw W. 48th and 49th Sts., tel. 212/265–8181. Subway: N or R to W. 49th St. Also: 1 or 9 to W. 50th St. Open daily 11–11. No credit cards.*

UNDER $10 **Chantale's Cajun Kitchen.** Looking weirdly out of place (it's next door to the Port Authority Bus Terminal), this homey New Orleans eatery serves authentic Cajun and Creole dishes ($3.50–$6.50) as well as meal-size salads ($4.25–$7). The house special, Chantale's Gumbo, is a stew of shrimp, sausage, scallops, fish, and chicken served in portions small ($3.50) and large ($6). *510 Ninth Ave., btw W. 38th and 39th Sts., tel. 212/967–2623. Subway: A, C, or E to W. 42nd St. (Port Authority). Open Mon.–Sat. 11–7:30. No credit cards.*

Cupcake Cafe. The Cupcake seems trapped in one of those sleepy Twilight Zones where things never seem to age, where pert wanna-be actresses pick daintily at their sandwiches ($4–$5.50), and where Billie Holiday drifts from the scratchy stereo. Indulge in lusciously frosted baked goods (60¢–$2) or fill up on decent diner fare. *522 Ninth Ave., at W. 39th St., tel. 212/465–1530. Subway: A, C, or E to W. 42nd St. (Port Authority). Open weekdays 7 AM–7:30 PM, Sat. 8–6, Sun. 9–5. No credit cards.*

What do Madonna and Martha Stewart have in common? They both love cakes from the Cupcake Cafe.

Sapporo. At Sapporo, a big bowl of *hiyashi chuka* (cold noodle soup) is perfect on hot summer days. Or try any of the filling ramen noodle and teriyaki dishes ($5–$8) that keep this place packed with a mostly Japanese clientele. *152 W. 49th St., btw Sixth and Seventh Aves., tel. 212/869–8972. Subway: N or R to W. 49th St. Also: B, D, F, or Q to Rockefeller Center (W. 47–50th Sts.). Open daily 11 AM–1 AM (Sun. until 11 PM). Wheelchair access. No credit cards.*

Soul Fixin's. This small restaurant cranks out an enormous, outstanding Country Lunch ($6): your choice of barbecued, fried, baked, or smothered chicken; barbecued spare ribs or fried whiting fish; plus corn bread and two side dishes, such as candied yams or black-eyed peas. Vegetarians can get four meatless side dishes for $5.50. *371 W. 34th St., near Ninth Ave., tel. 212/736–1345. Subway: A, C, or E to Penn Station (W. 34th St.). Open weekdays 11 AM–7 PM. Wheelchair access. No credit cards.*

Soup Kitchen International. Soup Man Al Yeganeh, who came to the States to study physics, probably never could have guessed that Jerry Seinfeld would be his rocket ride to fame. New Yorkers and tourists alike now line up willingly for a take-out taste (small $6, large $8, extra large $13) of his excellent vegetable, bean, nut, seafood, or meat soups (about 15 daily varieties, both hot and cold). If you hope to get bread and fruit with your seafood bisque, you've gotta move: Know what you want (ask no questions and speak quickly) and have your money ready. Don't loiter and *don't* call him the Soup Nazi. *259-A W. 55th St., near Eighth Ave., tel. 212/757–7730. Subway: A, C, D, or 1 to 59th St./Columbus Circle. Also: C or E to 50th St. Open weekdays noon–7 PM, Sat. 1–6. Wheelchair access. No credit cards.*

Vegetarian Heaven. The specially trained Chinese chefs work wonders with tofu and wheat gluten, creating vegetarian "beef" lo mein ($6.50) and sweet and sour "chicken" ($8). Seafood dishes, like the crispy veggie eel ($12), are made with arrowroot flour and bean-curd skin. There's also matzoh-ball soup ($2.50) and occasional live Jewish folk music. *304 W.*

Park It

On a sunny day, the best place to eat lunch in midtown Manhattan is in beautiful Bryant Park (see Parks and Gardens, in Chapter 2). The charming folding chairs sprinkled across its startlingly green, flower-trimmed lawn are free for you to use—if you can snag a few before legions of pallid office types monopolize them. It also frequently hosts free noontime concerts, poetry readings, and comedy performances.

58th St., btw Eighth and Ninth Aves., tel. 212/956–4678. Subway: A, B, C, D, 1, or 9 to Columbus Circle (W. 59th St.). Also: N or R to W. 57th St. Open Mon.–Thurs. 11–11, Fri. 11– sundown, Sat. sundown–1 AM, Sun. noon–11 PM. Lunch special ($4.25–$5.50) weekdays 11 AM–3:30 PM.

Westside Cottage II. The Westside Cottage's menu could be considered the Good Book of Asian food—it lists more than 200 Hunan, Szechuan, and Cantonese dishes (most priced $5–$12). On top of this are about 50 three-course lunch specials ($5) and, at dinner, several dozen chef's specials ($8–$10). 689 Ninth Ave., btw W. 47th and 48th Sts., tel. 212/245–0800. Subway: C or E to W. 50th St. Open Mon.–Thurs. 11:15–11, Fri. and Sat. 11:30 AM–midnight, Sun. 11:30–11:30. Lunch special ($5) weekdays 11–4. AE only.

UNDER $15 **Arroz y Feijão.** White or yellow rice? Black or red beans? Once you've decided, sit back and enjoy a Brazilian feast. Try feijoada ($9.75), a stew of black beans, pork loin, sausage, bacon, and spare ribs, or the peixe amazonas ($11.25), a fish stew with onions, tomatoes, green peppers, and coconut milk. For dessert, the Romeo & Juliet (guava paste and cheese) is a mere $2.50. 744 Ninth Ave., btw W. 50th and 51st Sts., tel. 212/265–4444. Subway: C or E to W. 50th St. Open weekdays 11 AM–10:30 PM, Sat. 1 PM–10:30. Lunch special ($6.50) weekdays 11–4.

MIDTOWN EAST OF FIFTH AVENUE

Unless you have an AmEx Corporate Card, the food situation is fairly grim east of Fifth Avenue. Most of Midtown East is prime big-business country, and nearly all its restaurants are slavishly devoted to the power lunch. On the upside, even the "nice" restaurants offer cheap weekday lunch specials—a good way to sample some of Manhattan's finer eateries without paying $45 for a dinner entrée. If you've absolutely gotta eat in Midtown East, check out the row of Indian and Pakistani restaurants along **Lexington Avenue** between East 27th and 28th streets. Though it's not as vibrant as the East Village's Little India (see below), you should be able to suss out a few all-you-can-eat buffets.

UNDER $5 **Fresco Tortilla Grill.** Despite its ghastly resemblance to Mickey D's, this place produces fresh, wholesome, tasty Cal-Mex food ($1–$5). Big burritos in homemade tortillas, tostada salads, and steak tacos are all fresh and free of nasty additives. 546 Third Ave., near E. 36th St., tel. 212/685–3886. Subway: 6 to E. 33rd St. Open daily 11–11. Wheelchair access. No credit cards.

UNDER $10 **Beit Eddine.** Lunch is the reason to visit this Lebanese restaurant, when $7 buys an all-you-can-eat buffet of tabouleh, hummus, baba ghanoush, falafel, spinach pie, okra, moussaka, and other Lebanese dishes. On Thursday, Friday, and Saturday nights live music starts around 10 PM, belly dancing at midnight. 308 E. 49th St., btw First and Second Aves., tel. 212/759–5386. Subway: 6 to E. 51st St. Open weekdays 11 AM–midnight (Fri. until 2 AM), Sat. noon–4 AM, Sun. 2 PM–11 PM. Lunch buffet weekdays 11:30–3:30.

Madras Mahal. A letter posted outside this kosher and 100% vegetarian Indian restaurant— part of Lexington Avenue's "Little India"—informs doubting customers that VEGETABLES ARE CLEANED UNDER SUPERVISION. NO BUGS OR INSECTS. How reassuring. Curries and such are $5.50– $9, but the real deal is the all-you-can-eat lunch ($7). 104 Lexington Ave., btw E. 27th and 28th Sts., tel. 212/684–4010. Subway: 6 to E. 27th St. Open weekdays 11:30–3 and 5– 10:15, weekends noon–11. Lunch special ($7) weekdays 11:30–3. Wheelchair access.

Sam's Noodle Shop & Grill Bar. Attitude and atmosphere are minimal here; at least you get plenty of well-priced food. Mandarin noodle soups are $4.75–$6, sizzling platters like pan-fried tofu with vegetables $9–$12. You can also pick your own vegetables, meat, or seafood to skewer and grill ($1.25–$2.75 per item). 411 Third Ave., at E. 29th St., tel. 212/213–2288. Subway: 6 to E. 28th St. Open daily 11:30–midnight. Lunch special ($4.25) weekdays 11:30–4. Wheelchair access.

UNDER $15 **Tivoli.** Stolid and weathered, the Tivoli looks like it's been around for centuries. In reality, it's no older than Donald Trump, with typical coffee-shop fare (sandwiches, salads, and pastas) for both lunch ($4–$7.50) and dinner ($8–$12). *515 Third Ave., btw E. 34th and 35th Sts., tel. 212/532–3300. Subway: 6 to E. 33rd St. Open daily 6 AM–1 AM (and sometimes until 4 AM or 5 AM; call ahead). Wheelchair access.*

CHELSEA

Chelsea was once a warehouse wasteland; nowadays it's truly trendy, a fave of hip twentysomethings and the hangout of choice among gays and lesbians. As a result, **Eighth Avenue**, between West 30th and 14th streets, and **West 18th Street**, between Sixth and Ninth avenues, are crammed with stylish bistros, cafés, revamped diners, natural-food restaurants, bakeries, and juice bars. At the heart of it all is **Taylor's** (228 W. 18th St., btw Seventh and Eighth Aves., tel. 212/366–9081; 523 Hudson St., btw W. 10th and Charles Sts., tel. 212/645–8200; 175 Second Ave., btw E. 10th and 11th Sts., tel. 212/674–9501)—scope out the scene from the front porch while enjoying one of their mouthwatering muffins or donuts ($1.50–$2.25), three dozen types of salads ($2.50–$7), or sandwiches ($4–$5).

UNDER $5 **The Donut Pub.** When in Manhattan, never pass up a turkey sandwich for $2.40, a large coffee for 95¢, or a bagel for 55¢. *203 W. 14th St., at Seventh Ave., tel. 212/929–0126. Subway: A, C, E, or L to W. 14th St. (Eighth Ave.). Also: 1, 2, 3, or 9 to W. 14th St. (Seventh Ave.). Open 24 hrs. Wheelchair access. No credit cards.*

UNDER $10 **Bendix Diner.** The menu here is exotic in a strange sort of way, blending American comfort food with Thai dishes. Translation: You can have meat loaf ($6.50) while your date chows on *yaki meshi* (stir-fried chicken teriyaki with soybean sprouts, broccoli, zucchini, and brown rice; $7.25). The crowd is hip and gay, the servings are huge, and the music kicks. *219 Eighth Ave., at W. 21st St., tel. 212/366–0560. Subway: C or E to W. 23rd St. BYOB. Open Mon.–Thurs. 8 AM–11:30 PM, Fri. and Sat. 8–midnight, Sun. 8–11. Wheelchair access.*

Uncle Mo's. A family of Sasquatches could feed for a week on one of Uncle Mo's monstrous burritos ($4.75–$7), stuffed with *barbacoa* (slow-cooked shredded beef), *pollo verde* (chicken in a mild green chile sauce), or *carne asada* (marinated steak). Less massive but still filling are the tacos ($2.75–$4) and quesadillas ($4.75–$5.50). *14 W. 19th St., btw Fifth and Sixth Aves., tel. 212/727–9400. Subway: F to W. 23rd St. Also: N or R to W. 23rd St. Open weekdays 11:30–9:30, Sat. noon–7:30. Wheelchair access. No credit cards.*

UNDER $15 **Cajun.** This place masquerades as a New Orleans riverboat, with smartly dressed waiters serving up hearty but pricey Southern dishes, notably boiled whole crab ($8), jambalaya ($11), and mustard-fried catfish ($14). Dig the live, no-cover jazz on Wednesdays (12:30–2 PM), Sundays (noon–4), and most evenings (7:30–10 PM). *129 Eighth Ave., btw W. 16th and 17th Sts., tel. 212/691–6174. Subway: A, C, E, or L to W. 14th St. (Eighth Ave.). Open weekdays 11:45–11 (Fri. until midnight), Sat. 5 PM–midnight, Sun. noon–11.*

Prix-Fixe Madness

When you're on a shoestring budget, a $70 meal at a world-class restaurant might seem like a sick joke. Happily, impoverished gourmets can score big-time at more than 100 of New York's top restaurants during the annual New York Restaurant Week (mid-June). It all started with $19.92 meals offered during the 1992 Democratic National Convention, which the city hosted. This year, participating restaurants will sell their prix-fixe lunches for $19.97—still a bang-up deal. And some restaurants now offer these prices through Labor Day, or even year-round. Past participants have included such way-outta-your-league joints as Le Cirque, Bouley, Lutèce, the Rainbow Room, and the Four Seasons; for more info, check the city's weekly magazines during June. And make reservations far in advance.

Food Bar. Try, just for a minute, to keep your eyes from straying to the incredibly good-looking gay clientele at this lively café. Focus instead on your delicious grilled-vegetable sandwich ($8.50) or your spicy fried chicken with black beans and hominy salad ($9.50). Dinner specials range from pastas ($9–$11.25) to seafood ($13). *149 Eighth Ave., btw W. 17th and 18th Sts., tel. 212/243–2020. Subway: A, C, E, or L to W. 14th St. (Eighth Ave.). Open weekdays noon–midnight, weekends 11 AM–midnight. Wheelchair access.*

Mr. D's. The "D," they'll tell you, stands for "delicious" and "delightful." And perhaps even "demented," because they do some funky things here to traditional Chinese dishes ($7–$13), be it pairing roast duck with linguine and cream sauce or stir-frying chicken with bananas and vegetables. Of course, you can still get chop suey. *199 Eighth Ave., btw W. 20th and 21st Sts., tel. 212/989–1116. Subway: C or E to W. 23rd St. Open daily 11:30–11 (Fri. and Sat until midnight). Lunch special ($5) Mon.-Sat. 11:30–4. Wheelchair access.*

Regional Thai Taste. The cool thing about this funky Thai joint is that instead of serving the same old pad thai, it explores recipes from around the country: Try *kow pad rot fie* (fried rice with shrimp and chicken; $9), traditionally sold on Thai trains; *yum ta lay* (marinated seafood salad; $7), from the island of Phuket; or the Bangkok favorite *kow mun som tum* (shredded beef with coconut rice and green papaya; $13). Prices are $2–$4 cheaper before 4 PM. *208 Seventh Ave., at W. 22nd St., tel. 212/807–9872. Subway: 1 or 9 to W. 23rd St. Open daily noon–11 PM (Fri. and Sat. until 11:30 PM).*

GRAMERCY AND UNION SQUARE

Some of New York's finest five-star restaurants are tucked between the million-dollar town homes that surround Gramercy Park and Union Square. If you have money to burn, a meal at **Union Square Cafe** (*see box* Serious Splurges, *below*) is a truly uplifting, ur–New York experience. Don't have the cash? Then meander over to the **Union Square greenmarket** (*see* Greenmarkets, *below*), a great place to pick up snacks and fresh produce.

Your best bet for cheap eats is along **Third Avenue**, lined with no-frills ethnic restaurants, pizza places, bagel shops, and delis. **Irving Place** between East 19th and 14th streets is lined with moderately priced restaurants and sweet shops like **Mio Pane, Mio Dulce Bakery** (77 Irving Pl., btw E. 18th and 19th Sts., tel. 212/677–1905). **Park Avenue South** in the 20s and 30s has a sizzling dinner scene, with wall-to-wall stylish restaurants. The hot spot of the moment is **Lemon** (230 Park Ave. S, near E. 18th St., tel. 212/614–1200), possibly because investors include the Ford modeling agency and David Lee Roth.

UNDER $5 **Palace.** Despite its proximity to the Union Square greenmarket, this joint goes heavy on the grease and forsakes sissy steamed vegetables. It's strictly diner fare, like the meat loaf sandwich ($3.50) and the ham-and-two-egg breakfast ($4.75). *36 Union Square, at Park Ave. and E. 16th St., tel. 212/505–6411 or 212/673–0452. Subway: L, N, R, 4, 5, or 6 to Union Sq. Open 24 hrs. Wheelchair access.*

UNDER $10 **America.** Been to Madison Square Garden yet? This noisy restaurant is just as vast, and the food is better (no Knicks, though). Try one of 25 salads—we like the Omaha ($8.50), which comes with warm bacon and spinach—or one of about 20 sandwiches; our fave is the Berkeley ($8), with avocado, sprouts, and cucumber. *9 E. 18th St., btw Fifth Ave. and Broadway, tel. 212/505–2110. Subway: L, N, R, 4, 5, or 6 to Union Sq. Open daily 11:30 AM–1 AMish. Wheelchair access.*

Friend of a Farmer. New Yorkers willingly endure Friend of a Farmer's ultra-cute decor to indulge their hankerings for country cooking (even if they look incredibly sheepish doing it). Entrées ($7.50–$9) are steamed or broiled, never fried. Menu highlights include the old-fashioned chicken pot pie and the hefty Farmer's Sandwich. *77 Irving Pl., btw E. 18th and 19th Sts., tel. 212/477–2188. Subway: N, R, L, 4, 5, or 6 to Union Sq. Open weekdays 8 AM–11 PM, weekends 10 AM–11 PM.*

Heartland Brewery. Heartland is one of the city's newest microbreweries, which means it's the latest watering hole for big, meaty Wall Street guys. There are six microbrews ($4.25 per pint) on tap and a menu full of inventive pub grub ($6–$9). *35 Union Sq. W, btw E. 16th and 17th Sts., tel. 212/645-3400. Subway: L, N, R, 4, 5, or 6 to Union Sq. Open daily 11 AM–2 AM. Kitchen open Sun.–Thurs. until 11, Fri. and Sat. until midnight. Wheelchair access.*

Add a Ted Danson look-alike to the Old Town Bar and you'd have "Cheers."

Old Town Bar. A zillion people—from cops to picky newspaper food critics to David Letterman—claim that this 1892 saloon serves some of the best burgers ($6) in the city. Just beware the weekend crowds. Salads and fancy grilled sandwiches are about $7. *45 E. 18th St., btw Broadway and Park Ave. S, tel. 212/529-6732. Subway: L, N, R, 4, 5, or 6 to Union Sq. Open weekdays 11:30–3 and 5–11:30, Sat. 12:30–11:30, Sun. 1–10. Bar open daily until 2 AM.*

UNDER $15 **Chat 'n' Chew.** Simply put: sassy home cookin'. Gorge yourself on Roseanne-size portions of macaroni and cheese "with the crunchy top" ($7), Not Your Mother's Meatloaf ($11.25), or Thanksgiving on a Roll (roast turkey, stuffing, cranberry sauce, and mayo on chiabatta bread; $9.25). And enjoy that trailer-park ambience. *10 E. 16th St., btw Fifth Ave. and Union Sq. W, tel. 212/243-1616. Subway: L, N, R, 4, 5, or 6 to Union Sq. Open weekdays 11:30–11 (Fri. until 11:30), Sat. 10 AM–11:30 PM, Sun. 10 AM–11 PM.*

Park Avalon. From the outside, the Avalon looks like all the other overpriced restaurants on Park Avenue South. Happily, the Avalon's New American/Mediterranean cuisine is surprisingly affordable (entrées $8–$11). The beautiful clientele is included at no extra charge. *225 Park Ave. S, btw E. 18th and 19th Sts., tel. 212/533-2500. Subway: L, N, R, 4, 5, or 6 to Union Sq. Open daily 11 AM–midnight. Reservations recommended for dinner. Wheelchair access.*

Serious Splurges

When your rich uncle and aunt come to town with an empty stomach and a fat wallet, suggest one of the following restaurants. They're among the top 10 in New York, according to the annual Zagat Survey (leaving the list are big-name restaurants Bouley's and Le Cirque, which have closed temporarily). What you're getting isn't just fancy food, but a piece of the True New York Experience: stunning decor, impeccable service (by the friendliest New Yorkers you'll ever meet), and elbow-to-elbow proximity with the rich and famous. The average price for such pampering is about $65. Per person.

- *Four Seasons. Its Grill Room has been the deal makers' power-lunch destination for decades. The Pool Room is simply fabulous. 99 E. 52nd St., btw Lexington and Park Aves., Midtown East, tel. 212/754-9494.*

- *Gotham Bar and Grill. The American cuisine served here often arrives at your table in fantastically engineered towers. The prix-fixe lunch is $19.97. 12 E. 12th St., btw Fifth Ave. and University Pl., West Village, tel. 212/620-4020.*

- *Peter Luger Steak House. Though it's in a sketchy neighborhood, this is regarded as the best steak house in the country. 178 Broadway, at Driggs Ave., Brooklyn, tel. 718/387-7400.*

- *Union Square Cafe. The New American cuisine is slightly less expensive than at other five-star restaurants, but the service is still slavish. 21 E. 16th St., btw Fifth Ave. and Union Square W, tel. 212/243-4020.*

Rungsit. Wedge yourself into one of Rungsit's tightly packed tables and reward yourself with excellent Thai soups ($3), curries ($8–$10), and seafood dishes ($11–$15). The platter of pad thai ($8.25) is big enough to feed all the drunken yokels in Gramercy Tavern. And don't forget: It's BYOB. *161 E. 23rd St., btw Lexington and Third Aves., tel. 212/260–0704. Subway: 6 to E. 23rd St. Open Mon.–Thurs. 11:30–10:30, Fri. and Sat. 11:30–11, Sun. 4–10:30. Wheelchair access. No credit cards.*

Zen Palate. You are more likely to see a banker than a Buddhist in this starkly beautiful restaurant. The tone is set with Asian-influenced vegetarian dishes like the Oceanic Treasure (veggie "squid" sautéed with peppers), Harvest Delight (vegetables in sesame sauce), and Sweet and Sour Sensation (fried soy protein and steamed broccoli). Entrées average $5–$9 in the café or $12–$15 in the fancy dining room upstairs. *34 Union Sq. E, at E. 16th St., tel. 212/614–9345. Subway: L, N, R, 4, 5, or 6 to Union Sq. BYOB. Open daily 11:30–11 (Fri. and Sat. until 11:30). Wheelchair access. Other locations: 663 Ninth Ave., at W. 46th St., Midtown West, tel. 212/582–1669; 2170 Broadway, btw W. 76th and 77th Sts., Upper West Side, tel. 212/501–7768.*

WEST VILLAGE

The restaurants on the West Village's narrow tree-lined streets are so tiny that their tables often spill onto sidewalks or into tranquil back gardens. If you think that's romantic, you're right. While the scene in the West Village proper has gotten a bit stale in recent years (gays prefer Chelsea, and hipsters have drifted over to the East Village), the neighborhood has plenty of reasonably priced options, especially on noisy **Sixth Avenue** and **Seventh Avenue South**. The cheapest eats, though, are on the blocks around **New York University (NYU)**; if you're looking for fast-food, **Broadway** between West 14th and Houston streets has your name all over it. If you want "charming" and "romantic" try **West 4th Street**, **Bleecker Street**, or **Greenwich Avenue**. To sample a few new cool crowd hangouts, check out the **meat-packing district**, way off to the west by the Hudson River—we highly recommend **Anglers & Writers** (420 Hudson St., at St. Luke's Pl., tel. 212/675–0810). Also, on **Washington Street**, trendy bistros alternate with refrigerated meat lockers. This is a rough commercial area, so use caution at night.

UNDER $10 **Aggie's** and **Aggie's Too.** Aggie herself says the eggs are the reason why breakfasts ($4.75–$6.25) taste so good at this hip restaurant duo. Yes, the eggs: fresh and double-A. Order those wonderful eggs (and any other breakfast food) daily until 3 PM. Or maybe you'd like one of the scrumptious sandwiches ($5.75–$9.75)? *146 W. Houston St., at MacDougal St., tel. 212/673–8994. Subway: 1 or 9 to Houston St. Also: C or E to Spring St. Open weekdays 7:30–5 and 6–10, Sat. 10–10, Sun. 10–4. Wheelchair access. No credit cards.*

The Bagel Restaurant. It's not just bagels: Delicious cheese omelets ($4.25), griddle cakes ($2.75), and even dinner dishes like pork chops with apple sauce ($6.50) are on the menu. Owner Mrs. Vitano (who works miracles with breaded fish) runs things from a seat at the counter. *170 W. 4th St., btw Jones and Cornelia Sts., tel. 212/255–0106. Subway: 1 or 9 to Christopher St. (Sheridan Sq.). Open weekdays 7:30 AM–midnight, Sat. 8 AM–midnight, Sun. 8 AM–11 PM.*

Benny's Burritos. Hip Benny's makes *healthy* Cal-Mex tacos, enchiladas, and burritos ($4–$7). And what exactly does that mean, you ask? Well, nothing has preservatives, lard, or MSG. You can even ask for non-dairy tofu sour cream, whole-wheat tortillas, and (for $2.50 extra) a few flatulence-fighting drops

> *At Benny's Burritos, ignore the sign in the window that says SAN FRANCISCO MISSION STYLE. Trust us, it just isn't true.*

of Beano. Nearby, **Harry's Burritos** (76 W. 3rd St., at Thompson St., tel. 212/260–5588) does practically the same thing with a little less flair. *113 Greenwich Ave., btw Jane and W. 12th Sts., tel. 212/633–9210. Subway: 1, 2, 3, or 9 to W. 14th St. Open daily 11:30 AM–midnight (Fri. and Sat. until 1 AM). Other location: 93 Ave. A, at E. 6th St., East Village, tel. 212/254–2054. No credit cards.*

Chez Brigitte. Charming chef and owner Rose Santos draws from her Spanish/French heritage, creating some deliciously spiced sandwiches ($3.50–$5) as well as savory entrées like beef bourguignon ($8). Don't skip the homemade pies ($2.25). *77 Greenwich Ave., at 11th St., tel.*

212/929–6736. Subway: 1, 2, 3, or 9 to W. 14th St. Open Mon.–Sat. 11 AM–10 PM. No credit cards.

Mappamondo I & II. These twin West Village Italian eateries, though sized like sardine cans, are wildly popular with young Manhattanites—which makes them pretty noisy and cramped. Even so, pastas ($6.50–$8) like *panzotti gratinati* (round ravioli filled with spinach and ricotta) and *farfalle al salmone* (bowtie pasta, smoked salmon, asparagus, and cream) are worth it. *581 Hudson St., at Bank St., tel. 212/675–7474. Subway: 1 or 9 to Christopher St. (Sheridan Sq.). Open daily noon–midnight (Fri. and Sat. until 1 AM). Other location: 11 Abingdon Sq., at Eighth Ave., tel. 212/675–3100. No credit cards.*

Marnie's Noodle Shop. Your noodle options include Thai glass-noodle salad ($8), noodles with Indonesian peanut sauce ($5), Korean beef noodles ($8), and Japanese *udon* noodle soup ($7). A few salads and sandwiches—believe it or not—feature no noodles at all! Despite attempts to look trendy, the atmosphere is friendly and relaxed. *466 Hudson St., at Barrow St., tel. 212/741–3214. Subway: 1 or 9 to Christopher St. (Sheridan Sq.). Open Mon.–Sat. noon–10 PM.*

Melanie's Natural Café. Those with a fear and loathing of fat will find comfort in Melanie's quiches, salads, casseroles, and stuffed baked potatoes, all priced $3.25–$6. Sandwiches ($4–$6.50) are made with whole-grain bread and lean, nitrate-free meat. *445 Sixth Ave., at W. 10th St., tel. 212/463–7744. Subway: F or L to W. 14th St. Open weekdays 8 AM–10 PM (Fri. until 9), Sat. 9–8, Sun. 11–8.*

Moustache. They bust out with some excellent Middle Eastern food ($3–$8) at this tiny restaurant on a beautiful residential street. Try the house specialty, *pitzza*, a large pita bread dressed up like a pizza with mushrooms, chicken, lamb, capers, artichokes, eggplant, and other toppings. Individual pitzzas start at $6.50. *90 Bedford St., at Grove St., tel. 212/229–2220. Subway: 1 or 9 to Christopher St. (Sheridan Sq.). Open Tues.–Sun. noon–midnight. Wheelchair access.*

Taquería de México. For half a sawbuck ($5), this mellow taco joint gives you a dandy lunch special: soup, mixed salad, and rice and beans; or a chicken burrito, rice and beans, and Mexican rice pudding. The regular menu won't break the bank, either, with tacos (2 for $4), enchiladas ($6.50), tamales ($3), and burritos ($4). *93 Greenwich Ave., btw Bank and W. 12th Sts., tel. 212/255–5212. Subway: 1, 2, 3, or 9 to W. 14th St. Open weekdays 11:30–11, Sat. noon–11, Sun. noon–10. Lunch special ($5) weekdays 11:30–4. No credit cards.*

Woody's. When it comes to Sunday brunch, Villagers are prepared to stampede for a seat next to Woody's big glass windows so they can watch the Seventh Avenue people-parade. The food is good but of secondary importance; try the poached eggs on toasted brioche ($6.50) or the applewood smoked chicken salad ($9). *140 Seventh Ave. S, btw 10th Ave. and Charles St., tel. 212/242–1200. Subway: 1 or 9 to Christopher St. Open daily noon–11:30 (Fri. and Sat. until midnight).*

UNDER $15 **Brothers Bar-B-Q.** Brothers is like a little piece of Dixie in the heart of Manhattan, dishing out North Carolina barbecued pork ($8.25), blackened catfish ($10), and chicken fried steak ($9.75) to soul food–less urbanites. Hungry folk should order the Pig-Out ($13.75); herbivores can nosh on the Veggie Delight ($6.25). Every Monday (4:30–11 PM) they throw an all-you-can-eat barbecue for $11. *225 Varick St., 1 block west of Houston St., tel. 212/727–2775. Subway: 1 or 9 to Houston St. Open weekdays 11:30–11 (Fri. until midnight), Sat. 5 PM–midnight, Sun. 5–11. AE only.*

Home. There's no place like Home for comfort food: chicken dumplings ($8), fresh grilled trout ($10), and hearty french toast breakfasts ($3–$5.50). Inside it's cozy and warm, and the garden patio out back is glorious. Dinners are $13–$16. *20 Cornelia St., btw W. 4th and Bleecker Sts., tel. 212/243–9579. Subway: A, B, C, D, E, F, or Q to Washington Sq. Open weekdays 9–3 and 6–11, Sat. 11–4 and 6–11, Sun. 11–4 and 5:30–10. AE only.*

Kun Paw. Let candlelight and reggae music put you in the mood for good lovin' and good Thai food at Kun Paw. The friendly young staff can help you select from the dozens of house specialties ($8–$14); our pick is the *pla katheam* (fried snapper and garlic sauce) with sticky rice.

In summer, the tables on Greenwich Avenue offer great people-watching. *39 Greenwich Ave., at Charles St., tel. 212/989–4100. Subway: 1, 2, 3, or 9 to W. 14th St. Open daily noon–11. Wheelchair access.*

Magic Carpet. A cut above your average falafel shack, Magic Carpet serves all sorts of Middle Eastern food—from vegetarian platters ($8.50–$10.50) to spicy dishes of lamb, chicken, or shrimp ($9.50–$14). It's not at all as formal and imposing as it looks. *54 Carmine St., btw Bleecker and Bedford Sts., tel. 212/627–9019. Subway: 1 or 9 to Houston St. Open weekdays 11–11 (Fri. until midnight), Sat. noon–midnight, Sun. 2–11.*

The Pink Tea Cup. Fans of diner food will appreciate the Big 3 (hamburger, pie, and coffee; $5) and the Big 5 (the same, plus french fries and soup; $7). Otherwise, entrées like fried chicken ($10.75), barbecued ribs ($14), and smothered pork chops ($11) all come with two vegetables, soup, salad, hot bread, and dessert. And yes, the decor is PINK. *42 Grove St., btw Bedford and Bleecker Sts., tel. 212/807–6755. Subway: 1 or 9 to Christopher St. (Sheridan Sq.). Open daily 8 AM–midnight (Fri. and Sat. until 1 AM).*

Rio Mar. One reason to make the trek out here is the Rio Mar's giant portions ($9–$13) of traditional Spanish dishes, such as paella or *mariscade en salsa verde* (seafood in green sauce); another is the potent sangria and lively bar scene. When the meal is over, head upstairs to the dance floor and salsa the night away. Budget alert: Tapas are served daily noon–6 and are all priced under $5. *7 Ninth Ave., at Little W. 12th St., tel. 212/243–9015. Subway: A, C, E, or L to W. 14th St. Open daily noon–2 AM (Fri. and Sat. until 4 AM).*

Sakura. This simple restaurant sells 20 kinds of sushi, either à la carte ($2.50–$4 each) or with miso soup and salad ($9–$13.50). Entrées include teriyaki chicken ($8.50–$11.50), *chirinabe* (Japanese-style stew; $9–$12.50), and all things tempura ($7.50–$12). *615½ Hudson St., btw W. 12th and Jane Sts., tel. 212/645–2128 or 212/645–2129. Subway: A, C, E, or L to W. 14th St. Open weekdays 11:30–3 and 5–11 (Fri. until midnight), Sat. 5–midnight, Sun. 4–11. Wheelchair access.*

Tartine. Vaguely French dishes like *bouchée à la reine* (chicken pot pie; $8.75), quiche ($6.75), and grilled polenta provençale ($12) are served with typical French surliness at this tiny, attractive restaurant. Local hipsters don't mind waiting up to an hour for a table, especially for weekend brunch. *253 W. 11th St., at W. 4th St., tel. 212/229–2611. Subway: 1 or 9 to Christopher St. (Sheridan Sq.). BYOB. Open Tues.–Fri. 9–4 and 5:30–10:30, weekends 9–10:30 and 5:30–10:30. No credit cards.*

Tortilla Flats. Come play some bingo or take the hula hoop for a spin at this loco meat-packing-district diner. It's loud, a bit drunken, and fun. Filling the menu are basic enchiladas, tacos, burritos, and tostadas ($4–$11), not to mention shrimp fajitas and chicken *mole* (in chocolate sauce). Plastic fruit garlands and Elvis paintings clutter the walls. *767 Washington St., at W. 12th St., tel. 212/243–1053. Subway: A, C, E, or L to W. 14th St. Open Mon.–Sat. noon–midnight (Fri. and Sat. until 1 AM), Sun. noon–11:30. AE only.*

Village Natural Health Food Restaurant. Everything about the Village Natural is simple, from the wood furnishings to the organic, unprocessed entrées (many of which are dairy- and wheat-free). Try spaghetti with "wheatballs" ($10) or shiitake mushrooms sautéed with tofu ($9). Omelets ($6) are served weekdays 11–2:30. *46 Greenwich Ave., btw Charles and Perry Sts., tel. 212/727–0968 or 212/727–2888. Subway: 1, 2, 3, or 9 to W. 14th St. Open Mon.–Thurs. 11–11, Fri. and Sat. 11–midnight, Sun. 11–10.*

UNDER $20 **Florent.** This hip meat-packing-district bistro is the late-night favorite of a surreal mix of drag queens, truckers, club kids, and stray couples from Jersey. French maps and flags cover the walls while French–American food ($8–$17) fills the menu. For the true Fellini-esque experience, arrive after midnight. Be warned that there's a minimum purchase of $10 between 6 PM and midnight. *69 Gansevoort St., btw Washington and Greenwich Sts., tel. 212/989–5779. Subway: A, C, E, or L to W. 14th St. Open Sun.–Thurs. 9 AM–5 AM, Fri. and Sat. 24 hrs. No credit cards.*

Pò. If the thought of eating another $3.99 diner special nauseates you, treat yourself at this airy Northern Italian bistro. The people are pretty and the food is scrumptious. Go hearty with grilled boar sausage ($16) and sautéed calamari with tomatoes and garlic ($13), or keep it light with white-bean ravioli tossed with balsamic vinegar ($10). *31 Cornelia St., btw Bleecker and W. 4th Sts., tel. 212/645–2189. Subway: A, B, C, D, E, F, or Q to Washington Sq. Open Tues. 5:30–11, Wed.–Sun. 11–3 and 5:30–11. Wheelchair access. AE only.*

EAST VILLAGE AND ALPHABET CITY

Budget diners, this is your Shangri-la: Nowhere in the city will you find as many funky and cheap restaurants as in the East Village, be they Italian, Middle Eastern, Cambodian, Tibetan, Korean, Mexican, Filipino, Cuban, Burmese, Jewish, Creole, Japanese, Spanish, or plain old American. Even better, most places stay open until the wee hours of the morning, especially in summer when the sidewalks are packed at all hours.

East 6th Street between First and Second avenues is know as "Little India" for its dozens of savory Indian, Bangladeshi, and Pakistani joints—many of which offer live, free traditional music in the evenings. Walk down the block and you'll score a handful of coupons worth up to 30% off your next meal. Most places here allow you to bring your own beer or wine, though some will charge a small corkage fee—even if you're drinking King Cobra. Eastern European (particularly Ukrainian) coffee shops are plentiful on **Second Avenue** from East 7th to 9th streets. **Avenue A** overflows with all sorts of interesting options, including a number of sushi bars just north of Houston Street. For superior people-watching, pick one of the sidewalk cafés lining **Tompkins Square Park**—try Stingy Lulu's or Life Cafe (*see below*). One practical note: The East Village is not easy to reach on the subway unless you take the L line to First or Third avenue. You're better off riding a bus or catching a cab, especially late at night.

A food critic once described the Ukrainian borscht soup ($2.75) at 24-hour Veselka (144 Second Ave., at E. 9th St., tel. 212/228–9682) as "tasting like something your grandmother would make if you came home with a black eye."

UNDER $5 **Dojo.** The hordes of East Villagers who favor this snack shack don't seem to mind that most of the burgers and salads ($3–$6) arrive smothered in "Japanese-style tahini" dressing (which is actually a carrot-based vinaigrette with not a hint of tahini). Neither should you: You can definitely chow here for less than $5. *24 St. Marks Pl., btw Second and Third Aves., tel. 212/674–9821. Subway: 6 to Astor Pl. Open daily 11 AM–1 AM (Fri. and Sat. until 2 AM). No credit cards.*

Elvie's Turo-Turo. Get in line at this tiny Filipino cafeteria and *turo* (point) to whatever looks good, from *lumpia* (a cousin to the Chinese egg roll) to *ginisang gulay* (shrimp and pork stir-fried with seasonal vegetables) to *adobo* (grilled meat marinated in soy sauce, vinegar, garlic, and bay leaves). It's $3.75 for one entrée, $5 for two. *214 First Ave., btw E. 12th and 13th Sts., tel. 212/473–7785. Subway: L to First Ave. Open daily 11–9 (Sun. until 8). No credit cards.*

Odessa. Sure, they've got omelets ($1.75–$3.50) and cheeseburgers ($3.25) at this Eastern European diner. But what really make this place famous are the *latkes* (potato pancakes), *pierogi* (dumplings stuffed with a combination of meat, cheese, cabbage, and mushrooms; $3.25), and giant cheese- or fruit-filled blintzes ($2.25). Just down the street, **Leshko's Coffee Shop** (111 Ave. A, at E. 7th St., tel. 212/473–9208) serves up the same gut-busting Eastern European home-cooking. *117 Ave. A, btw St. Marks Pl. and E. 9th St., tel. 212/473–8916. Subway: 6 to Astor Pl. Open 24 hrs. Wheelchair access. No credit cards.*

UNDER $10 **ACME Bar and Grill.** A self-proclaimed "okay place to eat," ACME serves Southern faves like chicken fried steak ($9), fried chicken ($8), and po'boy sandwiches ($7)—all of which are better than "okay." Spice things up with the house hot sauce, labeled ALMOST FLAMMABLE. The rock venue Under ACME (*see* Live Music, in Chapter 6) lies—surprise—under ACME. *9 Great Jones St., btw Broadway and Lafayette St., tel. 212/420–1934. Subway: 6 to Bleecker St. Open weekdays 11:30 AM–midnight, Sat. 11:30–1 AM, Sun. 11–11.*

Angelica Kitchen. What's the vegan definition of heaven? Probably a place like this, where the food is 100% organic and free of animal products. They even serve a funky barley brew in place of regular coffee. Dishes—try the Dragon Bowl, a plate of steamed seasonal veggies with rice, beans, and tofu—cost $6.50–$8. *300 E. 12th St., btw First and Second Aves., tel. 212/228– 2909. Subway: 6 to Astor Pl. Also: L to Third Ave. Open daily 11:30–10:30. Wheelchair access. No credit cards.*

Beyond Mickey D's

A number of citywide chains keep New Yorkers coming back for great, reliable, afford-able eats. At the places listed below (many of which have additional locations) you can eat well for less than $10.

- *Burritoville. Some of the best burritos in town—including tons of veggie options. UPPER WEST SIDE: 451 Amsterdam Ave., btw W. 81st and 82nd Sts., tel. 212/787– 8181. EAST VILLAGE: 141 Second Ave., btw 9th St. and St. Mark's Place, tel. 212/260–3300. TRIBECA: 144 Chambers St., at W. Broadway, tel. 212/571–1144. LOWER MANHATTAN: 36 Water St., at Broad St., tel. 212/747–1100.*

- *Daikichi Sushi. These take-out shops serve some of the freshest and cheapest sushi in town. UPPER WEST SIDE: 2345 Broadway, btw W. 85th and 86th Sts., tel. 212/362– 4283. MIDTOWN: 45 E. 45th St., btw Madison and Vanderbilt Aves., tel. 212/953–2468. WEST VILLAGE: 35 E. 8th St., at University Pl., tel. 212/254–1987. LOWER MANHAT-TAN: 32 Broadway, btw Beaver St. and Exchange Pl., tel. 212/747–0994.*

- *Dallas BBQ. Hungry carnivores come here to gorge on heaping plates of cheap bar-becue. UPPER WEST SIDE: 27 W. 72nd St., btw Columbus Ave. and Central Park W, tel. 212/873–2004. WEST VILLAGE: 21 University Pl., at E. 8th St., tel. 212/674– 4450. EAST VILLAGE: 132 Second Ave., at St. Marks Pl., tel. 212/777–5574.*

- *John's Pizzeria. Many New Yorkers claim John's makes the best pizzas in the city, bar none. UPPER WEST SIDE: 48 W. 65th St., btw Broadway and Central Park W, tel. 212/721–7001. WEST VILLAGE: 278 Bleecker St., btw Sixth Ave. and Seventh Ave. S, tel. 212/243–1680.*

- *Mary Ann's. The especials de la casa (house specials) at these kitschy Mexican joints are excellent. UPPER WEST SIDE: 2452 Broadway, at W. 91st St., tel. 212/877–0132. CHELSEA: 116 Eighth Ave., at W. 16th St., tel. 212/633–0877. EAST VILLAGE: 80 Second Ave., at E. 5th St., tel. 212/475–5939.*

- *Royal Canadian Pancake House. They make pancakes the size of tractor tires here. Think we're kidding? MIDTOWN: 1004 Second Ave., at E. 53rd St., tel. 212/980– 4131. GRAMERCY: 180 Third Ave., at E. 17th St., tel. 212/777–9288.*

- *Two Boots To Go. Like the Two Boots restaurant in the East Village, these take-out stands offer excellent Cajun–Italian pizzas and pastas. WEST VILLAGE: 75 Greenwich Ave., btw W. 11th St. and Seventh Ave. S, tel. 212/633–9096. EAST VILLAGE: 36 Ave. A, btw 2nd and 3rd Sts., tel. 212/505–5450.*

Baby Jakes. Even people who help old ladies across the street may lie, cheat, and steal to get more of the melt-in-your-mouth corn bread served with dinner at this cool Cajun eatery. Try the Jake Burger (with pepper jack cheese and maple barbecue sauce) or the blackened catfish poorboy, both $7. *14 First Ave., at E. 1st St., tel. 212/254–BABY. Subway: F to Second Ave. Open daily 11 AM–midnight (Fri. and Sat. until 4 AM). Wheelchair access. AE only.*

California Pizza Oven. God only knows why you'd ever tire of greasy, thin New York pizza. But just in case, the California Pizza Oven tosses crispy, brick-oven-baked pies that are quite unlike your average NYC slice. Most popular is Mike's Favorite ($5), with shiitake and Portobello mushrooms, roasted garlic, sun dried tomatoes, goat cheese, and pesto. Pies cost $12–$18. *122 University Pl., btw E. 13th and 14th Sts., tel. 212/989–4225. Subway: L, N, R, 4, 5, or 6 to Union Sq. Open daily 11:30–10. Wheelchair access. No credit cards.*

Esashi. At Esashi, visibly excited East Villagers sit next to visiting Japanese businessmen for superb and inexpensive sushi à la carte, both nigiri ($1.75–$2.50) and in rolls ($2.75–$5.50). Dinner specials (5–8 PM) include udon noodle soups ($7) and big sushi combos ($8.50). It's not very fancy, but then neither is a Zen garden. *32 Ave. A, btw E. 2nd and 3rd Sts., tel. 212/505–8726. Subway: F to Second Ave. Open daily 5 PM–11:30 PM (Sun. until 11 PM). Wheelchair access.*

Frutti de Mare. Savvy New Yorkers usually pass on the *frutti de mare* (seafood) in favor of tasty terrestrial entrées, notably the chicken with balsamic sauce ($8) and the homemade pumpkin ravioli in pesto cream sauce ($7). Though the decor is classy, the attitude is very low-key. *84 E. 4th St., at Second Ave., tel. 212/979–2034. Subway: 6 to Astor Pl. Open daily noon–midnight (Fri. and Sat. until 1 AM). Wheelchair access. No credit cards.*

Kiev. According to a rough-and-tumble crew of regulars, Kiev's got the best Eastern European cooking ($4.50–$7) west of the Volga. It serves breakfast round-the-clock and has a veggie dinner special (potato pancake, kasha varnishkes, and steamed vegetables; $6.50) that's bigger than a Yugo. *117 E. 7th St., at Second Ave., tel. 212/674–4040 or 212/674–4041. Subway: 6 to Astor Pl. Open 24 hrs. Wheelchair access. No credit cards.*

Life Cafe. On Sunday, slip on your shades and stumble over to Life Cafe for the huge breakfast ($8), coffee and mimosa or Bloody Mary included. Even on days when you don't feel like hell, their Tex-Mex grub ($5.25–$9) tastes pretty damn good. The outdoor tables are great for pondering the action in adjacent Tompkins Square Park. *343 E. 10th St., at Ave. B, tel. 212/477–8791. Subway: 6 to Astor Pl. Also: L to First Ave. Open weekdays noon–midnight (Fri. until 2 AM), Sat. 11 AM–2 AM, Sun. 11 AM–midnight. Other location: 1 Sheridan Sq., btw W. 4th St. and Washington Pl., West Village. MC, V only.*

National Cafe. This Cuban dive serves food that's delicious, filling, and cheap. Dishes cost $4.25–$7 and range from simple steak-and-onion sandwiches to roast pig to *mofongo* (a meatball the size of a bowling ball, cooked in chicken fricassee sauce). All meals come with sides of cassava and fried plantains. *210 First Ave., btw E. 12th and 13th Sts., tel. 212/473–9354. Subway: L to First Ave. Open Mon.–Sat. 10:30–10. Lunch special ($3.75) daily 10:30–3.*

Rose of India. So what if the dining room, festooned with silk flowers and Christmas lights, was seemingly decorated by Timothy Leary's Punjabi cousin? The food is excellent and the waitstaff chummy. Some of the better dishes are sizzling shrimp *korai* (they say "ask waiter for explanation"; $8) and chicken Bengal ($6.25). *308 E. 6th St., btw First and Second Aves., tel. 212/533–5011. Subway: F to Second Ave. BYOB. Open daily noon–midnight. No credit cards.*

Sahara East. If you think couscous can only be bought in small cardboard boxes marked "instant," you'll sit up and slap yourself after a spoonful from this upscale Middle Eastern restaurant. It's fluffy, soft, and delicious, and it comes with vegetables, grilled lamb, chicken, or fish ($6.25–$8). *184 First Ave., btw E. 11th. and 12th Sts., tel. 212/353–9000. Subway: L to First Ave. Open daily noon–1 AM. No credit cards.*

Stingy Lulu's. This restaurant/bar is best in summer, when crowds linger until 4 AM at the outside tables. Inside, Stingy Lulu's is festooned with a museum-quality array of primo 1950s diner decor. Sunday brunch (with your choice of screwdriver, Bloody Mary, or mimosa; $7) is a major event. Otherwise tuck into pork chops with mashed potatoes ($7.95) or a hefty salad ($4–$7). Cocktails are served at all hours. *129 St. Marks Pl., btw First Ave. and Ave. A, tel. 212/674–3545. Subway: 6 to Astor Pl. Open daily 10 AM–2 AM (Fri. and Sat. until 4 AM).*

Village Mingala. You're greeted with the words *min ga la ba* ("pleasant day") at this Burmese restaurant, then served succulent southeast Asian specialties like squid salad ($4.75), duck with green and hot red peppers ($9), or Burmese chicken curry with potatoes ($7). The wood-paneled dining room is a bit dark, but not unpleasantly so. *21–23 E. 7th St., btw Second and Third Aves., tel. 212/529–3656 or 212/260–0457. Subway: 6 to Astor Pl. Open weekdays 11:30–10:30 (Fri. until 11:30), Sat. 2–11:30, Sun. 2–10:30. Lunch special ($4.25) weekdays 11:30–4.*

Yaffa Café. If you've been given only one meal on Planet Earth, and you happen to be in the East Village, eat it here. The kitschy decor is cool, the patrons are cool, and the waiters and waitresses bedecked in black are just too cool. Filling the five-page menu are cool foods like Berber chicken (with spicy lemon-basil sauce; $8) and the prodigious Yaffa Salad ($5.25). In summer grab a seat in the huge, leafy back garden. *97 St. Marks Pl., btw First Ave. and Ave. A, tel. 212/674–9302. Subway: 6 to Astor Pl. Open 24 hrs. AE only.*

UNDER $15 **Avenue A.** This is not your father's sushi joint. In addition to the standard Japanese tempura and teriyaki dishes ($8.50–$13), it's got whacked-out sushi rolls ($4.50–$6) like the Panic (softshell crab tempura and plum paste) and the Dragon (eel, roe, and avocado). Best of all, it sports the ambience of a Tokyo nightclub, including black walls, a DJ spinning house music, and an achingly hip crowd. *103 Ave. A, btw E. 6th and 7th Sts., tel. 212/982–8109. Subway: 6 to Astor Pl. Open daily 6 PM–1 AM (Fri. and Sat. until 2 AM).*

Caravan of Dreams. Neo-hippies and P.C. punk rockers flock to this subterranean restaurant for heaping plates of meatless, organic, multi-ethnic food—plus live Middle Eastern music. Entrées range from the steamed Vegetable Medley ($9) to Angel's Pig-Out (vegetarian burger, polenta in sweet potato sauce, steamed vegetables, and salad; $12.50). *405 E. 6th St., btw First Ave. and Ave. A, tel. 212/254–1613. Subway: F to Second Ave. Also: 6 to Astor Pl. Open Tues.–Thurs. noon–11, Fri. noon–midnight, Sat. 11 AM–midnight, Sun. 11–11.*

Great Jones Cafe. It's got a jukebox with one of the best selections in the world and only 10 tables, so you can bet your weight in okra that this Cajun diner (entrées $8.50–$12) is always crowded. A summer favorite is the Crayfish Boil ($5.95), a pound of the spicy crustaceans that you shell yourself. *54 Great Jones St., btw Lafayette St. and Bowery, tel. 212/674–9304. Subway: 6 to Bleecker St. Open daily 5 PM–midnight (Fri. and Sat. until 1 AM). No credit cards.*

La Paella. If you're unfamiliar with Spanish cuisine, here's what you need to do: (1) Arrive with a large group of friends; (2) drink several pitchers of sangria; (3) order up a mess of hot or cold tapas ($3–$5.50); and (4) come back another day for paella (smallest serving feeds two for $20–$32), a traditional stew of rice, saffron, garlic, sausage, and seafood. *214 E. 9th St., btw Second and Third Aves., tel. 212/598–4321. Subway: 6 to Astor Pl. Open daily noon–midnight (Mon. from 5 PM). Wheelchair access.*

Second Avenue Deli. Though it's completely charmless, this has long been one of the city's premier spots for kosher noshes. Try Jewish favorites like gefilte fish ($9) and Chicken in the Pot (noodles, carrots, and a matzoh ball; $12.75), or sink your teeth into a mammoth pastrami sandwich ($7.50). *156 Second Ave., at E. 10th St., tel. 212/677–0606. Subway: 6 to Astor Pl. Open daily 10 AM–9 PM.*

Two Boots. This popular spot mixes Cajun and Italian cuisines to produce delicious dishes like pizza with andouille sausage and barbecued shrimp ($18 for large) or Linguine Dominique (blackened chicken with spinach linguine; $10). It's popular with families as well as with cool Village types; arrive early on weekend nights. The "boots" in question are Louisiana and Italy, if you hadn't already guessed. *37 Ave. A, btw E. 2nd and 3rd Sts., tel. 212/505–2276. Subway: F to Second Ave. Open daily noon–midnight. For take-out only locations, see box Beyond Mickey D's, above. Wheelchair access. AE only.*

LOWER EAST SIDE

The Lower East Side is an awkward mix of old and new, of ancient kosher delis and new hipster hangouts. Some areas have remained largely unchanged since the first Jewish immigrants settled here around the turn of the century, though bagel shops and delis are sadly becoming scarce. **Ludlow** and **Houston streets** are being steadily colonized by East Village types looking to expand their turf of grunge bars and slacker cafés. Fortunately, **Moishe's** (181 E. Houston St., tel. 212/475–9624), an Old World Jewish bakery, is still turning out delicious bagels and bialys. The Puerto Rican community has a Lower East Side toehold, a cluster of super-cheap take-out stands near the intersection of **Delancey** and **Clinton streets**. If you crave falafel at 4 AM, **Bereket** (187 E. Houston St., at Orchard St., tel. 212/475–7700) sells kebabs and other Turkish goodies "just like the ones in Istanbul" for less than $5.

UNDER $5 **Yonah Schimmel's Knishery.** The Schimmel family has been making *knishes* (fried or baked turnovers; $1.35) for more than 100 years; some folks even claim that they invented 'em. Choose from 12 varieties, including potato, mushroom, kasha, and chocolate cream cheese. *Fressers* (Yiddish for "gluttons") should start with a bowl of borscht (cold beet soup; 85¢) and a half-dozen potato pancakes ($1 each). *137 E. Houston St., at Second Ave., tel. 212/477–2858. Subway: F to Second Ave. Open daily 8–6. No credit cards.*

UNDER $10 **Festival Mexicana.** This authentic, above-average bean slinger serves Mexican favorites like chile rellenos ($5.25), quesadillas ($2.50), and burritos ($6), plus novelties like lamb tacos (3 for $5.50). *120 Rivington St., btw Essex and Suffolk Sts., tel. 212/995–0154. Subway: F to Delancey St. Also: J, M, or Z to Essex St. Open daily 10–7. No credit cards.*

Katz's Delicatessen. Katz's has been serving knishes ($1.75) and hefty deli sandwiches ($6–$9) to Lower East Siders—including magic guy Harry Houdini, who was once a regular—since

Bagels: The Hole Story

Most cafés and corner stores sell plastic-wrapped bagels, but these are usually too tough or just plain stale. For the real deal, visit one of the popular bagel bakeries listed below. Just don't ask which one is best—no two New Yorkers can agree on how to eat a bagel or where to buy one.

- *TRADITIONAL BAGELS: H&H Bagels (2239 Broadway, at W. 80th St., Upper West Side, tel. 212/595–8003 or 800/NYBAGEL for U.S. deliveries; 639 W. 46th St., tel. 212/595–8000).*

- *BIGGEST BAGELS: Ess-a-Bagel (831 Third Ave., at E. 50th St., Midtown, tel. 212/980–1010; 359 First Ave., at E. 21st St., Gramercy, tel. 212/260–2252).*

- *24-HOUR BAGELS: Columbia Hot Bagels (2836 Broadway, btw W. 110th and W. 111th Sts., Morningside Heights, tel. 212/222–3200).*

- *BAGELS OF MANY FLAVORS: Bagels on the Square (7 Carmine St., btw Bleecker St. and Sixth Ave., West Village, tel. 212/691–3041).*

- *LARGEST SELECTION OF SHMEARS: Bagels on Amsterdam (see Upper West Side, above).*

- *BEST SHOP NAME: Kossar's Bialystoker Kuchen Bakery (367 Grand St., btw Essex and Norfolk Sts., Lower East Side, tel. 212/473–4810).*

1888. You'll need to shout your order, since the staff is usually bickering behind the counter in thick New Yawk accents. *205 E. Houston St., at Ludlow St., tel. 212/254–2246. Subway: F to Second Ave. Open weekdays 8–8, weekends 10–7. Wheelchair access.*

Ratner's. This dairy (i.e., no meat) kosher restaurant is a Lower East Side institution. It's got some of the best blintzes ($7) and vegetarian noshes in town. *138 Delancey St., btw Norfolk and Suffolk Sts., tel. 212/677–5588. Subway: F to Delancey St. Also: J, M, or Z to Essex St. Open Sun.–Thurs. 6 AM–11:30 PM, Fri. 6 AM–3 PM, Sat. 1 hr after sundown–1:30 AM.*

LITTLE ITALY

If you think that Little Italy is the best place in town for Italian food, you need to stop reading Mario Puzo and go get some fresh air. True, the *ristoranti* here serve authentic—if pricey—Italian food. It's just that you're paying to sit with a bunch of tourists gushing about how "Olde Worlde" Little Italy is—when, actually, it isn't. While Chinatown continues to boom, Little Italy has shrunken to just one lonely little avenue, **Mulberry Street**. Walk its length and you'll be accosted by a jacket-wearing waiter at every door, bidding you *buon giorno* and tempting you inside with discounts or unbelievably cheap lunch specials. At some point you may think, why fight this? That's when it's time to suck down a plate of spaghetti, order a cappuccino and tiramisù, squint your eyes, and imagine you're in Rome. A couple of glasses of Chianti will help. For something a tad cheaper, try one of Little Italy's many coffeehouses (*see* Cafés and Coffee Bars, *below*).

UNDER $5 **Bella's Coffee Shop and Luncheonette.** Bella's is a no-nonsense spot to sit reading the paper at the counter with an un-Italian breakfast (two eggs, toast, and potatoes; $2.25) or an un-Italian lunch (grilled cheese sandwich; $2.50). *Elizabeth St., at Prince St., no phone. Subway: 6 to Spring St. Open daily 7 AM–3 PM. No credit cards.*

UNDER $10 **Il Fornaio.** It's the only place in Little Italy where you can dine like a Mafia don without needing the fortune of a Bertolucci. Dive into a generous plate of *pollo alla parmigiana* (chicken with spaghetti and Parmesan cheese; $8) or *rigatoni con zucchini* ($7). *132 Mulberry St., btw Hester and Grand Sts., tel. 212/226–8306. Subway: J, M, N, R, Z, or 6 to Canal St. Open daily 11:30–11 (Fri. and Sat. until midnight). Lunch special ($5) daily noon–4. No credit cards.*

Luna's. The peeling murals of Sicily and the sagging floorboards make it clear this ain't Brunelleschi's Duomo. Despite all that, the food ($9–$17) is good and the line often snakes out the door and around the corner. Come early or wait it out. *112 Mulberry St., near Canal St., tel. 212/226–8657. Subway: J, M, N, R, Z, or 6 to Canal St. Open daily noon–11:30 PM. Wheelchair access. No credit cards.*

The waiters at Luna's are famously rude: Don't be startled if you're greeted with a snarl and told to "quit fooling around and order some food."

Puglia. People come to Puglia in large groups for two reasons: to gorge on decent pastas ($5.50–$9) and to drink prodigious quantities of vino at one of the communal tables. By the end of the night, most folks are sloshed and singing along with Jorge (a man with a serious Elvis fixation), who croons in Italian while noodling on a cheesy Casio keyboard. *189 Hester St., btw Mott and Mulberry Sts., tel. 212/966–6006. Subway: J, M, N, R, Z, or 6 to Canal St. Open daily noon–midnight (Fri. and Sat. until 1 AM). Lunch special ($7.25) daily noon–4. No credit cards.*

UNDER $15 **Umberto's Clam House.** Umberto's is famous for being the place where mobster Joey "Crazy" Gallo had his last supper in 1973: He was whacked by the mob while eating a birthday dinner of scungili ($9.50). Pastas are pricey ($9–$13.50) but good. *129 Mulberry St., at Hester St., tel. 212/431–7545. Subway: J, M, N, R, Z, or 6 to Canal St. Open daily 11 AM–4 AM (Fri. and Sat. until 6 AM). AE only.*

CHINATOWN

Ask 100 New Yorkers what their favorite Chinatown restaurant is, and you'll get 100 different answers. This is a crowded, bustling, vibrant neighborhood, and restaurants come and go at a manic pace. But don't be deterred: Hit the streets, ponder the live-fish markets, and search out your own favorite pork-bun bakery. And know that Chinatown is more diverse than the name suggests: You'll find dishes from Hong Kong, Shanghai, Bangkok, Seoul, and Taipei, all within walking distance of one another. Whatever else you can say about it, Chinatown isn't dull.

Though Chinatown restaurants often aren't much to look at and rarely cater to tourists, they do offer phenomenally cheap lunch specials. Most are clustered around the intersection of **Bayard** and **Mott streets**. For a quick snack (like yummy coconut rolls), try bakeries **New Lung Fung** (41 Mott St., btw Pell and Bayard Sts., tel. 212/233–7447) or **Manna 2** (87 East Broadway, near Forsyth St., tel. 212/267–6200). Both offer a dizzying array of delectable Chinese pastries, cakes, and sweet breads for under $1. The **Chinatown Ice Cream Factory** (65 Bayard St., btw Mott and Elizabeth Sts., tel. 212/608–4170) has old standbys like vanilla and chocolate, as well as more exotic flavors like red bean, lychee, ginger, green tea, and taro ($1.80 for one scoop, $2.40 for two).

UNDER $5 **Bo Ky.** At this spartan joint you can select from over 25 Vietnamese and Chinese soups ($2–$3.50), all loaded with tasty morsels like shrimp balls, squid, roast duck, and various noodles. Service is speedy and polite. *80 Bayard St., btw Mulberry and Mott Sts., tel. 212/406–2292. Subway: J, M, N, E, Z, or 6 to Canal St. Open daily 11–11. No credit cards.*

Excellent Dumpling House. The green tile walls give it the look of a public rest room, but get over it—the dumplings (8 for $4) really are excellent. So are the Shanghai-style noodle soups ($4) and stir-frys. At lunchtime the place is packed. *111 Lafayette St., btw Canal and Walker Sts., tel. 212/219–0212. Subway: J, M, N, R, Z, or 6 to Canal St. Open daily 11–9. Wheelchair access. No credit cards.*

Sweet 'n' Tart Cafe. Restore your inner harmony at this crowded snack shop with a few *tong shui* (Chinese sweets believed to have healing properties). The most popular are double-boiled Chinese pears with almonds ($3.75), licorice-infused gelatin ($2.50), and walnut broth ($2). The delicious dumplings ($1–$2) and noodle soups ($3–$5) have no curative properties; they simply taste great. *76 Mott St., at Canal St., tel. 212/334–8088. Subway: J, M, N, R, Z, or 6 to Canal St. Open daily 8 AM–midnight. No credit cards.*

Suffering from migraine headaches, achy joints, or just a case of down-in-the-dumps blahs? A few "tong shui" from the Sweet 'n' Tart Cafe should set you right.

UNDER $10 **31 Division Dim Sum House.** You need to be sociable at this spartan dim sum diner: Waiters will lead you to

Act Locally, Eat Globally

AFGHANI: Afghan Kebab House (764 Ninth Ave., btw W. 51st and 52nd Sts., Hell's Kitchen, tel. 212/307–1612). **ARGENTINEAN:** La Portena (7425 37th Ave., btw 74th and 75th Sts., Jackson Heights, Queens, tel. 718/458–8111). **CAMBODIAN:** Cambodian Cuisine (87 S. Elliot Pl., btw Fulton St. and Lafayette Ave., Fort Greene, Brooklyn, tel. 718/858–3262). **CHILEAN:** Pomaire (371 W. 46th St., btw Eighth and Ninth Aves., Theater District, tel. 212/956–3056). **HUNGARIAN:** Mocca Hungarian (see Upper East Side, above). **PERSIAN:** Kabul Cafe (265 W. 54th St., btw Broadway and Eighth Ave., Midtown, tel. 212/757–2037). **ROMANIAN:** Sammy's Roumanian (157 Chrystie St., at Delancey St., Lower East Side, tel. 212/673–0330). **SRI LANKAN:** Taprobane (234 W. 56th St., btw Broadway and Eighth Ave., Midtown, tel. 212/333–4203). **TIBETAN:** Angry Monk (96 Second Ave., btw E. 5th and 6th Sts., East Village, tel. 212/979–9202). **TUNISIAN:** La Baraka (255–09 Northern Blvd., at Little Neck Pkwy., Queens, tel. 718/428–1461). **TURKISH:** Bereket (187 E. Houston St., at Orchard St., tel. 212/475–7700).

the first open seat, often at an already occupied table. On weekend afternoons expect long lines of locals eager for *har gow* (steamed shrimp dumplings). *31 Division St., btw Bowery and East Broadway, tel. 212/431–9063. Subway: B, D, or Q to Grand St. Open daily 7:30 AM–11 PM. Dim sum served daily 7:30–4.*

House of Vegetarian. The devilish chefs here concoct faux animal flesh out of vegetable gluten, which allows vegetarians to keep their karma intact while tearing into Chinese dishes like lemon "chicken" or Peking "spareribs." Most entrées are $7–$9. *68 Mott St., btw Canal and Bayard Sts., tel. 212/226–6572. Subway: J, M, N, R, Z, or 6 to Canal St. Open daily 11–11. No credit cards.*

Nha Trang. You can make a complete meal from Nha Trang's Vietnamese rice-noodle soups, called *pho* ($3.50–$4.50). But then you'd miss out on all the zesty, unusual entrées made with barbecued beef, pork, curry chicken, or frogs' legs. Rice and noodle dishes are under $6. *87 Baxter St., btw Canal and White Sts., tel. 212/233–5948. Subway: J, M, N, R, Z, or 6 to Canal St. Open daily 10–10. No credit cards.*

Thailand Restaurant. Why bother flying to Bangkok when the chef here is a genius, producing authentic Thai curries ($6.50–$9), noodles ($5), and rice dishes? The dining room—decorated with dolls and masks from Thailand—is one of the most elegant in Chinatown. *106 Bayard St., at Baxter St., tel. 212/349–3132. Subway: J, M, N, R, Z, or 6 to Canal St. Open daily 11–11:30. Lunch special ($3–$6) daily 11:30–4. AE only.*

Triple Eight Palace. Chinatown's most popular place for dim sum is a chaotic restaurant the size of a football field, crowded from 8 AM on with Cantonese-speaking customers. Rolling by on squeaky carts are 45 varieties of dim sum ($2–$4 per plate), from which you'll select *without* the aid of an English menu (just smile and point politely). Only tourists come here for dinner ($10–$16). *88 East Broadway, near Market St., tel. 212/941–8886. Subway: F to East Broadway. Open daily 8 AM–10 PM. Dim sum served daily 8–4.*

UNDER $15 New Viet Huong. The *bo la nho* (barbecued beef wrapped in grape leaves; $3.50) at this Vietnamese restaurant is 100% delicious. Entrées like *com tom cari dau que* (curry shrimp and rice; $6) or *ca chien chua ngot* (sweet and sour fish; $13.50) are equally excellent. Save room for guava ice cream. *73 Mulberry St., btw Bayard and Canal Sts., tel. 212/233–8988. Subway: J, M, N, R, Z, or 6 to Canal St. Open daily 10:30–10:30.*

SOHO

Most of the restaurants in glamorous, gallery-filled SoHo are too expensive for budget travelers. After all, if you're closing a deal on a $85,000 Stella, you'd look gauche taking your prospective buyer to a greasy spoon. Your options? You can join the Beautiful People and damn the costs. Or you can forsake ambience for a good feed at the smattering of delis and health-food stores in SoHo, notably **Whole Foods** (117 Prince St., btw Greene and Wooster Sts., tel. 212/982–1000). SoHo also has two of the city's favorite fancy marketplaces—**Gourmet Garage** (453 Broome St., at Mercer St., tel. 212/941–5850; open daily 8 AM–8:30 PM) and **Dean & Deluca** (*see* Markets and Specialty Shops, *below*)—which offer affordable take-out sandwiches. The biggest SoHo scene is along **West Broadway**, especially on late-summer evenings: A sophisticated crowd packs every sidewalk table between Houston and Canal streets.

Stock up on heavenly fresh bread ($2) at SoHo's charming, 75-year-old Vesuvio Bakery (160 Prince St., btw Thompson St. and West Broadway, tel. 212/925–8248), a favorite backdrop of fashion photographers.

UNDER $5 Spring Street Market and Deli. When they're not busy catering to movie crews and MTV stars, darling, the folks at Spring Street will feed you sandwiches, salads, and gourmet pizzas, all priced around $5. You can eat at one of the back tables or get takeout. By the way, Woody Allen shot part of *Husbands and Wives* here. *111 Spring St., btw Greene and Mercer Sts., tel. 212/226–4410. Subway: B, D, F, or Q to Houston St. Open weekdays 7 AM–8 PM, weekends 8–8. AE only.*

UNDER $10 **Bell Caffe.** Many people describe Bell Caffe as "relaxed." After all, the couches sag and the tables are battered—and it's one of few places in SoHo where you can simply hang out. But ever since Drew "Firestarter" Barrymore was spotted here recently, it's been in danger of being upgraded to "trendy." Besides serving an eclectic menu of steamed mussels, gazpacho, and chicken dumplings ($3–$8), it's got live music nightly, cover-free. Also, *see* Bars, in Chapter 6. *310 Spring St., near Greenwich St., tel. 212/334–2355. Subway: C or E to Spring St. Open daily noon–2 AM (Fri. and Sat. until 4 AM).*

Cafe 12 Chairs. The sandwiches ($3–$7), omelets ($3.50), blintzes ($5.50), and gargantuan bowls full of salad ($3.50–$5.25) are satisfying. But save room for apricot cookies and mixed-berry mousse ($3). Oddly, Cafe 12 Chairs has 15 chairs. *56 MacDougal St., btw Houston and King Sts., tel. 212/254–8640. Subway: C or E to Spring St. Open daily 8 AM–midnight. No credit cards.*

Fanelli's Cafe. This 1872 relic couldn't be more British, with its dark wood, chummy barflies, and permanent reek of spilled ale. Join the crowd with a brew and a snack: chicken wings ($5), stuffed potato skins ($5), or Cuban black bean salad ($6.50). *94 Prince St., at Mercer St., tel. 212/226–9412. Subway: N or R to Prince St. Open daily 10 AM–2 AM (Fri. and Sat. until 3 AM). Kitchen open weekdays until midnight, weekends until 1 AM.*

Herban Kitchen. The focus at this cool warehouse-style restaurant is on extraordinary organic and vegan dishes, like the grilled free-range chicken breast (with egg-free mayonnaise), the smoked tofu club sandwich, and vegetarian pizza with rosemary crust. Everything's around $7. *290 Hudson St., at Spring St., tel. 212/627–2257. Subway: C or E to Spring St. Open weekdays 8:30–8, weekends 11–8.*

Jerry's. At lunch, loudly dressed art connoisseurs and unknown teenage models nibble tuna salad on greens ($7.50) or sliced chicken breast with roasted-tomato mayonnaise ($8). Oh so nice. The decor—red vinyl booths, zebra-striped walls, and glaring green-framed mirrors—has as much attitude as the patrons. *101 Prince St., btw Greene and Mercer Sts., tel. 212/966–9464. Subway: N or R to Prince St. Also: 6 to Spring St. Open daily weekdays 9–5 and 6–11, Sat. 11–5 and 6–11:30, Sun. 11–5.*

Kelley and Ping. All day long, black-clad artists and vintage-clothing store clerks pop into this chaotic noodle house/Asian grocery/tea shop for stir-fry ($7), spring rolls ($4.25), and Vietnamese, Japanese, Cantonese, or Thai noodles ($5–$7.50). Stacked sacks of Thai black rice and huge jars of tea enhance the *feng shui. 127 Greene St., btw Houston and Prince Sts., tel. 212/228–1212. Subway: N or R to Prince St. Also: B, D, F, or Q to Broadway–Lafayette St. Open daily 11:30–5 and 6–11.*

Lupe's East L.A. Kitchen. Okay, so it's no longer a secret—but this laid-back, divey little Mexican joint is still an un-SoHo haven for delicious quesadillas with rice, beans, and salad ($8) or large burritos ($6.50–$8), all served with killer salsa. *110 Sixth Ave., at Watts St., tel. 212/966–1326. Subway: A, C, or E to Canal St. Also: 1 or 9 to Canal St. Open daily 11:30–11 (Wed.–Sat. until midnight). Lunch special ($4.50–$7) weekdays 11:30–4. No credit cards.*

Moondance Diner. Rod Serling could have filmed a *Twilight Zone* in this renovated railroad car on a desolate block. Inside is a 1950s diner with sparkly, blue, plastic booths and a big selection of glorious greasy food ($5–$9). Thick milk shakes and root beer floats are $3.50. *80 Sixth Ave., at Grand St., tel. 212/226–1191. Subway: A, C, E, 1, or 9 to Canal St. Open Mon.–Wed. 8:30 AM–midnight, Thurs.–Sun. 24 hrs. Breakfast special ($2.50) weekdays 8:30–11 AM.*

Once Upon a Tart. Tarts (the pastry kind) as well as cookies, pies, and breads ($1.75–$4) dominate this stylish Parisian-style bistro and adjoining bakeshop. Fancy sandwiches and salads are $5–$8. *135 Sullivan St., btw Houston and Prince Sts., tel. 212/387–8869. Subway: C or E to Spring St. Open weekdays 8–8, Sat. 9–8, Sun. 9–6.*

UNDER $15 **Abyssinia.** At this Ethiopian restaurant, patrons sit on traditional tiny woven stools and enjoy authentic dishes like *ye'beg alitcha* (lamb in ginger-garlic sauce; $10), which you scoop up with sweet and spongy *injera* bread. Combination plates ($15–$17) are made for two or more to share. *35 Grand St., at Thompson St., tel. 212/226–5959. Subway: A, C, or E to Canal St. Open daily 6 PM–11 PM. AE only.*

Chez Bernard. Bernard is no common butcher but rather an artiste, a man in a spotless smock who saws sides of beef into perfect sculpture. His restaurant serves everything from basic sandwiches ($4.50–$6) to pâtés ($4) and full-blown French meals ($10–$14). *323 West Broadway, btw Grant Ave. and Canal St., tel. 212/343–2583. Subway: A, C, E, 1, or 9 to Canal St. Open weekdays 6:30 AM–11 PM, Sat. 8 AM–11 PM, Sun. 8 AM–9 PM.*

Helianthus. Tuck into that Lamb of Happiness ($11) or Sweet and Sour Delight ($7.50) without guilt, because all the food at this happy, happy, happy vegetarian café is 100% meat-free. Amazing what you can do with soy protein, wheat gluten, and a Chinese wok. *48 MacDougal St., btw Houston and Prince Sts., tel. 212/598–0387. Subway: C or E to Spring St. Open daily 11–11. Lunch special ($5.25) daily 11–5.*

Jean Claude. It's smaller than a Left Bank apartment, but somehow this small, elegant bistro puts out platefuls of truly inspired French cooking. Check out the Atlantic salmon in fennel broth; pan-seared monkfish with potato puree and eggplant rounds; or roast Cornish game hen with herb risotto. Most entrées start at $12. *137 Sullivan St., btw Prince and Houston Sts., tel. 212/475–9232. Subway: C or E to Spring St. Open daily 6:30 PM–11 PM. Wheelchair access. No credit cards.*

SoHo Kitchen and Bar. People don't come here for the gourmet pizzas ($10) with toppings like Thai chicken, or even for the salads ($4–$9) and grilled specialties. The main draw is wine: 110 vintages sold by the glass ($4.50 and up). *103 Greene St., btw Prince and Spring Sts., tel. 212/925–1866. Subway: B, D, F, or Q to Broadway–Lafayette St. Also: 6 to Spring St. Open Mon.–Thurs. 11:30 AM–2 AM, Fri. and Sat. 11:30 AM–4 AM, Sun. noon–11.*

UNDER $20 **L'Ecole.** You're dying for a grossly extravagant French meal. You can't afford Bouley or Chantarelle (where you're lucky to escape for less than $75). Luckily there's L'Ecole, the 100% student-run restaurant at the French Culinary Institute, where aspiring chefs are taught by masters from New York's top restaurants. L'Ecole's prix-fixe lunches (three courses; $16) and dinners (four courses; $22) are worth every penny. Note that same-day reservations are required Monday–Thursday; for Friday and Saturday reserve at least one week in advance. *462 Broadway, at Grand St., tel. 212/219–3300. Subway: J, M, Z, N, R, or 6 to Canal St. Open weekdays noon–1:45 and 6–9 (Fri. until 10), Sat. 6–10.*

Penang. This place follows a simple recipe: Take traditional Malaysian dishes—from *tuland gunung api* (fried pork ribs; $13) to *ikan bakar* (sea bass wrapped in banana leaves; $19)—and combine them with over-the-top tiki decor, including a waterfall and waving palm fronds. Then stir in a hip crowd that's heavy on drag queens. *109 Spring St., btw Greene and Mercer Sts., tel. 212/274–8883. Subway: C or E to Spring St. Open Mon.–Thurs. 11:30 AM–midnight, Fri. and Sat. 11:30–1 AM, Sun. 1 PM–midnight. Lunch special ($6–$8) daily noon–5.*

TRIBECA

TriBeCa residents have conflicting feelings about their neighborhood's paucity of restaurants: After all, there are only so many times you can eat in Bob DeNiro's posh **Tribeca Grill** (375 Greenwich St., at Franklin St., tel. 212/941–3900). On the other hand, people here don't want SoHo's trendy bistros and high prices. The end result is that on nights and weekends, TriBeCa's streets are empty and . . . even a little creepy. **Broadway** is the place to go if you're looking for fast food. For snacks and such, **Greenwich Street** offers some interesting options, notably **Bazzini's** (339 Greenwich St., at Jay St., tel. 212/334–1280), which has been selling mixed nuts, candy, and ice cream since 1886. The **Pennsylvania Pretzel Co.** (295 Greenwich St., at Chambers St., tel. 212/587–5938) does nothing but hot pretzels, topped with garlic, cinnamon, cheese, or chocolate.

UNDER $10 **Bubby's.** If you can overlook the trendiness and the ridiculous name, Bubby's offers great people-watching and an eclectic menu of fine food. Most everything (besides a few dinner specials) is around $8. *120 Hudson St., at N. Moore St., tel. 212/219–0666. Subway: 1 or 9 to Franklin St. Open daily 7 AM–11 PM.*

Le Roy's Restaurant and Coffee Shop. Le Roy's may have been around since 1940, but they're not out of touch with the health-food thing. They've got everything covered, from vegetarian carrot burgers ($7.50) and organic vegetables with brown rice ($7.25) to meat loaf ($4) and egg-and-salami sandwiches ($3). *247 West Broadway, at Sixth Ave., tel. 212/966–3370. Subway: 1 or 9 to Franklin St. Open Mon.–Sat. 6 AM–4:30 PM.*

R-Bar. Students from nearby law schools are frequently spied in R-Bar's cozy, dark-wood booths, guzzling beers and gnawing giant R-Burgers ($6.50). Standard pub grub costs $4–$8. *273 Church St., btw Franklin and White Sts., tel. 212/966–7769. Subway: 1 or 9 to Franklin St. Open Mon.–Thurs. noon–1 AM, Fri. and Sat. noon–4 AM, Sun. noon–11 PM. No credit cards.*

Yaffa's Bar and Restaurant. At this sprawling boho lair—furnished with vintage couches and weird abstract sculptures—the food is a multi-ethnic medley of Spanish tapas ($2.50–$4), sandwiches, and Mediterranean entrées ($8–$11). They offer a big bargain brunch ($10) on weekends. Next door, **Yaffa's Tea Room** (tel. 212/966–0577) serves the same stuff in addition to high tea ($15 per person) weekdays 2–5; reservations are required. *353 Greenwich St., at Harrison St., tel. 212/274–9403. Subway: 1, 2, 3, or 9 to Chambers St. Open daily 10 AM–midnight (bar open until 4 AM).*

UNDER $15 **Franklin Station Cafe.** Nothing in the name suggests that this is a warehouse-turned-bistro that plays French rock, pours café au lait, and serves Malaysian dishes like satay chicken and eggplant curry fish ($12.50) along with more prosaic sandwiches ($6–$8). Well, it is, and it does. For breakfast, try a curry chicken puff ($1.75) and mango milk shake ($2.50). *222 West Broadway, btw Franklin and White Sts., tel. 212/274–8525. Subway: 1 or 9 to Franklin St. BYOB. Open daily 10–10.*

Restaurant Delphi. This family-owned diner has won a large and loyal following over the last 25 years for its authentic Greek dishes; come sample the grape leaves stuffed with hummus ($7), the chicken kebabs ($11), or the hefty calamari stew ($10). *109 West Broadway, at Reade St., tel. 212/227–6322. Subway: 1, 2, 3, or 9 to Chambers St. Open daily 11:30 AM–midnight.*

LOWER MANHATTAN

This is Manhattan's mighty financial district, and something about its skyscrapers and canyon-like streets make good restaurants wither and die (either it's the lack of sun or the superabundance of bond traders). While high-rolling types motor uptown for their two-martini lunches, regular working stiffs simply trod over to **Broadway** between Pine and Liberty streets to pick up a $1.25 hot dog or $2.75 take-out carton of chow mein from the weekday-only jumble of street carts. There's an amazing variety of cuisines represented, and all the chefs are pretty talented with their mobile steam trays. When the weather is fair, take your lunch over to **Liberty Park** (Liberty St., btw Trinity Pl. and Broadway). Keep in mind that most people flee Lower Manhattan right after work, and that restaurants tend to close early.

UNDER $5 **McDonald's.** If you're one of those people who thinks the McDonald's at the Spanish Steps in Rome is really cool because it has a waterfall and salad bar, you're gonna flip when you check out this Wall Street branch. It's got a tuxedoed doorman, table service, a coffee bar, an orchid-filled dining room, and even a pianist at a baby grand. You'd think that all this swank would make your Happy Meal ($3.50–$5.50) taste like filet mignon. *160 Broadway, at Liberty St., tel. 212/385–2063. Subway: N or R to Cortlandt St. Also: 4 or 5 to Wall St. Open daily 6 AM–8 PM. Wheelchair access. No credit cards.*

Fans of Ronald McDonald and his hamburger friends will of course want a McDonald's tie ($15–$30), T-shirt, or stuffed animal from the Wall Street branch gift boutique.

Smiler's Delicatessen Store. Everything at Smiler's gigantic salad bar—an intimidating array of fresh vegetables, fruit, sushi, stir-fry, dim sum, roast beef, fried chicken, and macaroni 'n' cheese—is $5 per pound. Also on the premises are a juice bar, deli, bakery, and pizzeria. *49 Broadway, btw Exchange Pl.*

and Morris St., tel. 212/425–5000. Subway: 4 or 5 to Bowling Green. Open weekdays 6 AM–7 PM, Sat. 11 AM–7 PM. Wheelchair access. No credit cards.

UNDER $10 **Pearl Street Diner.** Professionals who play with other people's millions but don't want to waste a penny of their own come here for tasty and cheap diner food. You'll pay less than $6 for charbroiled burgers and big breakfast specials. 212 Pearl St., near Maiden Ln., tel. 212/344–6620. Subway: 2 or 3 to Wall St. Open daily 6:30 AM–9 PM. AE only.

Radio Mexico. This gringos-only joint serves Southwestern specialties like burritos, chimichangas, fajitas, and *carnitas asadas* (shredded pork tacos), each about $8. Pound a few Coronas, shoot some pool, and slip a little Bonnie Raitt on the jukebox. 259 Front St., at Dover St., tel. 212/791–5416. Subway: J, M, Z, 2, 3, 4, or 5 to Fulton St. Open daily 11:30–11 (Fri. and Sat. until midnight). Wheelchair access.

UNDER $20 **Bridge Café.** This cozy bistro in a 19th-century town house is a stone's throw from the majestic Brooklyn Bridge. Seasonal entrées include fresh black linguine with shrimp ($16) and roast duck in red wine sauce ($17). 279 Water St., at Dover St., tel. 212/227–3344. Subway: J, M, Z, 2, 3, 4, or 5 to Fulton St. Open Sun. and Mon. 11:45 AM–10 PM, Tues.–Fri. 11:45–midnight, Sat. 5 PM–midnight.

Outer Borough Restaurants

BROOKLYN

The neighborhoods of **Brooklyn Heights**, **Cobble Hill**, and **Park Slope** cater to people who think they still live in Manhattan. They're packed with all kinds of eateries, from dirt-cheap falafel stands to pricey French bistros. Also in Brooklyn Heights, on **Atlantic Avenue**, you'll find dozens of Middle Eastern and Moroccan restaurants. Just south of that begins the very Italian neighborhood of **Carroll Gardens**. Farther afield, **Williamsburg** has lots of Kosher bakeries and a number of cheap, natural-food joints catering to its growing artist community. When in **Sheepshead Bay**, think "clam bars" and "pasta shops." Meanwhile, **Greenpoint** is rife with Polish coffee shops serving very cheap kielbasa and borscht, and **Brighton Beach** supports a thriving community of Jewish/Russian immigrants.

BROOKLYN HEIGHTS, COBBLE HILL, CARROLL GARDENS, AND DOWNTOWN
Fatoosh Barbecue. This Syrian joint serves two things, both of which taste terrific: barbecued meats ($4.50) and *meze* ($3), a vegetarian appetizer made with pita bread and your choice of hummus, baba ghanoush, or pureed red pepper with walnuts. 311 Henry St., btw State St. and Atlantic Ave., tel. 718/596–0030. Subway: M, N, or R to Court St. Also: 2, 3, 4, or 5 to Borough Hall. Open daily 11–10. Wheelchair access. No credit cards.

La Bouillabaisse. Every now and then we at the Berkeley Guides find a restaurant so good we want to keep it to ourselves—for example, La Bouillabaisse. The delicious French cuisine, notably the seafood, induces drool like Pavlov's bell. Of course the place is incredibly tiny, so the wait is sometimes an hour or more. Please, if your idea of a fine time has never included gorging yourself for less than $15, wine included (provided that you bring a bottle from the liquor store up the street), stay away from here. 145 Atlantic Ave., btw Henry and Clinton Sts., tel. 718/522–8275. Subway: 2, 3, 4, or 5 to Borough Hall. BYOB. Open weekdays noon–3 and 5–10:45, weekends 5–11. No credit cards.

Mélange. If you can only afford one meal a day, this is the place to go: Mélange's all-you-can-eat buffet costs only $5.95 ($6.95 after 5 PM) and includes more than 20 hot and cold entrées. The country-style dining room is actually pleasant. 444 Atlantic Ave., btw Bond and Nevins Sts., tel. 718/935–1220. Subway: B, M, N, or R to Pacific St. Open daily 9–9 (Mon. until 3 PM).

Moroccan Star. If you stayed awake during history class, you would know that the French gave Moroccans a fondness for seafood crepes ($3) and their pesky, difficult-to-speak Romance language. But for a taste of something truly Moroccan, try the *patella* (spicy chicken pie;

$8.75) or *glaba* (sautéed lamb with okra; $9), both of which are big enough for two. Be warned: This place looks more like a Kansas City pool hall than anything out of *Casablanca*. *205 Atlantic Ave., btw Clinton and Court Sts., tel. 718/643–0800. Subway: 2, 3, 4, or 5 to Borough Hall. Open Sun.–Thurs. 11–10, Fri. and Sat. noon–11.*

New City Café. Most people come to this très chic bistro before a performance at the nearby Brooklyn Academy of Music (*see* Arts Centers, in Chapter 7). Lunch is $6.50–$10, while fancy dinner entrées run $16–$20. *246 DeKalb Ave., at Vanderbilt Ave., tel. 718/622–5607. Subway: G to Clinton–Washington Aves. Open Tues.–Fri. noon–2:30 and 5:30–10:30, Sat. 5:30–11, Sun. 4–9.*

Nino's Cafe. This no-nonsense cafeteria is a big favorite with the local Italian community, and here's why: You get huge portions of eggplant Parmesan, veal, fried calamari, or roast beef, all served either with a roll ($3.50), in a hero sandwich ($5), or over a plate of pasta ($7). *531 Henry St., at Union St., tel. 718/834–0863. Subway: F or G to Carroll St. Open Mon.–Sat. 10–10. Wheelchair access. No credit cards.*

Ozzie's Coffee and Tea. While nestled in a deep wicker chair beneath the bay windows of this posh Brooklyn Heights café, you can discreetly place hexes on the yuppies strolling by outside. *136 Montague St., btw Henry and Clinton Sts., Brooklyn, tel. 718/852–1553. Subway: M, N, or R to Court St. Open daily 7 AM–11 PM (Fri. and Sat. until midnight).*

Patsy's Pizza. While all those cheesy pizza joints in Manhattan scramble to call themselves "the original" and "number one," Patsy's keeps pulling the crispiest, best-tasting pizza pies ($11–$15) in New York City out of their coal-fired oven. It's in a weird no-man's-land below the Brooklyn Bridge, but don't let that stop you. *19 Old Fulton St., btw Water and Front Sts., tel. 718/858–4300. Subway: A or C to High St. (Brooklyn Bridge). Open Mon., Wed., and Thurs. 11:30–10:30, Fri. and Sat. 2 PM–midnight, Sun. 2–10:30. No credit cards.*

Tripoli Restaurant. Bring some friends to Tripoli if you're going to order *maza* ($39), a traditional Lebanese feast with 20 different entrées. Authentic dishes such as *azhi* (an omelet with herbs, onions, pine nuts, and lamb) and *ma'ani* (a spicy sausage) are $7–$11. *156 Atlantic Ave., at Clinton St., tel. 718/596–5800. Subway: 2, 3, 4, or 5 to Borough Hall. Open daily 11 AM–11:30 PM.*

PARK SLOPE **Cucina.** They serve incredible gourmet Italian cuisine in Cucina's elegant dining room; try the lobster ravioli with saffron ($17), roast rosemary chicken ($15), or a terrific brick-oven pizza ($9–$12). Eat at a place like this in Manhattan and you'd pay double or triple the price. *256 Fifth Ave., btw Carroll St. and Garfield Pl., tel. 718/230–0711. Subway: M, N, or R to Union St. Open daily 5:30–10:30 PM (Fri. and Sat. until 11). Reservations required. Wheelchair access.*

Lemongrass Grill. There's always a line of folks outside this plain little restaurant, waiting to do battle with the sweat-inducing Thai spices. Menu highlights here include *gaiton krai* (Siam chicken; $7), *kae-panang* (lamb with green curry sauce; $8.50), and the lemongrass pork chops ($8). *61A Seventh Ave., at Lincoln Pl., tel. 718/399–7100. Subway: D or Q to Seventh Ave. Also: 2 or 3 to Grand Army Plaza. Open Mon.–Thurs. noon–10:30, Fri. and Sat. noon–11, Sun. 1–10:30. Wheelchair access. No credit cards.*

Nam. This fashionable addition to Seventh Avenue—Park Slope's "restaurant row"—serves fiery and authentic Vietnamese dishes. The menu is heavy on vegetarian ($5–$7) and noodle ($8) entrées. *222 Seventh Ave., btw 3rd and 4th Sts., tel. 718/788–5036. Subway: F to Seventh Ave. Open daily noon–10:30. Wheelchair access.*

Two Boots. Artsy types and slumming professionals come to drink copiously over a plate of cheap Cajun/Italian food. It's got the same menu as the Two Boots in the East Village (*see above*), plus live music on Friday and Saturday nights. *514 2nd St., btw Seventh and Eighth Aves., tel. 718/499–3253. Subway: F to Seventh Ave. Open weekdays 5 PM–11 PM, weekends 11–3:30 and 5–11.*

WILLIAMSBURG AND GREENPOINT **bean.** California transplants usually get very tense and huffy when New York restaurants claim to serve "authentic" Cal-Mex food. But it's not so bad at bean, a funky Williamsburg eatery that serves huge, delicious burritos, enchiladas, and quesadillas. Most dishes are vegetarian and cost $5–$6. *172 N. 8th St., near Bedford Ave., tel. 718/387–8222. Subway: L to Bedford Ave. Open daily noon–midnight. No credit cards.*

Park Luncheonette. At the Park Luncheonette they don't want to hear your sob stories about high cholesterol, because they make their living with fried-egg sandwiches ($1.25), frankfurters with sauerkraut and chili ($1.75), and pork chops ($5.50). *334 Driggs Ave., at Lorimer St., no phone. Subway: G to Nassau Ave. Open daily 11–6. No credit cards.*

Egg-cream sodas have brought Park Luncheonette fame and fortune for more than 50 years.

RBBQ. A cross between a barbecue pit, bar, and art gallery—just what you'd expect in wacky Williamsburg. Everything off the grill—from Portobello mushrooms and half-pound hamburgers to Romanian steaks and spiced tofu—costs $5 and includes two big helpings of vegetables. *409 Kent Ave., at Broadway, tel. 718/388–3929. Subway: J, M, or Z to Marcy Ave. Open daily 11–11. No credit cards.*

CONEY ISLAND, BRIGHTON BEACH, AND SHEEPSHEAD BAY **Aiello's.** This family-run Italian eatery whips up unbelievable pizzas with homemade mozzarella cheese and imported Italian tomato sauce. Slices are $1.25, large pies $10. Also try the hearty pastas ($5) and hero sandwiches ($2.75–$4.50). *1406 Neptune Ave., at Stillwell Ave., tel. 718/373–1155. Subway: B, D, or F to Coney Island (Stillwell Ave.). Open weekdays 7 AM–9 PM, Sat. 8 AM–9 PM. No credit cards.*

Cafe Tatiana. Look beyond the Coney Island rides and you might mistake this boardwalk café as part of an exclusive Russian resort on the Black Sea: Everyone is speaking Russian, eating Russian food (heavy on the sausage, potatoes, and onions), and drinking from large carafes of iced vodka. Full meals run $4–$9. *On Boardwalk, near Brighton 3 St., no phone. Subway: D or Q to Brighton Beach. Open daily 11–11. Wheelchair access.*

Nathan's Famous. Yup, these are the same Nathan's Famous Hot Dogs that live in the freezer at your local supermarket. Nathan Handwerker started selling these franks back in 1916 for 5¢ each (undercutting competitors who charged a dime); today they're $1.85. And the menu now includes cheese fries ($2) and frogs' legs ($7). *Cnr Surf and Stillwell Aves., Coney Island, tel. 718/946–2202. Subway: B, D, or F to Coney Island (Stillwell Ave.). Open daily 11 AM–2 AM.*

Primorski. Hordes of Russian immigrants flock to this restaurant/nightclub to feast on food from the Motherland, toss back some ice-cold vodka, and dance to a big band fronted by a Russian Sinatra. Entrées like *salyanka* (lamb stew; $8.50) are great, but those in the know just fill up on appetizers ($1.75–$3.50). *282 Brighton Beach Ave., btw Brighton 2 and Brighton 3 Sts., tel. 718/891–3111. Subway: D or Q to Brighton Beach. Open daily 11 AM–midnight. Lunch special ($4) weekdays 11–5. Wheelchair access.*

Randazzo's Clam Bar. The best Italian seafood restaurant in Sheepshead Bay serves monster-size oysters on the half shell (6 for $6.50), not to mention Little Neck clams ($10 per dozen) so fresh they were probably living off the coast of Long Island only hours before hitting your plate. Pastas are $6–$13. *2017 Emmons Ave., 1 block from Ocean Ave., tel. 718/615–0010. Subway: D or Q to Sheepshead Bay. Open daily 11 AM–midnight (Fri. and Sat. until 2 AM). Wheelchair access.*

Randazzo's Clam Bar is the real deal; just ask the locals sitting at the counter, loudly conversing in Brooklyn–Italian accents and wondering how dem Yanks ah doin'.

QUEENS

Eating in Queens is less a two-hour commitment to dinner than an evening's odyssey to a foreign land. Almost every neighborhood hosts a different ethnic group, and every restaurant offers a chance to sample a new cuisine. In **Astoria** you'll find Greek tavernas and cafés, while **Flushing** boasts restaurants from virtually every nation in Asia. **Jackson Heights** is the place to go for South American, Caribbean, and East Indian cooking.

ASTORIA Walk down **Broadway** or **30th Avenue** between 31st and 36th streets and you'll find more Greek restaurants, cafés, and food stores than you can count on two hands and an abacus.

Al Dewan. The ersatz marble walls and plastic ivy set the mood, sort of, for feasting on Middle Eastern dishes like chicken kebabs ($8.50) and lamb stuffed with nuts and ground meat ($9.75). Come by Saturday night for belly dancing ($5 cover). *29–36 30th Ave., at 30th St., tel. 718/545–1700. Subway: N to 31 St. BYOB. Open daily 11 AM–midnight. All-you-can-eat buffet ($9.95) weekdays 11:30–3.*

La Espiga. This tiny grocer/bakery churns out some of the best Mexican food north of the Rio Grande. Beside the usual tacos and burritos ($2–$3.50), they make *huaraches* (giant tacos; $2–$3.50) and *tortas* ($3), which are grilled sandwiches made with sliced jalapeños, avocados, beans, and your choice of 13 different fillings—including fried pork and head cheese. Eat at the counter and watch Spanish TV, or take your grub to go. *32–44 31st St., at Broadway, tel. 718/777–1993. Subway: N to Broadway. Open daily 9 AM–10 PM. No credit cards.*

La Fonda Antioqueña. A mere $7.50 buys you a big plate of broiled beef, cornmeal cakes, rice-and-beans, fried pork, fried plantains, and fried egg at this tiny Colombian restaurant. If that makes your arteries shriek, plunk down $5 for a bowl of oxtail, chicken, vegetable, or tripe soup, served with rice and avocado. *32–25 Steinway St., at Broadway, tel. 718/726–9857. Subway: R to Steinway St. Open weekdays 9 AM–11 PM, weekends 9 AM–midnight. Wheelchair access. No credit cards.*

Omonia. In the center of Astoria's Greek community, Omonia always has a crowd lingering over its authentic Greek pastries ($3.50), such as *kadaifi* (shredded wheat with nuts and honey), *ek mek kadaifi* (the same, layered with custard and whipped cream), and sticky, sweet baklava. *32–20 Broadway, at 33rd St., Astoria, Queens, tel. 718/274–6650. Subway: N to Broadway. Open daily 8 AM–2:30 AM.*

Uncle George's. The menu here runs the gamut from authentic Greek entrées—like the roast lamb with lemon-drizzled potatoes ($8) or the octopus sautéed with vinegar ($6)—to, uh, "Greek-style" burgers and spaghetti ($3–$5). The house drink is *retsina*, a Greek wine stronger than paint thinner and, at $1 per glass, cheaper than mouthwash. *33–19 Broadway, at 34th St., tel. 718/626–0593. Subway: N to Broadway. Open 24 hrs. No credit cards.*

Zenon. Make that annoying friend of yours, the one who always agonizes over the menu for hours, order *meze* ($14). It's a sampler with 16 different salads, cheeses, and grilled meats. For yourself, try the Cyprus meatballs ($7.50) or spinach pie ($5). On Wednesdays, Greek singers and dancers entertain with traditional folk tunes on electric guitar. *34–10 31st Ave., btw 34th and 35th Sts., tel. 718/956–0133. Subway: N to 30th Ave. Open daily noon–midnight. No credit cards.*

FLUSHING The blocks around the **Main Street** subway station are crowded with wall-to-wall Asian restaurants, including Hunan, Szechuan, Cantonese, Japanese, Korean, Taiwanese, Vietnamese, and Malaysian. Farther south on Main Street (near the Queens Botanical Gardens), a handful of cheap Indian restaurants rounds out the cultural stew.

Joe's Shanghai. If you don't mind the sardine-like seating, you're in for a treat when you eat at Joe's. Start with their famous soup dumplings (yes, filled with soup; $6.25), experiment with one of 20 kinds of soup ($4.25), and finally ease into a food coma with one of the totally unique entrées ($9–$12). *136–21 37th Ave., near Main St., tel. 718/539–3838. Subway: 7 to Main St. Open daily 11–10:30. Wheelchair access. No credit cards.*

Penang. Penang brings the flavors and cooking styles of China, Thailand, India, and Malaysia to a menu that reads like exotic poetry. There's Buddhist yam pot ($9), fish wrapped in lotus leaves ($11), and pearl noodle soup ($5.25). The yam pot is, in fact, a yam stuffed like a

Twinkie with chicken, shrimp, and vegetables. *38–04 Prince St., btw Main St. and Roosevelt Ave., tel. 718/321–2078. Subway: 7 to Main St. Open daily 11:30–11:30. No credit cards.*

JACKSON HEIGHTS Around **Roosevelt Avenue** and **82nd Street**, Colombian, Cuban, Brazilian, Puerto Rican, Argentinean, and Peruvian restaurants churn out chorizo, tripe stew, and other South American fare. Just a few blocks down, at **74th Street**, chile peppers give way to cumin and curry, and cheap Indian food abounds.

Jackson Diner. Order tandoori ($7.50–$8) or anything cooked in a *kadai* (a type of earthenware pan) and you will understand, with blinding clarity, how a restaurant painted pink and decorated garishly with fake crystal chandeliers can do such booming business. *37–03 74th St., at 37th Ave., tel. 718/672–1232. Subway: 7 to 74th St. BYOB, Open daily 11:30–10. Lunch special ($4.50–$6) weekdays 11:30–4. Wheelchair access. No credit cards.*

> *On Jackson Heights streets, look for East Indian stands selling "pan" (rhymes with lawn), a mystery concoction of seeds and herbs rolled in a beetlenut leaf. Locals swear the stuff aids digestion; some folks claim it's psychoactive.*

Tierras Colombianas. Arrive hungry if you're planning to tackle a "mountain plate" ($8–$9) of South American staples like stewed beef, fried pork, rice-and-beans, plantains, or cassava. Finish up with a thick, sweet tropical juice ($3). *82–18 Roosevelt Ave., near 82nd St., tel. 718/426–8868. Subway: 7 to 82nd St./Jackson Heights. Open daily 11–11. Wheelchair access. No credit cards.*

LONG ISLAND CITY **Stick to Your Ribs.** Feel like picking a fight with a couple of renegade Texans? Simply walk into this Lone Star barbecue house and tell 'em their hot sauce ($3 per pint) ain't. Tell 'em their barbecued beef, pork, chicken, and sausage ($4–$13 per pound) tastes like Arby's. Then insult the masculinity of their chile-pepper beer ($3). Go on now. We'll wait outside. *5–16 51st Ave., btw Vernon Blvd. and 2nd St., tel. 718/937–3030. Subway: 7 to Vernon Blvd./Jackson Ave. Open Mon.–Sat. 11–9. No credit cards.*

THE BRONX

Not many Bronx-bound tourists get beyond the zoo, but those who do will find some rewarding restaurant choices. In the Italian-American neighborhood of **Belmont**, trattorias, pizzerias, caffès, pastry shops, salumerias, fish markets, and cheese stores line the streets. Across the Long Island Sound on **City Island**, you can gorge yourself to the gills on deep-fried seafood—and worry about your health later.

BELMONT For a truly gluttonous experience, stroll Bronx's "Little Italy" around **Arthur Avenue** and **187th Street**, stopping at **Madonia Brothers Bakery** (2348 Arthur Ave., tel. 718/295–5573), where fresh loaves of bread have come laced with prosciutto, provolone, pesto, and olives since 1918. **Cosenza's Fish Market** (2354 Arthur Ave., tel. 718/364–8510) has an outdoor fish stand that sells six clams on the half-shell for $3. At **Calabria Pork Store** (2338 Arthur Ave., tel. 718/367–5145), dried meats hang from the ceiling and huge blocks of cheese chill on the sidelines.

Ann and Tony's. They've been making a mean plate of spaghetti carbonara, veal Parmesan, and chicken marsala at this family-owned restaurant since 1927. Entrées are $12–$14; students get a 10%, cash-only discount. *2407 Arthur Ave., at E. 187th St., tel. 718/933–1469. Subway: C or D to Fordham Rd. Also: Metro-North to Fordham station. Open daily 11–10. Lunch special ($10) Mon.–Sat. 11–3. Wheelchair access.*

Dominick's. This place is about as unpretentious as it gets, with communal tables, jugs of wine, and a point-and-shout approach to ordering. Locals love it, and on weekends the line stretches out the door. A big Italian dinner costs $8–$15. *2335 Arthur Ave., near 187th St., tel. 718/733–2807. Subway: C or D to Fordham Rd. Also: Metro-North to Fordham station. Open Mon. and Wed.–Sat. noon–10, Sun. 1–9.*

Ristorante Egidio. Everything at this snazzy lunch spot costs less than $10, so indulge in one of the hearty pastas, soups, or sandwiches. For dessert and espresso, head next door to **Caffè Egidio** (tel. 718/295–6077), which has outlasted two World Wars and the Great Depression, and is still Belmont's favorite Italian café. Gelato costs $1.50 and their 55 kinds of pastries run 75¢–$1.75 each. *622 E. 187th St., at Hughes Ave., tel. 718/364–3157. Subway: D to Fordham Rd. Also: Metro-North to Fordham station. Open Mon.–Sat. 8–8, Sun. 7–3 PM.*

CITY ISLAND **Johnny's Reef Restaurant.** This simple chant will help you through a meal at Johnny's: FRIED FOODS ARE MY FRIEND, FRIED FOODS WILL NOT HURT ME. And, really, the delicious fried shrimp, oysters, and other sea critters (all $8–$10) are virtually greaseless. *2 City Island Ave., tel. 718/885–2086. Subway: 6 to Pelham Bay (25 min), then Bus BX12 to end of City Island Ave. (25 min). Open daily 11 AM–midnight (Fri. and Sat. until 2 AM). No credit cards.*

The bar at Rhodes is a good place to chat with old salts who look like they could show Hemingway a thing or two about hooking giant marlin.

Rhodes. Around the turn of the century, Rhodes was a sailor's home, inn, and whorehouse. Now it's a pub with live music, good burgers, and pub grub ($5–$12). There's even a moose head on the wall. *288 City Island Ave., at Fordham Rd., tel. 718/885–1538. Subway: 6 to Pelham Bay, then Bus BX12 to City Island Ave. Open daily 11 AM–3 AM.*

RIVERDALE, WILLIAMSBRIDGE, AND MORRIS HEIGHTS **African and American Restaurant.** Ever had Ghanian food? If not, here's the scoop: Ghanian mashes ($7.50) are brick-like blocks of steamed *fufu* (mashed cassava), *gari* (fermented cassava), or *emu-tuw* (kneaded glutinous rice), spiced with toasted melon seeds, peanut, ginger, or garlic and eaten with the right hand. Get in line and point to whatever looks good: There's southern-style grub for the less brazen of palate. *1987 University Ave., at Burnside Ave., Morris Heights, tel. 718/731–8595). Subway: 4 to Burnside Ave. BYOB. Open 24 hrs. No credit cards.*

An Bēal Bocht. This Irish pub ("The Poor Mouth" in Gaelic) has a funky, bohemian spirit and hosts poetry readings (Tuesday) and live Irish bands (Wednesday–Saturday). The crowd's a cool mix of Irish folk and students from nearby Manhattan College. Foodwise, fill up on Irish stew and soda bread ($7) or chicken pot pie ($6.50). Pints of Guinness and Harp are $4. On Sunday they serve a traditional Irish breakfast for $7, with black-and-white pudding, sausage, rashers, eggs, and fried tomatoes. *445 W. 238th St., btw Greystone and Waldo Aves., Riverdale, tel. 718/884–7127. Subway: 1 or 9 to 238th St.; walk up 238th St. to steep flight of stairs and start climbing. Open daily 9 AM–3 AM.*

In 1996 "New York" magazine voted An Bēal Bocht best joint in the city for a pint o' Guinness.

Burrito Kelly. Once again, those pushy New Yorkers have taken a beautiful concept—the Cal-Mex burrito—and messed it up with frou-frou ingredients like sauteed tofu, wild mushrooms, and spinach. Still, this is a pleasant place to kick back after a day at Wave Hill (*see* Museums and Galleries, in Chapter 2), and the gringo food is cheap enough ($5–$7). *430 W. 238th St., at Waldo Ave., Riverdale, tel. 718/549–4898. Subway: 1 or 9 to 238th St.; walk along 238th St. to steep flight of stairs and climb 'em. Open daily noon–11. Wheelchair access. No credit cards.*

STATEN ISLAND

Though you won't find crowds rushing across the Verrazano-Narrows bridge for Staten Island grub, there's no need to pack a lunch when you take a day trip to the Snug Harbor Cultural Center. The best Chinese food around is at **Lum Chin** (4326 Amboy Rd., btw Armstrong and Richmond Aves., tel. 718/984–8044; 1640 Forest Ave., near Willow Brook Rd., tel. 718/442–1707). For a splurge, the most popular place is **Aesop's Tables** (1233 Bay St., at Maryland St., tel. 718/720–2005), which serves gourmet French bistro food in the $15 range.

Adobe Blues. You wouldn't haul ass out to Staten Island just to visit a restaurant—but you might for this place. They've got great Southwestern dishes—chili con carne ($4–$5.50) and Drunken Mexican Shrimp ($12)—and more than 200 beers. There's even a roaring fireplace perfect for winters. *63 Lafayette Ave., New Brighton, tel. 718/720–2583. From ferry terminal, take Bus S40 to Lafayette Ave. (10 min). Open Mon.–Thurs. 11 AM–midnight, Fri. and Sat. 11 AM–2 AM, Sun. noon–midnight. Kitchen open daily until 11 PM (Fri. and Sat. until 1:45 AM).*

M. Bennet Refreshments. At this quaint little restaurant in an historic 1840s building, the food is named after famous Staten Island people and places. Order a Tottenville if you want a tuna sandwich, or an Alice Austen for a tomato and basil pizza. You can lunch here for less than $7; dinner is another story, with "sherry sauce" this and "corn crusted" that, costing up to $19. *3730 Richmond Rd., at St. Patrick's Rd., tel. 718/980–3410. From ferry terminal, take Bus S78 to Richmondtown Restoration (25 min). Open Wed.–Sat. noon–4 and 5–11, Sun. 10–9.*

Cafés and Coffee Bars

Excluding the West Village and Little Italy, decent coffee—much less café au lait and triple cappuccinos—didn't exist in Manhattan until the early '90s. Around that time a few New Yorkers noticed they'd missed the boat on the whole Seattle coffee craze, and imitation Left-Coast cafés started cropping up like pay-per-view wrestling matches. By 1994, the *New York Times* was moved to explain to its poor, confused readers that these new **coffee bars** were not to be confused with the old **coffee shops**. The distinction is subtle but real, so keep this axiom in mind: At coffee shops the grease is on your plate, while at coffee bars the grease is in the hair of the slacker employees.

While it's now impossible to go a single block without bumping into some sort of espresso bar, not all are the kind of place you'd want to hole up with a pack of smokes and a David Foster Wallace novel. Some, the Type-A cafés, are sterile outlets where the furniture is uncomfortable and the lighting fluorescent. These are sadly common in Midtown. The others, more common in the East Village and Chelsea, are cool and funky and often furnished with comfy thrift-store couches. Many do a lot more than just crank out coffee, like displaying the works of neighborhood artists, holding poetry and fiction readings, hosting live music, or providing access to the Internet. And unlike the Type A's, they won't go ballistic if you decide to linger all afternoon over your $1 purchase. You can count on either kind of café to fill you up with a menu of sandwiches, salads, soups, and desserts when you're down to your last $5. Some even serve beer or wine. Typically, a regular coffee costs $1, fancy caffeine brews $2–$4. One final note: If you really want to assimilate into the city's café culture, pick up a copy of the sassy East Village 'zine, *Java Journal.*

COFFEE-BAR CHAINS A few coffee-bar chains are worth checking out. If you need a CNN fix or want to browse a rack of 450 (yes, 450) foreign and domestic publications, try **News Bar** (2 W. 19th St., near Fifth Ave., Chelsea, tel. 212/255–3996; 107 University Pl., btw 12th and 13th Sts., West Village, tel. 212/260–4192). The ubiquitous **Barnes and Noble** (4 Astor Pl., btw Broadway and Lafayette St., East Village, tel. 212/420–1322) has cafés in all its Manhattan superstores; they've become legendary cruising zones for literary types who feel most glib and chatty when they're clutching a copy of *Sansho the Bailiff.* And finally, the Seattle chain that started it all is regarded by many as having New York's Best-Tasting Cuppa Joe: **Starbucks** (2379 Broadway, at 87th Street, tel. 212/875–8470; Waverly Pl., at E. 6th St., tel. 212/477–7776; and many, many more).

UPTOWN

Café Mozart. Pound out your own *Requiem* on this funky café's baby grand piano, right beneath an incredibly ugly framed likeness of its Austrian namesake. The café is a hangout for foreign journalists and literary types who enjoy decent sandwiches ($6–$7). *154 W. 70th St., btw Broadway and Columbus Ave., tel. 212/595–9797. Subway: 1, 2, 3, or 9 to W. 72nd St. Open weekdays 11 AM–2 AM, Sat. 10 AM–3 AM, Sun. 10–2 AM.*

The Hungarian Pastry Shop. Columbia University's alternative crowd comes here to think Deep Thoughts while refueling their physical beings with a selection of sugary confections ($2 each). *1030 Amsterdam Ave., btw W. 110th and 111th Sts., tel. 212/866–4230. Subway: 1 or 9 to*

W. 110th St. Open weekdays 8 AM–11:30 PM, Sat. 9 AM–11:30 PM, Sun. 9 AM–10:30 PM. No credit cards.

Muffin Man. On warm days they throw the French doors wide open at the popular Muffin Man. Besides sandwiches ($3–$5) and cheap breakfasts ($3), they have a vast array of sinful baked goodies. *1638 Third Ave., btw E. 91st and 92nd Sts., tel. 212/987–2404. Subway: 6 to E. 96th St. Open daily 6:30 AM–10 PM. No credit cards.*

Positively 104th Street. This place is whatever you want it to be: gourmet coffee emporium, art gallery, or café. And they offer free coffee refills—try finding that anywhere else in Manhattan. *2725 Broadway, at W. 104th St., tel. 212/316–0372. Subway: 1 or 9 to W. 103rd St. Open daily 7:30 AM–11 PM. Wheelchair access.*

MIDTOWN

The Coffee Pot. Professional types come here to practice social mergers and acquisitions. Drinks run the gamut from house blend (90¢) to a lethal 16-ounce cappuccino with a shot of vanilla ($3.35). *350 W. 49th St., at Ninth Ave., tel. 212/265–3566. Subway: C or E to W. 50th St. Open weekdays 8 AM–11 PM, Sat. 9 AM–midnight, Sun. 9 AM–11 PM. Wheelchair access. No credit cards.*

Palm reading, handwriting analysis, bingo, board games, and live music are some of the nightly happenings at the café Heaven.

Heaven. This ethereal hipster hangout is next door to the artsy Carlton Arms Hotel (*see* Chapter 3). The furniture is funky, the crowd cool. *62 E. 25th St., near Third Ave., tel. 212/889–8305. Subway: 6 to E. 23rd St. Open Mon.–Wed. 8 AM–10 PM, Thurs.–Sat. 8 AM–11 PM, Sun. 10–7. No credit cards.*

Jonathan Morr Espresso Bar. Don't blow your cover at this suave joint by asking for plain ol' coffee. They serve only the *finest* organic coffees (92¢–$3.50), plus gourmet sandwiches ($4–$6), soups, and baked goods. *1394 Sixth Ave., btw W. 56th and 57th Sts., tel. 212/757–6677. Subway: B or Q to W. 57th St. Open daily 7 AM–9 PM (weekends from 8 AM). Wheelchair access.*

Uncommon Grounds. Strong coffee, friendly staff, and great music make this one of the best coffeehouses in Midtown. Lunch is $5–$6.25; delicious fruit shakes and smoothies are $2–$4. *533 Third Ave., btw E. 35th and 36th Sts., tel. 212/889–5037. Subway: 6 to E. 33rd St. Open Mon.–Thurs. 7:30 AM–10 PM, Fri. and Sat. 8:30 AM–midnight, Sun. 8:30 AM–10 PM. Wheelchair access.*

CHELSEA

Big Cup Tea & Coffeehouse. Sip coffee ($1) or slam a triple cappuccino ($4) with a hip, gay crowd. Lavender flowers blossom with psychedelic radiance on the Big Cup's lime green walls—very Alice in Wonderland. *228 Eighth Ave., btw W. 21st and 22nd Sts., tel. 212/206–0059. Subway: C or E to W. 23rd St. Open weekdays 7 AM–2 AM, weekends 8 AM–3 AM. Wheelchair access. No credit cards.*

Eureka Joe. Part dentist's office, part Pee Wee's Playhouse, Eureka Joe has gigantic stuffed chairs and couches strewn randomly around a characterless room. Literary hipsters come for the usual café fare as well as beer and wine. *168 Fifth Ave., at 22nd St., tel. 212/741–7500. Subway: N or R to W. 23rd St. Open weekdays 7 AM–11 PM, Sat. 9 AM–11 PM, Sun. 10–6. Wheelchair access. No credit cards.*

Kaffeehaus. Coffee and desserts seem suave choices at this dark Viennese coffeehouse. The Icekaffee (coffee with vanilla ice cream; $3.95) is a must. *131 Eighth Ave., btw 16th and 17th Aves., tel. 212/229–9702. Subway: A, C, E, or L to W. 14th St. Open Mon.–Thurs. 11–11, Fri.–Sun. 11 AM–midnight.*

Paradise Cafe. Hip Chelseans crowd Paradise—while their pooches wait dutifully outside. Try the mysterious Euro-Ice Nutrition Drink ($1.50), which could prolong your life and make you enjoy house music. *139 Eighth Ave., at W. 17th St., tel. 212/647–0066. Subway: A, C, E, or L to W. 14th St. Open Mon.–Thurs. 7 AM–10 PM, Fri. and Sat. 7 AM–midnight, Sun. 8 AM–10 PM. Wheelchair access. No credit cards.*

WEST VILLAGE

Bleecker Street Pastry Shop. This Italian bakery and café, opened in 1966, doubles as a social club for Sicilian matriarchs. Try the Lobster Tail ($1), an Italian sweet with rum-flavored filling. *245 Bleecker St., at Carmine St., tel. 212/242–4959. Subway: A, B, C, D, E, F, or Q to W. 4th St. (Washington Sq.). Open Mon.–Thurs. 7:30 AM–10:30 PM, Fri. and Sat. 7:30 AM–midnight, Sun. 8 AM–10 PM. No credit cards.*

Cafe Borgia. The students of New York University come here in droves for delicious Italian desserts and free-flowing cappuccinos. *185 Bleecker St., at MacDougal St., tel. 212/674–9589. Subway: A, B, C, D, E, F, or Q to W. 4th St. (Washington Sq.). Open daily 10:30 AM–2 AM (Fri. and Sat. until 4 AM).*

Cafe Mona Lisa. You may wish your date were as gorgeous as this café. Arrive in the evening, when the lights are low and some singer's rich baritone is turned on high. Coffee drinks are $1.25–$2.50. *282 Bleecker St., btw Jones St. and Seventh Ave. S, tel. 212/929–1262 or 212/929–1347. Subway: 1 or 9 to Christopher St. (Sheridan Sq.). Open Sun.–Thurs. 11 AM–2 AM, Fri. 10 AM–2 AM, Sat. 10 AM–3 AM. No credit cards.*

Cafe Reggio. In the '50s this was a favorite hangout of the Beats (at the time, it had the only espresso machine in the Village). Today it's a great place to watch tourists dorking along MacDougal Street. *119 MacDougal St., btw W. 3rd and Bleecker Sts., tel. 212/475–9557. Subway: A, B, C, D, E, F, or Q to W. 4th St. (Washington Sq.). Open daily 9:30 AM–2 AM (Fri. and Sat. until 4 AM).*

Caffe Dell Artista. Caffe Dell Artista is a terrific place for a tête-à-tête—if you don't mind shouting a bit to be heard over the French show tunes. Salads, sandwiches, and delicious desserts are less than $6. *46 Greenwich Ave., btw Charles St. and Seventh Ave., tel. 212/645–4431. Subway: 1, 2, 3, or 9 to W. 14th St. Open daily noon–1 AM (Fri. and Sat. until 2 AM). No credit cards.*

Caffe Lucca. Notice something? All the people here are *Italian* tourists, which should tell you a thing or two about how good the cappuccinos and gelatos ($3.75) taste. *228 Bleecker St., btw Carmine St. and Sixth Ave., tel. 212/243–8385. Subway: A, B, C, D, E, F, or Q to W. 4th St. (Washington Sq.). Open daily 9 AM–3 AM.*

The Peacock. The Peacock—like every other Italian coffeehouse on MacDougal Street—claims it was the first in the Village to serve cappuccino. The excellence of their rum cake and tiramisù ($4), however, is undisputed. *24 Greenwich Ave., at W. 10th St., tel. 212/242–9395. Subway: 1 or 9 to Christopher St. (Sheridan Sq.). Open daily 1–1. No credit cards.*

EAST VILLAGE AND THE LOWER EAST SIDE

9A Coffee House. The nouveau Beats who hang at this café/art gallery sometimes skip the coffee thing in favor of cold microbrews ($3–$3.50), accompanied by slices from the pizza place next door. *110 St. Marks Pl., btw First Ave. and Ave. A, tel. 212/982–7129. Subway: 6 to Astor Pl. Open Sun.–Thurs. 9 AM–midnight, Fri. and Sat. 10 AM–1 AM.*

@Cafe. Fifteen Macs and PCs ($5 per half hour; instruction available) fill this cavernous space. They've got a long menu of coffee drinks and international eats, plus a weekday happy hour (5–7 PM) when draft beers are two-for-one. Also, hit their web site (http://www.fly.net). *12 St. Marks Pl., btw Second*

If drinking heavily while surfing the Internet is your idea of great time, @Cafe is your East Village hangout.

and Third Aves., tel. 212/979–5439. Subway: 6 to Astor Pl. Open daily 11:30 AM–midnight (Fri. and Sat. until 2 AM). Wheelchair access.

Café Pick Me Up. What could be better than slurping coffee ($1) while watching the skate punks, flannel-clad nihilists, hippies, and vinyl fetishists do their thing in Tompkins Square Park? Well, perhaps a $2.25 breakfast that's served until noon. 145 Ave. A, at E. 9th St., tel. 212/673–7231. Subway: L to First Ave. Also: 6 to Astor Pl. Open weekdays 8 AM–11 PM, weekends 8 AM–1 AM. Wheelchair access. No credit cards.

First Street Cafe. In size it's somewhere between "closet" and "shoe box," but this is the café of choice for East Village slackers looking to ponder life's meaning over coffee and cheap, tasty eats ($3–$8). Check out the Elvis bathroom. 72 1st St., btw First and Second Aves., tel. 212/420–0701. Subway: F to Second Ave. Open weekdays 8 AM–midnight, weekends 9 AM–2 AM. No credit cards.

Internet Cafe. E-mail an Armenian bass-fishing expert or chat with foot worshipers from around the globe while sipping espresso. Computers here cost $3 per half hour ($25 per month for unlimited use). The café even sponsors classes; peruse the listings at their web site (http://www.bigmagic.com). 82 E. 3rd St., btw First and Second Aves., tel. 212/614–0747. Subway: F to Second Ave. Open daily 11 AM–2 AM.

Limbo. Intellectuals dressed like Dieter smirk, smoke, and drink cappuccino at the city's most hyped café, run by Vassar grads and founded by a Bergdorf-Goodman heiress. Daytime is for book reading, nighttime for loud conversations about Flaubert and cybersex. On Wednesday evening, big-name and upcoming writers alike read their prose and poetry. 47 Ave. A, btw E. 3rd and 4th Sts., tel. 212/477–5271. Subway: F to Second Ave. Open daily 8 AM–1 AM (Fri. and Sat. until 2 AM). Wheelchair access. No credit cards.

Rumbul's. The Rumbul's empire once included three cozy downtown shops, but this is the only installation left. They still offer strong coffee, light snacks, and intoxicating sugar confections ($3–$6). 128 E. 7th St., btw First Ave. and Ave. A, tel. 212/473–8696. Subway: F to Second Ave. Also: 6 to Astor Pl. Open Sun.–Thurs. 8 AM–1 AM, Fri. and Sat. 24 hours. Wheelchair access. AE only.

Sin-é. The days when MTV used to drop by are long gone, but this wee Irish café is still an excellent choice for an afternoon cup of tea. Evenings bring live music, mornings a massive Irish breakfast (eggs, rashers, sausage, beans, and potatoes; $5.50). 122 St. Marks Pl., btw First Ave. and Ave. A, tel. 212/982–0370. Subway: 6 to Astor Pl. Open daily 10 AM–1 AM.

LITTLE ITALY

Caffé Roma. More Italian than Michelangelo or World Cup soccer, this Old World transplant has marble-topped tables, an ancient brass espresso machine, and killer cannoli ($6.50). 385 Broome St., at Mulberry St., tel. 212/226–8413. Subway: 6 to Spring St. Open daily 10 AM–midnight. Wheelchair access. No credit cards.

Ferrara. Your plan of attack at this century-old institution is simple: Keep eating desserts. We recommend the tartufo (chocolate-covered Bavarian cream puff; $2.50) and cannoli (fried pastry roll with sweet cream filling; $3.50). In fact, actor Tony Danza (think "Taxi") liked the cannoli so much that in return he left a few nice framed photos of himself. 195 Grand St., btw Mott and Mulberry Sts., tel. 212/226–6150. Subway: B, D, or Q to Grand St. Open daily 8 AM–midnight. No credit cards.

SOHO AND TRIBECA

Basset Coffee and Tea Co. A genuinely relaxed atmosphere and pleasant outdoor patio make this TriBeCa coffee and tea emporium a fine place to enjoy a light sandwich or salad ($5.25–$6.50). 123 W. Broadway, at Duane St., tel. 212/349–1662. Subway: 1, 2, 3, or 9 to Chambers St. Open weekdays 7:30 AM–10 PM, Sat. 9 AM–10 PM, Sun. 9–6.

Cyber Café. SoHo's Cyber Café, spacious and slick, offers organic foods, gourmet coffees, and all-fruit "Cyber Shakes" ($3), plus full Internet access, e-mail, and web surfing ($10 per hour). Their web address is http://www.cyber-cafe.com. *273A Lafayette St., at Prince St., tel. 212/334–5140. Subway: N or R to Price St. Also: 6 to Spring St. Open Mon.–Thurs. 11 AM–midnight, Fri. and Sat. 11 AM–1 AM, Sun. 11–10. Wheelchair access.*

Duane Park Patisserie. Hidden among TriBeCa's warehouses is a bakery/café selling the kind of cheesecakes ($2 per slice), chocolate tortes ($2.50), and custard tarts ($3.50) for which you'd gladly hock your trousers. *179 Duane St., btw Greenwich and Hudson Sts., tel. 212/274–8447. Subway: 1, 2, 3, or 9 to Chambers St. Open Tues.–Sat. 8–6:30, Sun. 9–5.*

In the Black. Come to this lushly appointed café to confirm all those clichés about SoHo people . . . like their fondness for all-black clothing, neatly clipped goatees, and incisive comments about art. *180 Varick St., btw King and Charlton Sts., tel. 212/807–8322. Subway: 1 or 9 to Houston St. Open weekdays 7–7, Sat. 10–5.*

Le Gamin. Just as you'd expect from a French café, Le Gamin serves superb crepes and magnificent crème brûlée. And the café au lait comes European-style, in a great big bowl ($2.75). *50 MacDougal St., btw Houston and Prince Sts., tel. 212/254–4678. Subway: C or E to Spring St. Open daily 8 AM–midnight. Other locations: 183 Ninth Ave., at W. 21st St., Chelsea, tel. 212/243–8864.*

Scharmann's. This spacious, loftlike café is decorated with mismatched Victorian furniture and populated by well-manicured SoHoers. It's certainly not a smoke-free environment. *386 West Broadway, btw Spring and Broome Sts., tel. 212/219–2561. Subway: C or E to Spring St. Open Sun. and Mon. 10 AM–midnight, Tues. and Wed. 10 AM–4 AM, Thurs. 10 AM–1 AM, Fri. and Sat. 10 AM–2 AM.*

T Salon. Fashionable types close a day of museum- and gallery-hopping at T Salon (it's under the SoHo Guggenheim), sipping teas like *grand bois cheri bop* and *ftgopi darjeeling mim* by the glass ($2.50) or pot ($4.50–$6). Avoid the overpriced entrées ($12–$18). *142 Mercer St., at Prince St., tel. 212/925–3700. Subway: N or R to Prince St. Open Mon. 11–9, Tues.–Thurs. 11–10, Fri. and Sat. 11 AM–midnight, Sun. 11–7.*

Markets and Specialty Shops

Most New Yorkers treat their kitchens with the same sort of kindly, solicitous dread that St. Augustine extended to leper colonies. They really don't like to deal with cooking, and why should they? The pizza and Thai guys will always deliver—even in a blizzard at 4 AM. That said, there are tons of places to buy the fixings for a do-it-yourself gourmet meal or a glorious picnic. If the selection below leaves you wanting, pick up *New York Eats* by Ed Levine (St. Martin's Press, $16.95); it lists every lox shop and knishery in the five boroughs, and more.

GENERAL MARKETS **Dean & Deluca.** SoHo's epicurean fantasyland isn't really a market—it's an art gallery for food. They sell the best in produce, fresh fish, breads, cheeses, desserts, candies, and strangely beautiful kitchen utensils. *560 Broadway, at Prince St., SoHo, tel. 212/431–1691. Subway: N or R to Prince St. Open Mon.–Sat. 8–8, Sun. 9–7.*

Fairway. This suburban-style warehouse/megamarket (complete with a 200-car parking lot) is a one-stop shopper's wet dream. In addition to a large, cheap selection of produce and baked goods, it abounds with fresh meats, poultry, fish, and dairy products—all displayed in a 38°F former meat-packing room. They even supply jackets so you won't catch cold while picking out the perfect flank steak. *2328 12th Ave., btw 132nd and 133rd Sts., Harlem, tel. 212/234–3883. Subway: 1 to 125th St. Open Mon.–Thurs. 8 AM–10 PM, Fri.–Sun. 8 AM–midnight. Other location: 2127 Broadway, at W. 74th St., Upper West Side, tel. 212/595–1888. Subway: 1, 2, or 3 to 72nd St. Open daily 7 AM–midnight.*

Russ and Daughters. Although many neighboring stores are run down or boarded up, Russ and Daughters is spit-shined and orderly. Just about everything is made on the premises, from barrels of pickled cucumbers, onions, tomatoes, and peppers to the variety of smoked fishes and

The lox at Russ and Daughters routinely wins praises as "best in New York." Which is nothing to sneeze at in a city where smoked salmon is, to some, more important than national defense.

spreads. *179 E. Houston St., btw Orchard and Allen Sts., Lower East Side, tel. 212/475–4880 or 800/787-7229. Subway: F to Second Ave. Open Mon.-Wed. 9–6, Thurs.-Sat. 9–7, Sun. 8–6. Wheelchair access.*

Zabar's. A real New York institution, Zabar's is a crowded and popular food emporium with, among other things, delicious fresh breads, meats, smoked fish, and candy. If you're shopping for housewares, browse the huge selection upstairs. Prices are surprisingly good and often downright cheap. Next door is Zabar's café (*see* Manhattan Restaurants, *above*). *2245 Broadway, at W. 80th St., Upper West Side, tel. 212/787-2000. Subway: 1 or 9 to W. 79th St. Open weekdays 8–7:30, Sat. 8–8, Sun. 9–6.*

ETHNIC FOODS **Italian Food Center.** They have Italian flags on the walls and a great selection of olive oils, salamis, prosciuttos, focaccia breads, and hero sandwiches. The food here is delizioso, but not exactly low-cal—notice that the employees are prone to overindulgence, too. *186 Grand St., at Mulberry St., Little Italy, tel. 212/925-2954. Subway: B, D, Q to Grand St. Open daily 8–7.*

Kam Man. This Chinese food and housewares emporium is unparalleled in the city. The main floor has foodstuffs—from ginseng to dried eel to hard candies—while downstairs there's a wide variety of teas, porcelain, noodles, and pots and pans. *200 Canal St., at Elizabeth St., Chinatown, tel. 212/571–0330. Subway: J, M, N, R, Z, or 6 to Canal St. Open daily 9–9.*

M & I International. This is the Brighton Beach community's equivalent to Zabar's—a gourmet store and supermarket with a decidedly Russian flavor (note the jaunty Russian pop blaring from the P.A. system). Browse the vast deli cases filled with sausages, salads, and smoked fish, and have lunch on the nearby beach. *249 Brighton Beach Ave., btw Brighton 2 and Brighton 3 Sts., tel. 718/615–1011. Subway: D to Ocean Pkwy. Open daily 9–9. Wheelchair access. No credit cards.*

Sahadi Importing Company. This is New York's best Middle Eastern market. In addition to exotic spices, Sahadi's sells grains, olives (nearly two dozen varieties), chickpeas, and standbys like hummus and leban. *187 Atlantic Ave., btw Court and Clinton Sts., Brooklyn Heights, tel. 718/624–4550. Subway: M, N, or R to Court St. Open Mon.-Sat. 9 AM–7 PM.*

SPECIALTY SHOPS **D&G Bakery.** Many food critics think the Italian peasant's bread that comes from this hole-in-the-wall bakery is the best in town. The secret is the coal-fire oven, one of the few remaining in the city. If you can't afford a meal at one of Little Italy's overpriced restaurants, try D&G's prosciutto bread—it's a meal in itself. Try to get here early, as the bread is usually snapped up by noon. *45 Spring St., btw Mulberry and Mott Sts., Little Italy, tel. 212/226–6688. Subway: 6 to Spring St. Open daily 8 AM–2 PM.*

East Village Cheese. Signs proclaiming ROCK-BOTTOM PRICES cover the entire front window of this dairy mecca. The gimmick is low prices on more cheese than you can shake a stick at, including Camembert and fontina for $2.99 per pound. It also sells fresh breads and low-cost pâtés ($5.99 per lb). *40 Third Ave., at E. 9th St., tel. 212/477–2601. Subway: 6 to Astor Pl. Open weekdays 9–6:30, weekends 9–5:30.*

Essex Street Pickles. If you can't imagine why anyone would trek to the sticks of the Lower East Side for a pickle, you've never been to this 80-year-old institution, which regulars still call Guss Pickles (its original name). Coming here is a quintessential New York experience—you can watch old men stand about gabbing in the doorway while you browse the pickles, sauerkraut, and other vinegar-cured treasures all displayed in brawny wooden barrels. *35 Essex St., btw Hester and Grand Sts., Lower East Side, tel. 212/254–4477. Subway: F to East Broadway. Open Sun.-Thurs. 10–6, Fri. 10–2.*

Joe's Dairy. Pungent wafts of smoked mozzarella lure unsuspecting passersby into Joe's, an old-world emporium packed floor to ceiling with wheels of cheese. *156 Sullivan St., btw Prince St. and Houston St., tel. 212/677–8780. Subway: C or E to Spring St. Also: 1 or 9 to Houston St. Open Tues.-Sat. 9–6:30.*

WINE AND SPIRITS **Astor Wines & Spirits.** A wide selection of wines, spirits, liqueurs, and sake at very nice prices. Astor stocks "good" wines for less than $10, and the prices on hard liquor are some of the best in the city. There's little reason to shop anywhere else. *12 Astor Pl., at Lafayette St., East Village, tel. 212/674–7500. Subway: 6 to Astor Pl. Also: N or R to E. 8th St. Open Mon.–Sat. 9–9.*

Greenmarkets

Open-air farmers' markets in New York City? Though it sounds like an oxymoron, it's true. And it comes as no surprise that they are the best places to stock up on organic vegetables and fruit, baked goods, fresh fish, flowers, and wine—all sold by real, honest-to-goodness farmers from New Jersey and upstate New York. A few of the best and most centrally located greenmarkets are listed below; unless indicated otherwise, their hours are 8 AM–5 PM rain or shine. For more info contact the city's **Greenmarket Program** (130 E. 16th St., NY 10003, tel. 212/477–3220).

Though you wouldn't expect it in a city where cigarettes and coffee qualify as "lunch," there are approximately 25 greenmarkets in New York, and 10 of them operate year-round.

MANHATTAN MARKETS **Union Square.** This is the largest of New York's greenmarkets, a place where epicurians (including some of Manhattan's best chefs) swarm around stalls filled with fresh fruit, vegetables, meat, fish, bread, and flowers. Look for **Tweefontein Herb Farm** (Saturday), which makes sorbets from lavender, lemon verbeno, and rosemary. On Saturday afternoon between June and December, star chefs sign copies of their cookbooks, give cooking demonstrations, and dispense free samples. *E. 17th St., at Broadway. Subway: L, N, R, 4, 5, or 6 to Union Sq. (E. 14th St.). Open Mon., Wed., Fri., and Sat.*

Abingdon Square. *W. 12th St., at Eighth Ave., West Village. Subway: A, C, E, or L to W. 14th St. (Eighth Ave.). Open May–Dec., Sat. 8–3.*

City Hall. *Chambers St., at Centre St., Lower Manhattan. Subway: 4, 5, or 6 to Brooklyn Bridge–City Hall. Open Tues. and Fri. 8–3:30.*

I. S. 44. *W. 77th St., at Columbus Ave., Upper West Side. Subway: B or C to W. 72nd St. Also: 1, 2, 3, or 9 to W. 72nd St. Open Sun. 10–5.*

Minisink Townhouse. *W. 143rd St., at Malcom X Blvd., Harlem. Subway: 3 to W. 145th St. Open mid-July–Oct., Tues. 8–4:30.*

St. Mark's Church. *E. 10th St., at Second Ave., East Village. Subway: 6 to Astor Pl. Also: L to Third Ave. Open June–Nov., Tues. 8–5.*

Sheffield Plaza. *W. 57th St., at Ninth Ave., Midtown. Subway: A, B, C, D, 1, or 9 to Columbus Circle (W. 59th St.). Open Wed. and Sat.*

Washington Market Park. *Greenwich St., at Reade St., TriBeCa. Subway: 1, 2, 3, or 9 to Chambers St. Open Sat.*

World Trade Center. *Church St., at Fulton St., Lower Manhattan. Subway: C or E to World Trade Center. Open Thurs. (also Tues. June–Nov.).*

OUTER BOROUGH MARKETS **Borough Hall.** *Court St., at Remsen St., Brooklyn Heights. Subway: 2, 3, 4, or 5 to Borough Hall. Open Tues. and Sat.*

Grand Army Plaza. *At entrance to Prospect Park, Park Slope, Brooklyn. Subway: 2 or 3 to Grand Army Plaza. Open Sat. (also Wed. May–Nov.).*

Poe Park. *E. 192nd St., at Grand Concourse, Bronx. Subway: C or D to Fordham Rd. Open mid-July–Nov., Tues.*

St. George. *St. Marks Pl., at Hyatt St., St. George, Staten Island. From ferry terminal, walk 3 blocks inland on Hyatt St. Open July–Nov., Sat.*

Reference Listings

BY TYPE OF CUISINE

AFRICAN

UNDER $10
African and American Restaurant (Bronx)
Darou Minan (Harlem)
Moroccan Star (Brooklyn)
Obaa Koryoe (Columbia University)

UNDER $15
Abyssinia (SoHo)

AMERICAN/DINER FOOD

UNDER $5
Bella's Coffee Shop and Luncheonette (Little Italy)
Dojo (East Village)
The Donut Pub (Chelsea)
Gray's Papaya (Upper West Side)
McDonald's (Lower Manhattan)
Nathan's Famous (Brooklyn)
Palace (Gramercy)
Park Luncheonette (Brooklyn)
Smiler's Delicatessen Store (Lower Manahattan)
Soup Burg (Upper East Side)
Spring Street Market and Deli (SoHo)
Zabar's (Upper West Side)

UNDER $10
Aggie's and Aggie's Too (West Village)
America (Gramercy)
The Bagel Restaurant (West Village)
Bell Caffe (SoHo)
Bendix Diner (Chelsea)
Big Nick's Burger/Pizza Joint (Upper West Side)
Cafe 12 Chairs (SoHo)
Cupcake Cafe (Midtown West)
Eclair Bakery Cafe (Upper West Side)
EJ's Luncheonette (Upper East Side)
Grandma's Kitchen (Columbia University)
Jerry's (SoHo)

M. Bennet Refreshments (Staten Island)
Mélange (Brooklyn)
Moondance Diner (SoHo)
Pearl Street Diner (Lower Manhattan)
Riverside Church Cafeteria (Columbia University)
Soup Kitchen International (Midtown West)
Stingy Lulu's (East Village)
Tom's Restaurant (Columbia University)
Wilson's Bakery and Restaurant (Washington Heights)

UNDER $15
Barking Dog Luncheonette (Upper East Side)
Food Bar (Chelsea)
Johnny's Reef Restaurant (Bronx)
Josie's (Upper West Side)
The Pink Tea Cup (West Village)
Tivoli (Midtown East)
Viand (Upper East Side)

UNDER $20
Florent (West Village)
Good Enough to Eat (Upper West Side)

CARIBBEAN/CUBAN

UNDER $10
Café con Leche (Upper West Side)
La Rosita (Columbia University)
National Cafe (East Village)

CHINESE

UNDER $5
Bo Ky (Chinatown)
Excellent Dumpling House (Chinatown)
Sweet 'n' Tart Cafe (Chinatown)

UNDER $10
31 Division Dim Sum House (Chinatown)

The Cottage (Upper West Side)
House of Vegetarian (Chinatown)
Joe's Shanghai (Queens)
La Caridad (Upper West Side)
Sam's Noodle Shop & Grill Bar (Midtown East)
Triple Eight Palace (Chinatown)
Vegetarian Heaven (Midtown West)
Westside Cottage II (Midtown West)

UNDER $15
Helianthus (SoHo)
Mr. D's (Chelsea)
Penang (Queens)

CONTINENTAL

UNDER $10
Bubby's (TriBeCa)
Chez Brigitte (West Village)
Woody's (West Village)
Yaffa Café (East Village)
Yaffa's Bar and Restaurant (TriBeCa)

UNDER $15
Park Avalon (Gramercy)
SoHo Kitchen and Bar (SoHo)

UNDER $20
Bridge Café (Lower Manhattan)
New City Café (Brooklyn)
The Velvet Room (Upper East Side)

EAST EUROPEAN

UNDER $5
Odessa (East Village)

UNDER $10
Cafe Tatiana (Brooklyn)
Kiev (East Village)
Primorski (Brooklyn)

UNDER $15
Mocca Hungarian (Upper East Side)

FRENCH

UNDER $10
Once Upon a Tart (SoHo)

UNDER $15
Chez Bernard (SoHo)
Jean Claude (SoHo)
La Bouillabaisse (Brooklyn)
Tartine (West Village)

UNDER $20
Florent (West Village)
L'Ecole (SoHo)

GREEK

UNDER $5
Omonia (Queens)

UNDER $10
Uncle George's (Queens)

UNDER $15
Restaurant Delphi (TriBeCa)
Viand (Upper East Side)
Zenon (Queens)

HEALTH FOOD

UNDER $5
Fresco Tortilla Grill (Midtown East)
Joseph's Food Basket (Harlem)
Tamarind Seed Health Food Store (Columbia University)

UNDER $10
Angelica Kitchen (East Village)
Benny's Burritos (West Village)
Candle Cafe (Upper East Side)
Friend of a Farmer (Gramercy)
Herban Kitchen (SoHo)
Le Roy's Restaurant and Coffee Shop (TriBeCa)
Melanie's Natural Café (West Village)

UNDER $15
Caravan of Dreams (East Village)
Good Health Cafe (Upper East Side)
Josie's (Upper West Side)
Village Natural Health Food Restaurant (West Village)

HOME COOKIN'

UNDER $10
Aggie's and Aggie's Too (West Village)
The Bagel Restaurant (West Village)
Friend of a Farmer (Gramercy)

UNDER $15
Chat 'n' Chew (Gramercy)
Home (West Village)

UNDER $20
Good Enough to Eat (Upper West Side)

INDIAN

UNDER $10
Bengal Cafe (Columbia University)
Jackson Diner (Queens)
Madras Mahal (Midtown East)
Rose of India (East Village)

ITALIAN/PIZZA

UNDER $5
The Bread Shop (Columbia University)
Manganaro's Hero-Boy (Midtown West)

UNDER $10
Aiello's (Brooklyn)
Big Nick's Burger/Pizza Joint (Upper West Side)
California Pizza Oven (East Village)
Frutti de Mare (East Village)
Garlic Bob's (Upper East Side)
Il Fornaio (Little Italy)
Luna's (Little Italy)
Mappamondo I & II (West Village)
Nino's Cafe (Brooklyn)
Puglia (Little Italy)
Ristorante Egidio (Bronx)

UNDER $15
Ann and Tony's (Bronx)
Bella Donna (Upper East Side)
Dominick's (Bronx)
Patsy's Pizza (Brooklyn)
Randazzo's Clam Bar (Brooklyn)

Two Boots (East Village and Brooklyn)
Umberto's Clam House (Little Italy)
Viand (Upper East Side)

UNDER $20
Cucina (Brooklyn)
Pò (West Village)

JAPANESE/KOREAN/SUSHI

UNDER $5
Tachigui-Soba (Midtown West)
Teriyaki Boy (Upper East Side)

UNDER $10
Esashi (East Village)
Sapporo (Midtown West)

UNDER $15
Avenue A (East Village)
The Mill (Columbia University)
Sakura (West Village)

UNDER $20
Fujiyama Mama's (Upper West Side)

KOSHER/JEWISH

UNDER $5
Bagels on Amsterdam (Upper West Side)
Yonah Schimmel's Knishery (Lower East Side)

UNDER $10
Katz's Delicatessen (Lower East Side)
Madras Mahal (Midtown East)
Ratner's (Lower East Side)
Vegetarian Heaven (Midtown West)

UNDER $15
Second Avenue Deli (East Village)

LATIN AND SOUTH AMERICAN

UNDER $10
El Pollo (Upper East Side)
La Cabaña Salvadoreña (Washington Heights)
La Fonda Antioqueña (Queens)

207

FOOD

Mambi #1 (Washington Heights)
Tierras Colombianas (Queens)

UNDER $15
Arroz y Feijão (Midtown West)

MEXICAN/TEX-MEX

UNDER $5
Fresco Tortilla Grill (Midtown East)
La Espiga (Queens)

UNDER $10
Adobe Blues (Staten Island)
bean (Brooklyn)
Benny's Burritos (West Village)
Burrito Kelly (Bronx)
Festival Mexicana (Lower East Side)
Life Cafe (East Village)
Lupe's East L.A. Kitchen (SoHo)
Radio Mexico (Lower Manhattan)
Samalita's Tortilla Factory (Upper East Side)
Taquería de México (West Village)
Uncle Mo's (Chelsea)

UNDER $15
Tortilla Flats (West Village)

MIDDLE EASTERN

UNDER $5
Amir's Falafel (Columbia University)
Fatoosh Barbecue (Brooklyn)

UNDER $10
Al Dewan (Queens)
Beit Eddine (Midtown East)
Moustache (West Village)
Sahara East (East Village)

UNDER $15
Magic Carpet (West Village)
Tripoli Restaurant (Brooklyn)

PUB GRUB

UNDER $10
An Béal Bocht (Bronx)
Fanelli's Cafe (SoHo)
Heartland Brewery (Gramercy)
Old Town Bar (Gramercy)
R-Bar (TriBeCa)
Rhodes (Bronx)

SOUTHEAST ASIAN

UNDER $5
Bo Ky (Chinatown)
Elvie's Turo-Turo (East Village)

UNDER $10
Bendix Diner (Chelsea)
Kelley and Ping (SoHo)
Lemongrass Grill (Brooklyn)
Marnie's Noodle Shop (West Village)
Monsoon (Upper West Side)
Nam (Brooklyn)
Nha Trang (Chinatown)
Thailand Restaurant (Chinatown)
Village Mingala (East Village)

UNDER $15
Franklin Station Cafe (TriBeCa)
Kun Paw (West Village)
New Viet Huong (Chinatown)
Regional Thai Taste (Chelsea)
Rungsit (Gramercy)
Zen Palate (Gramercy)

UNDER $20
Penang (SoHo)

SOUTHERN AND BARBECUE

UNDER $10
ACME Bar and Grill (East Village)
Baby Jakes (East Village)
Chantale's Cajun Kitchen (Midtown West)
Ethel's Southern Quarters (Harlem)
La Caridad (Upper West Side)

RBBQ (Brooklyn)
The Reliable (Harlem)
Singleton's Bar-B-Que (Harlem)
Soul Fixin's (Midtown West)
Wilson's Bakery and Restaurant (Washington Heights)

UNDER $15
Brothers Bar-B-Q (West Village)
Cajun (Chelsea)
Great Jones Cafe (East Village)
Stick to Your Ribs (Queens)
Sylvia's (Harlem)
Two Boots (East Village and Brooklyn)

SPANISH/PORTUGUESE

UNDER $10
Café con Leche (Upper West Side)
Mambi #1 (Washington Heights)
Yaffa's Bar and Restaurant (TriBeCa)

UNDER $15
La Paella (East Village)
Luzia's (Upper West Side)
Rio Mar (West Village)

VEGETARIAN

UNDER $5
Joseph's Food Basket (Harlem)
Tamarind Seed Health Food Store (Columbia University)

UNDER $10
Angelica Kitchen (East Village)
bean (Brooklyn)
Candle Cafe (Upper East Side)
Herban Kitchen (SoHo)
House of Vegetarian (Chinatown)
Le Roy's Restaurant and Coffee Shop (TriBeCa)
Madras Mahal (Midtown East)
Nam (Brooklyn)
Ratner's (Lower East Side)
Vegetarian Heaven (Midtown West)

UNDER $15
Caravan of Dreams (East Village)

Good Health Cafe (Upper East Side)
Helianthus (SoHo)

Village Natural Health Food Restaurant (West Village)
Zen Palate (Gramercy)

SPECIAL FEATURES

ALL YOU CAN EAT

Al Dewan (Queens)
Beit Eddine (Midtown East)
Brothers Bar-B-Q (West Village)
Madras Mahal (Midtown East)
Mélange (Brooklyn)

BRUNCH

UNDER $10
31 Division Dim Sum House (Chinatown)
Aggie's and Aggie's Two (West Village)
An Béal Bocht (Bronx)
Life Cafe (East Village)
Stingy Lulu's (East Village)
Triple Eight Palace (Chinatown)
Wilson's Bakery and Restaurant (Washington Heights)
Woody's (West Village)
Yaffa's Bar and Restaurant (TriBeCa)

UNDER $15
Good Enough to Eat (Upper West Side)
Good Health Cafe (Upper East Side)
Luzia's (Upper West Side)
Sylvia's (Harlem)
Tartine (West Village)

EATING AT 4 AM

UNDER $5
The Donut Pub (Chelsea)
Gray's Papaya (Upper West Side)
Odessa (East Village)
Palace (Gramercy)

UNDER $10
African and American Restaurant (Bronx)
Bell Caffe (SoHo)

Big Nick's Burger/Pizza Joint (Upper West Side)
Darou Minan (Harlem)
Grandma's Kitchen (Columbia University)
Kiev (East Village)
Mambi #1 (Washington Heights)
Moondance Diner (SoHo)
R-Bar (TriBeCa)
Singleton's Bar-B-Que (Harlem)
Stingy Lulu's (East Village)
Tom's Restaurant (Columbia University)
Uncle George's (Queens)
Yaffa Café (East Village)

UNDER $15
Rio Mar (West Village)
SoHo Kitchen and Bar (SoHo)
Tivoli (Midtown East)
Umberto's Clam House (Little Italy)

UNDER $20
Florent (West Village)

MUSIC WITH YOUR MEAL

UNDER $10
ACME Bar and Grill (East Village)
Al Dewan (Queens)
An Béal Bocht (Bronx)
Beit Eddine (Midtown East)
Bell Caffe (SoHo)
Obaa Koryoe (Columbia University)
Puglia (Little Italy)
Primorski (Brooklyn)
Rhodes (Bronx)
Two Boots (Brooklyn)
Vegetarian Heaven (Midtown West)

UNDER $15
Avenue A (East Village)
Cajun (Chelsea)

Caravan of Dreams (East Village)
Rio Mar (West Village)
Sylvia's (Harlem)
Zenon (Queens)

UNDER $20
Fujiyama Mama's (Upper West Side)

NOODLE BARS

UNDER $5
Excellent Dumpling House (Chinatown)
Sweet 'n' Tart Cafe (Chinatown)

UNDER $10
Esashi (East Village)
Kelley and Ping (SoHo)
Marnie's Noodle Shop (West Village)
Nam (Brooklyn)
Nha Trang (Chinatown)
Sam's Noodle Shop & Grill Bar (Midtown East)
Sapporo (Midtown West)

OUTDOOR SEATING

UNDER $10
Bell Caffe (SoHo)
Life Cafe (East Village)
Stingy Lulu's (East Village)
Yaffa Café (East Village)

UNDER $15
Home (West Village)
Kun Paw (West Village)
Sylvia's (Harlem)

SWEETS AND DESSERTS

UNDER $5
The Bread Shop (Columbia University)

FOOD

Omonia (Queens)
Sweet 'n' Tart Cafe (China-town)

UNDER $10
Cafe 12 Chairs (SoHo)
Cupcake Cafe (Midtown West)
Eclair Bakery Cafe (Upper West Side)
Once Upon a Tart (SoHo)
Ozzie's Coffee and Tea (Brooklyn)

VERY NEW YORK

UNDER $10
Luna's (Little Italy)
RBBQ (Brooklyn)
Soup Kitchen International (Midtown West)
Tom's Restaurant (Columbia University)

UNDER $15
Avenue A (East Village)

Barking Dog Luncheonette (Upper East Side)
Tortilla Flats (West Village)

UNDER $20
Florent (West Village)
Fujiyama Mama's (Upper West Side)
Penang (SoHo)
The Velvet Room (Upper East Side)

SHOPPING 5

The thrill of shopping in New York City is all in the pursuit. **There are no malls (well,** there is one, the **Manhattan Mall** in Herald Square, and it sucks), so to find that perfect pair of Docs, that discount stereolab CD, or that out-of-print Dos Passos novel, you'll need to be ready, willing, and able to travel the length and breadth of Manhattan. For despite the damnedest efforts of developers, this sprawling metropolis is still just a bunch of distinct neighborhoods patched together into one big beautiful whole.

Some of the more famous shopping neighborhoods include the **Flower District** (Sixth and Seventh Aves., btw W. 25th and 30th Sts.), where shops sell everything from tiny cacti to 20-foot-tall ficus trees; the **Garment District** (*see* Clothes, *below*); the **lamp district** (Bowery, btw Spring and Hester Sts.); the **restaurant equipment neighborhood** (Bowery, btw Houston and Delancey Sts.), with great buys on knives and cookware; the **secondhand jeans ghetto** (Broadway, btw St. Marks Pl. and Canal St.); the **Shoe Street** (*see* Shoes, *below*); the historic **Orchard Street bargain district** (*see* Manhattan Neighborhoods, The Lower East Side, in Chapter 2); the **semicheap antiques street** (Bond St., around Lafayette St.); and the **even cheaper antiques street** (Atlantic Ave., btw Clinton and Smith Sts., Brooklyn), where prices average 10% less than in Manhattan boutiques.

Tired yet? There's more: **Madison Avenue** between East 57th and 92nd streets is lined with the glitzy, overpriced shops of major designers like Giorgio Armani and Calvin Klein, while **East 9th Street** between Second Avenue and Avenue A is chockablock with super-hip, sorta-cheap antiques, collectibles, and nouveau-fashion shops. And on **Lafayette Street** (btw Spring and Houston Sts.) the streetscape alternates between classy antiques stores and Riot Grrl fashion boutiques. When you're done with all that, you've still got shops waiting in artsy **SoHo** and the rich ethnic neighborhoods of **Chinatown**, **Harlem**, and the **Lower East Side** (*see* Chapter 2).

Shops in New York City that close early on weekdays often stay open until 7 or 8 PM on Thursday nights.

Of course, you'll also have to deal with crowds during the holiday season, skirt chain stores threatening to bring the suburbs to Manhattan streets, and put up with prices that are almost always higher than in other American cities (and don't forget to add in that 8¼% sales tax). Nobody said this was going to be easy. So what are you waiting for? Start shopping, already.

Department Stores

New York City's department stores rival the best in Paris. And they leave those of London, Rome, and Tokyo in the dust. At no other stores in the world can you find lingerie displays more overwhelming, perfume sprayers more dogged, or customers (and mannequins) more lavishly dressed. This is, after all, the town where the modern American department store was born—and it all began around the time when R. H. Macy opened a shop on Sixth Avenue at 14th Street in 1858. By the end of the century, the stretch of Sixth Avenue between 14th and 23rd streets, called **Ladies' Mile**, was lined with huge department stores in beautiful cast-iron buildings. Fifteen years later most stores had moved uptown, with Macy's (*see below*) landing at 34th Street and most of the higher-fashion stores drifting up Fifth Avenue, but the concept was here to stay.

You can avoid instant depression by treating an afternoon in the department stores like a visit to the museums. They're excellent for an afternoon of harmless fawning, especially around the holiday season, when most bust out with outrageous and whimsical window displays—like the little nativity scene one year at Barneys, which cast pop chanteuse Madonna as the Virgin Mary and Bart Simpson as baby Jesus. Year-round, most department stores offer fancy **cafés** that are great for latte-drinking and people-watching—just like at the Met and MoMA.

The classiest department stores would never stoop to holding a "sale," but their "price reduced" racks do hide the occasional bargain.

Barneys New York. Barneys has floor upon museumlike floor of beautiful clothes for men and women, including all the major (and many minor) European and American designers. It's not cheap, so New Yorkers line up around the block for the semi-annual warehouse sales (late August and January). **Mad. 61**, the ritzy café at Barneys Uptown, is excellent for celebrity-spotting. *106 Seventh Ave., at W. 17th St., Chelsea, tel. 212/593–7800. Subway: 1 or 9 to W. 18th St. Open Mon.–Thurs. 10–9, Fri. 10–8, Sat. 10–7, Sun. noon–6. Barneys Uptown: 660 Madison Ave., at E. 61st St., Upper East Side, tel. 212/826–8900; open weekdays 10–8, Sat. 10–7, Sun. noon–6.*

Bloomingdale's. Bloomingdale's is to Midwestern visitors what Mecca is to devout Muslims. Its 11 floors of nice but ho-hum clothing and housewares are perpetually crowded with out-of-towners toting Bloomie's shopping bags. *1000 Third Ave., at E. 59th St., Upper East Side, tel. 212/705–2000. Subway: 4, 5, or 6 to E. 59th St. Open weekdays 10–8:30, Sat. 10–7, Sun. 11–7.*

Henri Bendel. Small, chic Henri Bendel is filled with whimsical, expensive clothing like outrageously *AbFab* hats and $150 silk pajamas. The store itself is a maze of tiny rooms and narrow passageways built around a central staircase; climb to the top for a dizzying look at the perfume pit below. *712 Fifth Ave., btw 55th and 56th Sts., Midtown, tel. 212/247–1100. Subway: E or F to Fifth Ave. Open Mon.–Sat. 10–7 (Thurs. until 8), Sun. noon–5.*

Macy's. Macy's at Herald Square claims to be the largest department store on earth, and who's gonna argue? They've got 2.1 million square feet of selling space on nine floors, and that includes a bookstore, beauty spa, estate jewelry department, and two coffee bars. Check out the Cellar marketplace, which sells everything from pizza slices and deli sandwiches to gourmet chocolates and coffees. On the Balcony level, you'll find a visitors center where you can buy theater tickets or ask for help getting into men's pants (they're on the 2nd floor). If the size of the beast's got you a bit overwhelmed, make a quick call to Macy's By Appointment (tel. 212/494–4181), which will furnish you with a personal shopping companion—free of charge, no minimum purchase. *151 W. 34th St., btw Broadway and Seventh Ave., Midtown, tel. 212/695–4400. Subway: B, D, F, N, Q, or R to W. 34th St. (Herald Sq.). Open Mon., Thurs., and Fri. 10–8:30, Tues., Wed., and Sat. 10–7, Sun. 11–7.*

Saks Fifth Avenue. In addition to excellent people-watching, courtly service, fabulous holiday window displays, and acres of haute couture, you'll find surprisingly good bargains on just-out-of-season clothes: Would you believe silk blouses for $20? *611 Fifth Ave., at 50th St., Midtown, tel. 212/753–4000. Subway: B, D, F, or Q to Rockefeller Center. Open Mon.–Sat. 10–6:30 (Thurs. until 8), Sun. noon–6.*

Clothes

Not surprisingly for a city that calls itself the fashion capital of the country, New York has a lot of places to buy clothes. And we're not just talking Jack Kerouac's khakis, here, either; if you want studded black leather jeans, you'll find them. What is surprising is how many of these places are actually affordable, though most (of course) are not. Check out **discount outlets** and **used-clothing shops** (*see below*) unless you're independently wealthy.

One way to buy clothes cheaply in New York is to head to the **Garment District** (Seventh Avenue and Broadway, from 34th to 42nd streets), where you can sometimes hit a few **sample sales**. Besides selling the samples (worn by models) of next year's fashion hopefuls, they usually offer overstock of stuff already in the stores. The best times for sample sales are April–June and November–December, and the best way to find out about them is to look for men handing out flyers on Garment District street corners. Just keep in mind that most sales are cash only, no returns and no exchanges, and that not every designer is as gifted as Donna Karan.

NEW CLOTHES

New York has all the same chain stores as your hometown mall, and a few are actually worth checking out: Midtown's über **Gap** (60 W. 34th St., at Broadway, Midtown, tel. 212/643–8960) is the world's largest—it covers 53,000 square feet. The hoity-toity **Polo/Ralph Lauren** (867 Madison Ave., at E. 72nd St., Upper East Side, tel. 212/606–2100) store occupies a former mansion, while across the street the **Polo Sport** (tel. 212/434–8000) store flogs "activewear." At any of several **Original Levi's Stores** (1492 Third Ave., at E. 84th St., Upper East Side, tel. 212/249–5045; 750 Lexington Ave., btw E. 59th and 60th Sts., Upper East Side, tel. 212/826–5957; 3 E. 57th St., at Fifth Ave., Midtown, tel. 212/838–2188), women can order **custom-made 501s**, which cost about $15 more than a regular pair. They're ready in three weeks, and Levi's will even ship them to your home.

Many young, hip clothing designers have set up tiny boutiques in the East Village, along 7th and 9th streets between Second Avenue and Avenue A, making this the place to shop when you're tired of dressing exactly like all of your friends. Often, the person who waits on you is the same one who drew up the design and then sewed it all together. A few to check out: **No XS** (80 E. 7th St., tel. 212/674–6753); **Eileen Fisher** (314 E. 9th St., tel. 212/529–5715); and **Mark Montano** (434 E. 9th St., tel. 212/505–0325).

Window-Shopping with the Rich and Famous

The couture houses, ritzy jewelers, and designer boutiques lining Madison Avenue, Fifth Avenue, and 57th Street make them (according to the people who care about these kinds of things) three of the 10 most expensive shopping avenues in the world. More costly, even, than the Champs-Elysées in Paris, Bond Street in London, or Rodeo Drive in Los Angeles. Naturally, this is where you'll find the world's wealthiest 1% sucking up the high-priced goodies while the rest of us stand around waiting for some trickle-down. The least you can do, really, is go make some smudge marks on a few of those windows: Cartier (2 E. 52nd St., at Fifth Ave., tel. 212/753–0111); Tiffany & Co. (727 Fifth Ave., at E. 57th St., tel. 212/755–8000); Chanel (5 E. 57th St., at Fifth Ave., tel. 212/355–5050); Prada (45 E. 57th St., at Madison Ave., tel. 212/308–2332); Calvin Klein (654 Madison Ave., btw E. 60th and 61st Sts., tel. 212/292–9000); and Gianni Versace (816 Madison Ave., at E. 68th St., tel. 212/744–5572).

Time your shopping sprees to coincide with end-of-season-sales, which most department stores and clothing shops hold July–August and again January–February, and you'll save 30%–50%.

Canal Jeans. If you can wear it, it's here—and it's cheap. Besides cheap T-shirts ($6) and baggy jeans ($25), Canal offers discounts on cool brands like French Connection, plus military surplus stuff and a ton of used Levi's ($5–$29). *504 Broadway, btw Spring and Broome Sts., SoHo, tel. 212/226–1130. Subway: N or R to Prince St. Open Mon.–Thurs. 10:30–8, Fri. and Sat. 10:30–9, Sun. 11–8.*

Medici. This store stocks hip, dressy women's clothes like you'll never see in the suburbs, from simple frocks to suits to frilly things. Half-price sales are almost constant. *163 Fifth Ave., at 22nd St., Gramercy, tel. 212/260–4253. Subway: N or R to W. 23rd St. Open weekdays 10–8, Sun. 11–7.*

New Republic. Men who want to look sharp but are allergic to cookie-cutter suits and ties can shop here without fear. The fine fabrics and styles translate into steep prices, so watch for sales. *93 Spring St., btw Mercer St. and Broadway, SoHo, tel. 212/219–3005. Subway: N or R to Prince St. Open daily noon–7 (Sun. until 6).*

O.M.G. The laid-back atmosphere makes this a great place to shop for those clothes fashion wags call "wardrobe basics." They've got some of the lowest prices in town on Levi's and other jeans. *546 Broadway, btw Prince and Spring Sts., SoHo, tel. 212/925–9513. Subway: N or R to Prince St. Other locations: 217 Seventh Ave., btw W. 20th and 21st Sts., Chelsea, tel. 212/807–8650. Subway: 1 or 9 to W. 23rd St. 301 E. 45th St., at Second Ave., Midtown, tel. 212/661–6495. Subway: 4, 5, 6, or 7 to E. 42nd St. All open Mon.–Sat. 9:30–9, Sun. 10–8.*

You know that X-Large (151 Ave. A, btw E. 9th and 10th Sts., East Village, tel. 212/477–0012) and x-girl (248 Lafayette St., btw Prince and Spring Sts., SoHo, tel. 212/226–0151) are gonna have cool clothes, 'cuz they're fronted by Beastie Boy Mike D, and Sonic Youth bassist Kim Gordon helps design the chick threads.

DISCOUNT CLOTHES

Discount outlets are the bottom of the city's fashion food chain, the final resting place for three-armed jackets and other designer bombs. To find that little $25 Calvin Klein dress takes patience and luck; serious discount hounds arrive early and shop often. Though it's a trek, **Loehmann's** (236th St. and Broadway, Bronx, tel. 718/543–6420) is a favorite of shopaholics. Hundreds of city dwellers search here for their own Lycra holy grail, at up to 75% off.

Century 21. You'll find three vast floors of in-season name-brand and designer fashions for men and women, like beautiful blouses by Paul Smith for $65 (originally $130), or a perfect Calvin Klein men's coat for $300 (originally $900). They also offer shoes, bedding, and cosmetics. *22 Cortlandt St., at Trinity Pl., Lower Manhattan, tel. 212/227–9092. Subway: N, R, 1, or 9 to Cortlandt St. Open Mon.–Wed. 7:45–7, Thurs. 7:45–8:30, Fri. 7:45–8, Sat. 10–7.*

Daffy's. They don't get the designer stuff you find at Century 21 and Syms, but Daffy's deals in plenty of plain ol' clothes like sport jackets and khakis. Men's pants and women's shirts sell for as little as $10. *111 Fifth Avenue, at 18th St., Gramercy, tel. 212/529–4477. Subway: L, N, R, 4, 5, or 6 to Union Sq. Open Mon.–Sat. 10–9, Sun. 11–6. Other locations: 335 Madison Avenue, at E. 44th St., Midtown, tel. 212/557–4422; open weekdays 8–8, Sat. 10–6, Sun. noon–6. 1411 Broadway, btw W. 33rd and 34th Sts., Midtown, tel. 212/736–4477; open weekdays 10–9, Sat. 10–8, Sun. 11–7.*

Moe Ginsberg. Moe has five floors of men's suits, sport jackets, trousers, and formal wear that's just as good as the stuff at Saks, and at prices that won't kill you. *162 Fifth Ave., at 21st St., Gramercy, tel. 212/242–3482. Subway: N or R to W. 23rd St. Open weekdays 9:30–7 (Thurs. until 8), weekends 9:30–6.*

Syms. Syms is a lot like Century 21 (*see above*), with more of an emphasis on work clothes. Recently seen on the final discount rack: A $5 sport jacket that could be worn *without embarrassment or fear.* Amazing. *42 Trinity Pl., at Rector St., Lower Manhattan, tel. 212/797–*

1199. Subway: N, R, 1, or 9 to Rector St. Open Mon.–Wed. 9–6:30, Thurs. and Fri. 9–8, Sat. 10–6:30, Sun. noon–5:30.

SECONDHAND CLOTHES

The cheapest way to dress yourself in New York City is to get into someone else's pants. Literally. **Domsey's** (*see below*) even sells them by the pound. The flagship store of the **Salvation Army** (536 W. 46th St., btw Tenth and Eleventh Aves., Hell's Kitchen, tel. 212/644–8563; many other locations throughout the city), like Salvation Armys everywhere, is rich on bargains and poor on ambience. But if you like to thrift it's worth the trip.

Of course, the older the clothes the higher the price tag: If it's vintage stuff from the '20s and '40s you seek, expect to pay a pretty penny. **The 1909 Company** (63 Thompson St., btw Spring and Broome Sts., SoHo, tel. 212/343–1658) deals with *luxe* items like vintage cashmere sweaters ($60 and up). A few new-clothes shops also carry secondhand stuff, especially used Levi's; *see* New Clothes, *above*.

Alice Underground. The selection varies at this pair of shops: Uptown you'll find dresses, trousers, suits, and shoes from the '40s through the '60s. The downtown store carries more '70s stuff, plus a frightening quantity of soccer-style shirts. *Uptown: 380 Columbus Ave., at W. 78th St., Upper West Side, tel. 212/724–6682. Subway: C to W. 81st St. Also: 1 or 9 to W. 79th St. Open Sun.–Fri. 11–7, Sat. 11–8. Downtown: 481 Broadway, btw Grand and Broome Sts., SoHo, tel. 212/431–9067. Subway: N or R to Prince St. Open daily 11–7:30.*

Cheap Jack's. Rarely cheap (and where's Jack?), this store carries tons of used denim, leather, suede, '70s warm-up gear, sweaters, coats, men's suits, whatever. For cash-only sales they slash prices by up to 50%. *841 Broadway, btw E. 13th and 14th Sts., Gramercy, tel. 212/777–9564. Subway: L, N, R, 4, 5, or 6 to Union Sq. Open Mon.–Sat. 11–8, Sun. noon–7.*

Domsey's. This legendary Brooklyn warehouse is worth the 20-minute subway ride from midtown Manhattan. Scrap with old Polish women over bins of clothes sold by the pound, or stroll forever through three floors of clean, well-organized (albeit heavy on the Brady Bunch–era) merchandise. Recent finds include $3 windbreakers and $8 dresses. *431 Kent Ave., btw S. 9th and 10th Sts., Williamsburg, Brooklyn, tel. 718/384–6000. Subway: J, M, or Z to Marcy Ave.; walk west on Broadway to S. 10th St. then turn left. Open weekdays 8–5:30, Sat. 8–6:30, Sun. 11–5:30.*

Housing Works. This is the best pair of thrift stores in the city, bar none. You can get a dress for $40 from one of their designer boutiques or browse the racks of cheaper stuff. Donations of unworn overstock (especially from Tommy Hilfiger) are frequent. *143 W. 17th St., btw Sixth and Seventh Aves., Chelsea, tel. 212/366–0820. Subway: 1 or 9 to W. 18th St. Open Mon.–Sat. 10–6, Sun. noon–4. Other location: 202 E. 77th St., at Third Ave., Upper East Side, tel. 212/772–8461; open weekdays 10–7, Sat. 10–6, Sun. 1–5.*

Repeat Performance. As you'd expect from a thrift shop that benefits the New York Metropolitan Opera, Repeat Performance gets good-as-new women's suits ($45) and other high-quality clothes. Call ahead and they'll happily describe the latest arrival of designer overstock. *220 E. 23rd St., btw Second and Third Aves., Gramercy, tel. 212/684–5344. Subway: 6 to E. 23rd St. Open Mon.–Sat. 10–5.*

Screaming Mimi's. Mimi's is stocked with cool stuff from the '60s and '70s, like plaid kilt skirts ($25 and up), Puma tennis shoes, and sparkly party dresses ($30 and up). They've got a great selection of vintage lingerie, ties, and housewares, too. *382 Lafayette St., at E. 4th St., East Village, tel. 212/677–6464. Subway: 6 to Bleecker St. Open weekdays 11–8, Sat. noon–8, Sun. 1–7.*

Smylonylon. It's wall-to-wall man-made fibers here, with lots of groovy skintight shirts, slinky skirts, wide pants, and platform shoes in bizarre combos of nylon, Dacron, Orlon, and polyester. Prices start around $10. *222-B Lafayette St., btw Spring and Broome Sts., SoHo, tel. 212/431–0342. Subway: 6 to Spring St. Open daily noon–7.*

SHOES

West 8th Street between University Place and Sixth Avenue is the city's **Shoe Street**, with more than 20 shops selling every kind of footwear from sneaks to Docs to thigh-high, patent-leather dominatrix boots. And prices are pretty cheap. Try **Bootéro** (10 Fifth Ave., at W. 8th St., tel. 212/529–7515) or **Here & Now** (56 W. 8th St., btw Fifth and Sixth Aves., tel. 212/979–2142). For much less, you can pick up a pair of stylish knock-offs made from genuine 100% "pleather" on **West 34th Street** between Sixth and Seventh avenues.

99X. Seeking the perfect pair of Docs? Check out the biggest and best selection in the city. 99X also has lots of cool sneakers and boots, plus hipster clothes like Fred Perry shirts and flippy little Catholic-schoolgirl skirts. *84 E. 10th St., btw Third and Fourth Aves., East Village, tel. 212/460–8599. Subway: 6 to Astor Pl. Also: N or R to E. 8th St. (NYU). Open daily noon–8 (Sun. until 7).*

Ritz. Ritz always stocks the Next Big Shoe Thing, plus lots more women's shoes that are hip but not so wickedly fashionable they require painkillers and a masochistic attitude to wear. *123 Prince St., btw Wooster and Greene Sts., SoHo, tel. 212/529–6885. Subway: N or R to Prince St. Open Mon.–Sat. 11:30–7, Sun. noon–6:30. Other location: 505 Park Ave., at E. 59th St., Upper East Side, tel. 212/838–3319.*

Tootsie Plohound. This shop's all about groovy shoes—some for work, some for dancing. Most cost $100, but sale stuff lurks at half that price. *137 Fifth Ave., at 19th St., Gramercy, tel. 212/460–8560. Subway: N or R to W. 23rd St. Open weekdays 11:30–7:30, Sat. 11–7, Sun. noon–6. Other location: 413 W. Broadway, btw Prince and Springs Sts., SoHo, tel. 212/925–8931; open weekdays 11:30–7:30, Sat. 11–8, Sun. noon–7.*

Books

Books are a big deal in New York City. Quite a few residents write them, and even more read them. Many of the bookstores hold regular **author appearances** and **readings** (listed in city weeklies like *Time Out* and *The New Yorker*), kindly tolerate magazine browsing, and even offer in-store cafés. Practically the only time you'll need to leave is to change your underwear.

In Chelsea, a half-dozen or so bookstores line West 18th Street between Fifth and Sixth avenues. Elsewhere, along busy streets like St. Marks Place and Broadway (near the 72nd Street subway station), look for folks hawking brand-spanking-new hardbacks (usually publishers' overstock) for a few measly bucks. The whole island of Manhattan becomes one big book-lover's paradise during the three-day **New York Is Book Country** fair (*see* Festivals and Annual Events, in Chapter 1), held every September.

NEW BOOKS

Mega-chain store **Barnes & Noble** (4 Astor Pl., at Lafayette St., East Village, tel. 212/420–1322; 33 E. 17th St., btw Broadway and Park Ave. S, Union Square, tel. 212/253–0810; 675 Sixth Ave., at 22nd St., Chelsea, tel. 212/727–1227; 2289 Broadway, at W. 82nd St., Upper West Side, tel. 212/362–8835; and an exponentially increasing number of other locations) has invaded Manhattan. Some of their in-store cafés have become legendary pickup spots for the city's literati. Be sure to stray from the superstore path—there may not be as many couches, and you might pay a couple bucks more, but you'll find some gems.

Coliseum. Scant blocks from the book-free zone of Planet Hollywood and the Hard Rock Cafe is this great bookstore with a helpful staff and wide selection of literature, nonfiction (including lots of music, travel, and gift books), and paperbacks. *1771 Broadway, at W. 57th St., Midtown, tel. 212/757–8381. Subway: N or R to W. 57th St. Open Mon. 8 AM–10 PM, Tues.–Thurs. 8 AM–11 PM, Fri. 8 AM–11:30 PM, Sat. 10 AM–11:30 PM, Sun. noon–8.*

St. Mark's Bookshop. Neo-beatniks will love the great selection of avant-garde and popular works on art, literature, and history. Young intellectuals should check out the exhaustive criticism and philosophy sections. *31 Third Ave., at E. 9th St., East Village, tel. 212/260–7853. Subway: 6 to Astor Pl. Open daily 10 AM–midnight (Sun. from 11 AM).*

Shakespeare & Co. At this pleasant shop, book displays are always thoughtfully selected from the latest in literature, poetry, and nonfiction. And the staff (full of moonlighting writers and junior editors) has probably even read them. *716 Broadway, at Washington Pl., West Village, tel. 212/529–1330. Subway: N or R to 8th St. (NYU). Open daily 10 AM–midnight.*

Tower Books. Around the corner from Tower Records (*see* Records, Tapes, and CDs, *below*) and just as overwhelming, Tower Books carries tons of books, 'zines, and other word-oriented things. *383 Lafayette St., at E. 4th St., East Village, tel. 212/228–5100. Subway: B, D, F, or Q to Broadway–Lafayette St. Open daily 11–11.*

From latex how-to guides to American folk erotica, Tower Books' recently expanded "Outpost" section has the latest on alternative literature, art, and lifestyles.

USED AND RARE BOOKS

Biggest and best of all the used bookstores is the **Strand** (*see below*). The Strand and most of the other shops listed below will be happy to buy any used books you've got laying around, though the prices they pay are ridiculously low. Call ahead for buyers' hours—and try not to draw from the experience any general ideas about the State of Literature Today. Several dozen sellers of used and rare books are set up on the ninth floor of the **Chelsea Antiques Building** (*see* Flea Markets, *below*).

Academy. Academy is packed with cheap, interesting books about art, philosophy, history, and psychology. There's a long-hair feeding frenzy here whenever they open a new shipment. Across the street, **Skyline** (13 W. 18th St., tel. 212/759–5463) deals in literature, poetry, and used LPs, with an emphasis on the '50s and '60s. *10 W. 18th St., btw Fifth and Sixth Aves., Chelsea, tel. 212/242–4848. Subway: L, N, R, 4, 5, or 6 to Union Sq. Open Mon.–Sat. 9:30–9, Sun. 11–7.*

Argosy. At this tony establishment you'll find an extensive stock of used and rare books, some beautiful prints and maps, and a friendly, helpful staff. The cheap stuff's stacked outside. *116 E. 59th St., btw Park and Lexington Aves., Upper East Side, tel. 212/753–4455. Subway: 4, 5, or 6 to E. 59th St. Open weekdays 9–6 (also Sat. 10–6 in summer).*

Books and Binding. The stock at this large and friendly shop ranges from 19th-century religious texts to big, glossy photography books, but it's heavy on the big, glossy photography books. *33 W. 17th St., btw Fifth and Sixth Aves., Chelsea, tel. 212/229–0004. Subway: L, N, R, 4, 5, or 6 to Union Sq. Open weekdays 9:30–8, Sat. 11–7, Sun. 11–5.*

Gotham Book Mart. Like the sign outside says, WISE MEN FISH HERE. Gotham's held the title as New York's most literary bookstore for decades; it's probably got the best-read staff, too. Check out the stacks of used literature, poetry, drama, and film books, and don't be afraid to ask for a second opinion. *41 W. 47th St., btw Fifth and Sixth Aves., Midtown, tel. 212/719–4448. Subway: B, D, F, or Q to Rockefeller Center. Open weekdays 9:30–6:30, Sat. 9:30–6.*

Strand. The Strand boasts 8 miles of books, but sometimes it feels like 80. In addition to hundreds of rare books, first editions, and just-plain-old-used books, they carry reviewers' copies of hot-off-the-presses stuff for 50% off retail. The $1 and 48¢ carts outside offer selections weird and wonderful. *828 Broadway, at E. 12th St., West Village, tel. 212/473–1452. Subway: L, N, R, 4, 5, or 6 to Union Sq. Open daily 9:30–9:30 (Sun. from 11 AM).*

SPECIALTY BOOKSTORES

The city has several excellent shops for foreign-language books: **Kinokuniya Bookstore** (10 W. 49th St., at Fifth Ave., Midtown, tel. 212/765–1461) stocks books in Japanese; the **Librairie de France** and **Libreria Hispanica** (610 Fifth Ave., in Rockefeller Center, tel. 212/581–8810) stock books in French and Spanish. For works on fine art, architecture, and photography, **museum bookstores** (particularly those at the Met and MoMA) can't be beat; *see* Major Attractions, in Chapter 2. For **gay and lesbian bookstores,** *see* Chapter 8.

Biography Bookstore. Famous artists, rock stars, politicians, dictators, ballerinas, religious figures, and TV show hosts just love to publish their fascinating life stories. This shop sells them. *400 Bleecker St., at W. 11th St., West Village, tel. 212/807–8655. Subway: A, C, E, or L to W. 14th St. (Eighth Ave.). Also: 1 or 9 to Christopher St. (Sheridan Sq.). Open Mon.–Thurs. noon–8, Fri. noon–10, Sat. 11–11, Sun. 11–7.*

Books of Wonder. The friendly staff at Books of Wonder can help you choose the perfect pop-up or picture book for your niece or nephew back home. They've also got a wonderful selection of classic and rare children's literature. *132 Seventh Ave., at W. 18th St., Chelsea, tel. 212/989–2370. Subway: 1 or 9 to W. 18th St. Open Mon.–Sat. 11–7, Sun. noon–6.*

The Drama Bookshop. At this tiny Theater-District shop, you'll find books on drama, TV, film, and dance, and more unemployed actors than you can shake a *Playbill* at. *723 Seventh Ave., at W. 48th St., Midtown, tel. 212/944–0595. Subway: N or R to W. 49th St. Open weekdays 9:30–7 (Wed. until 8 PM), Sat. 10:30–5:30, Sun. noon–5.*

Forbidden Planet. Come here ye teenage Wookies, fantasy fans, and Star Trek addicts, to the mother of all sci-fi stores. They've got new, used, and foreign comics; plenty of sci-fi paperbacks; and an assortment of space toys. *840 Broadway, at E. 13th St., West Village, tel. 212/473–1576. Subway: L, N, R, 4, 5, or 6 to Union Sq. Open daily 10–8:30.*

Partners & Crime. Offering both new and out-of-print mysteries (and loads of British imports), this bright little shop also has a rental library and spooky fireplace. *44 Greenwich Ave., near W. 10th St., West Village, tel. 212/243–0440. Subway: A, B, C, D, E, F, or Q to Washington Sq. Open Mon.–Thurs. noon–10, Fri. and Sat. noon–11, Sun. noon–8.*

A Photographer's Place. This tiny book shop/photo gallery sells new and out-of-print photography books, plus a small number of prints from the 19th and early 20th centuries. *133 Mercer St., at Prince St., SoHo, tel. 212/431–9358. Subway: N or R to Prince St. Open Mon.–Sat. 11–8, Sun. noon–6.*

Printed Matter. Maybe it's not an art gallery, but a lot of the stuff here qualifies as art: handmade and small-press books, text-based objets d'art, and art-related 'zines. *77 Wooster St., btw Spring and Broome Sts., SoHo, tel. 212/925–0325. Subway: N or R to Prince St. Open Tues.–Fri. 10–6, Sat. 11–7.*

St. Marks Comics. Comics of all kinds—new, used, foreign, x-rated, vintage, disgusting, heroic, and weird—make this a must for any comics fiend. They've also got a fine selection of trading cards, from X-Men to serial killers. *11 St. Marks Pl., btw Second and Third Aves., East Village, tel. 212/598–9439. Subway: 6 to Astor Pl. Open Sun. and Mon. 10 AM–11 PM, Tues.–Sat. 10 AM–1 AM.*

Records, Tapes, and CDs

New York's club scene supports an endless number of 12″ shops, and the city's legions of hipsters and rockers and assorted hangers-on keep CD and indie shops stocked with every imaginable American and European release. On **Bleecker Street** in the West Village and **St. Marks Place** in the East Village you'll find plenty of shops competing to offer the lowest prices and largest selection for stuff new and used. As if that weren't enough, the city's superstore chain **HMV** (2081 Broadway, at W. 72nd St., Upper West Side, tel. 212/721–5900; 1280 Lexington Ave., at E. 86th St., Upper East Side, tel. 212/348–0800) actually ain't bad. For the ultimate overload, try the **Virgin Megastore Times Square** (1540 Broadway, btw 45th and 46th Sts., tel. 212/921–1020). Opened in April 1996 amid much hoopla and foofaraw, the 75,000-square-foot behemoth has been described as the biggest record, video, book, and multimedia store in the world.

So, maybe you're sick of traveling with your Abba collection and are ready for something new? That's terrific, because many stores in the city buy used CDs. The going rate is $3–$5 per (resellable) disc, and trade value is usually 10%–20% more than cash value. **Venus Records** (*see below*) has a reputation for good prices and fair trades.

Academy. In Academy's well-organized bins of used records and CDs you'll find tons of bargains on classical music, rock, and jazz. Almost everything is less than $10. *12 W. 18th St., btw Fifth and Sixth Aves., Chelsea, tel. 212/242–4848. Subway: L, N, R, 4, 5, or 6 to Union Sq. Open Mon.–Sat. 9:30–9, Sun. 11–7.*

Adult Crash. Every new independent release on the planet is here on CD, LP, and 7″. The hipper-than-thou atmosphere can be a little chilly, and prices are definitely not discount. *66 Ave. A, btw E. 4th and 5th Sts., East Village, tel. 212/387–0558. Subway: F to Second Ave. Open Sun.–Thurs. noon–11, Fri. and Sat. noon–midnight.*

Bleecker Bob's. Your prototypical New York record store, this place is cluttered with nasty rock and roll and punk (including some rare older stuff) and rock junk like stickers and T-shirts. *118 W. 3rd St., btw Sixth Ave. and MacDougal St., West Village, tel. 212/475–9677. Subway: A, B, C, D, E, F, or Q to Washington Sq. Open Sun.–Thurs. noon–1 AM, Fri. and Sat. noon–3 AM.*

Dance Tracks. You've got two big couches for chillin' and four turntables for sampling the wares: 12″ house, plus some hip-hop, soul, and ambient. *91 E. 3rd St., at First Ave., East Village, tel. 212/260–8729. Subway: F to Second Ave. Open weekdays noon–9 (Fri. until 10), Sat. noon–8, Sun. 1–6:30.*

From the Department of Recent Weird Celebrity Sightings: rocker David Lee Roth at Footlight Records buying biker movies and Fellini soundtracks.

Footlight. Movie and Broadway soundtracks, R&B, jazz, big band, and early rock and roll await at this used vinyl/new CD shop. The good stuff's more than $10. The rest is $2. *113 E. 12th St., btw Third and Fourth Aves., East Village, tel. 212/533–1572. Subway: L, N, R, 4, 5, or 6 to Union Sq. Open weekdays 11–7, Sat. 10–6, Sun. noon–5.*

Generation. Most people come here for the astounding collection of live bootlegs, covering bands from Pavement to White Zombie. *210 Thompson St., btw Bleecker and W. Houston Sts., West Village, tel. 212/254–1100. Subway: A, B, C, D, E, F, or Q to Washington Sq. Open Mon.–Thurs. 11–10, Fri.–Sat. 11–midnight, Sun. noon–10.*

Gryphon. You might, understandably, find a room packed with 90,000 LPs (many classical) overwhelming. But give the staff a few minutes and they'll unearth that rare recording you've been seeking. *251 W. 72nd St., Suite 2F, btw West End Ave. and Broadway, tel. 212/874–1588. Subway: 1, 2, 3, or 9 to W. 72nd St. Open Mon.–Sat. 11–7, Sun. noon–6.*

Kim's Underground/Kim's Video & Audio/Mondo Kim's. These three shops (attached to the Village's favorite video-rental stores) stock well-priced indie rock CDs, LPs, and 7″s. Don't think your taste's too obscure—if you've heard it, they have it. *Kim's Underground: 133 Bleecker St., at La Guardia Pl., West Village, tel. 212/260–1010. Subway: A, B, C, D, E, F, or Q to Washington Sq. Open daily 9 AM–midnight. Kim's Video & Audio: 350 Bleecker, at W. 10th St., West Village, tel. 212/675–8996. Subway: 1 or 9 to Christopher St. (Sheridan Sq.). Open daily 9 AM–midnight. Mondo Kim's: 6 St. Marks Pl., at 3rd Ave., East Village, tel. 212/505–0311. Subway: N or R to E. 8th St. or 6 to Astor Pl. Open daily 9 AM–midnight.*

Rebel Rebel. All your American and Brit rock, techno, and dance faves are here on new and used vinyl, 12″s, and CDs. There's some great acid jazz, too. *319 Bleecker St., btw Grove and Christopher Sts., West Village, tel. 212/989–0770. Subway: A, B, C, D, E, F, or Q to Washington Sq. Open Mon.–Wed. 12:30–8, Thurs.–Sat. 12:30–9, Sun. 12:30–7.*

Rocks in Your Head. An entire section of this store is devoted to '70s art rock. No kidding. They've also got indie rock and classic soul, with some surf, dub, and international thrown in. *157 Prince St., btw Thompson St. and W. Broadway, SoHo, tel. 212/475–6729. Subway: N or R to Prince St. Open Mon.–Thurs. noon–9, Fri. and Sat. noon–10, Sun. 1–9.*

Sounds. Sounds is heavy on hipster rock, jazz, hip-hop, and dance; new releases are always priced $2–$3 below the competition. They only accept cash. *16 St. Marks Pl., btw Second and Third Aves., East Village, tel. 212/598–4459. Subway: 6 to Astor Pl. Open Mon.–Thurs. noon–10, Fri. and Sat. noon–11, Sun. noon–9.*

Changing trains at Times Square? Pop into Record Mart (1470 Broadway, in Times Sq. subway station, tel. 212/840–0580) for Latin and Caribbean recordings as you fly between the 1/9 and the N/R.

Throb. From jungle to techno to trip-hop to ambient, this small store stocks it all on CDs and 12"s. At your service are two turntables and a CD player. *211 E. 14th St., btw Second and Third Aves., East Village, tel. 212/533–2328. Subway: L, N, R, 4, 5, or 6 to Union Sq. Open Mon.–Sat. noon–9, Sun. 1–7.*

Tower Records. This is just like the Tower Records in your hometown, except it's bigger and more crowded. *692 Broadway, at E. 4th St., West Village, tel. 212/505–1500. Subway: N or R to E. 8th St. (NYU). Open daily 9 AM–midnight.*

Venus Records. Venus is the best in the East Village for recent CDs and unused promos. They carry indie rock, acid jazz, hip-hop, techno, and a ton of used '80s vinyl. *13 St. Marks Pl., btw Second and Third Aves., East Village, tel. 212/598–4459. Subway: 6 to Astor Pl. Open Sun.–Thurs. noon–8, Fri. and Sat. noon–11.*

Vinylmania. For serious DJ types, this is *the* place to buy groovy dance 12"s. *41 Carmine St., btw Sixth Ave. and Seventh Ave. S, West Village, tel. 212/924–3309. Subway: A, B, C, D, E, F, or Q to Washington Sq. Open weekdays 11–9, weekends 11–7.*

Household Furnishings

The stores listed below are just a smattering of what New York has to offer in the way of beautiful furniture and linens and housewares 'n' stuff for your home or (more likely) your squalid, cramped apartment. Should none of these tickle your fancy, wander East 9th Street in the East Village—or just about anywhere in SoHo—where cool new purveyors of knickknacks are always setting up shop. And don't forget to check the curbsides in your wanderings: People will throw anything out in New York, like perfect Art Deco love seats, unopened bottles of wine, and, according to legend, a Jean Michel Basquiat painting presumably worth millions. If you're determined, you can furnish an entire apartment with castaways found on the streets.

For peddlers of homey stuff cheap and used, New York City has several options: **Housing Works**, **Repeat Performance**, and **Salvation Army** (*see* Secondhand Clothing, *above*). At Housing Works, you'll find lots of housewares, as well as appealing tables ($20) and sofas ($100–$150). Repeat Performance is always full of well-priced, clean furniture from the 1980s (i.e., chunky and ugly), and has a small but good selection of housewares. Salvation Army's got the usual array of ugly chairs and veneered coffee tables; occasional surprises include pleasant couches for less than $100. You can also find home-furnishing bargains at flea markets (*see below*) and auction houses (*see box, below*).

If you're into feathering your nest with a decidedly Scandinavian flavor, there're plenty of cheap but bland options at superstore IKEA: In Manhattan, the **IKEA Outpost** (135 E. 57th St., at Lexington Ave., Midtown, tel. 212/308–4532) focuses on a different section of the house (e.g., kitchens or bathrooms) every two months. You can also catch a free **IKEA shuttle bus** to the behemoth IKEA warehouse store in Elizabeth, New Jersey. Shuttles depart from the IKEA Marketing Outpost weekends 11–6; pick up a shuttle pass inside the store.

ABC Carpet & Home. Exquisite (and expensive) new and antique furniture, lamps, linens, rugs, and bric-a-brac are displayed in heaps and jumbles at this vast household emporium masquerading as a dowager queen's attic. *888 Broadway, at E. 19th St., Gramercy, tel. 212/473–3000. Subway: L, N, R, 4, 5, or 6 to Union Sq. Open weekdays 10–8, Sat. 10–7, Sun. 11–6:30.*

The Apartment Store. The things in this gallery store—whimsical chairs, hockey stick–size spatulas, alien lamps—are created by artists and can double as art. *548 Broadway, btw Spring and Broome Sts., SoHo, tel. 212/066–7745. Subway: N or R to Prince St. Open Tues.–Thurs. 10–6, Fri. and Sat. 11–8.*

The Apartment Store is for that special, trend-defying individual who likes furniture made of whiskey bottles.

DOM. The translucent plastic lamps ($30), hanging bead curtains, and futuristic, chrome-intensive housewares at DOM are guaranteed to please your sassy, postmodernist friends. *382 W. Broadway, btw Spring and Broome Sts., SoHo, tel. 212/334–5580. Subway: N or R to Prince St. Open Sun.–Fri. 11–8, Sat. 11 AM–midnight.*

Fish's Eddy. This hip citywide chain sells leftover custom china from big corporations like Chrysler. They've also got lots of weird pieces like finger bowls and porcelain glove molds. At the Hudson Street store everything is 50% off. *551 Hudson St., at Perry St., West Village, tel. 212/627–3956. Subway: 1 or 9 to Christopher St. (Sheridan Sq.). Open daily noon–9 (Sun. until 7). Other locations: 889 Broadway, at E. 19th St., Gramercy, tel. 212/420–9020; open weekdays 10–9, Sat. 10–8, Sun. 11–7. 2176 Broadway, at W. 77th St., Upper West Side, tel. 212/873–8819; open Mon.–Sat. 10–9, Sun. 11–7.*

Sammy's. Sammy's is crammed with secondhand oddities and antiques, from crystal doorknobs ($18–$23 per pair) to medicine cabinets to the occasional suit of armor. *484 Broome St., btw W. Broadway and Wooster St., SoHo, tel. 212/343–2357. Subway: A, C, or E to Canal St. Open Tues.–Sat. noon–6, Sun. noon–5.*

Bidding for Fun and Furniture

New York's auction houses are great spectacles, and the cheaper ones are even smart places to shop. Sales are advertised in Friday's "Weekend" and Sunday's "Arts & Leisure" sections of the "New York Times"; most houses hold auctions several times a month. Your strategy should include checking out the merchandise during the preview (a few days before the sale) and setting a limit for yourself (in case bidding gets hairy). If you do want to bid, be aggressive, as the pace can be very quick.

- *Tepper Galleries. You'll find real bargains at this no-frills joint dealing in everything from furniture to furs to really ugly sculptures of elephants. Stuff goes for as little as $25. 110 E. 25th St., near Park Ave. S, Gramercy, tel. 212/677–5300.*

- *William Doyle Galleries. Though their main auction room deals with stuff you can't afford, at Doyle's twice-a-month "Treasure Auctions" you can score quality sofas for $50 and '50s dresses for $20. 175 E. 87th St., near Lexington Ave., Upper East Side, tel. 212/427–2730.*

- *Christie's East and Sotheby's Arcade. The second-string divisions of the city's two famous auction houses are still pretty pricey, with furniture, decorative arts, and paintings starting around $200. But if you've moved beyond milk crates, they can't be beat. Christie's East: 219 E. 67th St., btw Second and Third Aves., Upper East Side, tel. 212/606–0400. Sotheby's Arcade: 1334 York Ave., at E. 72nd St., Upper East Side, tel. 212/606–7000.*

Terra Verde. Eco-friendly furniture, sheets, towels, toys, soaps, and household cleaning products fill this airy "ecological department store," where even the selection of menstrual pads are washable and landfill friendly. *120 Wooster St., btw Prince and Spring Sts., SoHo, tel. 212/925–4533. Subway: N or R to Prince St. Open Mon.–Sat. 11–7, Sun. noon–6.*

Williams-Sonoma Outlet Center. Seconds, returns, and overstocks from Williams-Sonoma, Pottery Barn, Hold Everything, Gardener's Eden, and Chambers include essentials like glassware, dishes, cookware, and cardboard dressers at 30%–70% off original prices. They occasionally get furniture and linens, too. *231 Tenth Ave., btw W. 23rd and 24th Sts., Chelsea, tel. 212/206–8118. Subway: A, C, or E to W. 23rd St. Open daily 11–6 (weekends until 5).*

Zona. From wrought-iron candlesticks to dining tables, the housewares and furniture at Zona are simply beautiful. You'll buy them even if you don't need them. *99 Greene St., btw Prince and Spring Sts., SoHo, tel. 212/925–6750. Subway: N or R to Prince St. Open Mon.–Sat. 11:30–6:30 (Thurs. until 7), Sun. noon–6.*

Specialty Stores

CAMERAS **47th Street Photo.** Though the name is misleading (it moved from 47th to 45th Street in 1995), this reliable shop has great prices on computers and stereos as well as cameras. *115 W. 45th St., btw Sixth Ave. and Broadway, Midtown, tel. 212/921–1287. Subway: N or R to W. 49th St. Open Mon.–Wed. 8:30–7, Thurs. 8:30–8, Fri. 8:30–2, Sun. 10–5.*

COSMETICS AND BODY PRODUCTS **Cosmetic Show.** This place carries famous-name perfumes and cosmetics at unbeatable discounts, plus department store rejects like Sexation perfume and *Beverly Hills 90210* lip gloss. *919 Third Ave., at E. 56th St., Midtown, tel. 212/750–8418. Subway: 4, 5, or 6 to E. 59th St. Open weekdays 8–7, Sat. 10–5, Sun. 11–5.*

Kiehl's. Makeup artists and fashion editors swear by Kiehl's own line of shampoos, soaps, and cosmetics. And the friendly staff can answer all your itching, burning skin-care questions. *109 Third Ave., btw E. 13th and 14th Sts., East Village, tel. 212/677–3171. Subway: L, N, R, 4, 5, or 6 to Union Sq. Open weekdays 10–6:30, Sat. 10–6.*

HERBAL MEDICINE **C. O. Bigelow Chemists.** From their stock of more than 700 remedies—like pulsatilla (a kind of flower) for cold symptoms—this 150-year-old homeopathic drug store can cure whatever ails you. *414 Sixth Ave., at W. 9th St., West Village, tel. 212/533–2700. Subway: F to W. 14th St. Open weekdays 9–9, Sat. 10–7, Sun. 10–5:30.*

Enchantments. Come to this aromatic little shop for lots of friendly advice on how to heal, change, or reach the goddess; and to stock up on incense, crystals, herbal tonics, and essential oils. *341 E. 9th St., btw First and Second Aves., East Village, tel. 212/228–4394. Subway: 6 to Astor Pl. Open Mon.–Sat. noon–9, Sun. 1–8.*

KITSCH-O-RAMA **Little Rickie.** Little Rickie is all about weird toys and kitsch items like Elvis air fresheners, magnetic poetry kits (great for composing odes on the refrigerator door), and St. Theresa commemorative spoons. *49½ First Ave., at E. 3rd St., East Village, tel. 212/505–6467. Subway: F to Second Ave. Open Mon.–Sat. 11–8, Sun. noon–7.*

For a cool souvenir, pop into the black-and-white photo booth at Little Rickie. For $2 you get four pictures of you 'n' your buds.

Love Saves the Day. At Love Saves the Day, you'll find all your old toys from the '60s and '70s, like the *Charlie's Angels* board game ($39), the Bionic Woman, and '60s Barbie dolls ($1.95 and up). *119 Second Ave., E. 7th St., East Village, tel. 212/228–3802. Subway: 6 to Astor Pl. Open daily noon–9.*

PAPER, CARDS, AND STATIONERY **Kate's Paperie.** From wrapping paper and handmade stationery to hatboxes, if it's made of paper, then this shop sells it. *561 Broadway, at Prince St., SoHo, tel. 212/941–9816. Subway: N or R to Prince St. Open weekdays 10:30–7, Sat. 10–6, Sun. noon–6. Other location: 8 W. 13th St., at Fifth Ave., West Village, tel. 212/633–0570; open weekdays 10–7, Sat. 10–6.*

SEX ACCESSORIES **Condomania.** If your condom-buying experiences have been previously limited to a few furtive moments in the local drug store, Condomania's selection of more than 100 (including glow-in-the-dark condoms and "Moby Dick" condoms) should rock your world. *351 Bleecker St., at W. 10th St., West Village, tel. 212/691–9442. Subway: 1 or 9 to Christopher St. (Sheridan Sq.). Open daily 11–10:45 (Fri. and Sat. until 11:45).*

TATTOOS AND PIERCINGS **East Side Inc.** Satisfied customers at this superior East Village tattoo parlor include Ace Frehley of the '70s glam-band Kiss. Note: They won't give out their address unless you have an appointment, so call in advance. *Tel. 212/388–0693. Open Tues.–Sat. noon–8.*

Gauntlet. This no-attitude shop has been doing the three N's—noses ($25), nipples ($35), and navels ($35)—for more than two decades. They pierce other body parts, too—just ask. *144 Fifth Ave., at 19th St., 2nd Floor, Chelsea, tel. 212/229–0180. Subway: N or R to W. 23rd St. Open Sat.–Weds. 12:30–7:30, Thurs. and Fri. 2–9 PM.*

TOYS AND GAMES **F.A.O. Schwarz.** If life is not like a giant toy store, at least F.A.O. Schwarz is. The world-famous toy-o-rama is as expensive and crowded as it is cool. *767 Fifth Ave., at 58th St., Midtown, tel. 212/644–9400. Subway: N, R, 4, 5, or 6 to E. 59th St. Open Mon.–Sat. 10–6 (Thurs. until 8), Sun. 11–6.*

Game Show. From "Careers" to Chinese checkers to "Post Office," Game Show has all the board games, backgammon sets, and fancy dice you'll ever need. And then some. *474 Sixth Ave., btw W. 12th and 13th Sts., West Village, tel. 212/633–6328. Subway: F or L to W. 14th St. (Sixth Ave.). Open Mon.–Sat. noon–7 (Thurs. until 8), Sun. noon–5. Other location: 1240 Lexington Ave., btw. E. 83rd and 84th Sts., Upper East Side, tel. 212/472–8011; open Mon.–Sat. 11–6 (Thurs. until 7), Sun. noon–5.*

ONE·OF·A·KINDS **The How To Video Source.** Whatever you're doing you could probably do just a little bit better with help from an instructional video, like *Handgun Basics, Intense Rock,* or *Making Sex Fun (With Games and Toys). 953 Third Ave., at E. 57th St., Midtown, tel. 212/486–8155. Subway: N, R, 4, 5, or 6 to E. 59th St. Open weekdays 10–8, weekends 11–7.*

New York Firefighter's Friend. They sell those famous FDNY shirts ($12–$26) here, as well as books, posters, patches, and hats celebrating the New York City Fire Department. *263 Lafayette St., btw Prince and Spring Sts., SoHo, tel. 212/226–3142. Subway: N or R to Prince St. Open Mon.–Sat. 10–6.*

Flea Markets

The city's **flea markets**, which are good things, are not to be confused with its **street fairs**, which are bad, bad, bad things. Flea markets are held in established locations (usually vacant lots) almost year-round. They're full of stuff that's weird, old, cool, and kitschy. Street fairs pop up randomly all over town during the summer and fall, and no matter where they are, they sell the same damn things—block after hellish block of ugly houseplants, ugly clothes, and smelly sausage sandwiches. The street fairs cause traffic to snarl for miles and legitimate merchants to lose business. For several years now, many New Yorkers have been hoping the street fairs will just go away. You don't want to piss them off, now, do you?

MOSTLY ANTIQUES

Every weekend several hundred vendors from as far away as Pennsylvania unpack their wares around the intersection of **West 26th Street and Sixth Avenue** for the mammoth Annex Flea Market (*see below*). This is where Andy Warhol used to show up in his black limousine. This is where people like Ralph Lauren and Martha Stewart send their lackeys to find all those old saddles and romantic black-and-white photos they use as props. What started out as a single parking lot has at last count grown to four lots plus three buildings.

Look no farther than Fabulous Fanny's flea market stand for cool eyeglasses frames ($35) from the '50s and '60s. Fanny's stand is at The Garage (25th St., west of Sixth Ave.) on Saturdays and The Annex (outdoors, on the corner of Sixth Ave. and 25th St.) on Sundays.

ANNEX ANTIQUES FAIR AND FLEA MARKET The mother of all New York City flea markets now takes up two lots on Saturdays and four lots on Sundays. More than 400 dealers display wares ranging from vintage wallpaper and Fiestaware to chandeliers and mismatched spoons. *Sixth Ave., btw W. 24th and 27th Sts., Chelsea, tel. 212/243–5343. Subway: F to W. 23rd St. Admission: $1 (free before 9 AM). Open weekends.*

CHELSEA ANTIQUES BUILDING Looking for World War II photographs? Russian cookie jars? Or out-of-print Austrian poetry books? This 12-story building is filled with specialized dealers, though prices can be steep. The best bargaining happens on weekends. *110 W. 25th St., at Sixth Ave., Chelsea, tel. 212/929–0909. Subway: F to W. 23rd St. Open daily.*

THE GARAGE The newest flea market in town is indoors, in a 23,000-square-foot, two-story former parking garage. *112 W. 25th St., btw Sixth and Seventh Aves., Chelsea, tel. 212/647–0707. Subway: F to W. 23rd St. Open weekends.*

GRAND STREET ANTIQUES FAIR Good deals and a great SoHo location are what make this smallish flea market so popular. It's heavy on household items, records, old toys, and vintage clothes. *Grand St., at Broadway, SoHo. Subway: N or R to Canal St. Open weekends.*

STUFF AND JUNK

Yeah, yeah, "one man's junk..."—we've all heard that before. In addition to the purveyors of priceless treasure listed below, on weekends the empty lot next to **Tower Records** (*see* Records, Tapes, and CDs, *above*) is a great place to pick up street-market staples like obnoxious and arty T-shirts, cut-rate cosmetics, and handmade jewelry.

CONEY ISLAND FAIR About 45 minutes from Manhattan by subway, Russians and other immigrants set up shop every weekend in the shadow of the Cyclone roller coaster. You'll find true junk like rotary dial telephones, acrylic socks, and signed photos of Hulk Hogan. *Surf Ave., at Stillwell Ave., Coney Island, Brooklyn. Subway: B, D, F, or N to Coney Island. Open weekends.*

I.S. 44 MARKET More than 300 dealers of handmade jewelry, vintage clothing, and bric-a-brac (plus a farmer's market) jam this Upper West Side schoolyard and gym. *Columbus Ave., btw W. 76th and 77th Sts., Upper West Side. Subway: 1, 2, 3, or 9 to W. 72nd St. Open Sun.*

MALCOLM SHABAZZ OUTDOOR MARKET Sellers of African-themed clothing, leather goods, jewelry, incense, and books used to line 125th Street until the city moved them several blocks south to this little plot of land. It's not as vibrant, but still worth the trip uptown. *W. 116th St., at Lenox Ave., Harlem. Subway: 2 or 3 to W. 116th St. Open daily.*

WOOSTER STREET CORNER MARKET Handcrafted jewelry, T-shirts, cheap clothing, and a preponderance of hats are what you'll find on this tiny corner lot. *Wooster St., at Spring St., SoHo. Subway: 6 to Spring St. Open daily.*

AFTER DARK   6

By Shon Bayer, Matthew Jalbert, Amy McConnell, and Mira Schwirtz

Manhattan's nightlife is the most garish, brazen, and brilliant show on planet Earth— and true to every cliché, it never stops. Bars stay open until 4 AM, dance clubs wind down around dawn, and the concept of "weeknight" just doesn't exist. The scene varies by neighborhood. On the **Upper West Side** and **East Side**, you'll find Ivy League grads drinking off another market-driven day. The **West Village** is a center for gay nightlife—even if Bleecker Street near Washington Square is typically saturated with straight, horny, beer-guzzling NYU students. **SoHo** is a Beautiful People brew of dance clubs and funky bars, while the **East Village** and **Lower East Side** are populated by less pretentious packs of the young, pierced, and hip. Whether it's jazz in a basement dive, a crowded club throbbing with a house-happy beat, or a spoken-word show in a smoky bar, New York is where it's at.

If you're new in town, get off your butt and grab a weekly events magazine: *Time Out New York* ($1.95), the *Village Voice* (free), *New York* magazine ($2.95), *The New Yorker* ($2.95), the *New York Press* (free) and the *New York Observer* ($1) all have listings. The most thorough is *Time Out*, though the *Voice* has long been considered the bible of the downtown scene. The *Observer*'s "Eight-Day Week" captures quirky society, fashion, and arts stuff. Note that clubs and bars can draw hugely different crowds on different nights: dykes one day, dweebs the next. To add to the confusion, many bars function as clubs, with live bands and dancing one or two nights a week. And dance clubs frequently showcase live bands. But who's complaining? It sure beats navel-gazing in suburbia. A final note: Wherever you go at night, walk on main streets and use designated off-hour subway platforms, especially if you're alone. Or, better yet, catch a cab.

Bars

In Seattle it may be chic to make coffee into a social event, but this Starbuck's-fueled trend has yet to subvert nightlife in the Big Apple. Whether you're going out with friends, a blind date, business associates, or even your parents, you're bound to end up at one of New York's bars—especially since they're legally allowed to serve alcohol until 4 AM. Throughout New York you can have a cocktail with glorious drag queens, drink single-malt with exiled IRA supporters, or just have an anonymous beer in a dark corner. If your idea of good drinking company is the cast of *Friends*, try the **Upper West Side**. If Dee-Lite or Sonic Youth are more your style, try the **East Village** or **Chelsea**;

For the dope on local gay and lesbian nightlife—bars, clubs, you name it—see Chapter 7.

if you'd rather hang with a slightly more sophisticated (read: rich and sometimes snooty) crowd, try **SoHo** and the **West Village**; nearby Bleecker Street is the place to be if you want to experience New York's version of Collegetown U.S.A.

UPPER WEST SIDE AND AROUND COLUMBIA UNIVERSITY

Theme bars are big with the Upper West Side's post-college crowd. Take a happy-hour crawl along Broadway in the 70s and 80s and you'll visit plenty of alcohol-serving jungle huts, hunting lodges, and surf shacks. Much farther north, the blocks around Columbia University naturally support a number of cheap and divey student hangouts: Undergrads on the five- to seven-year plan pack **Augie's Pub** (2751 Broadway, btw W. 105th and 106th Sts., Morningside Heights, tel. 212/864–9834) nightly for cheap beer and occasional live jazz.

511 Lounge. This swank den has several floors full of upscale types in wire-rimmed glasses. When conversation falters, reach for one of the backgammon boards—there's one at every table. *511 Amsterdam Ave., btw W. 84th and 85th Sts., tel. 212/799–4643. Subway: 1 or 9 to W. 86th St.*

1020 Amsterdam. The snip, snip, snip of scissors has been replaced by the thwock of billiard balls at this barbershop turned watering hole (a few old salon chairs remain). Don't lose your shirt to the grad students who shoot pool here; they play to win. *1020 Amsterdam Ave., at 110th St., tel. 212/961–9224. Subway: 1 or 9 to Cathedral Pkwy.*

Jake's Dilemma. While this Jake fellow wrestles his inner demons, join the throng having a fabulous time rehashing favorite *Melrose* episodes in the roomy bar. On Monday, drafts are $1, pitchers $6. *430 Amsterdam Ave., at W. 80th St., tel. 212/580–0556. Subway: 1 or 9 to W. 79th St.*

Raccoon Lodge. Come to observe wild, rugby-striped Upper West Siders drink beer, think beer-induced romantic thoughts, and drink more beer. The bar itself is an Elks Club knockoff with all the trimmings: stuffed moose head, fireplace, and plenty of scrimmaging for the seats at the bar. *480 Amsterdam Ave., at W. 83rd St., tel. 212/874–9984. Subway: 1 or 9 to W. 86th St.*

Rack 'Em

The city that never sleeps has a couple of pool halls that never close (literally). Tables cost $10–$15 per hour and are usually cheaper before 5 PM.

- **CHELSEA BILLIARDS.** *This classy, crowded joint has 45 pool tables, six snooker tables, and two billiard tables, all spread over two floors. 54 W. 21st St., btw Fifth and Sixth Aves., Chelsea, tel. 212/989–0096. Subway: N or R to W. 23rd St.*

- **JULIAN'S FAMOUS POOLROOM.** *Look familiar? This smoky joint (with 28 tables plus a few of the Ping-Pong variety) was the setting for "The Hustler" and dozens of music videos. 138 E. 14th St., Second Floor, btw Third and Fourth Aves., East Village, tel. 212/598–9884 or 800/JULIANS. Subway: L, N, R, 4, 5, or 6 to Union Sq.*

- **LE Q.** *It has 32 tables and some of the lowest rates in town: $3 per person per hour, any time of day. 36 E. 12th St., near University Pl., East Village, tel. 212/995–8512. Subway: Subway: L, N, R, 4, 5, or 6 to Union Sq.*

Zoo Bar. What can you say about a place that's decorated like the Amazon jungle and specializes in Slurpee-style vodka and tequila concoctions? Try the Jungle Juice or Shark Attack; both come in glasses bigger than your head. *2268 Broadway, btw W. 81st and 82nd Sts., tel. 212/580–0200. Subway: 1 or 9 to W. 79th St.*

What do you get when you suspend a 300-pound mechanical gorilla above a herd of randy young lawyers and investment bankers? Zoo Bar.

UPPER EAST SIDE

Here single yuppies troll for Mr. and Ms. Right–Now in the sanitized Irish bars of Second and Third avenues, like the eternally popular **Pat O'Brien's** (1497 Third Ave., btw E. 84th and 85th Sts., tel. 212/628–7242). West of Lexington Avenue is the land of the $15 martini—don't say we didn't warn you. Also note that during summer the entire Upper East Side shuts down, mostly because everyone is socializing at their beach houses in the Hamptons. So grab a can of malt liquor and pretend.

American Trash. Though true bikers would rather eat asphalt than party on the Upper East Side, this thrashed bar at least *looks* like a Hell's Angel hangout. Happy hour (daily 4–7) gets you $2 pints and other cheap drinks. *1471 First Ave., btw E. 76th and 77th Sts., tel. 212/988-9008. Subway: 6 to E. 77th St.*

Ruby's Taphouse. The two frat brothers who got together and opened this joint are proud to be your buds. They've got 26 microbrews on tap and decent pub grub. *1754 Second Ave., btw E. 91st and 92nd Sts., tel. 212/987–8179. Subway: 4, 5, or 6 to E. 86th St.*

MIDTOWN

Midtown bars are a weird (and occasionally overwhelming) mix of sleazy Times Square XXX dives, swank hotel bars, and cheesy tourist traps. One small comfort: Virtually every Irish pub you'll see is a winner.

On alternate Wednesday evenings, the New York Beer Appreciation Club convenes at Ruby's Taphouse to swill new brews.

44. Don your least scuzzy duds and slip into the Royalton Hotel's outrageously chic cocktail lounge. Must-sees include the padded circular bar and the too-fabulous bathrooms. *44 W. 44th St., btw Fifth and Sixth Aves., tel. 212/869–4400. Subway: B, D, F, or Q to W. 42nd St.*

Full Moon Saloon. This tiny Theater District dive boasts a 100% country-and-western video jukebox, which most customers treat as if it were a dispenser of bubonic plague. A laid-back attitude and lotsa local color make it worth a visit, despite the country tunes. *735 Eighth Ave., btw W. 46th and 47th Sts., no phone. Subway: A, C, or E to W. 42nd St. (Port Authority).*

Howard Johnson's. The HoJo cocktail lounge, surrounded by Times Square sleaze, is so tacky it's beautiful. There is no place better to sip highballs with complimentary egg-salad sandwiches. The daily happy hour is 3:30–7. *1551 Broadway, at W. 46th St., tel. 212/354–1445. Subway: 1 or 9 to W. 50th St.*

Monkey Bar. Take a peek at how the other half drinks at the posh Monkey Bar, which has a big, hairless ape at the door and lots of cool jungle murals inside (bring a flashlight to see them; it's dark). *60 E. 54th St., btw Park and Madison Aves., tel. 212/838–2600. Subway: 6 to E. 51st St.*

Penn Bar & Grill. This old-time bar near Madison Square Garden and Penn Station is not hip or cool or popular—just a terrific spot to wait for that last train to Memphis or contemplate the latest Knicks' loss. *416 Eighth Ave., at W. 31st St., tel. 212/502–5874. Subway: A, C, E to W. 34th St. (Penn Station).*

Pen Top Bar and Terrace. Atop the 23rd floor of the Peninsula Hotel you'll find indoor and outdoor seating with fab views of Fifth Avenue. It's patronized by a youngish cocktail-drinking crowd. *700 Fifth Ave., btw 54th and 55th Sts., tel. 212/903–3902. Subway: E or F to Fifth Ave.*

Sardi's. Come to this landmark spot if you want to be a tourist in the Theater District: The walls are covered with caricatures of past and present Broadway stars. Sometimes celebs even occupy Sardi's red-leather booths. *234 W. 44th St., near Eighth Ave., tel. 212/221–8440. Subway: A, C, or E to W. 42nd St. (Port Authority).*

Whiskey Bar. With the purchase of an expensive drink you get hours of people-watching at this hyper-trendy bar in the swank Paramount Hotel (*see* Hotels, in Chapter 3). *235 W. 46th St., btw Broadway and Eighth Ave., tel. 212/764–5500. Subway: C or E to W. 50th St.*

At the Whiskey Bar, waitresses dressed like Catwoman prowl and purr, while the men are, if nothing else, convinced of their own prowess.

CHELSEA AND UNION SQUARE

Take a look at the crowds on **Eighth Avenue**, especially around **East 18th Street**, and you'll see that this once blah neighborhood is newly hip—especially among gays. The action spills over into the Union Square area, though things here tend to get pricey. At revamped warehouses on Chelsea's western fringe, bawdy crowds keep things going way past 3 AM.

Chelsea Commons. Construction workers mingle with Chelsea dandies at this longtime neighborhood fave. It's got a lamp-lit brick courtyard straight out of olde London, as well as live music on Saturdays. *242 Tenth Ave., at W. 24th St., tel. 212/929–9424. Subway: C or E to W. 23rd St.*

Ciel Rouge. Sip titillating cocktails like Lady Love Fizz and Bitches Brew ($6–$8) in a wicked all-red room straight out of *Amityville Horror*. And don't miss cool happenings like live jazz and piano evenings, as well as the Marquis de Sade's birthday bash. *176 Seventh Ave., btw W. 20th and 21st Sts., tel. 212/929–5542. Subway: 1 or 9 to W. 23rd St.*

Coffee Shop. Arrive way, way, way after midnight to catch the action at this hip, model-owned bar and diner. Attendance is mandatory for club crawlers. *29 Union Sq. W, at E. 16th St., tel. 212/243–7969. Subway: L, N, R, 4, 5, or 6 to Union Sq.*

Flower's. This pitch-dark bar and rooftop patio is crowded with rich and beautiful people. What saves it are the jazz and tango bands that play weekly free of charge. *21 W. 17th St., btw Fifth and Sixth Aves., tel. 212/691–8888. Subway: F to W. 14th St. Also: L to Sixth Ave.*

Rebar. Rebar offers every kind of entertainment except ice-skating polar bears: open-mike nights, stand-up comedy, live bands, and a DJ spinning house and salsa on weekends. *127 Eighth Ave., at W. 16th St., tel. 212/627–1680. Subway: A, C, E, or L to W. 14th St.*

Zip City Brewing Co. After long days at the office, crowds come to this cavernous microbrewery/restaurant to gossip, snack, and guzzle Zip City's own beers. *3 W. 18th St., btw Fifth and Sixth Aves., tel. 212/366–6333. Subway: F to W. 23rd St.*

WEST VILLAGE

Gays and straights, drag queens and rockers, and just plain folks all mix in the West Village's myriad bars and clubs. **Christopher Street** is a center for gay nightlife, while **Hudson Street** is leather-and-chains territory. On **West 4th** and **Bleecker streets** there are scores of cheesy, tourist-filled bars—great if you just wanna have fun with buffalo wings and cheap beer. Otherwise, avoid them.

On cold, wintry evenings cozy up to the Art Bar's fireplace and luxuriate in the plushness of it all.

Art Bar. Sip your scotch-and-soda on one of the plush couches by the fireplace at this popular Village bar. It's a great place for a romantic cocktail during the week; on weekends it's really, really crowded. *52 Eighth Ave., btw Horatio and Jane Sts., tel. 212/727–0244. Subway: A, C, E, or L to W. 14th St.*

Bar D'O. At this dimly lit lounge, beautiful young things cradle cocktails and get cozy on the low-slung couches. On Wednesday nights crooners entertain cover-free. *29 Bedford St., at Downing St., tel. 212/627–1580. Subway: 1 or 9 to W. Houston St.*

Chumley's. Once a speakeasy, this still-secret pub is great for a civilized pint of ale or a debauched night with old chums. To find the unmarked wooden doorway, listen for boisterous conversation and peals of laughter as you walk past Bedford Street's brick row houses. *86 Bedford St., at Barrow St., tel. 212/675–4449. Subway: 1 or 9 to Christopher St. (Sheridan Sq.).*

Down the Hatch. This subterranean space gives half the West Village a buzz and full belly on weekends with their $14 all-you-can-drink-and-eat draft beer and wings special (1–6 PM). *179 W. 4th St., btw Sixth Ave. and Seventh Ave. S, tel. 212/627–9747. Subway: A, B, C, D, E, F, or Q to W. 4th St. (Washington Sq.).*

Hogs and Heifers. Sure, this roughneck bar has seen a few fistfights. But most of the time its crew of wanna-be Harley-riding hard-asses is just having a damn good, hard-rockin', Pabst-drinkin' time. *859 Washington St., btw W. 13th and 14th Sts., tel. 212/929–0655. Subway: A, C, E, or L to W. 14th St.*

Hudson Bar and Books. Satisfy your hankering for brandy and a big fat stogie at this cigar bar, done up like a billionaire's library. Cigars range from $9 (merely stinky) to $16 (Dominican Allone). *636 Hudson St., btw Horatio and Jane Sts., tel. 212/229–2642. Subway: A, C, E, or L to W. 14th St.*

Kettle of Fish. This mellow neighborhood joint draws a friendly crowd of NYU students and others for a few games of darts. *130 W. 3rd St., btw Sixth Ave. and MacDougal St., tel. 212/533–4790. Subway: A, B, C, D, E, F, or Q to W. 4th St. (Washington Sq.).*

Peculier Pub. From Aass Amber to Zywiec, the Peculier Pub stocks more than 400 beers representing 43 countries, including Vietnam, Nicaragua, and the Ivory Coast. The besotted crowd is half as interesting. Pints are $3.25–$7.50. *145 Bleecker St., btw Thompson St. and La Guardia Pl., tel. 212/353–1327. Subway: 6 to Bleecker St.*

Rio Mar. This throwback to Spain sits hidden on a corner in the meat-packing district. Though they stop serving tapas ($3.50–$5) around 6 PM, the bar stays open (and packed) into the wee

Red Death and Buffalo Sweat

Did you know that cocktails were invented in New York? Well, according to legend, an 18th-century New York tavern keeper used the tail feather from a rooster to stir drinks, inspiring the name. Two hundred years later, even bars that qualify as "dives" know how to make martinis, cosmos, and Manhattans. Yet when you need something more exotic and perhaps downright toxic, try one of the following at your own risk.

The West Village's BAR D'O (see above) is famous for its glow-in-the-dark cocktails. SoHo's MERC BAR (151 Mercer St., btw Houston and Prince Sts., tel. 212/966–2727) specializes in Cement Mixers ($7), a combo of Bailey's Irish Cream and Rose's Lime Juice that solidifies after you swish it around in your mouth for a few seconds. Also in SoHo, NAKED LUNCH (17 Thompson St., at Grand St., tel. 212/343–0828) makes a mean Red Death for $7: vodka, Rose's Lime Juice, Triple Sec, Southern Comfort, Amaretto, sloe gin, and orange juice, topped with Sambuca. In the East Village, the NO-TELL MOTEL (see below) is proud of their Safe-Sex Drink ($6), which comes with a condom.

hours. If you're really hungry, check out the adjoining dining room (*see* Chapter 4). *7 Ninth Ave., at Little W. 12th St., tel. 212/243–9015. Subway: A, C, E, or L to W. 14th St.*

The Slaughtered Lamb Pub. This English pub packs 'em in, despite such "spooky" gimmicks as paintings with roving eyes and taped howls that are played intermittently. Maybe it's the 12 beers on tap and 100 in stock. *182 W. 4th St., btw Sixth Ave. and Seventh Ave. S, tel. 212/627–LAMB. Subway: A, B, C, D, E, F, or Q to W. 4th St. (Washington Sq.).*

White Horse Tavern. Go gentle into this good pub, where Dylan Thomas drank himself to death in 1953. A mix of mournful poets and uncaring yuppies carry on the wake at this historic 110-year-old tavern. But unless you want to booze with Jerseyites, come weeknights for a more authentic feel. *560 Hudson St., btw W. 11th and Perry Sts., tel. 212/243–9260. Subway: 1 or 9 to Christopher St. (Sheridan Sq.).*

EAST VILLAGE, ALPHABET CITY, AND THE LOWER EAST SIDE

In the East Village and Alphabet City there are a zillion bars and clubs per block, each one different. And whether you wear cowboy boots, wing tips, Doc Martens, platform shoes, or go-go boots, you'll have no problem finding something suitable. The big new scene is currently on the Lower East Side, on **East Houston** and **Ludlow streets**. Bars here are hip and nearly unpretentious, frequented by Gen X-ers with lots of style and little cash. If you fall into this category, two mandatory Alphabet City stops are **7B** (E. 7th St., at Ave. B, no phone) for cheap Genesee beer on tap ($1), and **Sophie's** (507 E. 5th St., btw Aves. A and B, tel. 212/228–5680) for pinball machines, a jukebox heavy into alternative music, and endless cheap beer—not to mention major crowds on weekend nights.

2A. Take two dark floors and add a few couches, bar stools, and boozy-looking characters, and you've got 2A. Free weekend entertainment includes a bizarre collection of movies and TV clips (*La Strada, Starsky and Hutch*) projected on the side of a neighboring building. *25 Ave. A, at E. 2nd St., no phone. Subway: F to Second Ave.*

Bowery Bar. The celebrities and general scenesters who habitually appear on the *Post*'s "Page Six" hold court at this revamped gas station, though its reputation is cooling—a recent drug bust yielded six arrestees, *none* of them famous. *40 E. 4th St., btw Bowery and Lafayette, tel. 212/475–2220. Subway: 6 to Astor Pl.*

Cafe Tabac. Madonna, Drew Barrymore, Francis Coppola, and Keith Richards have been known to drink at this chic boîte. Drinks are weak and cost a fortune. The in-crowd sits upstairs. *232 E. 9th St., btw Second and Third Aves., tel. 212/674–7072. Subway: 6 to Astor Pl.*

d.b.a. The name means "doing business as," a legal term that reflects the owners' inability to choose a name when filing the bar's paperwork at City Hall. Employees say it means "don't bother asking" and "drink beer always." Which is easy to do with 40 beers in bottles ($3–$7) and 13 on tap ($3.75–$5). It also has one of the largest collections of single-malt whiskeys outside Scotland. *41 First Ave., btw E. 2nd and 3rd Sts., tel. 212/475–5097. Subway: F to Second Ave.*

Decibel Sake Bar. Decibel takes care of business with a small sign outside announcing NO SUSHI, NO KARAOKE. Instead, you'll find 40 kinds of sake ($5–$9) and dozens of delicious Japanese appetizers ($3–$5). *210 E. 9th St., btw Second and Third Aves., tel. 212/473–3327. Subway: 6 to Astor Pl.*

Fez. Brass tables, pillow-strewn divans, and gorgeous Arabic tiles fill this dark and smoky room beneath Time Cafe. Nightly events include everything from big band to hip-hop to spoken word. For big-name bands you should make reservations in advance. *380 Lafayette St., at Great Jones St., tel. 212/533–2680. Subway: 6 to Astor Pl.*

K.G.B. East Villagers saddened by the fall of the Wall (Berlin's, not Pink Floyd's) boozily discuss the state of the Revolution in this crimson room hung with old CCCP posters. It's a favorite hangout of literary types and frequently hosts readings. *85 E. 4th St., btw First and Second Aves., tel. 212/505–3360. Subway: F to Second Ave.*

Lucky Cheng's. Drag queens (and the men and women who love them) fill this gay bathhouse turned trendy Chinese bar/restaurant. On weekends, a house DJ takes over the lower level. *24 First Ave., btw E. 1st and 2nd Sts., tel. 212/473–0516. Subway: F to Second Ave.*

Buy fish food ($1) from the bartender at Lucky Cheng's, a former gay bathhouse, to feed the snapping turtles and koi carp that live in the basement pools.

Marion's Continental Restaurant and Lounge. Discover the meaning of *swank* in this fabulous '60s-style cocktail lounge, a onetime fave of Gable and Sinatra. There's also a signed photo from John F. Kennedy. Marion's is still ideal for celeb-watching over a cosmopolitan or Stoli Gibson. The food is tip-top, if a bit expensive (entrées $9–$17). *354 Bowery, at E. 4th St., tel. 212/475–7621. Subway: 6 to Astor Pl.*

Max Fish. The Lower East Side's trendiest bar is always ultracrowded with black-clad slackers, seemingly underaged skaters, and the odd raving bum or two. There's no place to sit, so everyone mills around like it's a junior high dance. If you want a scene, Max Fish is fine; if you want a quiet drink, go elsewhere. *178 Ludlow St., btw E. Houston and Stanton Sts., tel. 212/529–3959. Subway: F to Second Ave.*

McSorley's Old Ale House. Not much has changed at this saw-dust-carpeted saloon since it opened in 1854. By 11 AM on any given day there's a long line of NYU regulars and curious tourists waiting to doublefist mugs of McSorley's own brew (two mugs for $3). *15 E. 7th St., btw Second and Third Aves., tel. 212/473–9148. Subway: 6 to Astor Pl.*

Diehard geezers at McSorley's Old Ale House still complain about the decision (under court order) to admit women in 1971.

Mona's. The Ultimate Neighborhood Dive Bar is the place to drink and play pool with low-key East Villagers. Crowds show for live Irish folk music (Monday), rockabilly DJs (Wednesday), and $2.50 pints of Guinness (Thursday). The neighborhood isn't the greatest, so don't go wandering alone at 4 AM. *224 Ave. B, btw E. 13th and 14th Sts., tel. 212/353–3780. Subway: L to First Ave.*

No-Tell Motel. Slumming college students and East Village wanna-bes flock to this kitschy nightspot to sin anonymously. Though the bar in the front is cool, the truly hellbound slink into the back room, where couches await under walls plastered with '50s porn. *167 Ave. A, btw E. 10th and 11th Sts., tel. 212/475–2172. Subway: L to First Ave.*

Psycho Mongo's House of Sublimation. The early afternoon crowd here is always a trip: stoned punks with Irish brogues, red-faced senior citizens, and construction workers drinking their lunches. *7 Ave. A, at Houston, tel. 212/533–2209. Subway: F to Second Ave.*

Sidewalk Café. Most people come here to fight over a bar stool, down a few beers, and leave, though the kitchen's open 24 hours. East Village barhoppers roll through around 10 PM and again at dawn. *94 Ave. A, at E. 6th St., tel. 212/473–7373. Subway: L to First Ave.*

Z Bar. If you've got tattoos, copious body piercings, and a no-bullshit attitude, then you're already in the door at Z Bar. Shoot some pool, scan the room for Madonna, get a pint of ale ($3.25), or just crank the jukebox with Fugazi and the Beastie Boys. *206 Ave. A, btw E. 12th and 13th Sts., tel. 212/982–9173. Subway: L to First Ave.*

CHINATOWN AND LITTLE ITALY

If you're looking for an Italian-American watering hole à la *Goodfellas*, rent the movie—you won't find it in Little Italy. Opium dens are likewise scarce in Chinatown. Sorry, kids.

Marechiaro Tavern. Sometimes known as Tony's, this gruff no-nonsense bar is Little Italy's only authentic spot for a drink. Note the mural-size photo of Frank Sinatra and the barkeep, looking swell together. *176½ Mulberry St., btw Broome and Grand Sts., no phone. Subway: 6 to Spring St.*

Spring Lounge. Nurse a glass of beer with elderly Italian men reminiscing about the way things used to be. Or play a game of Q*Bert (if they still have it). Drinks are all under $4. Some people know this place as the "Shark Bar" because of the awning out front. *48 Spring St., at Mulberry St., tel. 212/226–9347. Subway: 6 to Spring St.*

SOHO AND TRIBECA

SoHo is the center of glam New York nightlife, and **West Broadway**'s bars and bistros are always packed, especially when they set up outdoor tables in summer. Along **Greenwich** and **Hudson streets** there are some fine places that happily don't charge the steep prices you'll find at bars in SoHo's center (i.e., along Spring and Mercer streets). TriBeCa has more restaurants than bars, though you will find a few watering holes off Broadway above **Chambers Street**.

Bell Caffe. If any struggling artists still lived in SoHo, they would drown their sorrows in this funky pub filled with lumpy couches and weird kitsch items. Sit outside on summer nights or dive on in for some free live music: acid jazz on Fridays, straight jazz on Saturdays. *310 Spring St., btw Hudson and Greenwich Sts., tel. 212/334–2355. Subway: C or E to Spring St.*

Café Noir. You'll wonder if you're still in SoHo at this chic French–Moroccan oasis: The waiters, waitresses, and bartenders all speak French (and not much English). *32 Grand St., at Thompson St., tel. 212/431–7910. Subway: A, C, or E to Canal St.*

Ear Inn. Rumor has it that this used to be the Bear Inn, until the B fell off the sign. Regardless, this self-described "dump with dignity" draws a crowd of friendly folk to its long, old-fashioned bar for leisurely pints of stout. If it's crowded, head across the way to Bell Caffe (*see above*). *326 Spring St., at Greenwich St., tel. 212/226–9060. Subway: C or E to Spring St.*

Fanelli. This 1872 relic couldn't be more authentic, with its dark wood, chummy barflies, and permanent smell of spilled ale. If you're hungry, the big burgers ($5) and other pub snacks will set you right. *94 Prince St., at Mercer St., tel. 212/226–9412. Subway: N or R to Prince St.*

Lucky Strike. This über-cool bistro has started quieting down now that the supermodels party elsewhere. Even so, its weekend dance parties are still crowded affairs, with DJs playing funky tunes for the young Euro types boozing it up at the cozy back tables. *59 Grand St., btw Wooster St. and West Broadway, tel. 212/941–0479. Subway: A, C, or E to Canal St.*

Match. A hip crowd checks in at this beautifully understated restaurant/bar in between gallery openings, AIDS benefits, loft parties, spoken-word performances, sexual dalliances, etc., etc.,

Disco Bowl

- *BOWLMOR LANES. A cool Village crowd plays on Bowlmor's busy 44 lanes; grab a beer at the bar while you wait. The best night is Monday, when you get disco lights, a DJ, and bowling until 4 AM—all for $10. 110 University Pl., btw E. 12th and 13th Sts., East Village, tel. 212/255–8188. Subway: L, N, R, 4, 5, or 6 to Union Sq. Open daily 10 AM–1 AM (Mon., Fri., and Sat. until 4 AM).*

- *LEISURE TIME. While you're waiting for a bus outta town, catch a game ($3.75 per person) at the Port Authority Bus Terminal's 30-lane bowling alley. Once a month (usually on Saturday) they host a "Moonlight Bowl" ($19), which includes food, cheap beer, raffle prizes, a DJ, disco lights, and as many games as you can play until 3:30 AM. W. 42nd St. and Eighth Ave., Midtown, tel. 212/268–6909. Subway: A, C, or E to W. 42nd St. Open daily 10 AM–11 PM (Fri. and Sat. until 2 AM).*

etc. *160 Mercer St., btw Houston and Prince Sts., tel. 212/343–0020. Subway: N or R to Prince St. Also: B, D, F, or Q to Broadway/Lafayette St.*

Novecento. A lively crowd and good music (usually acid jazz or salsa) make this Argentinean café/bar an adventure any night of the week. The downstairs is spacious and airy; upstairs it's intimate, with deep couches and dim lighting. *343 West Broadway, btw Broome and Grand Sts., tel. 212/925–4706. Subway: A, C, E, 1, or 9 to Canal St.*

Red Bench. SoHo's trendiest (and tiniest) late-night bar draws downtown scenesters, club kids, street artists, and nouvelle hippie chicks. Definitely a place to be seen. *107 Sullivan St., btw Prince and Spring Sts., tel. 212/274–9120. Subway: C or E to Spring St.*

Toad Hall. This tribute to *Wind in the Willows* is surprisingly mellow for SoHo, and completely bereft of talking moles, toads, and water rats. Most patrons drink quietly at the bar and form an orderly line for the single pool table. *57 Grand St., btw Wooster St. and West Broadway, tel. 212/431–8145. Subway: A, C, E, 1, or 9 to Canal St.*

Zinc Bar. It's currently the white-hot center of the downtown social scene, a subterranean space oozing sexy ambience (gilt mirrors, flickering candles, and velvet-curtained walls). Catch live jazz Thursday–Saturday and Brazilian music on Sunday. *90 W. Houston St., btw West Broadway and Thompson St., tel. 212/477–8337. Subway: 1 or 9 to Houston St.*

The Zone. If you have neither a modeling contract nor a demo tape, mellow Zone is one of the best places to drink in SoHo—few tourists, lots of locals, and just the right number of dark nooks. *357 West Broadway, btw Broome and Grand Sts., tel. 212/431–9172. Subway: A, C, E, 1 or 9 to Canal St.*

LOWER MANHATTAN

New Yorkers who work on Wall Street don't stick around Lower Manhattan much past 6 PM. As a result, most bars here cater to tourists (and hardcore drunks), close early on weeknights, and shut down completely on weekends. That said, pubs around the **South Street Seaport** keep their doors open relatively late to accommodate the Nikon-toting hordes.

Jeremy's Ale House. Enjoy two-pint styrofoam "buckets" of beer ($5–$6.75) and the ultimate in frat-party ambience (e.g., stacked kegs and bras in the rafters). The crowd is heavy on tourists from the Seaport, with a few Wall Streeters nostalgic for their Ivy days. *254 Front St., at Dover St., tel. 212/964–3537. Subway: J, M, Z, 2, 3, 4, or 5 to Fulton St.*

North Star Pub. This snug London-style pub is one of the only places at South Street Seaport not completely overrun by tourists. Have a pint of Guinness ($4.25), but skip the greasy, expensive bar food. *93 South St., at Fulton St., tel. 212/509–6757. Subway: J, M, Z, 2, 3, 4, or 5 to Fulton St.*

OUTER BOROUGHS

The sign over the door at Peter's Waterfront Alehouse proclaims it's the home of WARM BEER, LOUSY FOOD, AND AN UGLY OWNER.

BROOKLYN **Henry's End.** Here's a cozy little spot to take a pint after a day's exploration in Brooklyn Heights. They serve a good dinner, too, with entrées around $8. *44 Henry St., at Cranberry St., tel. 718/834–1776. Subway: A or C to High St./Brooklyn Bridge.*

Odessa. Come to this Brighton Beach joint to toss back iced vodka with old Russian men. *282 Brighton Beach Ave., btw Brighton 2 and Brighton 3 Sts., tel. 718/891–3111. Subway: D or Q to Brighton Beach.*

Peter's Waterfront Alehouse. It's not exactly on the waterfront, but the cozy booths, mellow atmosphere, and fine selection of ice-cold beers—50 in bottles, 12 on tap—merit a trip across the East River. *136 Atlantic Ave., btw Henry and Clinton Sts., Cobble Hill, tel. 718/522–3794. Subway: 2, 3, 4, or 5 to Borough Hall.*

RBBQ. This is where Williamsburg artists, too smart and too poor to pay Manhattan rents, get together to talk abstract expressionism. They serve barbecued everything (*see* Chapter 4). *409 Kent Ave., at Broadway, tel. 718/388-3929. Subway: J, M, or Z to Marcy Ave.*

BRONX An Bēal Bocht. The crowd at this authentic Irish pub (the name means "The Poor Mouth" in Gaelic) is a cool mix of Irish immigrants and students from nearby Manhattan College. Offerings include poetry readings (Tuesday) and live Irish bands (Wednesday–Saturday). *445 W. 238th St., btw Greystone and Waldo Aves., Riverdale, tel. 718/884-7127. Subway: 1 or 9 to 238th St.; walk up 238th St. to steep flight of stairs and climb 'em.*

QUEENS Amnesia. Local bohemians gather at this lavender-lit, artsy café/bar for live music (European and house) and loud conversation. During summer its outdoor tables are *the* place to scope out Astoria's streetlife. *32-02 Broadway, at 31st St., Astoria, tel. 718/721-1969. Subway: N to Broadway.*

STATEN ISLAND Adobe Blues. Choose from more than 200 international beers and 33 kinds of tequila at this kitschy but cozy Old West–style bar. On Wednesday, Friday, and Saturday nights you also get live jazz and blues, free of charge. The adjoining dining room serves up southwestern and Mexican fare (*see* Chapter 4). *63 Lafayette Ave., at Fillmore St., New Brighton, tel. 718/720-2583. From Ferry Terminal, take Bus S40 to Lafayette Ave. (10 min).*

Dance Clubs

The city's myriad dance clubs encompass every type of music, fashion, sexual preference, ego, and bank account. Biggies, like the **Palladium** and **Limelight** (*see below*), are fantasylands with thousands of dollars' worth of strobe lights, lasers, and smoke machines, rooms full of foam or slides or bouncy castles, and a cast of characters dressed like space men and dominatrixes. House, techno, and ambient are currently in vogue, although plenty of clubs stick to soul, hip-hop, dance-hall reggae, and acid jazz.

To visitors with small-town sensibilities, the city's dance scene might seem more shocking than glamorous: Cover for an A-list club costs up to $20 (even more for men). At many clubs you'll encounter the cursed Velvet Rope, cordoning off the rabble from celebrities and hard-core club kids; keep in mind that flashy up-to-the-minute style is what really matters here. Age limits and dress codes may be selectively enforced to keep out those whom the bouncer deems undesirable. If you get rejected, don't take it personally. Also note: Unless we say otherwise, assume that all of the following clubs are for people 21 and over (sometimes they check, sometimes they don't).

Some of America's finest DJs tear up the turntables in New York. Watch for Keoki, Dimitri, Frankie Bones, Junior Vasquez, and "Little" Louie Vega, all of whom have strong followings not only in New York but around the world.

New York's dance scene is notoriously fickle, and this week's hottest club may get boarded up a month later. Likewise, a place can host completely different crowds depending on night of the week—drag ball on Tuesdays, punk "battle of the bands" on Wednesdays—or even shut its doors temporarily to throw a private party. And many places are only open one or two (rotating) nights a week. Call ahead to avoid any nasty surprises. Or check the huge stacks of flyers at one of the city's several dance-record stores for upcoming events and—this is key—big discounts (*see* Records, Tapes, and CDs, in Chapter 5). Finally, turn to the **New York Press**, **Urb**, or **Project X** for decent (but selective) listings and reviews; the **Village Voice** is the most comprehensive.

The Bank. Wear black—lots and lots of black—to New York's premier industrial and Gothic club. It's the best place in the city to see Trent Reznor look-alikes getting sweaty in a former bank lobby. *225 E. Houston St., at Essex St., Lower East Side, tel. 212/505-5033. Subway: J, M, or Z to Essex St. Cover: $4–$10.*

bOb. If you don't want to dance, relax; it's no big deal at this mellow club. The music's mostly soul and jazz. P.S.: the bOb in question is a small religious doll that sits on the bar. *235 Eldridge St., at E. Houston St., Lower East Side, tel. 212/777-0588. Subway: F to Second Ave. Cover: $5 or less.*

Buddha Bar. It's SoHo-on-the-Bosphorus at this glam Turkish nightspot peopled with leggy hostesses and expert DJs. *150 Varick St., at Vandam St., SoHo, tel. 212/255–4433. Subway: 1 or 9 to W. Houston St. Cover: $10.*

Club Expo. At this former theater, scantily clad go-go girls do their thing on stage while a crowd fresh from New Jersey stands around waiting for something to happen. Check out the giant pillows on the upper balcony. *124 W. 43rd St., btw Sixth Ave. and Broadway, Theater District, tel. 212/819–0377. Subway: N, R, 1, 2, 3, 7, or 9 to Times Sq. Cover: $15 ($20 on Fri. and Sat.).*

Den of Thieves. They spin everything from new wave to reggae to trip-hop to acid jazz at this tiny, sleazy club. Most nights it's bathed in red lights and filled with East Villagers harboring lurid pasts. *145 E. Houston St., btw Eldridge and Forsyth Sts., Lower East Side, tel. 212/477–5005. Subway: F to Second Ave. Cover: $5 or less.*

Don Hill's. This old warehouse has been converted into a hangout for go-go trash; come for one of the cool weekend dance parties. *511 Greenwich St., at Spring St., SoHo, tel. 212/219–2850. Subway: C or E to Spring St. Cover: $10.*

Jackie 60. Jackie 60 is the famous domain of drag queens who strut their stuff for an appreciative crowd of gays and straights. Expect glitter and spectacle with undercurrents of fetish and bondage. *432 W. 14th St., at Washington St., West Village, tel. 212/677–6060. Subway: A, C, E, or L to W. 14th St. Cover: $10.*

Les Poulets. Stylish latinos and latinas come to this spacious supper club to dance to salsa, hip-hop, and disco. *16 W. 22nd St., btw Fifth and Sixth Aves., Chelsea, tel. 212/229–2000. Subway: N or R to W. 23rd St. Cover: $5–$15.*

Limelight. A landmark 19th-century church turned temple-to-dance, the Limelight has five themed dance floors (cathedral, library, topiary, chapel, and arcade) and dozens of bizarre rooms. The music is different on each dance floor (so is the crowd) and often features a live band. Don't leave without experiencing the foam bath on the back patio or the big bed in the French Burlesque room. *660 Sixth Ave., at W. 20th St., Chelsea, tel. 212/807–7850. Subway: F to W. 23rd St. Cover: $15 ($20 on Fri. and Sat.). Ages 18 and over.*

Nell's. Years ago, this dark and elegant club was *the* haunt of the demimonde. These days a cool multicultural crowd blends in with a few dorks in Bermuda shorts. *246 W. 14th St., btw Seventh and Eighth Aves., West Village, tel. 212/675–1567. Subway: 1, 2, 3, or 9 to W. 14th St. Cover: $8.*

Palladium. Opened in the 1920s as a burlesque house, the Palladium mutated into the Club of the Decade during the '80s (it's where Michael J. Fox bought drinks and more in *Bright Lights, Big City,* and where Club MTV was filmed). Perennially long lines signal that there's life yet in this 104,000-square-foot megaclub. The crowd is a bizarre mix of drag queens and kids from Brooklyn. *126 E. 14th St., btw Third and Fourth Aves., East Village, tel. 212/473–7171. Subway: L to Third Ave. Cover: $8–$15. Ages 18 and up.*

Roxy. Cavernous Roxy has cool raves and occasional live bands—and don't miss the roller-skating dance fest on Tuesdays (gay) and Wednesdays (mixed). Rental skates are $4, blades $10. *515 W. 18th St., btw Tenth and Eleventh Aves., Chelsea, tel. 212/645–5156. Subway: A, C, E, or L to W. 14th St. Cover: $20.*

System. For house and techno, this is the best club in New York. Be prepared to look *very* trendy to get in. *76 E. 13th St., btw Broadway and 4th Ave., East Village, tel. 212/388–1060. Subway: L, N, R, 4, 5, or 6 to E. 14th St. (Union Sq.). Cover: $20.*

Tunnel. Tunnel has achieved the impossible in clubland: perpetual coolness. It also manages to attract an ultra-diverse crowd of more than 3,000 each night. The party ends around,

At Tunnel, top DJs spin techno on five dance floors, skate rats do their moves on the U-ramp, and the bar inside the coed bathroom is its own nonstop scene.

oh, 10 or 11 AM the next day. *220 Twelfth Ave., at W. 27th St., Chelsea, tel. 212/695–4682. Subway: C or E to W. 23rd St. Cover: $20. Ages 18 and over.*

Vertigo. Hip-hop and house rattle bones at this low-grade disco, favored by crowds in XXXXL baggy pants and baseball caps. Special bonus: a full-body frisk upon entry, under the gaze of bouncer-thugs. *27 W. 20th St., btw Fifth and Sixth Aves., Chelsea, tel. 212/366–4181. Subway: N or R to W. 23rd St. Cover: $15. Ages 18 and over on Sun.*

Webster Hall. Even the truly jaded will find something to do at this 40,000-square-foot mega-club. All kinds, from rastas to transvestites, hang at Webster Hall's four diversion-filled dance floors. *125 E. 11th St., btw Third and Fourth Aves., East Village, tel. 212/353–1600. Subway: 6 to Astor Pl. Cover: $15–$20.*

Live Music

Strike up a conversation with most New Yorkers, and they'll tell you about the time when Bono or Eddie Vedder or Sean McGowan, then totally obscure, cruised into their favorite dump and jammed for six hours straight. This is New York City, and you can see the best of everything here, be it cutting-edge indie bands or arena rockers. Bars also host live bands, usually on weekends, sometimes for a cover and sometimes for free. If you're broke, check the *Village Voice* for listings of free shows. To find out what's going on at venues like Central Park's Summerstage, Irving Plaza, the Beacon Theatre, the Academy, and Roseland, call the **Concert Hotline** (tel. 212/249–8870).

Sin City

New York has always been oversexed; in the mid–19th century a traveler from Norway called it "the Gomorra of the New World." Today you can choose between strip joints, 24-hour video booths, and sex clubs. Yes, kids, you read right—sex clubs, dens of iniquity, places where it's actually legal to have protected sex with whomever you like. Rules vary from club to club, so either call in advance or watch and learn. Also note: You can sometimes get discounts for the strangest of things (coming naked, shaving your pubic hair, having pierced nipples, you get the idea), but no club condones alcohol or illegal drugs of any sort. You'll be refused entry if you show up intoxicated.

- *The Blue Angel. This is a strip club with a twist, featuring monologuists, and a, um, fascinating genitalia puppet show. The crowd's heavy on downtown artsy types; Drew Barrymore has reportedly taken it off here. 44½ Walker St., btw Church St. and Broadway, TriBeCa, tel. 212/226–4977. Subway: 1 or 9 to Franklin St. Open daily 5 PM–2 AM.*

- *Pandora's Box. This cozy S&M house offers a dungeon, schoolroom, and 14 experienced mistresses. The location is given by appointment only. Tel. 212/242–4577.*

- *The Vault. Anything goes at New York's most famous sex club. Most nights women pay $15, "single gentlemen" pay $40, and couples who arrive together pay $50. 28 Tenth Ave., at 13th St., tel. 212/255–6758. Subway: A, C, E, or L to W. 14th St. Open Sun. and Tues.–Thurs. 8 PM–3 AM, Fri. and Sat. 11 PM–6 AM.*

Summer is the perfect time for free concerts. Central Park offers its **Summerstage** series (tel. 212/360–2777) from June through August, featuring opera performances, rock, world music, and spoken word by some big names. Past performers have included Patti Smith, the Indigo Girls, Steel Pulse, and Paul Simon. For more on Summerstage, *see* Summer Arts, in Chapter 7. **Coney Island** offers its own indie-rock version of these events every Friday night in summer at Steeplechase Park; for information contact the New York City Parks Department (tel. 718/946–1350). You'll hear the best in jazz at the prestigious **JVC Jazz Festival** (tel. 212/501–1390), held for 10 days in late June at larger venues (with free shows in Bryant Park) and during the **Jazz at Lincoln Center** series (tel. 212/875–5599 or 212/875–5299), which runs September 12–May 18.

Two gigantic annual music festivals give you a chance to scope up-and-comers in every genre. The **Macintosh Music Festival** (July), playing at clubs around Manhattan, features rock and blues by both little-known and signed bands. Two or three computers are placed at each club so patrons can access the festival web site on the Internet for a schedule of performances as well as constantly updated visuals of the action. The *College Music Journal* hosts a major festival every September, featuring college talent, with forums for students and industry people. If you're in town during one of these fests, grab a city weekly for more info.

For big events, purchase tickets in advance from one of three agencies—if you don't mind paying a service charge (a big "if"). **Ticket Central** (tel. 212/279–4200) deals with some rock venues and charges $4 per order for its services. **Tele-Charge** (tel. 212/239–6200) deals with most shows and charges $4.75 per ticket. Corporate monster **Ticketmaster** (tel. 212/307–7171) has outlets all over the city and charges $3–$5 per ticket (depending on the show and venue), plus an additional $1.50 if you charge by phone. The moral: Avoid ticket agencies (and their service charges) by purchasing tickets in cash at a record store (*see* Records, Tapes, and CDs, in Chapter 5).

MAJOR VENUES

Beacon. Built in 1928 as a vaudeville theater, the Beacon has an interior to rival Radio City Music Hall. It seats around 3,000 and usually hosts big-name music acts. *2124 Broadway, btw W. 74th and 75th Sts., Upper West Side, tel. 212/496–7070. Subway: 1, 2, 3, or 9 to W. 72nd St.*

Carnegie Hall. This landmark music hall, built in 1891, features mostly classical and jazz (October–June). Occasionally, major pop and rock acts like Natalie Merchant or Crosby, Stills, and Nash also fill the hall's 2,800 seats. *154 W. 57th St., at Seventh Ave., Midtown, tel. 212/247–7800. Subway: N or R to W. 57th St. Also: A, B, C, D, 1, or 9 to 59th St./Columbus Circle. Closed Aug.*

Madison Square Garden. This giant 20,000-seat indoor arena hosts mega-major rock and pop concerts, not to mention Knicks and Rangers games (*see* Spectator Sports, in Chapter 9). *Seventh Ave., btw W. 31st and 33rd Sts., Midtown, tel. 212/465–6741. Subway: A, C, or E to W. 34th St. (Penn Station).*

Paramount. It's adjacent to Madison Square Garden and handles slightly smaller affairs. Capacity is 5,600. *Seventh Ave., btw W. 31st and 33rd Sts., Midtown, tel. 212/465–6741. Subway: A, C, or E to W. 34th St. (Penn Station).*

Radio City Music Hall. Besides the hokey annual "Christmas Spectacular" and the "Easter Show," Rockefeller Center's stylish music hall puts on national music acts of all kinds. Seating capacity is 6,000. *1260 Sixth Ave., btw W. 50th and 51st Sts., Midtown, tel. 212/247–4777. Subway: B, D, F, or Q to W. 47–50th Sts. (Rockefeller Center).*

Roseland. Tickets for touring rock shows average $15–$20 at this stellar open-floor hall. Seating capacity is 3,200. *239 W. 52nd St., btw Broadway and Eighth Ave., Midtown, tel. 212/247–0200. Subway: 1 or 9 to W. 50th St.*

If Latin and American ballroom dancing is your thing, come to Roseland on Thursdays ($7 for DJ music) or Sundays ($11 for live bands).

Town Hall. This landmark 1921 auditorium seats 1,500 for every imaginable kind of show, from classical to rock to spoken word. *123 W. 43rd St., btw Sixth and Seventh Aves., Midtown, tel. 212/840–2824. Subway: N, R, 1, 2, 3, 7, or 9 to W. 42nd St. (Times Sq.).*

Tramps. Tramps's spacious, table-filled floor is one of the better places in the city to catch live bands. Shows range from record-company freebies to big-name, big-ticket ($70) items. Some shows are all ages, some are 21 and over; call for details. Seating capacity is 700. *51 W. 21st St., btw Fifth and Sixth Aves., Chelsea, tel. 212/727–7788. Subway: N or R to W. 23rd St.*

CLUBS AND OTHER VENUES

ALL SORTS OF MUSIC **Brownies.** Every night there seems to be a different group of people lined up outside this East Village favorite: sometimes grunge kids and New Jersey skate rats, sometimes NYU freshmen, sometimes drunken punks smoking cloves. Needless to say, the music varies from night to night. *169 Ave. A, btw E. 10th and 11th Sts., East Village, tel. 212/420–8392. Subway: L to First Ave. Cover: $6–$8.*

Knitting Factory. What started as a crude '80s punk venue has grown to include two slick bars and three stages. Shows include everything from jazz to punk to Gothic/industrial, with both big names and local talent. In the front room, pick up a calendar of events or buy a CD of whomever or whatever the hell you just heard. The **AlterKnit Theatre**, downstairs, books folksier artists and cool spoken-word stuff. *74 Leonard St., btw Broadway and Church St., TriBeCa, tel. 212/219–3055. Subway: 1 or 9 to Franklin St. Cover: $5–$16.*

Mercury Lounge. Yet another reason to head to the Lower East Side for music. The Mercury's reputation has been built on its eclectic music and great sound system. *217 E. Houston St., at Essex St., Lower East Side, tel. 212/260–4700. Subway: F to Delancey St. Also: J, M, or Z to Essex St. Cover: $6–$8.*

Rainy Days Cafe. Come here because nobody else does. This crash-pad café has mellow live music (reggae, acoustic folk, whatever) almost every night, plus a limited health-food menu. Tuesday is "musical chairs night," with poetry reading and a band. *149 W. 21st St., btw Sixth and Seventh Aves., Chelsea, tel. 212/620–4101. Subway: F to W. 23rd St. Cover: $5 or less. Closed Sun.*

ROCK, PUNK, AND ALTERNATIVE **CBGB's & OMFUG.** CBGB's may be the most famous rock club in the world. During the 1970s and early '80s, it *was* American Punk and post-Punk, with alumni including the Ramones, Blondie, the Talking Heads, and Sonic Youth. It still is a great—if smoky and seriously crowded—place to see a show; there are usually about four or five bands a night. Not to be missed is the graffiti-covered bathroom, which has never, ever been painted. Next door is **CB's 313 Gallery** (313 Bowery, tel. 212/677–0455), serving up more folksy musical offerings. *315 Bowery, at Bleecker St., East Village, tel. 212/982–4052. Subway: 6 to Bleecker St. Also: F to Second Ave. Cover: $3–$10.*

Coney Island High. This is the kind of place that your mama warned you about: sleazy crowds listening to alternative bands singing songs about debauchery and destitution. But how can you not love a club whose bar is called the Detention Lounge? *15 St. Marks Pl., btw Second and Third Aves., East Village, tel. 212/674–7959. Subway: 6 to Astor Pl. Cover: $6–$20.*

The Cooler. This former meat locker (look for stray hooks on the walls, once used to hang sides of beef) has become a slick, black-and-stainless-steel club. It draws a hip and tattooed crowd for punk, spoken word, and the occasional dance party. *416 W. 14th St., btw Ninth and Tenth Aves., West Village, tel. 212/229–0785. Subway: A, C, E, or L to W. 14th St. Cover: $10 (free Mon.). Advance tickets ($6) available at Kim's Underground (144 Bleecker St., tel. 212/387–8250).*

Downtime. There are live bands downstairs, a pool room on the second floor, and a steamy industrial dance floor on top. A big drawback: a crowd that takes Goth far too seriously. *251 W. 30th St., btw Seventh and Eighth Aves., Chelsea, tel. 212/695–2747. Subway: 1 or 9 to W. 28th St. Cover: $5–$10.*

Lion's Den. The Den is a great place to catch a ton of rock bands. It's cheap, and the cavernous space means good views and plenty of room for dancing. *214 Sullivan St., btw W. 3rd and Bleecker Sts., West Village, tel. 212/477-2782. Subway: A, B, C, D, E, F, or Q to W. 4th St. (Washington Sq.). Cover: $3 and up.*

Under ACME. This basement club is slowly building a reputation as one of the city's great alternative-rock venues. The cover is never more than $5, so you can afford to splurge upstairs at the trendy ACME restaurant (*see* Chapter 4). *9 Great Jones St., btw Broadway and Lafayette St., East Village, tel. 212/420-1934. Subway: 6 to Bleecker St.*

Wetlands. This joint rock venue and environmental action center has helped launch big names like Phish, Blues Traveler, the Spin Doctors, and Hootie and the Blowfish. "Save the Rainforest" info is posted on an old VW hippie bus parked next to the dance floor. *161 Hudson St., at Laight St., TriBeCa, tel. 212/966-4225. Subway: 1 or 9 to Franklin St. Cover: $5-$15 (free Tues.). Ages 18 and over.*

FUNK, BLUES, AND REGGAE **The Bitter End.** This prominent blues joint draws a cool, mixed-aged crowd. During the '70s it was the place to see folks like Billy Joel, Linda Ronstadt, and Stevie Wonder. *147 Bleecker St., btw Thompson St. and La Guardia Pl., West Village, tel. 212/673-7030. Subway: A, B, C, D, E, F, or Q to W. 4th St. (Washington Sq.). Cover: $5 (women free).*

Manny's Car Wash. Manny's is your crowded, grungy outpost for blues on the Upper East Side. It's heavy on bridge-and-tunnel types too meek to tackle the downtown scene. *1558 Third Ave., btw E. 87th and 88th Sts., Upper East Side, tel. 212/369-BLUES. Subway: 4, 5, or 6 to E. 86th St. Cover: $12 or less.*

Mondo Perso. Every night of the week there's a different sound at this sweaty, smoke-filled West Village club. Monday is world beat, Tuesday is reggae, Wednesday is blues, and Thursday is funk/blues. Weekend shows are predominantly blues. In lieu of a cover Mondo Perso has a two-drink minimum per set. *167 Bleecker St., btw Thompson and Sullivan Sts., West Village, tel. 212/477-3770. Subway: A, B, C, D, E, F, or Q to W. 4th St. (Washington Sq.).*

S.O.B.'s (Sounds of Brazil). Now 15 years old, S.O.B.'s brings in bands playing African, reggae, Caribbean, Latin, jazz, funk, and soul. *200 Varick St., at W. Houston St., SoHo, tel. 212/243-4940. Subway: 1 or 9 to W. Houston St. Cover: $17.*

JAZZ **Arthur's Tavern.** This tiny club, once the stomping ground of Charlie Parker, has been hosting Dixieland jazz for almost 50 years. The stage is so small that patrons can mill around right next to the performers. Best of all, there's rarely a cover. *57 Grove St., at Seventh Ave. S, West Village, tel. 212/675-6879. Subway: 1 or 9 to Christopher St. (Sheridan Sq.).*

Birdland. A baby grand piano dominates the stage at this chic upscale club. You'll hear tip-top jazz from at least three bands each night. Call for the schedule before making the long trek uptown. *2745 Broadway, at W. 105th St., Upper West Side, tel. 212/749-2228. Subway: 1 or 9 to W. 103rd St. Cover: $12 ($20 Fri. and Sat.).*

Take note: Many jazz clubs are not late-night affairs, and bands typically play from 8 PM to around midnight.

The Blue Note. Without a doubt, this is one of New York's most famous jazz clubs (Charlie Parker and Duke Ellington have played here), showcasing local and big-name talent almost every night of the week. Now the bad news: The cover charge can be as high as $40. *131 W. 3rd St., btw MacDougal St. and Sixth Ave., West Village, tel. 212/475-8592. Subway: A, B, C, D, E, F, or Q to West 4th St. (Washington Sq.).*

Deanna's. Jazz buffs with savvy (and no cash) skip the Blue Note in favor of this club-cum-Gatsby-era-bachelor's-pad, where the crowd spills out onto the street on warm summer nights. The owner, Deanna, is a not-too-bad jazz singer who sometimes belts a few out. *130 E. 7th St., btw First Ave. and Ave. A, East Village, tel. 212/505-5288. Subway: 6 to Astor Pl. No cover.*

Red Blazer Too. Among the uppity eateries on Restaurant Row, this jazz club is a genuine find. Every night of the week, combos play New Orleans or Chicago Dixieland, swing, and traditional jazz to an older audience in the mood for a post-*Phantom* party. *349 W. 46th St., btw Eighth and Ninth Aves., Theater District, tel. 212/262–3112. Subway: A, C, or E to W. 42nd St. (Port Authority). Cover: $5 (free Mon. and Tues.).*

Smalls. Owner Mitchell Borden (a jazz man from San Francisco, and no relation to Lizzie) keeps the coolest joint in the city: Non-alcoholic beverages are free (BYO stronger stuff), and you get two smokin' sets followed by a jam session stretching into the wee hours of the morning. *183 W. 10th St., at Seventh Ave. S, West Village, tel. 212/929–7565. Subway: 1 or 9 to Christopher St. (Sheridan Sq.). Cover: $10. BYOB.*

Sweet Basil. For almost 20 years, Sweet Basil has been winning praises as one of the city's top spots for jazz. Just don't do any talking: Patrons here want to listen to the *music*, okay? Friday and Saturday feature three shows; on other nights there are two. *88 Seventh Ave. S, btw Bleecker and Grove Sts., West Village, tel. 212/242–1785. Subway: 1 or 9 to Christopher St. (Sheridan Sq.). Cover: $24.*

Village Vanguard. The Vanguard isn't a jazz club, it's a jazz institution, presided over by owner Max Gordon. Some of the biggest names in the business have played here since it opened in 1935—Miles Davis, John Coltrane, Sonny Rollins, Charlie Mingus, Dexter Gordon, and Thelonious Monk. *178 Seventh Ave. S, at W. 11th St., West Village, tel. 212/255–4037. Subway: 1 or 9 to Christopher St. (Sheridan Sq.). Cover: $25.*

Movie Houses

New York City is a movie town, and when New Yorkers aren't watching movies, they're making them. Remember that this is where greats such as Spike Lee, Ang Lee, and Martin Scorsese went to school (at New York University) and where dozens of other filmmakers come each year to shoot their next big flick. Walk around Manhattan and you'll eventually stumble upon a camera crew. Not surprisingly, independent- and foreign-film buffs will find quite a few theaters and museums devoted exclusively to screening the cool stuff, both new and revival. For philistines, there's a movie house showing the latest Stallone flick in just about every neighborhood. The going rate for a first-run film is a sky-high $8, though the **Cineplex Odeon Worldwide Cinema** (340 W. 50th St., btw Eighth and Ninth Aves., Midtown, tel. 212/504–0960) shows second-run and non-blockbuster movies for $2.

Call MovieFone (tel. 212/777–FILM) to get theater locations and current schedules, or to make an advance purchase with a credit card—a good idea, since recent releases often sell out quickly.

ALTERNATIVE VENUES Beyond theaters, you've got a few exotic options for movie-watching: The **Knitting Factory** (*see* Live Music, *above*) houses a tiny theater that shows alternative videos and, on Sundays, old or underground films. On weekdays **A Different Light Bookstore** (*see* Bookstores, in Chapter 8) shows films with a gay or lesbian angle. Ever seen a 3-D IMAX film? Even if the $9 films are sometimes hokey, the space-age 3-D headsets are pretty cool; check one out at the **Sony Theaters Lincoln Square** (1998 Broadway, at W. 68th St., Upper West Side, tel. 212/336–5000). The **American Museum of Natural History** screens science and nature films in its IMAX theater ($10, $7 students), while the **Museum of Television and Radio** hosts regular screenings of vintage TV programs (for both, *see* Museums and Galleries, in Chapter 2). Finally, during summer, you can bring a picnic and blankets to **Bryant Park** (Sixth Ave., at W. 42nd St., Midtown, tel. 212/512–5700) on Mondays just after sunset, when classics like *Sunset Boulevard*, *Adam's Rib*, and *King Kong* are shown for free. There's always a crowd, so arrive early.

FILM FESTIVALS If you're in town in late September and early October don't miss the annual **New York Film Festival**, which acts as the premier showcase for dozens of feature films and shorts from around the world; it's also one of your best bets for spotting famous directors and actors. The **New York Video Festival**, founded in 1995, runs simultaneously and features video premiers. For either, check listings in local papers and buy tickets a few days in advance. Additionally, dozens of smaller festivals—like the Human Rights Film Festival, the Asian American International Film Festival, and presentations by film-school students at Columbia and New York universities—pop up year-round. For info on the city's gay and lesbian film festivals, *see* Chapter 8.

MAJOR VENUES **American Museum of the Moving Image.** The museum itself is housed in the historic Kaufman-Astoria studios in Queens. The theater screens Hollywood classics, experimental videos, documentaries, and major retrospectives of artists' works (sometimes with personal appearances). *Tel. 718/784–0077. For hours and directions, see Museums and Galleries, in Chapter 2.*

Angelika Film Center. The Angelika is revered among hip New York movie buffs as a mecca of exceptional independent and foreign films (cult classics screen weekends at midnight). The six screens (some tiny) and cool lobby café inspire lines around the block. The Midtown annex, **Angelika 57** (225 W. 57th St., btw Broadway and Seventh Ave., tel. 212/586–1900), shows the same stuff. *18 W. Houston St., at Mercer St., SoHo, tel. 212/995–2000. Subway: B, D, F, or Q to Broadway–Lafayette St.*

New York's most famous resident filmmaker, Woody Allen, debuts almost all his movies at the Beekman Theater (1254 Second Ave., btw E. 65th and 66th Sts., tel. 212/737–2622) on the Upper East Side. Too bad getting tickets to premieres is almost impossible.

Anthology Film Archives. Anthology's vaults hold more than 10,000 experimental and avant-garde films by artists like Cocteau, Flaherty, Eisenstein, and all those other directors whose movies you've never heard of. It also hosts the Underground Film Festival and part of the NY Lesbian and Gay Experimental Film Festival. *32 Second Ave., at E. 2nd St., East Village, tel. 212/505–5181. Subway: F to Second Ave.*

Cinema Village. This aging theater shows stuff outside the mainstream. It's home to the annual NY Gay and Lesbian Film Festival and a wildly popular annual tribute to the films of Hong Kong. *22 E. 12th St., btw Fifth Ave. and University Pl., East Village, tel. 212/924–3363. Subway: L, N, R, 4, 5, or 6 to Union Sq.*

The Film Forum. The Film Forum can't be beat for recent independents, cult classics, and rare uncut versions of old favorites. There's always some sort of tribute on one of the three screens. *209 W. Houston St., at Sixth Ave., SoHo, tel. 212/727–8110. Subway: 1 or 9 to Houston St.*

Museum of Modern Art (MoMA). The MoMA is a treasure house of films dating from cinema's earliest days and covering just about every country that makes 'em. They have screenings almost daily, and your ticket is free once you've paid admission to the museum. Complimentary tickets are available at the main desk beginning at 11 AM for the afternoon show and at 1 PM for the evening show, and they disappear quickly. *11 W. 53rd St., btw Fifth and Sixth Aves., Midtown, tel. 212/708–9480. For hours and directions, see Major Attractions, in Chapter 2.*

Quad Cinema. Count on funky stuff like blaxploitation revivals and French works on sexual politics on the Quad's four small screens. One recent offering: a film about phone sex by Vincent van Gogh's great-grandnephew, Theo. *34 W. 13th St., near Fifth Ave., West Village, tel. 212/255–8800. Subway: L, N, R, 4, 5, or 6 to E. 14th St.*

Walter Reade Theater. This cinema, part of Lincoln Center, specializes in foreign films and often highlights the work of a single director. *70 Lincoln Center Plaza, at W. 65th St. and Broadway, Upper West Side, tel. 212/875–5600. Subway: 1 or 9 to W. 66th St.*

THE PERFORMING ARTS   7

By Matthew Jalbert and Mira Schwirtz, with Shon Bayer

From Eric Bogosian to the Metropolitan Opera, New York City is like no other when it comes to the performing arts, be it name-brand or cutting-edge dance, theater, music, or opera: It's got all the big names and about a million small ones. On any given night you'll wrestle to choose among the world-famous American Ballet Theatre, the renowned New York Philharmonic, and maybe a few Pulitzer Prize–winning plays. Or you can chuck it all to cruise the alterna-arts scene downtown, maybe take in a poetry slam at the Nuyorican, or catch the Naked Angels' latest spoof on granola-chewing lesbian poetesses. Sounds fabulous, right? Can't wait to see it all? Reality check: These days, a pair of tickets to a Broadway show can cost you up to $150. That's right, *$150*. Major concerts and recitals don't come so cheap, either. And of course ticket agencies like **Tele-Charge** (tel. 212/239–6200 or 800/233–3123) and **Ticketmaster** (tel. 212/307–4100), which handle most of the city's big theaters and concert halls, slap a hefty $4–$6 per-ticket surcharge on top of that (and sometimes a $2–$3 per-order fee).

There are, thankfully, a few ways to beat high ticket prices (*see below*). And lots of the really cool, funky arts centers downtown (particularly on the Lower East Side, in TriBeCa, and the East and West Village) will charge you $10 or less for a full night's entertainment. Remember, just because the folks in the federal government have done their red-tape best to snuff out the arts doesn't mean you have to sit around watching reruns of *Friends*.

PUBLICATIONS To find out who or what's playing where, your first stop should be a newsstand. Consult *Time Out*, the *New York Times* (particularly Friday's "Weekend" section), the "Goings on About Town" section of *The New Yorker*, the "Cue" listings at the back of *New York* magazine, and the *Village Voice*. The most thorough is *Time Out*, though the *Voice* has long been considered the bible of the downtown scene. For listings of just the free stuff—free concerts, free plays, free festivals, free happenings—look for *The Skinny* ($1) at downtown bookstores and newsstands.

HOTLINES You can get updated info by phone from the **NYC/ON STAGE Hotline** (tel. 212/768–1818), the Theatre Development Fund's (TDF) 24-hour performing arts info service. The free, 24-hour, interactive **Arts Hotline** (tel. 212/765–ARTS) lists the week's events at more than 750 of the city's theaters, museums, and concert halls. For wheelchair accessibility info, call either of the two major ticket companies mentioned above. Additionally, the TDF runs a **Theatre Access Project** (tel. 212/221–1103) for city residents with disabilities. Membership (free) gives you access to special seating and discount tickets for some of the city's hottest shows.

FINDING A CHEAP SEAT Whether your interest is in the theater, symphony, or ballet, there are more ways to get a deal on tickets than there are runaway Andrew Lloyd Webber musicals. The best plan, of course, is to buy your tickets at the theater's or concert hall's own box office, where they'll help you choose the best seats and, thankfully, won't stick you with a service charge. You can go the day of the performance, or you can go a few days earlier to avoid crushing disappointment. Occasionally, box offices offer same-day standing-room tickets ($10–$20) for sold-out shows; check with the particular theater for more info.

➤ **TICKET AGENCIES** • The city's two **TKTS** booths offer day-of-performance tickets for selected Broadway and Off-Broadway shows at 25%–50% off (cash or traveler's check only), plus a $2.50 per-ticket service charge. The crowded **Times Square** TKTS booth (W. 47th St. and Broadway) is open Monday–Saturday 3–8 and Sunday noon–8, with additional hours Wednesday and Saturday 10–2. Expect lines to form an hour before the booth opens. The TKTS booth at the **World Trade Center** (Mezzanine Level, 2 World Trade Center; open weekdays 11–5:30, Sat. 11–3:30) is worth the trek downtown: It's indoors, it's rarely crowded, and (unlike the Times Square booth) it sells matinee and Sunday tickets one day in advance. For more info, call the NYC/ON STAGE hotline (tel. 212/768–1818).

The **Music and Dance Half-Price Ticket Booth** is the outlet for day-of-performance tickets to all the city's music and dance performances, from the New York Philharmonic to Korean dancing at La MaMa E.T.C. Tickets are 50% off, but you can pay only with cash or traveler's checks. *Bryant Park, W. 42nd St. just east of Sixth Ave., tel. 212/382–2323. Subway: B, D, F, or Q to W. 42nd St. Open Tues.–Sun. noon–2 and 3–7.*

➤ **COUPONS AND VOUCHERS** • Look for **"two-fer" coupons**—which offer two tickets for the price of one, or at least some sort of discount—at the New York Visitors and Convention Bureau, and in bookstores, department stores, banks, restaurants, and hotel lobbies. Unfortunately, they're generally available only for the long-running Broadway extravaganzas that probably came to your home town several years ago. Another option is a **Theatre Development Fund (TDF)** voucher, which are sold in sets of five ($20) and are redeemable at Off- and Off-Off-Broadway theaters as well as at many music and dance spaces. They're available to students (and other limited-income types) only. For an application send a SASE to: TDF, 1501 Broadway, Suite 2110, NY 10036, and allow six to eight weeks for processing. For more info, call the TDF's 24-hour info line (tel. 212/221–0013) or the NYC/ON STAGE hotline (tel. 212/768–1818).

Arts Centers

At the city's arts centers you can catch performance art, classical music, serious drama, modern dance, or a poetry reading. Whether you're in the mood to see David Byrne or Kathleen Battle, you can probably find the performance you're looking for at one of these cultural clearinghouses.

LINCOLN CENTER From the moment it opened on the Upper West Side 30 years ago, the 14-acre Lincoln Center for the Performing Arts has been the undisputed heart of the city's arts scene. This is where you'll find **Alice Tully Hall** (*see* Concert Halls, *below*), home to the Chamber Music Society; **Avery Fisher Hall** (*see* Concert Halls, *below*), home to the New York Philharmonic; the acclaimed **Julliard School** (*see* Music Schools, *below*), which frequently puts on free concerts, theatrical performances, and operas; the grand **Metropolitan Opera House** (tel. 212/362–6000), home to the Metropolitan Opera (*see* Opera, *below*) and the American Ballet Theatre (*see* Dance, *below*); the **New York State Theater** (tel. 212/870–5570), home to the New York City Opera (*see* Opera, *below*) and New York City Ballet (*see* Dance, *below*); and two theaters, the **Vivian Beaumont** and **Mitzi Newhouse**. The Center's **Damrosch Park and Bandshell** are frequently the site of Lincoln Center's many outdoor festivals and concerts, such as **Mostly Mozart, Mostly Vienna, Lincoln Center Out of Doors**, and **Serious Fun** (for more info on festivals, *see* Summer Arts, *below*). Its year-round series, **Great Performers at Lincoln Center**, features visits from the world's greatest talents, including Luciano Pavarotti, Dame Joan Sutherland, the Vienna Philharmonic, and the Boston Symphony. For info on Lincoln Center's excellent jazz offerings, *see* Jazz, in Chapter 6. For more on Lincoln Center, including tours of the grounds, *see* Manhattan Neighborhoods, Upper West Side, in Chapter 2. All Lincoln Center venues are wheelchair accessible. *Mailing address: 70 Lincoln Center Plaza, NY 10023–6583, tel. 212/875–5400 for general info and daily calendar. Subway: 1 or 9 to W. 66th St. (Lincoln Center).*

OTHER VENUES **92nd Street Y.** The Y's Kaufmann Hall, the city's most prestigious site for readings and lectures by poets, artists, writers, and scholars, also has a lively menu of music and dance. At its Unterberg Poetry Center are tapes dating back to the 1940s of the greatest poets of this century reading their work for Y audiences. *1395 Lexington Ave., at E. 92nd St., Upper East Side, tel. 212/415–5440. Subway: 4, 5, or 6 to E. 86th St. Ticket prices vary. Wheelchair access.*

Brooklyn Academy of Music (BAM). America's oldest performing arts center (opened in 1859) has a sizzling reputation for daring and innovative dance, music, opera, performance art, and theater productions. Its fall festival of new music, theater, and dance, **Next Wave**, brings artists from around the globe. The main hall is the Opera House; other spaces at BAM are the Majestic Theatre, the Helen Owen Carey Playhouse, and Lepercq Square. Student rush tickets ($10) are available for some BAM shows; call on the day of performance for info. *30 Lafayette Ave., btw Ashland Pl. and St. Felix St., Fort Greene, Brooklyn, tel. 718/636–4100. Subway: D, Q, 2, 3, 4, or 5 to Atlantic Ave.; walk 2 blocks north to Fulton St. and turn left. Tickets: $15–$50. Wheelchair access.*

The (ex) Princess of Wales's first official visit to the United States was to the Brooklyn Academy of Music, to hear the Welsh National Opera perform Verdi's "Falstaff" in its American debut.

City Center. Under City Center's eccentric Spanish dome (built in 1923 by the Ancient and Accepted Order of the Mystic Shrine) you'll find the Manhattan Theatre Club, where you can see innovative new dramas, modern dance troupes such as the Alvin Ailey American Dance Theater and the Martha Graham Dance Company, and concert versions of American musicals. *131 W. 55th St., btw Sixth and Seventh Aves., Midtown, tel. 212/581–7907. Subway: N or R to W. 57th St. Tickets: $15–$35. Wheelchair access.*

Joseph Papp Public Theater. The Joseph Papp Public Theater, a complex of five theaters and one film house, is the year-round home of the New York Shakespeare Festival. Despite the name, performances are not limited to the bard and are anything but staid: Bring In 'Da Noise, Bring in 'Da Funk premiered here in 1995. Each summer, the financially challenged wait for hours at its box office to catch their free Shakespeare performances in Central Park (*see* Summer Arts, *below*). *425 Lafayette St., at Astor Pl., East Village, tel. 212/539–8500. Subway: 6 to Astor Pl. Ticket prices vary. Wheelchair access.*

The Kitchen. This is *the* Manhattan center for performance art, although video, dance, and music have their moments here, too. It's where unclassifiable artists like Philip Glass, Meredith Monk, and Laurie Anderson got their start. *512 W. 19th St., btw Tenth and Eleventh Aves., Chelsea, tel. 212/255–5793. Subway: A, C, E, or L to W. 14th St. Tickets: $10–$15.*

New Victory. After a stint as a burlesque theater, the New Victory reopened in 1995 as New York City's first performing-arts center for children. The ornate 500-seat venue underwent $11 million worth of restoration before groups like the Metropolitan Opera Guild and the Canadian Cirque Eloize took the stage. *209 W. 42nd St., btw Seventh and Eighth Aves., Midtown, tel. 212/564–4222. Subway: N, R, 1, 2, 3, 7, or 9 to Times Sq. Also: A, C, or E to W. 42nd St. (Eighth Ave.). Tickets: $10–$25.*

The Performing Garage. This small space has a reputation as being the best in the city for performance art, dance, and experimental theater, often by up-and-comers. Alumni of the Performing Garage's resident company, Wooster Grove, include actor Willem Dafoe and monologuist nonpareil Spalding Grey. *33 Wooster St., btw Broome and Grand Sts., SoHo, tel. 212/966–9796. Subway: A, C, or E to Canal St. Tickets: $8–$25. Wheelchair access.*

P.S. 122. Performances here are so cutting-edge that the *Village Voice* once called it "the petri dish of downtown culture." Plays, concerts, and exhibits all breed here, especially during their February marathon. *150 First Ave., at E. 9th St., East Village, tel. 212/477–5288. Subway: L to First Ave. Tickets: $12–$15.*

Theater

There are roughly 250 legitimate theaters in New York, and many more ad hoc venues—lofts, galleries, streets, rooftops—where performances ranging from Shakespeare to sword-dancing take place. Theaters can be divided into three categories: **Broadway**, **Off-Broadway**, and **Off-Off-Broadway**, based on size, price, and attitude. Count on Broadway theaters for long-running, flashy shows with big casts, big budgets, and big hair—the majority these days are recycled Golden Age musicals. Off-Broadway and Off-Off-Broadway theaters stage performances that can be pretentious, incendiary, or obscure, but rarely boring.

Don't overlook tomorrow's hits and today's flops—there's something special about seeing a show in previews, or seeing an already-panned play before it bites the dust.

Theaters with fewer than 100 seats are Off-Off; those with 100–500 seats are considered Off-Broadway. More seats than that and it's big-time Broadway, no two ways about it. Most theaters are dark on Mondays. Matinees (afternoon shows) are typically staged on Wednesdays, Saturdays, and Sundays.

You can get the latest info on Broadway and Off-Broadway shows with one of the arts hotlines or city weeklies, or by phoning **The Broadway Show Line** (tel. 212/563–2929). For extensive reviews and listings of Off-Broadway and Off-Off-Broadway, your best bets are the *Village Voice* and *Time Out*.

BROADWAY

Dozens of magnificent theaters sprang up around Times Square between 1899 and 1925, drawing actors and audiences like no other place on earth. Many have since been gutted or converted to porn palaces, but those that survived are gathered in a section of Midtown known as the **Theater District** (West 42nd–53rd streets, btw Sixth and Ninth avenues). It's the heart and soul of that state of mind, Broadway. Come here to find marquees emblazoned with Hollywood names like Julie Andrews, Michael J. Fox, and Glenn Close. And carry plenty of cash, since seats regularly cost $20–$75 and continue to inch towards the $100 mark as the millennium approaches. Broadway theaters typically don't have telephones (possibly to avoid flak about those ticket prices), so for up-to-date show times call a ticket agency, check magazine listings, or visit the box office. Some prominent Broadway theaters are listed below.

Booth. The Booth has hosted four Pulitzer prize–winning productions over the last few decades, including *The Time of Your Life* and *You Can't Take It With You. 222 W. 45th St., btw Broadway and Eighth Ave. Subway: N, R, 1, 2, 3, 7, or 9 to Times Sq. Also: A, C, or E to W. 42nd St. (Eighth Ave.). Wheelchair access.*

Broadhurst. This was home to seven-time Tony award winner *Kiss of the Spider Woman*, as well as Patrick "Jean-Luc Picard" Stewart performing the role of Prospero in Shakespeare's *The Tempest. 235 W. 44th St., btw Broadway and Eighth Ave. Subway: N, R, 1, 2, 3, 7, or 9 to Times Sq. Also: A, C, or E to W. 42nd St. (Eighth Ave.). Wheelchair access.*

Broadway. *Miss Saigon*, a regurgitation of Puccini's *Madama Butterfly*, is currently parked at this gargantuan theater. *1681 Broadway, at W. 53rd St. Subway: 1 or 9 to W. 50th St. Wheelchair access.*

Cort. Some of the most daring shows on Broadway have turned up here, including the Pulitzer prize–winning *Diary of Anne Frank*. Katharine Hepburn had her debut here in *These Days* (1928), a flop. *138 W. 48th St., btw Broadway and Sixth Ave. Subway: N or R to W. 49th St. Wheelchair access.*

Ethel Barrymore. Marlon Brando and Jessica Tandy started their careers here in *A Streetcar Named Desire*, and Sidney Poitier started his in Lorraine Hansberry's *Raisin in the Sun. 243 W. 47th St., btw Broadway and Eighth Ave. Subway: C or E to W. 50th St. Also: 1 or 9 to W. 50th St. Wheelchair access.*

Eugene O'Neill. Neil Simon premiered a half dozen of his plays here in the '60s and '70s, when he was its owner. *230 W. 49th St., btw Broadway and Eighth Ave. Subway: C or E to W. 50th St. Also: 1 or 9 to W. 50th St. Wheelchair access.*

Gershwin. This is one of the newest theaters (1972) on Broadway, but it's already had scores of hits—including *Sweeney Todd*, Stephen Sondheim's romp about cannibalism. *1633 Broadway, at W. 51st St. Subway: 1 or 9 to W. 50th St. Wheelchair access.*

Imperial. Shows at the Imperial (*Peter Pan*, *Fiddler on the Roof*, *Annie Get Your Gun*) rarely flop, earning it the nickname "The Lucky House." *249 W. 45th St., btw Broadway and Eighth Ave. Subway: N, R, 1, 2, 3, 7, or 9 to Times Sq. Also: A, C, or E to W. 42nd St. (Eighth Ave.). Wheelchair access.*

Majestic. The Majestic is famous for having premiered Rodgers and Hammerstein musicals like *Carousel* and *South Pacific*. *245 W. 44th St., btw Broadway and Eighth Ave. Subway: N, R, 1, 2, 3, 7, or 9 to Times Sq. Also: A, C, or E to W. 42nd St. (Eighth Ave.). Wheelchair access.*

Neil Simon. It's not just about Neil Simon here. Other playwrights can use the theater, too. *250 W. 52nd St., btw Broadway and Eighth Ave. Subway: C or E to W. 50th St. Also: 1 or 9 to W. 50th St. Wheelchair access.*

Shubert. *A Chorus Line* had its record-breaking 15-year (1975–1990) run here. *225 West 44th St., btw Broadway and Eighth Ave. Subway: N, R, 1, 2, 3, 7, or 9 to Times Sq. Also: A, C, or E to W. 42nd St. (Eighth Ave.). Wheelchair access.*

Brothers Lee, JJ, and Sam Shubert ruled Broadway in the early 1900s. Now they have to share one lousy theater named after them.

Walter Kerr. Tony Kushner's moving two-part epic about gay life, *Angels in America: Millennium Approaches* and *Perestroika*, recently played here. *219 W. 48th St., btw Broadway and Eighth Ave. Subway: C or E to W. 50th St. Also: 1 or 9 to W. 50th St. Wheelchair access.*

Winter Garden. In the Roaring '20s this was *the* place to catch vaudeville extravaganzas by the Shubert brothers. For the last decade it's been inhabited by singing, dancing, jellicle *Cats*. *1634 Broadway, at W. 50th St. Subway: 1 or 9 to W. 50th St. Wheelchair access.*

OFF-BROADWAY

Off-Broadway is a good place to catch Broadway smashes in the making—like *A Chorus Line*, which opened at the Public Theater, or Wendy Wasserstein's *The Heidi Chronicles*, which first appeared at Playwrights Horizons—before they relocate to the Great White Way and ticket prices hit the stratosphere. The biggest clusters of Off-Broadway theaters can be found in the West Village (around Sheridan Square) and in Midtown on **Theater Row** (42nd Street, between Ninth and Tenth avenues).

Off-Off-Broadway, which came of age in the '60s, offers an in-your-face, the-hell-with-it alternative to everything else. Depending on which night you show up, you'll find everything from cabaret and comedy to serious drama at Off-Off-Broadway theaters. They're also the birthplace of **performance art** (a mix of dance, drama, music, and video, usually expressing Very Deep Thoughts). Catch a performance-art piece in New York and you'll really impress those snooty friends of yours back home. Of the theaters listed below, **Franklin Furnace**, **The Kitchen**, and **La MaMa E.T.C.** are known for their devotion to performance art. So are the **Brooklyn Academy of Music**, the **Joseph Papp Public Theater**, and **P.S. 122** (*see* Arts Centers, *above*). Ticket prices for Off-Broadway shows typically run $15–$45, for Off-Off-Broadway $10–$25.

Actor's Studio. Tickets are free ($5 donation suggested), but reservations are required. *432 W. 44th St., btw Ninth and Tenth Aves., Midtown, tel. 212/757–0870. Subway: A, C, or E to W. 42nd St. (Port Authority).*

Jean Cocteau Repertory. Specializes in the sort of obscure plays that drama geeks rave about. *Bouwerie Lane Theatre, 330 Bowery, at Bond St., East Village, tel. 212/677–0060. Subway: 6 to Bleecker St.*

La MaMa E.T.C. Famous alumni of this "MGM of experimental theater" include Sam Shepard, Bette Midler, Andy Warhol, Nick Nolte, and Meatloaf. *74 E. 4th St., btw Second and Third Aves., East Village, tel. 212/475–7710. Subway: F to Second Ave. Wheelchair access to 1st-floor theater.*

Naked Angels. This is one of the hottest theater groups of the '90s, with famous faces like Marisa Tomei, Fisher Stevens, Matthew Broderick, Sarah Jessica Parker, and Rob Morrow. And John F. Kennedy Jr. is on the board of directors. *The Space, 114 W. 17th St., btw Sixth and Seventh Aves., Chelsea, tel. 212/594–5147. Subway: 1 or 9 to W. 18th St. Wheelchair access.*

National Black Theater. Produces new works by contemporary African-American writers. *2033 5th Ave., Harlem, tel. 212/722–3800. Subway: 2, 3, or 4 to 125th St. Wheelchair access.*

New Dramatists. Playwrights bring their shows here to iron out kinks before moving to Broadway. Tickets are free, so reserve far in advance. Readings, too, are popular here. *424 W. 44th St., btw Ninth and Tenth Aves., Midtown, tel. 212/757–6960. Subway: A, C, or E to W. 42nd St. (Port Authority).*

Pan-Asian Repertory Theatre. A forum for Asian American actors and plays. *47 Great Jones St., btw Lafayette St. and Third Ave., tel. 212/505–5655. Subway: 6 to Bleecker St.*

Playhouse 91. The Jewish Repertory Theater and the Riverside Shakespeare Company make their home here. *316 E. 91st St., btw First and Second Aves., Upper East Side, tel. 212/831–2001. Subway: 6 to E. 96th St.*

Playwrights Horizons. This theater is dedicated to developing the talents of new playwrights. *Sunday in the Park with George* and *The Heidi Chronicles* both started out here. *416 W. 42nd St., btw Ninth and Tenth Aves., Midtown, tel. 212/564–1235. Subway: A, C, or E to W. 42nd St. (Port Authority).*

Pregones Theater. This nationally acclaimed Latin American theater offers bilingual productions. *295 St. Ann's Ave., at 140th St., Bronx, tel. 212/585–1202. Subway: 6 to Brook Ave.; walk 1 block east and 2 blocks north. Wheelchair access.*

Repertorio Español. Those who can't follow the action in Spanish can often listen to a simultaneous translation though a nifty cordless headset. *Gramercy Arts Theatre, 138 E. 27th St., btw Lexington and Third Aves., Gramercy, tel. 212/889–2850. Subway: 6 to E. 28th St.*

Ridiculous Theatrical Company. Count on the Ridiculous for campy, outré comedies: One of their latest smashes was a Nancy Drew/Hardy Boys–style mystery done entirely in drag. *Charles Ludlam Theater, 1 Sheridan Sq., btw Sixth and Seventh Aves., West Village, tel. 212/387–7717. Subway: 1 or 9 to Christopher St. (Sheridan Sq.). Wheelchair access.*

Sullivan Street Playhouse. Home to *The Fantasticks*, the world's longest-running musical. *181 Sullivan St., btw Houston and Bleecker Sts., West Village, tel. 212/674–3838. Subway: A, B, C, D, E, F, or Q to W. 4th St. (Washington Sq.).*

Ubu Repertory. At the Ubu, français is what you'll find, though many performances are in English (c'est la vie, non?). *15 W. 28th St., btw Broadway and Fifth Ave., Chelsea, tel. 212/679–7562. Subway: N or R to W. 28th St. Wheelchair access.*

Music

Even if you're not a big fan of classical music, you've probably seen *Live at Lincoln Center* on PBS, know that Julliard is the world's most prestigious music school, and have heard the lame joke about "practice" being the only way to get to Carnegie Hall. If these three institutions were all that New York had going for it, its music scene would still surpass the combined efforts of most major U.S. cities. Luckily, though, they represent only the tip of the iceberg. New York City is home to several major orchestras and three of the country's finest music schools; it's also a favorite stop for touring musicians from all over the world. And if this all smacks of too much big money for your taste, perhaps you should scout out the city's museums, churches, and other small venues, which frequently host musical performances both traditional and avant-garde. At these spaces concerts are often free.

CONCERT HALLS

New York concert halls are constantly filled with world-class musicians. Lincoln Center's 2,700-seat Avery Fisher Hall (*see below*) is one of the grandest venues in the city, though nit-pickers will tell you that the 1976 renovations didn't entirely repair the hall's dreadful acoustics. In addition to those listed below, venues noted for classical music include the Brooklyn Academy of Music, City Center, The Kitchen, the 92nd Street Y, and P.S. 122; for more info on each, *see* Arts Centers, *above*.

Aaron Davis Hall. The World Music Institute stages a wide variety of contemporary and classical concerts and theater productions, including a number of events designed for children. One of their theaters holds 750, another 250. Tickets start at $3 for children's shows and go up to $18 for other performances. *City College, W. 134th St., Harlem, tel. 212/650–6900. Subway: 1 or 9 to 137th St. (City College). Wheelchair access.*

Alice Tully Hall. The Chamber Music Society of Lincoln Center performs at this intimate, acoustically perfect space, along with promising Julliard students, small ensembles such as the Guarneri and Kronos quartets, musicians using period instruments, famous soloists, and choirs. Seats for the Chamber Music Society's performances are $22–$30 (students $11–$15). *Lincoln Center (see Arts Centers, above), tel. 212/875–5050 for box office or 212/721–6500 for CenterCharge. Ticket prices vary. Wheelchair access.*

Avery Fisher Hall. Playing at Avery Fisher is the 150-year-old New York Philharmonic, considered one of the world's premiere symphony orchestras. It's currently led by Kurt Masur; the great Leonard Bernstein was musical director from 1958 to 1970. Weeknight "Rush Hour" Concerts (6:45 PM) and "Casual Saturday" Concerts (2 PM) last one hour and are less expensive than regular concerts. Student rush tickets ($10) are available 30 minutes before performances, as are occasional seats in the orchestra ($25). Weekly rehearsals (Wednesdays and Thursdays at 9:45 AM) are open to the public for a bargain $10. *Lincoln Center (see Arts Centers, above), tel. 212/875–5030 for box office, 212/721–6500 for CenterCharge, or 212/875–5656 for info on rehearsals. Tickets: $15–$60. Season Sept.–early June. Wheelchair access.*

Bargemusic. This 102-foot former Erie Lackawanna coffee barge, now tethered along the East River, holds a concert hall that seats 125. Bargemusic's resident artists recruit soloists from around the world and throw them together to make impromptu chamber groups. Tickets are $23, $15 for students. *Fulton Ferry Landing, Brooklyn, tel. 718/624–4061. Subway: A to High St. Wheelchair access.*

Carnegie Hall. This granddaddy of concert halls has hosted some of the 20th century's greatest orchestras and musicians, including Isaac Stern, Leonard Bernstein, Yo-Yo Ma, Frank Sinatra, Tchaikovsky, and the Beatles (not all at the same time). Though the emphasis is on classical music, it also hosts jazz, cabaret, and folk-music series. The Opera Orchestra of New York puts on concerts of rarely performed works here, and the city's music schools debut their star students in its Weill Recital Hall. Acoustics in the main auditorium are sounding better than ever, thanks to the 1995 discovery and removal of several tons of cement lurking below the stage (nobody knows how it got there, but musicians claimed it ruined the sound). *881 Seventh Ave., at W. 57th St., Midtown, tel. 212/247–7800. Subway: N or R to W. 57th St. Ticket prices vary. Wheelchair access.*

Merkin Concert Hall. This relatively new concert hall is doing an admirable job of keeping up with the Joneses, especially considering that the Joneses are the Merkin's near neighbor, Lincoln Center. Lots of famous soloists and chamber groups perform at this 457-seat hall, which also occasionally hosts the New York Philharmonic Ensemble, the Mendelssohn String Quartet, and the Boston Camerata. *Abraham Goodman House, 129 W. 67th St., btw Broadway and Amsterdam Ave., Upper West Side, tel. 212/501–3330. Subway: 1 or 9 to W. 66th St. (Lincoln Center). Tickets: $10–$20. Wheelchair access.*

OTHER SPACES

Stray outside the city's concert halls and you'll find venues where the sight lines may be imperfect or the acoustics may be less than ideal, but where the experience is still somehow grand. Nothing can rival a summer evening's concert in the Metropolitan Museum's rooftop garden. And you can't complain about the cost (often free) of performances at the city's top-ranked music schools.

CHURCHES Musical offerings at churches take place during worship services and afternoon vespers, or frequently as separate concerts. During the Christmas holidays every church and cathedral in the city breaks out the Bach.

Cathedral of St. John the Divine. Mammoth St. John has a lively arts calendar, including music and drama. *1047 Amsterdam Ave., at W. 112th St., Morningside Heights, tel. 212/662–2133. Subway: 1 or 9 to W. 110th St. Tickets: $25 or less. Wheelchair access.*

St. Paul's Chapel. Together with nearby **Trinity Church** (Broadway at Wall St., tel. 212/602–0800), St. Paul's offers free lunchtime concerts (Mondays and Thursdays at noon) of everything from Beethoven's symphonies to the traditional music of Zimbabwe. *Broadway, at Fulton St., Lower Manhattan, tel. 212/602–0747. Subway: 4 or 5 to Fulton St. Admission: $2 (suggested).*

Theater at Riverside Church. Chamber music concerts, dance productions, drama, and one of the largest organs in the country make this a great place to catch a performance. *490 Riverside Dr., at W. 122 St., Morningside Heights, tel. 212/222–5900. Subway: 1 or 9 to W. 125th St. Tickets: $10–$15. Wheelchair access.*

MUSEUMS For open hours, subway directions, and other info on the museums mentioned below, *see* Major Attractions and Museums and Galleries, in Chapter 2.

The Cloisters Museum. Well-known early music groups perform most Sunday afternoons in the museum's fabulously atmospheric medieval chapel. For tickets send a SASE to: Concerts at the Cloisters, Fort Tryon Park, NY 10040, or call to order by credit card. Traditional Christmas concerts performed by the Waverly Consort sell out fast, so plan ahead. *Fort Tryon Park, tel. 212/923–3700 or 212/650–2290 to order tickets. Tickets: $18–$35. Wheelchair access.*

The Frick Collection. Sundays bring classical concerts, from Norwegian violinists playing Brahms to quartets performing 16th-century Spanish works. For tickets, send a SASE several weeks in advance to: Concerts Dept., The Frick Collection, 1 E. 70th St., NY 10021. *1 E. 70th St., at Fifth Ave., tel. 212/288–0700. Tickets free. Wheelchair access*

Metropolitan Museum of Art. The Met offers a wide variety of classical music concerts weekends at its Grace Rainey Rogers Auditorium, priced $20–$40. Additionally, Friday and Saturday evening concerts on its Great Hall Balcony are free (you pay for the wine). On warm summer evenings, head to the museum's roof, where classical guitar accompanies the view. Half-price student rush tickets are available 30 minutes before most performances. *Fifth Ave., at E. 82nd St., tel. 212/570–3949. Wheelchair access.*

Museum of Modern Art. The MoMA's Summergarden concert series take place in its beautiful sculpture garden. Performances (free) are Friday and Saturday evenings, July–August. *11 W. 53rd St., btw Fifth and Sixth Aves., tel. 212/708–9480.*

MUSIC SCHOOLS If student recitals make you think of 20 third-graders hacking away at "Chopsticks," think again. New York City's three major music schools are the launching pads for many of the nation's most respected musicians. Best of all, performances by the schools' celebrity wanna-bes are usually inexpensive or free.

More than half of the New York Philharmonic's musicians graduated from The Juilliard School.

The Juilliard School. Juilliard offers exceptional orchestral, opera, dance, and theater performances in Lincoln Center's Avery Fisher and Alice Tully halls, as well as in its own Paul Recital Hall (also at Lincoln Center). Many performances are free; those that aren't generally cost $15, $7 for students. *Lincoln Center (see Arts Centers, above), tel. 212/799–5000. Wheelchair access.*

Manhattan School of Music. Four concert spaces mean hundreds of classical and jazz performances (some free) throughout the year. *120 Claremont Ave., at W. 122nd St., Morningside Heights, tel. 212/749–2802 or 212/749–3300 for concert hotline. Subway: 1 or 9 to W. 116th St. Tickets: $25 or less. Wheelchair access.*

Mannes College of Music. The emphasis at Mannes is on early music and classic opera. The Mannes Orchestra performs (free) at halls around the city. *150 W. 85th St., btw Amsterdam and Columbus Aves., Upper West Side, tel. 212/580–0210 or 212/496–8524 for box office. Subway: 1 or 9 to W. 86th St. Wheelchair access.*

Dance

Naysayers will tell you that dance in New York City is dead—or at least seriously ailing. But despite the disheartening 1995 relocation of the revered Joffrey Ballet Company (founded here in 1956) to the more dance-friendly city of Chicago, some 140 dance troupes, classic and modern, soldier on. Of those, the New York City Ballet, the American Ballet Theatre, and the Dance Theatre of Harlem are the most celebrated. And, as if that weren't enough, New York continuously attracts troupes from around the globe: the Bolshoi, the Kirov, the Royal Danish, the Stuttgart. See, there must be New Yorkers out there somewhere who will gladly pay to watch men gamboling in tights.

If you're not a by-the-books balletomane, a few venues that feature up-and-coming dance companies and dance/performance art are worth checking out: **Playhouse 91** (*see* Theater, *above*), **Dia Center for the Arts** (155 Mercer St., btw Houston and Prince Sts., SoHo, tel. 212/431–9233), **Merce Cunningham Studio** (55 Bethune St., near Washington St., West Village, tel. 212/691–9751), and **Danspace Project** (St. Marks-in-the-Bowery Church, 131 E. 10th St., at Second Ave., East Village, tel. 212/674–8112).

American Ballet Theatre. In its 50-plus years, the American Ballet has included some of the greatest dancers of the century: Mikhail Baryshnikov, Natalia Makarova, Rudolf Nureyev, and Cynthia Gregory. It's famous for its brilliant renditions of the great 19th-century classics—*Swan Lake, Giselle, The Sleeping Beauty*—and increasingly for its eclectic repertoire of works by 20th-century masters like Balanchine, Robbins, and de Mille. Two of its newest members, Angel Corella (from Spain) and Vladimir Malakhov (from Russia) have wowed audiences with their spirit and grace. *Metropolitan Opera House, at Lincoln Center (see Arts Centers, above), tel. 212/362–6000. Tickets: $15–$110. Season Apr.–June.*

The annual Workshop Performances of the School of American Ballet (tel. 212/877–0600), whose students eventually graduate into the New York City Ballet's prestigious corps de ballet, are held the first week in June. Tickets are $25–$40.

Dance Theater Workshop. The Workshop, on the second floor of a converted warehouse, began in 1965 as a choreographers' cooperative. It now showcases some of the city's freshest dance talent, as well as contemporary music, video, theater, and readings. *219 W. 19th St., btw Seventh and Eighth Aves., Chelsea, tel. 212/924–0077. Subway: 1 or 9 to W. 18th St. Tickets: $12, $6 students.*

Joyce Theater. This art deco former movie theater has become a major center for dance. It's the permanent home of the **Feld Ballet Company** (founded in 1974 by an upstart American Ballet Theatre dancer), which performs during the spring and summer, and a favorite for visiting companies. The eclectic year-round program also includes tap, jazz, ballroom, and ethnic dance. Discount student tickets ($12) are available for some performances. *175 Eighth Ave., at W. 19th St., Chelsea, tel. 212/242–0800. Subway: C or E to W. 23rd St. Tickets: $25–$30. Wheelchair access.*

New York City Ballet. The City, started in 1948 by Lincoln Kirstein and George Balanchine, has become one of the most highly praised ballet companies in the world. Its repertoire of 20th-century works is unmatched anywhere, and of its 88 or so dancers several—including Kyra Nichols, Darci Kistler, Damian Woetzel, and Jock Soto—have become stars in their own right.

Currently under the direction of Peter Martins (formerly one of Balanchine's best dancers), the company offers a wide range of works, from the brand-new to the classics, just as the great Balanchine choreographed them. Their production of Balanchine's *The Nutcracker* plays to sellout crowds every holiday season. *New York State Theater, at Lincoln Center (see Arts Centers, above), tel. 212/870–5570. Tickets: $20–$62. Season mid-Nov.–Feb. and late Apr.–June. Wheelchair access.*

Modern Dance: You Just Might Like It

If you're at all interested in modern dance, New York City is a great place to broaden your horizons: Its resident companies are some of the most innovative in the world (and many, like the Dance Theater of Harlem, are also facing budget crunches and could really use your help). Companies perform for a few weeks or months each year at one of the city's dance theaters.

- *Alvin Ailey American Dance Theater. One of the city's most gorgeous dance troupes carries on the work of the late Alvin Ailey, a brilliant choreographer who blended ballet, modern dance, and jazz (Duke Ellington composed "Les trois rois noirs" for him in 1970). Many of his works, including the well-known "Revelations" and "Blues Suite," pay homage to black culture. Tel. 212/767–0590. Performs Dec. at City Center.*

- *Ballet Hispanico. The nation's leading Latin-influenced modern dance company has been delighting New York audiences for a quarter-century with works inspired by the cultures of the Caribbean, Latin America, and the land of the flamenco, Spain. Tel. 212/362–6710. Performs Nov.–Dec. at the Joyce Theater.*

- *Dance Theatre of Harlem. The Dance Theatre of Harlem is famous for taking a traditionally all-white art and standing it on its ear. Led by Arthur Mitchell, the first African-American principal dancer in the New York City Ballet, the company has reworked classics ("Giselle" in a Creole setting, for example) and trained several generations of black dancers and choreographers. Tel. 212/690–2800.*

- *Mark Morris Dance Group. Mark Morris, one of the most creative choreographers alive today, draws on everything from Roland Barthes and Indian ragas to Yoko Ono and 18th-century opera to create pieces blending humor with serious social commentary. Tel. 212/219–3660.*

- *Martha Graham Dance Company. For most of its 65 years, this revered company was headed by the founder of modern dance herself, Martha Graham. It continues to perform some 200 of Graham's works, while former dancers like Alvin Ailey and Merce Cunningham have gone on to form troupes of their own. Tel. 212/838–5886 or 212/832–9166.*

- *Merce Cunningham Dance Company. The unfailingly avant-garde works of Merce Cunningham have included collaborations with John Cage, David Tudor, Paul Taylor, Jasper Johns, Robert Rauschenberg, and Andy Warhol. Tel. 212/255–8240.*

Opera

If you can't consider your trip to New York over until you've heard the fat lady belt out a few arias, you've got a plethora of options—and for an art pegged as highbrow the prices are shockingly plebian. Small and ethnic opera groups are constantly forming in New York, performing cutting-edge and classical operas for a song (sorry). Check out the **National Opera Ebony** (Aaron Davis Hall, City College, Convent Ave. at W. 138th St., Harlem, tel. 212/877–2110) for performances by up-and-coming African-American, Hispanic, and Asian singers. The students of the Julliard American Opera Center, the Manhattan School of Music, and the Mannes College of Music (*see* Music Schools, *above*) perform operas—often for free—on a par with the pros in other cities. At the other end of the spectrum, even the hoity-toity Metropolitan Opera Company will squeeze you in for as little as $11.

Two additional venues for opera are **Carnegie Hall** (*see* Concert Halls, *above*), where the Opera Orchestra of New York performs, and the **Brooklyn Academy of Music** (*see* Arts Centers, *above*). During summer, you can catch an opera under the stars for free (*see* Summer Arts, *below*).

Amato Opera Theater. You've never seen *The Marriage of Figaro* performed more passionately than at the Amato, where up to 70 performers (most of them young, unpaid, and yearning to be discovered) at a time have been known to squeeze onto its 20-foot-wide stage. *319 Bowery, at E. 2nd St., East Village, tel. 212/228–8200. Subway: F to Second Ave. Tickets: $18.*

Blue Door Studio. Come to this miniscule (75 seats) SoHo loft/theater to hear short, experimental new operas by American composers. *463 Broome St., btw Greene and Mercer Sts., SoHo, tel. 212/431–8102. Subway: N or R to Prince St. Tickets: $15–$30, $8–$12 students. Wheelchair access.*

Metropolitan Opera Company. One of the most lauded opera companies in the world performs on a stage the size of a football field. Since 1883, it's given 16,000 performances of 235 different works, and it continues to crank out four major new productions (with extravagant touches like live horses and falling snow) each season. It attracts the finest singers, like Jessye Norman and Marilyn Horne—and plenty of criticism for a tendency to stick with opera's greatest hits rather than trying anything adventurous. Although tickets can cost more than $100, many less expensive seats (including 600 sold at $23) and standing room ($11–$15) are available. Weekday prices are lower than weekend prices. Standing-room tickets for the week's performances go on sale (cash only) on Saturday at 10 AM. *The Metropolitan Opera House, at Lincoln Center (see Arts Centers, above), tel. 212/362–6000. Tickets: $11–$137. Season Oct.–mid-Apr.*

New York City Opera. In addition to classics like *Carmen*, *Madama Butterfly*, and *The Magic Flute*, the renowned New York City Opera has a penchant for unusual and rarely performed works like *The Times of Harvey Milk* and *The Mostly Happy Fella*. It was one of the first opera houses in the country to introduce "supertitling" (line-by-line English translation displayed electronically over the stage) and has helped start the careers of some of the world's finest singers, including Placido Domingo, José Carreras, and Beverly Sills. Tickets are much cheaper than those at the Met, ranging from $17 to $78. Student-rush ($10) and standing-room tickets ($7) are sold on the day of performance starting at 10 AM, cash only. *New York State Theater, at Lincoln Center (see Arts Centers, above), tel. 212/870–5570. Tickets: $7–$78. Season Sept.–Nov. and Mar.–Apr.*

Comedy

There's something sad and a little desperate about forcing people to pay upwards of $15 (and don't forget that two-drink minimum!) for a few hours of yuks. But that's the state of comedy in most New York clubs today, so consider yourself warned. Luckily, the recent explosion of clubs featuring "alternative comedy" keep the scene from being a total wash. Comics at these clubs perform a manic mix of stand-up comedy, sketch comedy, and performance art, sometimes to hilarious effect, and sometimes, well, not. Best of all, alternative comedy clubs usually impose little or no cover charge and practically never have a drink minimum. As well as Luna Lounge and Surf Reality (*see below*), try Chelsea's **Rebar** (*see* Bars, in Chapter 6) to see some of this cutting-edge stuff. Most clubs (unless otherwise noted) offer one show nightly Sunday–Thursday and two or more shows Friday and Saturday nights.

Those comedians you're paying to watch will seem much funnier if you've cut the cost of the cover charge by checking for coupons in the "Village Voice."

The "Sunday Night Improv" show (7 PM) at **West End Gate Café** (2911 Broadway, btw W. 114th and 115 Sts., Morningside Heights, tel. 212/662–8830) draws funny groups like Chicago City Limits (*see below*) and Ms. Dee's Comedy Ice Tea. If you don't laugh at the jokes, you'll laugh at the price: Cover is $5 (students $4), with no drink minimum.

Boston Comedy Club. The young and the raunchy bring their gags to this NYU favorite. (It's named the Boston because the owner likes Boston. Funny, huh?) Wednesdays bring an all-women lineup. *82 W. 3rd St., btw Thompson and Sullivan Sts., West Village, tel. 212/477–1000. Subway: A, B, C, D, E, F, or Q to W. 4th St. (Washington Sq.). Cover: $5, $3 students Sun.–Thurs.; $10 Fri. and Sat. 2-drink minimum.*

Chicago City Limits. The oldest comedy and improvisational theater company in the city busts out with outrageous off-the-cuff skits and skewering of celebrities, based entirely on *your* insane suggestions. Okay, they do pre-write some of their material—but it doesn't make it any less funny. *1105 First Ave., at E. 61st St., Upper East Side, tel. 212/888–LAFF. Subway: 4, 5, or 6 to E. 59th St. Also: N or R to Lexington Ave. Cover: $17.50.*

Comedy Cellar. Beneath the Olive Tree Café is this dim and smoky throwback to the Village coffeehouses of the '60s. The nightly lineup features pros from *Letterman*, HBO, and *Conan O'Brien*. Newer talent slinks in after midnight. *117 MacDougal St., btw W. 3rd and Bleecker Sts., West Village, tel. 212/254–3480. Subway: A, B, C, D, E, F, or Q to W. 4th St. (Washington Sq.). Cover: $5 Sun.–Thurs., $10–$15 Fri. and Sat. 2-drink minimum.*

Dangerfield's. Rodney "No Respect" Dangerfield and pal opened this kitschy Vegas-style club in '69 so Rodney could become famous. And somehow (don't ask us), he did. It's also served as a springboard to stardom for guys like Jay Leno, Jim Carrey, Andrew Dice Clay, and Sam Kinison (R.I.P.). *1118 First Ave., btw E. 61st and 62nd Sts., Upper East Side, tel. 212/593–1650. Subway: 4, 5, or 6 to E. 59th St. Also: N or R to Lexington Ave. Cover: $12.50 Sun.–Thurs., $15 Fri. and Sat. Wheelchair access.*

Luna Lounge. Comics both well known and obscure try out performance-art comedy skits at this newly hip club. Expect experimental stuff that's uproariously funny or just plain strange. *171 Ludlow St., at Houston St., Lower East Side, tel. 212/260–2323. Subway: F to First Ave. Cover free.*

New York Comedy Club. Friday is "New York's Best African-American and Latino Comics"; Wednesday and Thursday there's sketch comedy. *241 E. 24th St., btw Second and Third Aves., Gramercy, tel. 212/696–LAFF. Subway: 6 to E. 23rd St. Cover: $5 Sun.–Thurs., $10 Fri. and Sat. 2-drink minimum.*

Stand-up New York. Robin Williams is known to drop by this swank joint to warm up for his *Letterman* appearances. Unannounced. Maybe you'll get lucky. *236 W. 78th St., at Broadway, Upper West Side, tel. 212/595–0850. Subway: 1 or 9 to W. 79th St. Cover: $7 Sun.–Thurs., $12 Fri. and Sat. 2-drink minimum. Wheelchair access.*

Surf Reality. Surf Reality is, no joke, the coolest performance space south of Houston, with some of the most outré comedy. Other offerings include folk music, performance art, and spoken word. *172 Allen St., btw Stanton and Rivington Sts., Lower East Side, tel. 212/673–4182. Subway: F to Second Ave. Cover: $3–$10. Closed Mon. and Tues.*

Spoken Word

Only in New York City do novelists, poets, historians, journalists, and other intellectuals get treated with the sort of adulation and respect normally reserved for American sports heroes. Dozens of readings, workshops, and lectures take place nightly at bookstores, museums, universities, galleries, theaters, and cafés around the city; check one of the weeklies for listings. The city's two most distinguished venues for readings and lectures are the **92nd Street Y** (*see* Arts Centers, *above*) and **Symphony Space** (2537 Broadway, at W. 95th St., Upper West Side, tel. 212/864–5400), which hosts the National Public Radio program "Selected Shorts" (short story readings by notable authors and actors) twice monthly.

A few other venues to watch for: **New Dramatists Headquarters** (*see* Theater, Off-Broadway, *above*) holds regular readings of works by up-and-coming playwrights; the Alterknit Theater at the **Knitting Factory** (*see* Live Music, in Chapter 6) holds a weekly poetry series and open mike Fridays ($5); **Limbo** (*see* Cafés and Coffee Bars, in Chapter 4) snares the latest authors of the very hippest fiction; and literary watering hole **K.G.B.** (*see* Bars, in Chapter 6) hosts frequent readings of cool new fiction. For odes and sonnets and such, look for events at **The Poetry Project** (St. Mark's-in-the-Bowery Church, 131 E. 10th St., at Second Ave., East Village, tel. 212/674–0910) and **Poets House** (72 Spring St., btw Crosby and Lafayette Sts., SoHo, tel. 212/431–7920). At **Summerstage** (*see* Summer Arts, *below*), the Central Park arts festival, big-time authors read from their latest and greatest works.

Nuyorican Poets Cafe. This is home of the "poetry slam," ground zero for the whole '90s urban poetry *thing*. Nuyorican poets—not your typical mush-mouthed, whey-faced spewers of wispy sonnets—have even busted rhyme on MTV. A typical night is packed with in-your-face urban rap and hip-hop jams; performing bards are scored by a panel of judges. *236 E. 3rd St., btw Aves. B and C, Alphabet City, tel. 212/505–8183. Subway: F to Second Ave. Cover: $5–$9. Wheelchair access.*

Summer Arts

As faithfully as the swallows of San Juan Capistrano, theater groups, orchestras, and opera companies alight in the city's parks come summer for various festivals and freebie concerts. Those noted for their musical offerings include **Bryant Park**, **Hudson River Park**, **Washington Square Park**, **Riverside Park**, the **World Trade Center Plaza**, and, of course, sprawling **Central Park**. Additionally, many museums, like the **Cooper-Hewitt Museum** and the **Museum of Modern Art**, hold summertime concerts in their gardens and courtyards. For more info on parks and museums, *see* Chapter 2, or check the city weeklies. To find out about concerts and other goings-on in the city's parks, you can also call the **Parks and Recreation Special Events Hotline** (tel. 212/360–3456). For info on the city's summer **jazz festivals**, *see* Jazz, in Chapter 6.

A hint for the uninitiated: Getting a swatch of lawn at a free summer concert—particularly performances by the New York Philharmonic, which are followed by fireworks—can be as fun and easy as scoring a cab on 42nd Street in rush hour during a snowstorm. Arrive at least an hour before curtain time with a bottle of wine and a blanket and you'll do just fine.

One unorthodox, but very popular, stage is the World Trade Center Plaza, where classical, jazz, oldies, and R&B are staged at least three days a week at 12:15 and 1:15 during the summer.

Celebrate Brooklyn. The free Shakespeare, opera, and dance productions and all kinds of concerts at Prospect Park bring Manhattanites across the Brooklyn Bridge in droves. *9th St. Bandshell, Prospect Park, Brooklyn, tel. 718/855–7882 or 718/965–8969. Subway: F to Seventh Ave. Also: 2 or 3 to Grand Army Plaza. Season June–Sept.*

Central Park Summerstage. Central Park's free performing arts mega-festival features something different just about every day of the week: Verdi operas performed by the New York Grand Opera; readings and performances by novelists and poets like Tom Robbins, Dorothy Allison, and Walter Mosley; modern dance performances; and concerts of just about every sort, includ-

55555555

ing blues, country, folk, jazz, polka, indie rock, and world music. *Rumsey Playfield, mid-park at 72nd St., tel. 212/360–CPSS. Subway: B or C to W. 72nd St. Season mid-June–early Aug.*

Lincoln Center Out-of-Doors. During summer, as many as 300,000 people attend some 100 events at stages set up in Lincoln Center's plaza. Offerings include free performances of theater, modern dance and ballet, symphonic and chamber music, jazz and blues, and even clowns and mimes. *At Lincoln Center (see Arts Centers, above). Season Aug.*

Mostly Mozart. At this indoor festival it's Mozart, Mozart, Mozart, and when you think you've heard it all, more Mozart, by the world's best music groups as well as the finest solo performers and opera singers. Recently it's grown to include an additional two-week series, **Mostly Vienna**. *At Lincoln Center's Avery Fisher Hall (see Concert Halls, above). Season July–mid-Aug.*

New York Shakespeare Festival. Each summer brings two plays by you-know-who, outdoors and under the stars. Pick up tickets (free, limit two per person) from 1 PM onwards the day of the show at the Delacorte Theater in Central Park, or from 1 to 3 PM the day of the show at the Joseph Papp Public Theater box office (425 Lafayette St., at Astor Pl., tel. 212/539–8500). *Delacorte Theater, mid-park at 80th St., tel. 212/861–7277. Subway: B or C to W. 81st St.*

Serious Fun! Hear classically trained musicians play milk bottles, car parts, and squeaky balloons! See performance artists like "East Village cult goddess" Ann Magnuson! *At Lincoln Center's Alice Tully Hall (see Concert Halls, above). Season July–Aug.*

GAY AND LESBIAN NEW YORK

8

By Matthew Lore

Fran Lebowitz, New York's wittiest resident, once commented, "if you removed all of the homosexuals and homosexual influence from what is generally regarded as American culture, you would be pretty much left with *Let's Make a Deal*." Nowhere is this more obvious than in her hometown. Lesbians and gay men participate in huge numbers in every major New York industry: magazine and book publishing, advertising, fashion, art, design, architecture, theater, dance, restaurants, law. To be lesbian or gay and to walk New York's streets is a singular experience.

New York is the capital of cruising, of mentally noting what people are wearing today, of how their hair is cut, of checking out asses and faces, cleavage and baskets. "The eyes, the eyes, they're a dead giveaway," a gay resident once said about walking New York's streets. Unless you're a queer wilderness fanatic (in which case you're probably not reading this), you should be able to find in this grand and miraculous city whatever it is that enlarges your spirit and pleases your senses. This chapter teases New York's lesbian and gay whirl from the overall fabric of the city, as much as it's possible to do. If you're new to New York and need a place to crash, check out the gay- and lesbian-friendly suggestions *below*. Beyond that, we list dozens of bars and cafés where you can experience the highs and lows of the city's gay and lesbian scene. The section on Resident Resources focuses on hotlines, health services, and gay-oriented media in the city. Either way, a good place to visit if you're new in town is the **Lesbian and Gay Community Services Center** (*see below*), your single greatest resource in New York City.

Resident Resources

USEFUL ORGANIZATIONS Center for Lesbian and Gay Studies (CLAGS). Contact CLAGS, the nation's foremost gay and lesbian academic organization, for the latest on the city's queer academic scene. Call with any questions; they're not usually open for drop-in visitors. *Graduate Center of the City University of New York, 33 W. 42nd St., btw Fifth and Sixth Aves., tel. 212/642–2924. Subway: 4, 5, 6, or 7 to Grand Central.*

Gay and Lesbian Alliance Against Defamation (GLAAD). When you want to congratulate *Time* for running a lesbian couple on its cover or thank Fox TV for taking the bold step of letting a gay sitcom character actually *kiss* his lover, call GLAAD. Meetings are the first Wednesday of the month (8 PM) at the Lesbian and Gay Community Services Center (*see below*). *150 W. 26th St., Suite 503, btw Sixth and Seventh Aves., Chelsea, tel. 212/807–1700, fax 212/807–1806. Subway: 1 or 9 to W. 28th St. Open weekdays 9–6.*

257

Lesbian and Gay Community Services Center. New York City's gay men and lesbians come together at "the Center" as they do nowhere else. A mind-boggling 400+ organizations meet here, from FIRE-FLAG (gay firefighters) to ACT UP. It also holds special monthly events like movies, readings, panel discussions, potluck dinners, dances, and more. Pick up the free monthly *Center Happenings* or ask to be placed on the mailing list. Also here is a low-cost health clinic (*see* Health and Safety Resources, *below*). *208 W. 13th St., btw Greenwich Ave. and Seventh Ave. S, West Village, tel. 212/620–7310. Subway: 1, 2, 3, or 9 to W. 14th St.; walk 1 block south and ½ block west. Also: A, C, E, or L to W. 14th St.; walk 1 block south and ½ block east. Open Mon.–Sun. 9 AM–11 PM.*

Check out the bathroom on the second floor of the Lesbian and Gay Community Services Center; it was decorated by Keith Haring. Also know that the Center's Pat Parker/Vito Russo Library holds a benefit sale during the first week of every month, with hundreds of used books, CDs, and videos.

Social Activities for Lesbians (SAL). SAL sponsors dozens of lesbian-only events year-round, including softball games, Sunday brunches, biking and in-line skating excursions, museum trips, and book discussion groups. Call or write for the monthly newsletter. *Box 150118, Brooklyn, NY 11215, tel. 718/630–9505.*

TELEPHONE HOTLINES **Gay and Lesbian Anti-Violence Project.** Call this 24-hour hotline if you are ever a victim of a gay- or lesbian-related bashing or harassment, physical *or* verbal. Services—including counseling, referrals, and self-defense workshops—are all free and confidential. *Tel. 212/807–0197.*

Gay and Lesbian Switchboard of New York. Volunteers at the Switchboard give advice about all aspects of lesbian and gay life in NYC, including safe-sex and AIDS info, emergency numbers, and bar and dance club info. *Tel. 212/777–1800. Staffed daily 10 AM–midnight.*

Lesbian Switchboard The all-girl Switchboard, run by the chicks at SAL (*see above*), has nightlife info, makes medical referrals, can help you find a 12-step group, et cetera. *Tel. 212/741–2610. Staffed weekdays 6 PM–10 PM.*

HEALTH AND SAFETY RESOURCES For health care info, the New York City Department of Health's **Office of Gay and Lesbian Health Concerns** (tel. 212/788–4310) should be your starting point. Ask for the free "Health and Social Services Referral Guide," published annually for the lesbian, gay, bisexual, and transgender communities. It includes a list of agencies specializing in the health care of people with HIV and AIDS.

The Department of Health's **HIV Program Services** agency administers an **AIDS Hotline** (tel. 212/447–8200 or 800/TALK–HIV), staffed daily 9–9. Counselors provide info about HIV and AIDS, make referrals to other organizations, and set up appointments for free and anonymous HIV testing at a DOH clinic. Of these clinics, **ACT 1 Chelsea** (303 Ninth Ave., at W. 28th St., Chelsea, tel. 212/239–1744 or 212/447–8200 for advance appointments) is the most lesbian- and gay-friendly. The DOH's **Client Notification Assistance Program** (tel. 212/447–2498) helps people who have tested positive for HIV and want advice about methods of notifying their sex partners or needle-sharing acquaintances.

The **Community Health Project**, at the Lesbian and Gay Community Services Center (*see* Useful Organizations, *above*), is a vital resource for those who don't have private health coverage and want low-cost care in a friendly, comfortable environment. It provides routine physical exams, STD screening and treatment, vaccinations, and gynecological services. The downside? Popularity and limited hours make immediate attention hard to come by.

Gay Men's Health Crisis (GMHC). The oldest and largest AIDS service organization in the nation, GMHC offers direct assistance for people with AIDS, plus peer counseling, financial advocacy, legal services, and recreational activities. Their frequent safe-sex workshops double as social scenes. *129 W. 20th St., btw Sixth and Seventh Aves., Chelsea, tel. 212/807–6664 or 212/807–6655 for HIV/AIDS-related referrals and counseling. Subway: 1 or 9 to W. 18th St. Open weekdays 10–6.*

Institute for Human Identity. This counseling center for gays, lesbians, and bisexuals was founded more than 20 years ago by Bernice Goodman and Charles Silverstein, co-authors of *The Joy of Gay Sex* and *Gay Couples*. Fees are on a sliding scale ($25–$95 per hour). *160 W. 24th St., btw Sixth and Seventh Aves., Chelsea, tel. 212/243–2830. Subway: F to W. 23rd St. Also: 1 or 9 to W. 23rd St. Open weekdays 10–9, Sat. 10–5.*

BOOKSTORES **Creative Visions.** This modest store carries gay and lesbian books; its affiliate next door, Gay Pleasures (*see* Sex, *below*), handles the rest. *548 Hudson St., btw Perry and Charles Sts., West Village, tel. 212/645–7573. Subway: 1 or 9 to Christopher St. (Sheridan Sq.). Open Sun.–Thurs. noon–11, Fri. and Sat. noon–midnight.*

A Different Light. Nationally renowned ADL has a mind-boggling 17,000 gay and lesbian titles, as well as videos, T-shirts, magazines from seven continents, and a knowledgeable staff to help sort it all out. Free events—including readings, movies, and musical performances—are held nightly at 7 PM in the store's art gallery. Socializing takes place continuously at A Different Bite (*see* Cafés, *below*), the in-store café. *151 W. 19th St., btw Sixth and Seventh Aves., Chelsea, tel. 212/989–4850. Subway: 1 or 9 to W. 18th St. Open daily 10 AM–midnight.*

Oscar Wilde Memorial Bookstore. When it opened in 1967, this postage-stamp-size store faced bomb threats and had its windows smashed. It's now the oldest lesbian and gay bookstore in the nation. A plaque by the front door remembers founder Craig Rodwell (who died of AIDS in 1993), organizer of the first Gay Pride Parade. *15 Christopher St., at Gay St., West Village, tel. 212/255–8097. Subway: 1 or 9 to Christopher St. (Sheridan Sq.). Open daily 10:30 AM–8:30 PM, Sat. until 9 PM.*

MEDIA Gone, finally, are the days when the *New York Times* refused to use *gay* (not to mention the "L" word) in its pages, and the *Village Voice* was the only place for openly lesbian and gay journalists. These days, you'll find 10 or more nightly television shows by and for lesbians and gay men. New Yorkers are especially devoted to **Groove TV** (Channel 69, Tuesday at midnight), the gay music video station that plays bands too queer for MTV; **Dyke TV** (Channel 34, Wednesday at 1 PM); **Men and Films** (Channel 35, Thursday at midnight), which reviews new porn films; and **Gay USA** (Channel 35, Thursday at 11 PM), a weekly gay news show.

➤ **PUBLICATIONS** • Though there is no single, authoritative, widely read gay and lesbian newspaper focusing on New York City, **Christopher Street** is worth glancing at for movie reviews by the inimitable Quentin Crisp and inspired essays on AIDS, friendship, and love in the '90s by Andrew Holleran. The bar rags—**HX (Homo Xtra), Next Magazine**, and, in Queens, **On the Wilde Side**—are available everywhere and filled with phone-sex ads and shots of beefy, hairless torsos; love 'em or hate 'em, they're best for up-to-the-minute listings of gay bars, clubs, parties, restaurants, TV programs, movies, theater, and sex clubs; HX has the best listings for dykes.

Queer 'zine fanatics can find the latest issues of "Teen Fag," "OutPunk," and "Lezzie Smut" at New York's 'zine headquarters, See Hear (59 E. 7th St., btw First and Second Aves., East Village, tel. 212/ 505–9781).

Other options to watch for on newsstands and in cafés include **Lesbian & Gay New York (LGNY)** (tel. 212/995–9100), which offers a good mix of hard news from all the boroughs, features, cultural coverage, a calendar, and Alison Bechdel's "Dykes to Watch Out For." **Metrosource** (tel. 212/691–5127) is an upscale mag that shuns sex-related advertisements—though you'd be surprised how many naked bodies still turn up in the ads. Features and listings are geared toward both men and women with gupster sensibilities. **Sappho's Isle** (tel. 516/747–5417) is the city's only all-lesbian newspaper, with news, reviews, a calendar of city events, and classified ads.

Neighborhoods

While New York City's gay men and lesbians live, work, and play all over town, a few neighborhoods—Chelsea, the East and West Village, and Park Slope in Brooklyn—are undoubtedly the "gayest." The sights and attractions that follow are highlights. For full coverage of the city's neighborhoods, *see* Chapter 2.

CHELSEA "A clone corridor crowded with handsome men" is what novelist Andrew Holleran calls Chelsea's **Eighth Avenue** between West 14th and 23rd streets. Dozens of gay and lesbian (but mostly gay) restaurants, cafés, clothing stores, tchotchke boutiques, video shops, gyms, and bars make this the city's current Gay Main Street (the title belonged to the West Village's Christopher Street until the early '90s). You'll find more gay enterprises on side streets stretching east to Sixth Avenue and west to 10th Avenue.

One of the major players in Chelsea's revitalization is **Barneys** (106 Seventh Ave., at W. 17th St., tel. 212/929–9000), New York's premiere men's clothing store (which seems to be doing business as usual, despite a recent bankruptcy filing). Try not to yelp too loudly when you look at the price tags. For something more affordable, try **Housing Works** (143 W. 17th St., btw

Queers in Print

New York City has long been the epicenter of gay and, to a lesser extent, lesbian writers. With astonishing variety, they have fabricated novels, plays, mysteries, histories, memoirs, and essays out of the raw material of life in "the gay capital of the world," as writer Larry Kramer calls the city. Here's a highly selective list of their works with a New York City slant:

- *ANGELS IN AMERICA: PART ONE: MILLENIUM APPROACHES and PART TWO: PERESTROIKA. Tony Kushner's two-part play is the grandest epic vision of America in the age of AIDS ever fashioned. Sure there are scenes in Utah, San Francisco, and Heaven, but New York is its primary setting—from the South Bronx to the Bethesda Fountain in Central Park, site of the play's indelible final words.*

- *DANCER FROM THE DANCE and GROUND ZERO. A work that, in a moment, defined the gay '70s, Andrew Holleran's "Dancer" follows Malone, more god than man, and the all-knowing drag queen Sutherland through days and nights of dancing, drugs, and sex. "Ground Zero" is its coda, a book of essays mostly reprinted from Holleran's long-running "Christopher Street" column.*

- *GAY NEW YORK: GENDER, URBAN CULTURE, AND THE MAKING OF THE GAY MALE WORLD, 1890–1940. Urban archaeology rarely yields news as astonishing as what George Chauncey turns up in this study. Decades before Stonewall, New York was home to a "forgotten gay world" that thrived until it was forced into hiding in the late '30s, a time that bears an eerie likeness to our own.*

- *THE LURE. A cop goes undercover into New York's gay demimonde and discovers he's gay himself in this thriller by Felice Picano, one of the surviving members of the Violet Quill Club, the now legendary gay writing group that also included Andrew Holleran and Edmund White.*

- *RUBYFRUIT JUNGLE. Rita Mae Brown's rousing, fiercely feminist first novel is the story of Molly Bolt's journey from the "rural dot" of Coffee Hollow, Pennsylvania, to New York City. It's the ur–coming out book, a breathless depiction of Molly's trajectory of wit- and intellect-fueled success.*

Sixth and Seventh Aves., tel. 212/366–0820); proceeds help homeless people with HIV or AIDS. At the epicenter of Eighth Avenue gaydom is Chelsea's neighborhood coffee shop, **Eighteenth and Eighth** (159 Eighth Ave., at W. 18th St., tel. 212/242–5000), which is crowded with gay boys and girls just back from the gym. **Food Bar** (149 Eighth Ave., btw W. 17th and 18th Sts., tel. 212/243–2020) draws a 99.9% gay clientele (the male–female ratio is 50/50 at lunch, but by dinner it's virtually all men) that noshes on lemon risotto, seared tuna au poivre, and all those other dishes that will eventually seem as dated as baked Alaska.

WEST VILLAGE Stonewall . . . Sheridan Square . . . Christopher Street. The West Village is home to all the major landmarks of lesbian and gay liberation, with sites familiar to everyone from Brooklyn to Budapest. More than New York's other, more recently gay-colonized neighborhoods (such as Chelsea and the East Village), the West Village boasts a long and colorful history as the home and stomping ground to generations of lesbians and gay men. In the 1920s, queer speakeasies were as numerous as today's cafés and coffee bars, although more discreet. By the '50s, when jazz and beatnik clubs moved in, the Village had entered the popular consciousness as "queer" to such a degree that many of the era's lesbian pulp novels (with their lurid covers and coded cover copy) were set here. The fact that it used to be a cheap place to live is unfathomable today, but low rents once drew the likes of Willa Cather, who spent many of her New York years at 5 Bank Street; *Nightwood*'s Djuna Barnes, who lived in a small apartment at 5 Patchin Place from 1940 until her death in 1981; Hart Crane, who started to write his masterwork, *The Bridge*, while subletting an apartment at 45 Grove Street; James Baldwin, who, when he moved back from Paris in the late '50s, landed at 81 Horatio Street, where he rented three large rooms for $100 a month; and Berenice Abbott, who worked out of her studio at 50 Commerce Street.

No trip to the West Village is complete without an homage-paying visit to the **Stonewall Inn** (53 Christopher St., btw Seventh Ave. S and Waverly Pl., at Sheridan Sq.). The Stonewall of today doesn't *look* like a landmark—and in fact it's not really. The original bar is long gone, and today's Stonewall is a much later incarnation, but look for a plaque in memory of the original. The western end of Christopher Street (from Hudson Street west to the river, including what's known as the Christopher Street Pier) brings you to a zone popular with young African-American gay men, who gravitate here from all over the New York area. But the future of this strip is anyone's guess, as a recently enacted—though hotly contested—new law threatens the sex-related businesses that dominate here.

The Stonewall Riots exploded on the night of June 27, 1969 (the same day Judy Garland was buried), and are now universally recognized as the start of the lesbian and gay liberation movement. Read Martin Duberman's "Stonewall" for the definitive account of the riots.

Some observers claim the West Village is in irreversible decline: a revolving door of mediocre restaurants, too many stores selling skimpy Spandex girdles to gym bunnies, dive bars with sticky floors and petrified customers. If you're overwhelmed by the mobs on Seventh Avenue South and the griminess of Christopher Street, walk a few blocks up Bleecker, hang a left on Jane, Bank, or Charles streets, and you'll be brought back—fast—to better days, when bohemians really knew how and where to live.

If you just want a drink, head to **Orbit** (46 Bedford St., at Seventh Ave. S, tel. 212/463–8717) or its next-door neighbor, **Universal Grill** (44 Bedford St., at Leroy St., tel. 212/989–5621), both as gay as it gets. Featuring burgers and bar food, Orbit attracts its share of glamour dykes; at Universal—widely considered to be the gayest restaurant in the city—tambourine-toting waiters serve up home-cooked food and lip sync "Dancing Queen" as they help the constant flow of birthday revelers usher in another year. Another spot to check out is the **meat-packing district** (at the southwest corner of the West Village), the unlikely home of **Florent** (*see* West Village, in Chapter 4), a gay-owned, 24-hour French bistro clothed as a diner. It draws a crowd so perfectly multiculti you might think you've stumbled into a Benetton ad.

EAST VILLAGE The East Village—long a hotbed of radical social, political, and artistic activity—has been home to many of New York's most important gay citizens: artists like Robert Mapplethorpe, Keith Haring, and David Wojnarowicz; poets and writers, including W. H.

Auden, Frank O'Hara, Allen Ginsberg, Audre Lorde, and Samuel Delaney; and activists from Susan B. Anthony to Sarah Schulman. Gay history buffs will want to walk by **Columbia Hall** (32 Cooper Sq./392 Bowery), the leading gay bar and club of the late 1800s. Although the now-defunct **St. Marks Baths** (6 St. Marks Pl.) are currently home to an ultra-hip video store, during the 1970s and '80s one could have sex upstairs, then get a peanut-butter sandwich in the cafeteria.

Today, East Village gay bars and cafés continue to attract activists and artists. For hipster queers, they're good places to meet interesting souls and get a fix on the Zeitgeist. **Lucky Cheng's** (24 First Ave., btw E. 1st and 2nd Sts., tel. 212/473–0516), once home to the infamous Club Baths, is a nightspot serving pricey California-inflected Chinese food. The waitresses are Asian drag queens. **Flamingo East** (219 Second Ave., btw E. 13th and 14th Sts., tel. 212/533–2860) looks like it could have been a set for *Pulp Fiction*, with its low purple ceiling, long swoosh of a bar, and '50s lounge furniture. The weekly gay salon (Wed. at 10 PM) draws a strong crowd.

MIDTOWN From yesterday's burlesque shows to today's hustler bars, porn palaces, and peep shows, the theaters of **Times Square** have proffered sex in one form or another since at least the 1920s. Wander its blocks and you'll find "adult entertainment" both straight and gay—that is, until Walt Disney moves in and replaces XXX with Goofy. Just two blocks east but seemingly a world away is the gloriously revitalized **Bryant Park** (*see* Parks and Gardens, in Chapter 2); it started as a hangout for the "fairies" of the 1920s and '30s, later served as the site of sexual encounters in John Rechy's *City of Night*, and is now the best place in the city to lunch on a sunny day. Look for the Buddha-like statue of lesbian factotum Gertrude Stein near the park's fancy restaurant, the Bryant Park Grill (tel. 212/840–6500).

PARK SLOPE, BROOKLYN Known affectionately as "Dyke Slope," this neighborhood, 20 minutes by subway from downtown Manhattan, is the lesbian version of Chelsea (though a fair number of gay men also live here). The Slope is home to the nation's only exclusively lesbian archive, the **Lesbian Herstory Archives** (tel. 718/768–3953; open by appointment only), with a vast collection of documents and memorabilia begun by lesbian activist and writer Joan Nestle and her partner. If you're in the area, don't miss a stroll through the 3,000-acre, lushly landscaped **Brooklyn Botanical Garden** (*see* Parks and Gardens, in Chapter 2) and its Brooklyn Walk of Fame, where Brooklyn born-and-bred celebs like Harvey Fierstein, Barbra Streisand, and Mary Tyler Moore are honored with bronze-and-flagstone markers. You'll be amazed at how many celebs are known, or at least widely rumored, to be gay or lesbian.

Where to Sleep

FINDING AN APARTMENT The best place to start searching is the **Housing Notices Bulletin Board** at the Lesbian and Gay Community Services Center (*see* Useful Organizations, *above*). You can bring your own flyer or fill out a card at the front desk. If you can afford to, offer a reward—something like $100 to anyone who helps you find and move into a decent apartment. There is also a bulletin board at **A Different Light** (*see* Bookstores, *above*). And watch for flyers at gay-friendly cafés and health-food stores. For more hints, *see* Longer Stays, in Chapter 3.

Gay Roommate Service. Though this is strictly a one-man-and-an-index-card-file operation, your $100 will get you six months' access to 120 or so listings. Most listings are placed by gay men, though women-only listings are also available. *133 W. 72nd St., Suite 504, btw Columbus and Amsterdam Aves., Upper West Side, tel. 212/580–7696. Subway: 1, 2, 3, or 9 to W. 72nd St. Open weekdays noon–7:30. Appointment required.*

HOTELS AND HOSTELS Decent, inexpensive hotels and hostels are scarce in the city; decent, inexpensive, gay-oriented lodging is even rarer. The citywide network of **YMCA**s (*see* Hostels, in Chapter 3) have functioned for decades as well-priced centers of gay life, long before John Rechy waxed about their "never-stopping showers" in *City of Night*. In Harlem, the gay-owned **Sugar Hill International House** and **Blue Rabbit International House** (*see* Hostels, in Chapter 3) are pleasant, cheap, and worth the trek. If you're willing to splurge, the **Paramount**

(*see* Hotels, in Chapter 3) is the chic home-away-from-home for scenesters of all sexual orientations, offering dozens of porn videos for use in its in-room VCRs. If you're planning to spend Gay Pride Week or Halloween at any of the places mentioned here, reserve far in advance.

Brooklyn Bed & Breakfast. It's not exactly at the center of the action, but the charm of this B&B makes it worth the subway ride. It's housed in a grand old mansion built by a 19th-century shipping magnate. Rooms (some with fireplaces) are $35–$80, with lower weekly rates. *128 Kent St., btw Franklin St. and Manhattan Ave., Greenpoint, Brooklyn, tel. 718/383–3026 or 800/570–3026. Subway: G to Greenpoint Ave.; walk 1 block north to Kent St. and turn left. 6 rooms, 1 with bath. Air-conditioning, no smoking. No credit cards.*

Chelsea Pines Inn. Each of the recently renovated rooms in this temple to movie kitsch has a theme, including homages to Kim Novak, Rock Hudson, and Susan Hayward. Rooms are $55–$89; try to score one in the back, overlooking the garden. *317 W. 14th St., btw Eighth and Ninth Aves., Chelsea, tel. 212/929–1023, fax 212/645–9497. Subway: A, C, E, or L to W. 14th St. (Eighth Ave.); walk ½ block west. 21 rooms, some with bath. Air-conditioning.*

Colonial House Inn. This bed-and-breakfast is housed in an 1850s brownstone and feels like a private home, with homemade muffins for breakfast and cozy rooms ($65–$99) decorated with the owner's artwork. *318 W. 22nd St., btw Eighth and Ninth Aves., Chelsea, tel. 212/243–9669, fax 212/633–1612. Subway: A, C, or E to W. 23rd St.; walk 1 block south and ½ block west. 20 rooms, some with bath. Air-conditioning, concierge, laundry. No credit cards.*

At the Colonial House Inn, spend an afternoon sunbathing au naturel on the rooftop deck or wandering through the minigallery of gay art exhibits.

Incentra Village House. Though the rooms at this gay B&B (housed in twin West Village brownstones) are dusty and a bit run-down, they often come with kitchenettes and working fireplaces. Singles are $99, doubles $129. *32 Eighth Ave., btw W. 12th and Jane Sts., West Village, tel. 212/206–0007. Subway: A, C, E, or L to W. 14th St. (Eighth Ave.); walk 4 blocks south. Also: 1, 2, 3, or 9 to W. 14th St. (Seventh Ave.); walk 3 blocks west on W. 12th St. 12 rooms, all with bath. Air-conditioning, luggage storage.*

Cafés

The coffee bar onslaught of the mid-'90s has added a new twist to the city's social fabric, and gay men and lesbians (like everyone else) have embraced café tables and couches as fabulous places to meet, flirt, and have a cuppa joe. Listed below are some of the city's most gay-friendly and hippest cafés. For others, *see* Cafés and Coffee Bars, in Chapter 4.

Big Cup Tea and Coffeehouse. The center of Chelsea's café society is this popsicle-hued spot, where a mix of well-coiffed boys and girls pack the tables and cushy couches. Monday night features bingo. *228 Eighth Ave., btw W. 21st and 22nd Sts., Chelsea, tel. 212/206–0059. Subway: C or E to W. 23rd St. Open Sun.–Thurs. 7:30 AM–2 AM, Fri. and Sat. 7:30–3 AM.*

mi casa su casa

Think about it: Why spend money on a hotel room when you can shack up in the home of friendly lesbians or gay men? If you can afford to fork over the $78 annual membership to mi casa su casa, you're entitled to a listing of the 200 or so worldwide participants. Make arrangements as early as possible, as it takes a few weeks to get the list, contact your prospective host, and finalize an arrangement. And just so you know, lesbians comprise about 15% of the members. Contact mi casa su casa at 800/215–CASA or 510/268–8534, fax them at 510/268–0299, send 'em an e-mail (homeswap@aol.com), or check out their web page (http://www.well.com/user/homeswap/).

A Different Bite Café. Browse the latest gay books and magazines while sipping espresso or herbal tea at this cozy café, part of the legendary A Different Light (*see* Bookstores, *above*). *151 W. 19th St., btw Sixth and Seventh Aves, Chelsea, tel. 212/989–4850. Subway: 1 or 9 to W. 18th St. Open daily 10 AM–midnight.*

Kaffeehaus. Stopping here for espresso *mit schlag* (with whipped cream) and a fancy dessert ($3–$5) is heaps cheaper than schlepping to Vienna. And the crowd at the red velvet banquettes is very lesbian and gay. *131 Eighth Ave., btw W. 16th and 17th Sts., Chelsea, tel. 212/229–9702. Subway: A, C, E, or L to W. 14th St. (Eighth Ave.). Open Mon.–Thurs. 11:30 AM–midnight, Fri. and Sat. until 1 AM, Sun. 11 AM–midnight.*

Ozzie's Coffee Inc. The Slope's most popular café, Ozzie's has a large selection of coffee drinks and desserts, plus coffee beans, teas, and coffee paraphernalia. *57 Seventh Ave., at Lincoln Pl., Park Slope, Brooklyn, tel. 718/398–6695. Subway: B or Q to Seventh Ave.; walk 3 blocks south on Seventh Ave. Open daily 6 AM–midnight (Sun. until 11 PM).*

After Dark

Gay men have their pick of bars and clubs in Chelsea and the East and West Village—and even in Queens. Lesbians will find that though they have fewer bar options per se, dozens of clubs hold parties (*see* Dance Clubs, *below*) one or more nights a week, just for girls. The city's 60 or so gay and lesbian bars are also an essential part of life for queer New York and always have been: The birth of the modern lesbian and gay liberation movement took place in 1969 at a bar in the West Village, the Stonewall Inn. In all respects, you'll find tremendous diversity once the sun sets, from swank Midtown retreats for lipstick lesbians to the steamy Latino bars of Queens to strip joints in Times Square.

The much-publicized 1990 murder of a gay man, Julio Rivera, in Queens, was one of those periodic and unfortunate reminders that gay-bashers are still out there doing harm.

BARS

A few basics before you begin: Bars don't usually offer dancing (it requires a costly cabaret license), though in general they do feature drink specials Monday–Thursday. Check the listings and ads in the bar rags and get to work on your collection of little paper umbrellas. Very few bars charge covers; if they do, it's usually on weekends. But even then it's always much cheaper than paying a dance-club cover. Finally, unless noted otherwise, alcoholic beverage service stops at 4 AM.

CHELSEA **Barracuda Bar.** When the crowds at Big Cup (*see* Cafés, *above*) get a hankering for a cocktail, they make their way to this intimate den, which has the good sense to graft a bit of the East Village onto Chelsea. A long, cruisy bar in front turns into a swanky lounge in back, with low-slung couches and mood lighting. *275 W. 27th St., btw Seventh and Eighth Aves., Chelsea, tel. 212/645–8613. Subway: 1 or 9 to W. 28th St. Open daily from 4 PM.*

The Break. Your basic Chelsea neighborhood gay bar, the Break occasionally hosts drag shows and fills up Thursdays for $1 margaritas. The garden terrace is open on warm afternoons—on summer Fridays and Saturdays follow your nose to the barbecue. *232 Eighth Ave., btw W. 21st and 22nd Sts., tel. 212/627–0072. Subway: C or E to W. 23rd St. Open daily from 8 AM (Wed. and Sun. from 2 PM).*

Champs. The wrestling mats, lockers, and free-throw lines in this gay sports bar will summon up repressed memories of high-school gym horrors. Sunday's tea dance (free) usually draws a crowd. *17 W. 19th St., btw Fifth and Sixth Aves., tel. 212/633–1717. Subway: F to W. 23rd St. Open from 4 PM.*

Rawhide. Welcome back to the '70s, unironically. A fortyish leather-and-Levis crowd keeps the disco spinning on the jukebox while a huge papier-mâché face of what looks like one of the Village People presides over the bar. *212 Eighth Ave., at W. 21st St., tel. 212/242–9332. Subway: C or E to W. 23rd St. Open daily from 8 AM.*

The Spike. A no-nonsense, leather-and-Levis butch bar (the dress code is sporadically enforced) with good crowds, especially on Fridays. *120 Eleventh Ave., at W. 20th St., tel. 212/243–9688. Subway: C or E to W. 23rd St. Open Mon.–Sat from 9 PM, Sun. from 6 PM.*

Splash. This is guppie central, with suits and gym bunnies in "Look Better Naked" T-shirts mingling around the surfboard tables. Hunky dancers emerge nightly (10 PM–midnight) from the two center-stage showers. For a place with a hygienic theme, the atmosphere is strangely seedy. *50 W. 17th St., btw Fifth and Sixth Aves., tel. 212/691–0073. Subway: F or L to W. 14th St. (Sixth Ave.). Open daily from 3 PM.*

WEST VILLAGE **Crazy Nanny's.** The most racially mixed of the city's lesbian sit-down bars. Upstairs (past the *Forbidden Love* poster) there's a dance floor that hosts step dancing on Thursdays. *21 Seventh Ave. S, at LeRoy St., tel. 212/929–8356. Subway: 1 or 9 to Houston St. Open weekdays from 4 PM, weekends from 3 PM. Cover: $5 Fri. and Sat.*

Cubby Hole. At one of the loveliest corners in the West Village is this pint-sized neighborhood nook decorated with rainbow-hued paper puffballs, garlands of plastic grapes, and faux-leopard-skin chairs. On Tuesdays there's live music. *281 W. 12th St., at W. 4th St., tel. 212/243–9041. Subway: A, C, E, or L to W. 14th St. (Eighth Ave.). Open daily from 4 PM.*

Henrietta Hudson. This spacious bar has a *luxe*, woodsy feel that screams Ralph Lauren. Devotees include quite a few preppie-ish, thirtysomething dykes dressed for the Dinah Shore golf classic. *438 Hudson St., at Morton St., tel. 212/924–3347. Subway: 1 or 9 to Houston St. Open weekdays from 3 PM, weekends from 1 PM.*

Keller's. Keller's dates back to the '50s and is one of the oldest gay bars in the city. Cheap drinks, house music, pool, and blaxploitation flicks on the TVs make this a favorite among African-American men. *384 West St., at Barrow St., tel. 212/243–1907. Subway: 1 or 9 to Christopher St. (Sheridan Sq.). Open daily from 2 PM.*

The Lure. Bartenders with bare asses, an S&M floor show (Wednesday nights), and an in-house leather/fetish shop make this a destination for the adventurous. *409 W. 13th St., btw Ninth Ave. and Washington St., tel. 212/741–0218. Subway: A, C, E, or L to W. 14th St. (Eighth Ave.). Open Wed.–Fri. from 8 PM, weekends from 4 PM.*

Leather, steel-toed boots, and torn Levis get you in the door at The Lure; button-down oxfords, sneakers, and Dockers don't.

The Monster. Jean Baudrillard would have a field day at this schizophrenic two-tiered circus. Upstairs, it's a piano bar decorated by a high school home-ec teacher on acid. Downstairs, a young mixed crowd gets sweaty on the intimate dance floor. *80 Grove St., at W. 4th St., tel. 212/924–3558. Subway: 1 or 9 to Christopher St. (Sheridan Sq.). Open weekdays from 4 PM, weekends from 2 PM. Cover: $1 Thurs. and Sun., $5 Fri. and Sat.*

Uncle Charlie's. The nightlife equivalent of a junior college, Uncle Charlie's draws clusters of fresh-faced gay boys who haven't yet discovered Splash. The G-stringed dancers will make you feel like you're at a petting zoo. *56 Greenwich Ave., btw Charles and W. 10th Sts., tel. 212/255–8787. Subway: 1 or 9 to Christopher St. (Sheridan Sq.). Open daily from 3 PM.*

EAST VILLAGE **The Bar.** The subway-car-at-rush-hour crowds should tip you off that most gay men know *which* bar is *The Bar*. It's the first choice for many of the city's writers, artists, filmmakers, activists, and graduate students. *68 Second Ave., at E. 4th St., tel. 212/674–9714. Subway: F to Second Ave. Open daily from 4 PM.*

The Boiler Room. Particularly with the pierced and Adidas-wearing set—boys *and* girls, straight *and* gay—this is one of the hottest bars in town. Typically, Sunday is women's night (but call first; they like to shake things up regularly). *86 E. 4th St., at Second Ave., tel. 212/254–7536. Subway: F to Second Ave. Open daily from 4 PM.*

Crowbar. One of the few neighborhood bars where you can dance, Crowbar is many a gay boy's favorite, thanks to raucous theme nights such as "Crisco Disco" (Wednesday) and "1984." It's a good alternative for when you're just not up for navigating one of those mammoth dance clubs. *339 E. 10th St., btw Aves. A and B, tel. 212/420–0670. Subway: L to First Ave. Also: 6 to Astor Pl. Open daily from 9 PM.*

Dick's Bar. Comfy high-backed bar stools, great lighting, a low-key local crowd, and a decent jukebox make this a good two-drink bar. *192 Second Ave., at E. 12th St., tel. 212/475–2071. Subway: L to First Ave. Also: 6 to Astor Pl. Open daily from 2 PM.*

Wonder Bar. From the outside, cute blue shutters make this look like Dorothy's house in Kansas. Inside, it's the Brady rec room at Christmas. Wednesdays and Sundays are best, though it's almost always filled with an ethnically diverse East Village crowd, plus more women than in most other gay bars. *505 E. 6th St., btw Aves. B and C, tel. 212/777–9105. Subway: F to Second Ave. Also: 6 to Astor Pl. Open daily from 9:30 PM.*

MIDTOWN AND UPTOWN **Cleo's Ninth Avenue Saloon.** The only gay bar in Hell's Kitchen is filled with actors and off-duty waiters chatting about old Broadway musicals over bowls of free popcorn. *656 Ninth Ave., btw W. 45th and 46th Sts., tel. 212/307–1503. Subway: A, C, or E to W. 42nd St. (Port Authority). Open daily from 8 AM.*

Julie's. Done up with black-and-white photos of fabled Hollywood ladies like Garbo and Tallulah, Julie's is a tony refuge for the lipstick lesbians of Midtown. Fridays and Saturdays they haul out the piano, and on Sundays there's a tea dance. *204 E. 58th St., at Second Ave., tel. 212/688–1294. Subway: 4, 5, or 6 to E. 59th St. Also: N or R to Lexington Ave. Open daily from 5 PM.*

Gente del Ambiente

Adventurous souls bored with Manhattan nightlife will find nearly a dozen gay bars waiting in the Queens neighborhoods of Jackson Heights and Woodside—just 15 minutes by subway from Midtown Manhattan. Most cater to Queens's Latino population, so you'll find Selena on the jukebox and crowds who know how to salsa. To get here, take Subway E, F, G, or R to Roosevelt Avenue/Jackson Heights; the bars are on a 20-block strip of Roosevelt Avenue.

- **Bum Bum Bar. The friendly bartenders here will fill you in on Queens nightlife if you're a rookie. Note the dance contest (Thursday) and free barbecue (Sunday). 63–14 Roosevelt Ave., btw 63rd and 64th Sts., Woodside, tel. 718/651–4145.**

- **Lucho's Club. Nonstop Latin music will have you dancing with boys of all ages (and a few dykes) at the hottest Latino bar in Queens. You won't want to leave. 38–19 69th St., at Roosevelt Ave., Woodside, tel. 718/899–9048. Closed Tues.**

- **Magic Touch. A poem once posted above the bar lamented this joint's temporarily revoked liquor license: "Our booze is gone, and so is our beer./But we are serving soda, to those who come here./The dancers perform, and are somewhat more risqué./But since there's no booze, I guess that's OK." Fortunately, they've got a new license. 73–13 37th Rd., btw 73rd and 74th Sts., Jackson Heights, tel. 718/429–8605.**

- **Montana Saloon. If you've come to Queens to salsa, look elsewhere. This is strictly a neighborhood spot, with little attitude and a not-too-heavy-handed Western theme. 40–08 74th St., at Broadway, Jackson Heights, tel. 718/GAY-9356.**

M Bar & Lounge. New and slick and hyper-stylish, this place is either empty or home to an after-work gathering of gay professionals. *256 E. 49th St., at Second Ave., tel. 212/935–2150. Subway: 6 to E. 51st St. Open weekdays from 5 PM, weekends from 6 PM.*

The Townhouse. The hotel-lobby decor is just right for the suits who bust out of the corporate closet after work. Three bars, two floors, and a crowded piano make this Midtown's best nightly show. *326 E. 58th St., btw Second and Third Aves., tel. 212/754–4649. Subway: 4, 5, or 6 to E. 59th St. Also: N or R to Lexington Ave. Open daily from 4 PM.*

The Works. An uptown cousin of Chelsea's The Break, this is the Upper West Side's main neighborhood bar, heavy on friendly, scrubbed, and polished thirtysomethings. *428 Columbus Ave., btw W. 80th and 81st Sts., tel. 212/799–7365. Subway: 1 or 9 to W. 79th St. Open daily from 2 PM.*

PARK SLOPE, BROOKLYN **The Roost Pub.** In spring and summer, members of the lesbian softball league fill this no-frills bar (which sponsors a few of the teams) after games in Prospect Park. *309 Seventh Ave., at 8th St., tel. 718/788–9793. Subway: F to Seventh Ave.; walk 1 block north. Open Mon.–Wed. from 7 PM, Thurs.–Sat. from 8:30 AM, Sun. from 6 PM.*

DANCE CLUBS

More than any other aspect of New York's lesbian and gay social whirl, dance clubs are notoriously *du jour*, and new ones pop up daily. What's listed below (and in Chapter 6) are a few long-running faves; for the hottest and latest, scan the bar rags and look for party cards (which often offer discounts on cover charges) at lesbian and gay cafés, bookstores, and bars. Keep in mind that bars like The Monster (for men) and Julie's (for women) offer dancing one or more nights a week with no or low cover; for more info *see* Bars, *above.*

Quite a few clubs host weekly parties (*see below*), which all have a particular theme and crowd. The dance organized twice-monthly by the students of **Columbia University's Earl Hall** (tel. 212/854–1488) is better than the big clubs, with good music, a smoke-and-lights-enhanced dance floor, and a sexually and ethnically diverse crowd from all over the city. Likewise, the **Lesbian and Gay Community Services Center** (*see* Useful Organizations, *above*) is home to a popular dance held on the second and fourth Saturdays of the month.

Bar Room. This space is home to quite a few weekly parties beloved by clubsters: Clit Club (*see below*); Clit Club with Boys (Saturday, $5); and Jackie 60 (Tuesday, $10). All very *now*. *432 W. 14th St., at Tenth Ave., West Village, tel. 212/366–5680. Subway: A, C, E, or L to W. 14th St. (Eighth Ave.).*

Sound Factory Bar. This vast, two-tiered club (three bars, two dance floors) earns consistent raves for the quality of its DJ'd house music. The big nights are Thursday (Latino and Chelsea Boy) and Friday (Sound Factory Boys). Alternate Sundays there's a tea dance for HIV-positive men. *12 W. 21st St., btw Fifth and Sixth Aves., Chelsea, tel. 212/206–7770. Subway: N or R to W. 23rd St. Open daily 11 PM–5 AM.*

WEEKLY PARTIES **Clit Club.** Every Friday from 10 PM, legions of young, coiffed, tattooed, and pierced dykes revel at Gotham's oldest all-girl party. Girl porn and go-go girls add to the distractions. *At the Bar Room (see above). Cover: $5–$10.*

Eden. Every Saturday at 10 PM L'Udo, a vast Italian restaurant/garden, becomes a dance club, drawing the hottest crowd of youngster dykes anywhere in the city. *432 Lafayette St., btw Astor Pl. and E. 4th St., East Village, tel. 212/388–0978. Subway: 6 to Astor Pl. Cover: $5.*

Rollerballs. Every Tuesday at 8 PM, nonstop DJ dance music propels everyone around the Roxy's expansive dance floor on in-line skates ($10 for rental) or old-fashioned roller skates ($4). Don't panic: The skill level ranges from lock-kneed neophytes to daredevils who treat roller disco like an Olympic event. *515 W. 18th St., btw Tenth and Eleventh Aves., Chelsea, tel. 212/645–5156. Subway: A, C, E, or L to W. 14th St. (Eighth Ave.).*

Squeeze Box. This is *the* Friday night party, the quintessential queer New York experience for the '90s. The doors open at 10 PM, and lead acts (which go on after 2 AM) keep Don Hill's hop-

Squeeze Box at Don Hill's is not to be missed: a mix of shrilly hostesses in drag, 17-year-olds trying out punk aesthetics, and raging queer bands bellowing songs with unfathomable lyrics—at decibels one hopes might wake the gods from the prolonged slumber that has left us to amuse ourselves with scenes like this.

ping until breakfast. *511 Greenwich St., at Spring St., West Village, tel. 212/334–1390. Subway: 1 or 9 to Houston St. Cover: $10.*

THE SEX SCENE

You'll find sex in New York City in all the familiar places, and then some: peep shows, theaters, sex clubs, bathhouses, back rooms of bars, gym steam rooms, subway platforms, tearooms, parks, and at the beach. Keep in mind that city officials (spurred by a small but vocal contingent of gay activists) began strict monitoring of commercial sex establishments in 1995, and what the future holds is anyone's guess. No matter where you end up enjoying sex in New York, *follow safer-sex guidelines.*

All Male Jewel Theater. This place is just like the Bijou (*see below*), but with daytime hours. It's most crowded 11 PM–1 AM. *100 Third Ave., btw 12th and 13th Sts., East Village, tel. 212/505–7320. Subway: L to Third Ave. Open Sun.–Thurs. 10 AM–3 AM, Fri. and Sat. 10 AM–5 AM. Cover: $8–$10.*

Bijou Theater. Here you've got two dozen no-frills private rooms plus a theater showing your basic gay porn. A constant supply of pretzels, cookies, coffee, and sodas (sorry, no alcohol) lends the place a comfy, church-social feel. Just look for the unmarked door directly below the LA STRADA CAFÉ sign. *82 E. 4th St., btw Second Ave. and Bowery, East Village, no phone. Subway: F to Second Ave. Open Sun.–Thurs. 8 PM–6 AM, Fri. and Sat. 7 PM–7 AM. Cover: $8–$10.*

East Side Club and **West Side Club.** Patrons find sex the civilized way at this pair of gay bathhouses: No worries about pickpockets or having sex with their pants around their legs, since everyone wears towels, and showers, steam rooms, and saunas let everyone clean up after the excitement. The cost is $10–$25 for membership plus $10–$20 per visit. Most don't show up before midnight on weekends. *East Side Club: 227 E. 56th St., btw Second and Third Aves., Upper East Side, tel. 212/753–2222. Subway: 4, 5, 6 to E. 59th St. West Side Club: 27 W. 20th St., btw Fifth and Sixth Aves, Chelsea, tel. 212/691–2700. Subway: N or R to W. 23rd St. Both open 24 hrs.*

Eve's Garden. An office building in Midtown isn't the obvious place for the world's first feminist sex store; but this is a low-key, stress-free place for women to shop for dildos, vibrators, body oils and lotions, videos, books, and mags. *119 W. 57th St., Suite 420, btw Sixth and Seventh Aves., tel. 212/757–8651. Subway: N or R to W. 57th St. Open Mon.–Sat. noon–7 PM. Unescorted men admitted noon–2 PM only.*

Gay Pleasures. Gay Pleasures has the dignified charm of an old apothecary shop, making it the only sex emporium on the planet to which you could bring your grandmother. Offerings include videos ($5–$60); mags like *Torso, Drummer,* and *Stroke*; and plenty of pulpy paperbacks. Next door, **Creative Visions** (*see* Bookstores, *above*) stocks lesbian erotica. *546 Hudson St., btw Charles and Perry Sts., West Village, tel. 212/255–5756. Subway: 1 or 9 to Christopher St. (Sheridan Sq.). Open daily noon–midnight.*

The Arts

THE VISUAL ARTS The most gay-friendly of New York City's hundreds of galleries are listed below, but they're not the only ones that show works by queers. In fact, remove the works by lesbians and gay men from all of the city's art museums and galleries and you'd just have vast expanses of white space. For current shows, check the arts listings in the *Village Voice*, *New York Times*, *The New Yorker*, or in bar rags like *HX*.

Feature. You'll find lots of homoerotic art here, including Tom of Finland and Bastille. *75 Greene St., 2nd Floor, btw Spring and Broome Sts., SoHo, tel. 212/941–7077. Subway: 6 to Spring St. Open Tues.–Sat. 11–6.*

Leslie-Lohman Art Foundation. The main traffic at this volunteer-run gallery is in erotic art of all kinds, even cheesy beefcake. Watch for the annual all-lesbian show. *127 Prince St., Basement Level, at Wooster St., SoHo, tel. 212/673–7007. Subway: N or R to Prince St. Open Tues.–Sat. 1–6. Closed Aug.*

Wessel O'Connor Gallery. The exhibits at this TriBeCa gallery represent 30 lesbian and gay photographers, both historical and contemporary. *60 Thomas St., btw Church St. and W. Broadway, TriBeCa, tel. 212/406–0040. Subway: 1 or 9 to Franklin St. Open Tues.–Sat. noon–6.*

White Columns. Though it's not exclusively gay, White Columns hosts frequent queer shows. *154 Christopher St., btw Greenwich and Washington Sts., West Village, tel. 212/924–4212. Subway: 1 or 9 to Christopher St. (Sheridan Sq.). Open Wed.–Sat. noon–5.*

THEATER This decade has seen three "gay" plays—Harvey Fierstein's *Torch Song Trilogy*, Tony Kushner's *Angels in America*, and Terrence McNally's *Love! Valour! Compassion!*—win Tonys and enjoy extended Broadway runs. But consider moving beyond Broadway to the dozens of tiny theaters downtown. Here you'll find a staggering variety of gay- and lesbian-themed productions, from boys-in-underwear-talking-about-sex plays to sharply incisive works by lesbian performance artists. Check the bar rags or a weekly such as the *Village Voice*, *Time Out*, or *The New Yorker* for what's current. Note that many theater organizations go on hiatus during summer months.

$3 Bill Theatre. The $3 Bill is working hard to establish itself as New York's leading producer of highbrow lesbian and gay plays. *Tel. 212/463–7492. Venues and prices vary.*

Dixon Place. Almost nightly, New York's most innovative writers, performance artists, musicians, and dancers present works-in-progress in the loft/home of Dixon Place's artistic director. Every July it hosts "HOT: The New York City Celebration of Queer Culture." *258 Bowery, btw Houston and Prince Sts., Lower East Side, tel. 212/219–3088. Subway: J or M to Bowery. Also: 6 to Spring St. Tickets: $8.*

Don't Tell Mama. Multiple daily shows at the city's leading gay cabaret feature celebrity impersonators, drag queens, and even *female* female impersonators. *343 W. 46th St., btw Eighth and Ninth Aves., Times Square, tel. 212/757–0788. Subway: A, C, or E to W. 42nd St. (Port Authority). Cover: $8–$15. 2-drink minimum. Reservations advised.*

The Wild Side

The Ramble, one of New York's most popular alfresco sex playgrounds for men, is a maze of paths on the north side of the Lake in Central Park. Surprises lurk under every tree, but the peninsula that pokes out into the lake is particularly cruisy. As always, be watchful for those who look more antagonistic than randy.

Duplex. The Duplex is home to the long-running "Dressing Room Divas," plus other drag and comedy shows. Joan Rivers was discovered here. *61 Christopher St., at Seventh Ave. S, West Village, tel. 212/255–5438. Subway: 1 or 9 to Christopher St. (Sheridan Sq.). Cover: $6–$12. 2-drink minimum. Reservations advised.*

Lesbian Theater Project. This theater group puts on two monthlong productions annually, plus a monthly reading series. Its noble goal is to depict gay and lesbian life without dwelling on sex, sex, sex. *Tel. 212/243–5770. Tickets: $5–$10. Venues vary.*

If you want to catch outré downtown dykes before they turn up on the cover of "Deneuve," WOW is a good place to find them.

WOW (Women's One World). New York's oldest lesbian theater is the place to come for often-wild theatrical experiences, from plays and performance art to poetry readings and open-mike nights. *59 E. 4th St., btw Second Ave. and Bowery, East Village, tel. 212/460–8067. Subway: F to Second Ave. Tickets: $6 Tues.–Thurs., $8 Fri.–Sun.*

Festivals and Annual Events

SUMMER Endless parties and celebrations take place during Gay Pride month (June); look for the free *Pride Guide* (tel. 212/807–9839) for all those important dates and times.

The New Festival: The New York Lesbian and Gay Film Festival. During this 10-day extravaganza, you can catch several hundred feature films, shorts, documentaries, and videos by and about lesbians, gay men, bisexuals, and transgender folks. *Tel. 212/254–7228. Late May/early June.*

Stonewall. The anniversary of the 1969 riots at Greenwich Village's Stonewall Inn is the lesbian and gay version of the 4th of July. On the last Sunday in June there's a spectacular parade followed by a massive dance at the Christopher Street Piers. *Tel. 212/807–7433.*

FALL **National Coming Out Day** is October 11.

MIX: The New York Lesbian and Gay Experimental Film/Video Festival. The self-proclaimed world's largest avant-garde film festival includes hundreds of experimental works by notables like Todd Haynes, Barbara Hammer, and Thomas Allen Harris. *Tel. 212/501–2309. 2 weeks in Nov.*

Wigstock. Every drag queen and her princess sister heads to the Christopher Street Piers on Labor Day weekend for Wigstock, the zaniest drag party in the world. For a preview and inspiration on what to wear, check out the 1995 documentary *Wigstock*. *Tel. 212/213–2438, fax 212/213–0204, http://www.at-beam.com/Wigstock.*

SPORTS AND OUTDOOR ACTIVITIES 9

By Shon Bayer, Matthew Jalbert, and Mira Schwirtz

New Yorkers may love dining out, drinking cocktails, and smoking—but during summer you'll see zillions of ripped hardbodies on bikes and 'blades, slackers whacking around tennis and soccer balls, and old folks speed-walking through Central Park. Zillions more fill stadiums during biggie annual events like the U.S. Open, New York Marathon, and Gay Games, and to cheer on the city's pro sports teams. If you feel like joining in, *Time Out* ($1.95), available at most newsstands, is a great resource: Its "Sports" section lists upcoming events, times, dates, and ticket info. The *TripBuilder's Sports Guide* ($5), available at bookstores, also has up-to-date info on city sports leagues and places to play.

Gyms and Rec Centers

There are plenty of private health clubs in town that charge thousands of dollars for the privilege of sweating your patootie on their StairMasters. Thankfully, **Crunch Fitness** (tel. 212/475–2018) has four locations in Manhattan and only charges $850 for a yearly membership. That entitles you to as many yoga, kick boxing, aerobics, and karate classes as you can stand. Crunch Fitness also has a reputation as one of the most gay- and lesbian-friendly gyms in the city. The women-only gym **Living Well Lady** (tel. 212/582–8850) has four locations in Manhattan; it charges $20 per month for a two-year membership, good for three visits per week. For unlimited use it's $30 per month plus a $75 initiation fee.

PRIVATE GYMS **Asphalt Green.** This 5-acre, state-of-the-art facility features an Olympic-size indoor pool (with special features for swimmers with disabilities), indoor and outdoor tracks, basketball courts, an Astroturf field, and all kinds of exercise equipment and classes. The drop-in fee for the pool or gym is $14 ($25 for both). Membership is $50–$100 per month. *1750 York Ave., at E. 91st St., Upper East Side, tel. 212/369–8890. Subway: 4, 5, or 6 to E. 86th St. Open weekdays 5:30 AM–10 PM, weekends 8 AM–9 PM. Closed to nonmembers weekdays 3–8 PM. Wheelchair access.*

Chelsea Piers Sports Center. In this brand-new gym the size of three football fields, you'll find the city's longest indoor running track (¼ mi), a boxing ring, indoor sand volleyball courts, a rock-climbing wall, an indoor swimming pool, and just about everything else a sports fiend could want. A day pass ($26) gives you access to everything at the Sports Center, but you can only purchase six day passes per year. Annual membership is a pricey $100 per month with a $300 start-up fee. Chelsea Piers offers direct shuttle service ($1–$2) from many parts of the city; call for a schedule. Also at Chelsea Piers are an ice-skating rink and roller rink (*see* Participant Sports, *below*); a golf driving range; and indoor soccer, field hockey, and lacrosse fields. *W. 23rd St., at Hudson River, Chelsea, tel. 212/336–6000 or 212/336–6666 for recorded info. Subway: C or E to W. 23rd St.; walk 3 long blocks or catch a crosstown bus. Open weekdays 6 AM–11 PM, Sat. 7 AM–10 PM, Sun. 8–8.*

PUBLIC GYMS City-operated rec centers are an excellent deal. Pay the $25 annual membership fee at one and you have access to all eight Manhattan locations. Offerings include swimming pools (outdoor pools are free in summer), basketball and volleyball courts, weight-training equipment, all sorts of exercise bicycles and Nautilus machines, even salsa aerobics and classes in African martial arts; contact the **NYC Parks & Recreation Department** (tel. 212/360–8111 or 800/201–PARKS in NYC) for more info. Two of the best are:

Carmine Street. Offers indoor and outdoor pools, an indoor track, indoor volleyball and basketball courts, two gyms, a dance studio, and weight rooms. Classes include yoga, aerobics, fencing, and self-defense. *3 Carmine St., at Seventh Ave. S, West Village, tel. 212/242–5228. Subway: 1 or 9 to W. Houston St. Open weekdays 7–2 and 5:30–10, Sat. 10–5.*

West 59th Street. Facilities include an indoor pool, fitness rooms, a gym, and an indoor climbing wall. Classes include weight-training and climbing. *533 W. 59th St., btw Tenth and Eleventh Aves., Upper West Side, tel. 212/397–3166. Subway: A, B, C, D, 1, or 9 to W. 59th St. Open Mon.–Sat. 11–6:30 (hours for recreational swimming vary).*

Participant Sports

There is no lack of sportsy things to do in New York, be it ice skating at Rockefeller Center or mountain biking on Staten Island. No matter what you're into—jogging, biking, in-line skating, football, soccer, ultimate Frisbee, snoozing by a shady tree—the best place to start is **Central Park** (*see* Major Attractions, in Chapter 2). Most sports activities are free if you do it yourself or join a pickup game, though for only a few bucks you can also join a fairly organized local team. For info on participant sporting events throughout the city, call the **NYC Parks & Recreation Department** (tel. 212/360–8111 or 800/201–PARKS in NYC) and dial your way through their recorded choices.

New York's public recreation centers are amazing deals: $25 gets you unlimited access to all sorts of exercise equipment for a full year.

BASKETBALL For serious team players, the **New York Urban Professional Athletic League** (tel. 212/877–3614) sponsors league games starting in June and November. **Yorkville Sports** (tel. 212/645–6488) starts play in October. Both leagues have separate divisions for men and women, hold open tryouts, and charge $125 per person. It's a hefty investment, but worth it if you're heavy into hoops. Call a month or two before the season starts to register.

➤ **PICKUP GAMES** • There are hundreds of outdoor courts all over the city, where competition ranges from inept to life-threatening. Most players are men. Female hoopsters tend to gather at **Tompkins Square Park** (Ave. A, at St. Marks Pl.), while the courts on **West 4th Street** at Sixth Avenue draw hotshots from around the city (and even an audience). Lively play also takes place on the six half-courts at **West 76th Street** at Columbus Avenue (closed summer weekends) and at two courts in **Central Park**, near the Metropolitan Museum. On the Upper East Side, easygoing players fill three half-courts at **Carl Schurz Park** (E. 84th St., at East End Ave.) and the courts at the **Armory Building** (E. 94th St., at Madison Ave.). If you're looking to be absolutely humiliated, try **Riverbank State Park** (W. 145th St., at Riverside Dr.).

BIKING You won't get killed exploring the city by bike, but you'd be smarter to stick to cruising around Central Park, **Riverside Park** (Riverside Dr., btw W. 72nd and 135th Sts., Upper West Side), or the **Battery Park City Esplanade** (on the Hudson River, btw Chambers St. and Battery Pl., Lower Manhattan). Outside Manhattan, the best spots to explore on two wheels are **Forest Park**, Queens, which is fantastic for BMXers, and **The Greenbelt**, in Staten Island, which has a pleasant trail along the beach (for more on both, *see* Parks and Gardens, in Chapter 2). If you're into racing, you can hook up with the **Century Road Club Association** (tel. 212/222–8062), which meets weekend mornings (7 AM) in Central Park for four- or five-lap races around its 6-mile circular drive. If you prefer to pedal for pleasure, join **Time's Up** (*see* Cheap Thrills, in Chapter 2) for one of their moonlight rides.

➤ **BIKE RENTALS AND REPAIRS** • Plenty of bike shops in the city will rent you a pair of wheels on which to cruise around. Try **Bicycle Habitat** (244 Lafayette St., btw Prince and Spring Sts., SoHo, tel. 212/431–3315), which rents mountain bikes and hybrids for $25 per day (plus $250 deposit); **Bicycles Plus** (1690 Second Ave., btw E. 87th and 88th Sts., Upper East Side, tel. 212/722–2201), which rents the same for $7 per hour ($25 per day), with a $100–$150 deposit; or **Metro Bicycles** (332 E. 14th St., btw First and Second Aves., Upper East Side, tel. 212/228–4344; and six other locations citywide) rents hybrids for $6 per hour or $25 per day ($35 to keep bike overnight), plus a $150 deposit. In summer you can rent bikes ($6–$8 per hr, $32–$40 per day) inside Central Park at **AAA Bikes** (Loeb Boathouse, mid-park at 74th St., tel. 212/861–4137). Bike owners and would-be owners can't do better than **Frank's Bike Shop** (553 Grand St., btw Jackson and Lewis Sts., Lower East Side, tel. 212/533–6332), which charges $20 for a basic tune-up.

CLIMBING Rock climbers intent on climbing in Manhattan, but not ready to scale the Empire State Building, can test their mettle on one of three indoor walls at the **Manhattan Plaza Health Club** (482 W. 43rd St., btw Ninth and Tenth Aves., Midtown, tel. 212/563–7001). Day access is $10 plus $5 for equipment rental. In Central Park, the **North Meadow Rec Center** (mid-park at 97th St., tel. 212/348–4867) has a 13-foot indoor wall and a 25-foot outdoor wall. Their single-day introductory class is $75; the four-day comprehensive course costs $200. They'll also show you the two places you can climb in Central Park, **Rat Rock** and **Chess Rock**, or take you out to the 50-foot rock in **Fort Tryon Park** (*see* Parks and Gardens, in Chapter 2). Chelsea Piers and the West 59th Street rec centers (*see* Gyms and Rec Centers, *above*) also offer indoor climbing walls and instruction for beginners.

CROSS-COUNTRY SKIING When a heavy snowfall hits New York, Central Park's bridle paths and roadways make for spectacular treks, particularly in the woodsy wonderland above 86th Street. **Scandinavian Ski and Sports Shop** (40 W. 57th St., btw Fifth and Sixth Aves., Midtown West, tel. 212/757–8524) can set you up with boots, poles, and skis for $16 per day, though you'll need to move swiftly to score a pair.

FOOTBALL You can let Fox TV get under your helmet, or you can do what Jack Kennedy did (and what JFK, Jr. still does) every weekend in Manhattan: Grab family and friends and go play some touch football. Central Park's **Great Lawn** (mid-park, at 83rd St.) and **Sheep Meadow** (near Central Park W, at 66th St.) are the land of pickup games. Most start on weekends by 9 AM, year-round, and there's also action on weeknights in summer. **Yorkville Sports** (tel. 212/645–6488) has both men's and coed leagues that play a 10-game season starting in September. The cost to join is $100 per person.

HIKING Though hiking in New York City seems an odd concept, there are plenty of nearby places to worship Mother Nature and hug a tree. The obvious choice is Central Park—there are literally hundreds of trails crisscrossing its length, most of which are rarely crowded. In the outer boroughs, enormous parks like **Alley Pond Park**, **Forest Park**, **Pelham Bay Park**, **Van Cortlandt Park**, the **Staten Island Greenbelt**, and the **Jamaica Bay Wildlife Refuge** each offer acres of wilderness and plenty of picnic tables; *see* Parks and Gardens, in Chapter 2, for more info on each.

The **Urban Park Rangers** (tel. 212/427–4040 or 718/287–3400) organize guided walks throughout the New York area; they can also recommend the best spots for bird-watching, dog walking, jogging, you name it. The **Gateway National Recreation Area** (tel. 718/338–3338) in Brooklyn offers moonlight walks, wildflower walks, and dune hikes, all for under $20 per person (often for free). The **North Meadow Rec Center** (*see* Climbing, *above*), in Central Park, organizes park hikes, bird-watching expeditions, and other nature programs. **Shorewalkers** (tel. 212/330–7686) leads weekend tours of New York area shorelines.

HORSEBACK RIDING **Claremont Riding Academy** is a 100-year-old institution and the only stable in Manhattan. Experienced English riders can rent horses to explore 6 miles of bridle paths in nearby Central Park for $33 per hour. Claremont also offers classes in riding and jumping for all experience levels. *175 W. 89th St., at Amsterdam Ave., Upper West Side, tel. 212/724–5100. Open weekdays 6 AM–10 PM, weekends 6 AM–5 PM.*

ICE SKATING AND ICE HOCKEY If you want to play hockey, the Sky Rink (*see below*) at Chelsea Piers sponsors several year-round leagues, from beginner to expert. Games are $15 for members, $40 for nonmembers. On winter weekends, you can also drop in on a hockey game at Lasker Rink (*see below*) for $4. All ice skating rinks offer skate rentals, lockers, tacky music, and snack bars serving steaming cups of cocoa. Hockey players need to bring their own gear.

Lasker Rink. This newly revamped rink, at the northern end of Central Park near 106th Street, offers crowd-free skating late October–mid-March. Skate rentals are $3. *Tel. 212/534–7639. Subway: 2 or 3 to W. 110th St. (Central Park North). Admission: $4, $2.50 children. Open Sun. and Mon. 10–5, Tues.–Thurs. 10–9:30, Fri. and Sat. 10 AM–11 PM.*

Rockefeller Center Ice Skating Rink. The rink isn't huge, but there's still something amazing about skating in the heart of Manhattan on a crisp winter evening. Kids love this place. Skate rentals are $4–$5. *601 Fifth Ave., btw W. 49th and 50th Sts., Midtown, tel. 212/757–5731. Subway: B, D, F, or Q to W. 47–50th Sts. (Rockefeller Center). Admission: $7–$10, $6–$9 children. Open Oct.–Apr., weekdays 9 AM–10 PM (Fri. until midnight), Sat. 8:30–midnight, Sun. 8:30–10.*

Call it corny or call it magical, but a few turns around the ice at glitzy Rockefeller Center, under the city's fabled Christmas tree, is a true New York experience.

Sky Rink. This deluxe indoor rink (the size of Alaska) is located in the brand-new Chelsea Piers. It's open year-round. Rentals are $3.50. They also offer lessons in hockey, speed skating, and figure skating. *W. 23rd St., at the Hudson River, Chelsea, tel. 212/336–6100. Subway: A, C, or E to W. 23rd St. Admission: $9. Open Mon. noon–6:20 and 8–9:20, Tues. noon–6:20, Wed.–Fri. noon–9:20, Sat. 11:45–4:45 and 8–10:20, Sun. 12:30–4:45.*

Wollman Memorial Rink. Ice skaters pack this famously beautiful Central Park rink, near 59th Street, November–March. Skate rentals are $4–$6. *Tel. 212/517–4800. Subway: B or Q to W. 57th St. Also: N or R to Fifth Ave. Admission: $6, $3 children. Open Sun.–Thurs. 10–9:30, Fri. and Sat. 10 AM–11 PM.*

IN-LINE SKATING On weekends, city parks and roadways swarm with 'bladers oblivious to everything but their Walkmans. Evel Knieval types set up obstacle courses and jumps near **Tavern on the Green** (near Central Park W, at 66th St.) in Central Park. During warm months, the park's **Wollman Memorial Rink** (*see* Ice Skating and Ice Hockey, *above*) becomes a roller disco; rentals are $15 (2 hrs) or $25 (all day). Other popular outdoor spots include Hudson River Park, Riverside Park, and the concrete canyons and wide open plazas of **Wall Street** (which are nearly car-free on weekends). The brand-new **Chelsea Piers** (W. 23rd St., at the Hudson River, Chelsea, tel. 212/336–6200) has a giant indoor roller rink, which offers classes ($15) for beginner, expert, and hip-hop 'bladers; general skating ($3.50); and, on Friday and Saturday nights, DJ'd dance parties ($8). The **New York Road Skaters Association** (328 E. 94th St., at Second Ave., Upper East Side, tel. 212/534–7858) holds classes ($10 per session), organizes group skates, and publishes a booklet of safety tips for Central Park.

If you need to rent, head to one of the **Blades** branches. Full-day rentals (pads included) are $15 on weekdays, $25 on weekends, plus a credit-card deposit of $200. *120 W. 72nd St., btw Columbus Ave. and Broadway, Upper West Side, tel. 212/787–3911. Subway: 1, 2, 3, or 9 to W. 72nd St. Open daily 10–8 (Sun. until 6). Other locations: 160 E. 86th St., btw Lexington and Third Aves., Upper East Side, tel. 212/996–1644; Westside Hwy. and W. 23rd St., Chelsea, tel. 212/336–6199; 659 Broadway, btw. Bleecker and W. 3rd Sts., West Village, tel. 212/477–7350.*

➤ **IN-LINE SPORTS** • Not only does the New York Road Skaters Association (*see above*) offer basic lessons in the fine points of staying on your 'blades and off your bum, it also sponsors roller-hockey leagues. League games are held April–October, usually in the evenings. You pay $100 for the season, not including gear. Chelsea Piers (*see above*) also offers several levels of league play, year-round. If hockey isn't your fancy, the **National In-line Basketball League** (tel. 212/260–5698) sponsors *basketball* games on 'blades. Who'd have thunk it? Members pay $35 to compete three times a week at Tompkins Square Park.

New Yorkers aren't afraid to cross-check, so arrive well-padded wherever you go. The best place to play street in-line hockey is **Robert Moses Playground** (E. 41st St., at First Ave.), where the competition is pretty fierce. In summer you'll also find pickup games at **Riverbank State Park** (W. 145th St., at Riverside Dr., Harlem). Throughout the year on weekends, there are also games at **Tompkins Square Park** (Ave. A, at St. Marks Pl., East Village) and, on Sunday afternoons, at the north end of **Union Square** (E. 17th St., at Broadway).

If you've never been on Rollerblades before, proceed slowly and cautiously to one of the Central Park Skate Patrol's "Stopping Clinics." From April to October, these quick, free, knee-saving seminars are held daily 12:30–5:30 at the East and West 72nd Street park entrances.

RUNNING Though Manhattan streets are crowded with pedestrians, bicycle messengers, city buses, and curb-jumping taxis, there are plenty of places where you can run safely in New York. Most popular is the **Central Park Reservoir** (mid-park, btw 85th and 96th Sts.), where tenacious people in Lycra orbit the 1.58-mile track in every kind of weather. Roads within the park all have designated runners' lanes and close completely to traffic weekdays 10–3 and 7–10 and from Friday at 7 PM until Monday at 6 AM. The entire loop of the park—from 59th Street to 110th Street and back again—is 6 miles.

Other favorite Manhattan circuits are: **Riverside Park** (4½ mi), **Washington Square Park** (½ mi), **East River Park** (¼-mi track), the **Battery Park City Esplanade** (2 mi), and the **Hudson River Esplanade** (1½ mi). In Brooklyn, try either the **Brooklyn Heights Promenade** (1 mi), which offers stunning views of the lower Manhattan skyline, or the loop in **Prospect Park** (6 mi), which is closed to traffic on Sundays. For park locations, *see* Parks and Gardens, in Chapter 2.

➤ **RUNNING CLUBS** • New York has almost a dozen clubs geared exclusively toward runners; most organize group runs, provide safety info, plan races, and sponsor events throughout the year. Most clubs meet weekly in Central Park and charge a small annual membership fee. The **Achilles Track Club** (tel. 212/354–0300) is primarily for wheelchair racers and runners with disabilities. **Front Runners** (tel. 212/724–9700) is New York's main gay and lesbian running group. **Moving Comfort** (tel. 212/222–7216) is a highly competitive all-women team. The **Warren Street Social and Athletic Club** (tel. 212/807–7422) is known for its friendly attitude towards less-than-Olympic-caliber athletes.

Use caution wherever you run or jog, and don't go out alone in deserted areas or after dark. The New York Road Runners Club (tel. 212/860–4455) can match you with a running partner if you're new in town.

The **New York Road Runners Club** holds free 2-, 4-, and 6-mile group runs weekdays at 6:30 PM and 7:15 PM, Saturday at 10 AM, all starting near Central Park at the club headquarters.

What Has 54,000 Legs and Uses 642 Tubes of K-Y Jelly in a Single Day?

New York's marathon is one of city's most celebrated civic events, a 26-mile party that passes through all five boroughs before ending in front of Tavern on the Green in Central Park. In a single Sunday in early November, over 27,000 runners from 99 foreign countries and all 50 states will have passed 18,000 yards of barricade tape; 2 million spectators will have whizzed in 550 portable toilets; and 642 tubes of K-Y Jelly will keep the whole thing running smoothly. For further info or entry forms, contact the New York Road Runners' Club, 9 E. 89th St., New York, NY 10128, tel. 212/860–4455 or 212/423–2229, fax 212/423–2272.

They also sponsor classes, races, and "fun runs" year-round, and help to coordinate the annual New York Marathon. *9 E. 89th St., at Fifth Ave., Upper East Side, tel. 212/860–4455. Subway: 4, 5, or 6 to E. 86th St.*

SKATEBOARDING To check in with the New York skate scene, cruise to **Astor Cube** (Astor Pl. and Lafayette St.) in the East Village. You'll also find great obstacles—benches, stairs, fountains—at the **American Museum of Natural History** (W. 79th St., at Central Park W) and at the **Time-Life Building** (1271 Sixth Ave.), but sometimes you'll also find cops. **Brooklyn Banks** (on the Manhattan side of the Brooklyn Bridge), a.k.a. 'da Banks, is always crowded with skaters, both pros and newbies. The hippest skate shop in town (and it's just down the street from the Astor Place scene) is **Supreme** (274 Lafayette St., btw Houston and Prince Sts., SoHo, tel. 212/966–7799; open Mon.–Sat. 11:30–7:30, Sun. noon–6). Bettys should check out **Swish** (115 St. Marks Pl., btw First Ave. and Ave. A, East Village, tel. 212/673–8629), one of few shops in town that carries gear for the ladies.

SOCCER Alexi Lalas aspirants should cruise over to **Soccer Sport Supply** (1745 First Ave., at E. 90th St., tel. 212/427–6050), which can outfit you with cleats and Umbro shorts and give you the dope on soccer activities around the city. **Yorkville Sports** (tel. 212/645–6488) runs a year-round coed league, which costs $95 per person to join.

➤ **PICKUP GAMES** • You may have noticed that Manhattan isn't blessed with acres of open fields. Your best bet is to join a weekend game at Central Park's **Great Lawn** (mid-park, at 83rd St.), which has one soccer field, or **North Meadow** (mid-park, at 97th St.), which has three. Downtown diehards play on the narrow strips of grass and asphalt that constitute **Washington Square Park** (Waverly Pl., at University Pl.) and **Tompkins Square Park** (Ave. A, at St. Marks Pl.), though the latter is really too small to have a serious game.

SOFTBALL AND BASEBALL Between April and mid-September, softball dominates the city's parks on weekends and weekday evenings. Most games are sponsored by a league, either men's, women's, or coed and either fast- or slow-pitch. Most people hook up with a league through their employer or with an organization like **Corporate Sports** (tel. 212/245–4738), **Manhattan Indoor/Outdoor Sports** (tel. 718/712–0342), or **Yorkville Sports** (tel. 212/645–6488). It generally costs around $100 per person to join a private league. Otherwise, if you and your friends are all self- or unemployed, you'll need to buy a permit ($10–$40) from the **NYC Parks & Recreation Permit Office** (tel. 212/360–8133) to use one of the city's hundreds of baseball diamonds, even for a single game. Sorry.

SWIMMING If you're too poor to escape to the Italian Riviera—or even the south shore of Long Island—at least you can keep your cool at a city pool or nearby beach (*see box*, New York City, Land of Skyscrapers and Sunny Beaches?!, in Chapter 2). The pools at public rec centers (*see* Gyms and Rec Centers, *above*) are free during summer—and crammed with splashing pre-teens. You're better off at a private pool: The five-lane indoor pool at **John Jay College of Criminal Justice** (899 Tenth Ave., at W. 58th St., Midtown, tel. 212/237–8371) is open to the public weekdays until 5 PM; $25 buys you 100 visits to the pool. The eight-lane, 50-meter Olympic pool at **Asphalt Green** (*see* Gyms and Rec Centers, *above*) is members-only weekdays 3–8 PM; otherwise it's open to the public for $14 per visit. A $50 annual membership gives you access to the **Midtown YMCA**'s (610 Lexington Ave., at E. 53rd St., Upper East Side, tel. 212/735–9770) large six-lane pool, which is perfect for rigorous workouts. Your cheapest option is **Lasker Rink** (tel. 212/996–1184) in Central Park. In summer this skating rink becomes a swimming pool; you pay $3 for a full day of splashing around. To reach Lasker Rink, enter the park at 110th Street and Lenox Avenue.

TENNIS Whenever the weather is good, you'll find hundreds of people on the public courts in Central Park. Though pickup games are possible, most people arrive in pairs and aren't in the mood to share their courts with anyone. Reservations are a good idea. Also, you must get a permit to play on a city-owned court: $5 for a single-play permit or $50 for a full-season permit that's valid in all five boroughs. Call the **NYC Parks & Recreation Permit Office** (tel. 212/360–8133) for more info. Or pick up your permit in person at Room 1 in the Arsenal Building (Fifth Ave., at E. 64th St.). The courts at **East River Park** (East River Dr., at Delancey St., tel. 212/529–7185) are available on a first-come, first-served basis; they're never as busy as the courts in Central Park. If you have money to spare and don't mind the trek to Queens, reserve one of 38 outdoor/indoor courts at the **U.S.T.A. National Tennis Center** (Flushing Meadows–Corona Park, Queens, tel. 718/760–6200), site of the U.S. Open. You can make reservations up to an hour in advance; courts cost $28–$40 depending on the time of day. For directions to Flushing Meadow–Corona Park, *see* Queens, in Chapter 2.

VOLLEYBALL League volleyball is half sport and half social: Teams are coed and usually celebrate wins (and losses) with a postgame trip to a bar. The **Big City Volleyball League** (tel. 212/288–4240) fields over 90 teams at seven skill levels. The cost is $85 per person for a 10-week season starting in January, April, July, or October. The smaller **New York Urban Professional League** (tel. 212/877–3614) has similar schedules and prices. **Yorkville Sports** (tel. 212/645–6488) starts its league games in mid-September; membership is $70. If you want to hone that killer serve, try the three nets in Central Park or in one of New York's public rec centers (*see above*).

Spectator Sports

Even though they lost their beloved Dodgers to Los Angeles in 1958, sports-crazy New Yorkers still have great pro teams like the Yankees, Mets, Knicks, Islanders, and Rangers. Sure, the *Post* and *Daily News* seem to find more excitement chronicling off-field antics—like Yankee owner George Steinbrenner's bullying (and unending) threats to move his team to another planet or Spike Lee's latest courtside outburst—but, hey, a sunny day hangin' in the House that Ruth Built (New Yorkers' pet name for Yankee Stadium) while drinking beer with rowdy fans is still a singular New York experience.

The main venues for New York's pro teams are: **Giants Stadium** (*see* Football, *below*); **Meadowlands** (Rte. 3, East Rutherford, NJ, tel. 201/935–3900), accessible by bus from Port Authority; and **Madison Square Garden** (Seventh Ave., btw W. 31st and 33rd Sts., Midtown, tel. 212/465–6000) near the Penn Station subway stop (1, 2, 3, or 9). In addition to hosting the Knicks and Rangers, the Garden is the place to catch an endless parade of wrestling, boxing, rodeo, and monster-truck shows. Purchase tickets at a team's box office or through **Ticketmaster** (tel. 212/307–4100), which slaps a service charge (usually about $5 per ticket, depending on the game) on whatever you buy.

BASEBALL Nothing's better than hot dogs, beer, and baseball—except all of that *plus* a free pair of stylin' Yanks sunglasses. Annual freebie fests include the Mets' Beach Towel Night and Jersey (shirts, not cows) Day, and the Yankees' Sunglasses and Bat (the baseball-hitting kind, not the flying rodents) days. Regular baseball season runs April–October.

New York Yankees. In years past, greats like Babe Ruth, Joe DiMaggio, and Lou Gehrig led the Bronx Bombers to championship after championship. These days you never know what to expect, though rowdy bleacher bums guarantee a good time. Bleachers cost $6, reserved seating is $11.50–$16. *Yankee Stadium, Bronx, tel. 718/293–6000 or 718/293–4300 for automated tickets. Subway: C, D, or 4 to 161st St. (Yankee Stadium). Box office open weekdays 9–5 and during home games.*

New York Mets. The current team has youth and talent and Bobby Bonilla, one of the National League's dominant sluggers. So why have they sucked for most of this decade? Tickets cost $6.50–$15. *Shea Stadium, 123–01 Roosevelt Ave., at 126th St., Flushing, Queens, tel. 718/507–TIXX. Subway: 7 to Willets Point (Shea Stadium).*

BASKETBALL The **New York Knickerbockers** (Madison Square Garden, tel. 212/465–JUMP) suffered through several humiliating runs for the championship under Armani-clad coach and personality Pat Reily. Don Nelson (of Golden State Warriors fame) tried his hand as coach from 1995 until he got canned in early 1996, when finally Jeff Van Gundy took over the talented but geriatric crew that includes Patrick Ewing and John Starks. Tickets start at $17 and peak at $1,000. The **New Jersey Nets** (Meadowlands Arena, tel. 201/935–3900), who migrated from NY to NJ in 1977, perennially rank as one of the NBA's worst teams—despite star players like Kenny Anderson, Derek Coleman, and Kevin Edwards. Tickets sell for $16–

277

$55. In the spring, Madison Square Garden hosts the Big East and National Invitational college tournaments, both worth checking out. The pro-basketball season runs late October–April.

FOOTBALL If you've come to town expecting to see some football, try a sports bar. Tickets for both New York pro teams are almost impossible to get: You can scramble for single **New York Jets** (tel. 201/538–6600) tickets when they go on sale in August, join the waiting list for **New York Giants** (tel. 201/935–8222) tix, or hand a scalper your life savings. Both teams play in New Jersey at **Giants Stadium** (East Rutherford, tel. 201/935–8111 for the Giants; tel. 516/538–6600 for the Jets); catch a bus from Port Authority to reach the stadium. Big college matchups like Army–Navy occasionally come to Giants Stadium, too. Football season runs September–December.

As an alternative of sorts, check out the **Columbia Lions**, the Ivy League's perpetual doormat. Their losing streaks have hit 40-plus in a row, but they're not gonna dwell on it, OK? The Lions play at Columbia University's **Baker Field** (200 W. 118th St., tel. 212/854–2546) September–November. Tickets cost $13–$14.

ICE HOCKEY Fast paced, brutal, and full of fights, ice hockey is just like the subway at rush hour—no wonder New Yorkers love it. All three pro teams play in the notorious Patrick Division, and recent triumphs have made tickets (typically $15–$75) pretty scarce by game time. The season runs October–April.

Though they're wimps compared to their rabid fans, the **New York Rangers** (Madison Square Garden, tel. 212/456–6000) did manage to end a 54-year championship drought with a Stanley Cup win in 1994. The **New Jersey Devils** (Meadowlands Arena, tel. 201/935–3900) won the Stanley Cup in 1995 after enduring a lifetime as league losers (Wayne Gretzky once dissed them as "Mickey Mouse"). And the **New York Islanders** won four consecutive Stanley Cups in the early '80s, but unless new tough-guy coach Mike Milbury works a miracle, at least you won't have trouble getting tickets. The Islanders play at Nassau Coliseum (Hempstead Turnpike, Uniondale, Long Island, tel. 516/794–4100), accessible by train from Penn Station.

During the big weeks of the U.S. Open, shy guy Andre Agassi has been known to sneak off to the courts of Central Park for a little extra practice.

TENNIS The prestigious **United States Open Tennis Tournament** (tel. 914/696–7284) takes place late August–early September at the U.S.T.A. National Tennis Center (*see* Tennis, in Participant Sports, *above*). It's a hugely popular event with New Yorkers, and tickets ($18–$66) to the exciting matches go fast. You can purchase tickets by phone through **TeleCharge** (tel. 212/239–6250 or 800/524–8440) for a $5-per-ticket service fee. The WTA Tour **Championships** (tel. 212/465–6500) sponsored by Corel (it was formerly brought to you by Virginia Slims) brings together the top 16 women's singles and top eight women's doubles for over a million dollars in prizes. It's held at Madison Square Garden in mid-November, and tickets cost $25–$45.

Index